NURSES
and
THE LAW

NURSES
and
THE LAW
A Guide to Principles and Applications

Nancy J. Brent, JD, MS, RN
Attorney at Law
Chicago, Illinois

W.B. SAUNDERS COMPANY
A Division of Harcourt Brace & Company
Philadelphia   London   Toronto   Montreal   Syndey   Tokyo

W.B. SAUNDERS COMPANY
A Division of Harcourt Brace & Company

The Curtis Center
Independence Square West
Philadelphia, Pennsylvania 19106

This publication is designed to provide accurate and authoritative information in regard to the subject matter covered. In publishing this book neither the author nor the publisher is engaged in rendering legal, accounting or other professional service. If legal advice or other expert assistance is required, the services of a competent professional should be sought.

Library of Congress Cataloging-in-Publication Data

Brent, Nancy J.
Nurses and the law: a guide to principles and applications / Nancy J. Brent.

p.   cm.

Includes index.

ISBN 0–7216–3463–X

1. Nursing—Law and legislation—United States.   I. Title.   [DNLM:
   1. Legislation, Nursing—United States.   2. Liability, Legal—United
   States—nurses' instruction.   WY 33 AA1 B8n 1997]

KF2915.N8B74   1997   344.73'0414—dc20   [347.304414]

DNLM/DLC   96–30633

NURSES AND THE LAW   ISBN 0–7216–3463–X

Printed in the United States of America.

Last digit is the print number: 9   8   7   6   5   4   3   2   1

To the memory of my mother
Marian Maloney Weiss

To the honor of my father
Edward William Weiss
and my brother and sister
Terrill Weiss *and* **Elizabeth Weiss Martin**

and especially to my husband
George W. Brent
who never failed to inquire about the book's completion
by asking:
"When already???"

Nancy J. Brent received a Bachelor of Science degree with a major in nursing from Villa Maria College in Erie, Pennsylvania. Her Masters Degree in psychiatric-mental health nursing was obtained from the University of Connecticut in Storrs. After holding a number of clinical and teaching positions in nursing, Ms. Brent attended Loyola University of Chicago School of Law, graduating in 1981. Since 1986, Ms. Brent has practiced law as a sole practitioner in Chicago, concentrating her practice in legal representation, consultation, and education for health care practitioners, health care delivery systems, and school of nursing faculty. She has also published extensively in the area of law and nursing practice and has conducted many seminars across the country on law and health care delivery.

Penny Simpson Brooke, JD, MSN, RN
University of Utah
College of Nursing
Salt Lake City, Utah
The Nurse in the Community

Margaret R. Douglas, MS, RN
Saint Xavier University
School of Nursing
Chicago, Illinois
Ethics and Nursing Practice

Paula Henry, JD, NP-C, BSN, RN
Lewis, D'Amato, Brisbois & Bisgard
Costa Mesa, California
The Nurse in Advanced Practice

Lenore J. Boris, JD, MSN, RN
Samaritan Hospital
School of Nursing
Troy, New York

Carolyn Krauch Braudway, MS, RN
Columbia Union College
Department of Nursing
Takoma Park, Maryland

Penny Simpson Brook, JD, MSN, RN
University of Utah
College of Nursing
Salt Lake City, Utah

Shirley J. Bruenjes, MSN, RNC
Columbus, Indiana

Caroline Camuñas, EdD, RN
Columbia University
Teachers College
New York, New York

Michele Daniele, JD, RN
Harvey, Pennington, Herting, and
    Renneisen, Ltd.
Philadelphia, Pennsylvania

Gail Watkins Ford, EdD, CS, FNP, RN
Tuomey Family Health Center
Sumter, South Carolina

Catherine E. Graziano, PhD, RN
Salve Regina University
Newport, Rhode Island

Paula Henry, JD, NP-C, BSN, RN
Lewis, D'Amato, Brisbois & Bisgard
Costa Mesa, California

Patricia Iyer, MSN, CNA, RN
Medical League Support Services
Stockton, New Jersey

Maxine Musilli Knapp, PhD, RN
Ohio University
School of Nursing
Athens, Ohio

Adrienne Mayberry, DPA, RN
California State University
Long Beach, California

Anna Omery, DNSc, RN
UCLA, School of Nursing
University of Southern California,
    Hepatitis Research Center
Los Angeles, California

Carol M. Patton, Dr. PH, CCRN,
CRNP, CFNP
Carlow College
Pittsburgh, Pennsylvania

Jamie Richardson, JD, MSN, RN
Fulbright and Jaworski, L.L.P.
San Antonio, Texas

Lisa K. Anderson Shaw, MSN, MA, RNC
University of Illinois Medical Center
College of Nursing
Chicago, Illinois

Andrea J. Sloan, JD, RN
Private Practice
McLean, Virginia

Florence Nightingale, in her classic 1859 text, *Notes on Nursing: What It Is, And What It Is Not,* clearly understood the context within which nursing was practiced. Whether her timely observations and guidelines focus on providing variety in a patient's physical surroundings or admonish the nurse from engaging in "Chattering Hopes,"[1] Ms. Nightingale understood the importance of assessing and manipulating the context within which the patient existed in order to provide maximum nursing care.

As nursing continued to develop, other contextual factors were identified as important to its existence and growth. One of those factors was the law. As early as 1901, Ethel Manson Fenwick, who was attending the Third International Congress of Nurses in Buffalo, New York, identified the need of a system of registration, established and administered by nursing, in order to guarantee the qualifications of nurses.[2] Her voiced concerns helped to secure the first permissive nurse practice act's passage in North Carolina in 1903 and the first mandatory act in New York in 1938.[3]

Tort law, of which negligence and professional negligence is a part, was insignificant prior to the 1900s.[4] After the Industrial Revolution, tort law developed rapidly.[5] Even so, early tort law ignored nursing, due mainly to the fact that nursing was not seen as an accountable, responsible profession until nursing began to establish itself in the 1940s. With developments that included nurses in the U.S. Civil Service obtaining professional status classification in 1946, the founding of additional professional associations representing various specialties in nursing practice (e.g., the American Association of Operation Room Nurses in 1949), (the American Nurses' Association [ANA] and the National League for Nursing [NLN] had been in existence in some form since the late 1800s), and the expanded role responsibilities, specialization, and advanced practice of nurses,[6] the law eventually required the profession and its members to answer to alleged breaches of its duties of care to patients.

Despite the law's early oversight of nursing's legal accountability and responsibility to its consumers, nursing has always believed it was accountable and responsible to those it served. Florence Nightingale wrote about nursing responsibility to patients in 1859. Likewise, in its most recent Social Policy Statement, the American Nurses' Association states that the Statement is a document that "nurses can use as a framework for understanding nursing's relationship with society and nursing's obligation to those who receive nursing care."[7]

Nursing's relationship with society and the intricate intertwining of it with nursing's legal character and nursing's professional practice has never been more apparent. An early version of universal precautions was suggested by a nurse nearly 50 years ago.[8] Nurses were at the forefront of making needed changes in the identification and management of pain.[9] The ANA published its first statement on the care of the patient with HIV/AIDS in 1988.[10] Health care reform, access to quality, low-cost health care, and the efficient use of advanced practice nurses continue to be advocated by the nursing profession.[11]

The nursing profession and its members also identified the need to "flex legal muscles" in order to protect their collective and respective legal rights during the profession's growth and development. As early as 1934, the ANA was active in campaigning for an 8-hour work day instead of a 12-hour, 6-day week.[12] In 1975, eight nurses who worked at Denver General Hospital and the Denver Visiting Nurse Association sued the city of Denver, alleging sex discrimination in city and county policies concerning the payment of wages.[13] In *Wallace v. Veterans Administration*,[14] a recovering registered nurse successfully sued the VA for a violation of the Rehabilitation Act of 1973 after it refused to hire her solely because of her chemical addiction. Politically, professional organizations, including the ANA, have established their clout on both the federal and state levels.[15]

It is certain that nursing's relationship with society will continue. So, too, will nursing's involvement with the law and legal principles. This textbook is an attempt to help today's nurse become knowledgeable about the law and the legal principles of professional nursing practice. Legal principles and their application are not merely part of the title of the text. Rather, an attempt has been made to identify legal principles and apply them to current issues in nursing practice.

The text has been divided into three major parts. Part 1 contains an overview of the law as it pertains to nursing practice generally. Part 2 identifies legal issues of concern to any area of nursing practice. It also includes an important chapter on ethics and nursing practice. Part 3 applies specific legal concerns to identified roles of nursing in particular practice settings.

Each chapter contains key legal principles that are developed in the chapter and applied through the use of actual, analyzed court decisions or examples from clinical practice. Other chapters that are related and may help add to the reader's understanding are also identified at the beginning of each chapter. When possible, tables and other easy reference and study aids are used. Each chapter also ends with a list of topics for further inquiry.

Every attempt has been made to provide the reader with current, accurate, and up-to-date information concerning the legal issues in nursing practice. However, because the law is ever-changing, some of the content may not be current if a new decision has been reached by a particular court concerning a particular issue or if Congress or a state legislative body has passed a new piece of legislation. Therefore, it is incumbent upon the nurse reader to keep up with changes in the law that impact upon nursing practice.

Once you review the book, I think you will see that "keeping up" with the law is a never-ending responsibility. I trust that my effort to make the law understandable and interesting will make that responsibility at least an adventuresome one.

NANCY J. BRENT

1. See, Florence Nightingale. *Notes On Nursing: What It Is, And What It Is Not.* NY: Dover Publications, Inc., 1969 (Reprint Edition).

2. Shirley Fondiller, "Selections From U.S. Nursing History", 90(10) *American Journal of Nursing,* (October 1990), 18 (Anniversary Issue—*Progress And Promise: 1900–1990*).

3. "Nursing Practice And The Law", *Nurse's Handbook Of Law & Ethics.* Springhouse, PA: Springhouse Corporation, 1992, 3.

4. Lawrence Friedman, "Torts", *A History Of American Law.* 2nd Edition. NY: Simon and Schuster, Inc., 1985, 467.

5. *Id.*

6. See also, Barbara Brodie, "Nursing's Quest For Professionalism", *Current Issues In Nursing.* 4th Edition. Edited by Joanne McCloskey and Helen Grace. St. Louis: C.V. Mosby Company, 1994, 559–565.

7. American Nurses' Association. *Nursing's Social Policy Statement.* Washington, DC: ANA, 1995, 1.

8. Marguerite Jackson and Patricia Lyngh, "In Search Of A Rational Approach", 90(10) *AJN* (October 1990), 65–66, 68, 71, 72, 74.

9. Margo McCaffery, "Nurses Lead The Way To New Priorities", 90(10) *American Journal of Nursing* (October 1990), 45–48, 50.

10. American Nurses' Association. *Nursing and HIV: A Response To The Problem.* Kansas City, Missouri: ANA, 1988.

11. See, for example, Linda Heffernan, "Regulation Of Advanced Practice Nursing In Health Care Reform", 28(2) *Journal Of Health And Hospital Law* (March/April 1995), 73–84; Peter Buerhaus, "Creating A New Place In A Competitive Market: The Value of Nursing Care", 2(2) *Nursing Policy Forum* (March/April 1996), 13–16, 18–20.

12. Fondiller, *supra* note 2, at 46.

13. *Id.* The case, *Lemons v. City Of Denver,* 620 F. 2d 228 (10th Cir.), *cert. denied,* 449 U.S. 888 (1980), was based on the comparable worth theory. The nurses lost the suit.

14. 683 F. Supp. 758 (D. Kan. 1988).

15. See, for example, Kathleen Canavan, "Nurses Become Political 'Tour De Force'", 28(3) *The American Nurse* (April/May 1996), 1, 12; Diane Mason, Susan Talbott and Judith Leavitt. *Policy And Politics For Nurses: Action And Change In The Workplace, Government, Organizations And Community.* 2nd Edition. Philadelphia: W.B. Saunders Company, 1993.

acknowledgments

I have many, many people to thank who have helped me during the six (yes, six!) years this book was "in progress." To begin, I would not have been able to undertake and complete the task without the supportive and interested help of the research assistants who were my "eyes and ears" in the library. Whether they were "shepardizing" cases, checking citations for accuracy, or spending hours reviewing recent court decisions for updates for chapter material, their reliable and consistent concern for the completion of the book were greatly appreciated. Most of the assistants were law students, either in a J.D. or Masters in Health Law program, during the time they worked with me on the book. Early assistants included Ms. Dana Scher, Ms. Pepi Camerlingo, and Ms. Nanete Augustine. More recently, Mr. Doug Swill, now an attorney concentrating his practice in Health Law at Gardner, Carton & Douglas in Chicago, Illinois, and Ms. Kathleen Svanascini, now a sole practitioner in Palos Heights, Illinois, were of invaluable help. An added benefit has been the friendship and colleagual relationships with Doug Swill and Kathy Svanascini that have continued beyond the completion of the book.

My computer person for the book, Ms. Linda Semenzin, and I met quite by chance. After I had begun working on this book, I received a flyer in the mail describing Linda's typing and support services, Word Express. I was impressed with the quality of the flyer and the professional way in which the information concerning the service was presented. I began using Word Express for the book. The quality of Linda's work for the book manuscript was unbeatable and unfaltering. With my limited computer skills, I would hammer out a chapter, cut and paste it after it came back from a review, mark additional corrections and additions with red pencil, draw tables from scratch, and send the chapter disc and additions to Linda for completion. Each and every time, the end result was an organized, correctly footnoted, and professional-appearing manuscript. Moreover, when due dates became increasingly important, Linda never balked at getting a chapter completed by *my* deadline. This was true even though Linda had demands on her time due to family responsibilities, her typing service and the completion of her Masters Degree in Education. I will be indebted to her forever, which is OK with me, because we have also established a fine friendship as well.

I also want to thank my friends and my nursing and law colleagues for their unwavering interest in the book and its completion. Their genuine support, inquiries concerning its progress, and offers to do anything to help me finish the book were priceless encouragement.

The assistants to Thomas Eoyang, who is now Vice President and Editor-in-Chief of Nursing Books at Saunders, were also of great help to me during the writing of this book. Most recently, Ms. Melanie Nordlinger's invaluable assistance in working with me on all aspects of the book, including the many details of placing the book into production, has not gone unnoticed. Melanie's organizational skills and low-keyed manner have not gone unnoticed either.

Last, but by no means least, I owe Thomas Eoyang, the Editor of this book, my deepest gratitude. Thomas and I have known each other for over 10 years. When Thomas initially asked me to consider doing this book, I was hesitant to do so. However, because I had worked with him in the past as a contributing author to a nursing text, I decided to accept this project. Probably neither one of us believed it would take me this long to finish this text. Although the demands of a solo law practice, teaching, and family existed when I began this project, I somehow thought I could do it in a timely manner. But time became my enemy during the writing of the book. Fortunately, Thomas never became an enemy. His patient yet constant prodding to complete the book, along with his grace and humor, helped me to continue what I set out to do. I could not have done it without him.

NANCY J. BRENT

contents

1 Overview of the Law

2 Legal Issues

part one

Overview of
the Law

1

The Government and the Law

contents

The United States had its first constitution embodied in the Articles of Confederation, which was in effect from 1781 until 1789.[1] The Articles established a loose alliance of independent states with a central government. The powers of the government were limited, and there was no judiciary. Furthermore, the executive powers of the established system were weak at best.[2] As a result, Congress was given most of the power in the early system of government.

On March 4, 1789, the "new" federal Constitution, which had been formulated at the 1787 Constitutional Convention and eventually ratified by 11 states, became the second framework of the government. It was composed of a preamble stating its purpose, articles, and several amendments.[3] The articles governed such topics as (1) the legislative, executive, and judicial branches of the government; (2) the relationship of the states to each other and to the central government; and (3) ways in which the Constitution could be amended.[4]

Although the new Constitution was seen by many as an improvement over the Articles, for some it did not contain adequate protections for the continued sovereignty of the states and individual rights. Thus, specific amendments to the Constitution were proposed to "limit and qualify the powers of the government."[5] Those amendments, which were accepted by the states in 1792, became known as the Bill of Rights.

Despite the attempt to balance the powers of the federal government with those of individuals and states, the struggle did not end. Because the Constitution was established as the "supreme law of the land,"[6] the courts continued to further define and interpret the respective relationship between the federal government and the state governments and their citizens. Moreover, the Constitution itself continued to change. As of 1983, 26 amendments or articles to the federal Constitution had been ratified.[7]

Interestingly, before development of the federal Constitution, states tried to define their power by adopting their own constitutions. The definition of power by the states focused on several issues: their respective abilities to govern their particular state, limitations on the ability of the state government to usurp individual state citizens' rights, the interrelationship between the state governments, and where the federal government's power ends and a state's power is at least shared with the federal government or becomes supreme. Although each state eventually adopted its own constitution, these issues are still of concern today.

> *Clearly, the federal Constitution, and state constitutions, are ever-changing documents.*

Clearly, the federal Constitution, and state constitutions, are ever-changing documents. Their applicability to all aspects of life, whether in the 1800s or the twentieth century, is ever present, albeit in differing interpretations and applications of those charters. This chapter will present selected aspects of the United States Constitution and state constitutional principles as they apply to the nurse and health care delivery. The chapter illustrates the respective governments' abilities to directly or indirectly influence a nurse in his or her individual and professional life in two major areas: individual constitutional rights and the legislative process.

KEY PRINCIPLES

Constitution
Bill of Rights
Separation of Powers Doctrine
Right
Due Process of Law
Equal Protection of the Law

ESSENTIALS OF THE GOVERNMENT AND THE LAW

There is no question that the government influences a person's life, whether professional or private. What is unique about this influence is twofold. One distinctive aspect is the balancing of the state governments' power with federal governmental power. The second is the emphasis on the balancing of governmental power with the personal and collective liberties citizens possess.

The Constitution

A constitution is the primary law of a nation or state that establishes the character and organization of its government, limits and distributes power within the government, and establishes the extent and manner of the exercise of the government's power.[8]

Federal Constitution

The federal Constitution is composed of 7 articles and 26 amendments, the first 10 of which have traditionally been called the Bill of Rights.[9] However, all 26 amendments focus on individual rights that are protected against governmental intrusion.[10]

The Constitution's purpose, included in its Preamble, is to "form a more perfect Union, establish justice, insure domestic tranquility, provide for the common defence, promote the general welfare, and secure the blessings of Liberty to ourselves and our Posterity."[11] The original seven Articles are summarized in Table 1–1.

BILL OF RIGHTS. The American Bill of Rights (Table 1–2) is included in the United States Constitution and is composed of the first 10 amendments to the original articles. The first 10 amendments were ratified December 15, 1791, and the remaining amendments were enacted in the period from 1795 to 1971.

It is interesting to note that the Bill of Rights,

TABLE 1–1
Articles of United States Constitution

ARTICLE	ESSENCE OF ARTICLE
I	Establishes legislative branch of government, Congress, with a Senate and House of Representatives; powers and limitations of Congress listed, including promoting the general welfare, regulating interstate commerce, and establishing courts inferior to the Supreme Court
II	Establishes executive power in the U.S. President; spells out how President is elected; makes President commander in chief of Army and Navy; allows President to recommend legislation; provides for State of the Union reports to Congress
III	Bases judicial power in one Supreme Court and inferior courts established by Congress; provides for Supreme Court to review ''Article III'' lower court decisions where jurisdiction exists (e.g., constitutional questions, laws of the United States, and treaties)
IV	''Full Faith and Credit'' given by each state to other states' ''Acts, Records and Judicial Proceedings''; citizens in each state granted ''privileges and immunities'' of citizens in all states; guarantees to all states a ''Republican Form of Government''
V	Enumerates the manner in which amendments to the Constitution can occur
VI	Establishes the Constitution and the laws of the United States as the ''supreme Law of the Land''; Congress is bound by oath to uphold Constitution; no ''Religious Test'' can be required as a qualification for any U.S. office or public trust
VII	Ratification of the Convention of Nine States required to ''establish'' Constitution

TABLE 1–2

Amendments to the United States Constitution

AMENDMENT	ESSENCE OF AMENDMENT
I	Inability of Congress to pass laws concerning (1) establishment of religion or its free exercise; (2) limits on freedom of speech, the press, or the right of peaceful assembly; and (3) the right to petition the government for redress of grievances
II	States cannot be limited in their ability to establish their own military to maintain security, nor can states limit the people in their right to keep and bear arms
III	In peacetime, no soldier can be housed in any private home without the owner's consent; in war, housing soldiers in private homes may occur, but only by law
IV	No unreasonable search or seizure of property or person can take place; a warrant can be issued only for probable cause, supported by an oath or affirmation, and must include a description of the place to be searched and the person and property to be seized
V	Prosecution of criminal offenses must be initiated with an indictment of a grand jury (except for U.S. or state armed forces); protection against being tried for the same offense twice (double jeopardy); no individual can be compelled to be a witness against himself in criminal case; no deprivation of life, liberty, or property without due process of law; no private property taken for public use without just compensation
VI	In criminal cases, accused has right to (1) speedy and public jury trial; (2) notice of nature and cause of accusation; (3) face witnesses against him; (4) use established procedures to require favorable witnesses to be present at trial; (5) an attorney
VII	In common lawsuits in which the amount in controversy is more than $20, trial by jury shall exist; when a jury renders its verdict, no fact shall be re-examined except pursuant to established common law rules
VIII	In criminal cases, no excessive bail or fines can be imposed, nor cruel and unusual punishment inflicted upon prisoners
IX	The constitutional rights shall not be used to deny or disparage others retained by the people
X	The powers not delegated to the United States by the Constitution or prohibited by it are retained by the respective states or by the people
XI	Limits the power of the federal courts to hear cases in law or equity in which one state sues another or in which the case involves citizens of any foreign state
XII	Enumerates procedures for the election of President and Vice-President; limitations on presidential terms and the succession of the President in event of death, resignation, or incapacitation
XIII	Abolished slavery and involuntary servitude
XIV	Declares that persons born or naturalized in the United States and subject to its jurisdiction are U.S. citizens and citizens of the state where they live; prohibits a state from passing or enforcing any law that diminishes privileges or immunities of U.S. citizens; a state cannot deprive a person of life, liberty, or property without due process of law, or deny any person within its jurisdiction equal protection of the law; enumerates certain voting rights (male and over 21 years); grants Congress the power to pass legislation to enforce amendment
XV	Says that U.S. citizens' voting rights cannot be denied or limited by any state or the United States on account of race, color, or previous servitude
XVI	Establishes the ability of Congress to impose and collect taxes
XVII	Provides for the direct election of U.S. senators
XVIII	Prohibited manufacture, sale or transportation, importation and exportation of intoxicating liquors in U.S. and all territories
XIX	Prohibits denial or limitation by any state or United States of voting rights on account of sex; grants Congress the power to pass legislation to enforce amendment
XX	See comment for Amendment XII
XXI	Repealed the XVIII Amendment; transportation or importation of intoxicating liquors into a state in violation of state law prohibited
XXII	See comment for Amendment XII
XXIII	Grants District of Columbia residents the right to vote for President and Vice-President
XXIV	Eliminates poll tax in federal elections
XXV	See comment for Amendment XII
XXVI	Prohibits denial or limitation by a state or U.S. of voting rights on account of age for citizens 18 years of age and older

and the subsequent amendments, have essentially remained unchanged since their adoption. This fact is particularly interesting since the Bill of Rights was passed when the Constitution was less than 5 years old.[12] Furthermore, only three amendments—XI, XIV, and XVI—were enacted to overturn Supreme Court decisions.[13] Thus, although the character of the Constitution and the Bill of Rights may change with court decisions interpreting the "black letter language" of this document, its basic framework continues to survive.

State Constitutions

State constitutions vary in their organization and content, so it is difficult to summarize their contents. However, using the Illinois Constitution as an example, there are 14 articles covering such topics as a bill of rights (for example, freedom of speech, due process protections, and the rights of one accused of a crime) (Article I), powers of the state (Article II), the respective branches of the government (Articles IV, V, and VI), and the manner in which the state constitution can be revised (Article XIV). Clearly, a state constitution will include topics similar to those included in the federal Constitution. However, it is important to note that because the United States Constitution is the principal law, no state law (or court, for that matter) can reduce the guarantees afforded by that law.

Separation of Powers of Government

The Separation of Powers Doctrine is an essential foundation of constitutional law and the respective organization of the United States and state governments. Basically it is the practice of dividing the powers of a government among its constituent parts to avoid a concentration of power in any one part, which could lead to abuse.[14] In the United States Constitution there are two parts to the doctrine: a *functional* demarcation between the government and the governed and between the branches of the govern-

ment (the legislative, executive, and judicial); and a *regional* distinction between federal and state governments.[15]

State constitutions also utilize the functional demarcation. The regional distinction is also incorporated within state constitutions; however, its character is composed of a delineation between the state and local governments.

. . . on both the federal and state levels, there is a tripartite system of government, each branch having its own distinct powers.

Thus, on both the federal and state levels, there is a tripartite system of government, each branch having its own distinct powers. For example, the legislative division (Congress or a particular state legislature) passes laws. In contrast, the executive branch (the President or the Governor) is charged with carrying out the laws enacted by the legislature. The judicial division is responsible for interpreting, construing, applying, enforcing, and administering the laws of the state or federal government.[16]

This organization serves as a system of checks and balances within the three components of a particular government to ensure a balance of power among the three. For example, when a decision is made by the United States Supreme Court (judicial branch) that interprets a particular federal law contrary to Congress's (legislative branch) intent when that law was passed, Congress can, through its established processes, pass another amendment to the law in question that essentially nullifies the Supreme Court decision. Or, if the Governor of a particular state vetoes a particular bill the state legislature has passed, it can attempt to override the veto in a special legislative session.

Some of the powers exclusively given to one branch of government may be exercised by another branch as well. For example, on the state level, the Governor appoints heads of administrative agencies, such as the head of the department responsible for enforcing professional practice acts. In essence, the Governor delegates to the appointed head the power to carry out the acts. Any delegated power cannot be exceeded, however. If that does occur, then there can be a challenge to the actions of the agency, person, or department that has allegedly exceeded the powers delegated to perform the responsibilities of the position.

Also, the President of the United States (executive branch) can issue executive orders or regulations (legislative function) that provide guidance for the implementation of, interpretation of, or credence given to a particular provision of the Constitution, a law, or a treaty.[17] The power to issue the orders or regulations, published in the *Federal Register* and codified in Title 3 of the *Code of Federal Regulations*, illustrates a *unique* variation of the executive branch's traditional power.

Individual Rights and Governmental Powers

A right is a power or privilege to which a person is entitled.[18] There are various rights, including moral, human, and legal ones. Each right possesses a different basis and character. Human rights, for example, are basic and fundamental ones that every individual should enjoy. They are expressed in many documents, including the United Nations' Universal Declaration of Human Rights.

A right is a power or privilege to which a person is entitled.

Legal rights, in contrast, are those conveyed by constitution, statute, or common (case) law.[19] They include personal rights (e.g., personal liberty), civil rights (e.g., trial by jury and the equal

protection of the laws), constitutional protections (e.g., freedom of speech and the press), and political rights (e.g., voting and citizenship).

Furthermore, a right may be absolute or conditional.[20] Thus, a nurse has the right to believe whatever he or she wants to. However, when that belief impinges on another person's rights, as when the belief is used in a discriminatory manner not to provide care to a particular group of patients, then the right of acting on that belief becomes conditional.

Rights may also be substantive or procedural. Substantive rights are the rights themselves—that is, the essence of the particular power or privilege. Procedural rights are those that govern the process and methods whereby governmental policies are carried out and actions occur. For example, a nurse may have his or her First Amendment right of free speech violated, which is a substantive violation. In addition, however, if this violation took place without the government utilizing the required approach in limiting or restricting the speech (refusing to respond to the nurse's request for a rally permit, for example), then the nurse would be able to allege a procedural violation as well.

The individual rights guaranteed by the United States and the various state constitutions are numerous, complex, and ever changing in terms of their character. Although they will be discussed as they relate to the nurse as an individual and as a professional in various chapters throughout this book, a brief, general overview of selected rights follows. Such an approach will aid the reader in further developing knowledge about them when studying a particular right in subsequent chapters.

First Amendment Rights

First Amendment rights, such as freedom of religion, press, and speech, are self-explanatory. However, these individual rights can change their character in health care. For example, freedom of religion takes on a new meaning when an individual refuses treatment based on his or her religious beliefs. Moreover, the right becomes more complex when it is exercised by a parent on behalf of a minor child.

Likewise, when a nursing faculty member's ability to speak in class is limited in some way by a public institution, his or her First Amendment rights are potentially at risk. Similarly, if a public university limits a nursing student's ability to participate in a rally against restricting abortion rights, his or her right of association is threatened.

Fourth Amendment Rights

The freedom from unreasonable searches and seizures clearly includes protection from governmental invasion of one's home without justification and the rights afforded to one accused of a crime when there is an attempt to use evidence at trial in violation of these rights. This amendment, and parallel state constitutional protections, also protects the nursing student in a public university who may be asked to provide a urine or blood sample for drug screening or a patient in a governmental hospital who is searched for drugs in its emergency room.

Fifth and Fourteenth Amendment Rights

The Fifth and the Fourteenth Amendments to the United States Constitution protect certain individual rights from being restricted by the federal and state governments, respectively. Both amendments state, among other things, that no federal or state government can deprive a person of "life, liberty, or property" without due process of law. Throughout the Bill of Rights' history, this language has been at the center of a multitude of lawsuits that have attempted not only to define what due process is, but also to delineate what life, liberty, and property include.

What is clear is that life, liberty, and property protected in these amendments have literal interpretations as well as more abstract meanings.

For example, a criminal accused of a crime is afforded many protections during the legal process so that his or her liberty and, possibly, life are not taken without due process. Furthermore, a person's real property—a house or parcel of land—cannot be taken by the government for a state road or federal highway without due process. These amendments protect more conceptual rights as well, such as a nursing license (property) or one's reputation and ability to be accepted into an academic program (liberty).

In addition, the Fourteenth Amendment's protections have been extended by various court decisions to other situations not specifically mentioned in the amendment's language. One such protection is the right of privacy. Thus the protection of privacy has been interpreted to mean that one has a right to refuse treatment, to have an abortion, and to decide whether or not to use birth control without undue governmental restriction.

Procedural due process . . . has been defined by the courts as what is fair *under the circumstances.*

Although still far from clear, due process has generally been divided into two types: *procedural* and *substantive.* Procedural due process, like procedural rights, is composed of the methods used by the government in executing its policies. Thus, it has been defined by the courts as what is *fair* under the circumstances. To define each and every circumstance and each and every procedural protection that would be afforded in those circumstances would be difficult, however. Therefore, courts have customarily looked at the right that might be limited or eliminated by the particular government and then determined what process would be due to ensure fairness. Thus an individual charged with a crime would be afforded *more* due process protections than would an individual whose driver's license needed renewal.

Keep in mind that due process protections are mandated only when the federal or state government encroaches upon individual rights guaranteed by the two respective amendments. The requirement does not apply to private actions. When a state government is involved, the action is called "state action" or is referred to as being carried out "under color of state law."

Fourteenth Amendment's Equal Protection Clause

The Equal Protection Clause located in the Fourteenth Amendment to the United States Constitution prohibits state governments from making unreasonable classifications in its laws. The federal government is also prohibited from doing so in the Fifth Amendment's Due Process Clause.[21]

In essence, this mandate requires that all people similarly situated be treated the same under the law of the particular government. This mandate has also been tested in the courts throughout its history with varying results. Many of the differences in court decisions can be attributed to many factors, including (1) the existence of a *reasonable*, as opposed to an *unreasonable*, classification being passed by a government; and (2) individuals challenging a particular law not being "similarily situated" to the group or class they were comparing themselves to.

If there is an equal protection challenge to a particular governmental classification, the court will evaluate the distinction by utilizing several tests. If, for example, the categorization creates a "suspect class"—based on race or national origin—or impacts a *fundamental* right, the "compelling interest" or "strict scrutiny" test will be applied. The category would be upheld under this test only if it promoted a compelling interest or purpose of the government.

A second test applied by the courts to evaluate governmentally based classes is the "rational basis" test. This test is used for laws relating to economics and social welfare issues. If the questioned law is "rationally related to a legitimate governmental interest" and not arbitrary, it can be upheld.

A third test relates to those classes that are not included in the first two categories. It has been called the "rationality plus" test, and is often used by the court when interpreting a classification impacting sensitive classes, such as those of gender. So long as there is a "fair and substantial" relationship to a government's purpose, the classification is often found to be constitutional.

An example of the equal protection concept would be the state's ability to regulate the practice of nursing. Classifications exist in nurse practice acts regulating who can obtain a professional or practical nursing license and who cannot. This is a legitimate exercise of the state's police power in regulating the practice of the nursing profession. If that regulation became discriminatory, however, it could be challenged.

For example, if a state did not allow males who met the requisite requirements to apply for a nursing license, a male could try to challenge the classification and the way in which it was administered in his situation as a violation of his equal protection rights. Most probably, the court would apply a "rationality plus" test, and unless the state could show that gender was related to a particular governmental purpose, the classification would be struck down as unconstitutional.

THE LEGISLATIVE PROCESS

Federal Legislative Body

The legislative body of the federal government is Congress, which is composed of the House of Representatives and the Senate. Their composition and powers are spelled out in the United States Constitution. Each has a member who is the presiding "officer."

The Speaker of the House (of Representatives)

is elected by the majority party, and he or she conducts the House's business, appoints members of the select and house committees, and schedules legislation for floor action.[22] The Senate's presiding officer is the Vice-President of the United States. However, the majority leader, elected by the majority party, is the most powerful member of the Senate.[23] Both houses also have minority leaders and "whips," the latter serving to help in obtaining support for the particular party's legislation.

State Legislative Bodies

State legislative bodies, called a legislature or assembly, are similarly organized as in the federal system, although variations exist according to the state's constitution. For example, the Illinois General Assembly is composed of a senate and a house of representatives, whereas Nebraska's legislature consists of one house called a senate. In New Hampshire the legislature is called the General Court.

How a Bill Becomes Law

Initiation of the Process

Laws arise when a need or change is identified by someone. The impetus to initiate the legislative process can come from individuals, professional or voluntary groups, the Governor or President, or a legislator or assembly member. Once the idea concerning the proposed need or change is crystallized, the proposal is drafted into acceptable legislative form and language. Then a sponsor of the bill is obtained. The selection of a sponsor is critical to the success or defeat of the proposed bill, for the legislative sponsor's commitment to the proposal is vital if it is to survive the next step of the process.

Introduction of the Proposed Bill

Once drafted and prior to its introduction into the legislative body, a proposed bill is given a number. For example, if a bill is introduced into the House of Representatives, it is given an H.R.

designation and number (e.g., 1234). A proposed bill in the Senate is given an S. designation and number (1234). Proposed bills may also be the result of joint sponsorship from the two assemblies and would be denoted with an H.R.J. or S.J. title and number.

The impetus to initiate the legislative process can come from individuals, professional or voluntary groups, the Governor or President, or a legislator or assembly member.

Assignment to Committee

Once introduced into the "chamber of origin," the bill is assigned to a committee or subcommittee of that chamber. The assignment depends on the subject matter of the proposed legislation. For example, issues concerning Medicare Part B are shared by the Ways and Means Committee and the Energy and Commerce Committee.[24]

The work done while the bill is in committee is legion. Generally there are several actions that can be taken in reference to the proposal, including refusal to consider it; making major or minor changes; and approving and returning the proposal to the chamber floor.[25] If the bill is not rejected immediately, the committee work then involves four major activities: (public) hearings; "markups" (changes made in the legislation); voting on the proposal by the committee; and reporting back to the legislative body (to apprise the members so they can cast their votes).[26]

Floor Action

The proposed bill is sent to the "originating chamber" by the committee, and the bill is debated, amended, and voted upon. If it is defeated, then the proposed bill dies. If it is passed, it then goes to the other assembly, if one exists, and the entire process of committee work and floor action is repeated. Any differences in the proposed bill must be reconciled between the two chambers. If that does not occur, the proposed bill dies. If passed by the entire legislative body, the proposal is sent to the President or Governor for consideration.

Action by the President or the Governor

The chief executive has two options when proposed legislation reaches his or her desk. It can be signed or not signed within the applicable time frame (for example, the President of the United States has 10 days, excluding Sunday, to act upon the proposal); in either case, the proposal becomes law. The proposal can also be vetoed. If vetoed, the proposal is usually sent back to the legislative body with the chief executive's rationale for the veto.

If it so chooses, the state or federal legislative branch can attempt to override the veto pursuant to the respective constitution. For Congress, a two-thirds vote of each house will override the President's veto. For most state legislatures, a two-thirds or three-fifths majority of both houses is required.[27]

Bill Becomes Law

Many bills contain provisions that specify when the bill will become law. The provision may indicate that the effective date is 1 year from ratification or that enactment is immediate, or it may delineate some other time frame. If a bill does not contain an effective date provision, in the federal system a bill becomes law on the date it is signed by the President or on the date the veto is overriden. State procedures for effective dates vary if the date is not specified in the bill.

Once passed into law, the bill is given a public law designation and number. For example, Congress's designations indicate the Congress that passed the bill and what number the bill was. Thus, Public Law 101-625 indicates that the 101st Congress passed the 625th bill. Similar designations are given to state laws. For example, in Illinois, Act 87-806 indicates that the 87th General Assembly passed the 806th bill.

Implementation of the New Law

Once passed, the law must be carried out consistent with its stated purpose. A particular state or federal agency or agencies will have the responsibility to administer the act. This is most often done by passing rules and regulations consistent with the process established by state or federal law for doing so. This aspect of implementation is discussed at length in Chapter 7.

Budget/Revenue Concerns and the Legislative Process

The process of passing legislation in a state or the federal system is intricate. In addition to the logistics required in the procedure to pass a particular bill into law, there is also the need for revenue to carry out the newly passed law. State legislatures have varying powers to pass their own budgets, with or without executive oversight from the governor in the state. In Congress, appropriations bills originate in the House and must be passed by both chambers. Clearly, without revenues to carry out a particular piece of legislation, the newly passed law is truly a hollow victory.

Clearly, without revenues to carry out a particular piece of legislation, the newly passed law is truly a hollow victory.

SUMMARY OF PRINCIPLES AND APPLICATIONS

With all of its shortcomings, the United States Constitution has endured its initial test of time.

With its state counterparts, it has existed essentially unchanged since its inception. Likewise, the individual rights protected by the framers of the federal Constitution continue to exist, albeit in differing and ever changing ways. Whatever continues to occur with the various constitutions, the nurse must be constantly aware of how the state and federal charters affect his or her personal and professional life and the lives of patients. Thus the nurse needs to:

▼ Keep abreast of changes that occur in state and federal constitutions

▼ Identify constitutional concepts inherent in everyday life and professional practice

▼ Protect individual freedoms in all situations, but especially when delivering health care or teaching in any public institution

▼ Become involved in the legislative process by providing testimony at public hearings, writing legislators, participating in lobbying, and supporting bills that further health care and individual rights

▼ Actively support candidates for political office at the state or federal level who further individual rights and professional goals

▼ Consult with an attorney when individual rights are threatened to obtain both substantive and procedural protections

▼ Exercise the right to vote

▼ Be active in state and national nursing organizations, including Political Action Committees (PACs) that support individual and professional rights

▼ Never take individual freedoms or the United States' systems of government for granted

TOPICS FOR FURTHER INQUIRY

1. During a given period, identify constitutional rights that exist during the care of patients. Analyze how each right was protected or violated. Suggest ways in which the patients' rights could have been better protected.

2. Write a position paper on a patient right that conflicts with your belief(s) about that particular right. Identify the basis for your beliefs and suggest ways in which you can resolve the conflict between your beliefs and the patient's.

3. Track a bill affecting health care from its inception into the legislative process until its completion, either on the state or federal level. Evaluate nursing's participation, if any, in the process. Analyze how the bill would impact upon nursing practice if it became law. Suggest how nursing's involvement in the legislative process might have changed the process or the actual bill itself.

4. Interview a state or federal representative to determine his or her priority concerning a topic related to nursing practice. Identify the elected official's understanding of nursing practice and the profession. Discuss how many times nurses have contacted the representative concerning legislation affecting health care and the profession. Suggest ways in which communication between the representative and nurses could be improved.

REFERENCES

1. Ralph Chandler, Richard Enslen, and Peter Renstrom. *Constitutional Law Deskbook: Individual Rights.* 2nd Edition. Rochester, NY: The Lawyers Co-operative Publishing Company, 1993, 2 (with Cumulative Supplement issued April 1995).
2. *Id.* at 2–3.
3. *Id.* at 14.
4. *Id.* at 14.
5. John Neary, "Roots and Radicals," *Life Magazine* (Fall 1991), Bicentennial Issue: The Bill of Rights, 43, *quoting* James Madison.
6. See, generally, *Marbury v. Madison,* 1 Cranch 137 (1803).
7. Chandler, Enslen, and Renstrom, *supra* note 1, at 14.
8. Henry Campbell Black. *Black's Law Dictionary.* Abridged Sixth Edition. St. Paul, Minn: West Publishing Company, 1991, 214–215.
9. Chandler, Enstrom, and Renstrom, *supra* note 1, at 5.
10. *Id.*
11. U.S.C.A. Constitution of the United States, Preamble.

12. Ronald Rotunda, "Celebrating the Bicentennial of the Bill of Rights," 79 *Illinois Bar Journal* (December 1991), 610.

13. *Id.*

14. Chandler, Enslen, and Renstrom, *supra* note 1, at 60–64.

15. *Id.*

16. Black, *supra* note 8, at 591.

17. *Id.* at 395.

18. Chandler, Enslen, and Renstrom, *supra* note 1, at 691.

19. *Id.*

20. *Id.*

21. *Id.* at 308.

22. Marilyn Goldwater and Mary Jane Lloyd Zusy. *Prescription for Nurses: Effective Political Action.* St. Louis: C.V. Mosby Company, 1990, 85.

23. *Id.*

24. Pamela Mittelstadt and Mary Ann Hart, "Legislative and Regulatory Processes," in *Policy and Politics for Nurses: Action and Change in the Workplace, Government, Organizations and Community.* 2nd Edition. Diana Mason, Susan Talbott, and Judith Leavitt, Editors. Philadelphia: W.B. Saunders Company, 1993, 401–402.

25. *Id.* at 402.

26. *Id.* at 402–404.

27. Goldwater and Zusy, *supra* note 22, at 93.

2 The Nurse and the Judicial System

contents

The public views the judicial system and the law with many emotions: awe, confusion, mistrust, fear, and anxiety, to name a few. These emotions are probably the result of many factors, including prior experience with a particular aspect of the law or legal system or, alternatively, no exposure to the workings of the law.

Regardless of the basis of the emotions felt by the public, the law and the legal system are more intimately involved in each member's life, directly or indirectly, than is acknowledged. The law provides society with a set of rules to live by and highlights one's rights as well as responsibilities.[1] Thus, whether driving a car, starting a business, or practicing one's profession, the law and the judicial system are central to those activities. In fact, Lawrence Friedman, a well-known author on the historical development of American law, has described law ''as a mirror held up against life.''[2]

The American judicial system had its roots, as did much of the development of American law, in the English system.[3] Its character and structure have undergone immense changes from their early beginnings, including division of the system into civil and criminal courts, a separate system for federal and state courts, and development of special courts, such as juvenile and equity courts.

Despite its many changes, the roles of the judicial system have remained constant: dispute resolution, behavior modification, allocation of gains and losses, and policy making.

Despite its many changes, the roles of the judicial system have remained constant: dispute resolution, behavior modification, allocation of gains and losses, and policy making.[4] How those roles are carried out, and the ultimate decisions that are reached, do fluctuate by necessity, however, because the law—and its judicial system—reflect society's wishes and needs.[5]

This chapter will present an overview of the American judiciary, with particular emphasis on the civil trial system and its applicability to the nurse. Although some of the same information presented here is relevant to the criminal justice system, the latter is a distinct system with a distinct set of procedural, and other, rules.

THE JUDICIAL SYSTEM OR JUDICIARY

The judiciary is the branch of the government that interprets, construes, and applies the law.[6] It is composed of many parts and subparts or branches, including the state judicial system, the federal judicial system, respective trial and appellate courts, civil courts, criminal courts, and special courts.

The judiciary carries out its responsibilities with the help of prior decisions, federal and

---

KEY PRINCIPLES

Jurisdiction	Statute of Limitations
Pleadings	Legal Precedent
Summons	Stare Decisis
Subpoena	Res Judicata
Burden of Proof	

RELATED TOPICS

state statutes and their concomitant legislative history, and the federal and state constitutions. The various sources of law used by the judicial system are listed in Table 2–1.

There are also specific rules of procedure, both civil and criminal, both federal and state, that guide the courts and the various parties to a suit in relation to their conduct while a case is pending before the court.

Federal Judicial System

The federal system's basis for existence is Article III, Section 1, of the United States Constitution, which enables the United States judicial power to "vest in one Supreme Court, and in such inferior courts as the Congress may from time to time ordain and establish."[7] The federal system is composed of the federal district courts—the trial courts, the federal courts of appeals, and the Supreme Court. In addition, there are several special courts in the federal system that are analogous to the trial and appellate courts, but which hear specific types of cases, such as tax or military matters. Figure 2–1 depicts the organization of the federal courts.

There are 94 geographic federal district courts, or trial courts, with at least one in every judicial district.

There are 94 geographic federal district courts, or trial courts, with at least one in every judicial district. Most often, a judge, with or without a jury, hears cases in the district courts, although some of the trial courts use magistrates. A federal magistrate may try certain civil and misdemeanor criminal cases or may be given responsibilities such as pretrial hearings.[8] A decision by a federal district trial court is binding only on that district.

The actual trial process in a federal district court is the same as in a state trial court and is discussed in the section Essentials of the Civil Trial Process.

There are 13 United States Courts of Appeals, with only the District of Columbia comprising the 12th Circuit. The 11 geographic circuits are composed of varying numbers of states, as is illustrated in Figure 2–2. The 13th appeals court is the Court of Appeals for the Federal Circuit located in Washington, DC. It has 12 judges and hears appeals in patent law from all the other 12 federal trial courts.[9]

The appellate courts sit in review of cases appealed from the federal trial courts. The court's role is to ensure that the law was applied correctly by the trial court. Usually the cases are decided by a panel of three judges, although on special cases, the entire court can decide to re-

TABLE 2–1

Sources of Law

SOURCE	COMMENT
1. Federal Constitution	Balances powers of government and protects individual rights; includes Bill of Rights (first 10 amendments) and remaining amendments
2. Respective state constitutions	Balances powers of government and protects individual rights; may vary in terms of additional rights granted by each state over rights granted by federal Constitution
3. Statutes	Laws passed by Congress (federal), state, or local legislative bodies
4. Administrative law, rules, and decisions	Decided by agencies delegated this power by the respective legislative body
5. Common law	"Judge-made" or "court-made" decisions; based on precedent, custom, usage, and tradition; also called case law
6. Other	Executive orders from the President or the Governor; treaties; principles of equity

Data from: Persis Mary Hamilton and Nancy J. Brent, "Legal Issues," in *Realities in Contemporary Nursing*, by Persis Mary Hamilton. Menlo Park, Calif: Addison-Wesley Nursing, 1992, 218–223.

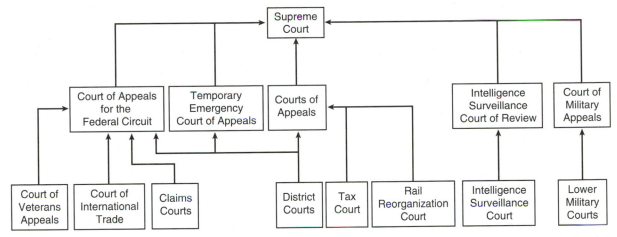

FIGURE 2–1 Organization chart of the federal court system. From Baum, Lawrence. American Courts: Process and Policy. 3rd Edition. Copyright © 1994 by Houghton Mifflin Company. Used with permission.

view a case *en banc* (full bench). Although the number of appellate judges in each district varies, the total number in the 12 appellate circuits is 156.[10]

A decision by a particular appellate court is not binding on any other judicial circuit, except for a decision by the Court of Appeals for the Federal Circuit, which, as stated above, reviews cases from *all* 12 circuits. Thus, only those states included in the particular circuit would be required to comply with a decision by its appellate court. If a decision that binds all states is sought, an appeal to the United States Supreme Court must occur.

> *The United States Supreme Court is the "supreme court of the land" and is therefore the final court to which a case can be appealed.*

The United States Supreme Court is the "supreme court of the land" and is therefore the final court to which a case can be appealed. The Court comprises nine justices. Most often, all of the justices participate in a decision *(en banc)*.

However, only four justices must agree to grant review of a case.[11]

One exception to the Court's full membership participating in a case is when a particular justice, in his or her role as a *circuit justice*, hears a special case from the circuit assigned to him or her when the Court itself has other matters pending before it. A common example of a special case that utilizes one justice to make a decision is a request for a stay of execution in criminal cases.

Like the appeals courts, the Supreme Court sits in review of cases from the lower federal and state courts.

It is important to note that federal judges and Supreme Court Justices are appointed by the President of the United States after being confirmed by Congress. This is in contrast to judges in the state system who are most often elected to their position.

State Judicial System

Because each state has its own judicial system, the state system has been described as really being a 50-state system as opposed to a unified, single one.[12] In addition, the District of Columbia and the territories of the United States also have their respective courts comparable to the

FIGURE 2–2 The eleven federal judicial circuits (see 28 U.S.C.A. § 41). Reprinted from *West's Law Finder: A Research Manual for Lawyers.* Copyright 1985 by West Publishing Company, with permission of the West Publishing Company.

state system. Because each state has the power to organize its own judicial system, each is unique, and no one system is representative of all of the others. Even so, there are some similarities that can be summarized.

> *. . . the state [judicial] system has been described as really being a 50-state system as opposed to a unified, single one.*

To begin with, the general framework of a state court system is identical to that of the federal system in that there are trial courts, appellate courts, and a state supreme court. However, the specifics of each state system may vary. For example, in regard to the trial courts, some states possess one level of trial court, as represented in Figure 2–3 (Illinois state court system), or there may be major and minor trial courts, meaning that they are divided in terms of the seriousness of the cases each division hears. If the latter structure exists, the major courts may function as appellate courts in reviewing some cases decided in the minor courts.[13]

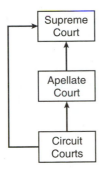

FIGURE 2–3 Organization chart of the Illinois Court System. From Baum, Lawrence. *American Courts: Process and Policy.* 3rd Edition. Copyright © 1994 by Houghton Mifflin Company. Used with permission.

Furthermore, some states have divided their trial courts into ones of general or limited jurisdiction. Illinois, for example, has given its trial courts general jurisdiction to hear all matters, despite the fact that the trial courts do have divisions, such as the traffic and the municipal courts.

The names of the state trial courts also vary. They may be called district courts, courts of common pleas, or circuit courts. In systems with limited jurisdiction or minor courts, they may be known as magistrate courts, justice of the peace courts, or juvenile courts.

State trial courts, or those considered "major" courts, can conduct jury and bench (in which the judge acts as the jury) trials, with a judge presiding. "Minor" courts and those with limited jurisdiction usually do not conduct jury trials.[14]

State appellate courts can be organized in either a one-tier or two-tier system.[15] Furthermore, some states divide their appeals courts into ones for criminal cases and ones for civil cases. How the appeals court hears their respective cases also varies; some use a panel of judges while others require the entire court to review an appealed case. Regardless of their structure, the appeals courts' jurisdiction is "mandatory"; that is, the court must hear each case appealed to it because of the fundamental doctrine in the judicial system that parties are entitled to one appeal.[16]

A state supreme court is the final court of appeal in the state system.[17] As such, its decision is binding only on the state in which it sits. The number of judges sitting on a state supreme court varies between five and nine.[18] How many state supreme court judges are needed to decide a case also varies from state to state. The jurisdiction of the court is generally discretionary, especially when lower appellate courts exist in the state system. As a result, the judges have the ability to decide which cases they will hear and which they will not decide. However, some cases must be heard by the state supreme court, including trial decisions from criminal courts that impose a life sentence or the death penalty.

Jurisdiction

Jurisdiction is the authority by which a court recognizes and decides cases.[19] The rules governing jurisdiction are set by respective state and federal constitutions and statutes, spelling out what kinds of cases a particular court can hear and which court is the correct forum for a particular case.[20] Jurisdiction can be defined as applied to one particular court (e.g., an Illinois criminal court) or the particular court system as a whole, such as the federal judicial system, including its organizational structure.[21]

Jurisdiction is the authority by which a court recognizes and decides cases.

The concept of jurisdiction is complex and varied, especially because of the two separate and distinct judiciaries in the United States, the state and federal systems. Even so, by analyzing each of these systems, certain common themes emerge. In doing so, it is helpful to think of jurisdiction both in terms of the two systems and in terms of a whole that incorporates both the essence and structure of the particular system.

Subject Matter Jurisdiction

Subject matter jurisdiction of the federal judicial system is predicated on the Constitution and various federal statutes. Thus a federal court hears criminal and civil cases such as those involving issues in which (1) the federal government is a party (federal party jurisdiction); (2) two or more states are parties (diversity jurisdiction); and (3) a challenge under federal law is raised (federal question jurisdiction).[22]

Subject matter jurisdiction in the state court system is defined by the state constitution and statutes and includes such issues as family matters, criminal matters, and the amount of money that is sought in the lawsuit.

Personal Jurisdiction

Personal jurisdiction in both the federal and state court systems is defined as the power of the court over the individual and is contrasted with *in rem* jurisdiction, meaning the court's power over one's property.[23] Depending on the nature of the suit—against the person, against a person's property, or both—the correct jurisdiction must be established for the court to render a judgment against the party or the party's property. Thus a suit in federal court could not be sustained if the particular court had no power over a nurse defendant, for example, located in Wyoming whose conduct was the subject of the suit.

Structural Jurisdiction

The structural jurisdiction of both the federal and state court systems is both vertical and horizontal.[24] In both systems the vertically organized courts are specified as either trial courts or appellate courts. The higher level courts function as courts of review or appeal from the courts

below.[25] Similarly, the horizontal courts, usually at the trial court level, possess specific jurisdiction to hear certain types of cases, such as domestic relations and probate (wills, guardianship) matters. Structural jurisdiction can be easily visualized by referring to Figures 2–1 and 2–2.

Venue

A particular concept related to the horizontal jurisdiction of a court system is that of venue. Although it is sometimes incorrectly referred to as jurisdiction, it involves the place or geographic area where a court with jurisdiction can hear and determine a case.[26] For example, depending on the particular state rules, if a nurse employee decides to sue her employer alleging a breach of an employment contract, the nurse must do so in the state court located where the case arose, where the nurse resides, or where the employer conducts business.

Legal Precedent

The American system of determining legal rights and responsibilities is based on prior case decisions, rulings, rationale, and custom. Thus, when a case, legal issue, or motion comes before the court, the judge must make a determination in *that* situation by reviewing prior case decisions and their rationale and applying those prior decisions to the case before the court. Generally the prior rulings are followed by the court. If either party is unhappy with reliance on the prior law, he or she can appeal the decision, particularly if it is believed there is a chance to "make new law" or challenge prior decisions because of some unique aspect of the case.

Stare decisis

In contrast to legal precedent, *stare decisis* ("to stand by cases decided") refers to the court following its own principles of law and those of inferior courts as applied to a particular set of facts.[27] Clearly, unless there is a superior court ruling or holding overturning decisions of the lower court, this doctrine binds the court hearing a particular case to apply the same ruling as has been reached before, so long as the facts of the current case fit within the principle of law decided earlier. Parties to the suit can always challenge a ruling based on *stare decisis* by appealing the decision to a higher court.

. . . stare decisis ("to stand by cases decided") refers to the court following its own principles of law and those of inferior courts as applied to a particular set of facts.

Res judicata

This rule stands for the principle that once a final decision in a case has been determined by a court having jurisdiction, it is binding on all of the parties and is therefore an absolute bar to any further legal action that involves the same claim, demand, or cause of action.[28] Thus, if a nurse is a defendant in a professional negligence claim and there is a final decision by a jury in his or her favor, the plaintiff in that case cannot file another case alleging the same causes of action against him or her for the same injury.

ESSENTIALS OF THE CIVIL TRIAL PROCESS

Despite the many variations that might exist among state court systems in organizational structure, there are certain common phases and steps in the trial process that exist in most state court systems. These phases and steps are helpful in many ways. Most important, they provide an organized and fair process for the resolution of the controversy that is the basis of the suit. Thus, one can determine how a case proceeds to trial and where in the judicial system a particular case may be—where it is pending—once it is filed.

Initiation of a Civil Suit

Evaluation of Possibility for Suit and Drafting Complaint

When an individual believes he or she has suffered a loss or injury because of someone else, whether the loss is bodily injury or property damage, the person will consult with an attorney concerning the possibility of filing a suit to compensate for the loss of injury. When the wrong suffered is allegedly the result of a health care professional's negligence, the attorney who is consulted will ask that the person obtain a copy of the medical record for review. If the potential cause of action (the grounds that serve as the basis for the suit) is based on another legal theory, such as a breach of contract, then any documents that would support the individual's theory would be reviewed by the attorney. In addition, the attorney would carefully interview the individual for additional information concerning the alleged wrong.

If the attorney determines that a suit can be initiated on behalf of the client, then a complaint is drafted and its accuracy is confirmed by the client. A complaint is one type of pleading. Pleadings are the formal, written allegations by parties in a case of their respective claims and defenses.[29] The state or federal rules of civil procedure—the procedures, methods, and practices to which attorneys and the court must adhere in civil cases—define, among other things, types of pleadings and their content. There are generally several pleadings utilized in civil cases. They are listed in Table 2–2.

The client who initiates the suit becomes the *plaintiff* (or *petitioner*) in the suit and those who are sued are the *defendants* (or *respondents*).

The complaint specifies with particularity the alleged wrongs of the defendants in paragraphs called *counts*. There may be one or several

TABLE 2–2

Common Pleadings in Civil Cases

NAME	PURPOSE
Complaint	To initiate case; must clearly inform defendant of allegations against him or her, relief requested; that plaintiff is entitled to relief; and that court has jurisdiction
Answer	Defendant's written assertion either denying plaintiff's allegations in the complaint or admitting them but then setting forth defenses against them
Counterclaim	Used by a defendant when a denial of the allegations in the complaint occurs and the defendant alleges his or her own causes of action against the plaintiff in the same case to defeat plaintiff's case
Reply	Plaintiff's response to defendant's counterclaim; can also be used after a motion is filed in a case (see Table 2–3) or at any other time the court orders either party to file one
Cross-claim	Used when co-parties—either co-plaintiffs or co-defendants—assert allegations against each other that are germane to the case and may avoid liability for that party
Third-Party Complaint	Used by defendant to bring third party into suit not originally sued by plaintiff, because third party may be liable for plaintiff's injury

Data from: Henry Campbell Black. *Black's Law Dictionary.* 6th Edition. St. Paul, Minn: West Publishing Company, 1991.

counts against a defendant or defendants. Figure 2–4 contains a portion of a sample complaint.

The plaintiff or petitioner who decides to bring the suit may also need to *verify* the complaint; that is, swear and sign under oath that it is accurate and truthful. If a complaint is verified, usually all other pleadings filed in the case must also be verified.

The attorney must also prepare a *summons.* A summons is the official notification to the defendant that a suit has been filed against him or her. The summons states that the defendant

is required to file his or her appearance, either himself or herself or through an attorney, and answer the complaint by a certain date. The summons must be attached to the complaint so that the defendant is appraised of the nature of the suit against him or her. A portion of a sample summons is contained in Figure 2–5.

A summons is the official notification to the defendant that a suit has been filed against him or her.

Filing the Suit

Once the evaluation and pleadings are complete, the suit must be filed with the court. This occurs by taking the summons and complaint to the clerk of the court's office where it is given a number that is required to be on all pleadings. For example, the case number often begins with the year the case is filed, followed by a designation as to the court division it is filed in, and is completed with the consecutive number of that particular case. Therefore, if a case were filed in the law division of a particular state court in the year 1992, it would have a number similar to 92 L 12345. The next case filed after it would have the number 92 L 12346.

The filed summons and complaint must then be *personally served* (delivered) to all of the defendants named in the suit. Service of the summons and complaint can take place in several ways, based on the state or federal civil practice rules, including by mail or by a sheriff or other agent delivering it to the defendant (or his or her agent) in the defendant's home or workplace. The defendant will not know about the case filed, or be required to respond to it, until receipt of the copy of the complaint and summons. The *service of process* formally begins the

IN THE CIRCUIT COURT OF COOK COUNTY
COUNTY DEPARTMENT-LAW DIVISION

Mary Jones,
        Plaintiff
 	
   v.
 	
ABC Hospital, Fred Free, M.D.,
and Susan Nega, R.N., M.S., individually
and as an employee of ABC Hospital,
        Defendants
	)
	)
	)
	) 92 L 1234
	)
	)
	)
	)
	)
	)
	)

COMPLAINT AT LAW

COUNT I

Now comes the Plaintiff, MARY JONES, by and through her attorney, SUSAN SMITH, and by way of her Complaint At Law against the Defendant, ABC HOSPITAL (hereinafter referred to as HOSPITAL), an Illinois not-for-profit corporation, alleges as follows:

1. On January 15, 1992, and for some time prior hereto, HOSPITAL operated a medical facility located in Chicago, Cook County, Illinois, for the care and treatment of patients.

2. On January 15, 1992, and for some time prior thereto, HOSPITAL undertook the care and treatment of the Plaintiff, MARY JONES.

3. Specifically, Plaintiff, MARY JONES came to HOSPITAL'S EMERGENCY ROOM on or about January 15, 1992, complaining of severe chest pain at about 10:45 a.m. . . . .

COUNT II

Now comes the Plaintiff, MARY JONES, by and through her attorney, SUSAN SMITH, and by way of her Complaint At Law against the Defendant, FRED FREE, M.D., alleges as follows:

1. On January 15, 1992, and for some time prior thereto, FRED FREE, M.D. was a licensed physician in the State of Illinois, having received his license in Illinois in 1967.

2. On January 15, 1992, and for some time prior thereto, FRED FREE, M.D. was employed by HOSPITAL as an Emergency Room physician. . . . .

COUNT III

Now comes the Plaintiff, MARY JONES, by and through her attorney, SUSAN SMITH, and by way of her Complaint At Law against the Defendant, SUSAN NEGA, R.N., M.S., alleges as follows. . . . .

1. On January 15, 1992 and for some time prior hereto, SUSAN NEGA, R.N., M.S. was a licensed professional registered nurse in the State of Illinois, having received that license in 1978.

2. On January 15, 1992, and for some time prior thereto, SUSAN NEGA, R.N., M.S. was employed by HOSPITAL as an emergency room nurse. . . . .

WHEREFORE, Plaintiff, MARY JONES, prays this honorable Court enter judgment in her favor and against the Defendant, SUSAN NEGA, in the amount of $30,000.00.

_____
Susan Smith, Attorney
for plaintiff, Mary Jones

FIGURE 2–4 Portion of sample complaint.

IN THE CIRCUIT COURT OF COOK COUNTY, ILLINOIS
COUNTY DEPARTMENT,   DIVISION

(Name all parties)   )
)
)
)
)
)
              v.   )   No. . . . .
)
)
)
)
)
)

SUMMONS

To each defendant:

   YOU ARE SUMMONED and required to file an answer to the complaint in this case, a copy of which is hereto attached, or otherwise file appearance in the office of the Clerk of this Court within 30 days after service of this summons, not counting the day of service. IF YOU FAIL TO DO SO, A JUDGMENT BY DEFAULT MAY BE TAKEN AGAINST YOU FOR THE RELIEF ASKED IN THE COMPLAINT, A COPY OF WHICH IS ATTACHED.

To the officer:

   This summons must be returned by the officer or other person to whom it was given for service, with endorsement of service and fees, if any, immediately after service. If service cannot be made, this summons shall be returned so endorsed. This summons may not be served later than 30 days after its date.

                                            WITNESS. . . . . 19. . .

                                            . . . .
                                            Clerk of court

Atty. No.
Name
Attorney for   Date of service. . . . . .19. . .
Address   (To be inserted by officer on copy
City   left with defendant or other
Phone   person)

FIGURE 2–5 Portion of sample summons. From: Cook County Circuit Court Form CCG-1 (7-90). Used with permission of the Clerk of the Circuit Court of Cook County, Aurelia Pucinski.

jurisdiction of the court over the defendant and the subject matter of the case.

It is important to remember that the case must be filed with the court within the applicable statute of limitations. A state or federal Statute of Limitations, along with the Statute of Repose included in the Statute of Limitations, specifies the time frames within which a case must be filed. For civil cases, the time limitations vary because of the nature of the suit and the various time frames adopted by the state or federal legislatures respectively in their civil practice rules and procedures. For example, an action alleging defamation must usually be brought within 1 year from the time the cause of action accrued, whereas a suit alleging professional negligence generally has a 2-year statutory limitation.

Filing of Appearance and Answer by Defendant

Once the defendant is properly served, a certain number of days—usually 30—is granted within which to respond to the complaint. The defendant's attorney will file an appearance with the court within the time frame so that the court has a record that the defendant is represented and has complied with the summons. A copy is also sent to the plaintiff's attorney.

In addition, if there are no objections raised by written motion as to the court's personal jurisdiction over the defendant or the subject matter, an answer to the allegations in the complaint is prepared, based on the defendant's discussions with his or her attorney. The answer is also filed with the court and a copy sent to the attorney for the plaintiff.

In addition to preparing an answer to the complaint, the attorney may determine that a counterclaim or a cross-claim is indicated (see Table 2–2). Either of those options would be filed with the answer.

It is important for the nurse to keep in mind that once served, he or she should not discuss anything about the case with anyone other than the attorney representing the nurse. The attorney representing the nurse sued for alleged professional negligence may use the attorney who works for the health care facility where the nurse is employed if, for example, the nurse is covered under the employer's professional liability insurance policy. Or the attorney may be one retained personally by the nurse if, for example, the nurse has purchased his or her own professional liability insurance.

A portion of a sample answer to the complaint in Figure 2–4 is illustrated in Figure 2–6.

Pretrial Phase

Period of Discovery

Once the court retains jurisdiction over the party or parties to a suit, the next step in the trial process is called the *period of discovery.* It is a time during which all the parties to a suit are given the opportunity to obtain information about the issues contained in the suit from the other parties, witnesses, or other sources. It also ensures a fair and equitable manner by which the parties obtain relevant information concerning the suit to avoid surprise concerning evidence should the case go to trial. It may also help settle a case prior to trial if adequate evidence indicates that a settlement might be an equitable manner of resolving the allegations in the suit.

Any of the parties in the suit has access to the same discovery methods. The more common ones will be addressed.

Written Interrogatories

These are questions that are directed at one party concerning information needed by the party who files them with the court and sends copies to all the other parties. The party to whom the questions are addressed must answer the questions in writing and under oath. The answers are also filed with the court and copies sent to all parties.

The questions would consist of information needed by the party who filed them. For exam-

IN THE CIRCUIT COURT OF COOK COUNTY
COUNTY DEPARTMENT-LAW DIVISION

Mary Jones, Plaintiff	)))
v.	)) 92 L 1234
ABC Hospital, Fred Free, M.D., and Susan Nega, R.N., M.S., individually and as an employee of ABC Hospital, Defendants	))))))))

ANSWER TO COMPLAINT AT LAW

Now comes the Defendant, SUSAN NEGA, R.N., M.S., by and through her attorney, NANCY J. BRENT, and by way of Answer to the Plaintiff's Complaint At Law, states:

COUNT I

Defendant, SUSAN NEGA, R.N., M.S., makes no response to Count I as Count I is not directed against her.

COUNT II

Defendant, SUSAN NEGA, R.N., M.S., makes no response to Count II as Count II is not directed against her.

COUNT III

1. Defendant admits the allegations in Paragraph 1 of Count III.
2. Defendant admits the allegations in Paragraph 2 of Count III.
3. Defendant . . . .

WHEREFORE, Defendant, SUSAN NEGA, R.N., M.S., denies that the Plaintiff is entitled to the relief prayed for or any relief whatsoever, and prays this honorable Court enter judgment in her favor and against the Plaintiff.

Nancy J. Brent, Attorney
for Defendant Susan Nega, R.N., M.S.

FIGURE 2–6 Portion of sample answer.

ple, in a professional negligence case against a nurse, the plaintiff might ask for information in the written interrogatories concerning the nurse's education, certifications, any involvement as a defendant in other professional negligence suits, and places of employment since graduation from his or her nursing program.

Deposition

A *deposition* is a procedure whereby a party in the case or a witness gives his or her statement concerning the case under oath with all parties and their attorneys present. If the deposition of a party to the case is requested, it is done by serving notice to the party's attorney. If, however, a non-party's deposition is requested, it is done by the court issuing a subpoena. The subpoena is used to ensure the presence of the person who is not named in the suit but whose testimony as a witness in a particular case is needed.

> *A deposition is a procedure whereby a party in the case or a witness gives his or her statement concerning the case under oath with all parties and their attorneys present.*

If the *subpoena* is a *subpoena duces tecum*, the person is required to appear *and* bring to the deposition (or trial) any specified documents in his or her possession that are relevant to the case.

The format in a deposition is a question and answer one; that is, the attorney who is taking the statement asks the deponent (the one giving the testimony) questions and the deponent answers them. A court reporter transcribes everything said during the deposition and reproduces the transcript of the deposition for use by the attorneys.

During the deposition, the other attorneys are given the chance to cross-examine the person giving the statement. In addition, throughout the deposition, objections to questions, answers, and other issues may be raised by any of the attorneys.

Depositions are an important method of discovery for several reasons. (1) Because the testimony is given under oath, any later deviation from the statement during trial can be used to impeach (question the credibility) the deponent. (2) Depositions provide the opportunity to "discover" the dependent; that is, to see how the deponent appears; how he or she responds to the questions asked; how credible he or she is; and other issues critical to the success or failure of the testimony at trial. (3) It can help obtain more information concerning the case in terms of potential additional witnesses (and defendants), in terms of whether settling the case may be more appropriate than proceeding to trial, and in terms of who might have been incorrectly included as a defendant.

Depositions can be taken as evidence depositions. If this is specified when the notice of the deposition is sent to all the attorneys involved, the statement will be introduced into evidence at the trial upon a motion by the attorney who asked that it be taken. Evidence depositions are used when there is a concern that a particular deponent may not be available at trial because of age, illness, or recently establishing residence in another state or country.

Request to Produce Certain Documents

A Request to Produce Certain Documents is used during the discovery phase to obtain materials and information from parties that are essential to the case. Most often, the Request will be filed prior to a deposition so that the materials and information can be utilized during the deposition.

A Request would be used, for example, when a nurse sues an employer alleging wrongful discharge. The nurse files the Request seeking copies of any and all material in his or her personnel file.

Request to Admit Facts

This type of discovery tool is used to ask that one of the parties admit or deny certain facts that are at issue in the case. The party to whom the Request is directed must file a response to the Request within a certain time frame and admit or deny what is asked in the Request. Most civil practice rules state that if the Request is not responded to, the information contained in the Request is admitted.

Like the Request to Produce Certain Documents, this tool is helpful in resolving many of the facts concerning the case as early as possible. Or, if facts are denied, it serves to crystallize the contested issues early in the pretrial process.

Court Motions and Orders

During the discovery phase, attorneys for all of the parties will seek orders from the court if it is determined that, for example, a party is not cooperating with the discovery process, if there are objections to the types or number of questions in the written interrogatories or deposition, or if a request for documents is unduly burdensome or irrelevant to the case. In addition, the court can dismiss a defendant from the suit during this phase if the results of discovery show that the particular defendant did not contribute to the injury or damages sustained by the plaintiff. A particular defendant might also ask for a judgment in his or her favor at this time, again because there was no liability for the alleged damages.

All of these requests are done through motions, in which the parties in a case, through their respective attorneys, ask that the court rule on a particular matter or order a party to do something or refrain from certain conduct. Most often they are written documents and are presented to the court after written notice has been given to all parties in the suit. Motions can, however, be oral, and these occur most often during a trial or hearing as legal issues and questions are raised for resolution by the court. Moreover, motions can take place *after* a trial;

for example, when a party asks the court to order a new trial.

Some of the more common motions in civil cases are presented in Table 2–3.

Pretrial Conference

The pretrial conference is the final step in the pretrial phase and is attended by the attorneys, the judge, and if they wish to be present, the parties to the case. Its purpose is to clarify and fairly resolve any pending issues in the controversy prior to trial. In addition, if possible, there is always the attempt to settle the case rather than have it proceed to trial. A settlement is not an admission of liability or fault; in fact, if a case is settled, any and all documents surrounding the settlement clearly state that the defendant admits no liability.

If a settlement is reached, the cause of action cannot be brought again against any of the defendants who participated in the settlement. It may be, however, that not all defendants settle with the plaintiff. If that occurs, the case would proceed to trial against any remaining defendants in the suit.

Factors that are evaluated in determining whether to settle a suit include the expense, both personal and financial, of continuing to trial; the credibility and strength of the evidence obtained during the discovery phase; and the uncertainty of what the jury's verdict will be at trial.

Trial Phase

Assignment of Case to Judge and Selection of Jury

When a case comes up on the trial calendar, it is immediately assigned to a trial judge. The trial judge is usually *not* the same judge who presided over the pretrial phase motions, period of discovery, and pretrial conference. If one of the parties has asked for a jury trial, the judge's role during the trial is that of "referee"; that is, he or she interprets the law as it pertains to the case before the trial court. The jury, after ruling on the facts of the case, renders a verdict.

TABLE 2–3

Common Motions in Civil Cases

NAME	PURPOSE
Quash service of summons	To render void the service of the summons and complaint on a party; if granted, requires another try at service because court does not have power over party unless properly served
Motion to Dismiss	Usually done before hearing or trial; attacks the suit by alleging insufficient legal basis to sustain suit
Motion for Summary Judgment	Asks court to dismiss case because there is no contest about the facts in the case and party making the motion entitled to ruling in his or her favor as a matter of law
Ex parte motion	Means "one side only"; may be used in rare circumstances in which giving notice to the other party may not be possible or helpful; is often used when one party seeks an injunction or restraining order against another
Discovery motions	Used during the discovery phase of a case when the parties are experiencing difficulties with each other in obtaining requested material or taking a deposition, for example; may also be used when unique discovery is needed or is not consistent with civil practice rules
Motion to Strike	Used when a party requests that biased, immaterial, or harmful information included in a pleading or in oral testimony be removed from the pleading or record and disregarded
Motion for Directed Verdict	Requested by either party during trial; asks that a verdict in his or her favor be granted because the party with the burden of proof did not meet that burden
Motion For Judgment Notwithstanding the Verdict	Requested by either party after judge or jury reaches decision; asks that despite decision, movant entitled to judgment in his or her favor
Motion for Mistrial	Requested by either party before the jury's verdict or judge's decision in order to render the trial void; can be due to a highly prejudicial remark or error; judge can also declare same if jury cannot make decision; a retrial must occur if mistrial granted

Data from: Henry Campbell Black. *Black's Law Dictionary.* 6th Edition. St. Paul, Minn: West Publishing Company, 1991.

If, on the other hand, there is no demand for a jury, then the judge also determines the facts at issue and renders a verdict. Jury trials are much more common than bench trials, however, and the selection of a jury usually follows the assignment of the trial judge.

Jury selection, the *voir dire*, is conducted by either the trial judge or the attorneys, depending on the state or federal civil practice requirements. In either case, questions are asked of the panel of potential jurors about matters relevant to the trial. Potential jurors may be dismissed (excused from jury duty) *for cause* (where prejudice or bias is found, for example) or *without cause* (preemptory challenges). Depending on the state or federal rules, each attorney in the case has a certain number of preemptory challenges.

The number of jurors needed in a civil trial varies. In federal courts and some state courts 12 jurors are required. Other state courts require only 6 jurors.[30]

Opening Statements

After the jury is selected, the trial begins with opening statements by all of the attorneys. The opening statement informs the jury of what that particular party intends to prove during the trial and what evidence will be used to do so. Most often, the plaintiff's attorney is the one who is the first to give his or her opening statement because the plaintiff has the burden of proving the case. The *burden of proof* means the obligation to affirmatively convince the judge or jury that the allegations contained in the complaint forming the basis of the suit are true. The burden is different, depending on the type of suit. For example, in a civil suit, the plaintiff must usually prove his or her case "by a preponderance of the evidence," whereas in a criminal case, the state must prove a criminal defendant guilty "beyond a reasonable doubt."

The burden of proof [for the plaintiff] means the obligation to affirmatively convince the judge or jury that the allegations contained in the complaint forming the basis of the suit are true.

Testimony of Parties and Witnesses

Plaintiff

The plaintiff is the first to present his or her case. Specifically, the plaintiff and any other witnesses are called individually to give their testimony under oath under the direct examination of the plaintiff's attorney. Witnesses that corroborate (strengthen or support) the plaintiff's testimony are usually called occurrence witnesses. However, other witnesses may be called, including an *expert witness.*

After each witness has testified under direct examination, the attorneys representing the defendants or other parties in the suit cross-examine the witness, each taking his or her turn individually. The purpose of cross-examination is to discount or render unimportant the witness' testimony in the eyes of the jury. After cross-examination, the attorney originally calling the witness, or the attorney for the party, can ask additional questions to rebut (refute) the testimony.

Once the plaintiff's attorney has called all witnesses, the attorney rests the case. The defendant's attorney then has a turn at presenting the case to the jury.

Defendant

Before beginning to call witnesses, the defendant's attorney will attempt to dispose of the case in his or her client's favor by asking the judge to grant a directed verdict (see Table 2–3) because the attorney will allege the plaintiff did not meet the burden of proof. If the judge grants the motion, the case is dismissed. Most often, however, such a motion is not granted by the judge, and the defendant then begins to present his or her case.

The attorney for the defendant then calls the defendant and witnesses to testify. As discussed, once each witness has testified, cross-examination takes place, and the ability to present rebuttal testimony also occurs. The defendant's attorney then rests the case once all the testimony and evidence has been presented to the court.

The defendant's attorney may again request that the court enter a directed verdict for his or her client. The plaintiff's attorney can also make the same request. If granted, the case is dismissed. If not, the next step in the trial process takes place.

Closing Arguments and Jury Instruction

Each side presents closing arguments, with the plaintiff doing so first. After all closing arguments have taken place, the judge then instructs the jury on the applicable law, how they are to determine money damages, and the burden of proof applicable to the hearing. In the federal judicial system and many state systems, the judge's instructions to the jury consist of suggestions from the attorneys in the case. In other states, model or pattern jury instructions exist that must be used, or substantially followed, by the judge.

The jury then retires to deliberate its verdict.

The Jury's Verdict

During its deliberations, the jury is sequestered (isolated from the public). Depending on the cause of action, or what the attorneys stipulated (agreed to), there may be a requirement for a unanimous verdict or a majority verdict. If no decision can be reached, a "hung jury" occurs, and a new trial would need to take place. If a decision is reached, however, and there are no challenges to that decision (e.g., tampering with the jury), then the jury announces its decision in open court and the judge enters a judgment and dismisses the jury.

Appeals Phase

If either party or parties are unsatisfied with the verdict, an appeal can be taken to the next highest court in the state or federal system. The party bringing the appeal is the *appellant*, and the one against whom the appeal is taken is the *appellee*. The appellant must file the notice of appeal in the manner and within the time specified in the applicable civil practice rules. Most often, appellants are required to file their notice within 30 days from the verdict.

The party bringing the appeal is the appellant, *and the one against whom the appeal is taken is the* appellee.

Depending on the subject matter of the case and the appeal, the appellate court may be *mandated* to review the case, or the review may be *discretionary*. If a discretionary review, it is often done through a petition asking the court to review the case. When such a request is made, it is called a *writ of certiorari*.

If the appellate court decides to review a decision of a lower court, it does so based upon the record in that hearing or trial, briefs, and other documents submitted by the appellant and appellee, and in some states, oral arguments by the attorneys. Once a decision is made, it is binding on the parties unless the next level of appeal is taken.

Appeals courts have the power to affirm lower court decisions (in which case the lower court ruling is final); to overturn the decision (in which case the lower court must render a verdict consistent with the higher court's decision); or to reverse, modify, or vacate a decision (in which instance the case is remanded [sent back] to the lower court for additional consideration).[31]

Ensuring Compliance with the Final Outcome

Once all appeals have been taken, the final outcome of the litigation must be complied with by the losing party or parties. Thus, if the case involved the professional negligence of a nurse and the judgment against the nurse was upheld, then the nurse must pay whatever monetary amount of damages he or she was found responsible for. If, in contrast, the nurse was a plaintiff who sued a former employer for wrongful discharge, and the court decision included the reinstatement to his or her position, that reinstatement would have to occur without delay.

If a defendant refuses to comply with the final outcome of the case, it is necessary to ensure it through various legal procedures. For example, if damages are not paid as ordered by the court, then an *execution of judgment* to enforce payment is filed. Or, an *injunction* may be sought to require a party to follow the judgment of the court or jury.

Role of the Nurse in the Trial Process

Obviously the nurse may be involved in the trial process in any of the roles discussed. The nurse may be a plaintiff in a suit if he or she, for example, sues an employer for wrongful discharge or defamation. However, the nurse's role as a defendant is perhaps the most familiar role, particularly in relation to professional negligence suits. Even so, the nurse may also be involved in the trial process as an *occurrence witness;* that is, someone who will be able to support or refute allegations against another nurse colleague or other party. Last, and by no means least, the nurse may be an expert witness (either the plaintiff or the defendant's expert) in a professional negligence suit against a nurse.

ALTERNATIVES TO THE CIVIL TRIAL PROCESS

Factors such as financial cost, length of time, and the adversarial nature of the litigation process had fueled dissatisfaction with the trial process as a means of settling controversies between litigants. Although alternatives to litigation (called alternative dispute resolution) existed in the United States since before the Declaration of Independence and the Constitution,[32] they were not utilized extensively by society as a whole (business and labor sectors being an exception).[33] As a result, in 1979, the alternative dispute resolution (ADR) movement began.[34] Its purpose was to identify alternatives to litigation when legal conflicts arose among parties. In 1982, then–Chief Justice Warren Burger challenged the legal community to develop methods to reduce the cost and time of litigation.[35]

Alternative dispute resolution (ADR) . . . include(s) but is not limited to mediation, arbitration, conciliation, and screening panels.

The end result of these, and other, efforts to establish and/or use alternatives to litigation has resulted in several options to the trial process. They include but are not limited to mediation, arbitration, conciliation, and screening panels. These alternative dispute resolution methods are used regularly today and are an effective means of deciding all kinds of disputes. Furthermore, in at least 20 states, including Illinois, court-mandated arbitration or mediation exists.[36]

In addition to the establishment of alternative dispute resolution methods discussed thus far, others have been established by state and federal laws for particular situations. In relation to health care, for example, on the federal level, the Federal Mediation and Conciliation Services (FMCS) has the power to conduct mandatory mediation of contract negotiation disputes when difficulties exist among employers, employees, and a union under the National Labor Relations Act (NLRA). In addition, some states have passed legislation providing for arbitration when a disagreement arises between a patient and a health care provider and the parties have a written agreement to submit the disagreement to binding arbitration.[37]

Although the purpose of each alternative dispute resolution method is to avoid litigation, the procedures vary. A comparison of the more common options is important for the reader to understand their commonalities and differences. It is important to keep in mind, however, that the methods may be combined or blended to form "hybrid" alternatives in a particular situation or state.

Mediation

Mediation is usually an informal process in which the parties in dispute will attempt to voluntarily resolve their differences by utilizing a private mediator or mediation service. Hopefully, the process ends with an agreement between the parties concerning the disputed issues.

Mediation may also occur, however, as part of the litigation process and is then termed court-annexed mediation. For example, in some state courts, parties contemplating divorce when children are involved are required to see a mediator to attempt to resolve such matters as child custody and support. In court-required mediation, the mediator cannot make a decision concerning the issues discussed in mediation. Rather, he or she aids the parties to reach agreement concerning the issues under consideration so that they do not have to be litigated. A final report concerning the mediation, whether successful or unsuccessful, is usually filed with the court.

Mediation may also be ordered by the court when a motion is presented to the judge during a pending lawsuit. For example, if a nurse has filed for divorce and custody issues are not being easily resolved, the nurse's attorney may file a motion asking that the parties submit to mediation.

Arbitration

Arbitration is defined as a more formal process in which a dispute is submitted to a third neutral party, or a panel of arbitrators, to hear arguments, review evidence, and render a decision.[38] In some arbitration agreements, the decision rendered—the award—is given the same weight as a court decision; that is, it is *binding*. If so, it is final, and the parties must abide by the decision.

Arbitration is defined as a more formal process in which a dispute is submitted to a third neutral party, or a panel of arbitrators, to hear arguments, review evidence, and render a decision.

Arbitration may be voluntary and done by a private organization and result in a binding resolution. This often occurs, for example, in grievance procedures established by employers for employees who want to challenge a disciplinary action taken against an employee. Binding arbitration is usually the last step of the procedure. Most often, the procedure clearly spells out the process for the selection of the arbitrator, who is required to pay for it, and how

the decision of the arbitrator will be treated. Binding arbitration is also included in many union contracts whereby the union agrees to have any union member–employee's work-related problems submitted to an arbitrator rather than be put through the nonunion employee's grievance procedure.

Arbitration may also be required before litigating the issues in court, but the decision of the arbitrator is nonbinding.[39] With this approach, arbitration is similar to mediation.

A third approach to arbitration is court-annexed arbitration. Court-annexed arbitration is governed by a state mandatory arbitration act that includes the procedures and process of arbitration, including the types of cases that will be heard (for example, civil cases), any jurisdiction amounts required (for example, cases asking for compensation between $2500 and $15,000), and qualifications for arbitrators. Usually, court-annexed arbitration is not binding, and a losing party may reject the arbitrator's decision within the time specified in the particular arbitration act and then move for a *de novo* trial (starting anew).[40]

When arbitration does not involve court-annexed arbitration, arbitors are often selected by the parties from a list of qualified arbitors compiled by the Board of the American Arbitration Association. Or, for state and federal organizations that require arbitration, such as the railroad and airline industries, The National Mediation Board was established to promote and select arbitrators for contract disputes in those industries.[41]

Conciliation

The purpose of conciliation is to improve communications and decrease tensions between the parties to a dispute. A third neutral party attempts to do so by interpreting issues, providing any technical assistance that may be needed, and suggesting solutions.[42] The process may be informal or formal. Conciliation is often a part of the mediation or arbitration process.

Screening Panels

Screening panels have been established in some states, such as Indiana,[43] to aid in reducing the number of cases that are filed in court by serving to determine if the proposed case has merit. They are most often used in professional negligence cases, and the panel is composed of a judge, an attorney, a physician, and perhaps a member of the public. Based on the evidence presented to the panel, it decides whether the health care provider acted or failed to act in accordance with standards of care. Screening panel decisions are binding in some states and in others serve only as an advisory opinion. When the latter is the case, certain penalties may occur. For example, the party who proceeds to trial when the panel has decided the case is without merit may have costs assessed against him or her if the case is lost at trial. Other states, such as Illinois, have ruled the joint panels unconstitutional because the judge sitting on the panel shares decision-making capacity with nonjudicial members, thus violating the Illinois constitutional mandate of vesting judicial power with the judiciary.[44]

SUMMARY OF PRINCIPLES
AND APPLICATIONS

The civil judicial system, both federal and state, can be confusing for the nurse because it is complex and foreign. In addition, alternative dispute resolutions provide options that may prove more beneficial in terms of time and cost, but add to the general confusion concerning resolving disputes. The nurse can attempt to resolve uncertainty about the civil judicial system by

▼ Becoming familiar with his or her state civil judicial system

▼ Comparing the state judicial system with the federal court system

▼ Comparing and contrasting the state civil justice system with its criminal justice system

▼ Serving as a juror when summoned to do so in his or her state

▼ Obtaining legal representation when contemplating the filing of a civil suit, when served with a summons and complaint as a named defendant, or when subpoenaed to testify at a deposition or at trial

▼ Cooperating with legal counsel when involved in a civil suit, regardless of the role

▼ Investigating alternative dispute resolution methods and, if possible and beneficial, incorporating them into any employment agreement, employee handbook, or other legal document governing the relationship between the parties

▼ Becoming involved in efforts to improve the civil judicial system, whether state or federal

TOPICS FOR FURTHER INQUIRY

1. Review at least three employee handbooks from health care delivery systems and analyze the type(s) of alternative dispute resolution methods they use for employee grievance resolution.

2. Analyze the types of cases, and the awards given to plaintiffs, in cases in which a nurse is a named defendant during a 2- or 3-month period in the state and federal court in your state.

3. Attend a nursing negligence trial, identify the role(s) of any nurse in the trial, and evaluate his or her effectiveness in that role.

4. Do a comparative study of the number of civil cases involving nurses with civil cases involving at least three other health care providers.

REFERENCES

1. Henry Campbell Black. *Black's Law Dictionary*. 6th Edition. St. Paul, Minn: West Publishing Company, 1991, 612.

2. Lawrence Friedman. *A History of American Law*. New York: Simon & Schuster, 1985, 695.
3. *Id*. at 19.
4. Lawrence Baum. *American Courts: Process and Policy*. 2nd Edition. Boston: Houghton Mifflin Company, 1990, 6–8.
5. Friedman, *supra* note 2, at 695.
6. Black, *supra* note 1, at 593.
7. U.S.C.A. Const. Article III Section 1.
8. Baum, *supra* note 4, at 30–31.
9. Ray Reynolds, "How The Legal System Works", in *You and the Law*. Lincolnwood, Ill: Publications International, Ltd., 1990, 46 (An American Bar Association Consumer Guide).
10. *Id*.
11. *Id*. at 48.
12. Baum, *supra* note 4, at 21.
13. *Id*. at 43.
14. Reynolds, *supra* note 9, at 43.
15. Baum, *supra* note 4, at 45–46.
16. *Id*.
17. Henry Abraham, *The Judicial Process*. 6th Edition. New York: Oxford University Press, 1993, 142.
18. *Id*. at 46.
19. Black, *supra* note 1, at 594.
20. Baum, *supra* note 4, at 22.
21. *Id*.
22. Ralph Chandler, Richard Enslen, and Peter Rentrom. *Constitutional Law Handbook: Individual Rights*. Rochester, NY: The Lawyers Cooperative Publishing Co., 1987, 521 (with April 1995 Cumulative Supplement).
23. Black, *supra* note 1, at 792.
24. Baum, *supra* note 4, at 24.
25. *Id*.
26. Black, *supra* note 1, at 1079–1080.
27. Black, *supra* note 1, at 978.
28. *Id*. at 905.
29. Black, *supra* note 1, at 798.
30. Baum, *supra* note 4, at 197.
31. *Id*. at 276.
32. Bette J. Roth, Randall Wulff, and Charles Cooper, Introduction, in *The Alternative Dispute Resolution Practice Guide*. Rochester NY: Lawyers Cooperative Publishing, 1993, Chapter 1:1, 2–3.
33. *Id*. at 3.
34. Larry Ray, "Emerging Options in Dispute Resolution," *American Bar Association Journal* (June 1989), 66.
35. Judge Robert Byrne, James Woodward, and John Lapinski, "Court Annexed Mandatory Arbitration Practice and Procedure in Illinois," *Chicago Bar Association Record* (May 1990), 14.
36. Reynolds, *supra* note 9, at 59.
37. See, for example, Smith Hurd Annotated 710 ICLS 15/1 *et seq*. (1976).
38. *Paths To Justice: Major Public Policy Issues of Dispute Resolution*. Report of the Ad Hoc Panel on Dispute Resolution and Public Policy. National Institute for Dispute Resolution. Appendix 2 (October 1983), *cited in* "Arbitration vs. Mediation—It's Time To Settle The Differences" by John Cooley. *Chicago Bar Record* (January/February 1990), 206.
39. Ray, *supra* note 34, at 67.
40. Roth, Wulff, and Cooper, "Judicial Arbitration", in *Dispute Resolution Guide, supra* note 32, Chapter 22:1, 2–3.
41. James Hunt and Patricia Strongin. *The Law of the Workplace: Rights of Employers and Employee*. 3rd Edition. Washington, D.C.: The Bureau of National Affairs (1994), 170.
42. Ray, *supra* note 34, at 60.
43. See, for example, Burns Indiana Statutes Annotated. Title 16, Chapter 9 Section 16-9, 5-9-1 *et seq* (1977).
44. *Bernier v. Burris*, 497 NE 2d 763 (Ill. 1986).

3

Concepts of Negligence, Professional Negligence, and Liability

contents

Negligence is a fairly familiar term to most individuals, whether they be professional nurses or laypeople. However, a clear understanding of what constitutes negligence and professional negligence or malpractice is elusive for many of those same individuals. Indeed, it has been only since the early part of the nineteenth century that the law has held negligence to be a distinct basis of liability, separate from other types of tort actions.[1] Since this separation, however, negligence has emerged as the "dominant cause of action for accidental injury in this nation today."[2]

This chapter will present the theory of negligence, professional negligence, and liability when negligence is found to be present. Information will focus on the elements, standards of care, and defenses to a cause of action in negligence. In addition, special considerations in this area of the law will be discussed, including Product Liability Law and Wrongful Death Actions.

ESSENTIALS OF NEGLIGENCE AND PROFESSIONAL NEGLIGENCE LAW

Definitions

Tort Law

Tort law includes negligence and professional negligence. The word *tort* is derived from the

RELATED TOPICS	
Chapter 2	The Nurse and the Judicial System
Chapter 4	Professional Negligence: Prevention and Defense
Chapter 5	Quality Assurance and Risk Management

Latin word "tortous." In the French language, a tort is a civil wrong, other than breach of contract, in which the law will provide a remedy by allowing the injured person to seek damages.[3] The definition describes the conduct that is the basis of a tort: conduct that is "twisted," "crooked," "not straight."[4] The law of torts seeks to protect others from unreasonable and foreseeable risks of harm by enforcing duties established by law that individuals have to each other. It does so by allowing compensation (money) to the victim of the injury "at the expense of the wrongdoer."[5]

> *A tort is a civil wrong, other than breach of contract, in which the law will provide a remedy by allowing the injured person to seek damages.*

KEY PRINCIPLES
Tort
Negligence/Professional Negligence
Personal Liability
Vicarious Liability
Respondeat superior
Corporate/Institutional Theory of Liability
Res ipsa loquitur
Expert Witness
Statute of Limitations
Immunity from Suit

Negligence

Negligence is defined as "conduct which falls below the standard established by law for the protection of others against unreasonable risk of harm."[6] The unreasonable risk of harm in negligence includes the concept of foreseeability. That is, the harm that occurred could be anticipated by the defendant at the time of injury because a reasonable likelihood existed that it could take place.[7] The conduct in question is measured by an objective standard of "due care" in the circumstances and has come to be known as "the ordinary, reasonable, and prudent" person standard (of care). In other words, when negligence is alleged, the conduct complained of is compared with what the ordinary, reasonable, and prudent person would have done in the same or similar circumstances. If the conduct being analyzed is in conformity with this objective gauge, then the individual is not negligent. If, however, the jury determines that the behavior was not consistent with this standard, then a verdict is returned against the person, supporting that he or she was negligent.

In every negligence action, four essential elements must be proven for a cause of action in tort to be successful:

1. A duty must exist between the injured party and the person who allegedly caused the injury
2. A breach of the duty must occur
3. The breach of duty must be the proximate (legal) cause of the injury (including the element that the defendant's conduct was the "cause-in-fact" of the injury)
4. Damages or injuries or both, which are recognized and compensable by law, must be experienced by the injured party[8]

In instances in which the defendant's or defendants' conduct was "evil," "outrageous," or intentional, damages may consist not only of compensatory payment, but "punitive" or "exemplary" damages as well. The latter serve as a deterrent, at least in theory, to warn others in society that such conduct will not be tolerated.

Negligent conduct can occur when acts of commission or omission take place. For example, negligent conduct can be alleged when an individual does something in a negligent manner or does something that an ordinary, reasonable, and prudent person *would not* do. This type of conduct is negligence by commission. In contrast, negligence by omission takes place when one fails to do something when a duty exists to do so. For example, a driver who fails to stop at a stop sign (duty exists) and runs into another car traveling through the intersection most probably would be found negligent. By not stopping at the sign, he or she could be found just as negligent as the driver who *does* stop, but who does not look carefully before proceeding into the intersection and hits the car.

It is important to be clear about the fact that in negligence the individual does not *intend* or *want* to bring about the injury or injuries that result from his or her behavior. Rather, the essence of the law of negligence is that the individual, knowing there is a risk of those results, has a duty to "anticipate them and guard against them."[9]

Nonprofessional negligence claims include suits filed for property damage (an improperly built garage, for example, which collapses on the car parked in it), personal injury (the improperly built garage collapses onto an individual in the garage at the time), or both. Most of the personal injury cases filed, however, result from injuries sustained in motor vehicle accidents.[10]

Professional Negligence

Professional negligence (or professional malpractice as it may also be called) involves the conduct of professionals (e.g., nurses, physicians, dentists, and lawyers) that falls below a professional standard of due care. Professionals possess knowledge, skill, and expertise upon which laypeople rely. Therefore, the law requires that their conduct be in conformity with the applicable standard of care for that professional group. The applicable standard includes a "standard minimum of special knowledge and ability."[11]

---

*Professional negligence . . .
involves the conduct of
professionals (e.g., nurses,
physicians, dentists, and lawyers)
that falls below a professional
standard of due care.*

Thus, for the professional nurse, when alleged negligent conduct occurs and a patient is injured, the nurse's conduct should be compared with that of other ordinary, reasonable, and prudent professional nurses in the same or similar circumstances. Furthermore, for professionals, generally, the standard of due care is framed in relation to what the reasonably well qualified professional(s) in the same or similar locality would do.

The latter standard, known as the locality rule, has been utilized less and less by many jurisdictions during the last several years. The justification for the application of a "national" standard, as opposed to a "local" one, has been the development of methods of communication and information exchange, the availability and use of new technologies and national licensing examinations, among other factors. Thus, the need for different standards of care for different geographic areas is no longer necessary. Even so, some jurisdictions still use the locality standard, or some remnant thereof.

In either event, the standard is established by an expert witness who testifies at the trial. An expert witness is an individual who, by training, education, and/or experience, is qualified by the court as able to assist the jury in understanding subjects not within the knowledge of the average layperson.[12] Many states have specific statutory provisions in their civil practice rules concerning who can function as an expert witness. In professional negligence suits, an expert witness is generally required because the jury's knowledge about health care and health care professionals is limited. Thus, the standard of care, and an opinion whether it was met in a case before the court, must be testified to by the expert witness.

The expert witness may come from another jurisdiction than the nurse defendant, or may be from the nurse's own state. He or she will be required to testify in accordance with whatever rule—local or national—is used in that state to establish the standard of care.

Liability

Although often defined in many diverse ways, liability, when the word is used liberally, means responsibility for a possible or actual loss, penalty, evil, expense, or burden for which law or justice requires the individual to do something for, pay, or otherwise compensate the victim.[13]

For example, the rule of personal liability holds everyone responsible for his or her own behavior, including negligent behavior. This rule makes it difficult, if not impossible, to shift liability totally to another person or entity.

. . . the rule of personal liability holds everyone responsible for his or her own behavior, including negligent behavior.

Vicarious liability, also called imputed liability or imputed negligence, refers to the responsibility one is found to have for the actions of other individuals because a special relationship exists between those individuals.[14] A common example of such a special relationship is that of employers and employees (master/servant). The basis of this theory is that when employees are hired to carry out the business of the employer, injuries may occur. When they do happen, the employer is in a better position to bear the financial cost of injuries to consumers than to assess it against the injured party.[15] Furthermore, if the employer may also be held responsible for employees' negligent acts, it is an incentive to the employer to hire, orient, and carefully supervise employees to reduce, insofar as it is possible, the employer's liability under this doctrine.[16]

Respondeat superior

Respondeat superior is a Latin term meaning "let the master speak," and is based on vicarious liability. It requires that, for the employer (master) to be vicariously liable for the negligent acts of employees (or its agents), the act must have occurred during the employment relationship *and* have been part of the employee's job responsibilities (that is, within the employee's scope of employment). Thus, if a nurse who is an employee of a particular hospital is providing care within the scope of his or her job responsibilities (e.g., giving an injection) and an injury takes place, the injured patient alleging negligence can sue the nurse *and/or* the hospital under this theory of liability.

There are two unique applications of the *respondeat superior* doctrine. One is called the borrowed servant doctrine and the other is titled the captain of the ship rule. Traditionally, both have been applied to the operating suite, but with the many changes in health care delivery today, their applicability to *any* service in the hospital is possible. What each doctrine does, briefly put, is to shift the employer-employee relationship from the hospital *to* another health care provider or entity vis-à-vis the nurse.

With the borrowed servant approach, the employer of the staff nurse in the operating suite becomes the physician, not the hospital. For the doctrine to apply, however, the staff nurse must technically become the physician or surgeon's "temporary employee"—that is, working under the direct control and supervision of that individual—during the operation. The individual who becomes the temporary employer of the employee must be in a position to exert specific control over the staff nurse in relation to the *specific* conduct that caused the injury. If this can be shown, then the hospital may be absolved of any vicarious liability for the staff employee for the injury, and the physician, surgeon, or other health care provider can be found liable for his or her temporary employee's acts.

It is important to note that this doctrine does not normally apply in most health care delivery situations where the staff nurse carries out orders of a physician or other health care provider. Likewise, when a nursing supervisor directs a nurse to perform certain functions, the nurse does not become the borrowed servant of that nurse supervisor. Rather, it arises in unique situ-

ations in which the nurse is clearly under the management of the surgeon. For example, if the surgeon utilizes his or her own nurse when performing surgery, or when an operating team utilizes its own nursing staff to assist during surgical procedures, this doctrine would most probably apply.

The captain of the ship rule is similar to the borrowed servant doctrine in that it holds the chief surgeon as the one who controls, and is thus responsible for, all individuals in the operating room. Thus, the employees of the operating suite become his or her temporary employees, and any injury during the course of that relationship becomes the vicarious responsibility of the chief surgeon.[17] It is important to note that neither doctrine has been widely embraced for various reasons, including the recent acknowledgment of nursing practice as an independent and accountable profession, regardless of the speciality area.

For example, in a 1990 case, *Franklin v. Gupta*,[18] the Maryland Court of Appeals upheld the trial court decision that the standard of care for the various defendants in the suit—a surgeon, a nurse anesthetist, and the anesthesiologist— would be based on their respective conduct that may have resulted in injury to the patient. The patient attempted to use the captain of the ship doctrine submitted as jury instructions in the hope of bringing the liability for his injuries to rest solely with the surgeon.

Although the case does not specifically utilize the doctrines by name, Key Case 3-4, discussed later in this chapter, illustrates the difficulty in identifying exactly *who* is a nurse's employer, especially in some of the newer practice arrangements. Nurses who are employed by nurse agencies or registries, or employed by a specific surgical group or other practice group, may face the legal question of who employs the nurse when a suit is filed.

Corporate or Institutional Theory of Liability

In the case *Darling v. Charleston Community Memorial Hospital*,[19] the Illinois Supreme Court formulated this theory concerning the liability of health care delivery systems. In essence, the theory states that the health care delivery system—whether a hospital or an ambulatory care center, for example—can be sued when it (allegedly) breaches any of its direct duties to its patients. Although there have been many duties specified in numerous court cases across the country, some of the direct duties that health care delivery systems have to health care consumers include (1) maintaining the facilities to avoid unreasonable and foreseeable risks of harm (this includes not only the physical plant of the entity but also in providing safe equipment for patient care); (2) providing qualified, trained, and licensed health care providers; (3) selecting competent medical staff; (4) proper orientation and supervision of staff; and (5) adopting adequate institutional policies.[20]

Because a health care delivery system is managed by its board of directors, chief executive officer (CEO), and his or her administrator(s), when determining if the health care delivery system was negligent, the standard of (due) care is measured by what other ordinary, reasonable, and prudent boards, CEOs, or administrators would have done in the same or similar circumstance(s).

Immunity from Suit

If applicable, immunity from suit exempts an individual or entity from liability in certain situations. At one time, the doctrines of charitable and sovereign immunity protected charitable (nonprofit) hospitals and governmental health care delivery systems from suit. Currently, however, only a handful of states apply the charitable immunity doctrine to health care. Those that do still embrace the doctrine increase the nurse's risk of inclusion in professional negligence suits.[21]

The sovereign immunity doctrine has also been somewhat eroded both on the state and federal level. Thus, under either state or federal law(s), when allowed, governmentally sponsored health care delivery systems can be sued pursuant to those laws.[22] As with charitable immunity, in those states still clinging to sovereign immunity, the nurse's risk of being named personally in a negligence suit is greatly increased.

It is important to note that immunity provisions in a state statute do not prevent a suit from being filed against a person who is immune. Rather, they provide the basis for dismissal of the suit against that defendant, if found by the court to apply. Also, immunity is never absolute. If, for example, an individual's alleged negligent conduct is determined to be willful, wanton, gross, or reckless, then immunity from suit would not apply.

Statute of Limitations

Whether passed by a state or federal legislature, a statute of limitations establishes the time periods within which a claim may be filed or within which certain rights can be enforced.[23] For negligence and professional negligence claims, that time period is a specified period (2 years, for example) from the date of the injury, or if the jurisdiction has adopted the discovery rule, a specified period from the discovery of the injury by the plaintiff, or from the time at which, using reasonable diligence, the plaintiff should have discovered the injury.[24]

. . . a statute of limitations establishes the time periods within which a claim may be filed or within which certain rights can be enforced.

There are often exceptions to these general statutory limitations placed on filing a suit. For example, a minor (as defined by state law) may be provided with a longer time within which to file a suit.

A statute of repose is often incorporated into a statute of limitations. This statutory language places an outermost limit on the time frame(s) within which a suit can be filed. The purpose of the statute of repose is to provide some mitigation of the hardship that is placed on defendants exposed to potential suits for negligent conduct under the "discovery rule."[25] Its application is often narrowly applied in certain cases, such as construction cases.

Res ipsa loquitur

Meaning, literally, "the thing speaks for itself," *Res ipsa loquitur* is a rule of evidence that allows for an inference of negligence on the part of the defendant due to the circumstances surrounding the injury. The inference is not automatic, however. It occurs because the plaintiff offers circumstantial evidence that allows the inference to be made. That evidence must consist of proof that (1) the injury normally does not occur in the absence of negligence; (2) the defendant(s) had exclusive control over the object that caused the injury; and (3) the injury cannot have occurred as a result of any voluntary action on the part of the injured party.[26]

Practically, what this rule does for the plaintiff depends on the jurisdiction. In some, it affects the strength of the inference that can be drawn by the jury concerning the injury. It allows the case to continue because the evidence concerning the injury, although inferred, is enough for the jury to make its decision. In others, it shifts the burden of proof to the defendant, requiring him or her to introduce evidence to rebut the inference of negligence.[27]

Examples of professional malpractice cases in which this doctrine was allowed by the court include (1) foreign bodies (sponges, surgical instruments) left in a patient after surgery[28]; (2) a (wrongful) pregnancy after bilateral tubal ligation[29]; and (3) wristdrop immediately after a nurse administered an injection to a patient.[30]

It is important to note that the doctrine can also be applied to multiple defendants. In the landmark case, *Ybarra v. Spangard*,[31] the operating room team refused to discuss what had taken place during an appendectomy that resulted in permanent injury to a patient's right arm. The team believed if they did not testify concerning what had occurred, the injured plaintiff would lose his suit because he could not prove who had exclusive control over him. The California Supreme Court held, however, that the team's silence would not deter a verdict in favor of the injured party. It decided in favor of the plaintiff. The court reasoned that a different decision would result in injured patients not being able to win a suit when health care providers simply decided not to disclose the facts of the incident.

PROFESSIONAL NEGLIGENCE CLAIMS AGAINST NURSES

Professional negligence claims against health care providers, including nurses, are based almost exclusively on *personal* injury. Examples of the types of personal injury allegations against nurses include death, limitation of the functioning of a body part (footdrop, for example),

---

TABLE 3–1

Common Allegations of Negligent Conduct Against Nurses

CONDUCT	CASE EXAMPLES
Medication errors (wrong dose, wrong route, wrong patient)	*Norton v. Argonaut Insurance Company*[32]
Improper monitoring or assessment	*Darling v. Charleston Community Hospital*[33]
Improper use of equipment	*Wagner v. York Hospital*[34]
Patient falls	*Daniel v. St. Francis Cabrini Hospital*[35]
Failure to communicate patient condition to MD or others	*George v. LDS Hospital*[36]
Failure to follow physician order(s)	*Pisel v. Stamford Hospital*[37]
Failure to follow hospital or other delivery system policies and procedures	*HCA Health Service v. National Bank*[38]
Failure to provide proper patient care or to deliver patient care properly	*Rutledge v. St. Anne's Hospital*[39]

injury to veins (when parenteral therapy is not properly supervised), injury to skin (burns and decubitus ulcers, for example), suicide (when a recipient of psychiatric services is not monitored carefully), stroke, and various types of brain damage (due to anoxia).

Furthermore, the types of personal injuries that occur when nurses provide patient care result from varied negligent conduct on the part of the nurse. Common allegations against nurses are summarized in Table 3–1.

Regardless of the type of conduct that ulti-

mately is determined to be negligent, however, the case alleging negligence must satisfy, to the court's satisfaction, the necessary components of the case. Simply put, the plaintiff must plead and prove his or her case, which includes meeting the burden of proof, that is, by affirmatively proving the facts in dispute.

Cases against nurses are no different. How the interplay of the essentials of professional negligence takes place in the courtroom is illustrated by analyzing selected early cases involving nurses.

KEY CASE 3–1   Fraijo v. Hartland Hospital et al. (1979)[40]

FACTS: Annette Boyd, 39 years old, married and the mother of three children from prior marriages, was not feeling well because of an asthmatic condition. She had sought medical help at an ER a number of times for her distress, and she was told to contact her regular physician about this but did not do so. On June 13, 1979, Ms. Boyd went to the ER of Hartland Hospital, where she was seen by one of the ER physicians. The doctor thought that she was in "moderate respiratory distress" but believed that she should be hospitalized because of the prior recent attacks. After standard treatment in the ER and the proper authorizations for admission were obtained, Ms. Boyd was admitted to a ward in the hospital.

The "backup" physician assigned to Ms. Boyd initiated a plan of care, including laboratory work, consultation with an asthma specialist, and the medications Demerol and Phenergan PRN for pain. In addition, he testified at the trial that he also ordered Solu-Cortef again (because it had not yet been given) and blood gas studies when he visited Ms. Boyd at about 10:15 P.M. According to the doctor, the patient was still dyspneic but "was not in peril." The RN assigned to care for Ms. Boyd testified at the trial that she saw no physician visit the patient between 10:00 and 11:00 P.M. but called the doctor shortly after 10:00 P.M. to inform him that Ms. Boyd's pulse and respiration were increased. He then ordered the Solu-Cortef and asked the nurse to call him later concerning the patient's condition.

Despite the provision of the care ordered, Ms. Boyd's condition continued to worsen (increased pulse, respiration, and increased blood pressure). In addition, she began to experience chest pain. The medication nurse administered the Demerol.

Shortly after the Demerol was administered IM, Ms. Boyd became cyanotic, and the nurse called for inhalation therapy. Ms. Boyd convulsed and stopped breathing. A Code Blue was called, but despite

KEY CASE 3–1   Fraijo v. Hartland Hospital et al. (1979)[40] Continued

efforts to save her from cardiopulmonary arrest, Ms. Boyd was declared dead at 12:15 A.M.

No autopsy was done. There was an investigation by the coroner's office, which concluded that death was caused by "heart and lung failure." The husband and other surviving family members filed a wrongful death suit against the hospital, the physicians, and the medication nurse alleging malpractice.

Plaintiff's experts testify that medical care was "substandard," and caused death

TRIAL COURT DECISION: At trial, the primary issue was the cause of Ms. Boyd's death. The plaintiffs' theory was that Ms. Boyd's care had been negligent from the beginning of her treatment. The expert witness also testified that the care given by the physicians was "too little, too late," and the Demerol, as the final example of "substandard medical practice," caused the patient's death. The defendants' two expert witnesses, both physicians, testified as to other theories concerning the death, stating that the medical care was "adequate"; that the death was probably caused by a pulmonary embolism, myocardial infarction, or spontaneous pneumothorax; and that the Demerol administered IM could not have acted within 5 minutes to cause the convulsion and apnea.

Defendants' expert witnesses testify as to different causes of death

Physician expert witness gives opinion about nursing care

One physician expert witness also testified about the medication nurse giving the Demerol. He believed her actions to be within the standard of care for a nurse in that situation.

The jury returned a verdict in favor of all of the defendants. The plaintiffs asked for a new trial, but that motion was denied by the court. They then appealed the judgment on the basis that the trial court made "serious errors" in the jury instructions. Specifically, they alleged that the instructions concerning the nurse's judgment when administering medications was not correct. They also alleged "serious errors" in an evidentiary ruling.

APPEALS COURT DECISION: The appellate court affirmed the trial court's decision. It held that the "serious errors" in the jury instructions, which involved the medication nurse's duty of care, did not exist because the instructions were modified to reflect the current practice of nursing, in which a nurse does make "independent" decisions concerning the care given a patient, which includes the administration of medications. Also, the court opined that a nurse's conduct is tested "with reference to other *nurses,* just as is the case with doctors."

Standard of care for professional nurse is to compare nurse's conduct with that of another nurse

As to the evidentiary issue, it concerned the court's denial of admitting the drug manufacturer's insert on Demerol as evidence during the testimony of one of the nurses, but later allowing it when one of the medical experts was testifying. The court held that the proper foundation had not been laid during the nurse's testimony.

Judge has discretion to select jury instructions about cause of death

Last, the appellate court held that the judge's choice of instructions given to the jury concerning the cause of Ms. Boyd's death (proximate cause vs. legal cause instructions) was within the discretion of the trial judge.

KEY CASE 3–1   Fraijo v. Hartland Hospital et al. (1979)[40] Continued

ANALYSIS: This case illustrates how important the standard of care is in a professional negligence case. Clearly the plaintiffs had hoped that by challenging what the court sanctioned as the *professional* standard for a nurse (comparing her conduct with that of other *nurses* in the same or similar situation) would bring them a new trial. The court's support of the expanded role of the nurse in its opinion, and specifically in relation to making judgments about medication administration, is also important. What is problematic about the case, however, is the use of a *physician,* as opposed to a nurse, as an expert witness concerning *nursing* roles. This case was decided before another California case, *Fein v. Permanente Medical Group,*[41] in which the California Supreme Court held that the standard of care for the professional nurse is that of another professional nurse, not a physician. With this decision firmly in place, it is doubtful that a California court today would allow a physician to be used as an expert witness to establish the standard of care for a professional nurse. Moreover, many courts have already held that to exclude a nurse expert witness' testimony concerning matters of *nursing* care is reversible error, requiring a new trial.[42]

KEY CASE 3–2   Mather v. Griffin Hospital (1988)[43]

FACTS: After Victor Mather's birth, his condition deteriorated rapidly, and he developed breathing problems. One of the nurses in the delivery room began suctioning the baby and administered oxygen. The baby stopped breathing. The physician inserted an endotracheal tube and attempted to suction the infant through the tube, but the nurse could not supply the doctor with the correct tubing to fit the endotracheal tube. The tube was removed, oxygen administered, and a second endotracheal tube inserted. Next, the doctor asked for an Ambu bag. The only one available had a mask attached to it, which could not be used with an endotracheal tube. Neither the doctor nor the nurse could remove the mask. The baby's condition continued to worsen. The doctor blew air into his lungs until appropriate equipment arrived. The infant survived, but suffered many injuries, including cerebral palsy.

The parents filed a suit against the hospital and the doctor, alleging professional negligence. The allegations against the hospital were based on the delivery room nurse's conduct, specifically that she failed to supply the delivery room with necessary equipment and supplies and that she could not operate the equipment needed in the situation.

KEY CASE 3–2   Mather v. Griffin Hospital (1988)[43] Continued

Nurse testifies to her conduct during incident

TRIAL COURT DECISION: The trial court jury returned a verdict against the hospital and found the physician not negligent. It did so based on the nurse's own testimony at trial. She testified that (1) it was her responsibility to equip the delivery room and know how to use the equipment there; (2) she failed to remove the mask, although she did not know why she failed to do so; (3) it was her responsibility to restock the supplies in the delivery room but she did not restock the suction tubes because she assumed she would not need them; (4) prior to the incident, she had not been working for 9 weeks; and (5) she had never assisted in a delivery room where an Ambu bag was used.

Experts testify that hospital breached its standard of care

Two experts, one for the plaintiff and one for the physician, also testified. Both concluded that failure to have proper equipment available and train employees in its use is a breach of the hospital's standard of care.

Doctor testifies nurse's conduct led to infant's injuries

The doctor's testimony also supported the fact that the nurse's conduct led to the injuries sustained by the infant.

The hospital appealed the $9 million verdict to the Connecticut Supreme Court.

Supreme Court affirms sufficient evidence for verdict against hospital

CONNECTICUT SUPREME COURT DECISION: The Connecticut Supreme Court upheld the trial court's verdict as well as the amount of the jury's award. It clearly stated that sufficient evidence existed in the transcript of the trial to support the breach of the standard of care by the hospital.

Furthermore, it held, there was sufficient evidence to link the cerebral palsy to the oxygen deprivation.

ANALYSIS: This case is interesting because it illustrates two important concepts: The first is that of corporate or institutional liability. Clearly, the hospital had duties of care to its patients. When the delivery room nurse's conduct was analyzed, the hospital's breach of its duties was clear. The trial court heard much testimony that indicated that if the hospital had provided an update or "refresher" orientation to the nurse regarding her responsibilities and the use of equipment in her position, the injuries that were sustained by the infant may have been avoided.

It is again important to emphasize that this case, if brought today, would most probably also name the delivery room nurse as an individual defendant under the theory of personal liability. A plaintiff's attorney will plead as many causes of action that he or she in good faith can plead. Therefore, the nurse employee must be clear about the fact that he or she is responsible for his or her own conduct. This, of course, includes continuing education updates and reorientation to equipment and responsibilities. However, an employer may also be named in a suit and liability assessed against it when it breaches one of its duties of care to the patient.

KEY CASE 3–3

Lenger v. Physician's General Hospital et al. (1970)[44]

FACTS: David Lenger underwent colon resection at defendant hospital by his surgeon for a cancerous growth in the colon. The operation and recovery were uneventful, and Mr. Lenger was transferred to a private room. The physician ordered morphine, intravenous therapy, a Levin tube, nothing by mouth, and private duty nursing around the clock. Because of an error by the night nurse, a food tray was sent to Mr. Lenger for all three meals 9 days after surgery. The patient challenged eating the solid food and demanded that the nurse, who was an agency nurse, call his physician. She refused to call the doctor, adding that the food would not have been sent to him unless he could eat it. Mr. Lenger ate breakfast and lunch, although he complained of discomfort after both meals. He therefore decided not to eat dinner.

The patient did not take anything more by mouth until the next day when he had some ice chips. The Levin tube was removed on August 14, and a liquid diet was started on August 16. Mr. Lenger began to feel "worse" on the 16th, however, and on August 20 surgery was initiated to determine the cause of his problems. During the operation it was discovered that the two ends of the colon had separated and could not be resutured. A double-barreled colostomy was done. A third operation to undo the initial colostomy, remove the remaining portion of the colon on the right side, and connect the small intestine to the descending colon on the left side was later performed. The patient left the hospital on October 30 and was unable to return to work until February of the following year.

The patient filed suit against the hospital, the nurse, and the nurse agency she worked for. He alleged that the solid food resulted in the separation of his colon. The separation necessitated further operations, additional medical expenses, and time lost from work.

Plaintiff fails to prove that solid food was proximate cause for bowel separation

TRIAL COURT DECISION: The jury returned a verdict in favor of the defendants, basing the ruling on the fact that the plaintiff did not prove that the solid food was the cause of the separation at the operative site. Only one medical expert testified at trial. He testified that he was unsure of what caused the separation. No evidence was presented to show when the separation occurred, what effect (if any) the *liquid* diet had on the separation, and whether the postoperative exercise regimen had any impact on the injury sustained by the plaintiff. Thus, he concluded, the eating of the solid food did not "establish a traceable chain of causation from the separation back to the solid food." Mr. Lenger appealed this decision to the Fort Worth Court of Civil Appeals.

Medical expert witness cannot testify as to what proximately caused separation

APPEALS COURT DECISION: The appellate court affirmed the lower court's decision. Mr. Lenger petitioned the state supreme court for a writ of error; that is, he asked that the verdict be reversed on (due to) the trial court's error.

KEY CASE 3-3	Lenger v. Physician's General Hospital et al. (1970)[44]
	Continued

STATE SUPREME COURT DECISION: The Texas Supreme Court affirmed the appeals court decision, stating again that one of the essential elements of a negligence case—proximate cause—was not proven at the trial level. The court clearly held that when a jury can only "speculate" as to the cause of injury, a verdict in favor of the defendants is not in error.

ANALYSIS: The element of proximate cause is the focus of this case. Without evidence to support that a specific action or a specific breach of duty *caused* the injury upon which the suit is based, no liability will be assessed against the defendant(s). Had expert testimony been offered that would have connected the separation with the intake of solid food, a different verdict may have been returned by the jury.

KEY CASE 3-4	Joyce v. National Medical Registry, Inc. (1988)[45]

FACTS: Daniel Joyce, a male infant, suffered cardiac arrest during the course of an operation. He went into a coma and subsequently died. The anesthesia was administered by a certified registered nurse anesthetist (CRNA) and an anesthesiologist. The parents of the deceased child, as the administrators of his estate, filed a suit against the surgeon, the anesthesiologist, the nurse anesthetist, the National Medical Registry (the nurse anesthetist's employment agency that provided temporary nursing services for the hospital), and Graham Hospital Association, where the surgery was done. They alleged negligence in administering the anesthesia and monitoring the deceased. In addition, the nurse anesthetist was alleged to have failed to notify the anesthesiologist when the infant's condition changed. The registry was brought into the suit under the *respondeat superior* theory because it was alleged that the nurse anesthetist was its employee. Last, the hospital was named under the theory that the nurse anesthetist was also an employee of the hospital.

Nurse registry brought into suit under respondeat superior *theory*

TRIAL COURT DECISION: The National Medical Registry, in a summary judgment motion, asked to be dismissed from the malpractice suit on the grounds that it was not the nurse anesthetist's employer. Therefore, its motion continued, there was no material issue of fact concerning its liability for the nurse anesthetist's alleged professional negligence. During the hearing on the motion, evidence was presented that supported this position, and specifically supported the fact that the

KEY CASE 3–4

Joyce v. National Medical Registry, Inc. (1988)[45] Continued

Court dismisses nurse registry from suit, as it had no control over nurse anesthetist

Registry only paid the nurse anesthetist's salary. The hospital, the anesthesiologist, and the nurse anesthetist herself had varying roles concerning the control of the nurse anesthetist's services. The court granted the summary judgment motion and dismissed the Registry from the suit. It based its holding on the fact that it had no control over the nurse anesthetist other than paying her salary, which was insufficient, as a matter of law, for imposing vicarious liability against the Registry. The plaintiffs appealed this decision.

APPEALS COURT DECISION: The appeals court affirmed the order of the trial court, discussing at length the Illinois law concerning master-servant relationships.

ANALYSIS: This case is an important one in health care delivery today, for traditional employer-employee relationships do not always exist. The use of "employer-retained employment agencies" (what National Medical Registry described itself as) is not new. This decision clearly supports a clear principle: Simply providing potential health care provider names to health care delivery system employers, who control the manner, time, place, and scope of the work, will not invoke the vicarious liability doctrine. It is fascinating to note that the Registry reimbursed the nurse anesthetist for her professional liability insurance premiums during her temporary assignment at the hospital. Apparently this did not affect the courts' decisions.

Professional nurses who obtain positions in an arrangement similar to the one involved in this case will need to be certain that they understand the legal ramifications. Whether the nurse is considered an employee has little impact on his or her *individual* liability. However, it may have an impact on who else is named in the suit. In addition, the purchase of one's own professional liability insurance is a must in this type of relationship. Relying on a perceived employer's policy, and then finding out that no employer-employee relationship exists, places the nurse in a precarious financial position if a verdict is entered against him or her.

The *Joyce* case does *not* deal with nurse registry situations in which the nurse is clearly an employee of that agency and the latter has much more control over the nurse in relation to performance, type of compensation arrangement, and the termination of employment. In such a situation, the agency would most probably be considered the employer. However, with unique and innovative employment agencies continuing to proliferate, their legal status, and that of the nurse obtaining work through them, will continue to be tested in the courts when patient injuries occur.

Undoubtedly, the few cases discussed do not illustrate each and every possible type of professional negligence case a nurse may be involved in. In fact, that would be difficult, at best, to do, for negligence *and* professional negligence cannot fit into any specific formula or rule.[46] Rather, it is "relative to the need and occasion."[47] Despite the impracticality of analyzing a myriad of cases concerning professional negligence, one thing is certain: The nurse must be ever vigilant in maintaining standards of care and providing patient care consistent with those standards. What the specific standard of care is will depend, again, on the circumstances and the area of nursing practice.

> *. . . The nurse must be ever vigilant in maintaining standards of care and providing patient care consistent with those standards.*

DEFENSES AGAINST NEGLIGENCE AND PROFESSIONAL NEGLIGENCE ACTIONS

Whenever an individual is sued, it is important for that person to defend himself or herself—that is, to attempt to establish that, by law or by fact, the plaintiff should not be awarded that which he or she seeks.[48] In defending oneself against allegations of negligence and professional negligence, there are several defenses that, if successful, would result in a verdict for the defendant(s) and against the plaintiff. It is important to note, however, that although it is not a guarantee, the *best* defense against inclusion in a lawsuit is to practice nonnegligently. Adherence to a risk-management approach when delivering patient care is also essential.

Failure of Plaintiff to Prove Essential Elements

One vital defense against allegations of any negligent conduct is the inability of the injured party to prove all of the elements of the cause of action—duty, breach of duty, proximate cause, and injuries/damages. Although this defense does not prohibit the case from being filed, it would prohibit a verdict against the defendant or nurse defendant.

Failure of Plaintiff to Prove Defendant(s) Acted Unreasonably

If the plaintiff cannot prove that the defendant acted unreasonably in the situation, then the plaintiff would be unable to have a verdict returned in his or her favor. Negligent behavior requires that the defendant place the injured party in danger of a "recognized" risk and then conduct himself or herself "unreasonably." Again, there are no guidelines or rules to follow concerning what conduct would satisfy these definitions. Rather, a risk-benefit form of analysis is used that takes into consideration, among other things, (1) the probability and extent of harm; (2) the social interest the actor is seeking to advance; and (3) what alternative actions are open to the actor.[49]

For example, when a nurse notifies all necessary staff who must be informed when a patient's condition worsens and initiates any and all actions needed to protect the patient from any further deterioration in condition, the nurse's conduct would be seen as reasonable. Thus, the nurse would not be found to be professionally negligent, even if injury or harm resulted to the patient.

Assumption of Risk by Plaintiff

This affirmative defense (meaning that the defendant(s) must plead it as a defense in the answer to the complaint) simply states that the defendant should not be held responsible for an injury the plaintiff received if the plaintiff (1) had knowledge of the facts that constituted the dangerous condition; (2) knew it was dangerous; (3) recognized the nature and extent of the danger; and (4) voluntarily chose to assume the danger.[50] The defendant(s) must prove all elements of the defense for it to be successful.

In nonprofessional negligence situations, this defense might be pleaded when, for example, someone is injured at a golf course by an uncontrolled golf ball or when a car accident occurs and the injured party was driving the car with faulty brakes for some time before the accident. In professional negligence actions, this defense may be used when the patient has been informed of specific, unavoidable results of a particular course of treatment but elects the treatment nonetheless.

However, under this defense, an individual *never* assumes the risk of negligent treatment.[51] Thus, injury to a patient's arm that is found to be the result of negligent administration of a chemotherapy agent by a nurse, rather than due to the propensities of the toxin itself (which had been discussed with the patient as an adverse result), would not fall under this defense.

At one time, the successful utilization of the assumption of risk defense barred any liability on the defendant's part. However, with the advent of the comparative negligence doctrine (see discussion below), the total prohibition against liability is being re-evaluated.[52] Currently, courts apply the defense differently with comparative negligence, some using it as a total bar to liability if the assumption of risk was "express," and others not using it as a bar when the defendant's negligence forced the plaintiff into a situation in which he "reasonably" assumed the risk.[53]

Plaintiff Filed Suit After the Statute of Limitations Has Run

This defense, if successful, requires a case filed after the required time to be dismissed, usually with prejudice, meaning that it cannot be filed again. Sometimes, however, by the time a layperson becomes aware that an injury suffered may be due to negligence of a health care provider, the period within which a person must file the case has already passed. Thus, the law allows extensions of time to file cases for those

individuals who find themselves in certain situations.

One such situation occurs when, for example, there has been an attempt by the health care provider or health care delivery system to conceal or act fraudulently with regard to an injury. When such behavior on the part of the defendant can be proven, courts have consistently held either that the defense is barred (cannot be used) or that the statute of limitations was tolled (stopped running) during the period of concealment or fraud. In either case, the court allows the case to proceed, despite the fact that the statute of limitations has, in actuality, passed.[54]

Another circumstance in which the statute of limitations defense may arise is when the plaintiff attempts to characterize a malpractice case as something else, for example, a breach of contract action. Because a contract action has a longer statute of limitations (5 years as opposed to 2 years, for example), the plaintiff may try to file the action long after the malpractice statute of limitations has run. The longer filing period for such actions is one reason that health care professionals, including nurses, and health care delivery systems are cautioned *not* to guarantee (specific) results in health care. Among other problems, it raises the possibility of a valid allegation that a contract was entered into. If this is proven, the longer filing period might then apply.[55]

Defendant's Immunity from Suit

Immunity from suit can occur in certain situations, as when the local, state, or federal legislature passes laws that protect entities from liability under certain circumstances. Thus, a nurse working for a county hospital and the county hospital (as the employer) who were sued for alleged negligence may be able to successfully obtain a dismissal of the suit if immunity were present for the alleged conduct.

Despite the gradual erosion of the doctrines of sovereign and charitable immunity, one possible area of immunity that exists for health care providers, including nurses, is the Good Samaritan acts or sections of specific practice acts (e.g., the state's nurse practice act or emergency medical systems act). This law provides immunity from suit for acts or omissions when the nurse provides care to an individual in an accident, in an emergency, or under other specified conditions. Most often, the care must be provided under certain circumstances: for example, without compensation, with no prior knowledge of the injury, and in good faith. Thus, a suit against the nurse would not be able to be sustained for any injuries unless the nurse's conduct was willfully or wantonly negligent (that is, intentional or with reckless disregard for the safety of another).[56] Similarly, some states allow immunity to the nurse who volunteers services at certain functions, such as a health fair or religious camp.[57]

. . . one. . . area of immunity that exists for health care providers, including nurses, is the Good Samaritan acts or sections of specific practice acts . . .

It is important to note that the immunity provided by Good Samaritan acts, in whatever form, was not traditionally applied to emergency room care by physician or nurse staff, or in any other emergency situation in a health care delivery setting in which staff provided care to patients. Recently, however, several state courts have begun to apply this doctrine to such situations, albeit under varying circumstances. Illinois and California are two states that have applied Good Samaritan immunity to physicians when they provided emergency care to hospital patients who were not under their personal care.[58]

Plaintiff's Contributory Negligence

This defense, one of the most common utilized against negligence allegations,[59] states that the plaintiff's conduct contributed to the injuries he or she sustained and that the conduct was below the standard that the plaintiff was to uphold for his or her own protection.[60] If the plaintiff is negligent, in most states he or she *cannot* recover any damages from the defendant. Rather than supporting the defendant's lack of negligence, this defense sees both parties as being "at fault," but because plaintiff did not act with reasonable care, he or she is barred from being enriched from it.[61]

This defense can be very successful in both negligence and professional negligence actions. For example, if a pedestrian is hit by the driver of a car and sues, and the defendant driver proves that the pedestrian had crossed the street against a no-walk sign, thus "contributing" to his or her injury, the driver can obtain a verdict in his or her own favor. Likewise, if a home health care nurse provides instructions concerning medications and diet and a patient is injured, he or she may sue the nurse under a negligent teaching theory. So long as the nurse can prove that it was not his or her instructions, but rather the patient's failure to follow the regimen presented, that caused the patient's injuries, a verdict would be returned in the nurse's favor as well.

Because of the obvious harshness of this defense—the plaintiff recovers nothing even though suffering injury—many states have modified the defense to that of comparative negligence.

Plaintiff's Comparative Negligence

Rather than operate as an absolute bar to a plaintiff's recovery of damages for injuries sustained, comparative negligence allows for the "comparing" of the negligence of the plaintiff *and* the defendant, and any damages awarded to the plaintiff are adjusted accordingly. Thus the plaintiff does recover for his or her injuries but only to the extent that he or she was not negligent. Three versions of comparative negligence exist: pure, modified (50%), and slight-gross.[62]

In a pure comparative negligence jurisdiction, the damages awarded to the plaintiff would be reduced by the respective negligence of the plaintiff and defendant. Thus, if a jury returned a $50,000 verdict against a nurse because his or her home care instructions to the plaintiff were negligent, but the plaintiff's failure to follow them were determined to be 20% of the reason for his injury, the verdict would be reduced by that 20%. The nurse's verdict amount, then, would be $40,000, a reduction of $10,000.

In a modified or 50% jurisdiction, the same example would result in reduction of the amount awarded to the plaintiff by whatever percentage his or her own conduct contributed to the injuries, so long as the negligence was less than the established "threshold" limit—usually 50%. If, however, the negligence exceeds that limit, then the plaintiff recovers nothing. Thus, if a patient's actions were found to be 35% responsible for the injuries and the defendant's conduct 65% responsible, the plaintiff could recover from the defendant because his or her negligence was under the threshold 50% "fault" limit. Even so, he or she could recover only 45% of the verdict amount. Using the above example, that would be $22,500.00.

The third version, slight-gross, allows recovery for the plaintiff only if his or her negligence is "slight" in comparison with the defendant's "gross" negligence. Reduction in the verdict based on the proportion of total negligence attributed to the plaintiff then occurs, as has already been illustrated.[63]

SPECIAL CONSIDERATIONS
Survival Actions

Historically, when a plaintiff or defendant died before completion of a suit based on a tort, the action died along with the person. Today, however, through survival statutes, a personal injury action can continue after the death of either party.[64] State survival statutes vary greatly, but they generally provide a "transfer" of the case to the personal representative, who can continue with a suit and recover the same damages the decedent would have been entitled to at his or her death.[65] Most survival statutes allow the cause of action to continue, whether or not death was due to the defendant's tort. Some, however, do not allow the action to continue if the cause of death was the defendant's tortious conduct. Rather, a "new" claim must be initiated on behalf of the beneficiaries under the wrongful death statute.[66]

Likewise, federal survival laws exist and include protections for civil rights violations, for federal employees, and perhaps even for those discriminated against in employment, especially when economic injury is alleged.[67]

Many states exclude certain torts, such as defamation, and specific damages, such as punitive or exemplary, from surviving the death of either party.

Wrongful Death Actions

As was the case historically with survival actions, the common law did not allow a deceased's heirs or dependents to sue, in their own behalf, for their loss due to the death of the family member. However, with the passage in England of the Fatal Accidents Act in 1846, English and American law, both in every state and at the federal level, provided statutory remedies for the wrongful death of a family member.[68] Generally speaking, the various statutes allow the action to be filed when death occurs as a result of negligent and intentional torts, under a strict liability theory, and, in some instances, for a breach of contract and a breach of warranty.[69]

Which family members are able to bring a wrongful death action are specified in each statute, usually by group. Thus, a spouse or children are examples of family members who can recover economic losses they might have reasonably expected to receive had the family member not died (e.g., the value of the decedent's companionship).[70]

Wrongful Pregnancy Actions

With the advances and developments in medicine and technology surrounding reproduction, pregnancy, and genetic counseling, new causes of actions are proliferating. Wrongful pregnancy actions are an example of these "new" torts. In a wrongful pregnancy suit, the plaintiff(s) seeks damages for the emotional, physical, and economic injuries allegedly sustained because the physician negligently performed a procedure that was to prevent further childbearing.[71] The injury sued for is the birth of a child who was not planned for.[72]

Wrongful pregnancy actions are an example of these "new" torts.

Wrongful pregnancy actions can be based on negligence (e.g., an improperly performed sterilization or abortion), on a lack of informed consent (e.g., the physician failed to inform the plaintiff fully of all risks concerning possible pregnancy *despite* the procedure), or on a breach of warranty action (the physician *guaranteed* that no pregnancy would occur after the procedure, for example).[73] Damages that can be awarded include the costs associated with the pregnancy and delivery, the costs of any medical complications due to the pregnancy, and, in some instances, the costs of raising and educating the child.[74]

Wrongful Birth Actions

This new tort is based on the idea that the *parents* of a child with congenital anomalies should be compensated for the birth of the child because the physician failed (1) to inform them of the risk(s) of giving birth to a deformed child

or (2) to advise them to undergo diagnostic tests that would have discovered the fetus's condition. In either case, the parents were not able to make a choice whether to forgo pregnancy altogether or, alternatively, to terminate the pregnancy once the defects were discovered.[75]

Damages recoverable under this cause of action generally include the costs determined to be necessary to care for the child as a result of his or her impairment. Many states do not allow the plaintiff to recover damages for his or her own emotional anguish in witnessing the child's birth or because he or she will experience suffering because the child is suffering.[76]

Although traditionally this cause of action has been filed against obstetricians, nurse-midwives may face inclusion in such suits if there is failure on their part to advise patients concerning genetic counseling and diagnostic testing. Nurse-midwives will need to ensure that an accurate and complete family history is taken when a new case is initiated. Referral of the client to the appropriate health care provider for counseling and testing is essential. Because nurse-midwives limit their practice to normal deliveries, the client should be referred to a physician if a complicated pregnancy is anticipated. This is also important to avoid inclusion in wrongful life suits.

Wrongful Life Actions

Wrongful life actions are brought by the parents of a child with congenital anomalies on behalf of the child who has been born with those deformities. Essentially, the gist of the action is based on the position that the child should never have been born at all, and thus the court must compensate the child for that harm. Because of the difficulty in measuring that "harm," as well as the philosophical difficulties in supporting a position that an individual should never have been born, most jurisdictions deny recovery to a child for general suffering in being born in a defective condition.[77]

Product Liability Actions

Product liability is an area of tort law that deals with the liability of a manufacturer, seller, and others in the "chain of distribution" who supply goods or products to the public and an injury occurs due to "defects" in those products.[78] The rationale for the development of a product liability law was to protect the public by requiring that a manufacturer and/or seller of goods introduced into the marketplace ("stream of commerce") bear the cost of any injury that might be sustained by the user of the product (or a bystander).

Several legal theories have developed under product liability, and the injured party, including a patient who alleges injury due to a product used in his or her care (medicine or patient care equipment, for example) can sue by alleging negligence, breach of an express or implied warranty, or strict liability in tort. Because negligence law (or the law of negligence) has been developed at length in this chapter, utilizing this theory in a products liability action will not be discussed, other than to remind the reader that all of the essential elements of a cause of action in negligence must also be pled in a products liability case based on it. The two other theories, warranty and strict liability, will be briefly addressed.

Warranty

Most goods/products are covered by a state's Uniform Commercial Code (UCC), which covers, among other things, express or implied warranties for goods/products manufactured, sold, and distributed. An express warranty is one that is given orally or in writing concerning a characteristic of the good/product, while an implied warranty is one that exists because of the operation of the law.[79] Under the UCC, there are two particular warranties important in relation to health care goods/products—the warranty of fitness and the warranty of merchantability.[80] Both are implied warranties.

The implied warranty of fitness states that the product sold is "fit" for its intended use, that the buyer (a hospital, for example) is relying on the skill of the seller to select and furnish the suitable good(s)/product(s), and that the seller, retailer, or manufacturer knows any particular purpose of the item.[81] The implied warranty of merchantability maintains that the item(s) purchased is adequately contained, packaged, and labeled; conforms to the promises of assertions on the container or label; is fit for the "ordinary purpose" the good/product is used for; and would successfully pass inspection by those in the "trade."[82]

When a patient is injured allegedly because of a product used in his or her care (a Stryker frame, for example), he or she may initially be unsure who is ultimately responsible for the injury: the manufacturer or seller of the product, because of a breach of the implied warranty of fitness or merchantability, or the hospital, for its failure to maintain the equipment properly or to adequately train staff to use the equipment. As a result, the patient will most probably include the manufacturer or seller in a products liability count in the suit. Moreover, although the hospital would be included in the malpractice suit under a liability theory other than product liability, it will need to provide testimony regarding the conditions discussed above concerning the implied warranty of fitness it relied on when it purchased the equipment.

It is important to note that some warranties may be disclaimed in certain situations. If allowed and properly worded, a disclaimer may defeat an individual's action against the manufacturer or others in the "chain of distribution."

Strict Liability

Strict liability in tort for products means that the manufacturer and others will be held for an injury without regard to the fault or intent of those individuals to harm or injure another. Although this is a sweeping liability theory, the injured person—the patient—must plead and prove all of the following: (1) the product was defective; (2) the defect existed at the time the product left the possession of the defendant(s) (e.g., the manufacturer or seller); (3) the product was unreasonably dangerous (e.g., defectively designed or manufactured, or bearing a defective warning); (4) injuries were sustained by the individual; and (5) the defect was the legal cause of injury to the plaintiff.[83]

If the defendant(s) can prove that a product alleged to be defective was "unavoidably unsafe"—that it could not be made "safe" for its ordinary and intended use—then no liability would be present under the strict liability theory. An example of such a product is a vaccine that may be needed to immunize the public, but which poses the inherent risk of the recipients' contracting the disease. Historically, the polio vaccine was one such product.[84]

Because nursing care is often delivered with equipment—monitors, surgical instruments, and syringes, for example—and most often with medications, products liability has more applicability to nursing than might be initially thought.

Because nursing care is often delivered with equipment—monitors, surgical instruments, and syringes, for example—and most often with medications, products liability has more applicability to nursing than might be initially thought. Although the provision of nursing care is usually considered a service and not the provision of a product, most nurses would not be involved in a strict liability suit as a defendant. However, implications do exist for both the nurse and the employer whenever a patient injury occurs with the use of a product. They are summarized in Table 3–2.

In addition to the implications noted in Table 3–2, it is important for the nurse to keep in mind that liability under a professional negligence theory may exist for the nurse who utilizes

---

TABLE 3–2
Implications for Nurses Utilizing Products in the Provision of Patient Care

- Membership on policy and procedure committees to ensure clear policies concerning product identification, evaluation, and repair
- Policies and procedures concerning actions to be taken when an injury or death occurs with equipment, including but not limited to whom to contact and preservation of the product
- Store medications, tubing, and other patient care equipment according to manufacturer's directions
- Administer medications, ointments, and other drugs according to manufacturer's instructions
- Adequate in-service and orientation to new patient care equipment
- If involved in purchasing equipment and other patient care products, obtain representations by company in writing
- Conduct a thorough assessment of the patient with regard to drug allergies and any previous problems when patient care equipment was used
- If a patient experiences a reaction to a particular medication, stop its use and notify the physician
- Document all instances of patient injury accurately and completely in the patient's record and other required forms

Data from Nancy J. Brent, "Assessing, Evaluating and Selecting Patient Care Products," 9(2) *Home Healthcare Nurse* (March/April 1991), 9–10.

---

equipment that is faulty or is used incorrectly. Thus, when equipment is not working properly, the nurse must inform those who are to be notified of the malfunction so the problem can be corrected immediately. Furthermore, adequate training on new equipment is essential so that no unreasonable and foreseeable injury is experienced by a patient because of the nurse's lack of expertise with that equipment.

Safe Medical Devices Act (SMDA)

The SMDA, effective November 28, 1991,[85] requires hospitals, nursing homes, and other medical "device-user facilities" to report a serious injury, illness, or death that "reasonably suggests" it took place because of the use of a medical device. The report is to be made to the Food and Drug Administration within 10 working days of awareness of the incident, and, if the identity of the manufacturer is known, to the manufacturer of the device.

All medical products except those absorbed into the body are included in the act's definition of "medical device." Thus, when a serious injury, illness, or death occurs with the use of a monitor, syringe, or other patient care product, the institution must report (1) its name; (2) the name, serial number, and model number of the medical device, if known; (3) the name and address of the manufacturer of the device; and (4) a brief description of the event.[86]

Although the duty to report is clearly the *institution's*, the nurse providing care with any medical device covered under the act should (1) follow agency policies when an injury, illness, or death occurs and a medical device is believed to be involved in some way; (2) document the incident accurately and completely in the medical record, incident report, and agency reporting forms; (3) discontinue the use of the medical device (and replace it immediately with another); and (4) record the ID number of patient equipment in the medical record and/or other forms on a regular basis.[87]

TORT REFORM

As a result of the spiraling costs of medical and nursing malpractice cases, rising premiums for professional liability insurance, and the time required to move a case through the civil courts, tort reform's "third wave" (the other two having begun in the mid 1970s and 1980s, respectively) became an important force on both the federal and state level after the 1994 legislative elections.[88]

. . . tort reform's "third wave" (the other two having begun in the mid 1970s and 1980s, respectively) became an important force on both the federal and state level after the 1994 legislative elections.

Although tort reform has been initiated on the federal level and completed in many states, it is still in progress, and therefore a complete discussion of its effects upon some of the principles presented in this chapter is impossible. However, four major areas of tort reform have been identified: (1) development of dispute resolution mechanisms that can minimize reliance on the traditional court system(s); (2) changes in the amounts of jury awards granted as well as changes in the way awards are paid to the plaintiff; (3) changes in the time within which a suit must be filed; and (4) other changes, including expansion of rules of discovery, nullification of the confidentiality of medical records when a plaintiff files a suit alleging malpractice, and the alteration of liability rules.[89]

It is too early to see how the tort reform changes will fare as court challenges to them occur. Until the changes are challenged and a resolution concerning their longevity occurs, the reader should constantly keep abreast of tort reform, on both the federal and state level.

SUMMARY OF PRINCIPLES AND APPLICATIONS

The law of negligence and professional negligence is complex and vast. The basic concepts and principles presented in this chapter are a framework that will be discussed in most of the other chapters in the book, especially in the following two chapters and those in Part III. In those chapters, the principles and concepts will be applied to the many roles and specialty areas of nursing practice. However, certain guidelines are important to review here:

▼ Negligence and professional negligence are examples of torts

▼ The essential elements of a cause of action in negligence are duty, breach of duty, proximate cause, and damages

▼ When professional negligence is alleged against a nurse, the nurse's conduct will be compared with that of other ordinary, reasonable, and prudent *nurses* in the same or similar circumstances in the same or similar community

▼ The use of an expert witness to establish the standard of care is essential in professional negligence cases

▼ Although the concept of personal liability is important for the nurse to be aware of, also important is the potential liability of the employer under two theories, the corporate theory and *respondeat superior*

▼ There are many defenses against allegations of negligence and professional negligence, including assumption of risk, untimely filing of the case, and immunity from suit

▼ "New tort" causes of action that may result in nurses being named as defendants include wrongful birth and life actions

▼ Survival actions allow a case to continue against a health care provider after the death of the plaintiff

▼ Although products liability cases may not include nurses as defendants unless they are involved in the "chain of distribution," providing patient care with any product—medications, monitors, or surgical tape—has clear implications for the nurse

▼ The *Safe Medical Devices Act* requires certain health care delivery systems to report serious injury, illness, or death that may have resulted from the use of a medical device to the Food and Drug Administration

▼ Tort reform may continue to result in changes affecting professional negligence, liability, and the practice of nursing

TOPICS FOR FURTHER INQUIRY

1. Analyze the process of tort reform in at least two states, one being the reader's own practice state. Compare and contrast topics introduced for reform, success and/or failure in achieving tort reform, and how the reforms have affected the practice of nursing in the states under review.

2. Do a statistical analysis of the types of cases in which nurses are named as defendants and compare them with cases involving another professional group providing direct patient care. Discuss the differences and similarities, if any.

3. Develop interview questions, and then interview nurses to evaluate their understanding of professional negligence.

4. Interview jurors who have served in a nursing malpractice case. Identify the issues that were important to them in deciding on a verdict in the case, such as the credibility of the expert witnesses, the injury involved, the length of time the nurse practiced, and the demeanor of the nurse defendant during his or her testimony.

REFERENCES

1. W. Page Keeton, General Editor. *Prosser and Keeton on The Law of Torts.* 5th Edition. St. Paul, Minn: West Publishing Company, 1984 (with updated pocket parts), 160–161.
2. *Id.* at 161.
3. Henry Campbell Black. *Black's Law Dictionary.* 6th Edition. St. Paul, Minn: West Publishing Company, 1991, 1036.
4. Keeton, *supra* note 1, at 2.
5. *Id.* at 7.
6. Restatment (Second) of Torts, Section 282 (1972) (with 1991 pocket parts).
7. Keeton, *supra* note 1, at 170, *citing Stewart v. Jefferson Plywood Co.,* 469 P2d 783, 786 (1970).
8. Keeton, *supra* note 1, at 164.
9. Keeton, *supra* note 1, at 169.
10. Lawrence Baum. *American Courts: Process and Policy.* 2nd Edition. Boston: Houghton Mifflin Company, 1990, 224.
11. Keeton, *supra* note 1, at 185.
12. Black, *supra* note 3, at 401.
13. Black, *supra* note 3, at 631.
14. Keeton, *supra* note 1, at 499.
15. *Id.* at 500.
16. *Id.*
17. Theodore LeBlang, Eugene Basanta, J. Douglas Peters, Keith Fineberg, and Donald Kroll, "Malpractice Law," in *The Law of Medical Practice in Illinois.* Rochester, NY:

Lawyers Cooperative Publishing Co., 1986 (with September 1993 Cumulative Supplement), 481–482.

18. 567 A.2d 524 (Md. Ct. App. 1990).

19. 211 N.E. 2d 253 (1965), *cert. denied,* 383 U.S. 946 (1966).

20. Christopher Kerns and Carol Gerner, Editors. *Health Care Liability Deskbook.* Deerfield, Ill: Clark Boardman Callaghan, 1995, 9–12; George Pozgar, *Legal Aspects of Health Care Administration.* 5th Edition. Gaithersburg, Md: Aspen Publishers, Inc., 1993, Chapter 5 ("Corporate Liability"), 143–169.

21. Eli Bernzweig, "Special Rules of Liability," in *The Nurse's Liability for Malpractice: A Programmed Course.* 5th Edition. St. Louis: C.V. Mosby Company, 1990, 109. Some states that adhere to the charitable immunity doctrine are Arkansas, Ohio, and Rhode Island. Kerns and Gerner, *supra* note 20, at 13.

22. The federal government has consented to be sued in certain situations under *The Federal Tort Claims Act* of 1946, originally enacted and found at 60 Stat. 843. State governmental consent for suit varies from state to state, but several states have adhered steadfastly to the doctrine of sovereign immunity. They are Alabama, Delaware, Maine, Maryland, North Dakota, South Dakota, Virginia, Wisconsin, and Wyoming. Bernzweig, *supra* note 21, at 111.

23. Black, *supra* note 3, at 639.

24. Keeton, *supra* note 1, at 166.

25. *Id.* at 167–168.

26. Keeton, *supra* note 1, at 244.

27. *Id.* at 257–259.

28. *Walker v. Rumer,* 381 NE 2d 689 (1978).

29. *Clay v. Brodsky,* 499 N.E. 2d 68 (1986).

30. *Bauer v. Otis,* 284 P. 2d 133 (Cal. App. 1962).

31. 154 P. 2d 687 (Cal. 1945).

32. 144 So. 2d 249 (La. App. 1962).

33. *Darling v. Charleston Community Hospital, supra* note 19.

34. 608 A. 2d 496 (Pa. 1992).

35. 415 So. 2d 586 (La. Ct. App. 1982).

36. 797 P. 2d 1117 (Utah 1990).

37. 430 A. 2d 1 (Conn. 1980).

38. 745 S.W. 2d 120 (Ark. 1988).

39. 595 N.E. 2d 1165 (Ill. 1992).

40. 160 Cal. Rptr. 246 (1979).

41. 211 Cal. Rptr. 368 (Cal. 1985), *Appeal dismissed,* 474 U.S. 892 (1985).

42. See, for example, *Maloney v. Wake Hospital Systems, Inc.,* 262 S.E. 2d 680 (N.C. App. 1980). This case involved the trial court's exclusion of testimony from a nurse expert witness who was qualified as an expert in the field of IV therapy. The hospital was sued by the plaintiff for injuries sustained when a nurse improperly administered potassium chloride that caused injury to the skin on the plaintiff's hand. The affected hand required cosmetic surgery, and the injury resulted in a loss of full use of the hand.

43. 540 A2d 666 (Conn. 1988).

44. 455 S.W. 2d 703 (1970).

45. 534 N.E. 2d 243 (Ill. App. 3 Dist. 1988).

46. Keeton, *supra* note 1, at 173.

47. *Id.*

48. Black, *supra* note 3, at 290.

49. Keeton, *supra* note 1, at 169–173.

50. Black, *supra* note 3, at 82.

51. Eli Bernzweig, "Proving the Nurse's Liability," in *The Nurse's Liability for Malpractice: A Programmed Course, supra* note 21, at 298.

52. Keeton, *supra* note 1, at 496.

53. *Id.* at 495–498.

54. See, for example, *Mueller v. Thaut,* 430 N.W. 2d 884 (Neb. 1988), in which the physician who negligently delivered the Muellers' child told the parents that their daughter's death was due to her "severe deformity." When the parents obtained the death certificate to file a life insurance claim and discovered the true cause of death was "traumatic injury" sustained at birth, they filed a wrongful death action against Dr. Thaut. He attempted to raise the statute of limitations as a defense, but the court held that his misrepresentation of the true cause of the child's death delayed the filing of the suit, and the parents were allowed to go forward with their cause of action.

55. See, for example, *Stanley v. Chastek,* 180 N.E. 2d 512 (2nd Dist. 1985); *Doerr v. Villate,* 220 N.E. 2d 767 (2nd Dist. 1966); *Murray v. University of Pennsylvania Hospital,* 490 A. 2d 839 (Pa. 1985).

56. Black, *supra* note 3, at 1103.

57. See, for example, 225 ILCS 65/5.1 (1988) (The Illinois Nursing Act of 1987).

58. See *McKenna v. Cedars of Lebanon Hospital,* 93 Cal. App. 3d 282, 155 Cal. Rptr. 631 (1979); *Burciaga v. St. John's Hospital,* 187 Cal. App. 3d 710, 232 Cal. Rptr. 75 (1986); *Johnson v. Mitaviuw,* 531 N.E. 2d 970 (Ill. App. 1st Dist.) (1988), *cert. denied.,* 125 Ill. 2d 566 (1989).

59. Keeton, *supra* note 1, at 451.

60. Pozgar, *supra* note 20, at 127.

61. *Id.* at 125.

62. Keeton, *supra* note 1, at 74.

63. *Id.* at 474.

64. *Id.* at 942.

65. *Id.* at 943.

66. *Id.*

67. *Id.* at 944.

68. *Id.* at 945.

69. *Id.* at 946–947.

70. Kerns and Gerner, *supra* note 20, at 8.

71. Pozgar, *supra* note 20, at 352–353.

72. LeBlang et al., *supra* note 17, at 876.

73. *Id.* at 877.

74. *Id.*

75. Keeton, *supra* note 1, at 370.

76. LeBlang et al., *supra* note 17, at 880.

77. Keeton, *supra* note 1, at 371. The case that brought wrongful life actions to the nation's attention was *Gleitman v. Cosgrove,* 227 A. 2d 689 (1967).

78. Keeton, *supra* note 1, at 677.

79. Black, *supra* note 3, at 1095–1097.

80. Uniform Commercial Code, Section 2–314 (1995).

81. *Id.*

82. *Id.*

83. *Restatement (Second) of Torts,* Section 402A (1965); Keeton, *supra* note 1, at 692–702.

84. *Restatement (Second) of Torts, Id.,* Comment K.

85. Public Law 101–629, 104 Stat. 4511 (November 28, 1990).

86. *Id.* at Section 8, Stat. 4511–4512.
87. Nancy J. Brent, "High Tech Care and Medical Devices: The Safe Medical Devices Act of 1990," 10(3) *Home Healthcare Nurse* (May/June 1992), 11–12.

88. Martha Middleton, "A Changing Landscape: The State Vanguard," 81 *ABA Journal* (August 1995), 56–61.
89. Robert D. Miller. *Problems in Hospital Law.* 6th Edition. Rockville, Md: Aspen Publishers, Inc. (1990), 196.

4

Professional Negligence: Prevention and Defense

In Chapter 3, general concepts of negligence and liability were presented. This chapter will focus on guidelines to aid the nurse in avoiding, insofar as humanly possible, unnecessary inclusion in lawsuits alleging professional negligence. It is important to keep in mind, however, that because professional negligence does not require the intent of a person to be negligent—that is, the intent to expose another to an unreasonable and foreseeable risk of harm—there is no absolute way to avoid being named in such a lawsuit. In fact, a study in the *Journal of the American Medical Association* indicates that even past professional negligence claims are not reliable tools in predicting future professional negligence.[1] The study, which focused on physicians included in lawsuits, concluded that it is easier to identify problem-prone procedures than negligence-prone physicians. Therefore, the information presented in this chapter consists only of suggestions that might preclude allegations of professional negligence against the nurse.

The guidelines presented—adequate orientation, adherence to job descriptions, and proper documentation in the patient's medical record, for example—are ones that are familiar to nurses in almost any health care delivery system and in whatever role they undertake in them. Even so, they bear highlighting within a preventive focus aimed at raising one's awareness of professional negligence.

In addition to discussion of guidelines, the defense of a lawsuit alleging professional negligence will also be examined.

KEY PRINCIPLES
Professional Liability Insurance
Defense
Deposition
Testimony at Trial

PREVENTION

Adherence to Standards of Care

It is important to keep in mind that the law *does not* require the nurse to protect against every possible harm to the patient. Rather, the law requires the nurse to carry out care in accordance with what other reasonably prudent nurses would do in the same or similar circumstances. Thus, the nurse's provision of high-quality care consistent with established standards is vital.

. . . the law requires the nurse to carry out care in accordance with what other reasonably prudent nurses would do in the same or similar circumstances.

Adhering to established standards of care requires that the nurse be knowledgeable about them. Attending continuing education courses that focus on established or new standards; continually evaluating skills through regular skills testing courses (whether employer sponsored or through other programs); and updating one's information concerning new developments in patient care are pivotal. These can be accomplished by reading journal articles and professional organization publications (American Nurses' Association, National Association of

Critical Care Nurses, and the Association of Women's Health, Obstetric and Neonatal Nurses, for example) and attending conferences sponsored by the professional groups.

Certification

Obtaining postbasic program certification in the nurse's area of practice is another way of providing quality care to patients. Certification recognizes that the individual nurse possesses advanced and specialized knowledge that the "general" practicing nurse does not.

The first type of certification—by a professional organization—is the most universal. Whatever organization certifies the nurse (there are approximately 30 nursing organizations with certification programs, including the American Nurses' Association, the Emergency Department Nurses' Association, and the American College of Nurse Midwives), the nurse must meet rigorous prerequisites to sit for the certification examination. The certification examination tests performance-based criteria in the area of specialty practice. Re-examination or continuing education is usually required to maintain certification, which is an additional way the provision of quality care to patients is maintained.

Although certification is often a voluntary means of credentialing, in many states it is required for a nurse to obtain a license to practice in advanced nurse practice as a nurse practitioner, a nurse-midwife, a nurse anesthetist, or a clinical nurse specialist. When certification and educational requirements are required by a state for licensure, the nurse is meeting the minimum legal requirements for the particular specialty practice area in that state.

A third type of certification—institutional—is done by academic entities. It acknowledges that the nurse has met the requirements of the particular program of study in the specialty area. For example, many colleges and universities offer a post-master's certificate program in gerontologic or trauma nursing.

Recent statistics indicate that of the 2.2 million nurses in the United States, 300,000 of them are certified in some nursing specialty.[2] However, the certification procedures requirements for those 300,000 are not uniform. A peer review program called the American Board of Nursing Specialties (ABNS) was established in 1991 to, among other things, set standards and establish policies and procedures concerning certification and education of the public relating to certified professional nursing care.[3] One issue being considered by this board and the current certification programs is whether or not a bachelor of science degree in nursing should be a requirement for any certification program.

Orientation to Job/Position

Adequate orientation to a new position or job in which patient care is given may be an important aspect in avoiding unnecessary inclusion in a lawsuit alleging professional negligence. This is particularly so with a new graduate nurse or when the new position is one in which the nurse has had no previous experience. It may be, for example, that a nurse with inpatient medical surgical nursing experience has been hired as a home health care nurse. Despite possessing excellent medical surgical nursing skills, the nurse's use of these skills is very different in the home setting. Health care delivery systems should require that all nurse employees successfully complete an orientation program before being assigned to provide care. In addition, the use of preceptors to work with the new employee for a specified period after orientation is helpful. The nurse can be given time to achieve a level of comfort in the new setting or position before working more independently with patients.

Once adequately oriented, the nurse will need to provide care consistent with patient care policies and procedures. If additional familiarization is needed by the nurse, he or she should voice that need. Furthermore, periodic evaluations of performance (performance appraisals) are important to substantiate quality care and identify areas in which improvement in patient care may be needed.

Job Descriptions

Whenever a nurse seeks a position, he or she should ask for and review carefully its job description. Job descriptions can provide a wealth of information to the nurse, for they include, among other things, the qualifications necessary to perform the job and define patient care responsibilities. If the nurse employee believes the job requirements are beyond his or her level of experience, the position should be rejected, or, at a minimum, the nurse should ask for additional orientation and supervision to fulfill the position responsibilities.

The acceptance of a position requires the nurse to perform his or her role responsibilities within the confines of its description. If there is an injury and professional negligence is alleged, the job description and other patient care documents, like policies and procedures and orientation information, may be introduced into evidence at trial to support conformity—or lack of conformity—with them.[4]

Conformity with a job description is important not only from a liability perspective, but also because of the position the nurse employee may be placed in vis-à-vis the employer. Not adhering to a job description, or performing a task that the nurse was not proficient in pursuant to the institution's internal monitoring system, can result in a theoretical, if not actual, adversarial posture between the employer and the nurse employee. Such a stance may prove quite beneficial to the plaintiff during the course of the trial, especially if the nurse and employer attempt to shift the "blame" for the injury to each other on the basis of the adopted policies, job descriptions, or skills proficiency evaluation.

Patient Care Policies and Procedures

Well-developed policies and procedures can be of great help in the provision of non-negligent care. Because they are based on current, accepted practice, adherence to them may help the nurse avoid omissions in patient care that might result in injury to a patient. Their development is influenced by many factors, including, but not limited to, accreditation standards, court decisions, patient care rights, and state and federal legislation. Health care delivery system policies and procedures are concerned with, among other things, the promotion of quality care, delineation of lines of authority and communication, and meeting accreditation requirements. As a result, they should be updated on a regular basis.[5]

Well-developed policies and procedures can be of great help in the provision of non-negligent care.

Although policies and procedures are used in conjunction with each other and are related, they have separate definitions. A policy is a declaration of the health care delivery system's expectations of staff and the philosophy of the entity, management, and specific departments within the system.[6] A policy does not eliminate the need for individual judgment and decision making, nor does it negate the nurse's accountability for decision making.[7]

A procedure, in contrast, is a detailed, step-by-step description of what is required for a particular situation; for example, in giving patient care, under what circumstances notification to administration must occur, and to whom a situation is to be reported. Procedures cannot be blindly followed by the nurse employee, however; individual decision-making and accountability still exist for the nurse employee.

Once oriented to the policies and procedures for the health care delivery system, the nurse needs to familiarize himself or herself with them and utilize them in the provision of patient care. Should changes be necessary because a procedure is out of date, or not consistent with the nurse's scope of practice, the nurse should discuss this with the Policy and Procedure Committee within the institution. In addition, membership on the committee is a responsibility of the nurse employee and nursing administration.

When deviation from established policies and procedures occurs, liability may result, as is illustrated in Key Case 4–1.

Accreditation, Licensing, and Other Standards

Knowledge of, and adherence to, accreditation, licensing, and other standards can help in reducing lawsuits by providing care consistent

---

KEY CASE 4–1   Czubinsky v. Doctors Hospital (1983)[8]

FACTS: Ms. Czubinsky was admitted to the hospital for "routine" removal of an ovarian cyst. After surgery, she suffered a cardiac arrest in the OR, which resulted in permanent and total paralysis and a semicomatose state. At the time of the arrest, the OR was staffed only by the anesthesiologist and an OR technician. The surgeon had left to prepare for another operation, and the circulating nurse left in response to a call from the surgeon.

Testimony at trial supported allegations of negligence in monitoring and caring for patient in operating room

TRIAL COURT DECISION: Plaintiff filed suit against the hospital alleging that the OR staff failed to properly monitor her and provide the care needed when the arrest occurred. Specifically, she alleged that the OR nurse and technician's "acts and omissions" were the proximate cause of her injuries. The testimony at trial supported this allegation. The surgeon testified to the importance of monitoring postoperatively; that CPR requires a joint effort of several people; and the brain damage that occurred would occur only after several minutes.

Likewise, the expert witness also provided similar testimony, adding that short of an emergency, it would be "inappropriate" for a surgeon to request the OR circulating nurse to leave the patient (no emergency existed here). The anesthesiologist testified that, among other things, he was alone for 2 to 3 minutes before the OR technician returned to the OR and therefore could not provide CPR adequately. The OR technician testified that he left the OR to get help and returned to observe CPR being administered by the anesthesiologist.

Nurse defendant testified she left plaintiff to assist doctor/surgeon on another case

The nurse testified that although she told the surgeon she could not leave the OR until the patient's condition was stable, she did leave and join the surgeon in another operating suite because she was being "yelled at."

Hospital procedure manual required that circulating nurse assist the anesthesiologist throughout entire surgical procedure

To further support her allegations, the plaintiff introduced into evidence the procedure manual of the hospital. It clearly stated that the circulating nurse is a member of the OR team and is to be on hand to assist the anesthesiologist "during the entire procedure." The jury returned a verdict in favor of the plaintiff. However, on a motion by the hospital for a judgment notwithstanding, the verdict (judgment NOV), the judge granted the motion. Ms. Czubinsky appealed.

KEY CASE 4–1   Czubinsky v. Doctors Hospital (1983)[8] Continued

Appeals court reverses trial court's granting of judgment to defendants and holds that the evidence at trial clearly supported jury's decision that the nurse's conduct was the proximate cause of plaintiff's injuries

APPEALS COURT DECISION: The appellate court reversed the trial court's grant of the judgment NOV and ordered the court to enter a judgment for the plaintiff that conformed to the jury verdict. The court did so for two reasons: (1) the lower court mistakenly applied the standard for a judgment NOV and (2) the OR staff was clearly negligent in its monitoring of the patient.

The court discussed at great length the conduct of the nurse and opined that her absence from the OR "was a patent, proximate, efficient cause of Czubinsky's injuries." Her conduct, then, was below the standard of care for the OR nurse. The hospital had therefore failed to provide adequate staff to assist the doctor(s) during the postoperative period.

ANALYSIS: This case illustrates how policies and procedures can be used at trial to support a deviation from the standard of care in a patient care situation. Although the oral testimony of all witnesses was important, the failure of the nurse employee to follow policies adopted by the hospital also aided the jury in finding the hospital negligent. Although it is not clear from the opinion whether the case alleged the hospital's negligence under *respondeat superior*, the corporate theory of liability, or both, it is clear that the court upheld the jury's verdict of negligence by hospital personnel. This case also illustrates the use of a post-trial motion by a losing party asking the court to grant it a verdict despite the jury returning a decision in favor of the other party. A judgment notwithstanding the verdict cannot be granted if the court determines that there is abundant evidence to support the verdict. The appellate court held there was clear and substantial evidence to support the jury's verdict, and therefore reversed the trial court's decision.

---

with those standards. Health care delivery systems are highly regulated by federal, state, and sometimes local laws. In addition, many private agencies also impact on those systems.

State Regulatory Laws

State laws such as a hospital licensing act and a home health care agency act grant a state administrative agency the power to adopt standards the entity must meet, grant licenses to conforming institutions, and enforce compliance with the laws and regulations promulgated by the agency.[9] Compliance with the act not only provides continued licensure, it also can provide guidelines for patient care, especially insofar as staffing requirements, qualifications, eligibility for staff membership, and other aspects of patient care delivery are concerned.

If compliance does not occur, and a patient is injured, he or she will attempt to prove that the noncompliance was the cause of the injury experienced. As a result of the *Darling v. Charles-*

ton Community Hospital case discussed in Chapter 3, applicable licensing standards can be utilized in a trial to support this allegation.

Accreditation Standards

Like licensing standards, accreditation standards for all types of health care delivery systems can provide precepts to adhere to when providing care. Accreditation is given by private organizations, such as the Joint Commission on the Accreditation of Health Care Organizations (JCAHO) and the American Osteopathic Association (osteopathic hospitals). Adherence to their standards is not legally mandated, as is the case with licensing requirements. However, submitting to the voluntary accreditation process speaks to the intent on the part of the health care delivery system to provide quality care to patients.

Furthermore, as with licensing standards, accreditation standards provide guidelines in the provision of acceptable care. They too can be utilized in a trial to prove conformity—or lack of conformity—with them when a patient injury occurs. For example, in a 1990 Illinois Appellate case, *Roberts v. Sisters of Saint Francis,*[10] the Appellate Court discussed the use of Joint Commission standards in relation to the case generally and to their use in the jury instructions against the physician named in that case. The court clearly stated that the Commission's standards could be used if they had been dealt with properly at the trial level.

Federal Regulatory Laws

Perhaps the best known federal law regulating health care delivery—and thus establishing patient care guidelines—is Medicare. Through its "Conditions of Participation,"[11] patient care guidelines are set that, if adhered to, can be helpful in proving the provision of acceptable, non-negligent care.

Continuing Education

Keeping abreast of the newest developments in patient care issues is another essential element in prevention of inclusion in a professional negligence suit. Participating in seminars and classes on the clinical care of patients, scope of practice issues, patient rights, and patient relations can be helpful in focusing the nurse's awareness on the issues and provide him or her with the updated skills to provide patient care safely and effectively. This is particularly so when clinical classes require an evaluation of the skills acquired during the course or workshop.

Keeping abreast of the newest developments in patient care issues is another essential element in prevention of inclusion in a professional negligence suit.

Also important to include in continuing education programs is information on risk management and the fundamentals of liability law.

Open Lines of Communication

It may seem simplistic to think that open lines of communication can be a preventive measure to inclusion in a lawsuit alleging professional negligence. However, communication is "essential for the provision of quality patient care."[12] Thus, the nurse must ensure open and ongoing lines of communication with other staff nurse colleagues, nursing management, hospital administration, risk management, physicians, and other health team members. If changes in a patient's condition are quickly communicated and intervention occurs, if a problem concerning disagreement with patient care is appropriately shared and resolved within the health care delivery system hierarchy, or if needed changes in patient care procedures are brought to the appropriate staff committee for needed revisions, patient injury may be avoided. In a 1986 study at George Washington University in Washington, D.C., data indicated that hospitals with good lines of communication between physicians and nurses had fewer deaths in the intensive care unit (ICU).[13]

Open and ongoing lines of communication with the patient and his or her family are also essential. This includes, of course, providing information to the patient and the family, informing them of changes in care, and keeping them abreast of hospital policy and procedures generally. It also includes more subtle ingredients, however, that lie at the heart of treating individuals with dignity and respect. Thus, establishing rapport, practicing "active listening," acknowledging feelings, and responding to the concerns of the patient or the family are essential.

Although it is difficult to say with certainty that being treated in a humane and caring manner will always avoid a lawsuit, especially when a "bad medical outcome" occurs, studies indicate that one factor used to evaluate medical care by patients is their level of satisfaction with the care. A well-known 1974 study indicated that patients are less critical of the technical aspects of their care than they are of its attitudinal and situational components.[14] Other commentators have said that the decision to file a suit as a result of an incident—real or imagined—is a socioeconomic process, not solely a legal or medical one.[15] In addition, indifference to the patient or family, anger experienced by the patient, and poor communication have all been identified as pivotal factors in the decisional process to sue.[16]

Documentation of Patient Care

The medical record is an essential and necessary part of patient care. The medical record is to be a complete and accurate account of the patient's care while receiving treatment in the health care delivery system. Its contents are regulated by many sources, including licensing, accrediting, and professional organization (for example, the American Nurses' Association)

standards, case law, and state practice acts. Common requirements from those sources include, but are not limited to, the medical history, physical examination results, reports of laboratory and other diagnostic tests, nursing assessments and care provided, informed consent for procedures, and the documentation of any patient and/or family teaching done.[17]

The uses of the medical record are as varied as the sources that impact on their contents. Within the health care delivery system, the record is used to communicate between and among staff, departments, and health care providers concerning the patient and his or her care. It is also used by the system's risk management department and utilization review and quality assurance committees to evaluate patient care and its need, and determine where improvements should occur.

Outside the health care delivery system itself, the medical record is used by third party payors, private and governmental, including Medicare and Medicaid, to ensure that they are paying for actual services provided; by researchers in health care; and for initial and continuing accreditation or licensing grants by health care administrative agencies.

The patient's medical record is also used in legal proceedings, whether by administrative agencies required to enforce social benefit programs, such as worker's compensation laws, by the state's attorney or other prosecutorial body to enforce criminal laws, or by a civil court to determine the extent of the injured person's injuries in a car accident or due to alleged negligence on the part of a health care provider.

The medical record is also used in litigation in which professional negligence is alleged (and is the first piece of potential evidence that is extensively evaluated by the plaintiff's attorney when consulted by an injured patient concerning a suit). Therefore, it must be viewed as a viable way in which to defend against allegations of professional negligence. If the medical record is complete and accurate and reflects the documentation of high-quality, non-negligent care, it can be the nurse's "best defense" against allegations of negligence. If, however, the documentation is incomplete, contains gaps, is not consistently done pursuant to policies, and is inaccurate, then the record can, and will, be used to support the allegations of negligence in the patient's complaint. One study indicated that one in four malpractice suits are decided from the patient's medical record.[18] Thus, adhering to guidelines for proper documentation is essential.

The following guidelines are general ones for the nurse to keep in mind when documenting in the medical record. They are not meant to be all-inclusive. Therefore, the nurse should consult other guidelines available, such as accreditation standards. In addition, review of the other chapters in the book in Parts 2 and 3 for specific DOCUMENTATION REMINDERS pertinent to those areas of practice is also recommended. Guidelines for computer documentation of patient care will be discussed separately.

Documentation Guidelines

1. Write legibly.
2. Use black, permanent ink for entries. Do not use colored pens, pencils, or felt-tip pens.
3. Date and time all entries.
4. Every entry must be accounted for; that is, the nurse must sign his or her name and list credentials and other required data for every entry reflecting patient care. No nurse should document in the medical record for another person, unless that practice is "standard" practice, as in emergency room nursing. Even so, when documenting for another, the nurse "scribe" must accurately reflect who is providing care and who is documenting the care. Under no circumstances, however, should the nurse sign another nurse's name in any portion of the record.
5. No blank spaces should be left in any area of the documentation. If space is left on a line after the entry is complete, the nurse should draw a line through the space to the end of the page. If larger areas are available on form sheets (e.g., comments section or other section) and are not used, a line should be drawn diagonally through them so it is clear that documentation in the section was not overlooked. Documenting something like N/A (for not applicable or not assessed), if documentation policies allow for this, is also acceptable.

6. There should be no erasures, obliterations, or "whiting out" on any portion of the medical record. If an error in the record must be corrected, it should be done by drawing one line through the error, initialing and dating the line, and continuing the documentation of the correct information on the next available space or line.

7. Factual entries are essential. The medical record is no place for opinions, assumptions, or meaningless words or statements ("Had a good day"). Rather, the entry should be factual, complete, accurate, and contain observations, clinical signs and symptoms, patient quotes, if applicable, interventions, and patient reactions.

Factual entries are essential. The medical record is no place for opinions, assumptions, or meaningless words or statements ("Had a good day").

---

8. The use of correct spelling, punctuation marks, and grammar is important.

9. Every medical record page should reflect the patient's correct name and other identifying information.

10. Abbreviations used in the medical record must be confined to ones adopted by the health care delivery system only, and used according to the meanings assigned them. If there is no adopted policy concerning abbreviations, then the nurse should not use them, but write out all words instead. Also, the nurse should not use his or her own abbreviations, however clever

and time saving they may be. Last, adopted abbreviations should be used consistently throughout the institution; for example, it would not be acceptable to use *pp* as "post partum" on the labor and delivery service, but use it for "pedal pulse" in other areas of the hospital.

11. Documentation in the record should occur as soon after the care given as possible. Entries should never be made before a procedure or medication is given.

12. When a physician, supervisor, or others (including other staff nurses) must be contacted concerning a patient's condition, that information should be entered in the record in a factual and accurate manner and include the manner of communication, the names of those contacted, what was discussed, and what response took place as a result of the contact. Any new orders must be documented according to policy, and the care provided, the patient's response to the newly ordered care, and any other necessary information documented. An incident or occurrence report may also need to be filled out.

13. Any order, narcotics count, narrative entry, or other documentation should not be countersigned unless the countersigner can attest to the accuracy of the information and that he or she has personal knowledge of it. If a nurse cannot speak to both of those issues, it is best to qualify the countersignature in some way; for example, documenting that the nurse has only reviewed the entry and signed it.

14. When an unusual incident occurs, such as a fall or other type of patient injury, in addition to documenting the information on an occurrence or incident report, the situation must also be documented in the patient's medical record. The filing of an incident report *does not* take the place of documenting the information in the record.

15. Whenever a patient leaves the nurse's care (for diagnostic work, for example) or the nurse leaves the patient (when a home health care nurse leaves the home after provision of care), an entry in the medical record should reflect the time, the condition of the patient upon leaving, and any other information necessary for the reader of the entry to be aware of.

16. A patient transfer requires that information concerning the transfer, including the date and time of transfer, patient condition when transferred, who (if anyone) accompanied the patient, who provided the transfer, where and to whom the patient is transferred, and manner of transfer (for example, wheelchair or ambulance) be documented in the record.

17. Consent for, or refusal of, treatment must be documented in the record, either by written consent or refusal forms or by the physician documenting this information in his or her progress notes. If the nurse is involved in a consent or refusal situation, the incident should be documented in his or her nursing notes.

18. Patient and/or family teaching, as well as discharge planning, must also be documented in the medical record. The use of teaching forms for the purpose of documenting the teaching that took place is an acceptable way of doing so, so long as the forms can withstand legal challenges to their completeness, accuracy, and the patient's ability to understand them. Likewise, discharge planning must be complete, specific to the needs of the patient and the family, and communicated to the patient and others who may be involved in his or her care.

19. The existence and disposition of any personal belongings of the patient—dentures, glasses, jewelry, and money, for example—need to be recorded. If, for example, the patient's glasses are placed in the bedside stand, or given to the family to take home, there must be factual documentation in the record.

20. Patient responses to medications, treatments, patient teaching, and any other interventions by the nursing staff should be documented. It *is* important to intervene with a patient care problem. It is equally important, however, to assess and document the patient's response to the care provided.

21. Agency or institution policies should be reviewed regularly and adhered to when documenting in the patient's record.

22. When it is necessary to add omitted information to an already existing entry, policies and procedures should be consulted to conform with them. Most often, the addition of information is coded on the next available line or space as a "late entry" or "addition to nursing note of _____," given the date and time of the information that is being added and then placed in the record.

Computer Documentation Guidelines

Electronic medical record (EMR) and *electronic medical charting* (EMC) are no longer strange or unknown terms to health care providers. Electronic or computer documentation is in use in many health care delivery systems across the United States, albeit in varying degrees. The variety is based mainly on the regulation of computers in health care by state regulatory agencies, such as the hospital licensing board. For example, some states may authorize health care institutions to utilize electronic documentation only for medical test results or nursing entries, while others have allowed electronic documentation for the entire patient care record. In either case, when the nurse must provide information concerning patient care by a computer, rather than by handwritten entries, additional concerns exist. Clearly, nurse managers must establish policies and procedures that address those concerns, including, but not limited to (1) internal and external data sharing, (2) monitoring and reporting of data, (3) periodic review of the data entered into the electronic system, and (4) methods for the patient to provide consent for the use and release of the stored information.[19] Including these points in policies and procedures can aid greatly in protecting the patient's right of privacy and confidentiality of the stored information.[20]

Electronic documentation guidelines include:

1. The nurse must protect the user identification code, name, and/or password given for documentation. They should not be given to anyone else for his or her "temporary" use or for another to document for the nurse who has been assigned those access identifiers.

2. The nurse should only access information and document where and how authorized to do so. For example, the nurse should not attempt to obtain information concerning a unit or patient if not authorized, as a breach of confidentiality and privacy clearly occurs (e.g., substance abuse or mental health care).

3. The nurse should not ignore any "expert reminders" that show up for a particular patient. For example, if the nurse did not code information correctly, or if important data were overlooked, the computer would alert the nurse to those omissions.[21]

4. Late entries will be handled differently than they would under a narrative format. The nurse will need to be clear about the procedure for adding information into the system *after* exiting a particular patient's file or the program itself.

5. Utilization of the correct user identification code of the nurse *and* the correct patient code (for the patient record itself) is essential.

6. Keeping current when changes in the documentation format occur will be important. This responsibility can be aided by the staff education department providing in-services to nursing staff when new formats are adopted.

DEFENSE

The defense of a case is the defendant's answer or response to a claim or suit that sets forth the reasons why the defendant is not liable and why the relief requested should not be granted.[22] The defense of a case includes, but is not limited to, the filing of an answer, raising specific, affirmative defenses against the allegations obtaining evidence to support one's position, and identifying the best strategic overall approach to the case.

The defense of any case alleging professional negligence against the nurse also involves proving, through the use of established rules of evidence and court procedures to a judge (bench trial) or jury (jury trial), that the relief requested by the plaintiff should not be granted. Several specific topics pertaining to the defense of professional negligence suits will be highlighted here. The reader is also encouraged to review Chapter 2 for further elaboration of the civil judicial system generally, especially in relation to the defense of any civil suit.

Selecting an Attorney

If the nurse's attorney is provided under the contract of insurance, the selection of the attorney remains with the insurer. If the nurse is not comfortable with the attorney assigned, or, if on the other hand, the nurse is not covered by a professional liability policy for whatever reason and must select an attorney for representation, Appendix A should be reviewed to aid the nurse in resolving his or her concerns surrounding the selection of an attorney.

Selecting an Expert Witness

The use of an expert witness in a professional negligence case is necessary in most jurisdictions. Thus, selecting the appropriate person who can best educate the jury concerning the nurse's conduct in the particular case and the applicable standard is important.

The selection of an expert witness can occur in various ways. First and foremost, it is important to retain a nurse expert who has had experience in testifying in that role. Those individuals can sometimes be identified through state nursing associations or through the national nurse attorney association (The American Association of Nurse Attorneys). In addition, local attorneys and nurse attorneys are good resources to obtain information concerning nurse expert witnesses.

Second, the nurse expert witness must possess the credentials necessary to qualify as an expert witness in the particular state. In addition, appropriate credentialing can be helpful in avoiding a successful attempt by opposing

counsel to question the nurse expert's credentials during cross-examination. Credentials would include educational preparation, experience, publications, and honors received by the nurse expert witness.

Third, the nurse expert witness must be able to testify accurately and with confidence. Guidelines for nurse expert testimony are discussed below.

Preparation for Trial

A civil suit has many phases, the last of which chronologically is the actual trial itself. Prior to trial, the discovery period is an active and intense time during which facts and information about the case are obtained from all the parties involved to assist in preparation for trial.[23] Guidelines for one specific tool used during the discovery phase, the deposition, and actual trial testimony will be briefly discussed.

A deposition is a type of pretrial discovery method whereby the statement of a party or witness is taken under oath.

A deposition is a type of pretrial discovery method whereby the statement of a party or witness is taken under oath. The deponent (person giving the deposition) may be asked questions by all attorneys for the named parties (plaintiff[s] and defendant[s]). If the deposition is a *discovery* deposition, it usually cannot be introduced into evidence at trial. It can, however, be used to impeach the deponent at trial if his or her testimony varies from the deposition testimony. In contrast, if the deposition is an *evidence* deposition, it can be introduced into evidence at the trial (thus eliminating the need for the witness to be present at trial). Evidence depositions are often used for parties or witnesses who may not be able to attend the trial for many reasons, including living in another state or terminal illness.

In contrast, testifying at the trial is the process of providing evidence, through one's statement under oath, for the purpose of establishing or proving a fact or facts in a judicial inquiry.[24]

The following suggestions are not meant to be all-inclusive or absolute. Rather, they provide ways in which the defense of a suit against the nurse can be better defended. As a general rule, these guidelines are important to consider whether giving a deposition or testifying at trial.

As a Named Party or Witness

1. Always be prepared for the testifying. This includes a thorough review of the situation that gave rise to the suit, and any and all documentation concerning the incident (e.g., the medical record). Talk with your attorney about what can be expected at the deposition or at trial.

2. Testifying truthfully is essential. Falsified or otherwise untrue testimony can create more problems than it helps in the defense of a case. In addition, perjury is a crime under federal and most state laws.

3. The nurse must be open and honest with his or her attorney. Although doing so may be "embarrassing" or uncomfortable for the nurse, the attorney must not be shielded from information that compromises his or her ability to defend the case to the fullest extent possible. This is particularly important if the nurse does not share information with his or her counsel and the attorney for the other party does discover it, and uses it during the deposition or at trial. This situation could result in the credibility of the nurse being compromised.

4. The nurse should dress conservatively and professionally when giving testimony. Because impressions will be important, whether during a deposition or at trial, the nurse's appearance is important. During the deposition, the others present want to "discover" how the deponent (the person providing the testimony)

looks and responds during the deposition *in addition to* hearing the actual testimony. Many times, cases are settled, or a decision made to go to trial, based on a witness's or party's demeanor during a deposition. And, at trial, how the jury perceives an individual and the testimony given can impact on their ultimate decision.

5. Controlling one's anger, anxiety, and frustration is important. During the deposition and trial, opposing counsel(s) may attempt to reduce the credibility of the nurse's testimony. Many times that attempt includes trying to manipulate the witness (being hostile, then nice); intentionally misstating prior testimony; appearing surprised at anything that is said; using hypothetical situations quite different from the incident that formed the basis of the suit; and questioning professional competence. Ignoring these, and other tactics, and answering as confidently, normally, and nondefensively as possible will weaken, if not totally destroy, these maneuvers.

Furthermore, questions involving a hypothetical situation should probably be objected to by the nurse's attorney as not relevant to the nurse's testimony. Although hypothetical situations are used by the expert witness in many states, their use with named parties or occurrence witnesses is questionable. If the nurse, however, is asked to respond to a hypothetical situation, he or she should do so only after differentiating it from the case before the court.

6. The nurse should answer only those questions asked of him or her. Many times, nurses involved in the legal system try to cooperate so fully that they do the work for the opposing side. It is the lawyer's responsibility and obligation to elicit testimony; make him or her do that job.

7. Waiting until the entire question is asked before answering is vital. Again, in an attempt to appear cooperative, or because of anxiety, the nurse involved in testifying may begin an answer before the question is clear. Doing so may volunteer information not asked, and once heard, whether by those attending the deposi-

tion or the trial jury, it is difficult to "disregard" the statement.

8. Waiting a few seconds before answering *after* the question is asked is also helpful, for it gives the nurse's attorney the opportunity to object to the question asked. Once an answer is given, an objection can still be made. However, as is true with an answer given before the question is completed, once heard, the jury may find it difficult to disregard the answer despite instructions by the judge to do so. Furthermore, only if an objection to a question is sustained is the answer stricken from the record. Thus a slight pause avoids the risk of an answer remaining in the record because the objection was overruled.

9. The nurse should not guess at any answers. If the nurse does not know an answer, does not remember something, or cannot estimate about a particular issue, he or she should say so. The attorney for the nurse can deal with these inabilities through various trial techniques. Also, if those techniques are not helpful to the nurse in providing the requested testimony, then it is best not to try to answer a question under oath when not as reasonably certain as can be about that answer.

10. Testifying as clearly as possible is important. Overusing "medicalese" can be problematic, although there must be a balance between using "appropriate" medical terms and descriptions and using it to excess. This is particularly important at trial, for the jury must be convinced that the nurse knows what he or she is testifying to—is a competent and non-negligent professional, in other words—but it cannot be "lost" in the process.

11. Although the nurse may want to appear friendly during the trial, it is important that the nurse defendant or witness *not* talk with the jury in any manner during the trial. Attempting to do so may lead to a mistrial being granted by the judge or charges of jury tampering being alleged against the nature.

12. The nurse must be careful not to personalize anything about the suit. Although the nurse's conduct is in question if a named defendant in the suit, the tendency to see himself or herself as a "bad nurse" or "doing something wrong" is a common, but not helpful, reaction.[25]

13. The nurse must rely on the advice his or her attorney provides. The defense of any lawsuit, including a professional negligence suit, is complicated, diverse, and foreign to most nurses. Although the advice the attorney provides may not seem "correct," the attorney is the one with the most knowledge in the situation concerning the law and its application. If the nurse simply cannot follow the attorney's advice and direction, however, he or she should discuss this with the attorney. It may be that another attorney will need to be assigned to the case, or perhaps the "differences" can be worked out when information and rationale are provided. In any event, the nurse must be clear about the fact that the attorney is *his or her advocate*. Advocacy depends on a relationship of mutual trust and honesty and open lines of communication.

Although the nurse may want to appear friendly during the trial, it is important that the nurse defendant or witness not talk with the jury in any manner during the trial.

As an Expert Witness

In addition to the suggestions given for the nurse defendant or witness, the nurse who functions as an expert witness has additional concerns in relation to his or her testimony and its impact on the defense of the case. The following general guidelines are also important during a deposition or trial in which the expert witness is testifying.

1. The nurse expert witness must testify accu-

rately and completely as to his or her qualifications. A thorough review of education, positions held, publications, and honors is vital, along with applicable dates.

2. Preparation is essential. Many sources of information must be reviewed to provide an opinion because the expert usually does not possess direct, actual knowledge concerning the case. Those sources include the medical record, nursing tests and articles, the state nurse practice act, national standards applicable to the case, the agency or institution policy and procedure manual, and depositions.

3. The nurse expert witness will need to be familiar with the law of the state where he or she will be testifying as it relates to the form the opinion will take. In some states the expert witness is asked directly to give his or her opinion after a review of the medical record and the testimony at trial. Other states present a hypothetical situation based on the case, and the expert witness is then asked to give an opinion based on the theoretical circumstance. In either case the nurse must testify honestly concerning whether or not the standard of care for the nurse in the case was maintained or breached.

4. The role of the expert witness is to educate the jury to the standard of care. Thus, his or her testimony must be clear, concise, and complete. This requires judicious use of medicalese so that the testimony can be understood by the jurors.

---

*The role of the expert witness
is to educate the jury
to the standard of care.*

Ramifications for Other Liability

The defense of any case, including the defense of a professional negligence case, must take into account the potential for other liability. Thus, the attorney who represents a nurse in a professional negligence suit must analyze the conduct that formed the basis of the suit to determine if potential criminal liability, or the possibility of a disciplinary action, is possible. If so, the defense of the professional negligence suit must be done with those other possible legal actions in mind. Consulting with attorneys who concentrate their respective practices in those areas initially is well advised so that the strategies of the suits can be planned. The nurse may need to raise this concern with his or her attorney at the beginning of the defense of the negligence suit so that additional problems can be planned for if further legal action is taken against the nurse.

INSURANCE ISSUES

Self-Insurance

Most nurses named in lawsuits are covered by some form of professional liability insurance. The insurance coverage may exist under the employer's self-insurance plan. With this type of self-insurance, the insurance statement/contract is drafted by the employer and establishes conditions under which the self-insurance applies (e.g., coverage and loss).[26] The institution's self-insurance may be in the form of a self-insurance fund, a trust fund, or disbursion from operating funds.[27] Self-insurance is seen as beneficial for several reasons, including the fact that the institution controls the claims and claims process, is less expensive than purchasing liability insurance from an insurer, and provides a sense of cohesion among the staff when a suit is filed.[28]

Professional Liability Insurance Policy

A professional liability insurance policy is a contract whereby an insurer agrees to enter into a policy of insurance with the insured (e.g., the hospital or the nurse) to provide coverage for delineated professional activities. If the hospital and/or nurse is found to be liable for the plaintiff's injuries or damages due to conduct covered under the insurance contract, the insurer (the insurance company) will pay that amount on behalf of the insured. Common language in liability insurance contracts specifying what is a covered event includes professional negligence (or malpractice), errors, omissions, and/or mistakes in rendering nursing services.

The nurse may carry his or her own professional liability insurance or may rely on coverage under the institutional liability policy. The latter will cover the nurse only when functioning as an employee and working within the scope of his or her employment. Regardless whether the nurse purchases his or her own professional liability insurance or relies on the employer's, certain factors should be evaluated by the nurse concerning the insurance policy, and these factors are summarized in Table 4–1.

Applicable Professional Liability Insurance

If the nurse named in a lawsuit is covered under a policy of professional liability insurance, the policy will usually stipulate that an attorney be employed by the insurer to represent

---

TABLE 4–1

Factors to Evaluate with Professional Liability Insurance Policies

TYPE OF POLICY—CLAIMS MADE (covers a claim only if injury occurs and claim filed while the policy is in effect) or OCCURRENCE (covers a claim regardless of when filed so long as the incident arose while the policy was in effect); if policy CLAIMS MADE, tail coverage needed to cover claim made after policy no longer in effect.

AMOUNT OF COVERAGE—Adequate coverage important. Based on type of practice, cost of coverage, any ceilings (caps) on the amount injured parties can recover for, and own assets that need protecting. Insurer will pay only for damages as specified in the insurance contract. Dollar limits are usually expressed as $A/$B; A represents the amount paid per claim and B the aggregate amount paid under the policy in a given year.

INSURED'S OBLIGATIONS UNDER POLICY—Full and honest disclosure concerning type of nursing practice and responsibilities; cooperating with the insurer in defending any suit; notifying the insurer if named in a suit, if a patient is injured as a result of care rendered, or if a suit is threatened against the nurse.

INSURER'S OBLIGATIONS UNDER POLICY—A general duty to defend any and all allegations against the insured that are covered by the policy; pay for any and all expenses to do so (unless limited by the terms of the policy); provide effective legal representation (if included in policy); and notify the insured within specified time frames if the insurance policy is going to be canceled.

EXCLUSIONS IN THE POLICY—Generally, no coverage for intentional torts, criminal charges, exceeding the scope of one's practice as defined by state nurse practice acts, or punitive damages.

INDEMNIFICATION AND CONTRIBUTION CLAUSES—Clauses in the contract of insurance covering the right of one of the parties to seek reimbursement for any costs and damages paid on behalf of the other party, and the right of the insurer to share a payment proportionally in accordance with the policy limits when more than one policy covers the loss. Although separate and distinct clauses, both are important to the insured and should be carefully reviewed. Depending on how they are written in the policy, the nurse may seek recovery from the insurance company for some or all monies paid personally to defend against a suit under the indemnification language. Or, with a contribution clause, if two liability insurance policies cover the same event, the two insurance companies will be determining each's respective "contribution" to any judgment entered against the nurse.

"OTHER INSURANCE" CLAUSE—A clause describing which policy of insurance will control if more than one exists. Terms such as *primary, excess,* and *secondary* will usually be present. Other clauses that control the contribution of the policy, once its role is established, are *excess* (no payment will occur until all other sources of coverage are expended); *pro rata* (sharing of the loss according to the contract); and *escape* (no coverage or payment if other insurance coverage exists). In addition, the insurance policy may have language in it allowing the company to settle a case without the consent of the insured (nurse). Although this is often a troubling requirement for the nurse defendant, it is important to remember that its inclusion in a policy is based not on the merits of the case, but rather on financial considerations of continuing a suit. In other words, if it is more beneficial for the insurance company to "cut its losses" and end the suit rather than proceeding further, it will do so.

Data from: The American Association of Nurse Attorneys. *Demonstrating Financial Responsibility for Nursing Practice.* Baltimore, MD: TAANA, 1989; University Hospital Consortium. *Nursing-Legal Survival: A Risk Management Guide for Nurses.* Oak Brook, IL: University Hospital Consortium, 1992, 95–103; American Medical Association. *The Guide to Medical Professional Liability Insurance.* Chicago, IL: AMA, 1991.

the insured. Although the insured may have the obligation to provide counsel, if the nurse is not satisfied with the selection of the attorney, he or she should make that dissatisfaction known to the insurer. Furthermore, if the nurse's concerns are not heeded by the insurer, the nurse may retain private counsel at his or her own cost to obtain effective representation. In such a situation, the insurance attorney would most probably withdraw from representing the nurse, and there may be another suit filed concerning the insurance contract and the potential breach of the insurer to provide competent counsel.

If the nurse named in a lawsuit is covered under a policy of professional liability insurance, the policy will usually stipulate that an attorney be employed by the insurer to represent the insured.

The insurance policy provisions will also include whether it is the "primary insurance," provides "secondary" coverage, or is an "excess" policy. Generally speaking, if only one policy is carried by the nurse, it will be the primary insurance policy. If, however, the nurse is covered by two professional liability insurance policies—one purchased by the employer and one purchased by the nurse personally, for example—one may become the secondary policy based on the language of the respective policies. If, in contrast, the nurse's employer is self-insured and the nurse covered in that manner, his or her own commercial policy would most probably become the primary coverage and the employer's self-insurance utilized as an excess fund.[29]

It is difficult to predict with certainty how coverage questions would be resolved, for each situation must be analyzed in view of the specific language of the policy and applicable state laws. Thus, if named in a suit, the nurse should obtain as much information as possible concerning the coverage issue and if needed, obtain an independent, objective opinion as to his or her rights and responsibilities in the situation.

SUMMARY OF PRINCIPLES AND APPLICATIONS

The defense of a professional negligence suit requires a great deal of time, effort, and strategy. Perhaps the best defense, however, is to avoid being included in such a suit. Although easier said than done, and although there is no absolute way to avoid being named in a suit that alleges professional negligence, the nurse can avoid unnecessary inclusion in such a suit by:

▼ Practicing nursing in accordance with licensing standards, professional standards, well-developed policies and procedures of the health care system, and accreditation standards

▼ Asking for orientation to a new position

▼ Reviewing the job description of the position hired for

▼ Documenting care in accordance with accreditation and licensing standards, agency policy, and applicable national standards of documentation of nursing care

▼ Maintaining open lines of communication with fellow health care workers and patients and their families

▼ Maintaining and updating credentials and certification for areas of nursing practice, including specialty areas of practice

▼ Keeping current on nursing practices, procedures, and other developments in the delivery of nursing care

▼ Carefully evaluating professional liability insurance coverage, including whether to purchase one's own policy, what type of policy is being purchased, and what the nurse's obligations are under the policy

▼ Practicing within the scope of nursing practice, including any specialty area of nursing

When inclusion in a suit does occur, the nurse can help in his or her own defense by:

▼ Cooperating fully with his or her attorney

▼ Testifying in a competent and professional manner

▼ Utilizing expert witness testimony by a nurse to establish the standard of care

▼ Not allowing the inclusion in a suit to undermine his or her confidence in one's professional abilities

TOPICS FOR FURTHER INQUIRY

1. Critically evaluate at least three different professional liability insurance policies. Look for similarities and differences in terms of coverage amounts, definitions of nursing in the policy, and exclusions and costs, as well as other provisions. Decide which policy provides the best protection for the nurse.

2. Interview a nurse who has been named in a suit and has had to go through at least a portion of the trial process. Ascertain the nurse's perception of her attorney's role during the deposition or trial testimony. Have the nurse identify ways in which he or she believed the attorney's role could have been different or more helpful.

3. Locate and interview several nurses who function as nurse experts in the reader's area of nursing specialty. Compare and contrast each nurse expert's experience as a part of the litigation team.

4. Analyze several documentation policies from health care facilities for how, if at all, the policies protect the nurse in documenting from a "defense" position. Identify ways in which the policies could be improved.

REFERENCES

1. John E. Rolph, "Malpractice Claims Data As A Quality Improvement Tool: Is Targeting Effective." 266(15) *JAMA* (October 16, 1991), 2093–2097.
2. Margaret Sloane, "Specialty Certification: Should A BSN Be Required?" 8(1) *The Nursing Spectrum* (January 23, 1995), 9–10.
3. *Id.* at 10.
4. *Darling v. Charleston Community Hospital*, 211 N.E.2d 253 (1965), *cert. denied*, 383 U.S. 946 (1966).
5. Janine Fresta, "Not Following Policies and Standards of Care," *20 Legal Pitfalls for Nurses to Avoid.* Albany, NY: Delmar Publishers, Inc. (1994), 24–30.
6. Anita Finkelman. *Policies and Procedures for Psychiatric Nursing.* Rockville, Md: Aspen Publishers, Inc., 1986, 8–9.
7. *Id.*
8. 188 Cal. Rptr. 685 (App. 1983).
9. Robert D. Miller. *Problems in Hospital Law.* 6th Edition. Rockville, Md: Aspen Publishers, Inc., 1990, 38.
10. 556 N.E.2d 662 (1st District 1990).
11. 42 U.S.C.A. Section 1395x(e) (1983 & 1989 Supp); 42 C.F.R. pt. 482 (1988).
12. Kay Meyers and Pauline Fergusson. *Nurse At Risk.* Des Moines, Iowa: HealthPro, 1988, 29.
13. *Id.* at 31.
14. J. L. Lebow, "Consumer Assessments of the Quality of Medical Care," 12 *Medical Care* (1974), 328.
15. Irwin Press, "The Predisposition to File Claims: The Patient's Perspective," in *Handbook of Health Care Risk Management.* Glenn Troyer and Steven Salman, Editors. Rockville, Md: Aspen Publishers, Inc., 1986, 443, citing W. Felsteiner, R. Abel, and A. Sarat. "The Emergence and Transformation of Disputes: Naming, Blaming, Claiming." 15 (3&4) *Law and Society Review*, (1980/1981), 631–654.
16. Gregory Lester and Susan Smith, "Listening and Talking to Patients: A Remedy for Lawsuits?" 158 *Western Journal of Medicine* (1993), 268–272.
17. William Roach and The Aspen Health Law Center, "Patient Record Requirements." *Medical Records and the Law.* 2nd Edition. Gaithersburg, Md: Aspen Publishers, Inc., 1994, 1–16.
18. Jacqueline Edelstein, "A Study of Nursing Documentation," 21(11) *Nursing Management* (November 1990), 301–302.
19. United States Congress. Office of Technology Assessment. *Protecting Privacy in Computerized Medical Information.* Washington, DC: U.S. Government Printing Office, September 1993 (OTA-TCT-567).
20. *Id.*
21. Ray Simpson, "Electronic Patient Charts: Beware The Hype." 22(4) *Nursing Management* (April 1991), 13.
22. Henry Campbell Black. *Black's Law Dictionary.* 6th Edition. St. Paul, Minn: West Publishing Company, 1991, 290.
23. Black, *supra* note 22, at 322.
24. *Id.* at 1028.
25. Nancy Johnson and Mary Wroblewski, "Litigation Stress

in Nurses," 20(10) *Nursing Management* (October 1989), 23.

26. Vickey Masta-Gornic. "A Basic Insurance Primer," *The Risk Manager's Desk Reference*. Barbara Youngberg, Editor. Gaithersburg, Md: Aspen Publishers, Inc., 1994, 173.

27. *Id.* at 174.

28. *Id.*

29. The American Association of Nurse Attorneys, Inc. *Demonstrating Financial Responsibility for Nursing Practice*. Baltimore: TAANA, 1989, 4.

5

Quality Assurance and Risk Management

The provision of quality patient care is of constant concern and a goal of most health care delivery systems and health care providers, especially in view of the legal obligation of both to provide reasonable, non-negligent care. That concern and goal can be thwarted, however, when additional factors exert equally compelling influences on their achievement. Such factors do exist and include economic concerns over the rising costs of health care; the proliferation of third-party payors in health care; increased regulation of health care delivery by state and federal governments, including diagnostic related groups (DRGs); the proliferation of "alternative delivery health care systems"; rising competition among health care systems; the "malpractice crisis" of the 1980s; the nursing and other health care provider "shortage;" and the increasingly sophisticated health care consumers who demand quality care.

It is clear that these factors have created a focus on cost containment, and that focus has impacted on the provision of quality patient care. Several authors have identified problems faced in providing quality care after diagnostic related groups were instituted, including access of patients to health care, "harried hospitals," "pressured professionals," and, of course, the financial impact of uncompensated care on the institution.[1] Another analyzed whether a lower standard of medical malpractice should exist because of the cost containment concerns in health care.[2] Certificate of need (CON) programs requiring justification for additional health facilities and services, especially when a cap on health care expenditures or a moratorium on approvals is established, has arguably reduced the availability of needed health care services and facilities.[3] Also, the ever-present question of the allocation of scarce resources has not been dissipated by cost containment.[4] If anything, the competition for limited resources has become more acute.

Although there may be general agreement that economic, and other, constraints may ad-versely affect patient care, there is little agreement on what quality patient care is. In its broadest sense, it may be best defined as "providing care in such a manner as to improve the health and functioning of the patient."[5] Using this definition, then, quality assurance can be seen as the ongoing, planned process that consistently and objectively monitors and evaluates the quality and appropriateness of patient care. The process also involves improving care and resolving identified problems.[6]

Cost containment will need to fit into the quality assurance process, as must the management of risk, both to the patient and others in the health care delivery system. Arguably, this can be successfully achieved through comprehensive, constant, and rigorous evaluation of patient care.[7]

This chapter will focus on examination of quality assurance and risk management programs in health care delivery systems.

ESSENTIALS OF MONITORING AND EVALUATING PATIENT CARE

Historical Overview

Quality assurance, utilization review, and risk management all had different developmental chronologies, but each of their distinctive developments can be traced to society's general con-

---

KEY PRINCIPLES

Quality Assurance

Utilization Review

Risk Management

Peer Review

Continuous Quality Improvement (CQI)/Total Quality Management (TQM)

Health Care Quality Improvement Act (HCQIA) of 1986

The National Council of State Boards of Nursing Data Bank

cern with the quality of health care. Nursing quality assurance most probably began with Florence Nightingale, who evaluated care given soldiers in the Crimean War in a systematic manner.[8] Quality assurance generally began as a response to the Joint Commission on the Accreditation of Health Care Organizations (JCAHO) establishment in 1953 (then JCAH) and its subsequent standards for accreditation.[9] The federal government, through its Medicare and Medicaid programs, also enhanced the development of quality assurance.

Nursing quality assurance most probably began with Florence Nightingale . . .

Likewise, utilization review was given a solid beginning with the establishment of the Medicare and Medicaid programs, especially in relation to payment for services rendered to patients under the two programs. DRGs, the initial Professional Standards Review Organizations (PSROs) established by the Social Security Act of 1972, and the current peer review organizations (PROs) are but three examples of aspects of the federal program that aided the development of utilization review activities.

Risk management's development and growth were clearly a result of the "malpractice crisis" experienced in the United States in the 1970s.[10] Although risk management in the health care industry did not exist until well after it was present in other industries, it has become an integral part of evaluating and maintaining quality care.

Definitions of Monitoring and Evaluating Patient Care

Quality Assurance

Quality assurance (QA) is the planned internal process of a health care delivery system established to continually and systematically monitor, assess, and improve the quality of patient care.[11] Quality assurance may involve numerous activities, including the establishment of policies and procedures for patient care, performance appraisals, and staff orientation. Regardless of the specific components, to be successful a good quality assurance program should include the following: (1) a requirement from the institution's board of directors that a quality assurance program be established; (2) a written plan of quality assurance that includes the program's objectives, scope, and method of evaluating the quality of patient care; (3) active involvement of leaders from nursing, medicine, administration, and other clinical areas in the formation and ongoing process of the quality assurance plan; and (4) documented improvement in patient care as a result of the monitoring established by the quality assurance program.[12]

Information utilized in the quality assurance process includes data from medical records, audits, measurement of patient care outcomes, incident reports, research, and infection control reports. Quality assurance activities have traditionally been carried out by a quality assurance committee, which is the "administrative and investigative arm" for the system's quality assurance overall program.[13] Thus, quality assurance can be seen as a process in and of itself. It can also be viewed as being composed of, and working in conjunction with, other important quality assessment processes, that is, utilization review, risk management, and peer review.

Utilization Review

Utilization review (UR) is performed by a utilization review committee of the institution or is contracted out to a private utilization review company. This internal process evaluates the provision of health care services in terms of medical necessity, the appropriate use of resources for the level of care needed, and if the care met adopted standards of care for health care professionals and quality care generally.[14] The review can occur before services begin, concurrently—while the patient is still receiving services—or retroactively (after the termination of services). Regardless of when it is done, it is helpful in many ways. For example, it can reduce costs and, at the same time, improve patient care by decreasing unnecessary services. Ultimately this can lead to reduction or avoidance of risks or complications that may occur as a result of that care.[15]

Utilization review . . . can reduce costs and . . . improve patient care by decreasing unnecessary services.

Utilization review is also done by the federal and state government through its Medicare and Medicaid programs and by private health insurance companies. These activities are seen more as "cost containment" methods than "quality control" procedures.[16]

Risk Management

Risk management (RM) is the internal process of a health care delivery system aimed at procuring liability insurance, improving patient care, and reducing financial loss for the health care entity.[17] This is accomplished by reducing risks

to the entity through "risk identification, risk analysis, risk treatment, and risk evaluation."[18]

Risk identification includes the use of occurrence or incident reports as well as anticipating the risks associated with the provision of services provided.[19] Risk analysis establishes the probability that a loss will occur and takes into account (1) the number of losses, (2) their frequency, and (3) the overall effect the losses would have for the health care system.[20] The analysis can occur through the use of a risk management committee, a statistical or mathematical evaluation, or a combination of the two.

Risk treatment includes controlling risks/losses and risk financing. It also may include loss prevention, loss reduction, and/or loss avoidance.[21]

Risk management's concern of reducing the financial losses to the organization clearly expands to losses other than those that might occur in delivering patient care. For example, the risk management department is also concerned with employee issues (resolving grievances in a fair and expeditious manner) and avoiding injuries to employees and injuries to visitors that might occur while on its premises.

Even so, risk management and quality assurance work hand in hand, for even though the two processes are separate, both "share the common concern of identifying substandard care, even if from two different perspectives."[22] In fact, this common concern is mandated by one accrediting body, the Joint Commission on the Accreditation of Health Care Organizations (JCAHO) standards. Risk management must be "operationally" linked to quality assessment and improvement when patient care and safety are at issue. Furthermore, information from risk management activities that may be helpful in improving the quality of patient care must be accessible to the quality assessment process.[23]

Peer Review

A component of quality assurance, utilization review, and risk management, peer review (PR) is carried out by the entity's practicing health care providers, including nurses. The purpose of peer review is to examine the quality of care provided by the health care provider group (physicians or nurses, for example) and the group's adherence to established standards of practice. Individual practitioner performance is also assessed.

Peer review may result in an individual health care provider's clinical practice being terminated or limited in some way (for example, placing the individual on a probationary status). In addition, peer review may result in the individual practitioner being reported to the National Practitioner Data Bank (NPDB) and other banks, such as the National Council of State Boards of Nursing Data Bank (NDB).

Peer review decisions may also result in liability for the Peer Review Committee. As a result, many states have provided immunity from civil suit for individuals participating in peer review activities as part of an institution's established process of internal quality control, improving patient care, and reducing patient morbidity or mortality. The immunity provided often extends to individuals in various health care delivery systems, such as hospitals and long-term care facilities. These state immunity protections are often found in the statutes governing the establishment, licensure, and operation of the health care delivery system, such as the hospital licensing act and the home health care licensing act.

In addition to the state protections afforded peer review and the evaluative procedures for improvement of patient care generally, the National Practitioner Data Bank also offers immunity from suit for health care delivery systems that participate in its procedures.

Peer review can also occur outside the health care delivery system's established procedures. One way this occurs is through the federal Peer Review Improvement Act (PRIA) of 1982.[24] The Peer Review Improvement Act authorizes the review of services provided to Medicare recipients to determine if care was reasonable, medically necessary, in conformity with national stan-

dards of care, and whether or not the care could have been provided on an outpatient basis or in another type of inpatient facility.[25] Peer review activities are carried out by the Health Care Financing Administration (HCFA).

If care is found to be in violation of the Act's objectives, sanctions can be imposed, including exclusion from participation in the Medicare program. Immunity from civil and criminal suit is granted those individuals who provide information pursuant to the stated objectives of the Act.

Paradigms of Monitoring and Evaluating Care

There are many models utilized to evaluate quality care. Some of the more general ones have been discussed in other chapters in this book, and include licensing, accreditation, and credentialing. Others focus on a specific manner in which the monitoring and evaluating take place. For example, the Donabedian approach centers on a structure-process-outcome evaluation.[26] The Hemenway model focuses on outcome measures from an economic perspective.[27]

A specific model is important in developing and implementing any quality assessment process. Regardless of the particular approach used, the model should include procedures for data collection, analysis, decision making, and implementation of changes that are identified and needed.[28]

Paradigms of Risk Management

Unlike quality assurance, utilization review, and peer review, risk management is not always performed by a separate committee composed of different staff members. In larger health care delivery systems or in teaching institutions, however, an interdisciplinary committee may exist, or a combined risk management/quality assurance committee may be formed.

When a separate risk management committee does exist, its composition can vary from entity to entity. However, in addition to the risk manager, it may include the administrator, medical staff president, chief financial officer, legal counsel, and representatives from nursing and quality assurance.[29]

Whether or not a risk management committee exists, most risk management functions are performed mainly by a risk manager or, in a larger health care system, by a risk management department. If an institution has a department of risk management, there are many models that are utilized. For example, in the chief executive officer (CEO) model, the risk manager serves as a staff member to the CEO with no direct line of authority over any department. In the department model, the office of risk management is a separate department reporting to an assistant administrator within the system. In the multi-institutional model, each component entity has its own risk manager. He or she is accountable to that entity's administrator and has a direct line to the corporation's risk manager. The corporate risk manager then reports to one of the top officers of the corporation.[30]

In any of the situations, it is imperative that the risk management department/committee or individual have excellent "interinstitutional relationships" and open lines of communication with the other departments, committees, and individuals in the health care delivery system. Without these two characteristics, the risk manager or department cannot easily facilitate and coordinate the many tasks and responsibilities necessary in limiting risks and reducing loss to the health care delivery system.

In relation to patient care issues, the importance of the exchange of information [within the health care facility] . . . is essential for risk management to fulfill its responsibilities.

In relation to patient care issues, the importance of the exchange of information, whether formal or informal, is essential for risk management to fulfill its responsibilities. Although information will come to risk management in many forms, including research findings, audit results, minutes of quality assurance, utilization review, and peer review committee meetings, one of the most helpful ways in which information concerning patient care reaches the risk manager is through the use of incident or occurrence screening and reporting.

Incident or Occurrence Screening and Reporting

Incident or occurrence screening is a systematic institution-wide process for identifying adverse patient care situations. In the screening process, the medical record is reviewed, either concurrent with the patient's stay or after discharge. The purpose is to "prevent" a patient care problem (if the patient is still being cared for) or prepare for the possibility of a suit (if the patient has been discharged).

Systematic screening is done regularly by utilizing a developed form with certain criteria listed for review. When a specific criterion is met, or a deviation from the criteria is discovered in the record, it is then referred to a second phase of screening.

During the second phase, assessment and appropriate interventions are discussed. If the screening is a retrospective review, the information is categorized and used to initiate changes prospectively. In contrast, if the screening is concurrent, changes may be implemented in the care of that patient immediately to avoid or at least lessen a further untoward result.

Examples of patient care situations that can be used for screening include the following[31]:

▼ Transfusion reactions

▼ Cardiopulmonary resuscitation (CPR)

▼ Return to intensive care unit (ICU)

▼ Break in sterile technique

In contrast to the screening process, incident or occurrence reporting is the way in which individual staff members communicate information concerning an adverse patient care situation to risk management utilizing the health care delivery system's policies and procedures for occurrence reporting. The incident or occurrence form is a formal document. It requests that certain objective information concerning the incident be supplied by staff so that appropriate screening can take place and necessary interventions instituted, if possible.

Although the forms vary greatly in format, size, shape, and comprehensiveness, they most often include information concerning the patient, a description of the incident, any injuries sustained, and the outcome of the situation.[32] Figures 5–1 and 5–2 are samples of a conventional incident form.

With the increasing use of computers in health care, the sample conventional form may be replaced with a form that can be easily converted to use in the institution's computerized system.[33]

For a comprehensive risk management program to work, especially in relation to risk screening and reporting, the health care delivery system staff should be encouraged to use the reports without fear of retribution, loss of job, or other negative results. Only when staff, risk management, quality assurance, utilization review, and peer review work closely together in an atmosphere of trust and cooperation can patient care monitoring and evaluation work successfully.

Standards in Quality Assurance, Utilization Review, Peer Review, and Risk Management

Most health care delivery systems will utilize accreditation standards developed by private accrediting bodies such as the Joint Commission or other applicable entity in monitoring and evaluating patient care. Although an institution may develop its own unique standards, it is hoped that working with a private accrediting entity's standards encourages compliance that leads to accreditation. Furthermore, because accrediting standards are often utilized by state licensing entities and in suits alleging negligence to establish standards of care, adherence to them can aid the health care delivery system in those situations as well.

Other standards that are utilized in quality assurance, utilization review, and peer review include Medicare and Medicaid (including the Health Care Financing Administration) guidelines and promulgated rules and regulations.

Guidelines utilized in risk management are not as well established as they are in quality assurance, utilization review, and peer review because of the unique nature of risk management and the possibility for many variations in its organization, scope, and functions within a health care delivery system. Even so, some standards do exist, and accreditation entity standards are one example.

Other standards for risk management come from standard forms used in occurrence screening developed by, as examples, the American Hospital Association and the Chicago Hospital Risk Pooling Programs. Also, through professional associations such as the American Society for Hospital Risk Managers (ASHRM) and the Risk Management Foundation, standards concerning education, credentialing, and the practice of risk managers have been established.

Ongoing Total System of Quality Assessment

Because quality assurance requires an ongoing process, one of the ways in which this can occur is through the use of the Quality Assurance Committee. The Committee obtains data from medical records, utilization review reports, peer review activities, and risk management, for example. It can then identify patient care issues, use "measurable objective and current clinical indicators" to monitor the issues, recommend solutions when problems occur or improvement would be prudent, implement proposed solu-

NAME:
PATIENT #:
ROOM #:
D.O.B.:
MARITAL STATUS:
   S M D W
SEX: M F

1.   Cause for hospitalization or treatment:

2.   Patient's mental condition before incident: ☐ Normal   ☐ Sedated   ☐ Disoriented   ☐ Other _____

3.   Date, Time & Place of Incident: /   / _____ hrs. _____

4.   Describe details of occurrence—what happened, how it occurred, patient's comments following; if an injury state part of body injured, describe property or equipment damaged, if applicable.

5.   Name of witness: _____

6.   Date & Time of Report: / / _____ hrs.   Bedrails: Up   Down   N/A

7.   Was physician notified: Yes   No   Did physician see patient after incident?   Yes   No
    If yes, name of physician & date/time seen: / / _____ hrs. _____

8.   Name of Responsible Resident: _____
    Name of Attending Physician: _____

9.   Findings of Examining Physician:

                                              Physician's Signature

10.   Name & title of person submitting report: _____

ROUTING OF REPORT	DATE & TIME RECEIVED	DISPOSITION	DATE SENT
Supervisior _____ RN	_____	Insurance _____	_____
Director _____ RN	_____	General Counsel _____	_____
Risk Manager _____	_____	Administration _____	_____

FIGURE 5–1 Sample incident report (front). From Gary Kraus: Health Care Risk Management: Organization and Claims Administration. Baltimore, MD: National Health Publishing/Rynd Communications, 1986. Reprinted with permission.

TO BE ANSWERED BY PERSON COMPLETING REPORT ONLY

11.   In your opinion, what caused this occurrence?

DO NOT USE

_____

_____

_____

12.   In your opinion, what can be done to prevent similar occurrences in the future?

TO BE COMPLETED BY SUPERVISOR ONLY

13.   Plan for followup:

Individual Counseling _____

Referral to Staff Development _____

Other corrective action (describe) _____

_____

DO NOT USE

_____

_____

_____

TO BE COMPLETED BY RISK MANAGER ONLY

14.   Action Taken: ☐ None   ☐ Follow-up Investigation
15.   Individuals Contacted:

16.   Investigative Findings:

F I G U R E   5 – 2 Sample incident report (back). From Gary Kraus: Health Care Risk Management: Organization and Claims Administration. Baltimore, MD: National Health Publishing/Rynd Communications, 1986. Reprinted with permission.

tions, and continually evaluate their effectiveness.

Similarly, the Utilization Review Committee, working with the Quality Assurance Committee and Peer Review Committee, meets the overall objective of utilizing the health care facility's resources appropriately through its members' participation in review activities. Evaluating such factors as the use of its facilities, if discharge was timely, and the initiation and proper use of discharge planning can help achieve its role in quality assessment.

In addition, the Peer Review Committee's constant focus is to ensure that professionals, including nurses, are practicing in accordance with national standards and providing quality patient care.

Recent Developments in Quality Assessment

Because of the dissatisfaction with "traditional" quality assurance methods and their results,[34] a focus on total quality management (TQM) or continuous quality improvement (CQI) has recently taken hold in many health care delivery systems.[35] Although defined in various ways, total quality management can be described as being a "structured" system for involving an entire organization in a continuous quality improvement process targeted to meet and exceed customer [patient] expectations.[36] All those in the organization responsible for customer satisfaction are equally accountable for ongoing improvement of results by improving the process of production.[37]

. . . total quality management (TQM) or continuous quality improvement (CQI) has recently taken hold in many health care delivery systems.

Total quality management/continuous quality improvement uses innovative tools to evaluate performance, identify reasons for poor performance, and develop methods for improvement. The tools include clinical protocols and "benchmarks"—internal and external measures of best performance used to set goals and improve the overall product.[38]

It is too early to evaluate the ramifications of total quality management/continuous quality improvement. Even so, its impact can already be seen on the delivery of health care. For example, accrediting standards from the Joint Commission on the Accreditation of Health Care Organizations have already incorporated total quality management methods and processes into its requirements for accreditation, with the realization that this evolution will be a gradual one.[39] Texts in nursing practice and nursing management contain chapters on incorporating total quality management/continuous quality improvement into traditional quality assurance activities for both processes to complement each other.[40] And, whatever the method, the ever-present questions of how quality in health care can truly be ensured continue.[41]

Implications for Nursing

Because the provision of quality patient care is a fundamental part of nursing practice, the monitoring and evaluation of patient care is a process that nursing must be consistently and actively involved in. Clearly, nurse executives, whether the chief nurse executive or those holding other positions in upper nursing management, should be vigorously involved in quality assessment in the health care delivery system. Likewise, nurse managers, as well as staff nurses, need to be involved as quality assurance, utilization review, or risk management committee members. In addition, participating in nursing audits, either as an auditor or one being audited, and conducting or participating in research that may ultimately improve patient care, is essential.

Participation in peer review activities is not only a way of contributing to the monitoring and evaluation of patient care, it also meets the need of the profession to monitor itself. Thus, when a nurse evaluates another nurse's performance within the context of their particular institution, he or she is also contributing to other overall regulation and improvement of the profession.

A nurse can contribute to quality assessment by being active on other committees as well. Membership on the Forms Committee, Policy and Procedure Committee, and Staff Development Committee, for example, directly impacts on the provision of quality patient care. If membership is not possible, each staff nurse can augment a committee's work by sharing concerns and making suggestions to a member of the committee.

Nursing must also ensure that the documentation of patient care is done in accordance with institution or agency policy and with guidelines for good documentation. Because the medical record is the common component in both quality appraisal and risk management, it is vital to the overall success of both programs.

Likewise, the use of incident or occurrence reports must be stressed as a necessary component of the process of improving patient care. In addition, the same guidelines for documentation in the patient's record should be followed for documenting on the incident form as well.

It is also important that the nurse feel comfortable in informally discussing potential patient care problems with fellow staff nurses, nurse managers, and committee members.[42] Because risk prevention is one of the elements of patient care evaluation, identifying a particular concern about patient care that has not yet become a problem is a valuable way to improve patient care and serve the institution's goals of QA as well.

Other factors can decrease poor patient care and reduce risks to patients, nursing staff, and the employer. They include, but are not limited to, the establishment and use of a good orienta-tion program for new staff; continual in-service programs for staff; support for attendance at continuing education programs; and establishment and updating of job descriptions.

SPECIAL CONSIDERATIONS

The Health Care Quality Improvement Act of 1986

The Health Care Quality Improvement Act (HCQIA) is a federal law passed by Congress in response to the increasing occurrence of malpractice in the United States and society's concern about the quality of health care.[43] The law's three stated purposes are to (1) improve the overall quality of health care; (2) limit the ability of incompetent physicians to move from state to state without disclosure or discovery of past performance; and (3) encourage and protect good faith involvement by physicians in peer review activities.[44]

To carry out its purposes, the act established the National Practitioner Data Bank (NPDB) to function as a national information system. Health care delivery systems, state medical and other boards, professional societies, and insurance companies are required to report certain activities and query the Bank under certain situations.

The National Practitioner Data Bank is operated by Paramax Systems Corporation, a UNISYS company, under a contract with the United States Department of Health and Human Services. Information that must be reported to the Bank by certain entities or groups include:

1. Any payment by a medical malpractice insurer (meaning an insurance company, self-insurance program(s), or self-insured individual practitioners, "or otherwise") on behalf of all licensed health care providers resulting from a written claim or judgment

2. Any disciplinary action taken by a state licensing board or agency against a physician or dentist for incompetence or professional misconduct

3. Any disciplinary action taken by a state licensing board or agency against other health care providers, including nurses, under the Medicare and Medicaid Patient Protection Act of 1987[45] for clinical incompetence or professional misconduct

4. Disciplinary actions by hospitals and health maintenance organizations adversely affecting clinical privileges of physicians and dentists (if the action denies, limits, revokes, or suspends privileges for 30 days or more)

5. Actions by a professional society that adversely affects membership in that society[46]

Hospitals are required to request information from the NPDB in two instances. One is when a health care practitioner, including, for example, a nurse anesthetist or nurse-midwife, applies for clinical or medical staff membership. The second situation is on the 2-year anniversary of the granting of privileges or membership, and then every 2 years thereafter.

Penalties for noncompliance with the Act exist. For example, failure of an insurance company to report a payment on behalf of a licensed health care provider can result in a $10,000 penalty.[47]

Certain benefits for compliance with the Act are also included. For example, a hospital, its agents and employees, and peer review committee members who make a report consistent with the Act and "in good faith" are immune from civil suit for damages and antitrust liability as a result of the professional review process.[48]

The National Council of State Boards of Nursing Data Bank

The National Council of State Boards of Nursing Data Bank (NDB) was established as a voluntary reporting system for member state boards of nursing to convey data concerning disciplinary actions taken against nurses by the particular state board. Information that may be reported to the National Council of State Boards of Nursing Data Bank includes the nurse's name and other biographic information, action taken,

and the type of violation (such as unprofessional conduct or incompetency). The Bank notifies all state board members and the certification body of nurse anesthetists of any information received by it. The branches of the military and the United States Public Health Service may query the Bank for information. Currently, no health care delivery systems have access to, or input into, the Bank.[49]

Liability Concerns

Negligence/Professional Negligence

Whenever monitoring or evaluation of patient care is undertaken, there is always concern that liability may be found to exist if the process is done negligently. The potential liability exists because of established legal principles of *respondeat superior*, the *corporate theory of liability*, and other laws, including case law (specifically, the *Darling* case), discussed in Chapter 3.

Whenever monitoring or evaluation of patient care is undertaken, there is always concern that liability may be found to exist if the process is done negligently.

Because potential liability might discourage health care providers and institutions from participating in patient care monitoring and evaluation, whether in the form of quality assurance, utilization review, or risk management, many states have passed statutes that provide civil immunity for those activities. It is important to note, however, that the immunity from suit applies only to conduct involved in the process and procedures of quality assessment. If the health care delivery system, or one of its employees, is negligent in the *treatment* of a patient, then no immunity exists for that alleged conduct.

Actions Involving Clinical Privileges

Peer review activities are protected from suit under the Health Care Quality Improvement Act (HCQIA) for covered institutions, the peer review committee, any member of the committee, or anyone assisting with the peer review process. However, for the immunity provisions to apply, certain conditions set forth in the Act must be met. They include "adequate" due process protections for the health care provider under review (e.g., notice of rights, hearing within 30 days); "reasonable" efforts to obtain the facts concerning the conduct under review; the review is believed to be in the interest of quality care; a person giving any information to the committee concerning the competence or professional conduct of a person must do so truthfully; and the review is believed warranted by the actual facts of the situation.[50] In addition, adherence to reporting mandates and query schedules and truth in providing information to the peer review body are required.

In addition to the Health Care Quality Improvement Act, some states have passed laws protecting health care entities other than hospitals for their peer review processes. For example, Illinois' Long-Term Care Peer Review and Quality Assessment and Assurance Protection Act[51] specifically provides for nonliability for civil damages as a result of conduct in peer review or quality assessment and assurance activities, unless the person or committee is involved in willful or wanton misconduct.

Defamation

A health care provider's concern that his or her reputation may be damaged during any process of monitoring and evaluating patient care is understandable. The law of defamation provides the protection of a qualified privilege to certain individuals or groups to speak what might otherwise be defamatory to protect the free flow of information necessary as part of that individual's official duties. Thus, unless the qualified privilege is abused, information given and exchanged during the quality assessment process would be protected from suit.

In addition, the courts have generally held that any exchange of information during quality assurance activities by the health care entity and its committees is not a publication to "a third party" for the purposes of defamation. So long as the information exchanged is within the entity, the communication is "only the corporation talking to itself."[52]

Even if the aforementioned two protections were not applicable in a particular situation, the general immunity provisions of the HCQIA and state statutes for the improvement of patient care activities would protect the free exchange of information concerning a specific health care provider so long as the protections were not abused.

Confidentiality of Quality Assurance, Utilization Review, Risk Management Reports, Data, Committee Meeting Minutes, and Other Information

The free exchange of information concerning quality assessment procedures also requires that the information reviewed, received, and generated remain confidential; that is, not subject to release to those outside the process. Although there is some controversy surrounding the availability of information to outsiders, the general rule is that material generated pursuant to quality assessment is confidential and can be disclosed only under limited circumstances.

The HCQIA, for example, severely restricts access to the Data Bank to ensure the information in it is used solely for the improvement of patient care. Thus, access to data reported to the Bank is limited to, for example, the individual health care provider who has been reported to the Bank; hospitals that query concerning an individual on staff or one applying for clinical privileges; state regulatory agencies responsible for licensing health care providers; and attorneys filing malpractice claims.[53]

Information in the possession of peer review organizations is also confidential, with a specific limitation on the release of the information concerning a particular patient or health care provider to the public.

State laws vary concerning the confidentiality of information received during patient care assessment and evaluation, but many states do provide statutory protection from disclosure as previously discussed. Additionally, some states, like Illinois, have enacted state statutes that protect any and all quality assessment data, including incident or occurrence reports, by prohibiting their release, discoverability, and introduction into evidence in any trial, administrative hearing, or judicial proceeding.[54]

It may seem clear that quality assessment materials are confidential. In reality, however, the interplay of the various state and federal laws, and the continued debate over whether the materials should be confidential, results in many cases being filed to test the ability of "outsiders" to obtain that information.

Moreover, other changes are taking place concerning the confidentiality of this kind of information. For example, JCAHO performance reports of hospitals, which include a rating by the Commission on a scale of 1–100, are now made available to the public for a fee of $30.00.[55] Its initial report listed all facilities evaluated by the Commission since January 1, 1994.[56] The Joint Commission on the Accreditation of Health Care Organizations reports also reportedly compare the health care facilities listed with other surveyed hospitals.[57]

These and other access issues will not be resolved quickly or easily in the near future, especially in view of the emphasis on meeting the needs and expectations of the customer [patient], as with the total quality management/ continuous quality improvement framework.

Antitrust Concerns

One of the unique concerns in quality assessment is the impact peer review may have on competition in health care. If the process impedes or eliminates the ability of health care providers from gaining access to clinical privileges in health care delivery systems, or maintaining those privileges, then those health care providers may be unfairly kept from providing their services. Furthermore, consumers would be unable to have a choice in seeking treatment from these health care providers. Because this issue most often arises when the health care provider does not obtain privileges in a particular system, the law has seen fit to protect health care entities and those involved in peer review from antitrust challenges in certain situations.

> *One of the unique concerns in quality assessment is the impact peer review may have on competition in health care.*

The Health Care Quality Improvement Act includes immunity for alleged antitrust violations, so long as the professional review activities comply with the Act. Thus, if an action is taken in furtherance of professional review, based on the health care provider's "competence or professional conduct," and is consistent with the requirements discussed earlier, then no antitrust violations would be likely.[58]

The Health Care Quality Improvement Act notwithstanding, federal antitrust laws also exempt certain peer review activities from its mandates. One such exemption is that of state action—when the review action can be attributed to the action of the state rather than a private organization. For this exemption or defense to apply, a health care entity must be certain its actions clearly conform with the federal law's requirements. Those requirements include the health care organization being a "sovereign branch" of state government (e.g., the state university hospital's actions) or, if a private facility, the challenged conduct is without question adopted by the state as state policy and the private conduct is supervised by the state itself.[59] Several court decisions have held that a private hospital's actions were not immune from the antitrust law because the peer review actions were not supervised by the state.[60] Thus, careful scrutiny by the courts will no doubt continue to take place when cases alleging a violation of federal antitrust laws are filed and the defense is that a particular peer review process is exempt from those federal antitrust laws under this exemption.

Managed Care

Managed care has been defined in many ways. One definition sees it as "a cost containment system that directs the utilization of health benefits by restricting the type, level and frequency of treatment; limiting the access to care; and controlling the level of reimbursement for services."[61] Regardless of the specific definition, it is, in reality, simply another name for cost control in health care.

Although this chapter has discussed various immunities for activities that might directly or indirectly be characterized as cost control measures, certain actions and their subsequent impact on patient care are being evaluated by the courts. Specifically, when compliance with limitations imposed by third-party payors by a health care delivery system or health care provider results in injury or death to the patient, courts are re-evaluating the liability for those limitations.

Two early particular cases bear mentioning. In the first case, *Wickline v. State of California*,[62] the California Appellate Court reversed a trial court decision in favor of Mrs. Wickline and against Medi-Cal, a state medical assistance program. After Medi-Cal denied a request for further hospital days following several surgical procedures for circulatory problems, the physician did not appeal that decision and discharged Mrs. Wickline. She developed additional problems at home, was readmitted to the hospital,

and two amputations were done on the affected leg—one below the knee and subsequently an above-the-knee procedure.

The appeals court clearly stated that "while a third party payor may be held legally accountable for medically inappropriate decisions, in this case plaintiff's treating physicians were ultimately responsible for the decision to release her, . . ."[63] especially when none of the physicians challenged the decision to discharge the patient.

In *Wilson v. Blue Cross of Southern California*,[64] a different result was reached, even though decided in the same California Appellate district and division as *Wickline*. The case involved a *private* health insurance company and its utilization review organization. The company denied additional days (only 10 days were allowed pursuant to the contract of insurance for psychiatric illness) for a psychiatric hospitalization for a severely emotionally ill young man, Harold Wilson, Jr. No appeal procedures for the denial existed, and the Wilsons had no money of their own to pay for additional hospitalization. The treating psychiatrist's evaluation indicated that 3 to 4 additional *weeks* of inpatient care were needed. Harold Wilson was discharged on March 11 and committed suicide on March 31.

In her suit against Blue Cross, the utilization review company, and others, Harold Wilson's mother was defeated at the trial level by a summary judgment motion. On appeal, the Appellate Court reversed the decision and remanded the case to the trial court. The Court stated that the case should go to trial against the utilization review company to determine its liability for "tortious interference with the contract of insurance between the decedent (Wilson) . . . and Blue Cross and its role in causing the wrongful death of the decedent."[65] Additionally, the Court held that the *Wickline* decision was not controlling in this case because of the many differences in the two cases. It also opined that language in *Wickline* concerning the liability of the physician was "overly broad" *dicta* (nonbinding language in a court opinion).

These two cases provide basic guidelines for

health care delivery systems and health care practitioners, including nurses, who may be involved in managed care decisions. Those guidelines include: (1) liability may be present for managed care decisions that result in injury or death to a health care consumer; (2) complete documentation is necessary concerning a patient's progress, or lack thereof, so that a managed care organization has all the information it needs to make a well-founded decision; (3) if the nurse is a reviewer, he or she will need to seek out as much information as possible concerning the patient to make a well-reasoned decision[66]; (4) the physician involved in a denial of additional days should vigorously exercise any established appeal procedures; (5) nurses functioning as utilization review employees should be licensed, and be competent in utilization review principles; and (6) each and every health care delivery system must regulate and oversee any outside managed care program, whether public or private.[67]

SUMMARY OF PRINCIPLES
AND APPLICATIONS

The importance of monitoring and evaluating patient care will not diminish. In fact, as health care resources continue to shrink, access to health care becomes even more restricted, cost control remains ever present, and the many other legal and ethical issues surrounding quality care persist, its importance will continue to be emphasized. Perhaps the following statement best describes the need for enduring scrutiny:

> We have granted the health professions access to the most secret and sensitive places in ourselves and entrusted to them matters that touch on our well-being, happiness and survival. In return, we have expected the professions to govern themselves so strictly that we need have no fear of exploitation or incompetence. The object of quality assessment is to determine how successful they have been in doing so; and the purpose of quality monitoring is to exercise constant surveillance so that departure from standards can be detected early and corrected.[68]

The nurse, then, must meet his or her responsibilities to ensure that quality assurance activities are successful by:

▼ Actively participating in quality assurance, utilization review, peer review, and risk management programs in the health care delivery system

▼ Understanding the different roles of quality assurance, utilization review, peer review, and risk management, but also appreciating the uncommon interdependence of one with the others

▼ Accepting responsibility to become skilled in quality assessment through continuing education courses, academic courses, and other methods of learning

▼ When a committee member is involved in quality assessment, adhering to the mandates of state and federal law concerning confidentiality, immunity, and good faith reviews

▼ Working with risk management to ensure, insofar as possible, risk identification and risk avoidance of patient care problems

▼ Remembering that the ethical ramifications of quality assurance activities are important

▼ When reviewing patient care situations for continued coverage if working as a third party utilization review employee, carefully analyzing the patient care situation to provide the best reasoned decision possible under the circumstances

▼ As a staff nurse, aiding risk management with its responsibilities by not documenting in the patient care record that an occurrence or incident report was filled out and by forwarding the report to designated personnel as indicated in the entity's policies

▼ As a nurse manager, providing leadership in the quality assessment and evaluation process

TOPICS FOR FURTHER INQUIRY

1. Develop a questionnaire for staff nurses in the health care facility where you work concern-

ing nurses' attitudes surrounding occurrence reports. Evaluate their opinions about the purpose of the reports, how many times they have filled one out pursuant to policy, any retaliation issues they fear as a result of their use of the reports, and other issues. Compare and contrast the results among the respondents and suggest ways for the facility to improve its occurrence reporting system.

2. Identify cases in your state that have been filed alleging a cause of action against a managed care organization. Determine what causes of action are the most predominant. Suggest ways in which such liability may be avoided in the future through the development of policies and procedures in a particular facility or type of facility (e.g., home health care agency, ambulatory clinic).

3. Interview nurses in your health care facility who have been members of the facility's quality assurance, utilization review, or peer review committee. Obtain information from the members as to how the committee functioned insofar as the nurses' input was concerned. How was their input used in comparison to others on the committee? What did the members see as their role on the committee? Was the committee as active as it could be with its responsibilities? Compare and contrast the results among the interviewees and suggest ways for the facility to improve the functioning of the committee.

4. Write an in-depth paper on total quality management/continuous quality improvement. Compare and contrast it with the current systems of quality assessment. Identify weaknesses and strengths of the process. Suggest how nurses can improve the system.

REFERENCES

1. Charles Dougherty, Robert Berenson, Kathleen Powderly, and Elaine Smith, "Cost Containment, DRGs and the Ethics of Health Care," 19 *Hastings Center Report* (January/February 1989), 5–18 (a series of three articles).

2. Mark A. Hall, "The Malpractice Standard under Health Care Cost Containment," 17 *Law, Medicine & Health Care* (Winter 1989), 347–355); see also, Barry Furrow, "Quality Control in Health Care: Developments in the Law of Medical Malpractice," 21(2) *The Journal Of Law, Medicine and Ethics* (1993), 173–192.

3. F. Shortell and T. Hughes, "The Effects of Regulation, Competition and Ownership on Mortality Rates among Hospital Inpatients," 318 *New England Journal of Medicine* 1100 (1988). See also Robert Miller, "Regulation and Accreditation," *in Problems in Hospital Law*. 7th Edition. Rockville, Md: Aspen Publishers, Inc., 1996, 43–44.

4. William D. Frazier, "Rationing of Health Care: Who Determines Who Gets the Cure, When and Why?" 2 *Annals of Health Law* (1993), 95–99.

5. Jesus Pena, Aiden Haffner, Bernard Rosen, and Donald Light, Editors. *Hospital Quality Assurance: Management and Program Evaluation*. Rockville, Md: Aspen Publishers, Inc., 1984, xiv.

6. Inge Winter and Claudette Krizek, "Integrating Quality Assurance and Risk Management," *The Risk Manager's Desk Reference*. Barbara J. Youngberg, Editor. Gaithersburg, Md: Aspen Publishers, Inc. (1994), 5.

7. *Id.*

8. Sarah Keating and Glenda Kelman, "Program Evaluation and Quality Assurance," *in Home Health Care Nursing: Concepts and Practice*. Philadelphia: J.B. Lippincott Company, 1988, 303.

9. Inge Winter and Claudette Krizek, "Integrating Quality Assurance and Risk Management," *supra*, note 6, at 6–7.

10. *Id.*, at 7.

11. *Accreditation Manual for Hospitals Volume I—Standards*. Oak Brook Terrace, Ill: Joint Commission on the Accreditation of Health Care Organizations, 1992, 137; Peggy Martin, "Quality Assurance," *Risk Management Handbook for Health Care Facilities*. Linda Harpster and Margaret Veach, Editors. Chicago: American Hospital Publishing Company, Inc. (1990), 101.

12. *Id.*, at 101–102.

13. Patricia Younger and Cynthia Conner, Editors. "Quality Assurance," *Nursing Administration and Law Manuals*. Volume 2. Rockville, Md: Aspen Publishers, Inc. (1989), 9:2.

14. Ann Helm, "Related Programs and Committees," *Risk Management Handbook for Health Care Facilities, supra* note 6, at 114.

15. *Id.*

16. G. Dans, B. Weiner, and S. Otter, "Peer Review Organizations," 313 *New England Journal of Medicine* 1136 (1985).

17. Nancy J. Brent, "Risk Management in Home Health Care: Focus on Patient Care Liabilities," 20 *Loyola University of Chicago Law Journal* (Spring 1989), 788.

18. Sheila Hagg, "Elements of a Risk Management Program," *Risk Management Handbook for Health Care Facilities, supra* note 6, at 28–31.

19. *Id.* at 28–29.

20. *Id.*

21. *Id.* at 29.

22. Brent, *supra* note 17 at 794, *citing* Steven Salman, "Quality Assurance and Risk Management" *in Handbook of*

Health Care Risk Management. Glenn Troyer and Steven Salman, Editors. Rockville, Md: Aspen Publishers, Inc., 1986, 153.

23. Howard S. Roland and Beatrice L. Rowland. *Nursing Administration Handbook.* 3rd Edition. Gaithersburg, Md: Aspen Publishers, Inc., 1992, 395.

24. 42 U.S.C. Section 1320c *et. seq.*

25. *Id.* at 1320c-3.

26. A. Donabedian. *A Guide to Medical Care Administration. Volume 2: Medical Care Appraisal—Quality and Utilization.* New York: American Public Health Association, 1969; Linda Hodges, Mary Louise Icenhour, and Starla Tate, "Measuring Quality: A Systematic Integrative Approach," *Current Issues in Nursing.* Joanne McCloskey and Helen Grace, Editors. St. Louis: C.V. Mosby Company, 1994, 296–297.

27. D. Hemenway, "Quality Assessment from an Economic Perspective," 6(4) *Evaluation and Health Professions* (1983), 379–396.

28. Keating and Kelman, *supra* note 8, at 310.

29. George Pozgar. *Legal Aspects of Health Care Administration.* 6th Edition. Gaithersburg, Md: Aspen Publishing, Inc., 1996, 674–675.

30. Thomas Gaudiosi, Gary Kraus, and Joan Rines, "Risk Management Program Design," *Health Care Risk Management: Organization and Claims Administration.* Gary Kraus, Editor. Owings Mills, Md: National Health Publishing, 1986, 28.

31. Inge Winter and Claudette Krizek, "Integrating Quality Assurance and Risk Management," *supra* note 6, at 11.

32. Gary P. Kraus, "The Risk Management Information System," in *Health Care Risk Management: Organization and Claims Management, supra* note 30, at 80.

33. Matthew Camden, "Computerizing Risk Management," *The Risk Manager's Desk Reference, supra* note 6, 89–95.

34. Joseph Truhe, "Quality Assessment in the '90's: Legal Implications For Hospitals", 26 *Journal Of Health And Hospital Law* (June 1993), 171.

35. *Id.*

36. Pamela K. Triolo, "TQM/CQI: What Is It? Does It Work?" *Current Issues in Nursing.* Joanne McCloskey and Helen Grace, Editors. 4th Edition. St. Louis: C.V. Mosby Company, 1994, 321.

37. Truhe, *supra* note 34, at 171–172.

38. *Id.* at 172.

39. *Id.* at 173, *citing* Joint Commission on the Accreditation of Health Care Organizations, *Accreditation Manual for Hospitals* (1992).

40. H. Roland and B. Roland, "Quality Care and Improvement" *Nursing Administration Handbook, supra* note 23, at 367–393.

41. Maria Mitchell, "How Can We Assure Health Care Quality," *Current Issues In Nursing, supra* note 36, 287–294.

42. Rosemary Luquire, "Nursing Risk Management," 20 *Nursing Management* (October 1989), 58.

43. 42 U.S.C. Section 11101 *et. seq.* (1986).

44. *Id.* Section 11101.

45. Pub. L. 100–93 (August 18, 1987), 42 U.S.C. Sections 1396a(a), 1396 v-2 (1989).

46. 42 U.S.C. Sections 11131, 11133 and 11132; 45 C.F.R. Sections 60.7, 60.9 and 60.8.

47. 42 U.S.C. Section 11131(a); 42 C.F.R. Section 1003. 102(c)(1).

48. Ila Rothschild, "The Health Care Quality Improvement Act and the National Practitioner Data Bank: Current Issues and Emerging Legal and Operational Trends," *1993 Health Law Handbook Series.* Alice Gosfield, Editor. Deerfield, Ill: Clark Boardman Callaghan, 1993, 321–330.

49. Nancy J. Brent, "The Impaired Nurse: Assisting Treatment to Achieve Continued Employment Status," 24 *Journal of Health and Hospital Law* (April 1991), 118, *citing* telephone interview with Ms. Vickie Sheets, RN, JD, Director for Public Policy, Nursing Practice and Education, National Council of State Boards of Nursing, Inc. (March 18, 1991).

50. 42 U.S.C. Section 11112 (a).

51. 745 ILCS 55/1. 55/3 (1990).

52. Younger and Conner, *supra* note 13, at 9:26.

53. Rothschild, *supra* note 48, at 341–345.

54. 735 ILCS 5/8-2101 (July 1, 1984).

55. Alice G. Gosfield, "Measuring Performance and Quality: The State of the Art and Legal Concerns," *1995 Health Law Handbook.* Edited by Alice G. Gosfield. Deerfield, Ill: Clark Boardman Callaghan, 1995, 48.

56. *Id.*, *citing* "Consumers Can Start Purchasing JCAHO Hospital Performance Reports," 3 *BNA's Health Law Reporter* 1841 (1994).

57. Gosfield, *supra* note 55, at 48.

58. Nathan Hershey, "Compensation and Accountability: The Way to Improve Peer Review," f(1) *Quality Assurance and Utilization Review* (Spring 1992), 23–29; Rothschild, *supra* note 48.

59. John Miles and Brian Henry, "Health Care Antitrust Law Developments—1991," *1992 Health Law Handbook.* Alice Gosfield, Editor. Deerfield, Ill: Clark Boardman Callaghan, 1992, 439.

60. *Patrick v. Burget,* 108 S.Ct. 1658 (1988); *Posner v. Lankenau Hospital,* 645 F. Supp. 1102 (E.D. PA. 1986); *Quinn v. Kent General Hospital, Inc.,* 617 F. Supp. 1226 (D.Del. 1985); *Miller v. Indiana Hospital,* 930 F. 2d 334 (3rd Cir. 1991).

61. Kathleen M. Todd, "Managed Care," *CDS Review* (January/February 1991), 32, *citing* House of Delegates, American Dental Association. Unofficial Report of Actions, 131st Annual Session, October 14–18, 1990.

62. 239 Cal. Rptr. 810 (July 1986).

63. *Id.* at 1630.

64. 271 Cal. Rptr 876 (Cal. App. 2d District 1990).

65. *Id.* at 885.

66. Nancy J. Brent, "Managed Care: Legal and Ethical Implications," 9 *Home HealthCare Nurse* (May/June 1991), 9–10.

67. See, generally, Christopher Kerns, and Carol Gerner, "Managed Care Organizations and Their Liability Exposure," *Health Care Liability Handbook.* Deerfield, Ill: Clark Boardman Callaghan, 1995, 59–98.

68. Alden Haffner, Stevan Jonas, and Burton Pollack, "Regulating the Quality of Patient Care," *Hospital Quality Assurance: Risk Management and Program Evaluation, supra* note 5, at 3, *quoting* Avedis Donabedian, *The Quality of Medical Care.* D.H.E.W. Pub. No. 78-1232 (P-H), Health: United States, 1978, at 11.

6

Other Torts and Civil Rights

The reader will recall that the tort of negligence and professional negligence did not require any *intent* on the part of the actor who caused injury to the victim. Rather, the liability, if determined to be present, was due to the actor's conduct not being in conformity with a standard of care. The law has defined other torts, however, that *do* require intent to be proven, albeit in varying ways. Despite this variety, there is one unifying quality of all the other torts—that of the defendant's purposeful conduct in interfering with an interest held by the plaintiff.[1] Because the intent of the defendant is an essential requirement in these torts, they have been identified as intentional and quasi-intentional torts. Some interests held by the plaintiff that, if violated, can result in liability include the protection of one's name and reputation (defamation), the ability to move freely without restriction as to place or time (false imprisonment), and privacy (invasion of privacy). A nurse may be involved in such suits when the nurse shares untrue information about a patient with another person, unlawfully prohibits a patient from leaving the institution, or shares private facts about the patient with others not involved in that patient's care. A nurse may also be involved as a plaintiff; that is, alleging that his or her own reputation was injured or his or her privacy invaded.

In addition to the requirement of intent, there are several other differences between negligence and professional negligence (many times referred to as negligent torts) and the other torts presented in this chapter. One difference is the damages that may be recovered. The reader will recall that when alleging professional negligence, the injured patient must prove that some injury occurred. In contrast, the intentional and quasi-intentional torts do not always require proof of injury or damages. The specific tort—defamation or an invasion of privacy, for example—is achieved when the required intent is present. If injury or damages take place, the extent of the injury or damages is taken into consideration by the court. If minimal or nonexistent, nominal damages will be awarded.

A second difference with torts other than negligent ones is that no expert witness testimony is necessary to prove the interference with the plaintiff's assailed interest. Unlike professional negligence, there is no standard of care that the health care professional—or private citizen—must meet.

In addition, punitive damages are more easily recoverable when a violation of the plaintiff's interest(s) takes place. Because the defendant's conduct is intended, assessing damages that punish that actor and deter others from engaging in the same behavior is justified.

Last, it is important to keep in mind that a defendant's actions may give rise to one or more violations of the plaintiff's interests. Thus, several violations can be alleged in a suit brought by the plaintiff, as many of the intentional and quasi-intentional torts are closely related. For example, restricting someone's freedom of movement (false imprisonment) may give rise to allegations of assault and battery as well.

Civil rights violations occur when an individual's rights are transgressed by the government or governmental entity. Because local, state, and federal governments often maintain health care delivery systems, a patient may allege a breach of his or her civil rights under federal law(s). Likewise, a nurse or other health care professional may file a suit alleging a violation of a particular right protected by those same laws.

This chapter will discuss intentional and quasi-intentional torts that are most common in health care. Likewise, the Civil Rights Act of 1871, codified at 42 U.S.C. Section 1983, as it applies to health care delivery, will be explored. Insofar as civil rights violations are concerned, this Civil Rights Act is only *one* way in which a person may sue for an alleged breach of rights guaranteed by the Constitution. Other avenues open to the plaintiff would include a suit alleging a violation of the Constitution itself as well as violations of other federal laws that protect civil rights.

Many of the intentional torts discussed in this chapter overlap with important consititutional rights. For example, the tort of invading one's privacy may affect one's constitutional right of freedom of speech when the action is based on a "false light" allegation.

INTENTIONAL TORTS

The concept of intent includes several basic elements. It is a state of mind about the results of a voluntary act (or the results of a voluntary failure to act) and includes not only having a desire to bring about the results but also knowing that the results are "substantially certain" to occur.[2] Intent must also exist when the act, or failure to act, takes place.[3] Insofar as tort liability is concerned, intent is not hostile or a desire "to do harm." Nor is it to be confused with motive, the reason a person acts. Rather, it is a design to

cause a specific outcome that unlawfully assails the interests of another.[4]

Intent can be "transferred." For example, even though the actor intended to harm victim A but harmed victim B instead, the actor would still be liable for the injury, as the intent to harm A is transferred to meet the requisite intent to harm B.[5] This increased liability is justified because of the greater burden the law places on "intentional wrongdoers."

The requirement that the act done be a voluntary one is fairly clear—liability will not exist if the conduct engaged in is not intended to bring about the result. For example, if a staff nurse faints and, in doing so, falls on a patient and injures him, the injury would not result in tort liability for assault and battery. The nurse did not *intend* to injure the patient.

Intentional torts most often seen in health care are assault, battery, false imprisonment . . . and conversion of property.

Intentional torts most often seen in health care are assault, battery, false imprisonment, intentional infliction of emotional distress, misrepresentation, and conversion of property. All but conversion of property involve interference with the individual himself or herself. All, of course, require intent and a voluntary act to take place.

Assault

This tort protects an individual's interest in the freedom from the apprehension of harmful or offensive contact.[6] There is no requirement of actual *touching* of the plaintiff; the intent to spur apprehension and the resulting fear that contact might occur in the victim satisfies this requirement. Thus, the damage or harm experienced by the individual is emotional—fright, fear, anxiety—in addition to any physical injury that may occur.[7] Therefore, the plaintiff can sue for those injuries, in addition to seeking punitive damages.

Although this tort has been described as a "touching of the mind . . . ,"[8] for assault to be actionable, the victim must be aware of the threat of harmful or offensive contact. A psychiatric nurse who comes toward an unconscious patient with leather restraints has not participated in an assault because the patient was not aware (conscious) of the potential harmful contact.

Mere words alone are usually not enough to satisfy the requirements that an assault took place, and an immediate harmful or offensive contact must be perceived by the potential victim. If the same psychiatric nurse simply threatens to place a patient in full leather restraints, probably no assault has occurred. If, however, the nurse shakes the leather restraints in front of the patient and threatens to place him in restraints immediately, an assault is more probable. It is important for the nurse to keep in mind, however, that the *threat* is the important component rather that the *manner* in which it is conveyed.[9]

An assault can occur without any other intentional tort. It usually takes place, however, with the intentional tort of battery.

Battery

This tort protects an individual's interest in freedom from an affirmative, intentional, and unpermitted contact with his or her body, any extension of it (such as clothing), or anything that is attached to it and "practically identified with it."[10] Unlike assault, actual contact is essential. The intent of the defendant can be either to carry out the offensive contact *or* to cause the apprehension that the contact is immediately going to take place.[11]

In contrast to assault, however, the victim does not need to be aware that the battery has occurred. Thus a patient who is unconscious and is treated without his or her consent can still sue for a battery, because his or her "personal integrity" is still entitled to protection.[12]

If physical harm is experienced by the plaintiff, the defendant would be liable for that injury. However, the defendant is also liable for those contacts that create no physical harm but result in insult, humiliation, and anxiety being experienced by the victim. Moreover, when there is no injury to the plaintiff, nominal damages are also possible.

It is also important for the nurse to keep in mind that whatever consequences, even if unintended and unforeseen, result from a battery will be the responsibility of the actor who initiated the conduct. Furthermore, although it can be said that individuals do "consent" to "customary and reasonable" contacts as members of society (a touching of the arm or a slight bump when passing through a crowd), the time, place, circumstances, and relationship of the parties will always be analyzed by the court when an unpermitted touching occurs.[13]

Therefore, when the nurse inserts a catheter over the patient's objections (*Roberson v. Provident House*[14]), encourages and aids a physician in performing surgery when no consent whatsoever was given by the patient (*Roberts v. Southwest Texas Methodist Hospital*[15]), initiates a game of tag with pediatric patients that results in an injury to one of the patient participants, or makes sexual advances toward a patient, he or she may be liable for assault as well as battery.

Assault and battery in medical care most often is alleged when there is a *lack of* consent for treatment, including surgery. Although a case alleging assault and battery is a perfectly viable way to seek damages for the unpermitted contact, the injured patient can seek redress by alleging lack of informed consent under a negligence theory; that is, alleging the practitioner was negligent in not providing all of the necessary information to make an informed choice about the treatment.

False Imprisonment

Freedom from a restriction of one's choice of movement is the interest protected by this tort.

If an intentional restriction of movement occurs, it must be against the will of the individual, for *any* length of time, however short, and the victim must be aware of the confinement.[16] Furthermore, the restraint must be with no means for the person to depart from the confinement, whether by physical barrier(s) or merely through the use of force. However, moral pressure ("Stay in the hospital and clear up your sexually transmitted disease so others will not suffer from your mistake") or future threats ("I will confine you to your room if you do not eat your meal immediately") are not actionable as false imprisonment.

If the plaintiff is successful, he or she can receive monetary damages for (1) any mental or physical injury to his or her well-being, (2) lost time, (3) humiliation, (4) damage to reputation, and (5) for other losses during the imprisonment (e.g., loss of property).

In the health care setting, false imprisonment is often alleged against nurses and institutions that hospitalize patients against their will, especially psychiatric nurses and hospitals. The allegations may also occur, however, when any health care delivery system keeps a patient after there is a duty to allow the patient to leave. Again, psychiatric facilities may be involved in such suits with voluntary patients, but other institutions may also commit this tort when, for example, a patient is not allowed to leave the emergency department when he or she has asked to leave, and there is no duty to hold the patient, or, as was true in a 1925 case, when a hospital confined a patient for 11 hours because he did not pay his bill.[17]

There is a distinct difference between the tort of false imprisonment and that of malicious prosecution, which is a quasi-intentional tort and will be discussed in that section.

Intentional Infliction of Emotional Distress

When a defendant's conduct is extreme and outrageous—exceeding the bounds of common decency—and it causes, or is fairly certain to cause, severe emotional distress, with or without causing concurrent physical results—this tort is satisfied.[18] It is clearly based on the plaintiff's interest in protecting his or her peace of mind.[19]

As with many of the other torts discussed thus far, the context within which the extreme and outrageous conduct takes place also has bearing on the severe mental distress experienced by the plaintiff. For example, when the defendant knows about a special sensitivity of, or has a special relationship with, the plaintiff and uses it to cause the mental anguish, the specific conduct may not be of paramount importance. Rather the improper use of that knowledge or interpersonal connection to create the emotional distress is what is evaluated by the court.

The plaintiff in an intentional infliction of emotional distress suit may also be a family member or close associate who observes another being treated in an offensive manner. In health care, family members who observe the death of a loved one, or who see continued medical treatment being administered to another when they have asked that it not be done, can sue for the mental anguish in witnessing that occurrence.[20]

Nurses are not immune from suits alleging their conduct resulted in intentional infliction of emotional distress.

Nurses are not immune from suits alleging their conduct resulted in intentional infliction of emotional distress. In one case, a nurse was sued for intentionally deactivating a patient's call button.[21] Nurses may also be plaintiffs in such suits, however, especially in relation to conduct by their superiors or colleagues. Thus, if sexually harassed, or a victim of false rumors about the nurse's family spread by colleagues, the nurse may file a case to seek redress for the emotional pain experienced by such conduct.

Conversion of Property

Unlike the other torts discussed thus far that involve the intentional interference with the individual, conversion involves an intentional interference with the *property* of another. Specifically, it requires that the defendant, with intent to affect the property in some way (e.g., exercise control over it, transfer it, alter it, or dispose of it), invades the owner's rights in that property.[22] The plaintiff must prove that at the time of the conversion, he or she had possession, or the right of possession, of the property.

In health care, conversion can take place when a nurse takes belongings from a patient without justification. This could occur when a search of a psychiatric patient's belongings results in certain items not being returned to the patient without justification. It could also take place when a nurse removes a patient's savings bank book from his or her bedside stand. The tort is complete simply by the nurse wrongfully taking the property; there is no need for a demand for its return.

Misrepresentation

This tort has become a very complicated one. This is mainly due to its flexible character and the ability to classify conduct depicting misrepresentation as the intent to deceive, as negligence, or simply as a "strict responsibility" an individual has to another.[23] It may also be viewed as a breach of an express or implied warranty in a contract.

Because of its complex nature, it will not be discussed as a tort except to state that it can easily be a component of the other intentional torts analyzed in this chapter. For example, misrepresentation by a nurse to a patient that he is drinking only orange juice when the juice contains medication can result in a battery. It can also occur by inducing consent for one particular type of treatment that turns out to be a different medical regimen altogether. Or, if the nurse maliciously lies to a patient about a contracted disease when, in fact, the patient is not suffering from it, an action for intentional infliction of emotional distress may be easily won by the patient.

Defenses to Intentional Torts

Defenses to the intentional torts presented are summarized in Table 6–1. It is important to keep in mind that an additional defense not included in the table, that of the statute of limitations, is also possible to raise when accused of interfering with the plaintiff's interest(s). Generally speaking, the time period within which an injured plaintiff can sue for suffering from any of the intentional torts presented is usually within 2 years from the date on which the tort occurred.

QUASI-INTENTIONAL TORTS

Quasi-intentional torts are those torts in which the intent of the actor may not be as clear as with the intentional torts, but a voluntary act on the defendant's part takes place, as does the subsequent interference with an individual's interest. Common quasi-intentional torts seen in health care are defamation, breach of confidentiality, invasion of privacy, and malicious prosecution.

Common quasi-intentional torts seen in health care are defamation, breach of confidentiality, invasion of privacy, and malicious prosecution.

A quasi-intentional tort may be experienced by itself, or it may occur in combination with any of the other torts. A patient whose privacy

TABLE 6–1
Defenses to Intentional Torts

TORT	DEFENSES	QUALIFICATIONS	OTHER COMMENTS	EXAMPLE
1. Assault and/or battery	Privilege	Justifiable motive	Court can inquire into motive	Nurse or patient acts in self-defense
	Mistake of law or fact	Usually goes in tandem with defense of privilege		Nurse or patient, erroneously believing he or she is being attacked, acts in self-defense
	Self-defense	Reasonable force must be used; no time to resort to other lawful remedies	No duty to retreat unless it can be done safely	Nurse in ER defends self when attacked by irate family member of patient
	Consent	Must be willingly given; no coercion or fraud used; capacity to consent must be present; no mistakes as to nature or quality of what consenting to; actor cannot exceed consent given	Consent can be manifested by conduct or words; also may be inferred; when emergency exists, consent for treatment, *absent direction to contrary,* implied	Patient, with full knowledge of procedure, gives informed consent for treatment
	Necessity	Need to interfere with property of another to protect victim or victims	Similar to privilege defense	Nurse pushes patient in clinic aside to take gun away from robber who is aiming gun at others in clinic
2. False Imprisonment	Privilege	Justifiable motive	Court can inquire into motive	Nurse places patient in seclusion room because he or she is combative and hits staff and patients
	Self-defense	Reasonable force must be used; no time to resort to other lawful remedies	No duty to retreat unless it can be done safely	See example under Privilege
	Defense of Others	Defense must be reasonably necessary	May be duty to defend where a legal or social duty is established by law	See example under Privilege
	Consent	Must be willingly given; no coercion or fraud used; capacity to consent must be present; no mistake as to nature or quality of what consenting to; actor cannot exceed consent given	Consent can be manifested by conduct or words; also may be inferred	Patient agrees to go to room voluntarily until control of behavior is regained
	Necessity	Need to interfere with property of another to protect victim or victims	Similar to privilege defense	See example under Privilege

TABLE 6–1
Defenses to Intentional Torts (Continued)

TORT	DEFENSES	QUALIFICATIONS	OTHER COMMENTS	EXAMPLE
3. Intentional Infliction of Emotional Distress	Privilege	Justifiable motive	Court can inquire into motive	Nurse, to prevent bodies of dead patients from burning up in fire in morgue, places bodies in a hallway
	Self-defense	Reasonable force must be used; no time to resort to other lawful remedies	No duty to retreat unless it can be done safely	See example under Privilege
	Defense of Others	Defense must be reasonably necessary	May be duty to defend when a legal or social duty is established by law	See example under Privilege
	Consent	Must be willingly given; no coercion or fraud used; capacity to consent must be present; no mistake as to nature or quality of what consenting to; actor cannot exceed consent given	Consent can be manifested by conduct or words; also may be inferred.	See example under Privilege
	Necessity	Need to interfere with property of another to protect victim or victims	Similar to privilege defense	See example under Privilege
4. Conversion of Property	Privilege	Justifiable motive	Court can inquire into motive	Nurse takes possession of medications when patient returns from pass
	Self-defense	Reasonable force must be used; no time to resort to other lawful remedies	No duty to retreat unless it can be done safely	Nurse takes possession of gun patient has in bedside stand
	Defense of Others	Defense must be reasonably necessary	May be duty to defend when a legal or social duty is established by law	See example under Self-Defense
	Consent	Must be willingly given; no coercion or fraud used; capacity to consent must be present; no mistake as to nature or quality of what consenting to; actor cannot exceed consent given	Consent can be manifested by conduct or words; also may be inferred	Patient agrees to give nurse gun or medications upon return from pass
	Necessity	Need to interfere with property of another to protect victim or victims	Similar to privilege defense	See example under Privilege

Data from W. Page Keeton, Editor. *Prosser and Keeton on the Law of Torts.* 5th Edition. St. Paul, Minn: West Publishing Company, 1984 (with 1988 Pocket Part).

is invaded, for example, may also sue for a breach of confidentiality and intentional infliction of emotional distress.

Defamation

Defamation includes the "twin torts" of libel (written word) and slander (spoken word).[24] The interest that is invaded is that of an individual's good name and reputation and, as such, is a "relational" interest.[25] Thus, for the tort to take place, there must be (1) a communication (publication) about the individual to a third party or parties; (2) that is so injurious that it tends to harm the victim's reputation; (3) to the point that others lower their estimation of the person and/or are deterred from associating with that person.[26]

The tort of defamation is a personal one; that is, with some narrow exceptions, only a living person may be defamed. Furthermore, "group defamation" ("All nurses are incompetent") is not actionable. Again, with narrow exceptions, there is no specific, identifiable person spoken about in the particular group.

In addition, the written or spoken words must be understood as defamatory. Whether or not this has occurred is a question for the jury. The jury will evaluate various circumstances to ascertain the interpretation of the information, including whether or not the communication was intended as a joke, or that no one who heard or read the information interpreted it in a defamatory manner. This principle was illustrated in a case in which the comment "whore's nest" was found to refer to unkempt surroundings and not to the "morals of the nurses" working there. Therefore, no defamation occurred.[27]

Liability for defamation can be found against the individual who initially communicates (publishes) the defamatory communication (primary publisher) and for those who repeat it (republisher).

In instances in which a defamatory statement is made about a "public figure" and is of "legitimate public interest," the injured public figure must prove that the statement was made with malice; that is, that it was communicated with the knowledge that it was false *or* with reckless disregard as to its truth or falsity.[28] This requirement is based on the First Amendment protection of freedom of speech and press. The right includes the news media's ability to provide information to the public concerning public figures without undue fear of being sued for an incorrect statement. It is also based on the idea that a public figure "voluntarily" enters into public life and, as a result, has lesser protection in his or her name or reputation.

Private individuals, however, have less of an opportunity to challenge defamatory statements (e.g., no access to the news media). Greater protection is therefore afforded "nonpublic" individuals by lessening the constitutional guarantees of free speech and press for publications about them. As a result, a private person need only show that the publication was negligently done. If successful, damages for "actual injuries" can be awarded.

The damages suffered by a person whose reputation has been injured can be legion and vary considerably. They include compensatory (general or special), punitive or exemplary, and nominal damages.[29] Because determining damages can be complicated, the law has developed rules to determine injury. These rules are based on whether or not the defamatory communication is written (libel) or spoken (slander) and whether the communication is "per se" defamatory.

Libel

As has been stated, libel is defamation in writing or in some other permanent form. It may sometimes occur when the publication occurs via television or radio, especially when there is a communication from a written script. If the published communication is libelous per se, that is, clearly defamatory, no special proof of damages by the plaintiff is necessary. If, however, the statement is not clearly libelous to the plaintiff, then the plaintiff must plead and prove special damages suffered (e.g., loss of a job or loss of an inheritance), unless the communication fits into one of the four exceptions discussed below.

Slander

Special damages due to slander, or spoken defamation, must generally be proven by the plaintiff because of its less permanent nature when compared to libelous communications. However, there are four exceptions to this rule, and when slander of this nature occurs (slander per se), damages are presumed:

▼ The plaintiff is, or was, guilty of a crime involving "moral turpitude"

▼ The plaintiff is suffering from a "loathsome disease"

▼ "Unchastity" in a woman

▼ Any defamatory statement bearing on the plaintiff in his or her business, trade, profession, or office[30]

A defamatory statement by a nurse can take place under most any circumstance. When a nurse falsely told another that a former patient was being treated for syphilis and the former patient's catering business failed as a result of the statement,[31] an action was filed against the nurse. The nurse may also be a defendant in a defamation action because of statements made about nurse colleagues or physicians, especially when they are made in relation to their professional performance. The nurse may also be a plaintiff in a defamation suit in which his or her own reputation is allegedly damaged.

Breach of Confidentiality

This tort protects a patient's sharing of information with a health care provider without fear that the information will be released to those not involved in his or her care. Initially, breach of confidentiality actions were mainly brought against physicians. As the role of other health care providers, including nurses, has developed professionally and they have become legally accountable for their actions, such suits have been filed against those providers as well.

In response to the expanded roles and legal accountability of health care providers generally, many states have included the mandate of protecting patient confidentiality in medical, social work, psychology, and other practice acts. Additionally, other state and federal laws, such as Illinois' *Medical Patients' Rights Act*,[32] require that the confidentiality of patient information be maintained. If breached, the acts provide for financial and other remedies to the injured patient. Also, in special areas of practice, such as mental health and chemical use treatment, federal and state laws prohibit disclosure to others without the patient's consent to only a few circumstances.

Invasion of Privacy

This tort is quite different from that of breach of confidentiality. Even so, a particular instance of conduct may give rise to allegations of a violation of each of these two protected rights.

With invasion of privacy, the interest protected is that of the individual's right to be free from unreasonable intrusions into his or her private affairs; in other words, "to be left alone."[33] It involves four separate possible invasions of this overall interest, which have greatly expanded the interest the tort originally protected.

Use of Plaintiff's Likeness or Name without Plaintiff's Consent for Commercial Advantage of Defendant

This occurs when the plaintiff's name, photograph, or other likeness is used as a symbol of his or her identity to further the product or service of another.[34] When a cosmetic surgeon used the photographs of a particular patient who had successful cosmetic surgery in a television program and department store presentation, an invasion of the patient's privacy occurred.[35] When the use does not identify the patient—for example, simply shows a hand or the back of the patient's head—no invasion of privacy takes place.

Unreasonable Intrusion into Plaintiff's Private Affairs and Seclusions

This category of an invasion of privacy takes place when there is conduct that pries or intrudes upon a person's private affairs or seclusions and is objectionable to a reasonable person.[36] The conduct can be physical intrusion by the defendant (e.g., entering one's home without consent), or it can be the result of less traditional intrusions, such as peering into the window of someone's home or eavesdropping upon private conversations with the use of wiretaps and microphones.[37]

It is important to note that no interference with privacy happens when one is in a public place or on a public street where there is no legal right to be left alone.

In the health care setting, this type of privacy invasion can be found actionable whenever an individual's care is observed by others, including medical, nursing, and other students, without the patient's consent.[38] It can also take place when unconsented-to photographs are taken of a patient after surgery, showing the patient's face to be distorted because of the pain being experienced.[39] It is important to note that in the latter case, the photographs were taken for the physician's files alone. Even so, the court held that because the patient did not consent to *any* photographs being taken, her right of privacy was assailed.

Public Disclosure of Private Facts about Plaintiff

To satisfy the elements of this invasion of privacy action, (1) there must be public disclosure of *private* facts; (2) it must be objectionable to someone of ordinary sensibilities; and (3) the information disclosed must be the type that the

public has no legitimate interest in knowing.[40] Information that is of public record, such as a person being divorced or a name and address, is generally not held to be private data.

A patient's right of privacy under this category may be intruded upon, for example, if the nurse or other health care provider releases information concerning the diagnosis and treatment of that patient to the press (especially when the patient is *not* a public figure). It may also occur when the discussion of an identified patient's treatment takes place during a seminar or workshop for the public.

An invasion of privacy can take place when an occupational health nurse shares medical information concerning an employee's mastectomy with "numerous other employees."[41] In that Illinois case, the court held that when there is a "special relationship" between the person and the "public" with whom the information is shared (e.g., fellow employees, church members, or neighbors), dissemination to that "public" group satisfies the elements of the tort.[42]

Placing a Person in a False Light in the Public's Eye

This tort occurs when an individual publishes false facts—attributing views not held or actions not taken—about another that would be objectionable to a person of ordinary sensibilities.[43] If the information published is a matter of "public interest," malice on the part of the defendant is also required; that is, the injured party must show that the defendant acted with knowledge of the falsity of the information or acted recklessly.

In health care, this tort could occur if a picture of a patient in the hospital, but not a recipient of its contagious disease services, appeared on a brochure advertising the newly renovated infectious disease unit for the treatment of AIDS.

Malicious Prosecution

The interest protected with this tort, as with abuse of process (which will not be covered), is the interest to be free from unjustifiable criminal and civil litigation.[44] The rules for a violation of this interest are different in relation to whether or not the case that is filed is a civil or a criminal one. However, certain elements must be satisfied in either instance: (1) the judicial proceeding terminated in favor of the injured party; (2) absence of probable cause; and (3) the presence of "malice," or a controlling reason other than seeking justice, in bringing the suit.[45]

The individual who suffers from malicious prosecution can recover damages to reputation, mental suffering, and humiliation, as well as for reasonable expenses, including attorneys fees, in defending against the suit. Clearly, punitive damages can also be awarded, especially when a jury finds "ill will or oppressive conduct" initiated the case.[46]

It is important to keep in mind that public policy favors access to the courts. Furthermore, fear of lawsuits alleging malicious prosecution and other torts of this nature would unduly hinder their initiation. Therefore, these types of suits are usually allowed to proceed, so long as they are initiated in good faith and with a reasonable basis.[47]

In the health care arena, malicious prosecution may be brought by a patient against a psychiatric nurse who maliciously initiates commitment proceedings against him or her, or a nurse may initiate this kind of suit.

In one such case, a registered nurse did bring a suit alleging malicious prosecution against her supervisor and employer for reporting her termination of employment due to unprofessional and unethical conduct to the Florida Board of Nursing.[48] The nurse was not successful, however, for several reasons. One reason was the absence of malice on the part of the home health care agency and supervisor in reporting the nurse to the board.

Defenses to Quasi-intentional Torts

The defenses to quasi-intentional torts are presented in Table 6–2. As was discussed with the defenses to intentional torts, the statute of limitations can be raised as an additional defense to any of the torts discussed. For the quasi-intentional torts, a defamation suit must usually be filed within one year after the cause of action occurred. For the others, a two-year time limitation is generally the rule.

CIVIL RIGHTS VIOLATIONS UNDER SECTION 1983 OF THE CIVIL RIGHTS ACT OF 1871

Section 1983 of the Civil Rights Act of 1871

Passed after the Civil War, Section 1983 of the Civil Rights Act of 1871 protects all of the rights encompassed in the Constitution (including life, liberty, property, privacy, due process, and equal protection) as well as federal statutory and administrative rights. It does so by stating that any violation of a federal right by governmental action can be sued for through a civil action requesting damages or equitable relief (e.g., an injunction) as a remedy.

A plaintiff bringing a suit alleging a violation of Section 1983 must prove that an individual acting under color of state law deprived the plaintiff of a specific, established federal right, whether substantive or procedural; in other words, discrimination of some kind occurred. Furthermore, there must be a causal connection between the violation and the injury alleged. Also, the injury that is the basis of the suit must be a closely related result of the violation.[49] It is important to note that the Act does not apply to infringement of rights granted by state law.

A plaintiff bringing a suit alleging a violation of Section 1983 must prove . . . discrimination of some kind occurred.

TABLE 6–2

Defenses to Quasi-intentional Torts

DEFENSES	QUALIFICATIONS	OTHER COMMENTS	EXAMPLE
1. Defamation Truth	Defendant must prove; entire statement must be truthful	If proven, an *absolute defense*	Nurse truthfully tells another patient that Mr. S. has AIDS
Absolute privilege (or immunity)	Limited to: (1) judicial proceedings and actors (judges, witnesses, attorneys); (2) legislative proceedings and actors (legislatures, witnesses, official records); (3) executive communications; (4) consent; (5) spousal communications (to each other); (6) political broadcasts	Based on protecting otherwise actionable conduct because it furthers societal purpose; privilege cannot be abused Must be knowing consent	Plaintiff's attorney calls nurse incompetent in malpractice case against nurse Mr. S. tells nurse it is OK to tell other patient he has AIDS
Qualified privilege	Based on interests:		
	1. interest of publisher	Cannot be abused or exceeded; used to protect self against defamation by another	Nurse, in response to a colleague saying she is incompetent, calls the colleague a liar
	2. interest of others	Publication justified by importance of interest; legal or moral duty may exist to share information; cannot be abused or exceeded	Former employer of nurse shares suspected drug diversion with prospective employer (*Judge Rockford Memorial Hospital* 150 N.E. 2d 202; *cert. denied,* 17 Ill. App. 2nd 365 [1958]); nurse anesthetist not slandered due to "less than desirable" reference given to prospective employer by former employer (*Gengler Phelps,* 589 P. 2d 1056 Ct. App N.M. 1978)
	3. common interest	When publisher speaks to another who has a common interest and sharing the information furthers that interest; may be legal and/or moral duty to speak; cannot be abused or exceeded	
	4. publishing to those who may act in public interest	Good faith required; cannot be abused or exceeded	Nurse reports unprofessional conduct of physician to state medical board
	5. fair comment on matters of public interest	Extends to matters in which public has legitimate interest; cannot be abused or exceeded	Nurse writes article for newspaper on poor patient care at local hospital
Partial defenses that mitigate (reduce) damages but do not avoid liability	1. retraction	Must immediately follow the publication; must be complete and without limitation; must be in same manner as publication	Nurse writes retraction of article on poor patient care at local hospital for same newspaper

TABLE 6–2

Defenses to Quasi-intentional Torts *(Continued)*

DEFENSES	QUALIFICATIONS	OTHER COMMENTS	EXAMPLE
	2. evidence of plaintiff's bad reputation	Defendant must prove reputation already "bad" as to what was published	Nurse defendant introduces evidence at administrative hearing that physician had problems with unprofessional conduct in other states
2. Breach of confidentiality Consent	Must be knowing, informed, voluntary	May be required to be in writing; cannot be abused or exceeded	Psychiatric nurse receives patient's written consent to release information about treatment to employer
Mandatory reporting requirements	Usually found in statutes or case law; basis is, in reality, that no confidential privilege exists in the identified situations	Cannot be abused or exceeded	Nurse reports to proper authorities child abuse or neglect or presence of a communicable disease; clear, imminent danger reported to third party
Other legal mandate to share information	Usually found in statutes or case law; also applies when required or ordered to testify in any judicial proceeding(s)	Cannot be abused or exceeded	Nurse is subpoenaed to testify as witness in case filed by former patient alleging malpractice against physician
3. Invasion of privacy Consent	Must be knowing, informed, voluntary	Cannot be abused or exceeded	Patient consents to nurse taking photographs of patient postoperatively
Mandatory reporting requirements	See comments under Breach of Confidentiality	Cannot be abused or exceeded	See example under Breach of Confidentiality
Other legal mandate to share information	See comments under Breach of Confidentiality	Cannot be abused or exceeded	See example under Breach of Confidentiality NOTE: *Truth is not a defense in invasion of privacy actions*
4. Malicious prosecution Any of the essential elements of the tort not satisfied	1. No malice 2. Termination of suit in favor of defendant 3. Presence of reasonable or probable cause to initiate suit		Employer, with reasonable basis, reports nurse to state agency or nursing board for violation of state nurse practice act
Guilt in fact	Must be proven by defendant; can be raised even if verdict in criminal case in favor of accused (not guilty)		

Data from W. Page Keeton, Editor. *Prosser and Keeton on the Law of Torts.* 5th Edition. St. Paul, Minn: West Publishing Company, 1984 (with 1988 Pocket Part).

Under color of state law has specific meaning in the law, and Section 1983's language is no exception. Generally this phrase means that an individual who deprives another of his or her rights and acts in this manner is a governmental official—state or local—or a private individual whose conduct is found to be "state action" rather than private conduct.

Health Care Delivery and Section 1983

In relation to health care delivery, governmental (state) action is easily satisfied when the hospital is a local or state hospital, a public health agency, or a prison health service. What is more difficult to determine is when a private entity or health care provider's conduct satisfied the state action requirement.

Although many tests have been applied by the courts to determine if conduct characterized as private is truly state action, no one specific criterion (e.g., receipt of state financial assistance) is indicative of how the action will be depicted. In fact, many of the reported cases filed by aggrieved plaintiffs alleging state action by a private entity or individuals have been decided in favor of the defendant—that is, depicting the conduct as "private action." Some examples include:

▼ Private hospital not acting under color of state law when reporting child abuse to state authorities and placing child under protective custody pursuant to juvenile court order for Section 1983 purposes.[50]

▼ Private hospital that denied ophthalmologist staff privileges not acting under color of state law when physician could not provide facts to support his allegations that the state regulated the personnel decisions of the hospital and discriminated against him in violation of Section 1983.[51]

▼ A private nursing home that exerted a great deal of control over a resident's existence is not a state actor even though it receives Medicare and Medicaid funds.[52]

It is important to note that in a Section 1983 action, an employer may be joined in the suit under the theory of *vicarious liability* discussed in Chapter 3. The plaintiff can do so by suing the employee individually and in his or her official role. The plaintiff can also directly name the entity, especially if the plaintiff can prove that the employer or entity violated his or her rights by the adoption of a policy ("custom or usage") that is in violation of the statute. Under the vicarious liability theory, the plaintiff need only prove that the employer indirectly or directly acquiesced in allowing the official's conduct to continue.

Damages that can be awarded to the successful plaintiff of a Section 1983 action are intended to compensate the person for the deprivation suffered and should therefore be governed by principles of compensation.[53] Thus, they include compensatory and punitive damages as well as nominal awards. Remedies also available may include reinstatement (when, for example, an employee is illegally discharged); the closure of a facility (when, for example, conditions at a jail are found to be unconstitutional); or an injunction prohibiting continuation of the conduct found to be in violation of the law.

To envision how this civil rights law actually protects an individual's right, the Boretti case (p. 121) involving two nurses is an interesting example.

Defenses to a Section 1983 Civil Rights Action

Alleged Conduct Not Violative of Civil Rights

There are several defenses to an allegation that one's civil rights under Section 1983 have been violated. Perhaps the most obvious is to prove that the conduct supposedly violative of one's constitutional right(s) did not occur. Thus, in the *Boretti* case discussed above, if the nurses are able to prove their conduct was not "deliberate inattention" to the incarcerated patient's medical needs, then that defense will be successful.

Boretti v. Wiscomb (1991)[54]

Prison nurse employees did not provide care ordered for prisoner

FACTS: Plaintiff, David Boretti, suffered a gunshot wound to the left thigh about 3 weeks before being transferred to the Oakland County Jail in Pontiac, Michigan. In December of 1987, he had surgery for the wound and was then taken to Jackson Prison and treated in its infirmary. When recovered, he was sent back to Oakland County Jail. The discharge instructions for the prisoner included dressing changes, ambulation, medication, and a follow-up appointment. Upon return to the jail on December 30, Boretti was placed in a holding cell with no bed. As a result, he had to sleep on the cement floor. His crutches were taken away, and no dressing changes were made for 6 days. No medications were given to the prisoner. Boretti asked two nurses, nurse Wiscomb and nurse Baldwin, to provide care to him, but both refused to do so. The prisoner was finally seen by the doctor at the scheduled appointment, and the wound healed properly.

Prisoner files a 1983 action, alleging his Eighth Amendment rights were violated

Boretti filed suit in federal court under 42 U.S.C. 1983 against both nurses, alleging violation of his Eighth Amendment right to be free from cruel and unusual punishment because (1) the nurses were acting "under color of state law" as employees of the prison and (2) were "deliberately indifferent" to his medical needs.

Trial court grants summary judgment motion of nurses

TRIAL COURT DECISION: Nurse Wiscomb filed a motion for summary judgment, stating that there was no material issue of fact that she had been indifferent to his needs. The court granted her motion, and Boretti appealed.

Court of appeals reverses trial decision in favor of nurses

APPEALS COURT DECISION: The Sixth Circuit Court of Appeals reversed the trial court's decision, holding that there was a material issue of fact as to whether the nurses named were deliberately indifferent to Boretti's medical needs. Testimony at the summary judgment hearing was that the prisoner's requests for treatment were met with comments such as "I'm too busy passing out medications . . . and can't be bothered with petty excuses" (Wiscomb) and "[I] don't have any time for you; you'll just have to make do until the doctor comes in" (Baldwin).

Question whether nurses' conduct was "inadvertent failure" or deliberate indifference to provide medical care a material fact issue that trial must resolve

Because of this testimony, the court held a jury must decide if the prisoner's Eighth Amendment rights were violated. If the nurses merely displayed "inadvertent failure to provide medical care," then no constitutional violations occurred. If, however, there was no compassion and reckless disregard of Boretti's medical needs, which included a total disregard for the medical regimen ordered, then the nurses' behavior clearly violated his Eighth Amendment rights.

ANALYSIS: The conduct of the two nurses in this case, if true, is far from exemplary, even if it does not rise to the test necessary for a constitutional violation. Furthermore, the alleged failure to provide for the medical needs of any patient, but most certainly a prisoner who has no other options for that care, is ethically unpermissible.

Immunity from Suit

The other defenses available to a 1983 case rest on the fact that the government enjoys immunity (freedom) from suit in some circumstances, as was discussed in Chapter 3. However, as a review, it is important to recall that such immunity is not absolute. Therefore, a suit will be filed if no immunity exists.

The nurse who is an employee of a governmental health care entity must also remember that as an employee, any immunities granted him or her may be eliminated if the nurse acts in "bad faith" or "malice," or otherwise abuses the immunity. In addition, many immunities are based on whether the conduct complained of was discretionary. If discretionary, immunity would exist in the absence of malice. If the conduct is ministerial, however, no immunity would be present because the individual is acting in obedience to a higher authority and without regard to his or her own judgment or discretion.[55]

Eleventh Amendment to the United States Constitution

The Eleventh Amendment provides another form of immunity from suit by prohibiting federal court suits, either in law or equity, against the states.[56] As a result, state treasuries are protected from being drained if there is a successful suit in federal court concerning a request for past injuries (retroactive relief) due to a violation of one's rights by state actors. However, the individual injured may be awarded other relief, such as an injunction or a declaratory judgment (nonmonetary and prospective) so that state actors comply with federal constitutional mandates.[57]

There are several exceptions to the general prohibition contained in the Eleventh Amendment. One is if the state actor is sued *personally* rather than in his or her "official capacity."[58] Only in the latter instance would the state treasury be in possible jeopardy and require application of the immunity provisions.

Common Law Immunities—Absolute or Qualified Immunity

As with many of the intentional and quasi-intentional suits discussed thus far, those involved in 1983 suits may have immunity from suit, either absolute or qualified, based on case law decisions rather than statutory law. For example, certain public officials—judges and legislators—are usually absolutely immune from suit for monetary damages under 1983 actions, but may be subject to prospective remedies sought by the plaintiff.[59]

Qualified immunity in 1983 actions rests upon the presence of "good faith" on the part of the defendant or defendants. For example, the defendant may try to prove that the conduct did not violate the plaintiff's civil rights because a reasonable person in that position would not have recognized the violation.[60] If successful, then the qualified immunity attaches, and the defendant is entitled to a dismissal of the suit.

SUMMARY OF PRINCIPLES
AND APPLICATIONS

The intentional and quasi-intentional torts, as well as civil rights violations, can be a potential quagmire of liability for the nurse if he or she does not consistently think about them. In addition to the defenses already presented, the following are some guidelines for the nurse to keep in mind.

Intentional Torts

Assault and Battery

▼ Always make sure the patient has consented to treatment before initiating it.

▼ If the patient refuses treatment, and there is no threat to the life or well-being of the patient, do not force treatment.

▼ Never hold a patient down to administer medications or treatment that the patient is refusing.

▼ Never act in a threatening manner toward a patient.

▼ Never hit, or threaten to hit, a patient.

False Imprisonment

- Never unlawfully restrict a patient's freedom.

- If a patient is committed to a psychiatric or other facility, be certain all papers are properly filled out and present upon admission.

- Use restraining devices (e.g., leather or posey belts) only when there is a clear clinical reason to do so and document well in the patient's record.

- If a patient chooses to leave the institution against medical advice (AMA), try to talk with the patient about staying; inform the patient that Medicare and other health insurance may not pay for the hospitalization if an AMA discharge occurs, and notify proper persons (doctor, nurse manager). If the patient refuses, ask him or her to sign the appropriate form. If he or she does not do so, simply let the patient go, document the incident well, and notify the proper individuals in the institution of the patient's leaving.

Intentional Infliction of Emotional Distress

- Always think before acting or speaking to patients and their families or significant others.

- Remember that when injury or death to a loved one occurs, friends and family are vulnerable and must be treated with an increased sense of empathy.

Conversion of Property

- Always ask a patient or family member if belongings can be removed, stored, or otherwise disposed of.

- Any belongings that are removed, stored, or disposed of should be properly documented in the patient's medical record or on other appropriate forms.

- Any patient belongings taken home by friends or family members should be documented in the patient's medical record.

- Never remove a patient's belongings without his or her consent.

Quasi-intentional Torts

Defamation

- Always be sure that what you are saying about a patient is the truth.

- If you must share information about a patient or another person and you may enjoy an absolute or qualified privilege to share what might be defamatory, be certain not to abuse or overstep the privilege.

- When disciplining a nurse colleague, or discussing something sensitive with a patient, be sure to do so in private so that what is discussed is not published to a third party.

- When asked to write a reference for a nurse colleague, be sure to adhere to the institution's policy concerning references. If uncertain about what you are sharing about the colleague, sending the reference to the nurse for review and asking him or her to send it on to whomever is asking for it will avoid any publication by the nurse giving the reference.

- Never repeat information received unless you know it to be true.

- Always adhere to the institution's policies concerning speaking with reporters or other news media personnel.

Breach of Confidentiality

- Adhere strictly to any obligations to maintain patient confidentiality.

- Do not discuss patients with those not involved directly with their care.

- Adhere to institution policies concerning confidentiality, especially in relation to information given over the phone about the patient and in speaking to reporters or other news media.

- If practicing in an area of nursing where special mandates concerning confidentiality exist—psychiatric nursing, for example—continually review and adhere to the obligations required to maintain confidentiality.

Invasion of Privacy

- See guidelines for Breach of Confidentiality, above.

▼ Always obtain consent for any photographs or use of the patient's name before disclosing either to another person.

▼ Provide patient care in a respectful and dignified way.

▼ Always ask the patient if observers of any kind can be present before care or treatment is initiated.

Malicious Prosecution

▼ Never initiate, or get involved in, a suit against another, including a patient, if there is not reasonable basis to do so.

Section 1983 Civil Rights Violations

▼ The nurse who is an employee of a local, state, or governmental health care delivery system must take great care to protect the patient's civil rights.

▼ If an absolute or qualified privilege exists, the nurse must make sure that no abuse of the privilege occurs.

▼ Good faith and knowledge of what a reasonable person would have known concerning the federal right are two tests that should also be kept in mind concerning the application of a qualified privilege.

TOPICS FOR FURTHER INQUIRY

1. Analyze at least two reported cases naming a nurse as a defendant in a breach of nurse–patient confidentiality. Compare and contrast the manner in which the breach occurred and any defenses raised by the nurse for the breach. Suggest how the nurse in each case might have handled the situation differently to avoid the breach of confidentiality.

2. Develop a patient care policy for obtaining consent for treatment with the specific concern of avoiding assault and battery allegations against a nurse who must provide care for patients in the institution or agency.

3. Write a research paper comparing and contrasting libel with slander. Focus specifically on how a nurse might be involved in libeling or slandering a fellow colleague or libeling or slandering a former patient. Discuss specific guidelines the nurse should follow to avoid these intentional torts.

4. Develop an interview instrument to question several nurses about their respective understanding of intentional or quasi-intentional torts. Utilize a situation-specific format that requires the nurse being interviewed to identify a particular tort or torts. Analyze the results and make suggestions for how to increase nurses' understanding of the tort or torts included in the interview instrument.

REFERENCES

1. W. Page Keeton, General Editor. *Prosser and Keeton on The Law of Torts.* St. Paul, Minn: West Publishing Company, 1984, 33 (with 1988 Pocket Part)
2. *Id.* at 34.
3. *Id.*
4. *Id., citing Baldinger v. Banks*, 201 N.Y.S. 2d 629 (1960); *Restatement of Torts*, Section 13, Comment e (1977).
5. Henry Campbell Black. *Black's Law Dictionary*, 6th Edition. St. Paul, Minn: West Publishing Company, 1991, 559–560.
6. Keeton, *supra* note 1, at 43.
7. *Id.*
8. *Id., citing Kline v. Kline*, 64 N.E. 9 (1902).
9. Keeton, *supra* note 1, at 45 *citing* Seavy, "Threats Inducing Emotional Reactions," 39 *North Carolina Law Review* 74 (1960).
10. Keeton, *supra* note 1, at 39, *citing Restatement of Torts*, Sections 13 and 18.
11. *Id.*
12. Keeton, *supra* note 1, at 40.
13. Keeton, *supra* note 1, at 41–42.
14. 576 So. 2d 992 (1991).
15. 811 S.W. 2d 141 (1991).
16. Keeton, *supra* note 1, at 47.
17. *Gadsen General Hospital v. Hamilton*, 103 So. 553 (1925).
18. Keeton, *supra* note 1, at 60, 64.
19. *Id.* at 56.
20. See, for example, *Austin v. Regents of the University of California*, 152 Cal. Rep. 420 (1979); *Grimsley v. Sampson*, 530 P.2d 291 (1975); *Strachan v. John F. Kennedy Memorial Hospital*, 538 A.2d 346 (N.J. 1988).
21. *Seitz v. Humana of Kentucky, Inc.*, 1988 Ky. App. LEXIS 164 (Ky. Court of Appeals November 4, 1988), *as discussed in* 17 *Health Law Digest*, January 1989, at 27.

22. Keeton, *supra* note 1, at 92–93.
23. Keeton, *supra* note 1, at 727.
24. Keeton, *supra* note 1, at 771.
25. *Id., citing* Green, "Relational Interests," 31 *Illinois Law Review* 35 (1936).
26. *Second Restatement of Torts* Section 559, Comment e.
27. *Funderburk v. Bechtel Power Corporation*, 698 P. 2d 556 (1985).
28. *New York Times v. Sullivan*, 376 U.S. 254 (1964).
29. Keeton, *supra* note 1, at 842.
30. Keeton, *supra* note 1, at 789–793.
31. *Schlessler v. Keck*, 271 P. 2d 588 (Cal. 1954).
32. 410 ILCS 50/0.01 *et seq.* (1993).
33. Keeton, *supra* note 1, at 851.
34. *Id.* at 853.
35. *Vassiliades v. Garfinkle's Brooks Brothers*, 492 A. 2d 580 (D.C. App. 1985).
36. *Id.* at 855.
37. *Id.*
38. See, for example, *Melvin v. Burling*, 490 N.E. 2d 1011 (3rd App. District 1986).
39. *Clayman v. Bernstein*, 38 PA D &C 543 (1940).
40. Keeton, *supra* note 1, at 856–857, *citing* Prosser and *The Second Restatement of Torts*, Section 652D, Comment d (1977).
41. *Miller v. Motorola*, 560 N.E. 2d 900 (App. Ct. 1st Dist. 1990).
42. *Id.* at 903.
43. Keeton, *supra* note 1, at 863–865.
44. Keeton, *supra* note 1, at 870.
45. *Id.* at 871.
46. *Id.* at 888.
47. Robert Miller, "General Principles of Civil Liability," in *Problems in Hospital Law*. 6th Edition. Rockville, Md: Aspen Publishers, Inc., 1990, 182.
48. *Northwest Florida Home Health Agency v. Merrill*, 469 So. 2d 893 (Fla. App. 1 Dist. 1985).
49. Ralph Chandler, Robert Enslen, and Peter Renstrom. *Constitutional Law Handbook: Individual Rights*. Rochester, NY: Lawyers Cooperative Publishing (1993), p. 116 of April, 1995 Pocket Part, *citing Albright v. Oliver*, 114 S.Ct. 807 (1994).
50. *Young v. Arkansas Children's Hospital*, 721 F. Supp. 197 (E.D. Ark. 1989).
51. *Pao v. Holy Redeemer Hospital*, 547 F. Supp. 484 (D.C. Pa. 1982).
52. *Hoyt v. St. Mary's Rehabilitation Center*, 711 F. 2d 864 (8th Cir. 1983).
53. *Carey v. Piphus*, 435 U.S. 247 (1978).
54. 930 F.2d 1150 (1991).
55. Henry Campbell Black. *Black's Law Dictionary*. 6th Edition. St. Paul, Minn: West Publishing Company, 1991, 689.
56. U.S. Constitution Amendment XI.
57. *Ex Parte Young*, 209 U.S. 123 (1908).
58. Keeton, *supra* note 1, at 1044, *citing Kentucky v. Graham*, 473 U.S. 159 (1985).
59. *Pulliam v. Allen*, 466 U.S. 522 (1984).
60. Keeton, *supra* note 1, *citing Harlow v. Fitzgerald*, 457 U.S. 800 (1982).

7

Administrative Law

contents

Administrative law is defined as the body of law—rules, regulations, orders, and decisions—created by administrative agencies to carry out their powers and duties.[1] Administrative agencies, whether state or federal, are created by respective state or federal (Congress) legislatures, which then delegate the responsibility of carrying out particular pieces of legislation, such as statutes, that are specific to the agency. In the health care field, and in nursing specifically, administrative law and administrative agencies have a great impact on the delivery of health care and on nursing practice.

The character, role, and powers of administrative agencies are varied and complex. Although an agency is created by a particular legislature with defined powers and roles, the ability of the agency to carry out those roles is also further defined. This further definition is found in the agency's authority to promulgate its own rules and regulations to enforce its responsibilities and is called formal or informal rule making. Furthermore, administrative bureaus also function as enforcers of the legislation they are empowered to oversee, often in a trial-type hearing. As a result, an administrative agency is often involved in sanctioning, limiting, or eliminating rights granted to citizens by the legislation when violations of an act occur. One such example is when a professional licensee (nurse or practical nurse) is disciplined. Rule making and enforcement roles are usually governed by the state or federal Administrative Procedure Act.

Other functions, however, although required to conform to certain rules of law and court decisions, are less readily defined. An example of such a role would be settlement powers of the agency.

This chapter will present a broad overview of administrative law and process and briefly discuss administrative agencies that most directly affect the health care field generally and nursing specifically. Although the focus of the content will be primarily federal in nature, some discussion of state laws will occur.

KEY PRINCIPLES

Administrative Procedure Act

Delegation of Authority to Administrative Agency

Rule Making

Rule-Making Procedure

Due Process

Property Interest

Liberty Interest

Judicial Review

ESSENTIALS OF ADMINISTRATIVE LAW

Origins and History of Administrative Law and Agencies

Administrative law deals with the body of law of governmental or public agencies, whether federal, state, or local. Most commentators mark the beginning of administrative law with the establishment of the Interstate Commerce Commission (ICC) in 1887.[2] The Interstate Commerce Commission like other early administrative agencies, was "regulatory" in nature, meaning that its primary purpose was to control the growth of large corporations and ensure that no undue influence or power was vested in a few companies. As the nation developed, other types of administrative agencies appeared, and their respective characters reflected what was happening in the country at the time. For example, when the country focused upon social reform

---

RELATED TOPICS

for its citizens, administrative laws and bureaus concentrated on benefit programs such as Medicare, unemployment insurance, and worker's compensation.[3]

Administrative law deals with the body of law of governmental or public agencies, whether federal, state, or local.

Despite the specific focus of an administrative agency, administrative bureaus became, and still are, a vital piece of the overall picture of a government's ability to function. Without them, the local, state, and/or federal government would virtually be at a standstill.[4] In addition to being a necessary vehicle for carrying out the goals of government, administrative agencies also serve other important goals that include managing issues with citizens fairly and in accordance with due process protections and deciding issues as accurately as possible by utilizing the best method to do so (trial-type hearing or informal notice, for example).

Essentially, two basic types of administrative agencies have emerged. The first, an executive department, agency, or bureau, is organized with a secretary appointed by the President as the head. Because these agencies are directly under the control of the President, he or she has the power to appoint and remove agency heads.

The second type of administrative agency is the commission or board, a more independent body in the sense that the head of a commission is appointed for a fixed term. Thus it is more difficult to remove commission heads unless there is a just reason for doing so. Furthermore, the commission is formed for a specific purpose, its members are appointed because of their expertise in a certain area, and, like the commission head, they cannot be removed from their position unless there is a clear reason to do so.

An example of a commission is the National Labor Relations Board, which administers the National Labor Relations Act.

Delegation, Accountability, and Control of Administrative Agencies

The United States Constitution (and respective state constitutions) establishes and protects a tripartite system of government—the legislative, executive, and judicial branches—to provide a system of checks and balances on the powers of each branch. Because specific powers and responsibilities are given to each branch of government, when the delegation of those powers and/or responsibilities to a governmental agency occurs, the delegation can raise serious constitutional questions.

Delegating powers and/or responsibilities to administrative agencies has always been controversial. Even so, the very language of the United States Constitution, Article I, Section 1 and Section 8, Paragraph 18, has been used to support the need for delegation to administrative agencies.[5] In addition, many cases have been decided by the federal courts supporting the ability of Congress to delegate to federally created administrative organizations.[6]

Accordingly, administrative agencies have been delegated powers through the so-called Delegation Doctrine that reflect the powers of all three branches of the government; that is, legislative powers (pass rules and regulations to which affected people and organizations must adhere or face civil and criminal penalties), judicial powers (to hear and resolve disputes when an alleged violation of an act or its rules and regulations occurs), and executive powers (to investigate, subpoena, and prosecute alleged violations).[7]

Despite the determination that delegation can occur, the judicial branch of the government—the courts, both federal and state—stands ready to carefully analyze and decide the propriety of any delegation of power to an agency that is challenged, including its constitutionality.

The reins on administrative agency functioning can be applied in many ways. One very strong control is "legislative oversight," whether formal or informal,[8] whereby Congress or a state legislature determines that an agency has overstepped its responsibilities. If that determination occurs, for example, the legislative body may "restructure" the agency.

A second means of control over administrative bureaus is by controlling the staff and employees of the agency.[9] When the President of the United States or governor of a particular state exercises his or her power to appoint heads of executive agencies, for example, it is a powerful way to ensure accountability and adherence to agency policy. Likewise, Congress, although it cannot make appointments to agencies, can establish qualifications for agency offices. These confirmation hearings can become very effective tools for ensuring that the person confirmed for a particular office will adhere to the mandates of the agency's delegated powers and responsibilities.[10]

A third effective means of control over administrative bureaus is "executive oversight," usually in the form of an executive order.[11] Other methods include the ability of the President to reorganize the agency and to control litigation involving administrative agencies through the Justice Department. Federal administrative bureaus must be represented by the Justice Department; if the Department refuses to defend or represent an agency policy, the practical effect of that refusal is that the policy is without force.[12]

Similarly, state agencies are represented by the state Attorney General's office. Again, if there is a decision to represent a particular state agency in a certain situation or, conversely, to settle a suit filed by a plaintiff, that decision effectively represents either support or nonsupport of the agency's performance.

ESSENTIALS OF ADMINISTRATIVE PROCEDURE

The Administrative Procedure Act

The federal or state Administrative Procedure Act is a statute that governs practice and pro-
ceedings before respective federal and state administrative agencies. The federal Act was passed in 1946 to provide minimum standards of procedures that all federal agencies were to follow. It also became a model for state legislatures contemplating their own acts. Areas included in the federal statute are (1) definitions of terms used; (2) access to, and publication of, agency rules, opinions, (public) records, and orders; (3) rule-making powers; (4) obligations of agencies to protect the privacy of individuals involved in administrative procedures (Privacy Act); (5) the requirement that specified agency meetings and proceedings be "open" (Government in the Sunshine Act); (6) adjudicatory practice and procedure (hearings, sanctions, and decision-making process; and (7) judicial review.[13]

Most states have adopted state administrative procedure acts that contain similar, if not identical, sections included in the federal law.

The federal or state Administrative Procedure Act is a statute that governs practice and proceedings before respective federal and state administrative agencies.

Rule Making

The process of rule making is a way for an administrative agency to deal with its responsibilities in carrying out a particular piece of legislation with clarity and efficiency. Rather than exercise its adjudicatory power(s) and issue an *order* each and every time there is an alleged violation of the act or its rules and regulations (which would apply only to those specific individuals or organizations), an adopted rule or regulation, if clear and well drafted, can provide guidance to the greatest number of individuals and organizations expected to comply with the particular act.

The Administrative Procedure Act defines the types of rules that can be passed, the process of rule making, and its scope. The types of rules that an agency is authorized to promulgate are (1) *legislative rules*, which have "the force and effect of law," are considered "binding" on all those affected by it, and must be adopted pursuant to established, "formal," or at a minimum, "informal," rule-making process; (2) *interpretive rules*, which indicate the agency's opinion on the act it administers; these are exempt from the rule-making process, but must be published; and (3) *procedural rules*, which regulate the agency's own practices and procedures, are legally binding on the agency (moreover, if not followed, can be challenged by persons adversely affected by the noncompliance), and although also exempt from the rule-making procedure, must be clearly articulated and published.[14]

There are two types of rule-making procedures authorized in the Administrative Procedure Act—"informal" (or "Notice and Comment" rule making) and "formal." The two types are summarized in Table 7–1. All federal agencies are required to follow these procedures. State agencies usually adopt similar informal and formal rule-making procedures. However, publication would occur in the particular state registry and code. For example, the state of Illinois utilizes the *Illinois Register* and the *Illinois Administrative Code*.

Protection of Individual Constitutional Rights

Due Process

In administrative law and procedure, due process protections are important to the individual or organization because the administrative agency, again an arm of the federal or state government, cannot deprive a citizen of "life, liberty, or property" without due process of law.[15] Although a threat to one's life is usually *not* an issue in administrative actions, liberty or property rights *are* often the central issues in

TABLE 7–1	
Informal and Formal Rule-Making Procedures Authorized by the Federal Administrative Procedure Act	
INFORMAL	**FORMAL**
1. Publish draft in *Federal Register*	1. Publish draft in *Federal Register*
2. Public can submit written comments concerning draft	2. Provide informal rule-making hearing for oral public comment or, if authorized by another act, trial-type hearing may be required
3. Review comments and revise draft, if necessary	3. Review oral comments and revise draft, if necessary
4. Publish final rule in *Federal Register* 30 days before effective date	4. Publish final rule in *Federal Register* 30 days before effective date; if trial-type hearing, hearing officer enters order that contains findings of facts based on evidence presented in the hearing
5. Include final regulation in *Code of Federal Regulations*	5. Include final regulation in *Code of Federal Regulations*

Data from: 5 U.S.C. 552, 553, 554 (1946).

such actions. Thus the Administrative Procedure Act, and its state counterparts, grant clear procedural protections to those individuals or organizations who face an infringement of liberty or property.

> *In administrative law and procedure, due process protections are important to the individual . . . because the administrative agency . . . cannot deprive a citizen of "life, liberty, or property" without due process of law.*

Property Interest

A property interest is liberally construed by the courts and defined in diverse ways based on the context in which they arise. In administrative law, property interest is interpreted to be any "legitimate claim of entitlement" to a benefit that may be adversely affected by an administrative action.[16] An example of a property interest in the context of administrative law is the possession of an occupational license to practice one's profession (e.g., RN or LPN).

Liberty Interest

Liberty interests are also liberally construed and defined in diverse ways by the courts. In criminal law, this interest clearly encompasses a potential restriction of movement if incarceration is contemplated as punishment. In administrative law, however, this interest has been expanded to also include "the right of the individual to contract, to engage in any of the common occupations of life, to acquire useful knowledge, to marry . . . and generally to enjoy those privileges long recognized . . . as essential to the orderly pursuit of happiness by free men."[17] An example of a liberty interest in the context of administrative law is the possession of an occupational license in good standing. If an RN or LPN is disciplined in a manner inconsistent with procedural protections, for example, his or her "freedom" to reinstate the license to one in good standing (not disciplined) is jeopardized. Likewise, the registered nurse or licensed practical nurse's ability to obtain licensure in another state ("freedom" to obtain licensure) is also threatened.

When a property or liberty interest is potentially at risk by an administrative agency action, the Administrative Procedure Act requires that the protections listed in Table 7–2 be afforded the individual or organization.

Judicial Review

Judicial review is a means by which parties affected by an agency decision can challenge the decision if it is believed to be arbitrary (unreasonable), not based on the law, illegal, or not based on the agency's power, procedures, or policies.[18] To do so, however, the party seeking review of an agency decision in the courts must meet certain requirements enumerated in the Administrative Procedure Act and delineated by many court decisions. They include "standing" to challenge the decision ("suffering legal wrong . . . or adversely affected or aggrieved . . . by agency action"[19]) and, with specific exceptions (e.g., when a party is challenging the jurisdiction of the agency to bring the action), a *final* administrative decision must have taken place for court review to occur. This latter requirement is often referred to as the exhaustion of administrative remedies rule. This rule is strictly adhered to by the courts, and the party seeking review must show that all agency appeal and review procedures have been used before seeking the court's decision.

The scope of the court's review is to include "relevant questions of law, interpret relevant constitutional and statutory provisions, and determine the meaning or applicability of the terms of an agency action."[20] The court is empowered to order an agency to act when the agency's action is "unlawfully withheld or unduly delayed." The court can also declare unlawful and set aside any agency "action, findings, and conclusions" found to be arbitrary, capricious, or an abuse of discretion, unconstitutional, in disregard of procedures required by law, or exceeding statutory authority, jurisdiction, or limitations.[21]

Other Aspects of Administrative Procedure

Information Gathering

For an agency to carry out whatever powers it has been delegated, it must have information upon which to rely when carrying out its responsibilities. Because the governmental agency or commission is an "arm" of the government, it is constrained by constitutional mandates when

TABLE 7–2

Due Process Rights Required by Federal Administrative Procedure Act When Protected Rights Threatened

RIGHT	SPECIFICS OF RIGHT	EXCEPTIONS
1. Notice	1. Inform party of action; time, place, and nature of hearing; basis of agency authority to take action	1. Need for immediate action to protect public from harm; or if a statute or "common law" already provides "process due"
2. Trial-type hearing	2. Present testimony; cross-examine witnesses; present evidence	2. If decision of agency "nonlegal" in nature; or if controversy can be decided by agency without hearing and denial of due process
3. Counsel	3. Attorney can "advise, represent, and accompany" party	3. If party is not compelled to appear before agency; if party cannot afford lawyer
4. Unbiased decision	4. Body or person making determination must not have direct or indirect conflict with merits of case	4. None
5. Complete record of decision	5. Record must set out "findings, conclusions, and basis of both from testimony and exhibits"	5. None

Data from: 5 U.S.C. Sections 554, 555, 556 (1946).

seeking out whatever information it needs from private individuals or entities, especially when the request for information is challenged. Thus, the Fourth, Fifth, *and* Fourteenth Amendment protections must be respected by the administrative bureau when it attempts to gather facts and evidence upon which to take action.

The Ability to Issue Subpoenas

An administrative organization generally has the power to issue subpoenas when seeking information, but the power is not unlimited. Rather, it is limited by four main constraints: (1) the inquiry must be within the powers of the agency and done for a lawful purpose or reason; (2) the information asked for must be "relevant" to the lawful purpose or reason; (3) the inquiry must be adequately sufficient and not unrealistically "burdensome"; and (4) the information requested cannot be privileged information (e.g., information obtained by the nurse from a patient during the course of providing patient care is generally treated as privileged by state law).[22]

The Ability to Compel Testimony

An administrative bureau may request that an individual testify about a matter that may have criminal law ramifications. For example, a nurse appearing before the licensing authority for an alleged violation of the nurse practice act may admit to behavior that is not only a violation of the practice act but also of the criminal statutes. If that is the case, the individual can refuse to incriminate himself or herself by relying on the Fifth Amendment's protections, but only under certain circumstances. One such circumstance is if the administrative hearing is truly criminal rather than civil in nature.[23]

Second, the protection against self-incrimination is *personal* in nature and does not extend to an organization, corporation, or association.[24] Thus the nurse entrepreneur who has formed her own nurse registry, is an officer or principal in that agency, and is asked to produce agency records when accused by the Office of the Inspector General of fraudulently billing Medicare cannot raise the Fifth Amendment as a protection. Furthermore, the nurse cannot rely on the fact that the records may incriminate her; by producing the nurse agency records, she is, as the record custodian, not performing a *personal* act. Rather, she is performing an act of the entity.[25]

Last, it is important to note that even if testimony given in an administrative hearing may be self-incriminating from the criminal law perspective, an individual may be forced to testify against himself or herself if granted immunity from prosecution. The immunity granted may be "use immunity" (prevents the testimony "and its fruits" from being used in *any* manner in connection with criminal law prosecution) or "transactional immunity" (prevents prosecution for violations to which the testimony relates).[26] In either case, the immunity would not prevent prosecution for *new* information obtained from sources independent of the compelled testimony, nor does it allow the individual any grant of immunity in the administrative hearing itself.[27]

The Ability to Conduct Inspections and Searches

Generally the constitutional prohibitions against warrantless searches apply to administrative agencies; that is, a warrant is generally required.[28] However, some important exceptions to that general rule have been established for administrative agencies by the United States Supreme Court. To begin with, so long as the search or inspection is based upon valid statutory authorization for the agency to conduct the search, there is no need to establish probable cause in the same manner that is required in criminal law, and a warrant is not required unless entry into the place to be searched is denied.[29]

Other exceptions to obtaining a search warrant include (1) when a particular type of business is heavily licensed/regulated by the administrative agency[30]; (2) when an emergency exists[31]; (3) when valid, voluntary consent is given, whether express or implied (e.g., not

objecting to an inspection)[32]; and (4) when the space or area to be searched is considered to be "in open view"; that is, consisting of what is "in plain view," so long as the inspector is legally on the premises, or consisting of "open fields," meaning outdoor property, even if privately owned.[33]

Examples of administrative searches or inspections that a nurse might experience include inspections by the Occupational Safety and Health Administration (OSHA) because, for example, a complaint had been filed with the local agency office concerning violations of the employer's duty to provide a healthful and safe workplace. Or, an inspection by state or local licensing officials may take place concerning compliance by the health care delivery system with that agency's licensing rules and regulations. In either case, the inspection might also involve the testing of materials found within the health care delivery system. For example, if a complaint alleged unhealthy air due to the presence of some toxin, samples could be taken by the inspector.

Examples of administrative searches or inspections that a nurse might experience include inspections by the Occupational Safety and Health Administration (OSHA) . . . concerning violations of the employer's duty to provide a healthful and safe workplace.

Administration of Benefit Programs

Federal programs (e.g., Social Security Disability and state programs [such as worker's compensation]) that provide financial benefits to citizens must be able to handle, in an expeditious manner, large volumes of applications for benefits and administer awards to those who are found to be eligible for the plan to which they applied. Thus the administrative agency charged with these responsibilities constantly makes unceremonious decisions concerning coverage on a daily basis. Some of the programs, such as the Social Security Disability program, do provide an "appeal" procedure, which includes a trial-type hearing before an administrative judge if benefits are initially denied. Even so, most of the initial decisions concerning coverage are made by first-level agency employees without a trial-type hearing, and they are not challenged by the applicant for many reasons, including but not limited to a lack of information concerning the appeal process and a lack of financial resources.

Summary Administrative Powers

Most administrative agencies have the power to act swiftly when an immediate threat to the public's health or safety exists. The Food and Drug Administration, for example, is empowered to confiscate any drug on the market that is adulterated or misbranded in violation of the Food, Drug, and Cosmetic Act.[34] Likewise, state licensing authorities often have the ability to suspend a licensing without a hearing when there is a need to protect the public's well-being.[35] Despite the authority to take these actions, the statute allowing summary powers or, if not present in the law, due process mandates, requires a postsuspension trial-type hearing within a certain time period so that the organization or individual has an opportunity to defend against the agency action.[36]

Settlement of Issues without Full Hearing

Because administrative agencies would be hopelessly inefficient if each were required to determine legal issues only through a trial-type hearing or some other more formalized process, administrative bureaus generally have the ability to utilize other methods of resolving con-

flicts. Those methods include negotiation, settlement, consent orders, and "alternative dispute resolution."[37] In addition to benefiting the agency, such methods often benefit the individual or organization alleged to have violated some provision, rule, or regulation of the agency because a resolution occurs with less cost, less time involved, and perhaps with less emotional strain to the respondent.

For example, if a union has accused an employer of committing an unfair labor practice by filing a complaint with the National Labor Relations Board (NLRB), the employer can enter into a consent order with the Board resolving the issues involved. Although the consent order will contain allegations, stipulations, and the specific terms of the agreement, there is no formal admission by the employer as to the allegations. Even so, once signed, the consent order has the same effect as a final agency order.[38]

Additional Considerations

Many of the additional aspects of administrative procedure overlap with those already discussed. They include, for example, the ability to issue advisory opinions and declaratory orders; the supervision of businesses over which the agency has jurisdiction; and the awarding of contracts and grants.[39]

Accountability of Agencies to the Public

Thus far, the discussion of administrative procedure has centered on the agency and its processes in getting its work done in a fair and equitable manner. There is another very important part of administrative procedure, however, which is the power the public possesses in ensuring that the administrative bureau is performing as mandated by federal and state law. Three important tools available to the public to determine agency compliance are the Privacy Act (and comparable state law, if any), the Freedom of Information Act (and comparable state law), and the Government in the Sunshine

Act (and comparable state law). It is important to note that although the titles of these three acts sound as though they are separate pieces of legislation, in the federal system they are all contained in the Administrative Procedure Act.

The Privacy Act[40]

The Privacy Act was an amendment to the Administrative Procedure Act because Congress was concerned that the privacy of individuals may be threatened by the "gathering, maintenance, use and dissemination" of personal information by federal agencies, especially when advanced technology, such as computers, was used to compile and use such information.[41] Furthermore, Congress stated that because the right of privacy is a personal and fundamental right protected by the Constitution of the United States, regulations concerning the personal information obtained and its use must be established.[42] The Office of Management and Budget was instructed to develop guidelines in accordance with the Act.

Basically the Act provides that no disclosure of any record in a (federal) system of records can occur except with the written request of, or consent of, the individual.[43] Exceptions to this general rule exist and include disclosure to officers and employees of the agency who maintain the records and who have a need for the information to perform their duties; when release is required under the Freedom of Information Act; to a person who shows "compelling circumstances" that affect the health or safety of an individual, so long as notice of the disclosure is sent to the last known address of that individual; release pursuant to a valid order of a court of competent jurisdiction; and disclosures for use as statistical research or reporting of statistics, so long as the individual cannot be identified.[44]

Furthermore, the Act requires that each agency (1) maintain an "accounting" of disclosures made; (2) when possible, obtain information from the subject (individual) himself or her-

self when the potential for adverse decisions for benefits under federal programs may flow from the information gathered; and (3) among other things, make an effort to ensure prior to release for any purpose other than a Freedom of Information Act request, that the records are accurate, timely, and relevant for agency purposes.[45]

. . . The [Federal Privacy] Act provides that no disclosure of any record in a (federal) system of records can occur except with the written request of, or consent of, the individual.

Another important provision of the Privacy Act is the ability of any individual, upon request, to have access to, review of, and copies of records about him or her contained in the agency's system.[46] Upon receiving such a request, the agency, pursuant to its established procedures, is required to search its system of records and produce nonexempt information to the requesting person. The agency *should* respond to the request within 10 business days and provide access within 30 days, unless "good cause" for further delay is shown. If the information is reproduced for the individual, the agency can charge for that reproduction, but not for its search.[47]

If a request is denied by the agency, an appeal process *can* be established by the agency, but no administrative appeal is mandated by the Act. In either case, the aggrieved individual can seek judicial review of the denial. If an appeal process is provided by the agency, it must be exhausted before seeking the court's decision concerning the denial.[48]

Amendments and corrections by the individual of agency records is also provided for in the Act, subject to the record's being inaccurate, untimely, not relevant, or not complete.[49] If requested and denied, the person can also seek judicial review of the denial of the agency to allow corrections. In this instance, the agency *must* provide an agency appeal process.[50]

Exceptions to an individual's ability to obtain access to his or her records consist of two general categories that have been described as up to agency "discretion" and that must be published in the Federal Register before being effective[51]: *general exceptions* (exemptions) and *specific exceptions*. Examples of the general exceptions include CIA records and any records kept by an agency that has criminal law enforcement as its main purpose.[52] Specific exemptions include "material required by statute to be maintained and used solely as statistical records. . . . and investigatory material compiled for law enforcement purposes" not included in the general exemption category.[53]

Other aspects of privacy are also governed by the Privacy Act. Because Social Security numbers can provide access to a wealth of information about an individual, since 1975 Social Security numbers cannot be required by a federal, state, or local government without notifying the individual (1) whether the disclosure is mandatory (required by federal law) or voluntary; (2) what the number will be used for; and (3) the authority for requesting the number.[54] In addition, generally no governmental entity can deny an individual a right, benefit, or privilege under federal law because the individual refuses to provide his or her social security number.[55]

Also, under the *Computer Matching and Privacy Protection Act of 1988*,[56] Congress amended the Privacy Act to regulate the sharing of private information about individuals between agencies through, among other things, the establishment of a "matching agreement" stating that data obtained may be subject to verification and disclosure through agency computer-matching programs.[57] Because computer matching consists of "side-by-side comparisons" of different agencies' data banks and information about a particular individual or individuals, the matching agreements are aimed to prevent agency abuse of access to personal information listed in the data banks.[58]

The Freedom of Information Act[59]

The Freedom of Information Act (FOIA) makes "all" agency records available to "any person" who requests them unless the records are exempt from disclosure.[60] Exempt agencies include Congress, the federal courts, and those divisions within the Presidential Executive Office whose only function is to advise and assist the President (e.g., the Chief of Staff).[61]

The Freedom of Information Act's (FOIA) purpose is to make "all" agency records available to "any person" who requests them unless the records are exempt from disclosure.

Agency records that must be made available (either for inspection and copying or release) from applicable agencies have been interpreted by the courts to include documents or any other materials that contain information (e.g., audio or computer tapes) that were "created or obtained by the agency and, at the time of the request, are in the possession and control of the agency."[62] If no record exists, the Act does not require the administrative agency to create one. Furthermore, if a record exists but is not in the possession of the agency when access is sought, there is no duty to obtain it.

Some agency records are exempt from mandatory release to the public. The Act contains nine exceptions. Among these are (1) national security information; (2) internal agency personnel rules and practices; (3) information clearly exempted from disclosure by statutes other than the Freedom of Information Act; (4) personnel, medical, or other files that would constitute a clear "unwarranted invasion of privacy"; and (5) records or information gathered for law enforcement purposes, if the disclosure would be harmful under several situations listed in the Act.[63] The Act also states that if an exemption does apply to a request for records, that information should be deleted and the remainder of the record released.

The procedures for obtaining access to agency records are clearly spelled out in the Act and in the *Federal Register*. The request should be in writing and "reasonably describe" the information sought. Although there is no need to justify a reason for the request, in some instances it may be helpful to do so; for example, when seeking a waiver of any fees that may be charged for the records request.[64] The request should also specify that the agency is expected to make an "agency determination" within the time frames spelled out in the Act; that is, within 10 working days of receipt of the request and within 20 working days of receipt of an appeal letter to contest the agency determination to the initial request.[65]

If the internal agency appeal process does not prove successful for the person requesting agency records, it is possible for that individual to seek help from the representative or senator in his or her district, although congressional members have no more power under the Act than other persons.[66] Another option is to seek judicial assistance by filing a suit for injunctive (asking the court to require the agency to release the requested records) and other relief. Such suits are costly and time consuming but may be successful if the specific situation is favorable to the plaintiff(s). In either case, all internal agency appeals must be exhausted before outside help or review is sought.

State Freedom of Information Acts are very similar in structure to the federal law; that is, they contain a general mandate that records be made available to the public; some records are exempt from disclosure; time guidelines for

agency response are listed; and the appeal process is spelled out.[67]

A nurse who is interested in obtaining records about himself or herself from a federal agency may be confused as to which act to utilize—the Privacy Act or the Freedom of Information Act. There are clear benefits and drawbacks to both, and they are listed in Table 7–3.

The Government in the Sunshine Act[68]

The Sunshine Act was passed by Congress to ensure that the government conducted the public's business in public.[69] It requires that federal agencies (and any subdivision authorized to act on behalf of an agency) subject to the Freedom of Information Act and headed by a "collegial" body of two or more members (the majority appointed by the President, with the advice and consent of the Senate) must hold their meetings "in the open."[70] Access to any agency meeting covered under the Act must be afforded to the public.

Ten narrow exceptions to the general rule of

TABLE 7–3	
Comparisons of the Privacy Act and the Freedom of Information Act (FOIA)	
PRIVACY ACT	**FOIA**
1. Applies to US citizens, permanent resident aliens	1. Applies to "any person"
2. Access to records kept by agency in its control and identifiable in some way (name, number, symbol)	2. Access to "any" agency records
3. Broader exemptions for most exempt records	3. Not as inclusive categories for exemptions
4. Does not specify time limits for agency response	4. Specified time limits for agency response
5. Does not mandate appeal procedures	5. Appeal procedures established
6. Agency can charge for copying, but not search, of records	6. Agency can charge for copying records

Data from: Allan Robert Adler. *Using The Freedom of Information Act: A Step by Step Guide.* Washington, DC: The American Civil Liberties Union Foundation, 1990.

open meetings are enumerated in the Act. These include meetings that (1) relate solely to the internal personnel rules and practices of the agency; (2) accuse any individual of a crime; (3) formally censure a person; (4) would disclose information of a personal nature that would result in unwarranted invasion of personal privacy; and (5) prematurely disclose implementation of a proposed agency action, thus frustrating its implementation.[71] The Act also requires the agency to carry out its nonexempt agenda items in the open.

The Act also contains procedures for administrative bureaus to follow when closing a meeting or portion thereof; notice requirements concerning meeting dates and times; maintaining minutes of *all* agency meetings; and procedures for challenging an agency action carried out in violation of the Act.[72]

State laws concerning open governmental meetings are very similar to the federal law. In fact, it may be that many of these state laws served as models for the federal legislation, because when the Sunshine Act was passed in 1972, 49 states had passed open-government laws, and 39 had constitutional provisions concerning open government.[73]

Nurses may need to ensure that a federal or state agency conducts its business in conformity with such public meeting acts, not only as private citizens but as health care professionals as well. If, for example, the state board of nursing considers an amendment to the state nurse practice act in a closed meeting rather than an open one if required by the Act, or does not keep minutes as mandated, those actions can be challenged in the courts. Such challenges cannot be made in an irresponsible or careless manner, but the opportunity to contest an agency's action lies at the very heart of ensuring that agency's accountability to the public.

SELECTED ADMINISTRATIVE AGENCIES THAT AFFECT HEALTH CARE

Federal Agencies

Numerous federal agencies affect health care. Because federal law most often preempts state law, familiarity with the following selected federal agencies is important:

▼ The Department of Health and Human Services—Social Security Administration

▼ The Department of Health and Human Services—Food and Drug Administration

▼ The Occupational Safety and Health Administration (OSHA)

▼ The Drug Enforcement Administration (DEA)

▼ The Department of Justice

▼ The Equal Employment Opportunity Commission (EEOC)

▼ The National Labor Relations Board (NLRB)

▼ The Labor Department

State Agencies

As has been discussed throughout this chapter, many states have counterparts to the federal agencies listed above, and additional state administrative bureaus exist that affect health care delivery. They include:

▼ Department of Public Health

▼ Board of Nursing or other body that regulates professions and occupations in the state

▼ State Labor Department

▼ Department of Protective Services (child abuse, elder abuse)

▼ Department of Aging

▼ Worker's Compensation Board

▼ Civil Rights Commission or Board

▼ Board of Education (school nursing)

▼ Department of Public Aid

▼ The Insurance Board or Commission

▼ Department of Alcohol and Substance Abuse

▼ Department of Human Rights

SUMMARY OF PRINCIPLES AND APPLICATIONS

Administrative law can be complex and confusing. In addition, because it is not governed by the more traditional rules that define civil and criminal law, it is often feared by those who must occasionally deal with it. Nurses have more exposure to administrative law than other individuals, mainly through their professional roles and responsibilities. Keeping certain guidelines in mind can be helpful in successfully getting through the administrative maze should that need arise. Those guidelines include:

▼ Consulting the federal and state Administrative Procedure Act

▼ Asking for agency accountability for agency actions

▼ Utilizing access to agency record laws

▼ Retaining counsel experienced in administrative law when representation or advice is needed

▼ Attending federal or state agency meetings, especially those that affect health care delivery

▼ Advising congressional and state legislative representatives of needed changes in the respective laws dealing with regulatory agencies

▼ Educating the public, especially patients, of their rights and responsibilities under administration laws that affect them and the delivery of health care

TOPICS FOR FURTHER INQUIRY

1. Develop a questionnaire to determine RNs' understanding of the Privacy Act and the Freedom of Information Act. Also ascertain whether or not the nurses surveyed have used either or both to obtain information about themselves, others, or a governmental agency. Analyze the data obtained, and if possible, utilize a similar questionnaire to obtain the same information from another professional group. Compare and contrast the data for the two groups.

2. File a Freedom of Information Act request under either the federal or a state statute for specific information and report on the success or failure experienced. Analyze how the procedure worked (if so) or where it could be improved.

3. Attend a public meeting in which proposed rules are being discussed by an agency, preferably an agency affecting nursing. Identify who provides testimony and whether or not the agency considered that testimony in the drafting of the final rule.

4. Write a paper comparing and contrasting due process rights protected in administrative hearings with those protected in criminal proceedings. Utilize actual reported cases in analyzing the differences and similarities. If possible, utilize cases involving a nurse or another health care provider.

REFERENCES

1. Henry Campbell Black. *Black's Law Dictionary*. 6th Edition. St. Paul, Minn: West Publishing Company, 1991, 29.
2. Lawrence Friedman, "Administrative Law and Regulation of Business," in *A History of American Law*. Second Edition. New York: Touchstone Books, 1985, 439.
3. *Id.* at 454–463.
4. Alfred Aman and William Mayton. *Administrative Law*. St. Paul, Minn: West Publishing Company, 1993, 10 (Hornbook Series).
5. This article and its sections read: "All legislative Powers herein granted shall be vested in a Congress of the United States, which shall consist of a Senate and House of Representatives. . . . The Congress shall have power . . . (18) To make all laws which shall be necessary and proper for carrying into Execution the foregoing Powers, and all other Powers vested by this Constitution in the Government of the United States, or in any Department or Officer thereof." United States Constitution, Article I, Section (1), Section 8 (18).
6. See, for example, *Field v. Clark*, 143 U.S. 649 (1892); *United States v. Grimaud*, 220 U.S. 506 (1911); *Crowell v. Benson*, 285 U.S. 22 (1932); *Amalgamated Meat Cutters v. Connally*, 337 F. Supp. 737 (D.D.C. 1971).
7. Ernest Gellhorn and Ronald Levin. *Administrative Law and Process*. 3rd Edition. St. Paul, Minn: West Publishing Company, 1990, 9 (Nutshell Series).
8. *Id.* at 607–610.
9. *Id.* at 576–582.
10. *Id.*
11. *Id.* at 561–563.
12. 28 U.S.C.A. Section 516 (1966).
13. 5 U.S.C. 551 *et seq.* (1946).
14. Administrative Procedure Act, *supra* note 13 at 552, 553, and 554.

15. Amendment V, United States Constitution (1791); Amendment IV, United States Constitution (1868).
16. *Board of Regents of State Colleges v. Roth*, 408 U.S. 564 (1972).
17. *Roth, Ibid., quoting Meyer v. Nebraska*, 262 U.S. 390, 399 (1923).
18. Gellhorn and Levin, *supra* note 7, at 357–358.
19. 5 U.S.C. Section 702 (1946).
20. *Id.* at Section 706.
21. *Id.*
22. Gellhorn and Levin, *supra* note 7, at 130–136; 5 U.S.C. Section 555(c).
23. Geoffrey Hazard and Cameron Beard, "A Lawyer's Privilege against Self-Incrimination in Professional Disciplinary Proceedings," 96 *The Yale Law Journal* 1060–1063 (1987). It has generally been held that, despite the fact that criminal ramifications may occur as a result of testimony in an administrative hearing, administrative hearings are *not* truly criminal in nature, but are more of a "quasi-criminal" or simply civil character. *Id.*
24. *Id.* See also *In Re Zisook*, 430 NE 2d 1037 (1982), *cert. denied*, 457 U.S. 1134 (1981); *Bellis v. United States*, 417 U.S. 85 (1974); *Fisher v. United States*, 425 U.S. 391 (1976).
25. *Braswell v. United States*, 487 U.S. 99 (1988). See also Aman and Mayton, *supra* note 4, at 714–722.
26. Black, *supra* note 1, at 383. See also Hazard and Beard, *supra* note 23, at 1068–1072. In the federal system, any immunity granted must be for testimony "necessary to the public interest" (18 U.S.C. 6004) and the Attorney General must approve the immunization before it is granted.
27. Hazard and Beard, *supra* note 23, at 1070–1072.
28. *Camara v. Municipal Court*, 387 U.S. 523 (1967); *See v. Seattle*, 387 U.S. 541 (1967).
29. Mark Rothstein. *Occupational Safety and Health Law*. Third Edition. St. Paul, Minn: West Publishing Company, 1990, 230–233 (with 1995 Pocket Part). See also, *United States v. Blanchard*, 495 F. 2d 1329 (1st Cir. 1974); *Camara and See, supra* note 28.
30. *United States v. Biswell*, 406 U.S. 311 (1972). In this case, the business involved was a pawn shop. Because the shop sold guns, the warrantless search, based on the Gun Control Act of 1968, was upheld. The Court reasoned that, among other things, the pawn shop owners waived their Fourth Amendment rights and gave their implied consent to warrantless administrative searches. Rothstein, *supra* note 29, *citing* 3 Wayne LaFave, *Search and Seizure*, Section 10.2 (1978) and Rothstein and Rothstein, "Administrative Searches and Seizures: What Happened to *Camara* and *See*?," 50 Washington Law Review 341 (1975).
31. Rothstein, *supra* note 29, at 234.
32. *Id.* at 236, *citing Stephenson Enterprises, Inc. v. Marshall*, 578 F. 2d 1021 1023–1024 (5th Cir. 1978) and *Stockwell Manufacturing Co. v. Usery*, 536 F. 2d 1306–1309, n. 6 (10th Cir. 1976).
33. Rothstein, *supra* note 29, *citing See v. Seattle, supra* note 28, at 545 and *Air Pollution Variance Board v. Western Alfalfa Corp.*, 416 U.S. 861 (1974).
34. 21 U.S.C. 301, 331, 334 (1938).
35. See, for example, 255 ILCS 65/27 (1987). This Illinois Nursing Act's section provides for immediate suspension of a license without a hearing when there is an immediate danger to the public by the licensee's conduct.
36. Illinois' Nursing Act, for example, mandates a hearing within 15 days after the suspension and is to be completed "without appreciable delay." *Id.*
37. Gellhorn and Levin, *supra* note 7, at 162–167.
38. *Id.* at 167, *citing NLRB v. Ochoa Fertilizer Corp.*, 368 U.S. 318, 322 (1961).
39. *Id.* at 187–192.
40. The Privacy Act of 1974, P.L. 93–579, 88 Stat. 1896 (September 27, 1975), codified at 5 U.S.C. Section 552a.
41. Section 2 of Public Law 93–579, *Congressional Findings and Statement of Purpose cited in* 5 U.S.C. Section 552a (Historical Note), 204.
42. *Id.*
43. 5 U.S.C. 552a(b) (1974).
44. *Id.*
45. 5 U.S.C. Section 552a(c) and 552a(e)(1)–(11).
46. 5 U.S.C. Section 552a(d)(1).
47. *Id.* at 552a(f)(1) through (5).
48. Allan Adler, Eric Glitzenstein, and Harry Hammitt, "The Privacy Act," in *Litigation under the Federal Freedom of Information Act and Privacy Act*. Edited by Allan Robert Adler. Washington, DC: The American Civil Liberties Union Foundation, 1990, 271, 278–284.
49. 5 U.S.C. 552a(d)(2), (f)(4).
50. *Id.* at 552a(d)(3).
51. Adler, Glitzenstein, and Hammitt, *supra* note 48, at 273.
52. 5 U.S.C. 552a(j)(1) and (2).
53. *Id.* at 552a(k)(1)–(7).
54. Adler, Glitzenstein, and Hammitt, *supra* note 48, at 284, *citing* Public Law 93–579 and 5 U.S.C. Section 552a note).
55. *Id.*
56. P.L. 100–503, 5 U.S.C. 55a(o).
57. *Id.*
58. Aman and Mayton, *supra* note 4, at 690–691.
59. 5 U.S.C. Section 552 *et seq.* (1966), as amended.
60. Allan Robert Adler. *Using The Freedom Of Information Act: A Step By Step Guide*. Washington, DC: The American Civil Liberties Union Foundation, 1990, 2.
61. Aman and Mayton, *supra* note 4, at 627 (citations omitted).
62. Adler, *supra* note 60, at 2.
63. 42 U.S.C. 552(b)(1)–(9).
64. Allan Adler, "Administrative Process," in *Litigation under the Federal Freedom of Information Act and Privacy Act, supra* note 48, 20.
65. 42 U.S.C. Sections 552(a)(6)(A)(i); 552(a)(6)(A)(ii).
66. Adler, *supra* note 60, at 10.
67. See, for example, 70 ILCS 405/11 *et. seq.* (1984).
68. Pub. L. No. 94-409, Section 2, Stat. 1241, 42 U.S.C. 552b (1977).
69. S. Rep. No. 354, 94th Cong., 1st Sess. 1, *reprinted in Government-in-the-Sunshine Source Book: Legislative History, Texts, and Other Documents, Committees on Government Operations*, U.S. Senate and House of Representatives, 94th Cong., 2nd Sess. (1976).
70. 5 U.S.C. 552b(a)(1).
71. *Id.* at 552b(c)(1)–(10).
72. *Id.* at 552b(d)(1)–(m).
73. S. Rep. 354, *supra* note 69, at 7.

8 Criminal Law

contents

A nurse may be involved as a defendant in the criminal justice system in one of two ways: either as a private citizen or as a professional. In either instance, the nurse has allegedly violated the state or federal criminal laws, and if those allegations are proven beyond a reasonable doubt (the standard of proof in criminal actions), the nurse is found guilty of the crime. In criminal cases, unlike civil cases in which monetary compensation is sought for injuries or damages sustained, a guilty verdict brings with it some sort of punishment. The form of the punishment varies according to the crime, but some examples include fines, incarceration, and the death penalty.

In addition to some sort of sanction being imposed when a criminal law is violated, criminal law is also very different from civil law because of the plaintiff who initiates the suit. With *civil* law, the person, or entity, initiating the suit is a private one. The plaintiff in criminal cases, however, is always the state or federal government and its respective citizens, represented by the prosecutor (called the US Attorney in the federal court system and the district attorney, county attorney, prosecuting attorney or state's attorney in the state system),[1] who, with the help of law enforcement officers, is able to bring the case against the accused. The prosecut-

RELATED TOPICS

ing attorney's responsibility is to ensure that when the public's safety or welfare is threatened or has been harmed, the guilty party is punished in some way for that behavior. Theories of punishment, and their specific effect on transgressors, have been the subject of much study in criminal law. Some include prevention of further criminal acts by the particular criminal ("particular deterrence"); prevention of further criminal acts by others who may be contemplating similar conduct ("general deterrence"); education of the public as to what conduct is good and bad; and retribution, making the offender "pay" for what he or she has done.[2]

This chapter will provide an overview of the criminal law and criminal justice system and its application to nurses and nursing practice, regardless of specialty area of practice or the health care delivery setting in which the nurse practices. It is important to keep in mind, however, that the information presented also applies to the nurse, or any other person, as a private citizen, that is, when not functioning in his or her professional role.

ESSENTIALS OF CRIMINAL LAW

As is the case with other types of law, criminal law did not develop, nor does it exist, in a vacuum. Rather, it is a creature of the state or federal legislature, both of which determine what kinds of behavior are criminal and what the punishment will be for a violation of the criminal statute or code.[3] In addition, behavior

KEY PRINCIPLES

Misdemeanor

Felony

Actus Reus

Mens Rea

Classification of Crimes

Beyond a Reasonable Doubt

Bail

Plea Bargain

Presumption of Innocence

Constitutional Protections of the Individual

Miranda Warning

that is a violation of criminal law may also be treated by the state or federal legislative body as a violation of respective civil or administrative statutes. For example, a nurse who falsifies narcotics records to "cover up" diversion of controlled substances from the employer faces not only potential criminal charges of forgery but also potential disciplinary action by the state nursing board or regulatory agency. Unlike civil law, and to a lesser extent administrative law, criminal law clearly involves all three branches of the government—legislative (passing laws), judicial (trying cases and hearing appeals, as well as determining sentences for those found guilty), and executive (issuing pardons and executive orders).

The criminal law cannot function without acknowledgment of constitutional—both federal and state—and jurisdictional limitations placed upon it. Insofar as constitutional limitations are concerned, they affect the power to pass laws that define criminal conduct (e.g., if the statute is vague or overly broad it will not be upheld), the power to treat an individual or individuals differently from others similarly situated unless there is a reasonable basis to do so (equal protection), the necessity for clarity in informing the public what conduct is prohibited, and the inability to establish "ex post facto" laws (making conduct a crime after it has occurred) and violating rights guaranteed by the Bill of Rights (see Table 8–1), to name a few.[4]

Jurisdiction is generally defined as the ability of the court to acknowledge and decide cases.[5] In constitutional terms, jurisdiction is limited in many ways. One important limitation deals with whether the federal or state government has the authority to prosecute a particular crime. An 1872 case[6] divided the powers of the government into four classes: (1) those belonging exclusively to the states; (2) those that can be exercised only by the federal government; (3) those that may be exercised concurrently and independently by both; and (4) those that the states can exercise, but only until Congress decides to exercise control over them.[7]

Thus, in any area involving criminal law where the federal government has taken control or "pre-empted" state law, it will be the federal government that will prosecute that alleged violation. An example would be any alleged violations of the many Medicare/Medicaid antifraud and abuse statutes. Conversely, when there is independent and concurrent jurisdiction, either the state or federal prosecutor may initiate criminal proceedings, so long as the state law does not conflict with the federal law. An example of criminal law in which both state and federal laws exist is in the area of controlled substances and their illegal possession and trafficking. In contrast, an example of a criminal law exclusively within state jurisdiction includes practicing a particular licensed profession without the requisite license.

Constitutional Protections

Because any action taken against a person alleged to have committed a crime is carried out by the state or federal government, clear constitutional mandates exist that protect the individual against arbitrary action by agents of the government, whether they be law enforcement officers or attorneys. Table 8–1 summarizes those protections mandated by the US Constitution and case law interpreting the Constitution. State constitutions may provide additional protections but cannot limit those granted by the federal government.

Actors

Whenever criminal conduct is alleged, all three branches of the government are involved in the case, from its initiation until its completion. Thus, various actors and roles exist throughout the process. State or federal law enforcement officers initiate the prosecution of an alleged offender by investigating him or her, and if adequate evidence is available, arresting the person alleged to have committed the crime. In the federal system, law enforcement officers may be agents of the Federal Bureau of Investi-

TABLE 8-1

Constitutional Protections of the Individual

RIGHT PROTECTED	SOURCE
Due process of law for government taking life, liberty, and property	5th Amendment (federal); 14th (states)
Establishment and exercise of religion, freedom of speech and press, peaceful assembly, and petition government for redress	1st Amendment
No unreasonable searches or seizures of self or property; search warrants issued upon "probable cause" only; illegally seized evidence excluded from trial	4th Amendment; *Draper v. U.S.; Stone v. Powell*
No self-incrimination or double jeopardy	5th Amendment
Counsel, speedy and public trial, impartial jury, notice of accusations, confront and cross-examine adverse witnesses, "compulsory process" for obtaining favorable witnesses	6th Amendment
No cruel or unusual punishment	8th Amendment

Draper v. U.S., 358 U.S. 307 (1959); *Stone v. Powell,* 428 U.S. 465, *on remand,* 539 F. 2d 693, *rehearing denied,* 429 U.S. 874. The right against self-incrimination protects one speaking about his or her involvement in a crime, and thus is "testimonial" in nature. The Supreme Court has ruled in many cases that it does not extend to the production of physical evidence, such as blood or hair samples. See, for example, *Schmerber v. California,* 384 U.S. 757 (1966); *Doe v. United States,* 487 U.S. 201 (1988). In *Baldwin v. New York,* 399 U.S. 66 (1970), the United States Supreme Court held that the right to trial by jury guaranteed by the Sixth Amendment was applicable to those crimes involving a potential sentence of greater than 6 months in prison, or "serious" crimes. *Blanton v. North Las Vegas,* 109 S. Ct. 1289 (1989).

gation (FBI) or the Drug Enforcement Agency (DEA). State officers include state and local police.

Prosecutor

Those who prosecute the case are probably "the most important actors" in the criminal justice system because of their ability to decide what cases will go to trial, what charges will be the basis of the trial, and whether or not a plea bargain will take place.[8] Federal and state prosecutors work closely with law enforcement officers and the other actors in the criminal justice system to ensure success with the case for which they are responsible.

Defense Attorney

The defense attorney also plays an important role in the criminal justice system. The attorney may be privately hired or be appointed by the court (public defender) when the accused is indigent and unable to afford an attorney.

Judge

The judge is a pivotal actor in any judicial system, and the criminal justice system is no exception. In addition to presiding over the trial, ruling on issues of law and determining sentence in jury trials, the judge is involved in pretrial determinations, such as setting bail. If there is no jury and a bench trial occurs, then the judge (or federal or state magistrate in some instances in which the crime is of a less serious nature) determines the innocence or guilt of the accused.

Jury

There are two types of juries in criminal law: the grand jury and the trial jury. In either case, the membership is theoretically to be composed of "impartial" individuals who represent a "cross section of the public."[9] Grand juries exist in most federal and state systems, and their role is to determine if there is adequate evidence to bring the accused to trial. In contrast, the trial jury's role is to determine issues of fact in the trial and determine the guilt or innocence of the defendant.

> *There are two types of juries in criminal law: the grand jury and the trial jury.*

Defendant

The defendant in a criminal trial is the individual accused of committing a certain crime or crimes. The defendant can be an individual, individuals, a corporation, a governmental agency, or the federal or state government itself.

Probation Officer and Other Personnel

One additional person with an important role is the probation officer, whose job it is to supervise the defendant who is placed on probation as a result of a determination of guilt or as a condition of release from jail or prison. The probation officer is mandated to report to the court regularly on the success of the probationer with the terms and conditions of the probation and must surrender the probationer to the court if those conditions are violated.[10]

Other actors in the criminal justice system include the same court personnel discussed in the chapter on the Judicial System.

Classification of Crimes

Crimes are classified in a manner that reflects the particular societal interest protected. Examples of interests protected include the integrity of the state or federal government (e.g., bribing a public official, perjury); protecting the public safety (e.g., assault, murder, and kidnapping); protection of property (e.g., burglary, robbery, and theft of services); and protection of honesty (e.g., forgery and falsification of legal documents and business records[11]).

Types of Crimes

There are essentially two types of crimes: misdemeanor and felony. A misdemeanor is a criminal offense punishable by a fine or imprisonment (usually a year or under) or both. Misdemeanors are considered less serious offenses than felonies. Examples of misdemeanors can include breaching patient confidentiality, failing to report suspected or actual child abuse to the proper authority, and disseminating any false information concerning the existence of any sexually transmitted disease.

There are essentially two types of crimes: misdemeanor and felony.

A felony is a more serious offense than a misdemeanor and therefore punishable by imprisonment for more than a year or by death. Examples of felonies include murder, diversion of controlled substances from a health care facility, and aggravated unlawful restraint.

Grades of Crimes

The state or federal statutes may also utilize different grades of crimes, such as Class A or Class B misdemeanors or felonies. The grading of the crimes reflects the seriousness of the offense and also aids the judge in sentencing the offender once the alleged defendant is found guilty of the crime.

Components of Crimes

Act ("Actus Reus") and Intent ("Mens Rea")

In criminal law, a bad thought in and of itself cannot constitute a crime. Thus, any conduct that is allegedly criminal must consist of a criminal act or a failure to act when there is a duty to do so, as when a nurse does not report suspected child abuse or neglect to the proper authorities, *and* criminal intent.

Intent has been traditionally defined to include consciously desiring a certain result as well as knowing a result is "practically certain" to occur as a result of certain conduct, regardless of the desire of a certain result.[12] Modern legal theory distinguishes intent from knowledge and calls it purpose or acting purposely.[13] Thus, crimes may require an individual to act intentionally or purposefully, or they may require that the perpetrator knowingly or intentionally caused a specific result of his or her act or failure to act.[14]

It is also important to note that not all crimes

require the intent or knowledge component to be applied exactly as discussed above. An individual can commit a criminal act if his or her conduct is reckless, if a reckless omission to act occurs, or if the person recklessly causes a particular result.[15] If a nurse acts in a reckless, or indifferent, manner and does not intervene when a patient is short of breath and a death occurs, for example, the nurse might be charged with involuntary manslaughter. Similarly, if an individual's conduct is such that an unreasonable risk of harm occurs to another and that conduct is "grossly negligent" or defined as "willfully and wantonly negligent," then a charge of criminal negligence may be sustained (e.g., negligent homicide).

Other Acts

An individual may be found guilty of a crime not only when he or she is directly violating a criminal statute, but also when involved in criminal conduct in a more ancillary manner. Traditionally called party to the crime, but now given the name accomplice(s), his or her conduct can occur in three main ways: a principal in the second degree, an accessory before the fact, and an accessory after the fact.[16] Regardless of the terminology, however, the main focus of determining the liability of others involved in a crime (felony) is to evaluate two issues: (1) whether the accomplice gave assistance or encouragement to the principal or failed to carry out a legal duty to prevent the crime; and (2) whether the accomplice acted with the intent to encourage or aid the commission of the crime.[17]

A nurse may be involved as a principal in the second degree if, for example, he or she "aids and abets" the unauthorized practice of nursing by one who is not licensed as a nurse. If the nurse leaves the narcotics keys in a prearranged place for a nurse colleague so the latter can obtain controlled substances from the hospital narcotics supply, a charge of accessory before the fact may be possible. If a nurse alters patients' narcotics records to indicate narcotics were given by a nurse colleague when the nurse colleague did not administer those drugs, the nurse's conduct may give rise to a charge of being an accomplice after the fact.

In addition to being named an accomplice, an individual may also become involved indirectly in a crime if a conspiracy takes place. A conspiracy is defined as an agreement between two or more individuals to intentionally carry out an act that is unlawful or to carry out a lawful act by unlawful means.[18] An example of a conspiracy is when two or more individuals or entities, or both, agree to limit the ability of a nurse-midwife to obtain admitting privileges on the staff of a particular hospital, in violation of the federal antitrust laws. This topic is discussed at length in Chapter 22.

Causation

Causation is just as important in the criminal law as it is in civil law. When criminal conduct is alleged, the prosecutor must be able to prove that the conduct of the accused was the "legal" or "proximate" cause of the specific result.[19] Although the conduct analyzed must meet the "but for this conduct, this result would not have occurred" test, it is also possible that an individual can be found guilty of a particular crime when his or her intended or reckless behavior does not specifically comply with that standard. In such instances, any variation in the actual result must be similar to, or create a risk of happening similar to, what the accused originally had in mind.[20] For example, if a nurse participates in an abusive search of a nursing home resident's pockets for missing money that results in that resident's death, the nurse can be found guilty of willfully violating state criminal statutory provisions prohibiting such conduct even though such searches took place frequently.[21]

Application of Components to Selected Cases and Crimes

Murder

Once defined as the killing of a human with malice aforethought,[22] murder is now defined by types: intent-to-kill murder, intent-to-do-serious-bodily-injury murder, depraved-heart murder, and felony murder.[23] Categories of murder may also be further delineated by degrees—first-degree and second-degree murder, for example—to provide guidelines for punishment. Unless the murder is justified, when, for example, one is defending himself or herself, it is subject to prosecution. Theoretically, a nurse may be charged with any type of murder, depending on the circumstances. Key Case 8–1 is one case involving murder charges against an LVN.

Other cases in which murder was alleged

KEY CASE 8–1   Jones v. Texas (1986)[24]

FACTS: Genene Jones, a licensed vocational nurse, was employed by a pediatrician as an office nurse in Kerrville, Texas. On August 24, 1982, a mother brought her daughter, Chelsea McClellan, to the doctor's office because of a cold. While Mrs. McClellan was describing her daughter's symptoms to the doctor, Ms. Jones took the child into another room, and shortly thereafter, called for the doctor, telling her that the child had just had a seizure. The child was admitted to the hospital for 8 days after being seen in the emergency room.

Mrs. McClellan returned to the doctor's office several weeks later to have her son examined, and decided that Chelsea should have her routine "baby shots" while there. Ms. Jones administered one injection to Chelsea in the upper left thigh, and Mrs. McClellan, who was present, noticed that her daughter was not breathing and her eyes looked abnormal. Ms. Jones told the mother not to worry, and injected a second shot in the upper right thigh, and Chelsea went "limp" with her eyes open. Ms. Jones then told the mother that the child was having another "seizure," called the doctor, and the child was sent to the ED of the same hospital where she had been seen a few weeks earlier.

The ED physician diagnosed the problem as symptoms of succinylcholine chloride (Anectine) and sent Chelsea to another hospital via ambulance. Prior to leaving the hospital ED, Ms. Jones gave Chelsea another shot and accompanied her in the ambulance. En route, Chelsea stopped breathing again, and she was pronounced dead by another hospital's ED physician.

Because of concern over this death, and an investigation that revealed that several other children experienced similar "seizures" after being seen at the office, Ms. Jones was charged with one count of murder and seven counts of causing injury to the other children.

Jury convicts defendant of murder

TRIAL COURT DECISION: The jury trial resulted in a conviction of murder, and Ms. Jones was sentenced to 99 years in prison. During the trial, evidence was presented that Ms. Jones had also been under investigation for the deaths of 10 infants and the "seizures" of other children at a hospital in San Antonio, Texas from 1980–1982. Although that investigation was hampered by many factors, including routine destruction of pharmaceutical records by the hospital, certain results of the investigation were used during the criminal trial.

KEY CASE 8–1 — Jones v. Texas (1986)[24] Continued

Evidence used by the court supported the Prosecutor's theory that the defendant had a motive for her criminal conduct

Of particular importance was Ms. Jones' apparent motive in the San Antonio situation—her desire to show the staff and parents of the children that she was an excellent nurse who tried to "save" or did "save" the children who had the seizures.

The prosecutor utilized that theory, as well as other findings of the investigation, to support a common plan or scheme, intent, and Ms. Jones' apparent motive in the Kerrville killings—"demonstrating a need for a pediatric intensive care unit" at the hospital where she could serve as its charge nurse and continue to "save" children through her "excellent" nursing care. Ms. Jones appealed her conviction on several grounds, including an allegation that the trial court convicted her without sufficient evidence of committing an act clearly dangerous to human life.

Ms. Jones appeals conviction

Appellate court upholds jury's conviction

APPEALS COURT DECISION: The appellate court upheld the conviction of Ms. Jones and overruled each and every issue brought by the appellant (Jones).

ANALYSIS: This case is interesting for several reasons. To begin with it deals not only with criminal intent and conduct, but also with the way in which evidence is utilized in a criminal case. The appellate court painstakingly analyzes Texas and federal law in relation to the prior incidents and in utilizing scientific evidence in use at the time—gas chromatography mass spectrometry test results done on the deceased child's blood to determine what drugs were present at death—to affirm the trial court's guilty verdict.

The case is also interesting in that it is an example of how hesitant individuals are in alleging criminal conduct against a colleague or peer. Ms. Jones was investigated not only by the authorities in San Antonio, but also by the hospital where she worked. For whatever reasons, no action was taken against her by any authority until the Kerrville case was filed.

The case has received a great deal of attention because of its interesting aspects. A 1990 book, *The Death Shift,* by Peter Elkind, painstakingly details Jones' life, the childrens' deaths, the investigations, and the trial. In 1991, a made-for-TV movie was also released.

---

against a nurse or nurses include *United States v. Narciso and Perez*[25] (two Filipino nurses accused of murdering Veterans Administration patients) and *Hargrave v. Landon*[26] (nurse's aide convicted of first-degree murder by injecting patients with lidocaine).

Manslaughter

This crime was once defined as the unlawful killing of another without malice aforethought.[27] Now, however, it is defined perhaps less distinctly as homicides not bad enough to be murder but too bad to be no crime whatever.[28]

Categories of manslaughter include voluntary manslaughter (killing another in the heat of passion or when provoked),[29] involuntary manslaughter (killing another when committing an unlawful act),[30] or criminal negligence involuntary manslaughter (conducting oneself in a lawful manner but without proper care or necessary skill).[31] A nurse may be charged with any of the three categories of this crime depending on the circumstances. Key Case 8–2 illustrates one case in which manslaughter charges were brought against an RN.

KEY CASE 8–2   State v. Winter (1984)[32]

Nurse administers wrong blood to patient

Patient dies and nurse is charged with aggravated manslaughter

Trial court jury returns verdict against the defendant, but she is guilty only of simple manslaughter, not aggravated manslaughter

FACTS: Laura Winter, a registered nurse, worked at Beth Israel Hospital in Newark, New Jersey. One of her patients, Anna Mudryj, required a blood transfusion. Unfortunately, blood for another patient who also needed a transfusion was sent to Ms. Mudryj's room, where she had been transferred after surgery. The incorrectly delivered blood had the other patient's name and blood type on it, as well as the same room number on it as Ms. Mudryj's. However, that room number, 608, was crossed out and the correct room number of the other patient written above it.

Nurse Winter administered the wrong blood to patient Mudryj. When a colleague of Ms. Winter found the patient "screaming in pain," pale, and lying in blood from incisional sites and chest tubes, the physician was contacted and a "transfusion routine" was ordered. The patient had been receiving Coumadin, so the physician questioned Ms. Winter about any bleeding around the Pleur-Evac. The nurse replied that it had been replaced because it "broke down." It could not be found; Ms. Winter told the doctor that she threw it away. No notation was made in the patient's chart concerning the failure. Because the doctor suspected a transfusion reaction, he asked for the empty bags of plasma, but Ms. Winter stated she had thrown them away, despite the hospital's policy of keeping them in the patient's room for 24 hours after a transfusion. The empty bags were never found, either. The patient died, and Nurse Winter was charged with aggravated manslaughter.

TRIAL COURT DECISION: The state attempted to prove that Nurse Winter killed the patient by transfusing the wrong blood; that the nurse concealed her conduct in many ways; and that she altered the chart to hide the effects of the transfusion reaction. Although Ms. Winter denied that she gave the transfusion, the jury returned a guilty verdict of the lesser-included offense of simple manslaughter, consisting of a recklessly committed criminal homicide. Winter was sentenced to 5 years in prison and fined 25 dollars, which was to be paid to the Violent Crimes Compensation Board.

Winter appealed the sentence to the Superior Court, Appellate Division.

APPEALS COURT DECISION: The appellate court reversed the trial court because of testimony of one of the trial witnesses, Dr. Goode, the Medical Examiner. He testified that he was told the deceased's family

KEY CASE 8–2   State v. Winter (1984)[32] Continued

Appeals court rules defendant was denied a fair trial due to comment made by medical examiner at trial

said that the deceased told them "she's trying to murder me." When he heard of this comment, Dr. Goode asked for all the documentation that could be obtained concerning the case, and based his opinion as to the cause of death on those statements and other documents.

Because Dr. Goode's testimony was considered prejudicial, despite admonitions by the trial judge to the jury to disregard the testimony, the appellate court reversed the verdict.

NEW JERSEY SUPREME COURT DECISION: The Supreme Court of New Jersey, in reversing the appellate court decision and remanding the case back to the trial court with instructions, held that there was no prejudice against the defendant due to Dr. Goode's testimony, especially in light of the trial judge's clear instructions to the jury to disregard the testimony. Furthermore, the court continued, there was enough other evidence in the record to support the verdict, which was the lesser offense than the original charge of aggravated manslaughter.

Supreme court reversed appeals court's holding that defendant did not have fair trial

ANALYSIS: The *Winter* case illustrates how a nurse's conduct that is careless can result in a criminal charge against that nurse. In addition to the "recklessness" of her behavior, Ms. Winter's attempt to conceal the results of her behavior did not help her in the situation. Also, in many states, both the death *and* the behavior might subject the nurse to disciplinary action by the state licensing agency or board and a civil suit alleging professional negligence.

Other cases involving nurses or physicians charged with manslaughter include an 1884 case, *Commonwealth v. Pierce*[33] (conviction for involuntary manslaughter for death of patient burned because of wrapping in kerosene-soaked bandages) and *State v. Weiner*[34] (physician convicted of involuntary manslaughter because of 12 patient deaths from hepatitis after receiving intravenous injections).

Nurses and other health care professionals have also been involved in the law, both criminal and civil, when the removal of life support systems, including food and/or fluids, is evaluated by a court. Several of these cases are discussed later in this chapter in the section Special Considerations.

Assault and Battery

Once classified as common law crimes (developed as a result of case law), assault and battery are now statutory crimes in all American jurisdictions.[35] The two are distinguishable by determining whether physical contact between the perpetrator and the victim occurred. An assault takes place when a person is fearful a battery may take place, but no actual touching occurs. A battery, on the other hand, requires that an offensive touching or bodily injury actually take place.[36] The two causes of action are further distinguished by degrees in many jurisdictions; in other words, classified as simple assault, or aggravated battery (e.g., battery with intent to kill) or criminal-negligence battery.

A nurse may be involved in a criminal case involving a charge of assault and battery when death of a patient occurs;[37] when unnecessary or unreasonable force is utilized against a patient (especially against an elderly citizen in some jurisdictions);[38] when a nurse, with a duty to act, simply omits that duty;[39] or when the nurse's conduct is directed against someone other than a patient.[40]

An assault takes place when a person is fearful a battery may take place, but no actual touching occurs. A battery . . . requires that an offensive touching or bodily injury actually take place.

Fraud

Conduct constituting fraud, and possibly other related crimes (such as false pretenses and forgery), involves an individual falsely representing a fact (by conduct, words, false or misleading allegations) or concealment of that which should have been disclosed to another person. The intent is to deceive the person and cause him or her to act upon the information to his or her legal detriment.[41] Although the actual conduct alleged to be fraudulent may not involve property in the traditional sense, fraud is a crime against property as opposed to a crime against a person, such as murder.

In health care, fraudulent conduct can take place in a number of ways. One fairly common example is falsification of medical records, either by entering information that is clearly false (e.g., recording treatments that did not take place, as in the *Winter* case), or by signing another nurse's name on the narcotic record as the nurse who gave a particular narcotic when that nurse did not administer it.

When the falsification of the medical record takes the form of making false claims to Medi-care to obtain payment for services not actually rendered, criminal penalties may occur under federal law.[42] If such false claims occur with other third party payors, whether public or private, additional criminal charges may be brought against the nurse.

Other examples of fraud include utilizing the US mail to carry out a fraudulent business activity (such as a school for practical nurses),[43] and practicing professional or practical nursing with a fraudulently obtained license, diploma, or record.[44]

Defenses to Crimes

The defendant in a criminal case has several defenses that can be raised to contest the allegations against him or her. For example, when criminal intent is a component of the crime, the defendant can attempt to deny the presence of that mental state. When the crime is such that intent is not an essential element, as in strict liability crimes, the mental state defense would not be helpful.

The Insanity Defense

This defense has undergone radical changes throughout the history of its existence. Generally, its purpose is not to provide an acquittal (finding of not guilty) and subsequent release of the person when tried for criminal conduct. Rather, the insanity defense provides a particular verdict (such as not guilty but mentally ill or not guilty by reason of insanity) that results in involuntary treatment in a mental institution.[45] The defense has been identified by various names; the *M'Naghten* rule (during the commission of the crime, the defendant did not know he was doing wrong, could not control his conduct because of mental illness or disease, or did not know the "nature and quality of the act he was doing");[46] the *Durham* rule (the crime was the result or "product" of a mental disease or defect);[47] and its most current rule, the *American Law Institute (A.L.I.) Substantial Capacity Test* (a person is not responsible for criminal conduct if, at the time of the criminal act resulting from a mental disease or defect, but not repeated criminal or otherwise antisocial conduct, the person lacked the substantial capacity to either appreciate the wrongfulness of his or her conduct or to conform to the requirements of the law.[48]

The use of the insanity defense has been the subject of much controversy and debate.[49] It is still a viable argument against many crimes, however, and will most likely continue to be unless there is a major change in the criminal justice or mental health system.

If the existence of a mental disease or defect inhibits the defendant in understanding the proceedings against him or her or prevents assistance with the attorney's defense against the charges (called incompetent to stand trial), then the defendant may not be tried, convicted, or sentenced until treatment renders him or her capable to stand trial. Similarly, if the defendant's mental illness does not allow an understanding of the nature and purpose of an imposed death sentence, then that punishment cannot occur until such understanding is present. As with the insanity defense generally, this protection has been the subject of dispute for some time.[50]

The Chromosome and Automatism Defenses

Two additional defenses that have surfaced in recent years that are separate from the insanity defense, but are often discussed along with it, are the XYY Chromosome Defense and the Automatism Defense.[51] The former involves the presence of a chromosomal abnormality (the "super male" or XYY configuration) that supposedly results in increased likelihood of antisocial or criminal conduct.

The automatism defense, on the other hand, basically rests on the fact that because the behavior that comprised the criminal act was done in an unconscious or semiconscious state, it could not be the result of a voluntary act. Exam-

ples of conditions that might give support to this defense include epilepsy, premenstrual syndrome (PMS), and post-traumatic stress disorder (PTSD).[52]

The Intoxication Defense

When a criminal defendant raises this defense, he or she is stating that because of the voluntary or involuntary presence of drugs or alcohol, the required intention to commit the crime, or knowledge that the behavior was illegal, is nonexistent. This defense, of course, is helpful only when the mental state of the accused is a component of the crime (e.g., forgery, when the intent to defraud is necessary for the prosecution to prove).[53] It would not be helpful, however, when being under the influence of drugs or alcohol was an essential element of the crime, as is the case in driving under the influence (DUI) cases.

In today's society, drug addiction and chronic alcoholism are often more the rule than the exception. As a result, this defense is receiving much scrutiny by the criminal justice system as a whole, especially when the defendant argues that the criminal act was the result of addiction or alcoholism. That argument has been treated with varying responses, but most successfully by resting it on the US Constitution's Eighth Amendment prohibition against cruel and unusual punishment.[54] When addiction or alcoholism is not successful as a defense against a crime committed, it *may* serve to mitigate (reduce) the punishment imposed. In addition, chemical use is currently viewed as a disease. Thus, requiring evaluation, treatment, and rehabilitation as part of the criminal's sentence or probation may be helpful in reducing the possibility of future use and the commission of future crimes due to chemical substances.

The Infancy Defense

Briefly, this common law defense squarely rests on three basic presumptions, although their application to specific instances of criminal conduct by minors has not been as easily resolved, especially since some legislatures have modified the assumptions by statute: Children 7 years old and younger are absolutely presumed to be without criminal capacity; those 7–14 have a rebuttable presumption (one that can be overturned if sufficient proof is presented) of criminal incapacity; and those minors 14 years of age and over are seen as fully responsible for their actions.[55] All states provide for the establishment of juvenile courts, which may have exclusive, or specified, jurisdiction over crimes committed by minors.

The Entrapment Defense

This defense can be used only against law enforcement officers or individuals cooperating with law enforcement officers or agencies who overstep their role in "encouraging" another to commit a crime, and instead initiate the criminal act and convince an otherwise uninterested individual to participate in that crime.[56] Moreover, the "otherwise uninterested individual" cannot have a predisposition to commit the crime. If he or she does have a propensity to engage in the proposed criminal conduct, and the law enforcement officer or agent simply provided the means for that crime to occur, then the defense will not be successful.

The Mistake or Ignorance Defense

This defense has been categorized into two specific types: a mistake of fact and one of law. The former allows the defendant to nullify any criminal intent requirement of a crime, and the latter, in some instances, allows an individual to raise ignorance as to the existence of the law or a belief that the conduct was not prohibited by law.

Usually, ignorance of the law is not a successful defense in the criminal law. However, a mistake of fact may be helpful in defending against criminal charges. For example, if the death of a patient occurs because a nurse mistakenly injected what she thought was a certain medication prepared and labeled in the pharmacy, but which turned out to be another medication altogether—one to which the patient was allergic—no liability would be present. No liability would exist because intent (mens rea) is an essential element of the crime of murder, and since no intent on the part of the nurse to kill the patient existed, there can be no criminal liability on the nurse's part for that crime.

The Necessity Defense

Based on the public policy premise that an individual in an emergency may be confronted with two choices (two "evils")—one to conform to the law and the other to break it—and either of them will produce a harmful result, this defense allows the individual to commit the crime, which is seen as the lesser of the two harms, and escape liability.[57] In other words, the criminal conduct is justified (or "necessitated") by the situation. Sometimes this defense is coupled with two others, the defense of others and the duress defenses.

If an ED nurse, for example, confronted with an individual who, pointing a gun at a patient taken hostage, demands that she "get drugs" for him or he will "blow the patient's head off and kill everyone in the ED," stabs and kills the perpetrator with one of the ED instruments, the nurse may be able to successfully utilize one or more of these defenses against murder charges. Or, if a nurse in an emergency situation administers a medication without an order to save a life, he or she may well be able to avoid any criminal charge of practicing medicine without a license because of the "necessity" of the situation.

It is important to note that the use of any of the defenses discussed in this section requires certain factors to be weighed for them to be effective as a defense. The factors analyzed include the harm done, intent to avoid the greater harm at the time of the incident, determination by the court that the individual did *indeed* avoid the greater evil, and determination that the individual had no part in bringing about the situation in which he or she was required to make a choice.[58]

The Self-Defense Defense

This defense allows a person who is not an aggressor to use *reasonable* force against another when of the belief that he or she is in immediate danger of unlawful bodily harm and that the use of force is necessary to avoid the bodily harm.[59] Generally the amount of force that can be used by the potential victim depends on the circumstances, with deadly force against the aggressor being justified when the person reasonably believes that deadly force (which can cause death or serious bodily injury) may be inflicted.[60]

Nurses may be involved in situations that require self-defense when, for example, the nurse is attacked by a violent patient or unruly family member.

Nurses may be involved in situations that require self-defense, when, for example, the nurse is attacked by a violent patient or an unruly family member. It may also occur, as was discussed in the case *People v. Clark*,[61] when a nurse or licensed practical nurse attempts to defend herself against an alleged beating by a hospital security guard. These types of situations are always difficult ones, for the nurse may be charged with some sort of criminal conduct when the self-defense occurs in a patient care situation. Factors that would probably be evaluated by the court in determining whether or not the actions taken by the nurse were truly ones of self-defense would include the details of the incident, whether the nurse reported the incident immediately to superiors, if the incident was documented in the patient record, if the nurse left or attempted to leave the scene, and whether the nurse attempted to obtain help from others, such as the police or hospital security.

ESSENTIALS OF CRIMINAL PROCEDURE

Criminal procedure is defined as the procedural steps through which a criminal case must pass.[62] It begins with the investigation of alleged criminal activity and terminates with the release of the offender, whether by return of a nonguilty verdict and release of the individual, by a guilty verdict and completion of the sentence imposed, or by dismissal of the charges against a person. Whatever the ultimate outcome of a case, the procedural aspects of criminal law must conform to state and federal constitutional mandates presented in Table 8–1. If they are not adhered to, the criminal defendant can attempt to challenge any part of the procedural process as a violation of those constitutional protections.

Pretrial Steps

Once a crime is reported to the police, the various phases of criminal procedure begin. It is important to note that the steps will be discussed in a sequential order, but in reality, several may be going on simultaneously.

Investigation

The investigation of a crime involves much footwork and results in the apprehension of a particular individual or individuals. When a specific individual's involvement in a crime is suspected, the investigation focuses on that particular person. The focus on a particular suspect may occur before arrest and booking of the individual. *When* the investigation takes place is important, for if the individual is questioned about the crime when "in custody" (in other words, involved in a custodial interrogation when he or she is not free to leave), clear protections are afforded the suspect that are based on Fourth, Fifth, Sixth, and Fourteenth Amendment rights. Furthermore, the individual must be reminded of his or her rights by being given a *Miranda* warning to avoid a coerced confession.

The United States Supreme Court, in its *Miranda v. Arizona*[63] decision, scrutinized custodial interrogation proceedings and practices. The opinion blended the Fifth Amendment right against self-incrimination with the Sixth Amendment's guarantee of the right to counsel before trial.[64] The Court held that, at the time of arrest and *before* interrogation by law enforcement officers occurred, the arrested person must be told (1) of the right to remain silent; (2) of the right to consult with an attorney and to have the attorney present during the interrogation; (3) that anything that is said can and will be utilized against him or her in court; and (4) if he or she is unable to afford an attorney, one will be provided. Furthermore, the Court held that if this warning is not given to the arrestee, any statements made by the accused are inadmissible at trial.[65]

The United States Supreme Court, in . . . Miranda v. Arizona . . . blended the Fifth Amendment right against self-incrimination with the Sixth Amendment's guarantee of the right to counsel before trial.

In addition to being interrogated, a suspect or an arrestee may be asked to participate in other investigative procedures including a lineup, provide writing samples, and provide blood or hair samples. In some instances, the suspect's attorney must be present during these procedures.

During the investigation phase, physical evidence may also be of importance in linking the suspect to criminal conduct. Therefore, searches of the individual and the individual's home or office, for example, and the confiscation of matter, such as a weapon or documents, may occur. The constitutional mandate of the federal and state constitutions that protect an individual against unreasonable and unwarranted searches and seizures must be adhered to by the investigators.

Briefly, the mandate generally requires that searches and seizures occur only after a warrant has been issued by a neutral party (e.g., a judge or magistrate) upon probable cause.[66] Some exceptions to the general rule of a warrant are when there is probable cause *and* an urgent situation exists (that is, when delaying the search and seizure to obtain a warrant would endanger the success of the search or pose a threat of harm to the investigators) and when valid consent for the search has been obtained. If evidence is obtained in violation of the individual's Fourth Amendment rights, it is inadmissible at trial. This is known as the exclusionary rule or the fruit(s) of the poisonous tree doctrine. The rule has been the subject of much debate and criticism, mainly because it is seen as rewarding criminal defendants.[67] Even so, it continues to survive in the criminal justice system, and most probably will, until a better alternative is found to replace it.[68]

A nurse who is, or may be, the focus of any investigation involving potential criminal liability must be very careful to protect his or her constitutional rights. The investigation may be conducted by police, state investigators from the licensing body (who are also police officers), or employer security personnel. To begin with, the nurse should not speak to any of these individuals without seeking advice from an attorney who is knowledgeable about criminal law *and* practice issues. Furthermore, no statement should be given to law enforcement officers without the attorney being present.

A nurse who is, or may be, the focus of any investigation involving potential criminal liability must be very careful to protect his or her constitutional rights.

If the nurse is asked to talk with any of these individuals, he or she should first ascertain whether or not an arrest is occurring or he or she is being detained. If neither is the case, the nurse should indicate that no interview or search will occur, that he or she is able to leave, and he or she should leave. If the request occurs in the nurse's home, he or she should state his or her position and ask that the investigators leave the home or the premises.

If, on the other hand, the nurse is informed he or she is being detained because of "reasonable suspicion" that the nurse was involved in a crime, or is being arrested, the nurse should not resist the detention or arrest but clearly inform the investigators that an attorney's presence and advice are requested and no statement will take place until that request is granted.

Likewise, if the law enforcement officers ask that a search of any belongings, such as the nurse's locker or home, or a body search be done, the nurse should ask if a search warrant has been obtained. If no search warrant is in the possession of the investigator, then the nurse is justified in refusing to participate in that search. If it takes place without the warrant, the nurse may have a basis for excluding any evidence obtained during that "illegal search," under the exclusionary rule. Of course, if the law enforcement officers can prove that the search or seizure was necessary even though no warrant existed (e.g., their concern that if the locker was not inspected at that time, any potential evidence might be removed from it), then the evidence may be able to be used against the nurse.

It is important to note that if the nurse, in an attempt to "cooperate" with the investigators, validly consents to a search when no warrant is present, then the law will not exclude any of the evidence obtained, for the valid consent is seen as a waiver of the right to have the search done only upon the issuance of a warrant.

In the workplace, nurses are not always initially investigated or questioned by the police but are sometimes examined by the employer's security staff or by a middle-level nurse man-

ager or nurse executive. If the employer is a governmental entity (e.g., Veterans Administration or county institution), constitutional protections exist for the nurse employee. If employed by a private entity, however, these individuals are considered *private* actors and are not constrained by the constitutional mandates discussed thus far. Therefore the nurse needs to be clear that when giving information to internal staff members, the information can, and most often is, shared with appropriate law enforcement personnel and can be used against the nurse in the criminal action as well as its own disciplinary proceedings. The need for legal counsel, not only for advice, but also for presence during any and all meetings with hospital administration, when possible, is imperative.

Grand Jury Indictment or Written Complaint and Information

When a crime involves a violation of federal law that is a felony, the Fifth Amendment requires that a grand jury be convened, and its role is to determine if there is "probable cause" to go forward with the prosecution of the suspect. Named so because of its size (usually more than 12 but no more than 23 members, as compared to a trial [petit] jury of 12 members), a grand jury has subpoena powers as well as the power to require witnesses to testify before it. If it determines that the suspect should be prosecuted, the grand jury issues an indictment (or "true bill") that formalizes, in writing, the accusations against the individual, and if the suspect has not yet been arrested, an arrest warrant is issued by a judge. If, on the other hand, the jury finds there is not probable cause to prosecute, then the case is dismissed upon the "no bill" being issued.

Thirty-two states also utilize the grand jury system for some portion of their criminal proceedings, and eight use it for all cases.[69] The utilization of the grand jury in the state system is not a requirement, however, and many states employ another form of determining probable cause, the written complaint and information.

With this approach, law enforcement personnel share the results of their investigation with the state prosecutor through a complaint, which is a sworn statement listing the crimes committed and the evidence to support the charges. Then, most often, an arrest warrant is issued, the suspect arrested, and an information—a formal, written accusation of the charges against the defendant—is drafted so that the arrestee can begin to develop his or her defense against the charges.

The determination of the grand jury and the decision by the prosecutor either to drop the charges or to issue the complaint are called the preliminary hearing phase.

Arrest and Booking

An arrest occurs when a person is taken into custody to obtain an answer to a criminal charge(s).[70] As was discussed above, it usually occurs after an arrest warrant has been issued by a judge pursuant to an indictment or complaint. However, an arrest can occur without a warrant if there is probable cause that a crime is being committed or had been committed. In any of the circumstances, however, the individual arrested is truly in custody, and a *Miranda* warning must be given by the law enforcement agents.

The booking procedure involves recording identifying and other information (e.g., name, address, age) about the person arrested in the police log or blotter. Also included, of course, is the crime committed. Booking also includes fingerprinting and photographing the arrestee.

Setting Bail

Because an alleged violation of criminal law, whether a misdemeanor or felony, results in an arrest and possible incarceration, a hearing is set to determine if bail can be set. Bail is used to ensure that the accused will remain in the state and be present in court for the trial of the alleged crime(s). Bail consists of money, and can be cash. Bail may also be arranged through a bail bondsman, where the accused enters into a contract with that bondsman to post the amount of the bail for a percentage of the bail amount. If the accused does not show up for court, or flees the state, then the court is paid the amount of the bond, and the defendant forfeits the money.

The amount of the bond is determined by many factors, including the type of crime, the accused's prior criminal record, if any, and the defendant's threat to public safety.[71] Sometimes the defendant is released on a personal recognizance bond because of his or her integrity and the court's belief that he or she will comply with all the proceedings.

In other instances, bond is not available at all, especially when the crime is a heinous one, such as the rape and murder of a child or elderly person. If bond is denied, the accused remains in the custody of law enforcement officers.

Arraignment

The arraignment is the first formalized court appearance for the accused in which he or she is informed of the charges, is informed of his or her rights, and is asked to plead guilty or not guilty to the charges. Most often, defendants plead not guilty at this pretrial stage. If a not guilty plea is made, the prosecutor is then required to prove every charge the defendant is accused of at trial.

If, however, the defendant pleads guilty, the judge must ascertain that he or she is doing so voluntarily and clearly understands the ramifications of the plea, for doing so waives all of the defendant's constitutional rights that would otherwise protect the defendant, including, of course, the right to a jury trial. If the judge accepts the guilty plea, then no trial occurs, and the defendant's sentence is decided and carried out.

Discovery, Motions, and Plea Bargaining

If the defendant has entered a not guilty plea during the arraignment and the case is to proceed to trial, a discovery period usually takes place during which the accused's attorney is given information in the possession of the prosecutor concerning the defendant and the crimes charged. Although state laws concerning discovery may vary, most provide for "reciprocal discovery," meaning that an exchange of information from both the prosecution *and* defense takes place.

The federal rules of criminal procedure clearly allow for ample discovery. Furthermore, under the *Brady* decision[72] and subsequent cases,[73] the United States Supreme Court has held that a prosecutor is required to provide the defense attorney with evidence "favorable to (the) accused" and "material to . . . guilt or punishment." If such existing evidence is not given to the defense, the accused's due process rights are violated. Examples of evidence that constitute discovery include statements to police officers, lists of property belonging to the defendant, reports of scientific tests or comparisons, and witness statements.

Also important at this step in the pretrial phase is the opportunity for defense counsel to attempt to exclude evidence that has been obtained in violation of his or her client's constitutional rights. Examples might include a statement of the defendant obtained without the required *Miranda* warning, evidence seized in violation of the accused's Fourth Amendment rights, and no assistance of counsel at any "critical stage" of prosecuting the crime. Or challenges may be made on the basis of imperfections in the statutory law under which the accused is charged; for example, that the statute is vague or that it violates the individual's other constitutional guarantees, such as freedom of religion or assembly.

It is important to note that in many states, criminal procedure statutes require the defendant to raise any defenses he or she may decide to use at trial at this time. Thus, if the defense decides to use the *necessity defense*, for example, it must be disclosed at this time, or its use may be barred at trial.

Plea bargaining also can take place at this time, although it may realistically occur at any time during the procedural phases. Plea bargaining is the process in which the accused, through his or her attorney, and the prosecuting attorney agree to a mutually satisfactory resolution of the case.[74] The final settlement is subject to court approval, either during its negotiation or before it will officially be accepted by the court. Plea bargaining can consist of the accused pleading guilty to a lesser crime, called a *charge bargain* (one less serious than the one he or she is charged with), or pleading guilty to some of the counts of a multicount complaint or indictment and, in return, receiving a lesser sentence, called a *sentence bargain*, or both.[75]

Although very much a controversial practice, there are many factors that enter into the decision to plea bargain on both the prosecuting and defense attorney's side. They include saving time by resolving a case without many man-hours of preparing for and participating in a lengthy trial; achieving desirable outcomes in which the prosecuting attorney is assured a conviction and the accused is guaranteed a lesser sentence than is probably possible at trial;[76] and saving taxpayers' dollars by avoiding unnecessary appeals of trial decisions.

Trial

The Sixth Amendment of the United States Constitution guarantees the criminal defendant certain rights during the trial (see Table 8–1) that make the criminal trial very different from a civil one. For example, the accused does not have to testify in his or her own defense unless it is decided by the defendant and his attorney to do so. A presumption of the innocence of the defendant is also unique to a criminal trial. More accurately described as an assumption,[77] this principle states that simply because an individual is charged with a crime does not mean he or she is guilty of that conduct. Thus the prosecuting attorney must meet his or her burden of proof—both in terms of the evidence presented and establishing the guilt of the accused—"beyond a reasonable doubt."

A presumption of the innocence of the defendant is . . . unique to a criminal trial.

The burden of proof is higher in a criminal case and requires the prosecution to prove each and every element of the crime(s) charged beyond a reasonable doubt. This burden of proof has been defined as requiring the evidence (facts) presented to the jury to be "clear, precise, and indubitable" *and* establish guilt entirely and to a moral certainty.[78] This standard is a much higher one than those in civil trials or administrative proceedings because the verdict of guilty in a criminal trial results in punishment that may include incarceration or death. Since deprivation of life, liberty, and property are constitutionally protected interests, a high degree of proof is necessary before these interests can be taken from the individual. Furthermore, in all but a few states, the jury must return a unanimous verdict in support of the defendant's guilt or innocence.[79]

The trial itself follows a format similar to civil trials in that there is:

1. Jury selection (voir dire)
2. Opening statements by each attorney
3. The prosecutor presenting his or her case (with cross-examination by defense counsel)
4. The defense presenting his or her case (again with cross-examination by the prosecutor)
5. Closing arguments
6. Jury instructions by the judge
7. Jury deliberation
8. Verdict

Sentencing

If the defendant is acquitted by the jury, the case is over, and the government is not able to retry the case. If, however, the defendant is found guilty, a sentencing hearing is held after the trial itself. The sentence imposed is usually dictated by Congress or the state legislature, thus allowing the judge little, if any, deviation from those guidelines. Furthermore, parole board decisions also are often carefully delineated in sentencing statutes.[80]

Post-trial Steps

Clearly, either before or after sentencing takes place, the criminal has many options to challenge his or her conviction and/or sentence. Some of those options include a motion for a new trial (alleging some violation of constitutional or other rights); an appeal of the decision of the state or federal trial court in which, if successful, the conviction may be overturned or a new trial ordered in certain situations; and filing a *writ of habeas corpus* ("you have the body"), which asks the court for immediate release of the criminal because he or she is being illegally imprisoned or detained. The court determines if the imprisonment is illegal and, if so, if the individual should be released. The court's decision concerning the *writ* can also be appealed.

SPECIAL CONSIDERATIONS

The criminal law has not generally been utilized to regulate nursing or medical practice.[81] This reluctance of the law to characterize "professional actions or tasks" as criminal is probably due to the difficulties in prosecuting "good faith" decisions by health care providers, especially when the conduct of the nurse or physician can be supported by expert testimony or was carried out at the request of the patient or the patient's family.[82] Even so, there are special situations when criminal conduct has been alleged against health care providers, health care delivery systems, and nurses in particular. Those areas include withholding and withdrawing treatment, practicing a profession without a license, and refusing to provide emergency care in the institution's emergency department.

The criminal law has not generally been utilized to regulate nursing or medical practice.

Withdrawing and Withholding Treatment

Several nurses have been indicted for withholding, withdrawing, or actively causing an individual's death without the patient's decision to refuse treatment and without an order from a physician who has determined that continued treatment was no longer medically helpful,[83] but none were convicted until 1990. In the case *State v. Shook*,[84] registered nurse Anthony Shook asked to care for patient Peggy Epley, who was admitted to the ICU unit because of renal failure. Her condition required a ventilator, dialysis, and blood pressure medications via IV lines. The patient died because of a huge drop in blood pressure. As a result of several statements that Shook had made to other nursing staff members ("One of these days her blood pressure is going to drop and she's not coming back"), the IV fluids administered by Shook before the patient's death were sent for analysis. The laboratory report indicated that none of the required medications were present in the IV fluid, and the medical examiner determined that death was due to the absence of the medications in the IV fluid, which caused the patient's blood pressure to drop.

Shook was charged with first-degree murder. Based on the evidence at trial, which included an admission by Shook that he had wanted to help her die because her husband could not "let her go," and the husband's testimony that he never indicated to nurse Shook that he hoped his wife would die, Shook was convicted of first-

degree murder. Shook appealed the conviction, but it was upheld by the appeals court and the North Carolina Supreme Court.

Only one case was prosecuted against two physicians in California, who were charged with murder and conspiracy to commit murder when they removed, at the family's request, ventilator support and IVs that caused the death of patient Clarence Herbert.[85] The California Appellate Court, in granting the physicians' request for writs of prohibition (which in essence dismissed the case), held that (1) although the Natural Death Act was one way an individual could direct the withholding or withdrawing of life-sustaining treatment, it was not the exclusive manner for such decisions; (2) a diagnosis of brain death was not a condition precedent to the cessation of life-sustaining treatment; (3) the fact that the physicians did not seek guardianship for the patient did not make the physicians' conduct illegal; and (4) although the physicians' decision not to continue treatment was intentional and was done with the knowledge that it would cause the patient's death, their conduct did not constitute an unlawful failure to perform a legal duty(ies).[86]

The *Barber and Nejdl* case is an important one for all health care providers for several reasons. First, it was a case of first impression for physicians in relation to the withholding and withdrawing of life-sustaining treatment—and specifically food and fluid—*and* potential liability for murder. Second, it is important to note that the case did not proceed to trial. Rather, the issue before the court was whether or not the facts of the case could support a charge of homicide; the court determined the facts could not do so. Third, and perhaps most important, the court clearly supported the physicians' decision,[87] leading one author to state that it would be difficult to prosecute any "good faith cessation of medical treatment, with the patient's or family concurrence" in this court's jurisdiction.[88]

Several other cases concerning the removal of life-sustaining treatment and their impact, albeit somewhat indirectly, on criminal liability are important to mention briefly here (these, and other cases, are discussed more at length in Chapter 13, Issues in Death and Dying). In two early cases, *In The Matter of Karen Quinlan*[89] and *In The Matter of Shirley Dinnerstein*,[90] respective civil courts held that no civil or criminal liability would occur for any participant involved in the removal of life-sustaining treatment when done in consultation with the physician (whose decision is done with "skill and care" and based on accepted medical standards), the patient and/or his legal representative, the family, and, clearly the case in *Quinlan*, an ethics committee. Furthermore, the courts held that no prior judicial approval of a decision based on those guidelines was necessary.[91]

In The Matter of Claire Conroy,[92] the New Jersey Supreme Court, in reversing the Appellate Court's decision that the removal of Ms. Conroy's feeding tube would be tantamount to killing her, held that removal of the tube could occur with an incompetent patient under specific guidelines drawn by the court, thus rebutting the lower court's ruling that removal of the nasogastric tube would be unlawful.[93] Also, in *John F. Kennedy Memorial Hospital v. Bludworth*,[94] the Supreme Court of Florida, in upholding the right of a terminally ill, comatose patient's choice to terminate treatment (in this case, a ventilator) through his "living" or "mercy" will, echoed the *Quinlan* and *Dinnerstein* decisions in holding that any individual, including a guardian, who participates in a good-faith decision to cease treatment will not be held civilly or criminally liable for that decision, and that prior judicial approval for it is not necessary.[95]

These, and other, cases do not provide *absolute* immunity from civil or criminal liability for decisions to withhold or withdraw treatment, for despite the best intentions of all of the individuals involved, disagreements concerning decisions to discontinue treatment may arise. Moreover, there may be questions as to the "good faith" of one or more individuals who participate in such decisions. Furthermore, there will be no protection from criminal charges when a

nurse or other health care provider decides on his or her own to withhold or withdraw treatment, particularly with no input from the patient, the legally recognized surrogate decision maker, and/or the family. Also, one must keep in mind that all of the cases discussed here were decided before the United States Supreme Court's decision in *Cruzan*, which has potentially far-reaching and yet unforeseen implications, both civilly and criminally.

Even so, the nurse who is involved with carrying out decisions to withhold or withdraw treatment can be somewhat comfortable in relying on these decisions in relation to criminal liability. However, the guidelines suggested are important to adhere to. They include obtaining written orders for any care decisions to withdraw or withhold treatment; physician documentation of the reasons for the decision to cease treatment; including the patient, or his legal representative, in such decisions; making any advance directive a part of the patient's medical record; informing the patient and family of any decisions that are made; adequate nursing documentation concerning the patient's care; utilizing ethics committees to confirm decisions to terminate treatment; and never making a unilateral decision to withdraw or withhold treatment from a patient. If possible, the nurse should participate as a member of an ethics committee, including, if possible, a nursing ethics committee, to provide invaluable input that aids in reasoned decision-making in patient/client care based on clear consideration of ethical dimensions.[96]

Practicing a Profession without a License

State practice acts contain provisions making the practice of a particular profession—nursing, medicine, and pharmacy, for example—without a license a criminal offense. Likewise, hiring someone to practice a specific profession without a valid, current license is also a crime. Moreover, aiding and assisting another to practice a licensed profession without a valid, current license is also considered criminal conduct. Some state statutory schemes make a first offense a misdemeanor with subsequent or second convictions a felony.[97]

State practice acts contain provisions making the practice of a particular profession . . . without a license a criminal offense.

Nurses in advanced practice—nurse-midwives, nurse practitioners, nurse anesthetists, and clinical specialists—probably face the most potential to be included in a criminal suit alleging the unlicensed practice of *medicine* because of their very independent and nontraditional roles and responsibilities. This was clearly the situation in the *Sermchief* case, discussed in Chapter 21, in which the nurse practitioners were functioning pursuant to physician-developed protocols for prescribing medications and performing other functions in rural obstetric and gynecologic clinics throughout Missouri. Although the Missouri Supreme Court decided in favor of the nurse practitioners and the physicians, this challenge to advanced practice continues today in many states across the country.

Nurses who are in advanced practice, those who are asked to perform nontraditional care in any health care delivery setting, and those who decide to initiate their own practice as an entrepreneur need to be aware of the potential criminal liability that may exist as a result of their expanded practice. To avoid unnecessary inclusion in a suit alleging the unauthorized practice of a particular profession, the nurse must know the state nurse practice act and its rules and regulations intimately. By conforming with the required conduct of both, the nurse can stay well within the scope of practice of *nursing* and his or her specialty. Furthermore, it is important for the nurse to be familiar with other state practice acts, including the medical practice act, pharmacy registration act, physical therapy practice act, and psychologist registration act to avoid an unknowing, but nonetheless clear, violation of one of those acts that may result in criminal liability for the nurse.

In addition, nurse administrators or nurse executives having the responsibility of hiring nursing staff need to ensure that each nurse considered for a position, whether an RN, an LPN, or a nurse with a specialty license, such as a nurse-midwife, has a valid and current license. If the state nurse practice act requires certain certification or credentialing for advanced practice, then the existence and validity of those additional criteria are also mandatory.

Also important for each RN or LPN is to adhere to renewal periods for the license and ensure that the license (and any required credentialing) does not expire. If expiration occurs, the nurse should not practice nursing until the license is renewed and is current and valid. Likewise, if the nurse moves to a new state and applies for licensure through endorsement, no nursing practice should occur until a valid license has been issued or, if the state practice act allows, until a temporary permit has been obtained.

Refusal to Provide Emergency Care

The refusal to provide emergency care to one whose medical condition is truly emergent has been the focus of many lawsuits, especially civil ones that have alleged that the refusal resulted in injury to, or death of, the person denied care. When the denial involves persons who do not have insurance or cannot pay for Emergency Department (ED) services themselves ("medically indigent" individuals) so that the "economic burden of care is transferred from private to public hospitals," the practice is called patient dumping.[98] To eradicate patient dumping, the federal government passed the Consolidated Omnibus Budget Reconciliation Act (COBRA) of

1985,[99] which provides for civil penalties and termination or suspension of Medicare Provider Agreements.[100] Patient dumping and implications for ED nurses are discussed in Chapter 17.

In addition to civil liability for refusing to provide care in an ED, criminal liability may also result when no emergency aid is rendered in an emergency.

KEY CASE 8–3   People v. Flushing Hospital and Medical Center (1983)[101]

Emergency Department nurse denies care to patient because "no beds are available"

Patient dies at another hospital

Hospital charged with misdemeanor for willfully refusing emergency medical care to patient

Hospital pleads guilty to offense, then asks for a vacation of judgment, saying the denial was not based on "bad intent"

Court denies motion to vacate judgment on basis that duty to provide emergency care is absolute, regardless of intent

FACTS: Around 10:20 PM on May 5, 1982, 89-year-old Katherine Streletsky, a nursing home resident, was taken to Flushing General Hospital for emergency treatment for congestive heart failure. When the private ambulance arrived at the hospital, a nurse on duty in the ER told the ambulance attendants that the patient would have to be taken to another hospital because no beds were available. Ms. Streletsky was immediately taken to another hospital where she died several hours later.

On July 2, 1982, the hospital was served with a summons and information charging it with a violation of New York's Public Health Law that made it a misdemeanor to willfully refuse to provide emergency care and service to one in need of such care and service. The Hospital pled guilty to the charge and was fined $2000.00, the maximum fine for the offense.

However, several days later, the hospital filed a motion to vacate the judgment of conviction and to withdraw its plea and based its motion on several legal points, including the fact that the hospital was not guilty of the crime charged and that although the denial of service was "willful," there was no "bad intent" on the hospital's part in denying the emergency care.

COURT DECISION ON MOTION: The court, after conducting a hearing on two separate days, denied the motion of the hospital. The court specifically held that the statutory language concerning a refusal of emergency care did not require a "bad intent." Rather, the court stated, it simply required a "willful denial for any reason whatsoever." The hospital's agent (the nurse) refused Ms. Streletsky treatment, which violated a statute meant to prohibit hospitals from "restricting access to emergency rooms and to prohibit the denial of treatment to patients brought to emergency rooms by volunteer ambulance corps." Therefore, for this and other reasons, the court concluded, the hospital's motion must be denied.

ANALYSIS: This case illustrates several principles of statutory construction, which deals with the interpretation of legislative laws. Here the court relied on the "plain language" of the statutory sections involved, and characterized it as imposing "strict liability" on the hospital when it refused treatment. In addition, it analyzed the legislative history of the act to determine its purpose. The case also illustrates the

KEY CASE 8–3

People v. Flushing Hospital and Medical Center (1983)[101]
Continued

importance of the conduct of a hospital agent—the nurse—and the criminal liability that can attach to that conduct. Any nurse functioning as a triage nurse in an ED who refuses treatment to a patient may find that conduct results not only in civil liability for the hospital (and perhaps the nurse individually) but also in criminal liability for the employer if a similar statute exists in the state where he or she works. Last, the hearing revealed marked differences in the nature of the instructions given to the nurse by the ED physician on duty. The physician testified that after he was told there were no beds available by the nurse, he instructed her to try to contact the ambulance and divert it en route. In contrast, the District Attorney's version of the physician's instructions was that if the ambulance could not be contacted by radio, the patient be admitted to the hospital and her condition at least stabilized. Although the discrepancy was not a controlling issue in the case because the "strict liability" to provide care *and* the fact that the nurse did not base her refusal on "per se" instructions from the physician, the differences in the physician's versions of what he allegedly said support the significance of accurately and immediately documenting any and all physician orders in the patient's ED record or other documentation system if no patient record is initiated. Had the instructions made a difference in this case, the end result may have been different, not only for the hospital but also for the nurse.

SUMMARY OF PRINCIPLES AND APPLICATIONS

Although nurses are more frequently involved in civil suits than in criminal ones, it is clear that the possibility exists for the RN or LPN to be a defendant in a criminal case. Because inclusion in a criminal case has far-reaching implications, including incarceration, it is vital that the nurse be ever mindful of professional and personal conduct that might result in criminal liability. Furthermore, if the nurse finds himself or herself the target of a criminal investigation or named in a criminal suit, the following guidelines can be helpful:

▼ Retain an attorney who concentrates his or her practice in criminal law and who is familiar with practice issues.

▼ Remember the constitutional protections afforded any individual who is accused of a crime and exercise them.

▼ Any statement made to a law enforcement officer can be used against the person.

▼ Statements made to health care delivery system security personnel can be turned over to law enforcement agents.

▼ Criminal liability may exist as a result of state *and* federal laws, so an understanding of both is essential.

▼ The elements of a crime include an act, intent, and causation.

▼ There are defenses to criminal conduct that may help in reducing a criminal charge or result in an acquittal.

▼ There are substantive and procedural protections afforded a person through the criminal justice system, including the right to counsel at any "critical stage" of the proceedings, which includes a detainment or arrest.

▼ If asked to speak to any law enforcement person when suspected of a crime or criminal conduct, remember that if detained or in custody or arrested, a *Miranda* warning must be given. If not being detained, or not in custody or not arrested, the nurse has a right to leave.

▼ When involved in decisions concerning the withdrawal or withholding of treatment, obtain written orders from the physician and provide good documentation concerning the care given and care not given pursuant to those orders.

▼ Never practice nursing without a current and valid license.

▼ Verify that nursing staff have current and valid licenses.

▼ Never refuse emergency treatment to a patient who is experiencing a true medical emergency and seeks help from the ED.

TOPICS FOR FURTHER INQUIRY

1. Analyze any filed cases against nurses involving the practice of nursing in the state in which you practice. Determine the differences and similarities of the charges against the respective nurse defendants. Based on the analysis, identify guidelines that could help nurses avoid future potential allegations of criminal conduct.

2. Critically evaluate one of the defenses to a crime. Attempt to use a reported case against a nurse involving the practice of nursing. If not available, then a "case" can be created. In either event, focus on such issues as whether the defense would aid the nurse defendant and why; what might be the potential difficulties in using the defense based on the case being evaluated; and suggest what other defenses may be possible.

3. With the consent of the facility and following privacy and confidentiality mandates, analyze the documentation done in patient medical records when medical care is withdrawn or withheld. Areas to evaluate include documentation of the existence of an advance directive; whether or not the advance directive is included in the chart; documentation by physician of orders consistent with the advance directive; if no advance directive exists, how the patient's consent for refusal of treatment was recorded.

4. Write a position paper on the presumption of innocence. Include ways to improve the presumption or why it should be eliminated altogether.

REFERENCES

1. Lawrence Baum. *American Courts: Process and Policy.* 2nd Edition. Boston: Houghton Mifflin Company, 1990, 172–174.
2. Wayne LaFave and Austine Scott. *Criminal Law.* 2nd Edition. St. Paul, Minn: West Publishing Company, 1986, 23–27 (with 1995 Pocket Part) (Hornbook Series).
3. Baum, *supra* note 1, at 170.
4. LaFave and Scott, *supra* note 2, at 90–190.
5. Henry Campbell Black. *Black's Law Dictionary.* 6th Edition. St. Paul, Minn: West Publishing Company, 1991, 594.
6. *Ex parte McNiel*, 80 U.S. (13 Wall.) 236 (1872).
7. *Id.*
8. David W. Neubauer. *Criminal Justice in Middle America.* Morristown, NJ: General Learning Press, 1974, 252.
9. Baum, *supra*, note 1, at 176.
10. Black, *supra* note 5, at 836.
11. LaFave and Scott, *supra* note 2, at 22–23.
12. *Id.* at 217.
13. *Id.* at 216.
14. *Id.* at 231.
15. *Id.*
16. LaFave and Scott, *supra* note 2, at 569.
17. *Id.* at 576.
18. *Id.* at 525.
19. *Id.* at 277.
20. *Id.* at 279.
21. *People v. Coe*, 501 N.Y.S. 2d (997) (Sup. 1986), *affirmed on appeal*, 510 N.Y.S. 2d 470 (1987).
22. *Id.* at 605.
23. *Id.*

24. 716 S.W.2d 142 (Tex. App. 1986).
25. 446 F. Supp. 252 (1977). The court ordered a new trial based on numerous due process violations by the prosecution, and shortly thereafter, the indictment against the nurses was dismissed. Beatrice Yorker, "An Analysis of Murder Charges Against Nurses," 1(3) *Journal of Nursing Law* (1995), 35–46.
26. 584 F. Supp. 302 (D.C. Va. 1984), *affirmed*, 751 F.2d 379, *cert. denied*, 473 U.S. 907 (1984).
27. LaFave and Scott, *supra* note 2, at 652.
28. *Id.*
29. Black, *supra* note 5, at 665.
30. *Id.* at 664.
31. LaFave and Scott, *supra* note 2, at 669.
32. 477 A. 2d 323 (N.J. 1984).
33. 138 Mass. 165, 52 Am. R. 264 (1884).
34. 194 A. 2d 467 (1963).
35. LaFave and Scott, *supra* note 2, at 684.
36. *Id.* at 685.
37. *Commonwealth v. Knowlton*, No. 84-7322 (Mass. 1984), *reported in The National Law Journal*, October 29, 1984, at 13. This case involved a nurse who allegedly turned off a patient's respirator while caring for the patient in his home. The patient died, and the nurse was charged with assault and attempted murder. The jury returned a verdict of not guilty. Also, in *People v. Nygren*, 696 P.2d 270 (Colorado 1985), a nursing home, its director of nursing, and charge nurse were charged with second-degree assault for giving a patient Thorazine that was not ordered for that patient and was used to sedate him. The patient died as a result of the injection.
38. See, for example, S.H.A. 720 IL CS 5/12–4.6 (1989), which provides for the crime of Aggravated Battery of a Senior Citizen. The crime is a Class 2 felony.
39. For example, if a nurse or other health care provider fails to warn a blind patient that he or she is walking toward an open window, and the patient falls out of the window and is injured, the nurse could be charged with intentionally or recklessly causing that battery. LaFave and Scott, *supra* note 2, at 686.
40. For example, in *People v. Clark*, 474 N.Y.S. 2d 409 (N.Y. City Criminal Ct. 1984), a licensed practical nurse was charged with assault in the third degree, criminal trespass, and menacing stemming from her refusal to show a hospital security guard her identification card when asked. In addition to refusing to show her ID, Ms. Clark also swore at the guard and kicked him. Although the case was ultimately dismissed because of a pending civil suit brought by the nurse against the security guard for injuries he inflicted upon her, it stands as an example of how a nurse may be involved in an assault case for conduct other than that involving the care of a patient.
41. Black, *supra* note 5, at 455–456.
42. 42 U.S.C. Section 1395nn *et seq.* (1977). These Amendments are called the *Medicare and Medicaid Anti-Fraud and Abuse Amendments of 1977*.
43. *Adams v. United States*, 347 F. 2d 665 (1965), *cert. denied*, 382 U.S. 975 (1965).
44. S.H.A., 225 ILCS 65/6(c) (1988).
45. LaFave and Scott, *supra* note 2, at 304.
46. *Id.* at 311.
47. *Id.* at 323.
48. American Law Institute. *Model Penal Code* Section 4.01 (1955).
49. See, for example, *Law, Psychiatry, and Morality: Essays and Analysis* by Alan A. Stone. Washington, DC: American Psychiatric Press, Inc., 1984.
50. See, for example, Thomas Szasz. *Psychiatric Justice*. New York: Collier Books, 1965; Stone, *supra* note 49.
51. LaFave and Scott, *supra* note 2, at 377–387.
52. *Id.* at 383.
53. *Id.* at 389.
54. *Id.* at 395–398. Some of the cases dealing with this issue are *Robinson v. California*, 370 U.S. 660 (1962) (one cannot be convicted of a criminal offense for "being addicted to the use of narcotics"—often called the "Status Case"), and *Powell v. Texas*, 392 U.S. 514 (1968), *rehearing denied*, 393 U.S. 898 (1968).
55. LaFave and Scott, *supra* note 2, at 398.
56. *Id.* at 420.
57. *Id.* at 441–443.
58. *Id.* at 441–450.
59. *Id.* at 454.
60. *Id.*
61. See note 40, *supra*.
62. Black, *supra* note 4, at 261.
63. 384 U.S. 436 (1966), *rehearing denied*, 385 U.S. 890 (1966).
64. Ralph Chandler, Richard Enslen, and Peter Renstrom. *Constitutional Law Deskbook: Individual Rights*. 2nd Edition. Rochester, NY: The Lawyers Co-Operative Publishing Company, 1993, 370 (April 1995 pocket part).
65. *Miranda v. Arizona, supra* note 63.
66. Chandler, Enslen, and Renstrom, *supra* note 64, at 703.
67. *Id.* at 652.
68. *Id.*
69. *Id.* at 661.
70. Black, *supra* note 5, at 72.
71. *Stack v. Boyle*, 342 U.S. 1 (1951); *U.S. v. Salerno*, 107 S. Ct. 2095 (1987).
72. *Brady v. Maryland*, 373 U.S. 83 (1963).
73. *U.S. v. Agurs*, 427 U.S. 97 (1976); *U.S. v. Bagley*, 473 U.S. 667 (1985).
74. Black, *supra* note 5, at 798.
75. *Id.*; see also Baum, *supra* note 1, at 187.
76. Baum, *supra* note 1, at 189–192.
77. LaFave and Scott, *supra* note 2, at 58.
78. Black, *supra* note 5, at 111.
79. Baum, *supra* note 1, at 197.
80. *Id.* at 203.
81. Leonard Glantz, "Withholding and Withdrawing Treatment: The Role of the Criminal Law," 15:4 *Law, Medicine & Health Care* (Winter 1987–1988), 231.
82. *Id.* at 232, *citing* G. Ginex, "A Prosecutor's View of Criminal Liability for Withholding or Withdrawing Medical Care: The Myth and Reality," in *Legal and Ethical Aspects of Treating Critically and Terminally Ill Patients*. Edward Doudera and J. Peters, Editors. Ann Arbor: AU-PHA Press, 1982, 209.
83. See, for example, Loy Wiley, "Liability for Death: Nine

Nurses' Legal Ordeals," 11(9) *Nursing 81* (September 1981), 34–43.

84. 393 S.E. 2d 819 (N.C. 1990).

85. *Barber and Nejdl v. Superior Court*, 195 Cal. Rptr. 484 (Cal. App. 2 Dist. 1983).

86. *Id.* at 484.

87. Leonard Glantz, "Withholding and Withdrawing Treatment: The Role of the Criminal Law," 15:4 231 *Law, Medicine & Health Care* (Winter 1987/1988), 236.

88. *Id.*

89. 355 A. 2d 647 (N.J. 1976).

90. 380 N.E. 2d 134 (Mass. 1978).

91. The *Quinlan* case dealt with the removal of a ventilator, while *Dinnerstein* focused on whether or not a Do Not Resuscitate (DNR) Order would result in liability.

92. 486 A. 2d 12099 (N.J. 1985).

93. George Pozgar and Nina Pozgar, "End of Life Decisions," *Legal Aspects of Health Care Administration.*

6th Edition. Gaithersburg, Md: Aspen Publishers, Inc., 1995, 513–515.

94. 452 So. 2d 921 (Fla. 1984).

95. *Id.* at 926.

96. George Miller, "A Look at Long Term Care Ethics: Dilemmas and Decisions," 16(12) *Provider for Long Term Care Professionals*, 1990, 13.

97. See, for example, The Illinois Nursing Act of 1987, S.H.A. 225 ILCS 65/6, 65/46 (1988).

98. Lisa Enfield and David Sklar, "Patient Dumping in the Hospital Emergency Department: Renewed Interest in an Old Problem," 13(4) *American Journal of Law & Medicine* 562–595 (1988).

99. Pub. L. No. 99–272, Section 9121, 1986 *U.S. Code Cong. & Admin. News* (100 Stat.) 82, 164–67 (codified as amended at 42 U.S.C. Section 1395dd (April 7, 1986).

100. *Id.* at 9121(b)(d)(2) and 9121(b)(d)(1)(a).

101. 471 N.Y.S.2d 745 (N.Y. City Crim. Ct. 1983).

9 Contract Law

contents

In addition to the potential civil liability that a nurse may experience under tort law or civil rights violations, liability under contract law may also exist for the nurse or other health care professional. Because an injured patient can bring a suit alleging many possible causes of action, a count alleging a breach of contract against a nurse anesthetist, for example, for misrepresenting the services to be rendered to the patient could accompany a count alleging negligence in the administration of the anesthesia.

Although the wrong allegedly suffered by the patient under contract law may be very different from that sought under tort law, many times the distinctions between the two become blurred because of the law's sometimes confusing treatment of the two areas of liability. For instance, in the example above, in addition to the patient alleging negligence in the administration of anesthesia because an injury occurred, he or she could also allege a breach of contract for the same injury because of the nurse anesthetist's failure to provide services with reasonable skill and care.[1]

Despite the blending of the two types of civil actions, the reader should try to keep the two separate by remembering that tort law involves obligations imposed by law to avoid injuries to another.[2] Contract law, in contast, deals with promises, either present or future, and the enforcement of them when a legal right has been created.[3] Therefore the nurse anesthetist in the example above could not legally contract with the patient not to exercise due care in the provision of anesthesia services. She could, however, contract to provide the services for a specific fee and on a specific date.

Contract law . . . deals with promises . . . and the enforcement of them when a legal right has been created.

Contract law is an important area of law for the nurse to be familiar with because it is often utilized by the nurse employee, nurse manager, or nurse entrepreneur in relation to respective rights and responsibilities within the job or business setting. For example, the nurse employee may allege a breach of an express or implied contract of employment when discharged from a position. Or a nurse entrepreneur may allege failure on the part of an independent contractor to provide services for the business the nurse has founded.

This chapter will address the basic principles of contract law and relate those principles to the delivery of health care in various settings and to the nurse who experiences a breach of his or her contract rights. Because the delivery of health care is a service, the focus of this chapter

---

KEY PRINCIPLES

Contract
Assignment and Delegation of a Contract
Statute of Frauds
Rules of Contract Interpretation
Parole Evidence Rule
Breach of Contract
Completion of Contract
Good Faith/Fair Dealing

RELATED TOPICS

will not be on contracts concerning goods. As a result, the Uniform Commercial Code (UCC), a uniform law adopted by states to cover the sale of goods in the state, will not be covered in any detail. Knowledge of this law, however, would be important if the nurse entrepreneur is involved in any way in the sale of goods or products in his or her business.

ESSENTIALS OF CONTRACT FORMATION

Elements of a Contract

A contract is a voluntary agreement between two or more individuals that creates an obligation to do or not do something and that creates enforceable rights or legal duties.[4] For a contract to be valid, certain elements must be present: (1) capacity to enter into the agreement; (2) mutual assent (includes an offer and acceptance); (3) legal consideration; and (4) no defenses that would void the agreement.[5]

Contracts exist in many forms, and the forms may overlap. For example, they may be (1) oral; (2) written; (3) express; (4) implied or quasi contracts; (5) unilateral; (6) bilateral; (7) void; (8) voidable; (9) adhesion (form); and (10) unenforceable.[6]

Generally a contract is entered into for the benefit of the two or more individuals who are parties to it. However, a contract can also be for the benefit of a third party. The third person, who is not directly involved in the formation of the contract, may have enforceable contract rights nonetheless.[7]

For example, assume agency A owed money to a nurse for nursing services rendered through that agency. Because of difficult financial times, the agency decides to enter into a contract with nurse agency B. The contract specifically requires agency B to hire the nurse and "perform agency A's obligations" (payment of the money owed) to the nurse. If agency B did not pay the money owed to the nurse as it contracted to, the nurse would have the right to sue for the money owed. The nurse would be a third party beneficiary to that contract in addition to being able to assert basic contract rights against agency A.[8]

Assignment and Delegation of Contract

If a valid contract is formed, one party may attempt to assign the rights under the contract to another. For example, a nurse who is under a contract of employment can "assign" the money to be received under the contract to her parents. The nurse continues to perform the work required by the terms of the contract, but transfers the right of payment under the contract to the parents. Generally one can assign whatever one wishes under a contract so long as there is no prohibition of assignment.[9]

Contracts may be delegated as well. A delegation most often occurs when the *duties* or responsibilities contracted for are transferred to another.[10] If a nurse educator, for example, contracts with a particular organization to do a full-day seminar, but cannot teach the program because of illness, he or she can substitute another colleague to do the program. However, if the contract restricted delegation to another, then the nurse educator would not be able to use a replacement. Instead, the nurse would have to reschedule the date of the seminar to fulfill the contract.

Questions Concerning the Validity of a Contract

Capacity to Enter into Agreement

For a contract to be valid and enforceable, the parties entering into it must have the legal qualifications to enter into the agreement. They must understand the nature of the contract, its effect, and their obligations under it. Although adults—persons who are 18 years of age and older—are presumed to possess the capacity or competency to enter into contracts, certain situations exist in which the presumption may be, or is, defeated.

It may be that an adult possesses a condition that might affect his or her cognitive ability to enter into and carry on a contract. For example, someone who has an IQ of 50 may not be able to appreciate the legal ramifications of entering into a contract to sell a house or perform certain personal services. Or someone who enters a contract when under the influence of a chemical substance or medication may not have the full mental capacity to do so at that time.

If an individual has been declared incompetent (or under a legal disability) and a guardian appointed for the person (ward), it may be that his or her capacity to enter contracts will be affected. If a guardian over the person's estate or finances has been found to be necessary, then clearly that individual would not be able to enter into any contracts concerning the sale or purchase of property, goods, or services. Likewise, a patient who signs an agreement to pay for care provided by a health care delivery system when such decisions have been turned over to the person's guardian does not enter into a valid and enforceable contract.

Some states have incorporated into their criminal statutes the suspension of a prisoner's civil rights upon conviction and until the sentence imposed by the court is completed. If so, then a prisoner could not enter into a contract during that time period because he or she has lost the ability to do so by law. Other states protect a criminal defendant's civil rights by limiting their loss and specifying when and how they are restored. Illinois, for example, presumes that a criminal defendant retains his or her civil rights, except the right to vote, during incarceration.[11]

Other losses, such as suspension or revocation of a license (for example, a nursing license) due to the conviction, can be restored after sentencing and after any probation has been completed, so long as there is no finding by the agency responsible for the licensing that the restoration is not in the public interest.[12]

Generally a minor (or an "infant" as is the term most often used in state statutes) is not seen by the law as possessing the capacity to

enter into a contract. Thus, until the minor reaches the age of majority—or adulthood—he or she would not be able to enter into a contract of any kind. Most states set the age of adulthood at 18 years, although there are some that set the age at 21.[13]

Exceptions exist in most states to the general rule that a minor is unable to enter into a contract.

Exceptions exist in most states to the general rule that a minor is unable to enter into a contract. The exceptions may include a minor declared an "emancipated minor" under state law,[14] or a minor parent who enters into a health care arbitration agreement on behalf of a minor child.[15]

Mutual Assent

Assent is legally defined as approving, ratifying, and confirming something.[16] Assent requires active participation by the party assenting to the issue or situation at hand. Therefore, mutual assent requires one or more parties to approve, ratify, and confirm something.

In relation to contract law, mutual assent has been termed a "meeting of the minds." It is composed of an offer and the acceptance of the offer.

Offer

An offer is a clear, direct, and precise communication in any form (in writing or orally) to another (the offeree) that the offeror intends to enter into a contract.[17] Generally an offer can be revoked at any time before acceptance so long as notice is given to the offeree. It can also be revoked if not accepted by the offeree within the time period set by the individual making the offer. If no time is set, the offer is considered revoked if not accepted within a reasonable amount of time.

Acceptance

Acceptance occurs when there is a voluntary, clear, definite communication to accept the offer as specified by the offeror.[18] Accepting the offer may need to be done in the same manner as the offer was communicated to the offeree. For example, if a nurse executive receives a proposed written severance agreement upon termination and is asked to respond in writing as to his or her acceptance or rejection on a date certain, the response must be in writing. Responding in any other manner would not conform with the terms of the agreement. Rather, any other response would be a counter-offer, and no agreement would be reached on either "offer" until acceptance by both parties took place.

It may be that the proposed contract terms do not specify a manner of acceptance. If so, then any form of communication of acceptance—words, a writing, or conduct—can satisfy this requirement. The nurse executive in the example above could then accept the proposed severance agreement by, for example, informing the employer of acceptance and tendering her resignation. It is important to note, though, that silence—not responding in some way—is not usually considered to be acceptance of a contract because it would be unfair to enforce a contract that was not clearly accepted in some manner by the offeree.[19]

Legal Consideration

Consideration is the cause, motive, "bargained for exchange," the *quid pro quo* (something for something) that motivates a person to enter into a contract.[20] Consideration includes both parties giving something of value. For example, a nurse faculty member is hired to provide academic instruction to students in a particular university and to forgo other faculty positions at other colleges. The university, in turn, agrees to pay the nurse faculty member a salary commensurate with his or her qualifications and retain the faculty member for a certain

period (e.g., a year contract of employment at a specific rank).

Consideration is *not* the same as a gratuitous promise to do something or to give something, because the one to whom the promise is made is not giving up anything of value. Furthermore, consideration does not exist when (1) past consideration is used for a future agreement; (2) an agreement is given by a party to the contract to do something he or she is already legally obligated to do; (3) the consideration is illegal or immoral; or (4) the consideration is inadequate, that is, not reasonable in light of what is contracted for.[21]

No Defenses That Would Void the Agreement

If a contract is to be valid and enforceable, no challenges (defenses) to its formation should be able to be successfully raised. If a defense is raised, the court will determine its validity and then determine what impact the existence of the defense has on the contract itself. If a defense is found to exist, the court can declare the contract (1) void (having no legal or binding effect); (2) voidable (declare the contract void at the election of the wronged party); (3) unenforceable; or (4) unconscionable.[22]

If a contract is to be valid and enforceable, no challenges (defenses) to its formation should be able to be successfully raised.

Defenses to Contract Formation

The challenges (defenses) that can be raised to question whether or not a contract was legally formed are varied and complex. Moreover, several challenges may be raised concerning one contract. Table 9–1 lists most of the defenses that may be utilized by one or both parties to a

TABLE 9–1

Defenses to Contract Formation

DEFENSE	COMMENT
No capacity to enter into contract (minor, mental illness)	Depending on circumstances, court may void entire contract or may make portions voidable; court will also look to nature of transaction
Undue influence	One party unfairly influences the other into contracting and other could not use free choice; often found in ''fiduciary relationships'' (e.g., where professional–client relationship exists, and client places trust and confidence in professional)
Duress	Party enters into contract because of improper express, implied or inferred threat
Mistake	Most successful if mutual; less so if unilateral
Misrepresentation	Defined as a claim that is not consistent with the facts; it must be substantial and cause the other to enter into the contract
Fraud	Person who is fraudulent must make misrepresentation with intent to have other rely on it and with knowledge that it was false
Unconscionability	Raised when there is a question as to the ability of one of the parties to understand the terms of the contract as a whole; is also used when the contract itself, or portions of it, are harsh or onerous; can be used when one party's capacity to enter into contract is questionable or when one party lacks equal bargaining power
Illegality/Violation of public policy	Used when contract is made for reason not in public's best interest or is illegal; examples include a contract to commit a criminal act, or an agreement that a health care consumer must waive the right to sue for any injuries suffered as a result of care; waiver is required *prior* to receiving care

Data from: Gordon Schaber and Claude Rohwer. *Contracts in a Nutshell.* 3rd Edition. St. Paul, Minn: West Publishing Company, 1990, 188–240.

contract in an attempt to avoid the obligations of the agreement.

An interesting example of one of the defenses, fraud, is discussed in Case 9–1.

Contract Interpretation

Rules of Interpretation

Guidelines have been adopted by the law to provide a set of rules for clarifying a contract when there is a challenge to its language. These general guidelines are: (1) a contract will be interpreted as a "whole," with specific clauses given less weight than the contract's general intent; (2) words in the contract will be given their "ordinary meaning"; (3) technical words and terms will be given those meanings when the contract covers a particular technical area (unless a different intent is clear in the contract); (4) custom and usage in the particular business and location where the contract is formed or performed are given considerable weight; (5) form ("adhesion") contracts will be scrutinized more closely than a typed or written contract drafted jointly by the parties, since adhesion contracts usually protect the interests of the drafter only rather than the interests of both parties.[24]

Good Faith/Fair Dealing

The duty of good faith and fair dealing to perform and enforce the contract is an implied term of all contracts.[25] Therefore, all parties to a contract are expected to conduct themselves accordingly once the contract has been entered into. Examples of bad faith and unfair dealing include a party not performing obligations diligently or performing them poorly, and failing to cooperate when the other party's obligations under the contract require participation from that individual.[26]

KEY CASE 9–1

Brindle v. West Allegheny Hospital (1991)[23]

Six nurse employees file a breach of employment contract and fraud claim against employer

FACTS: West Allegheny Hospital was under consideration to be sold by its owners, Greater Canonsburg Health Systems (GCHS). However, when asked about the proposed sale by six nurses and other employees, the hospital administration assured them that the hospital was not for sale and their jobs were not in jeopardy. Even so, statements by some staff members who knew about the proposed sale and the vice-president's resignation 6 weeks after assuring employees that the hospital was not for sale raised doubts in the employees' minds. Yet, because of the assurances received from administration, the nurses stayed at the hospital. The hospital was purchased by another hospital in the city, Allegheny General, which hired the vice-president from West Allegheny. West Allegheny closed a few months after the sale, and the employees were without jobs.

Six of the nurse employees filed a suit against the hospital alleging a breach of their employment contracts and for fraud and misrepresentation by the hospital that resulted in their staying in their jobs when the hospital knew the sale was to occur.

Breach of employment contract (allegations) found not to occur

TRIAL COURT DECISION: The hospital and GCHS asked the court for a summary judgment in their favor, stating that there was no material issue of fact concerning the breach of employment contract claim and the fraud or misrepresentation claim. The court granted the motion for all counts except the fraud and misrepresentation allegations. The nurses presented their case as to those allegations, and the court then granted a non-suit for the defendants and against the nurses. The nurses appealed that decision.

The nurses could not meet their proof burden concerning their fraud allegations

APPEALS COURT DECISION: The Superior Court of Pennsylvania held that the fact that negotiations were going on for the sale of West Allegheny Hospital did not mean that the hospital had "knowingly misrepresented" anything to the nurses, nor did it do so with the intent of keeping the nurses at West Allegheny. The Court held that intent means knowledge or recklessness concerning the statements at issue, and no proof was offered by the nurses that these elements existed. Furthermore, the Court held that the nurses offered no proof that West Allegheny would remain open.

Court found employer did not "knowingly misrepresent" anything to nurses

ANALYSIS: This case demonstrates the difficulty of proving two allegations: breach of an employee contract *and* fraud and misrepresentation. The case is particularly troublesome in view of the many hospital closings and unemployment. However, it is important to note that this is only one state court opinion. With the same or additional set of circumstances, it is possible that another court might find a breach of an express or implied employment contract and fraud, especially when it was known by many people other than the employees that the hospital was for sale.

The duty of good faith and fair dealing to perform and enforce the contract is an implied term of all contracts.

Many times the presence of bad faith and unfair dealing is alleged when a breach of the contract occurs. In fact, some jurisdictions recognize bad faith and unfair dealing not only as a contract action but also a tort action.[27] The court may also utilize the finding of bad faith or unfair dealing to support a finding that a breach has effectively taken place, even though that is not initially alleged.[28]

Parole Evidence Rule

This rule of contract interpretation is very important when challenging a contract and its terms. In its simplest form, the rule states that when a contract, will, or trust is a written one that both parties intend to represent the entire declaration of their agreement, the written document is legally binding on the parties. No other oral or written ("extrinsic") agreements made prior to, or contemporaneously with, that written contract can be used to modify or add to its terms.[29] For example, a nurse who attempts to challenge a contract term concerning a salary increase that did not take place will find it difficult to do so by attempting to rely on an earlier written promise concerning the salary when that promise did not end up in the final, written contract of employment.

The rule does not, however, forbid the use of prior written or oral evidence to challenge matters other than the contents of the contract. Therefore the nurse could use the earlier written promise as evidence to show that the employment agreement was affected by fraud, duress, mistake, misrepresentation, or prior custom or use.[30]

Statute of Frauds

The Statute of Frauds requires that certain contracts be in writing and signed by the party who must perform them. Its purpose is to ensure reliable, objective evidence of agreements. This is of particular importance after a substantial amount of time has passed since the contract was entered into and accurate recollection of its terms may have faded.

The Statute of Frauds requires that certain contracts be in writing and signed by the party who must perform them.

Each state in the United States except Louisiana has adopted in its respective statutes the *types* of contracts that must be in writing.[31] They are (1) an "agreement" in consideration of marriage; (2) a contract for the sale of goods amounting to $500 or more; (3) a promise to pay for the "debt, defaults or miscarriages" of another; (4) an "agreement" that cannot be performed within 1 year; and (5) a contract for the sale of interest in real estate, including a lease agreement, for more than 1 year.[32]

The requirement of a written instrument may be satisfied by a formal contract or a "written memorandum" that is sufficiently clear as to the subject matter of the contract and its terms.[33] In addition, the memorandum need not be one single document, but may consist of several documents.[34] The several documents must be referred to within the main or initial writing (called incorporating by reference).

The Statute of Frauds can affect a nurse in many ways. It may be used, for example, to defeat a nurse's claim when fired after 6 months of employment, that he or she had been offered a 5-year contract of employment, and there is no written document supporting the nurse's claim. Or, if a nurse entrepreneur enters into an agreement to purchase real estate to eventually open a clinic on that property, the agreement must be in writing in order not to be challenged under the Statute of Frauds.

COMPLETION OF CONTRACT

A contract can be ended in several ways. The most obvious is when the contract is performed; that is, the contract is adhered to, performance occurs, and the obligations under the contract are met. The result then is termination of the contract; no further obligations under the contract exist.

Sometimes, however, there is a need to end a contract because of problems that arise among and between the parties. When, for example, it is impossible for the contract to be performed, the contract is not seen as realistically enforceable. If the nurse lecturer, for example, contracted to do the 3-day workshop in a foreign country and war broke out in that country the day the nurse was to leave for the workshop, enforcing it would be foolish at best.

However, the nurse lecturer and the organization could renegotiate their agreement, thus ending the initial contract and entering into another. This is called accord and satisfaction.

The nurse lecturer and the entity may decide, however, that because of the unpredictability of the war, it would be unwise to end the initial contract and enter into another. They agree, then, to rescind the contract and end their respective obligations under it by treating it as though it never existed.[35] The two parties can do so because there are no third parties who have a vested interest in the contract or irrevocable assignments under it.

BREACH OF CONTRACT

A breach of contract occurs when one party to a contract fails to perform, without a legal justification, any major promise or obligation under the contract.[36] In addition to simply failing to perform one's obligations, a breach can also occur in other ways, such as making it impossible for the other party to perform his or her obligations or by declaring that one's obligations will not be carried out ("repudiation"). When the breach occurs, the nonbreaching party can sue for any damages, so long as that party can show that *but for* the breach, he or she is willing and able to perform the contract.

Table 9–2 lists the types of remedies the nonbreaching party can seek when a suit is filed alleging a breach of a contract.

SPECIAL CONSIDERATIONS

Express or Implied Promises Given in the Delivery of Health Care

One way contract law principles can be applied to the delivery of health care is by incorporating implied rules of conduct to the health care provider. Thus, when a nurse psychotherapist undertakes therapy with a depressed client, and recovery does not occur because of an alleged fault on the part of the nurse, the court may impose an implied contractual provision that governs the relationship. For example, a provision that might be applicable is that the nurse must provide therapy with the required skill and care in exchange for the payment of his or her fee by the client. Thus, if the nurse failed to provide such skill and care, the client can recover any amounts paid out pursuant to that treatment and the resulting breach (e.g., fees paid to the nurse for therapy). These types of damages are compensatory damages—those compensating the client/plaintiff as a result of the implied agreement.

A second way in which contract law can be applied to health care delivery is when an express promise or warranty is made by the health

TABLE 9–2
Breach of Contract Remedies

REMEDY	COMMENTS	EXAMPLE
Compensatory damages	Nonbreaching party must minimize losses, if possible, until contract dispute resolved	Nurse owns temporary nurse agency and has a contract with hospital; hospital does not abide by contract; agency must try to enter into contract with another hospital; agency also seeks attorney fees, punitive damages, and any other damages spelled out in contract ("liquidated damages")
Specific performance	Nonbreaching party asks that contract be carried out; court grants when goods are unique and not personal services; often requested when compensatory damages not adequate	Nurse-inventor does not deliver designed surgical instrument to manufacturing company; company sues for delivery
Injunction	Equitable remedy; court does not have to allow; can be prohibitory or mandatory injunction	Manufacturer asks court to prohibit nurse from giving instrument to other companies, or require nurse to deliver it to them
Reformation	Court can amend or remodel contract based on real or original intent of contract	Court says hospital in above example must use agency for 3 more months

Data from: Henry Campbell Black. *Black's Law Dictionary*. 6th Edition. St. Paul, Minn: West Publishing Company, 1991.

care provider to the patient. Using the above example, if the nurse psychotherapist promises to cure a client's depression and that does not happen, an express contract may be held to exist by the court when the cure does not occur. As with implied contract theory, damages that would be awarded would be based on any money the plaintiff expended as part of the express agreement.

It is important to note that generally the law is not fond of finding express contracts in the context of health care delivery.[37] Because much of what a health care provider says to a patient concerning his or her treatment is more in the form of opinion, reassurance, and optimistic prediction rather than a clear contract, the law requires the patient-plaintiff to clearly prove all the elements of the formation of an express contract.[38] Even so, with the changes in health care delivery today, including but not limited to the proliferation of PPOs, HMOs and other managed care delivery systems, the nurse is well advised to proceed cautiously when discussing health care treatment and results with patients.

Witnessing Special Contracts of Patients

No one comes into a hospital or other health care delivery system for care because he or she is well. Rather, consumers of health care are in need of health care services, whatever their nature. At times the condition that is present requires extensive treatment, and the survival of the individual may be in question. As a result, many times nurses are asked to witness various documents that the patient deems necessary to complete in the event of worsening of his or her condition and inability to speak for himself or herself, or in the event of death.

The documents most often needed by patients include a testamentary will (disposes of property), an advance directive(s) for health care (living will, durable power of attorney, or medical directive), and an advance directive for financial decisions. To ensure their validity and attest to the testator or declarant's soundness of mind when executing the documents, witnesses are helpful, sometimes required. Although it might seem natural, even helpful, for the nurse to witness these documents, it is prudent for the nurse to think carefully about doing so.

> *Although it might seem natural, even helpful, for the nurse to witness . . . documents, it is prudent for the nurse to think carefully about doing so.*

First of all, the nurse must check his or her institution or agency's policy concerning the witnessing of personal documents. Generally, most health care delivery systems have adopted a position that nursing staff should not do so. This prohibition is frequently based on state laws that restrict health care employees, including nurses, from witnessing certain documents. Such a policy may seem contrary to a policy that allows the nurse to witness a patient's signature on a consent, or refusal of consent, form for treatment. However, upon closer analysis, the distinction is somewhat logical because of the nature of the personal documents.

The testamentary will, for example, is clearly not something that is within the purview of the provision of nursing care. Furthermore, it is a highly personal document. Therefore, the rationale goes, the nurse need not be involved in its execution.

Although an advance directive is intimately connected to the delivery of health care, it is generally agreed—in fact, even mandated in some state statutes—that a health care provider *providing* care to a patient *should not* witness the signing of an advance directive. This prohibition eliminates any contest as to the influence the health care provider or the institution may have had on the patient in executing the advance directive.

If the nurse decides to witness a will or advance directive and the witnessing is not con-trary to agency or institution policy or state statutory law, then it is important for the nurse to understand that he or she may be called upon to testify to the following, and other issues, should the signing of the document be brought into question:

▼ In the case of a will, did the testator sign the document in his or her presence?

▼ What was the testator or the declarant's state of mind when signing the will or advance directive?

▼ Who, if anyone, was also present when the signing took place?

▼ What, if anything, did the testator or declarant say about the document and what he or she was asking the nurse to do?

▼ Did the testator or declarant seem to freely sign the document or was he or she coerced or under duress?

▼ Who took possession of the document once it was signed?

Also important for the nurse would be the necessity of documenting in the patient's record the event, who was present, the observed state of mind of the patient, and any comments made by the patient before, during, or after the document was signed.

SUMMARY OF PRINCIPLES AND APPLICATIONS

Contract law permeates a large part of health care delivery, whether directly or indirectly. It influences a nurse's purchase of professional liability insurance and governs a nurse's relationship with his or her union, as examples. Although it does not always receive the attention it may deserve when comparing it with other areas of health care law, such as professional negligence or refusal of treatment, it is nonetheless a key area of concern for the nurse. Furthermore, contract law can be a valuable tool to challenge employment and other decisions that are adverse to the nurse's interest if an express or implied contract governs the situation. Therefore the nurse should remember the following:

▼ To be valid, a contract must be formed with the capacity to enter into it, a "meeting of the minds," legal consideration, and no defenses that would void it.

▼ A contract can exist in many forms, including oral, written, express, implied, unilateral, bilateral, and adhesion.

▼ The Statute of Frauds requires that certain contracts must be in writing, and if they are not, no contract will be found to exist.

▼ Rules of contract interpretation exist to help reach a decision by the court as to the validity of a contract's terms.

▼ A contract is not fulfilled if a breach of the contract occurs. When that happens, remedies possible against the breaching party include money damages (compensation), specific performance, reformation of the contract, or an injunction.

▼ Good faith (or fair dealing) is an implied term of all contracts.

▼ The presence of certain factors—incapacity, minority—may render the contract void, voidable, unenforceable, or unconscionable.

▼ Defenses to contract formation include duress, fraud, mistake, and undue influence.

▼ The nurse must take care not to warrant or expressly state a specific cure, result, or outcome when providing care to patients.

▼ Witnessing patient contracts—testamentary wills or advance directives—may be against agency policy and state law.

▼ If the nurse believes that he or she has an express contract breached, or an implied one not adhered to, he or she should seek counsel and determine if the principles of contract law can aid the nurse in obtaining a remedy for the unfulfilled arrangement.

TOPICS FOR FURTHER INQUIRY

1. Analyze at least two employment contracts for health care providers. If possible, one should be for a nurse. Identify the various provisions in the contract, including provisions for a breach of contract, termination of the contract, and remedies specified (e.g., suit, arbitration, injunctive relief). Suggest additions to the contracts that might be beneficial to the health care provider. Draft language to include in the contracts.

2. Identify suits against health care providers in your state that allege breach of implied or express warranty. Analyze the data obtained as to types of health care providers sued; specific allegations in the suits; types of damages sought by the plaintiffs; and how the suits were resolved (e.g., settlement, verdict).

3. Write a paper on a specific remedy for breach of a contract. Discuss the mechanisms of the remedy and what types of damages can be obtained in your state. Suggest options for a resolution of the situation sued for other than the remedy selected for the paper.

4. Compare and contrast living will statutes in at least four states for language concerning the witnessing of the document by health care providers. Analyze the legislative history of the statute for reasons why the language was decided upon during the legislative process. Either support or reject the rationale in the paper and present reasons for either position.

REFERENCES

1. W. Page Keeton. *Prosser and Keeton On The Law of Torts.* 5th Edition. St. Paul, Minn: West Publishing Company, 1984, 657 (with 1988 Pocket Part), *citing DuBois v. Decker,* 29 N.E. 313 (1891); *McNevins v. Lowe,* 40 Ill. 209 (1866); *Napier v. Greenzweig,* 256 F. 196 (2nd Cir. 1919).
2. *Id.* at 655.
3. *Id.* at 656.
4. Henry Campbell Black. *Black's Law Dictionary.* 6th Edition. St. Paul, Minn: 1991, 224.

5. John Camamari and Joseph Perillo. *The Law of Contracts.* 3rd Edition. St. Paul, Minn: West Publishing Company (1987) (with updates).

6. Black, *supra* note 4, at 224–227.

7. Camamari and Perillo, *supra* note 5, at 691–719.

8. Example adopted from "Question 34," *in* Gordon Schaber and Claude Rohwer. *Contracts in a Nutshell.* 3rd Edition. St. Paul, Minn: West Publishing Company, 1990, 433.

9. Ron Coleman, "Contracts and Consumer Issues," *in You and the Law: The American Bar Association Consumer Guide.* Lincolnwood, Ill: Publications International, Ltd, 1990, 294.

10. *Id.* at 293.

11. 730 ILCS 5/5–5–5 (1990).

12. *Id.*

13. Camamari and Perillo, *supra* note 5, at 306.

14. 750 ILCS 30/5 (1980).

15. 710 ILCS 15/7 (1977).

16. Black, *supra* note 4, at 26.

17. Coleman, *supra* note 9, at 287.

18. *Id.* at 288.

19. *Id.* at 289.

20. Black, *supra* note 4, at 211.

21. *Id.*

22. Coleman, *supra* note 9, at 294–298.

23. 594 A. 2d 766 (1991).

24. Camamari and Perillo, *supra* note 5, at 418–424. See also *Restatement of Contracts, First,* Sections 230, 233, 236 (1932); *Restatement of Contracts, Second,* Sections 201, 202, 203, 211 (1981, with updated Supplements).

25. *Restatement of Contracts, Second,* Section 205 (1981, with updated Supplements); Schaber and Rower, *supra* note 8, at 175.

26. *Restatement of Contracts, Second,* Section 205, Comment d (1981, with updated Supplements).

27. Schaber and Rohwer, *supra* note 8, at 179–180.

28. Schaber and Rohwer, *supra* note 8, at 179.

29. Black, *supra* note 4, at 771.

30. *Id.* at 580.

31. *Id.* at 318.

32. Camamari and Perillo, *supra* note 5, at 770–844.

33. *Id.* at 816–817.

34. *Id.* at 825.

35. Coleman, *supra* note 9, at 905.

36. *Id.* at 318.

37. Theodore LeBlang, Eugene Basanta, Douglas Peters, Keith Fineberg, and Donald Kroll. *The Law of Medical Practice in Illinois.* Rochester, NY: The Lawyers Cooperative Publishing Company, 1986, 397 (with September 1993 Cumulative Supplement).

38. *Id.* at 397–398.

2

part two

Legal Issues

10

Ethics and Nursing Practice

Margaret R. Douglas, R.N., M.S.

contents

Today, perhaps more than ever before, nurses are going to the margins of their practice as they walk with clients through birth, suffering, death, and the moments between. As they enter the twenty-first century, nurses in the United States are practicing in what is simultaneously among the best and the worst of health care systems in the industrialized world. Nurses face incredibly complex situations as technology, morality, and economics interact within the context of human health. Nurses and patients together participate in the intricate dance among law, ethics, and economics, as ways of honoring life, health, and personhood unfold in a maze of paradoxes. Beliefs about the nature and development of human life and health are being challenged as never before. On the one hand, genetic and technologic innovations produce possibilities for creating and controlling new life. On the other hand, values about sanctity and quality of life compete with one another when persons are experiencing profound, unremitting suffering. Nurses collaborate in providing technologically superior care to some persons, while they seek to improve basic primary health care services in communities that are struggling with poverty and its correlates—inadequate housing, sanitation, nutrition, and education. Public health nurses at the turn of the twentieth century confronted similar issues of access to health care for unserved and underserved persons. Then, as now, ethics and issues of social justice were central concerns of nursing.

. . . nurses in the United States are practicing in what is simultaneously among the best and the worst of health care systems in the industrialized world.

It is not surprising, therefore, that ethics is regaining its place as a foundation of practice. The dominance of science or empirics as the essence of practice is being balanced by dialogue about what is right and what is just. Persons can justify extremely different ethical decisions through appeal to theories, principles, rules, and the "facts" of a given situation. Interpretation of ethical situations is grounded not only in ethical theories and moral principles, but also in moral reasoning and caring. Decades of philosophical, theoretical, empirical, and clinical work in ethics in nursing are coalescing into a new model of ethics that offers possibilities for informing and perhaps transforming nursing and health care. The ethics of care is at the heart of the emerging paradigm. This chapter will present an overview of nursing ethics as the ethics of care in relationship to ethical theories, moral principles, law, and nursing practice.

BIOETHICS, NURSING ETHICS, AND BIOMEDICAL ETHICS

What is nursing ethics, and how is it similar to and different from biomedical ethics and from law? Ethics, or moral philosophy, is concerned with the systematic study of morality—standards of moral conduct and moral judgment. Morality addresses traditions of belief about right and wrong human conduct.[1] Not all values or customs governing human conduct are moral

KEY PRINCIPLES

Relationships between Ethics and Law

Conflicts between Ethics and Law

Bioethics

Ethical Theories

Moral Principles

Moral Reasoning

Ethics of Care

Covenantal Relationships

values. Some customs or values may refer to other matters, such as economics, etiquette, esthetics, or culture. To differentiate morality from other norms of human conduct, Beauchamp[2] identified four properties that frequently are present in moral judgments. A judgment generally is considered to be a moral judgment if it has overriding social importance; prescribes a general course of action; is universalizable; and/or pertains to the general welfare of a social group.

Normative ethics refers to application of ethical theories, moral principles, and/or rules to specific situations or acts. Bioethics is the application of ethical theories and moral principles to life and to work. Nursing ethics, biomedical ethics, and ethics of other health care disciplines such as medical social work are dimensions of bioethics (Figure 10–1).

RELATIONSHIPS AMONG ETHICS, LAW, AND NURSING PRACTICE

The relationships between law and ethics is like some kind of free-spirited dance in which first one partner leads, then the other. Sometimes the partners dance in unison; sometimes they dance freely and simultaneously—disconnected from one another. At other times, one partner looks on as the other dances alone. Occasionally, as in the example of the Patient Self-

Determination Act[3] (PSDA), both partners dance a similar dance together as the audience of economics and special interests groups observes and tries to choreograph. Thus, law and ethics serve to inform one another in a relationship that occasionally is united and frequently is characterized by tension.

In an effort to clarify the interrelationships of ethics and law, Diane Kjervik,[4] a nurse-attorney, analyzed writings in both law and ethics to identify patterns of connection between the two. She concluded that there were at least three possible views: (1) *coextensive*, (2) *separate*, and (3) *partially overlapping*.

Patterns of Relationships between Law and Ethics

Coextensive Relationships

In the coextensive relationship (Figure 10–2), "law and ethics share the same scope in terms of matters considered."[4] In a pluralistic society such as contemporary United States society, the coextensive view more frequently represents the ideal than the actual relationship between ethics and law. In the coextensive relationship, law and ethics may inform one another in at least two ways. When there is genuine, principled dis-

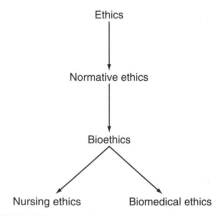

FIGURE 10–1 Nursing ethics as a component of normative ethics. (Data from: Goldstein DM Scope Note 19: Nursing ethics: a selected bibliography, 1987 to present. *Kennedy Institute of Ethics Journal* 1992; 2[2], 177–192.)

FIGURE 10-2 Coextensive relationship between ethics and law.

agreement about the "good" or "just" case, law may help to inform ethics. Conversely, values may need to be negotiated through persuasion so that an overriding moral value may be discerned. In this latter situation, ethics would inform law. Such a process would be cyclical and nonlinear. The Patient Self-Determination Act is a close, although not perfect, example of coextensive relationships. In the Patient Self-Determination Act, the moral principle of respect for autonomy is affirmed through legislation requiring health care entities and providers receiving Medicare and Medicaid funds to ask persons if they have an advance directive, and if not, if they wish to execute an advance directive to express their treatment preferences in certain situations.

Separate Relationships

A separate relationship between law and ethics identified by Kjervik is the second configuration in Figure 10–3. In the separate relationship, law and ethics are discrete and independent of one another. Each is concerned with "entirely distinct matters." If law and ethics were considered to be mutually exclusive, then one would not appeal to law for resolution of ethical issues. Furthermore, in instances in which existing legislation clearly conflicts with morality, civil disobedience may be argued to be morally required.

Partially Overlapping Relationships

The third possible relationship is a partially overlapping relationship described by Kjervik as represented symbolically in either of two ways, depending upon the context. One form of the relationships may be illustrated by two inter-

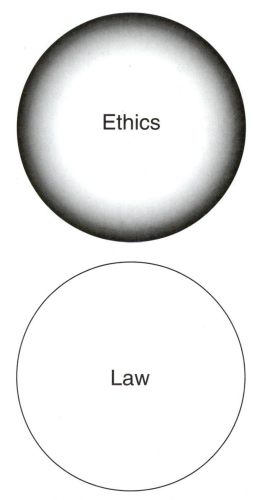

FIGURE 10-3 Separate relationship between ethics and law.

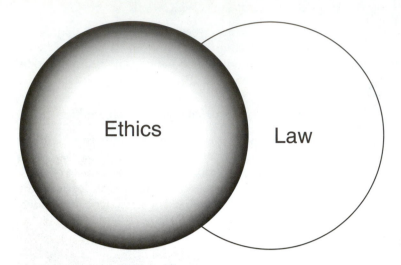

FIGURE 10–4 Overlapping relationship between ethics and law.

locking circles (Figure 10–4). The second form, by a circle within a larger circle (Figure 10–5). Of the two possibilities, Kjervik prefers the latter when the larger circle represents ethical matters and the smaller circle represents legal circumstances. This conception of law's being embedded within ethics is consistent with the observation that some ethical issues extend beyond the boundaries of law.

Complex Relationships

Although Kjervik's model may account adequately for the range of relationships between

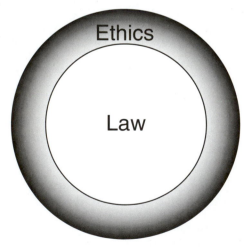

FIGURE 10–5 Overlapping relationship between ethics and law.

ethics and law, the full array of influences on both law and ethics is extremely complex. For example, values help to inform both law and ethics in intricate patterns of relationships. The values that interact with law and ethics include, but are not limited to, cultural, spiritual, religious, and economic values. In times of scarce or seemingly scarce economic resources, the relationship of economic values to law and morality becomes more critical than in times when resources are abundant. The current controversies and issues surrounding access to health care and health care reform highlight the interaction of economics with law and ethics. Law, ethics, and other values may interrelate in many ways, including the possibilities of coextension, separation, and overlapping described by Kjervik.

According to Schneider,[5] "the spirit of the law has penetrated into the bosom of bioethics" as law provides the languages of a "systematically disciplined language for thinking about bioethics . . . and a tool" for translating rhetoric into action. Schneider asserts that law is not wholly advantageous for bioethics, but has the disadvantages of inapt language and a penchant for failing to achieve its goals.

Bioethics, on the other hand, Schneider continues, is not entirely an academic discipline, but a political movement as well. The legal discourse of rights and the bioethical moral principle of autonomy illustrate the differences between the language of law and the language of bioethics. Bioethics can describe a principle of autonomy in a manner to assume the full range of relevant moral considerations. But the law is constrained because it is an agency of social regulation and therefore must find authority in legal precedent of the past, while at the same time, being always aware that it is setting legal precedent for the future.

This deliberative support of existing rights without establishing new rights is illustrated in the cases of *Roe v. Wade*[6] and *Cruzan*.[7] In *Cruzan*, the United States Supreme Court was asked to declare a constitutional right to die. Schneider contends that the Supreme Court might have supported a constitutional right to die had it not been for the right to abortion that was established by *Roe v. Wade*, a decision that has been contested for two decades.

. . . the language of law is designed to fulfill its task of social regulation, not to address the full and complex scope of morality . . .

Although "privacy" rights were at stake in both cases, the majority of the Court did not find a constitutional "right to die" in *Cruzan*. Citing Oliver Wendell Holmes,[8] Schneider illustrates that the language of law is designed to fulfill its task of social regulation, not to address the full and complex scope of morality: "The law is full of phraseology drawn from morals, and by the mere force of language continually invites us to pass from one domain to the other without perceiving it. . . . Manifestly, therefore, nothing but confusion of thought can result from assuming that the rights of man in a moral sense are equally rights in the sense of the Constitution and the law." Bioethicists who refer to the law as the moral minimum[9] also are ad-

dressing the usefulness of law in social regulation and its limitation in the complex, dynamic discourse of bioethics in which casuistry (case analysis) is a dominant model.

The extent of societal pluralism is a key factor in understanding which of the possible configurations best expresses the relationships between ethics and law in any given situation. In a pluralistic society, the prevailing moral values may be diverse and conflicting, thus making it difficult to discern whose values are being represented in any given legislation. The Patient Self-Determination Act assumes the high value for respect for autonomy that seems to dominate much of health care policy in the United States. Cross-culturally, however, interdependence and community may be of greater value than a given individual's rights. Among many indigenous people throughout the world, for example, decisions are made within the context of family and/or the community.

Abortion legislation also illustrates this phenomenon. Even in a predominantly Roman Catholic nation such as the Irish Republic, anti-abortion legislation that once represented the dominant moral values and religious beliefs of its male citizens is being challenged. The long-standing conflict between "pro-choice" and "pro-life" constituencies in the United States highlights the difficulties of attempting to enact legislation that is in harmony with the dominant values of a pluralistic society.

Time is another factor in the relationship among law, ethics, and values. There is a time lag, perhaps analogous to an incubation period, among changes in values, prevailing views of morality, and law. In the case of some civil rights legislation, the lag time required for congruence to occur between the ethical posture of the nation and the enactment of legislation was nearly a century—one that was punctuated by periods of civil disobedience.

Conflicts between Law and Ethics

Conflicts between legal and moral rights are common. Moral rights frequently are considered to exist independently of and form a basis for justifying or criticizing legal rights. In the United States, Congress generally is concerned with legal rights. The United Nations, on the other hand, focuses on human rights, moral rights that are intended to correct deficiencies in legal rights in various nations.

Health Care Law and Ethics

The right to health care is an example of a conflict between legal and moral conceptions of rights. In 1983, the *President's Commission for the Study of Ethical Problems in Medical and Behavioral Research*[10] held that a standard of "equitable access to health care requires that all citizens be able to secure an adequate level of care without excessive burdens." This finding provided only a weak statement of society's general obligation to provide access to health care and gave little direction for prospective legislation of health care entitlements. Childress[11] pointed out that there were "too many holes in the safety net; too many cracks in the floor" of the report of the President's Commission. Powers, an attorney, commented that Morris Abram, chairman of the President's Commission, "explicitly argued against adopting language recognizing a right to access to health care because of its potential influence upon future court decisions."[12] Individuals whose liberty interests have been curtailed, perhaps by imprisonment or institutionalization for mental illness, do have a positive legal right to health care.

Arguments supporting health care as a positive right sometimes contend that health care is a public good analogous to education and police or fire protection. Such arguments generally have not prevailed. In fact, according to Powers, opponents of health care as a positive right have countered with the argument that state and local governments have no constitutional obligation to provide *any* "substantive services within their borders."

Court decisions in the United States have tended to support negative rights with no cor-

responding entitlements. Negative rights require others to refrain from acting. The right to refuse treatment and the right to die are examples of negative rights that obligate professionals to not intervene. For example, in abortion decisions in the early 1980s, the Court held that even though women had a fundamental right to abortion without governmental interference, there was no corresponding obligation of the federal government to pay for the abortion procedures, except to save the mother's life or in cases of rape or incest.[13]

Ethical-Legal Influences on Nursing Practice

The dialogue between case law and casuistry (case analysis) in ethics has helped to clarify the position of nursing and other disciplines regarding a number of issues, especially those concerned with refusal of life-sustaining (or life-prolonging) measures. In the course of less than half a century, industrialized societies have needed to modify the goal of prolonging life through curative treatments for fatal or incapacitating diseases and/or injuries. As life-sustaining and/or prolonging technology has developed, questions of balancing the benefits and burdens of duration of life with those of quality of life have arisen. This plethora of technologic cures that both enhance and devastate human life is a relatively recent event, one that requires an interdisciplinary dialogue to address in a responsible, compassionate way.

The Patient Self-Determination Act and state advance directive and health care surrogacy legislation are examples of how the moral principles, such as respect for autonomy, are supported by laws that affirm individuals' positive right to have information about treatment options and to express those choices in advance directives, such as living wills or durable powers of attorney. In the Patient Self-Determination Act, there is a corollary obligation of institutions and other health care providers to provide clients with information about their rights regarding treatment alternatives and the right to refuse treatment. The political, economic, ethical, and legal positions represented in the Patient Self-Determination Act emerged, in part, from the widely publicized *Cruzan* case and the earlier *Quinlan* case.

Ethics Committees

The *In the Matter of Karen Quinlan*[14] case was among the first of the highly visible cases that raised questions about futility of treatment and resulted in the prognosis committees that were the precursors of today's ethics committees. Structure and membership of ethics committees vary. Some committees are called bioethics committees, and others are referred to as medical ethics committees. Some institutions have separate nursing ethics committees. Nurses generally serve on all types of committees along with representatives from other disciplines, such as pastoral care, medical social work, law, medicine, and community representatives.

Many of the first ethics committees were formed to offer consultation services on a case-by-case basis in hospitals and medical centers. A few of the early ethics committees served as ethical decision-making groups, although this decision-making or decision-recommending function was deliberately avoided by most committees. Most ethics committees reviewed specific cases either as they occurred or retrospectively. As the interfaces of personhood, ethics, law, professional practice, and technologic possibilities for treatment were revealed through case review, clients and health care personnel began to use the consultative services of representatives of the ethics committees for the ethics consultant, rather than requesting ad hoc review by the full committees.

Functions of contemporary ethics committees are changing from focus on case analysis and review to emphasis on teaching and policy development. Educational and policy-development initiatives address but are not limited to those relevant to health care rights legislation

and regulation, such as the Patient Self-Determination Act and Joint Commission on the Accreditation of Health Care Organizations (JCAHO) criteria regarding patient rights. Policies such as those related to informing patients about the *American Hospital Association Statement on a Patient's Bill of Rights*[15] advance directive legislation, "Do Not Resuscitate," and futile treatment generally are created and/or revised in ethics committees.

Functions of contemporary ethics committees are changing from focus on case analysis and review to emphasis on teaching and policy development.

As legislation and morality change, nursing's positions on related issues change as well. Nurses' rights and responsibilities are expressed in such documents as the *Code for Nurses: With Interpretive Statements*,[16] *Nursing's Social Policy Statement*,[17] and the American Nurses Association position statements on advance directives and withholding and/or withdrawal of artificially administered nutrition and/or hydration. Such codes, policies, and position statements are central to professional practice. The margins of practice are blurring still further as the dialogue extends to both extremes of treatment—from futile treatment to essential treatment. As managed care is emerging as an economically driven model of health care delivery, persons are concerned that they will not receive the type and quality of care that they believe is required.

Although nursing, with its focus on the ethics of care, has no comparable concept to that of the biomedical principle of medical futility, that is, there is not a time when competent care and comfort measures are deemed to be futile, nurses do have an advocacy role in helping people to secure the nature and quality of care that is essential to life and health. Nurses and other health care professionals need to be aware that some persons are executing advance directives that stipulate the nature and extent of treatment they want to receive, not only those measures that they wish to refuse. Cases such as that of *Helga Wanglie*[18] may help to clarify the boundaries between required and optional treatment and care. Whatever the structures of the relationships among ethics, law, and nursing practice, the processes are fluid and dynamic.

Whatever the structures of the relationships among ethics, law, and nursing practice, the processes are fluid and dynamic.

NURSING ETHICS AS THE ETHICS OF CARE

The dark side of rights to refuse treatment and respect for autonomy is the possibility of abandonment. Janet Quinn,[19] a noted nurse scholar and healer, spoke of the current trend toward assuming personal responsibility for one's own health and illness as a "thinly disguised form of abandonment" unless services and education directed toward helping persons assume responsibility for their own care are provided. The emerging nursing ethics as an ethics of care recognizes that even though health and healing are societal and personal responsibilities, people need another to walk with them on the healing journey. This is particularly important in today's rapidly changing health care environment in which managed care models are replacing fee-for-service as dominant models of health care delivery.

Although there may have been a tendency toward overtreatment in the fee-for-service models, there is a trend toward undertreatment with managed care. As people negotiate an ever more complicated health care system, the risks of abandonment are high. Nurses and their colleagues from other disciplines are coming together as part of a moral community that is committed to the health and well-being of all human beings. Nursing's work has been called invisible;[20] nursing ethics, more concerned with private aspects of care, with the in-between.[21] This tapestry of interwoven, sometimes invisible, yet essential threads that represent nursing's work and nursing's ethics, is in juxtaposition to the more visible public aspects of medical ethics. The newly emerging nursing ethics seeks to reveal the invisible work of nursing, to respect the private, the in-betweenness of nurse-patient relationships, thereby honoring personhood. Paradoxically, this emerging ethics is not really new. Travelbee's[22] work has long considered the interpersonal dimensions of human-to-human relationships to be at the heart of professional nursing practice.

Caring, Morality, and Nurse-Patient Relationships

Nursing ethics, although long embedded within the context of bioethics and biomedical ethics, is emerging as a distinct type of normative ethics, an ethics of care.[23] What does it mean to say that nursing ethics is an ethics of care? What is caring, and how is an ethics of care grounded in or related to other conceptions of ethical theories and/or moral principles? Definitions of caring vary so widely that a substantive discussion about what caring means is beyond the scope of this chapter. Nevertheless, common themes in the caring literature suggest that caring is concerned with reciprocal human connections and relationships,[24] preserving personhood in a world of objectivity,[25] and alleviating vulnerability.[26] The status of caring as a moral standard is still in a fluid, evolutionary state. Caring is argued to be a virtue, an imperative, or a moral ideal.[27, 28] Despite such ambiguity, caring is considered to be an emerging foundation for ethics in nursing.[29-31]

As nursing matures as a discipline and as the solutions of science simultaneously resolve and create health care problems, the need for an ethic of relationship that cherishes all persons has seldom been greater. The work of Carol Gilligan[32, 33] and nurse philosophers and theorists such as Patricia Benner,[34, 35] Barbara Carper,[36] Sally Gadow,[37] Madeleine Leininger,[38] and Jean Watson[39] explore how an ethics of care may serve to create moral community as nurses and others affirm the value of relationship in health care. Watson[40] proposes that "an ethic of care has a distinct moral position: caring is attending and relating to a person in such a way that the person is protected from being reduced to the moral status of objects . . . ." Nursing ethics as the ethics of care is grounded in the human-to-human relationships that are referred to as the nurse-patient/client relationship.

Covenantal Relationships

A variety of models of physician-patient relationship have been examined for their relevance to nurse-patient relationships.[41-44] In one view of the nurse-patient relationship, it is portrayed as a covenant.[45, 46] Covenantal relationships are characterized by (1) mutual exchange of gifts; (2) entrustment; and (3) endurance.[47] Patients give at least two kinds of gifts to nurses—the individual gift of participation and presence in the relationship and the social gift of support for education and regulation of professional practice. Nurses give patients the gift of competent, caring practice that is consistent with professional standards and statutory regulations.

Although patients and nurses are strangers when they first meet, they trust each other to fulfill the expectations that they have of each other. In most instances, nurses expect that patients will be open and honest in the information they share about their own health and experiences of illness. Patients expect that nurses will be competent to practice according to legal and professional standards. In addition, nurses expect that patients will engage in the health practices or treatments that are negotiated through the nursing process. Patients, in turn, expect that the nurse will provide care as long as it is needed. Covenantal relationships are not static. According to Beauchamp, they are a process of mutual discovery of those health practices that are *negotiated* within the context of ongoing developing relationship. Furthermore, the *mutuality of perspectives* is *constantly evolving* and must be re-evaluated as goals emerge that were not clearly seen before. Finally, and perhaps most importantly, each person is changed in the relationship. Table 10–1 illustrates the characteristics of covenantal nurse-patient relationships.

Covenantal Relationships and Conflict

Covenantal relationships are not idyllic connections in which everything always goes smoothly. The assumption that nurses will not abandon patients is being challenged as nursing practice is influenced by scarce financial resources. Societal patterns of drug use and violence against strangers limits patients' willingness to be open and honest in entrusting their well-being to strangers. Furthermore, some believe covenantal relationships contain seeds of conflict.

Allen,[47] in his book *Love & Conflict*, proposes two categories of covenants: inclusive and special. Inclusive covenants are open to all persons by virtue of their being human. Inclusive covenants are concerned with basic human rights and obligations. Special covenants are open only to those persons who meet specific criteria for membership. Examples of special covenants include marriage, family, and professional covenants. Parents, for example, have obligations for the health and safety of their own children that exceed the obligations they have for the children of strangers. People have a wide variety of covenantal relationships all at once. For instance, nurses are members of inclusive covenants that connect them with all other humans. In addition, they are in special covenantal relationships

TABLE 10–1
Characteristics of Covenantal Nurse-Patient Relationships

CHARACTERISTICS OF COVENANTAL RELATIONSHIPS	NURSES	PATIENTS
Exchange of gifts	Professional practice: competence in nursing knowledge and skills; commitment to attending and practicing according to legal and professional standards	Enabling privilege of professional practice: through willingness to participate in nurse-patient relationship and societal support of health care and educational institutions and regulation of practice
Entrustment	Willingness to enter as strangers into a continuing relationship	Willingness to entrust life and health to professional strangers
Endurance	Commitment to "walk with" patient through experiences of health—of wellness and illness; promise not to abandon	Commitment to follow through with recommended treatments or to be open with nurse about decision to refuse treatments

Data from: Allen JL. *Love & Conflict*. Lanham, Md: University Press of America, 1995.

with their families, their employers, and their professional organizations, for example.

Conflict occurs when the needs or obligations of some covenants are at odds with the needs or obligations of other covenants. When conflicts occur between two or more special covenants, creativity and negotiation skills can be used to preserve the integrity of the relationships. For example, nurses who are single mothers frequently experience such conflict when they are scheduled to work at the same time that one of their children is ill. Another family member, friend, or neighbor may care for the child, or another nurse may be willing to work an extra shift or work on a day off.

Earlier ways of examining ethical issues in health care, although necessary as reference points, are not sufficient to address the contextual complexities of health care possibilities and problems.

When conflicts occur between inclusive cove-

nants and special covenants, however, Allen argues that the commitment to the inclusive covenant should take precedence over the commitment to the special covenants. For example, a nurse who has witnessed the abuse of an elderly person is morally obligated to intervene to protect the person's safety and well-being even if a colleague or employer demands that the nurse overlook the situation.

Although it is emerging as a distinctive branch of bioethics and is clearly differentiated from biomedical ethics, nursing ethics, as the ethics of care, values ethical theories and moral principles as reference points and contexts within which to view specific actions and to arrive at moral choices together with patients. The technologic maze of possibilities for treatment offers a new challenge for everyone involved in life's journey—persons who are currently or potentially in need of treatment (this category includes everyone) and their families. Ethicists, lawyers, legislators, and health care professionals are struggling with the uncertainties about what is beneficial, burdensome, efficient, affordable, and compassionate. Earlier ways of examining ethical issues in health care, although necessary as reference points, are not sufficient to address the contextual complexities of health care possibilities and problems. Therefore, ethical theories and moral principles are necessary but not sufficient foundations for the moral life in nursing; such theories and principles offer structure and clarity to the covenantal dialogue. Together with a covenantal nurse-patient relationship, examination of relevant ethical theories and moral principles can help more fully to inform the moral life of nursing practice.

ETHICAL THEORIES, MORAL PRINCIPLES, AND MORAL REASONING

A variety of ethical theories and moral principles from philosophic and theologic ethics have offered a way of thinking about the moral life and ethical decision making in health care and nursing. Although each category of theories is useful in informing ethical decision making in nursing, all are limited in addressing the universe of ethical issues encountered in contemporary practice. Theories and moral principles serve as a reference point in the contextual, relational dimensions of nurse-patient covenants.

Ethical Theories

Three categories of theories in particular—virtue, consequentialist, and deontological—historically have served as a foundation for ethics in health care and nursing. Personalist theory, a fourth category of theories, is based in phenomenological philosophy and is emerging in concert with the current emphasis on caring as a central moral concept in nursing. Phenomenology is both a philosophy and a method that seeks to reveal the meaning of phenomena by describing them as accurately and completely as possible. The contemporary emphasis on caring as the moral foundation is grounded in a phenomenological world view. Table 10–2 lists selected ethical theories and their relationship to nursing.

Contractarian and rights-based theories sometimes are considered to be separate ethical theories. They will be considered here to be types of deontological theories. *Contractarian ethical theory* has some features in common with the Anglo-American legal system. In contract theory, the rules of ethics are a product of negotiated consensus. Contracts can be either formal or informal, individual or societal. Valid contracts hold that each party of the contract has duties to other parties.

Rights are the mirror images of duties or obligations. In their text, *Principles of Biomedical Ethics*, Beauchamp and Childress define rights as "justified claims that individuals can make upon others or upon society."[1] For each duty, there is a corresponding right. *Moral rights* are claims that are grounded in moral principles and/or rules. *Legal rights* are claims that are based upon legal principles and rules. Discussions of rights to health care, for example, may focus on health care as a moral right or as a legal right.

In addition to being categorized as moral or legal, rights also can be considered to be either *positive* or *negative*. A positive right is a claim that requires that some action be taken in behalf of individuals with justifiable claims. The right to information about health care treatment options is an example of a positive right that obligates health professionals to provide patients with the material necessary to make informed choices about treatment.

Moral Principles

Moral principles serve as a foundation for moral conduct and reference points for ethical decision making in nursing. Although less abstract and more context-specific than ethical theories, moral principles are at a higher level of abstraction than are rules or specific actions. For example, rules about informed consent are based on the moral principle of respect for autonomy.

What are the key moral principles and how many are there? There is disagreement among moral philosophers about the number of key moral principles. Some moral philosophers like Beauchamp and Childress argue that there are

TABLE 10–2

Selected Ethical Theories and Their Relationship to Nursing

ETHICAL THEORY	PHILOSOPHER/ ETHICIST	CENTRAL THESIS	RELEVANCE TO NURSING
Consequentialist (Teleological or Utilitarianism)	Jeremy Bentham John Stuart Mill	Outcome-oriented—from *telos* "end"—the principle of social utility, the greatest good or least harm for the greatest number	The principle of utility undergirds much of clinical nursing practice, social policy, and quantitative nursing research. Nursing process is goal-directed and outcome-oriented, as are critical pathways and Diagnostic Related Groups (DRGs)
Deontological	Immanuel Kant	Process-oriented—from *deon* "rule"—The rightness or wrongness of an act is determined by its inherent moral significance, not outcome	The *Code for Nurses: With Interpretive Statements* has a strong deontological focus. In early stages of nurse-patient relationships, standards of practice, institutional policies, etc., help to establish parameters of appropriate moral conduct
Virtue	Aristotle Alasdair MacIntyre	Person-oriented—Addresses moral life and values. Moral goodness or badness is discussed in terms of the moral value attached to the character trait or virtue	Historically, virtue theory was the basis for nursing's emphasis on the moral character of the nurse

Data from: Bentham J. *An Introduction to the Principles of Morals and Legislation.* New York: Hafner, 1948; Mill JS. *Utilitarianism,* Sher G, ed. Indianapolis: Hackett Publishing Company, 1979; Kant I. *Grounding for the Metaphysics of Morals,* Ellington, J, trans. Indianapolis: Hackett Publishing Company, 1981; ANA. *Code for Nurses: With Interpretive Statements.* Kansas City, Missouri: Author, 1985; Aristotle. *Nichomachean Ethics,* Book 2, Wardman AE, trans. In: Bambrough R. *The Philosophy of Aristotle.* New York: Mentor Books, 1966; MacIntyre A. *After Virtue.* Notre Dame: University of Notre Dame Press, 1981.

four moral principles. Others, such as Veatch,[48] identify six or more. The four principles of respect for autonomy, nonmaleficence, beneficence, and justice proposed by Beauchamp and Childress will be accepted for purposes of discussion in this chapter.

Other moral principles that generally are included in discussions of ethics in nursing include fidelity or promise-keeping, veracity or truth-telling, confidentiality, and privacy. These additional principles will be considered to be rules that are grounded in the four moral principles, especially in respect for autonomy.

The principles do not have a lexical, hierarchical order. Although there is a high value for autonomy in the United States and in the ANA's *Code for Nurses: With Interpretive Statements*, for example, there is no consensus about the rank ordering of moral principles. Ethicists frequently disagree about the overriding moral principles

that inform decisions in specific cases. The four moral principles relevant to nursing are defined in Table 10–3.

The Moral Principle of Respect for Autonomy

Respect for autonomy generally refers to individual freedom of choice or liberty interests. However, autonomy is not an "all-or-nothing" phenomenon. There are gradations of autonomy.[49, 50] Threats to autonomy arise from several sources, including uncertainty about how to interpret and respect autonomy. Two major ways that autonomy is threatened are by interfering too much (excessive control) and by not interfering enough (neglect). There is a fine line between respect for autonomy and abandonment, particularly in care of the chronically ill, mentally ill, physically disabled, adolescents, and the

TABLE 10–3	
Definitions of Moral Principles Relevant to Nursing	
MORAL PRINCIPLE	**DEFINITION**
Respect for autonomy	Self-determination—recognizes the right of persons to choose their actions freely without being constrained by the will or governance of others. Generally refers to individual freedom of choice or liberty interests. Three conditions of autonomous action are: (1) intentionality, (2) understanding, (3) absence of controlling influences.
Nonmaleficence	Doing no harm. Generally considered to be the first principle of human interaction (sometimes incorporated into the principle of beneficence)
Beneficence	Preventing harm, removing harm, and doing good
Justice	Fairness; giving to each his or her due (claim or entitlement)

Data from: Beauchamp TL, Childress JF. *Principles of Biomedical Ethics*, 4th Edition. New York: Oxford University Press, 1994.

elderly. Respect for autonomy also is threatened when the exercise of one person's autonomy rights interferes with another person's freedom of choice and action. This situation frequently occurs when ill persons are cared for at home by a family caregiver.

Much of the work on autonomy has been done in acute care settings. With managed care, prospective payment systems, and early hospital discharge, the ethics of community, home, and long-term care needs to be addressed more adequately than in the past. The predominant North American value for keeping patients out of nursing homes has the potential for threatening the autonomy of at least three categories of individuals: patients, their family caregivers, and their formal caregivers.

Patient autonomy is vulnerable to the gradual, unintended erosion of privacy rights and self-determination by caregivers. For example, family caregivers of persons with Alzheimer's disease (AD) reported that they were the sole decision makers for their relatives with AD.[51]

The autonomy of *family caregivers* may be endangered by society's expectation that the family has primary responsibility for providing health care to its own members.[52, 53] Patterns of decision-making about care of chronically ill persons have been based on the assumption that the welfare of the family is irrelevant to considerations about what is "the best thing to do" for their ill relative. This assumption is being challenged as ethicists call for a new view of autonomy and advocacy in long-term care. In addition, the high cost of nursing homes and the limited third-party reimbursement for long-term care place such an overwhelming financial burden on many families that they have few if any alternatives to caring for their ill family member at home. Finally, *formal caregivers* may find that their professional judgment is limited or overridden by the decisions of powerful family caregivers.[54]

Collopy, Dubler, and Zuckerman have explored issues of autonomy in home care and long-term care.[50, 55] They call for a model of autonomy that is collaborative or negotiated and is referred to as the "autonomy of accommodation." In negotiated autonomy, the liberty interests of all persons affected by a judgment are addressed in making decisions. This conception of autonomy is consistent with the idea of the moral community.

The Moral Principle of Nonmaleficence

The principle of nonmaleficence holds that one should do no harm. Discerning what is harmful is one of the most difficult problems in clinical practice. Although it is relatively easy to understand that some actions in and of themselves will be harmful to human life and/or health, it is less easy to determine when an action that is intended to be helpful actually harms. It is even more difficult to discern when refraining from action intentionally or unintentionally harms or risks harm to another. Few treatments are entirely beneficial and without risk of harm.

The dilemma of pain management in terminally ill clients illustrates the principle of nonmaleficence in both acting and refraining from acting.[56] As disease progresses and death becomes imminent, persons may experience excruciating pain, pain that is managed by increasingly large and potentially lethal doses of medication.[57–59] Nurses who struggle with the clinical judgment of whether and when to administer such treatments must consider the issue of harm, the standard of due care, and the ANA's *Code for Nurses: With Interpretive Statements*.

> Pro bono *or volunteer work is a professional obligation of beneficence. For example, some nurses and other health care professionals volunteer several hours per month at storefront clinics for homeless persons.*

The Moral Principle of Beneficence

Some ethicists consider that the principle of beneficence incorporates nonmaleficence. Beneficence, as explicated by Beauchamp and Childress, entails the obligations to (1) prevent harm, (2) remove harm, and (3) do good. The idea of balancing risks, harms, benefits, and effectiveness is grounded in the principle of be-

A PHYSICIAN SPEAKS OF SOCIAL JUSTICE

The United States ". . . is, first, a country morally imperiled, and those of us who care for patients cannot but do so in bad faith. This country and South Africa stand alone among industrial powers in having no national system of health care. Here, we have elected the commercialization of medicine rather than its socialization. The only aspect of our health policy which resembles a system is the systematic exclusion of millions. It is the fittest who benefit, not the frail, and not the vulnerable."

From: McGuire D. Forward: Medicine: a bedside view. *In*: McKenzie N., ed. *The Crisis in Health Care: Ethical Issues*. New York: Meridian (Penguin Group), 1990, pp. 11–18.

neficence. Although there is general agreement that beneficence involves personal, professional, and societal obligations, there is disagreement about what the strength and boundaries of those obligations are. *Pro bono* or volunteer work is a professional obligation of beneficence. For example, some nurses and other health care professionals volunteer several hours per month at storefront clinics for homeless persons.

The Moral Principle of Justice

Justice refers to fairness or to receiving one's due. Distributive justice, one type of justice, is concerned with the allocation and distribution of scarce benefits when there is competition for them. Theories of distributive justice typically address one or all of the following considerations about the distribution of benefits and burdens to each person: an equal share, according to individual need, according to individual effort, and according to societal contribution.

The language of justice frequently is used to discuss issues and policies concerning the allocation and distribution of scarce resources, including health care resources.[60–63] Table 10–4 lists several concepts of justice and their impact upon health care allocation.

JOHN RAWLS ON JUSTICE, INSTITUTIONS, AND LAW

". . . justice is the first virtue of social institutions as truth is of systems of thought. A theory, however elegant and economical, must be revised if it is untrue; likewise, laws and institutions, no matter how efficient and well-arranged, must be reformed or abolished if they are unjust."[64]

TABLE 10-4			
Conceptions of Distributive Justice that Inform Health Care Allocation			
CONCEPTION	**PHILOSOPHER**	**MAJOR IDEAS**	**HEALTH POLICY IMPLICATIONS**
Egalitarian	Aristotle	Equality in all respects of condition being considered (i.e., health care)	One-tier system. No one would be entitled to more or fewer benefits than anyone else in society.
Libertarian	John Stuart Mill Robert Nozick	Individual liberty should not be restricted on any grounds except that of harm to others (Mill) The minimal state is the most extensive state that can be justified (Nozick)	Two-tier system. Minimal health care benefits would be provided for those who have no resources to purchase more extensive goods and services. Goods and services beyond the minimum would depend upon one's ability to pay.
Decent minimum	John Rawls	Fairness: (1) Each person is to have an equal right to the most extensive basic liberty compatible with a similar liberty for others. (2) Social and economic inequalities are to be arranged so that they are both (a) reasonably expected to be to everyone's advantage, and (b) open to all.	A system that would define a standard of minimally decent health care that no one would fall below. Everyone would be able to compete for access to goods and services beyond the decent minimum.

Data from: Aristotle. *Nichomachean Ethics,* Book 2, Wardman AE, trans. In: Bambrough R, *The Philosophy of Aristotle,* New York: Mentor Books, 1966; Mill JS. *Utilitarianism,* G. Sher, Ed. Indianapolis: Hackett Publishing Company, 1979. (Original work published 1861); Nozick R. *Anarchy, State, and Utopia.* New York: Basic Books, Inc.; Rawls J. *A Theory of Justice.* Cambridge, Mass: The Belnap Press of Harvard University Press, 1971.

Rawls' *A Theory of Justice* is an example of a contractarian theory that sometimes is used to justify actual or proposed social policy. The recent and continuing issue of transforming the current health care system in the United States emerges, in part, from a question whether there is a moral right to access to health care goods and services. If so, then the question of how those goods and services can be fairly distributed among the population becomes a central concern.

Moral Reasoning

Moral reasoning is the interpretive process that helps to connect one's moral values with one's ethical choices. Through moral reasoning, one examines the salient features in an ethical situation and makes a judgment or chooses a course of action that is, presumably, congruent with one's moral beliefs and values. Moral values are not static, but change as persons mature.

Theorists of moral reasoning are attempting to discern the developmental patterns of moral values. Such developmental conceptions of moral reasoning include those of Piaget,[65] Kohlberg,[66, 67] Rest,[68] and Perry.[69, 70] Piaget was among the first psychologists to propose a developmental approach to the study of human values.

Kohlberg extended Piaget's work and proposed a linear, hierarchic model of three sequential levels, each of which contained two stages. In the first and lowest level, *preconventional morality,* moral behavior is grounded in external rules about right and wrong. In the second level, *conventional morality,* moral conduct is based on a sense of order and human relationships. In the third and highest level, *principled morality,* behavior is governed by a sense of social responsibility and justice.

Based on extensive comparative studies using Kohlberg's interviews and the *Defining Issues Test* (DIT), Rest and colleagues suggested that moral development was more complex than Piaget and Kohlberg had proposed. Rest proposed a four-component model of moral action that purports that four types of psychological processes are required for a person to take moral action: (1) moral sensitivity, (2) moral reasoning, (3) moral commitment, and (4) moral action.

Perry, another moral theorist, studied the development of undergraduate students' patterns of thought. From analysis of interview data, Perry and colleagues constructed a nine-position scheme of cognitive and ethical development that proceeded from *dualism* through *discovery of relativism* to *commitment in relativism*.

Gilligan, a moral psychologist, has discerned two moral orientations in human development. She argues that two moral visions—one of justice and one of care—recur in human experience.

The *justice orientation* focuses on oppression and inequality and values reciprocity and equal respect. The *care orientation* focuses on detachment or abandonment and values attention and response to need. Although both men and women evidence both justice and care concerns as they discuss moral issues, women tend to adopt a care perspective and men, a justice orientation.

Although both men and women evidence both justice and care concerns as they discuss moral issues, women tend to adopt a care perspective and men, a justice orientation.

Gilligan and her colleagues are discerning a different moral developmental pattern, one that reflects a high value for the contextual relevance of a situation. Gilligan's work, with its emphasis on human relationships and caring, resonates with nursing's contemporary focus on the ethics of care. Although several models of moral devel-

opment have been explored in nursing,[71] no one model of moral reasoning has adequately explained the complexities of ethical decision-making in the nursing profession. In addressing Gilligan's studies, Ray commented that Gilligan's work "reinforces the complexity of the ethical caring perspective."[72]

. . . no one model of moral reasoning has adequately explained the complexities of ethical decision-making in the nursing profession.

There is agreement among moral developmental theorists, however, that moral reasoning is linked to ethical decision-making. One's pattern of moral reasoning may help to determine the pattern of principles or values that is associated with ethical decision-making.

NARRATIVE AS A WAY OF REVEALING THE MORAL CORE OF NURSING

In ordinary moments of their everyday professional lives, nurses are privileged to participate in extraordinary moments in the lives of others. The ethics of care proposes a morally responsible way of sharing a person's journey through wellness, suffering, and illness. As technology, caring, and economics interact, nurses must reflect on the contemporary issues of practice and begin the conversation that will continue the development of a moral community. Chinn stated that community should be the context for exercising moral and practical reasoning that are founded on collectively formed values for, in this sense, the moral community becomes the crucible where collective "moral virtues, values, and principles guide interrelational behavior toward responsible choice-making for the good of the whole."[73] The controversial history of ethics committees[74] reflects one effort to ground decision-making within a moral community. Other efforts need to be made if all who participate in such decision making are to find moral peace, if not moral certainty.

Narrative discourse or story is at the heart of the ethics of care and of covenantal relationships. Narrative is a way of revealing community beliefs and values, of understanding which moral principles are operating and in what context.

The communal moral conversation will be fuller and richer if it acknowledges both the objective and subjective domains of human life, health, and values—the rational, analytic approaches of propositional discourse and the emotional, spiritual, and integrating approaches of narrative discourse. In addressing the need to value both types of discourse, Carson[75] remarked that in bioethics, propositional discourse is useful in selecting relevant ideas from the emotional array of deep feelings about life and death, suffering and healing, and arguing their merit, but propositional discourse has limitations because the link between sensibility and rationality has been severed. Bioethical rationality, he continues, has lost sight of the importance of imagination, which is composed of the emotions and the intellect.

Narrative discourse or story is at the heart of the ethics of care and of covenantal relationships. Narrative is a way of revealing community beliefs and values, of understanding which moral principles are operating and in what context. Benjamin commented that "narrative achieves an amplitude that information lacks."[76] Such narratives can appear in many forms—as prose, as poetry, and as other media. In the

foreword to *Remember Me*, Albert Anderson's book of poetry about his experience of syringomyelia, a paralyzing neurologic disorder, Edmund Pellegrino wrote:

> One man's mystery is too profound to be communicated to another man. And nowhere is this more true than with the universal experience of human illness. . . . Despite this, some singular humans can and do evoke, in all of us, the ability to feel some part of their experience. These are the poets, because poetry is, as May Sarton said, "the soul-making tool."[77]

Narrative and story are becoming increasingly important in nursing practice, education, and research. Diekelmann,[78] for example, has found that through the sharing of stories in clinical and educational settings, nurses are coming to a greater trust in their own clinical judgment and are valuing collaboration with colleagues and patients. Through story, nurses and their colleagues are creating multidimensional kaleidoscopic patterns that treasure the uniqueness of each person as he or she contributes to the intricate beauty of the group. Gadow[79] asserts that in nursing, story *is* truth.

ETHICAL DECISION-MAKING

From the perspective of truth as found in narrative, then, linear models of ethical decision-making have limits. Frequently what seems like an ethical conflict really is lack of information

---

A process of ethical decision-making that is grounded in an ethic of care and in covenantal relationships is contextual and communal. The kinds of questions asked and the alternatives proposed reflect an assumption that humans live in communities, not in isolation.

---

or understanding about the facts of the situation. Like the Sufi legend of the blind men describing an elephant, each person may possess different data and/or interpret the same data differently. A process of ethical decision-making that is grounded in an ethic of care and in covenantal relationships is contextual and communal. The kinds of questions asked and the alternatives proposed reflect an assumption that humans live in communities, not in isolation. Whenever possible, all persons who are involved in the decision are part of the process. The options proposed are not usually standard choices, but are creative alternatives that are unique to the persons and the communities involved. Some of the key questions are shown in Table 10–5.

IMPLICATIONS FOR NURSING PRACTICE

Morally responsible nursing practice requires that nurses know and examine their own values as well as the codified and emerging values of the discipline. Although it is important for nurses to be aware of the dramatic dilemmas that frequently accompany beginning- and end-of-life crises, nurses also must be sensitive to the more subtle ethical issues that are encountered every day. For example, changing staffing patterns in hospitals frequently raise issues of safety and effectiveness of nursing care. The use of a model of ethical decision-making that is consistent with their values and beliefs will help nurses to thoroughly and systematically review the complex aspects of ethical situations in clinical practice. Nurses must develop the habit of thinking systematically and regularly about the ethical dimensions of their practice not only at the level of nurse-patient relationships but at a broader social-system level as well. They must be visible and vocal when policies and practices related to moral situations are discussed or developed. For example, nursing should have representation on institutional ethics committees and be involved in developing and/or revising policies related to ethical concerns, such as advance directives and under what circumstances they are and are not honored. Nurses should know what the forum for discussing ethical issues is in their institutions and be aware of when and how to seek consultation from ethics committees or ethics consultants. They should develop comfort in discussing ethical issues with their patients and the patients' families. All nurses, especially those who are self-employed or employed in areas where there are no ethics committees, should cultivate a moral community, a safe haven for the discussion of the ethical issues they encounter in practice.

A STORY OF SUFFERING?

Bernard Gert, a philosopher and member of an ethics committee, shares a story about how he helped to identify the intent of a son's and daughter's request to continue to give morphine to their father, who was unconscious and dying from cancer:

"We started talking about the likelihood of their father actually suffering any pain or discomfort. The son was prepared to believe that their father was not suffering at all, but the daughter thought there was some slight possibility that he was suffering. However, when I pointed out to her that there was absolutely no change in his behavior before and after the morphine had been stopped, she admitted that this was correct. Eventually it became clear to all of us that the primary reason for their wanting morphine was to hasten death, that pain relief provided a rationalization for their insisting on the administration of morphine, but that neither of them had any firm conviction that their father was suffering."

From: Gert B. A philosophical consultation. *In*: Culver CM. *Ethics at the Bedside*. Dartmouth College, Hanover, NH: University Press of New England, 1990, pp. 29–39.

TOPICS FOR FURTHER INQUIRY

Until recently, research in nursing practice and nursing ethics has tended to focus on the characteristics of nurses and their moral reasoning processes and patterns with respect to their ethical decision-making. As the context and communal

TABLE 10–5
Considerations Relevant to Ethical Decision-Making

1. The facts:
   What are the facts of the situation? All too frequently, what appears to be an ethical issue is really misunderstanding of the information available, lack of information, lack of access to the information, and/or inadequate communication about the situation.

   What are the cognitive, emotional, spiritual, cultural, ethical, legal, and other decisional influences relevant to interpretation of the facts?

2. The persons:

   Who is/are/should be involved in the situation?
   What are their beliefs, values, knowledge, and decisional capacity with respect to the situation?

3. The institutions:

   What institutions are involved in the situation (consider many levels from family to national/international institutions).
   What norms, values, policies, regulations, laws, and economic considerations are relevant?

4. The relationships:

   What covenantal relationships have bearing on the situation?
   Of these, which are inclusive; which are special?
   Which of these relationships are in harmony; which are in conflict?

5. The issue(s):

   What is a clear, concise, communal statement of the issue(s) in the situation?
   Which of the issues is/are ethical? (Which are emotional, economic, legal, spiritual, cultural, etc?)

6. The options:

   What are the alternative courses of action? (Generate as many as possible. Try not to fall into the either/or trap; think of creative possibilities.)
   What are the consequences of each alternative?
   What are the benefits of each option?
   Who benefits?
   What are the burdens?
   Who bears the burdens?
   For which option(s) do the benefits most outweigh the burdens (or which options are least burdensome)—for whom: the client, the community, both client and community?

7. The choice(s):

   Who should decide?
   What should be decided?
   Who should communicate the decision?
   and
   Who should carry out the chosen action(s)?

8. The evaluation:
   Formative (Process):

   Is/are the action(s) as beneficial as anticipated?
   Is/are the burdens as onerous as anticipated?
   Are the actual benefits greater than the actual burdens (or is this actually the least burdensome alternative?)
   If not, what alternative courses of actions are available/preferable?

   Summative (Outcome):

   Was the intended benefit achieved? Were the anticipated burdens present?
   What can we learn from this situation that will help to inform our future decision-making, communication patterns, policies, and/or practices?

nature of ethics in nursing and other health care professions is emerging as an important dimension of nursing ethics, research should focus on questions that address but are not limited to:

1. Phenomenological inquiry, including but not limited to the lived experiences of communal moral relationships and/or decision making

2. Phenomenological and descriptive inquiry regarding moral and ethical issues in managed care, case management, and critical paths—for example, to what extent, if at all, is the quality of nursing care (with respect to professional norms and standards such as ANA *Standards of Nursing Practice*, state nurse practice acts, and professional credentialing criteria) altered for clients in managed care systems as compared with fee-for-service and/or other reimbursement/delivery models and questions regarding delegation to technicians, and the like

3. Phenomenological and descriptive studies of ethical considerations, issues, values, and the like in advanced nursing practice roles, such as clinical nurse specialists, nurse practitioners, nurse anesthetists, and nurse-midwives

4. Phenomenological and descriptive studies of interdisciplinary patterns of the moral professional life and decision-making

5. Phenomenological, descriptive, explanatory, predictive, and intervention studies to understand, describe, predict, and rectify such social justice concerns as restricted access to health care goods and services because of poverty and its consequences

6. Educational and evaluative research concerned with empowering students of nursing to act in accordance with their moral choices and to have a voice in interdisciplinary and community groups

7. Educational and evaluation research oriented toward heightening awareness of advance directives, consequences of managed care, and the like, among well persons to be done so that individuals, families, and communities are not confronted with the need to make critical health care decisions during times of crisis when they are most vulnerable

8. Replication of the fine array of existing studies in nursing so that the emerging knowledge in nursing ethics can be verified and used in practice

---

REFERENCES

1. Beauchamp TL, Childress JF. *Principles of Biomedical Ethics*, 4th Edition. New York: Oxford University Press, 1994.
2. Beauchamp T. *Philosophical Ethics: An Introduction to Moral Philosophy.* New York: McGraw-Hill Book Company, 1982.
3. Omnibus Budget Reconciliation Act (OBRA). (P. L. 101-158, Section 4205–5207; Section 4751–4752), 1990. (Patient Self-Determination Act passed November 6, 1990).
4. Kjervik D. Legal and ethical issues: The connection between law and ethics. *Journal of Professional Nursing* 6, 1990, 138, 185.
5. Schneider CE. Bioethics in the language of the law. *Hastings Center Report* (July-August), 16–22, 1994.
6. *Roe v. Wade*, 410 U.S. 113 (1973).
7. *Cruzan v. Director, Missouri Department of Health*, 497 U.S. 261 (1990).
8. Holmes OW. The path of the law, *in* Holmes OW. *Collected Legal Papers*. New York: Harcourt, Brace: 1920, p. 170.
9. Pellegrino E. Withholding treatment, surrogate decisions and rationing: some selected aspects. *In* Southby R, Hirsh J, eds. *Health Care Law and Ethics*. Washington, DC: George Washington University, 1989, 151–172.
10. President's Commission for the Study of Ethical Problems in Medical and Behavioral Research. *Securing Access to Health Care: Report on the Ethical Implications of Differences on the Availability of Health Services*. Washington, DC: U.S. Government Printing Office, 1983.
11. Childress J. *Moral Rights to Health Care.* Paper presented at the Advanced Bioethics Course II: Ethics and Health Care Allocation. Kennedy Institute of Ethics, Washington, DC, March, 1990.
12. Powers M. *Legal Rights to Health Care.* Paper presented at the Advanced Bioethics Course II: Ethics and Health Care Allocation. Kennedy Institute of Ethics, Washington, DC, March, 1990.
13. *Harris v. McRae*, 448 U.S. 297 (1980).
14. 70 N.J. 10 (1976), 355 A. 2d 647 (1976).
15. American Hospital Association. *American Hospital Association Statement on a Patient's Bill of Rights*, Chicago: American Hospital Association, 1972.
16. American Nurses Association. *Code for Nurses: With Interpretive Statements*. Kansas City, MO, 1985.

17. American Nurses Association. *Nursing's Social Policy Statement.* Washington, DC, 1995.

18. *In Re the Conservatorship of Wanglie*, No. PX-91-283 (Minn. Dist. Ct. Hennepin Co. July 1991).

19. National League for Nursing. *A conversation on caring with Jean Watson and Janet Quinn.* Videotape produced by NLN, 1989.

20. Reverby S. *Ordered to Care: The Dilemma of American Nursing*, 1850–1945. New York: Cambridge University Press, 1987.

21. Jameton A. *In* Achtenberg B, Sawyer J, *Code Gray: Ethical Dilemmas In Nursing.* Videotape production by Fanlight Productions, 1983.

22. Travelbee J. *Interpersonal Aspects of Nursing*, 2nd Edition. Philadelphia: F. A. Davis Company, 1971.

23. Goldstein DM. Scope note 19: Nursing ethics: A selected bibliography, 1987 to present. *Kennedy Institute of Ethics Journal* 2(2), 1992, 177–192.

24. Noddings N. *Caring: A Feminine Approach to Ethics and Moral Education.* Berkeley: University of California Press, 1984.

25. Watson J. *Human Science and Human Care.* Norwalk, Conn: Appleton-Century-Crofts, 1988.

26. Gadow S. Nurses and patient, the caring relationship. *In*: Bishop AH, Scudder JR, eds. *Caring, Curing, and Coping.* Tuscaloosa, Ala: University of Alabama Press, 1985, 31–43.

27. Brody JK. Virtue ethics, caring, and nursing. *Scholarly Inquiry for Nursing Practice* 2:87–96, 1988. Also see Fry ST. Response to "Virtue ethics, caring, and nursing." *Scholarly Inquiry for Nursing Practice*, 2, 97–101, 1988.

28. Watson J. Introduction: An ethic of caring/curing/nursing qua nursing, *in*: Watson J, Ray M, eds.). *The Ethics of Care and the Ethics of Cure: Synthesis in Chronicity.* New York: National League for Nursing, 1988.

29. Condon EH. Nursing and the caring metaphor: Gender and political influences on an ethics of care. *Nursing Outlook* 40(1):14–19, 1991.

30. Noddings N. In defense of caring. *Journal of Clinical Ethics* 3(1), 15–18, 1992.

31. Vezeau TM. Caring: From philosophical concerns to practice. *Journal of Clinical Ethics* 3(1), 18–20, 1992.

32. Gilligan C. *In a Different Voice: Psychological Theory and Women's Development.* Cambridge, Mass, Harvard University Press, 1982.

33. Gilligan C, Ward JV, Taylor, JMcL, eds. *Mapping the Moral Domain: A Contribution of Women's Thinking to Psychological Theory and Education.* Cambridge, Mass: Harvard University Press, 1988.

34. Benner P. *From Novice to Expert: Excellence and Power in Clinical Nursing Practice.* Menlo Park, Calif: Addison-Wesley, 1984.

35. Benner P, Wrubel J. *The Primacy of Caring: Stress and Coping in Health and Illness.* Menlo Park, Calif: Addison-Wesley, 1989.

36. Carper B. The ethics of caring. *Advances in Nursing Science* 3(3), 11–19, 1979.

37. Gadow S. Clinical subjectivity: Advocacy with silent patients. Ethics, Part I: Issues in nursing. *Nursing Clinics of North America*, 24(February), 535–541, 1989.

38. Leininger MM, ed. *Ethical and Moral Dimensions of Care.* Detroit: Wayne State University Press, 1990.

39. Watson Jean. *Nursing: Human Science and Human Care.* Norwalk, Conn: Appleton-Century-Crofts, 1985.

40. Watson Jean. *Nursing: Human Science and Human Care: A Theory of Nursing.* New York: National League for Nursing, 1988. (Publication Number 15–2236).

41. Gadow S. Existential advocacy: Philosophical foundations of nursing. *In*: Spicker S, Gadow S, eds. *Nursing: Images and Ideals.* New York: Springer, 1980, 102–124.

42. May W. *The Physician's Covenant.* Philadelphia: Westminster Press, 1983.

43. Pellegrino ED, Thomasma DC. *A Philosophical Basis of Medical Practice: Toward a Philosophy and Ethic of the Healing Professions.* New York: Oxford University Press, 1981.

44. Veatch R. *A Theory of Medical Ethics.* New York: Basic Books, 1981.

45. Cooper MC. Covenantal relationships: Grounding for the nursing ethic. *Advances in Nursing Science* 1988; 10(4):48–59.

46. Douglas M, Brent N. Substance abuse and the nurse manager: Ethical and legal issues. *Seminars for Nurse Managers* 2(1), 16–26, 1994.

47. Allen J. *Love & Conflict.* Lanham, MD: University Press of America, 1995.

48. Veatch R. Current Controversies in Theories of Distribution. Paper presented at the Advanced Bioethics Course II: Ethics and Health Care Allocation, Kennedy Institute of Ethics, Washington, DC, March, 1990.

49. Agich G. Reassessing autonomy in long-term care. *Hastings Center Report* (Special Suppl.) (March-April). 1–15, 1990.

50. Collopy B, Dubler N, Zuckerman C. The ethics of home care: Autonomy and accommodation. *Hastings Center Report* (March-April); 20(2), S1–S16, 1990.

51. Nick S, Douglas M. Alzheimer's families: Decisions for caring. *Journal of Home Health Care Practice* 3(4), 65–71, 1991.

52. Callahan D. Families as caregivers: The limits of morality. *Archives of Physical Medicine and Rehabilitation* 69,323–328, 1988.

53. Hardwig J. What about the family? *Hastings Center Report* (March-April), 12–17, 1990.

54. Collopy B, Boyle P, Jennings B. New directions in nursing home ethics. *Hastings Center Report* (March-April); 21 (2, Suppl.), S1–S15, 1991.

55. Collopy B. Autonomy in long term care: Some crucial distinctions. *Gerontologist* 28 (3,Suppl.),10–17, 1988.

56. Scanlon C, Fleming C. Ethical issues in caring for the patient with advanced cancer. *Nursing Clinics of North America* 24(4), 977–986, 1989.

57. Makielski M, Broom C. Administering pain medications for a terminal patient. (Case study and commentary). *Dimensions of Critical Care Nursing* 11(3),157–161, 1992.

58. Greipp ME. Undermedication for pain: an ethical model. *Advances in Nursing Science* 15(1),44–53, 1992.

59. Copp LA. An ethical responsibility for pain management. *Journal of Advanced Nursing* 18(1),1–3, 1993.

60. Aristotle. *Nichomachean Ethics*, Book 2, Wardman AE, trans. *In*: Bambrough R, *The Philosophy of Aristotle*, New York: Mentor Books, 1966.

61. Mill JS. *Utilitarianism.* Edited by G. Sher. Indianapolis: Hackett Publishing Company, 1979. (Original work published 1861.)

62. Nozick R. *Anarchy, State, and Utopia*. New York: Basic Books, 1974.

63. Rawls J. *A Theory of Justice*. Cambridge, Mass: Belnap Press of Harvard University Press, 1971.

64. Rawls J. *A Theory of Justice*. Cambridge, Mass: Belnap Press of Harvard University Press, 1971, 3.

65. Piaget J. *The Moral Judgment of the Child*. New York: Free Press, 1965.

66. Kohlberg L. *The Psychology of Moral Development: Essays on Moral Development*, 1. San Francisco: Harper & Row, 1981.

67. Kohlberg L. *The Psychology of Moral Development: Essays on Moral Development*, 2. San Francisco: Harper & Row, 1984.

68. Rest J. *Development in Judging Moral Issues*. Minneapolis: University of Minnesota Press, 1979.

69. Perry W. *Forms of Intellectual and Ethical Development in the College Years*. New York: Holt, Rinehart & Winston, 1968.

70. Perry W. Cognitive and ethical growth: The making of meaning. *In*: Chickering AW and associates, *The Modern American College*. San Francisco: Jossey-Bass, 1981.

71. Ketefian S, Ormond I. Moral reasoning and ethical practice in nursing: An integrative review (National League for Nursing Pub. No. 15–2250). New York: National League for Nursing, 1988.

72. Ray M. Communal moral experience as the starting point for research in health care ethics. *Nursing Outlook* 42(3),104–109, 1994.

73. Chinn PL. Toward the 21st Century: Nursing Theory, Research and Practice. Paper presented at the 1990 23rd Annual Communicating Nursing Research Conference, Western Institute of Nursing, Boulder, Colo; May 1990. 107.

74. Blake DC. The hospital ethics committee: health care's moral consciousness or white elephant? *Hastings Center Report* (January-February), 6–11, 1992.

75. Carson RA. Spirit, emotion, and meaning: The many voices of bioethics. *Hastings Center Report* (May-June), 23–24, 1994.

76. Benjamin W. *Illuminations*. New York: Schocken Books, 1968, p. 89.

77. Pellegrino ED. Foreword. *In*: Anderson AD, *Remember Me: A Collection of Poems*. New York: Albert D. Anderson, M.D., 1987, p. 7.

78. Diekelmann N. Behavioral pedagogy: A Heideggerian hermeneutical analysis of the lived-experiences of students and teachers in nursing. *Journal of Nursing Education* 32(6), 245–250, 1993.

79. Gadow S. Advocacy nursing and new meanings of aging. *Nursing Clinics of North America* 14, 81–91, 1979.

11

Reproductive and Family Concerns

contents

A lthough the right of privacy's initial beginnings were firmly planted in nonconstitutional ground—as a property right and when invaded, suing under a tort or contract theory—that viewpoint slowly changed. Privacy rights began to be rooted in several of the Bill of Rights' protections[1] and continued to further develop and change. In a 1928 United States Supreme Court case, for example, Justice Brandeis, in his dissenting opinion in the case that dealt with wiretapping, stated that the Fourth and Fifth Amendments provided a "right to be left alone."[2]

The First Amendment has also been cited as protecting privacy interests.[3] Also, the Fourteenth Amendment's Due Process and Equal Protection Clauses respectively have also been cited as the basis for the privacy of personal decisions such as reproductive choice. Clearly these and other case law decisions have expanded the right of privacy from "interpersonal relationships to the level of individual choice."[4]

The expansion of the right of privacy is based on two constitutional doctrines—the penumbra doctrine and the zone of privacy doctrine. The penumbra doctrine, contained in Article I, Section 8(18) ("Necessary and Proper Clause") of the Federal Constitution, states that when implied governmental powers exist in a charter, those powers can be "engrafted" on another.[5] The use of this doctrine, with the right of privacy, is important, since it is not specifically granted as a right in the United States Constitution. The right of privacy has been expanded by the courts in the penumbras of other clearly articulated constitutional rights, such as freedom of religion and association (First Amendment) and the protection against unreasonable searches and seizures (Fourth Amendment).

The zone of privacy is also an extension of the penumbra doctrine and expands clearly articulated rights to include the right of privacy. For example, the Ninth Amendment's language that the rights listed in the Constitution "shall not be construed to deny or disparage others retained by the people" has been used to include the right of privacy in the Fifth and Fourteenth Amendments' protection of liberty.[6]

Like other rights, the right of privacy is not absolute. As a result, an individual's privacy interest must always be balanced with another's interest and with those of the government, whether local, state, or federal. The balancing of respective privacy rights is based on the *Parens Patriae* Doctrine, meaning "the parent of the country." This doctrine originated from the English law in which the king was empowered to act as a guardian to individuals who were legally disabled, such as infants.[7] In the United States, this power was given to the states and has been long supported by the United States Supreme Court.[8] The doctrine is used to protect those individuals who cannot protect themselves, such as children and incompetent adults. If necessary, the state can intervene in that situation by initiating a suit on behalf of the person who needs protecting, or can become involved in a suit already in progress.

In either case, the state's purpose is to protect the individual or individuals involved because

---

KEY PRINCIPLES

Penumbra Doctrine

Privacy

Zones of Privacy

Parens Patriae Doctrine

Best-Interest-of-the-Individual Test

Substituted Judgment Test

RELATED TOPICS

it has an interest in maintaining the well-being and productivity of its citizens. Even so, the state's concerns are not absolute, and they must be balanced with the individual's constitutional and other rights. For example, when questions are raised, such as reproductive choice or who will be given the custody of a minor child when a divorce occurs, the state's interests and the individual rights of those involved are always compared by the court before a determination is made. That comparison must always conform to state and federal constitutional limitations on the ability of the government to unduly intervene in individual liberties.

To provide a consistent way in which respective rights can be carefully balanced, especially when one party cannot articulate his or her wishes, two tests are used in evaluating competing personal and state interests. One is "the best-interest-of-the-individual" test. In its pure form, it takes into account only the present welfare of the person and ignores societal, familial, or other secondary concerns that do not focus on what is best for the person at that time.[9]

> *. . . an individual's privacy interest must always be balanced with another's interest . . . and with those of the government . . .*

The second test, "substituted judgment," is based on the decision that would be made by the incompetent individual if he or she were able to do so. By its nature, this test requires clear, credible evidence of the individual's past preferences.[10] When such evidence is unreliable or unavailable, the use of this test is a legal fiction.[11]

Probably in no other area of the law is the balancing of such rights more delicate than in the exercise of such private decisions as procreation, choice of a mate, choice of living arrange-

ment, family matters, and what treatment one will select or refuse.

SELECTED CONSIDERATIONS IN REPRODUCTIVE AND FAMILY AFFAIRS

Reproductive Choice

Sterilization

Eugenic Sterilization

Eugenic sterilization—sterilizing those with certain "defects" to avoid offspring in society who might inherit those defects—was a popular practice in the early 1890s. The state of Indiana passed the first eugenic sterilization law in 1907.[12] This, and other, laws allowed sterilization of those who were found by the court to be insane, "feeble-minded," or moronic. Others with undesirable traits, including alcoholism, blindness, and deafness, were also included in these laws.

In a 1927 United States Supreme Court case, *Buck v. Bell*,[13] the Court upheld a Virginia law allowing the superintendent of a home for epileptics and the feeble-minded to sterilize inmates if it would be in the best interest of the inmate and society. However, in *Skinner v. Oklahoma*, 1942,[14] the United States Supreme Court held unconstitutional a law that allowed the state (under its Habitual Criminal Sterilization Act) to sterilize habitual criminals convicted of crimes involving moral turpitude. It is important to note that the act was struck down because of the success of an equal protection argument—all criminals were not treated the same under the law—rather than because of outrage over the sterilization issue.

After the *Skinner* decision, many states repealed their eugenic sterilization laws.[15]

Involuntary Sterilization

Involuntary sterilization laws exist in many states. The focus of these laws is not on the genetic impact of the offspring, but rather what is best for the individual(s) having the child and the offspring.[16] Many of these laws have been upheld by the courts under certain circumstances. Even so, they are subject to strict constitutional scrutiny, especially when the individual involved is not competent; that is, unable to give informed consent for the procedure.

> *Involuntary sterilization laws . . . are subject to strict constitutional scrutiny . . .*

Involuntary sterilization most often arises with those who are mentally disabled or mentally retarded and whose sexual activity, or its potential, is of concern to family members, a guardian (if one has been appointed), or facility staff. Regardless of the circumstance, specific due process and other protections are afforded the individual unable to provide informed consent for this procedure. Those protections include the right to a hearing, the right to counsel or a guardian *ad litem* (an attorney or other individual appointed by the court to represent the individual for the purposes of the hearing), the establishment of the need for the sterilization, and various medical and psychological examinations and opinions.[17]

Voluntary Sterilization

The decision to terminate the ability to procreate can take place under various circumstances. When that decision occurs because children are not wanted, the choice is of a different character than when the need arises because of the presence of a disease or injury that may necessitate removal of the reproductive organs. If the latter situation exists, it is probably not a voluntary choice in the sense that the removal of the reproductive organs is required for continued well-being. When the choice is truly voluntary, however, the most common method of sterilization

is vasectomy for men and tubal ligation for women.

For competent adult men and women, the only legal prerequisite for voluntary sterilization is the provision of informed consent for the procedure. Most often, *written* informed consent is mandated, either by state or federal law. Spousal consent for sterilization is currently not required in the United States.[18] Although private hospitals or clinics can establish policies requiring spousal consent to be obtained, public health care delivery systems cannot; doing so has been held to be a violation of the spouse's right of privacy and therefore unconstitutional.[19]

Unmarried minors—those under 18 years of age—have several restrictions on the right to sterilization. Some states, such as Georgia and Connecticut, prohibit sterilization of unmarried minors. Others, like Colorado, allow it only when a parent or guardian also gives permission for the procedure. When the parent or guardian consents to sterilization but the minor objects, then a suit must be filed to provide the minor with certain protections and a determination made as to which decision will prevail.

Married minors, as well as minors emancipated in other ways, can consent to all medical treatments including sterilization. Thus the only legal prerequisite for the married or otherwise emancipated minor in relation to sterilization would be the provision of informed consent.

Nursing Implications

The provision of care to one undergoing sterilization will vary depending on the circumstances surrounding that procedure. However, nurses who work in facilities for the developmentally disabled, those in home care, and those who provide nursing services for adult and minor women in ambulatory care and women's health centers will most probably be faced with patients who may undergo this procedure.

For the legally disabled patient or an unemancipated or unmarried minor, the nurse will be working with a guardian, other legally appointed consent giver or the parent, especially in terms of explaining procedures, discussing nursing care, and relaying information from the physician concerning the patient's progress. Even so, it is important to include the patient in those discussions to ensure that the patient's dignity remains intact and that he or she is treated in a caring and humane way. For those patients who are able to make the decision themselves, the nurse will need to listen and clarify and obtain any additional information the patient may need to make an informed choice concerning the procedure.

The nurse will also need to be certain that the institution's or agency's policies concerning written consent are adhered to. Although it is clearly the physician's responsibility to go through the process of obtaining the informed consent of the patient, it is the nurse's responsibility to see that it has occurred. If, for example, the nurse in the operating room determines that the required written consent has not been obtained, the nurse must inform the surgeon and the nurse manager that consent has not been obtained.

Furthermore, patients may request additional information from the nurse concerning the procedure. The nurse will need to ascertain what the patient had been told initially and, where possible, reinforce the information given by the physician. If necessary, the nurse may also need to contact the physician so that he or she can provide the additional details needed.

Any and all documentation that has taken place concerning the procedure should be a part of the medical record. Any communication to the physician, surgeon, or nursing administration concerning the patient and the procedure should be carefully and completely documented (See Documentation Reminder 11–1, p. 221).

Last, if the nurse assesses that the patient may not be able to make an informed choice about the procedure, it is vital that the nurse share this information with the nurse manager and the physician, so that whatever evaluations are necessary concerning the patient's neurologic and psychiatric status can be carried out before the procedure is undertaken.

Birth Control Services and Information

The ability to obtain information concerning birth control is another fundamental issue for any individual, whether male or female, whether married or unmarried. Although one's religious beliefs may prohibit the use of birth control, the state or federal government cannot easily restrict an adult's access to birth control information, devices, and medications. The United States Supreme Court in 1965 and 1972 invalidated two respective state laws that restricted access to birth control devices.

In the 1965 case, *Griswold v. Connecticut*,[20] Connecticut had a law that made it a crime for married couples to use contraceptives and for anyone to counsel another to use them. The Court held that the right of (marital) privacy was one guaranteed by the Constitution's penumbras and zones of privacy of the First, Third, Fourth, Fifth, and Ninth Amendments. Furthermore, the Court suggested that privacy was also protected by the Fourteenth Amendment's Due Process Clause.

. . . reasonable constraints on a minor's access to [birth control] services and information . . . can occur.

In *Eisenstadt v. Baird*,[21] the Court struck down a Massachusetts law that prohibited unmarried couples from obtaining or using contraceptives. Based on an equal protection argument, the Court held that married or unmarried adults have the same right to obtain and use birth control devices.

Although restrictions on birth control services and information for adults is not constitutional, reasonable constraints on a minor's access to the same services and information, especially unemancipated and unmarried minors, can occur. Most often, access to birth control services and information is limited as a result of the state's requirement of parental consent for medical treatment of the minor. Some states, however, such as Illinois, provide a minor access to these services through a specific statute authorizing a physician or other health care provider to provide services and information to the minor solely on the basis of his or her own consent.[22]

Nursing Implications

The nurse who works in a family planning or ambulatory care center where gynecologic services are offered will be the most directly involved in the provision of birth control services and information to clients. The information given must be clear, accurate, and in a manner the patient can understand. Patient teaching concerning birth control is best done not only by direct discussion with the patient, but also through evaluation of the patient's understanding of that information.

Nurse practitioners and nurses who are able to prescribe birth control medications in their particular state will need to do so only after careful and thorough assessment of the patient's physical status.

If the client is a minor, the nurse will need to be familiar with state law concerning consent and whether the minor needs parental consent for birth control information and devices. This need may depend on where the nurse is working. For example, a nurse who works in a public school clinic will most probably need to obtain the consent of the parent for any birth control services to the minor school child, even when state law might otherwise allow the minor himself or herself to consent. The requirement of parental consent is more a public relations issue and an attempt to avoid constitutional arguments; that is, the government might be seen to in some way be sanctioning sexual activity or

attempting to control the ability of minors to procreate, should they choose to do so.

Abortion

Abortion, the termination of pregnancy before the fetus reaches the stage of viability, can be spontaneous or induced, therapeutic or nontherapeutic.[23] Spontaneous abortions or miscarriages occur for many medical reasons, often without apparent cause.[24] Induced abortions, in contrast, are intentionally carried out for many reasons also, including the need to save the life of the mother. Although all of these situations raise controversial legal, ethical, and moral dilemmas, the focus of the development of the law has been on elective abortions that avoid a live birth.[25]

Abortion was a common form of birth control in England and America and was not considered a crime if it occurred before quickening.[26] However, after Connecticut passed the first law criminalizing abortion after quickening in 1821, other states followed. By 1900, abortion was illegal in all United States jurisdictions, and individuals who performed them were prosecuted as criminals.[27] In addition, medical licensing acts in most states allowed disciplinary proceedings to occur against physicians who participated in illegal abortions.[28]

In the late 60s and early 70s, many of the anti-abortion laws were amended to allow an abortion to occur when there was a threat to the mother (either physical or mental), when the pregnancy was due to incest or rape, or when fetal congenital anomalies were diagnosed. It was not until 1973, however, that the United States Supreme Court held that the right of a woman to obtain an abortion was included in the right of privacy.

Challenges to the *Roe* and *Doe* decisions were almost immediate. They centered not only on the holdings of the decisions, but also on who should finance abortions when the mother could not do so herself or through private health insurance. The latter clearly became an access to abortion issue, for many poor women were effectively unable to have an abortion if they could not pay for the procedure.

KEY CASE 11–1   Roe v. Wade (1973)[29]

Plaintiff alleges criminal statute a violation of her due process rights under the Fourteenth Amendment

Court holds statute vague and violates Ninth and Fourteenth Amendment rights

Fourteenth Amendment does protect personal liberty, which includes fundamental right of privacy to determine whether to terminate pregnancy

Court balances rights of mother with those of fetus

State does have interests, however, and court sets up trimester framework and state's ability to intervene in abortion decision within framework

FACTS: A Texas criminal statute made it a crime to "procure" or "attempt" an abortion, except to save the life of the mother. Plaintiff, a single, pregnant female, wanted her abortion to be performed by a competent physician under acceptable medical conditions. She did not have the money to seek the abortion in another state, nor did she qualify for any of the exceptions in the Texas statute.

She filed suit, alleging that the statute was unconstitutional because it violated Due Process Rights guaranteed under the Fourteenth Amendment of the United States Constitution.

DISTRICT COURT DECISION: The three-judge court held that the statute was void as vague and overly infringed on plaintiff's Ninth and Fourteenth Amendment Rights. A direct appeal to the United States Supreme Court was taken.

UNITED STATES SUPREME COURT DECISION: The Court held that, under the Fourteenth Amendment's protection of personal liberty, which includes a fundamental right of privacy, a woman had a right to determine whether or not to terminate a pregnancy. In balancing the mother's right with that of the fetus, the Court held that (1) the fetus was not a person and thus not protected by the Constitution; (2) excepting only life-threatening situations from criminal conduct does not consider other interest the female may have in terminating the pregnancy; and (3) although the decision to terminate a pregnancy is protected by the Constitution, the state *does* have legitimate interests in the general welfare of pregnant women, the unborn child, and the decision-making process after a certain point in time. Therefore, the Court held that during the first trimester of pregnancy, the decision to have an abortion was one between the mother and her physician. During the second trimester, the state may regulate the decision if the regulation(s) is reasonably related to the state's interest in the health of the mother. During the last trimester, when the viability of the fetus is a legitimate state interest, the state may regulate and/or prohibit abortion, except when necessary to save the life of the mother.

ANALYSIS: The *Roe* decision was a landmark one, and has been the subject of much controversy. In its companion case, *Doe v. Bolton*, the Court declared unconstitutional certain preabortion requirements in Georgia—state residency, approval by a hospital committee, and the procedure taking place only in a Joint Commission on Accreditation of Healthcare Organizations (JCAHO)–approved hospital. Although the two cases firmly rooted the right of a woman to make a choice about an abortion with limited governmental intervention, their respective parameters were tested by subsequent cases at both the federal and state levels (see discussion below).

KEY CASE 11-1	Roe v. Wade (1973)[29] Continued

It is also important to note that the *Roe* decision is an example of the use of the "strict scrutiny" test. Only when a "compelling state interest" exists can governmental intrusion into a "fundamental" right occur. As with many other constitutional rights, the right of privacy is not absolute. The Court's role here was to determine when the government can assert its interests and how an individual's rights may be narrowed.

Prerequisite procedures to obtain an abortion were also challenged, including procedural challenges involving a minor's access to abortion services. Table 11–1 summarizes several of the court challenges.

As Table 11–1 indicates, a clear trend began of retreating from the initial "strict scrutiny" test articulated in *Roe* and *Doe*. The *Rust* decision was particularly troubling to many health care providers, not only because it denied many poor women the right to counseling and abortion services, but also because of the restraints placed on the provider's right of free speech to counsel clients concerning what they determined to be sound medical advice. The regulations upheld by the court in *Rust* were dubbed as the "gag rules."

Because the regulations were so troublesome, the Department of Health and Human Services amended the rules to allow physicians to discuss abortion if based on "medical conditions." Nurses, counselors, and social workers, however, were still able to provide information on abortion to patients.[36] The United States Court of Appeals held that the revised gag rule was adopted in violation of the Department's required procedure for changing its rules.[37] It was not until President Clinton rescinded the gag rule during his first week in office, however, that family planning clinics were able to provide medical advice and counseling concerning abortion without fear of violating the rule.

In 1991, the most recent decision concerning abortion rights was decided by the United States Supreme Court. In *Planned Parenthood of Southeastern Pennsylvania v. Casey*,[38] the Court agreed to review a Pennsylvania law that (1) required physicians to tell women seeking an abortion about fetal development and alternatives to abortion; (2) had a 24-hour waiting period after the information is received; (3) required notification of spouses of the intent to have an abortion; (4) mandated unemancipated minors to obtain consent from a parent or the court before obtaining an abortion; and (5) required physicians to keep detailed records on all abortions performed, with the records being subject to public disclosure.[39] The information to be maintained included the age and weight of the fetus and information about the female's past pregnancies or abortions.[40]

The Third Circuit Court of Appeals upheld all aspects of the Pennsylvania law except the spousal notification requirement. In doing so, it opined that based on the *Webster* and *Hodgson* decisions, the "strict scrutiny" test was no longer embraced by the majority of the Supreme Court Justices. Rather, it continued, a lesser test—whether the law creates an "undue burden" on a woman's right to an abortion—was the appropriate standard.[41] Both sides appealed the Court of Appeals decision, asking for clarification on the law.

The United States Supreme Court upheld all of the Pennsylvania law's provisions except spousal notification as permissible ways in which a state's interest in the protection of fetal life and its preference for childbirth over abor-

TABLE 11–1

Court Cases After *Roe*

CASE NAME/YEAR	CHALLENGE(S)	UNITED STATES SUPREME COURT DECISION
Harris v. McRae (1980)[30]	Medicaid funding for abortions	No
Akron v. Akron Center for Reproductive Health, Inc. (1983)[31]	Restrictions on access: 24-hour waiting period, parental consent for unmarried minors, hospital procedure only for abortions after first trimester, detailed informed consent with MD's statement	Strikes down restrictions
Webster v. Reproductive Health Services (1989)[32]	Missouri statute stating life begins at conception; informed consent and information on abortions to patient; if pregnancy 20 or more weeks, MD must do tests to determine viability of fetus; and prohibition of abortions at public facilities unless pregnancy life threatening	Upholds restrictions with caveat that law's statement on life starting at conception cannot deny abortion rights; Court also discusses *Roe* as "rigid," "unsound," "unworkable"
Hodgson v. Minnesota (1990)[33] and *Ohio v. Akron Center for Reproductive Health* (1990)[34]	Parental notification for minors seeking abortion and provisions for court hearing to bypass parental notification to determine if minor capable of making decision	Upholds notification of *one* parent as constitutional and bypass provisions constitutionally permissible
Rust v. Sullivan (1991)[35]	Title X (funding for public and private nonprofit agencies providing family planning services) regulations interpreted by Secretary of HHS to mean: no counseling about abortion, no referral for abortion, referral for "appropriate" prenatal services only, no "advocacy, promotion or encouragement" of abortion as method of family planning, and clear physical and organizational separation of facilities and staff from abortion services for those receiving Title X funds	Upholds regulations and finds they do not violate 1st or 5th Amendment rights of patients or agencies

tion could be enforced.[42] The Court rejected the trimester approach established in *Roe*. In its place, the Court stated it would use the "undue burden" test in evaluating whether a state abortion law restricting abortion would be upheld or overturned. *Undue burden* is defined as whether a law restricting abortion has a purpose or effect of placing a substantial barrier on a woman's right to obtain an abortion.[43]

Although the *Casey* decision did not explicitly overrule *Roe v. Wade*, it effectively changed *Roe*'s protections by placing limits—either real or potential—on a woman's choice concerning abortion.

. . . the Casey *decision did not explicitly overrule* Roe v. Wade *[but] it effectively changed* Roe's *protections by placing limits . . . on a woman's choice concerning abortion.*

Nursing Implications

The decision to have an abortion under most any circumstance is difficult. Therefore, the nurse working with a patient who is faced with this choice needs to be especially sensitive to the patient's emotional stress during the time she is deciding what she will do. The provision of support, active listening, and information as needed will be very helpful to the patient during this process of decision-making.

The nurse can reinforce the patient's right in seeking the treatment to carry out the termination of pregnancy consistent with the state law. For the adult patient, this right includes the fact that the decision can be made without notifying any other person, including a spouse. It also includes the right of the patient to seek whatever medical information is necessary from the physician to fully understand the implications of her decision.

If working with minors, the nurse will need to comply with state law concerning the right(s) of the minor to seek information about an abortion. If the minor patient has decided to have an abortion, the nurse will need to focus particularly on the need for parental notification or consent and any waiting period that is required before the abortion can occur. This will require up-to-date understanding of the law in the state in which the nurse practices. Although not always possible or desired, a careful discussion of possibly seeking support and guidance from a parent can be explored with the minor.

Last, but by no means least, the nurse must explore his or her own feelings concerning abortion. This is important for the nurse so that personal values are clarified and owned.[44] Doing so also allows the provision of care to the patient without infringing on her legal rights in relation to the procedure.

If, however, the nurse has determined not to provide care to a patient seeking abortion information or services, it is possible under many state laws (New York and Illinois, for example) not to participate in those services. The state statutes are often based on abortion being contrary to the health care provider's religious beliefs. An employer is prohibited by the statutes from retaliatory action against the nurse who raises this issue in the employment setting.

DOCUMENTATION REMINDER 11–1
REPRODUCTIVE CHOICE

▼ Patient questions/comments/concerns

▼ Required forms—consent, notification of parent (if required for minor) and others—executed and in medical record

▼ Any and all patient teaching concerning procedure, follow-up care, discharge instructions

▼ Refusal of any part of procedure, follow-up care, discharge instructions

▼ Contact(s) with physician and others concerning care, nursing interventions, and patient response(s)

Reproductive Innovations

Artificial Insemination

Artificial insemination is the oldest reproductive technology and was first used in the United States in 1866.[45] Approximately 30 states have passed laws concerning artificial insemination.[46] It has been defined as the means of replacing, in part or in whole, the natural process of conception and in utero gestation.[47]

Artificial insemination is the oldest reproductive technology . . .

The process of artificially inseminating a female occurs by introducing viable sperm into the vagina, cervical canal, or uterus by artificial means.[48] Two processes exist—A.I.H. (homologous insemination), which utilizes the sperm of the female's spouse, and A.I.D. (donor insemination), which utilizes semen from a donor.[49]

A.I.H. insemination is the least legally problematic of the two. Even so, there are clear concerns that must be acknowledged. First and fore-most, the procedure must be done in accordance with whatever statute may exist in the state. When a statute exists, a physician is usually the health care provider required to perform the procedure. Furthermore, the written informed consent of the couple is required. It is important that no guarantee to a full-term pregnancy or live birth be given to the couple.[50]

A.I.D. insemination, in contrast, is fraught with legal issues. This is particularly so in relation to consent issues and the support of the child. Clearly, the written informed consent of the woman to be artificially inseminated is mandatory. If the woman is not married, this requirement is not unusually problematic. Problems may arise in relation to the donor, however, especially if a state does not have a law concerning the legitimacy of the child and the donor's responsibilities, if any, after its birth. Some states, including Florida, Oklahoma, Nevada, New Jersey, and Illinois have passed statutes specifying that a child from A.I.D. is legitimate, and the donor is not responsible for supporting the child because he is not considered the father. In those states that have not yet passed such statutes, issues of consent from the donor and support of the child will continue to exist.

If the woman is married and a decision is made to undergo A.I.D. without the consent of the husband, a legal battle may also occur. If a suit is initiated by the husband, he may challenge his obligation to provide care and support of the offspring of the A.I.D. insemination to which he did not agree. If, in contrast, that husband has consented to the procedure, most state statutes clearly indicate that the child is the legitimate offspring of the couple who consented to the procedure, thus decreasing challenges of support obligations by the husband.

The utilization of donor sperm adds the requirement by the physician and the sperm bank, if one is used, to screen the donor for infectious diseases (including AIDS and hepatitis), Rh factor incompatibility, and inheritable diseases.[51]

Nursing Implications

Because physicians have been identified as the health care provider who is to conduct the process of artificial insemination, the nurse will not be directly involved in the actual process. Even so, the nurse may participate by doing an initial physical assessment of the woman who is to undergo the procedure and obtaining other preliminary information from her or the couple. Furthermore, the nurse may provide some information to the female or couple concerning the procedure prior to the physician's doing so.

In addition, the nurse who works in any physician's office or a clinic providing artificial insemination services will need to be certain that all paperwork required for either procedure is in the patient's record (See Documentation Reminder 11–2). Furthermore, maintaining the privacy and confidentiality of the medical record, including the donor's identity in A.I.D. inseminations, is absolutely essential. Releases should be done only after written informed consent is obtained; records should be stored carefully and only certain staff granted access to them; and advice from legal counsel obtained whenever a subpoena is received for an individual record.

If the nurse is involved in the storage or handling of any semen, it must be done with care and caution. For example, policies and procedures should be developed and adhered to concerning receipt of semen from the donor; proper identification and storage of the sperm; and any treatment of the sperm (for example, centrifuge) prior to its use.[52] The development of policies and procedures should be based on guidelines established by such organizations as the American Association of Tissue Banks, the American Fertility Society, the Food and Drug Administration, and the Centers for Disease Control.[53]

Artificial insemination may be anxiety-provoking and frightening to the patient, her husband, or significant other. The nurse's ability to provide support and care during the process can be invaluable to those undergoing this reproductive technique.

In Vitro *Fertilization*

Also a procedure of artificial insemination, *in vitro* fertilization (IVF) involves removal of an ovum from the woman, fertilizing it *in vitro,* and then replacing the fertilized egg back into the uterus.[54] The procedure may take place with homologous or donor insemination. The birth of the first living child conceived as a result of this method occurred in 1978.[55] Since then, variations of the initial method have developed, including embryo transfer, gamete intrafallopian transfer (GIFT), and ovum donation.[56]

Many of the family, legal, and other concerns with this method of reproduction are similar to those discussed in the section on artificial insemination. However, an additional concern arises with IVF regardless of the method used. That concern is what is to be done with an ovum or ova not implanted until a future date or not used for implantation at all.

[In vitro fertilization] may take place with homologous or donor insemination.

The storage of ova not used immediately raises concerns as to proper storage, labeling, length of ability to survive storage techniques (usually freezing), and ownership. For example, in a 1983 case, a California couple were both killed in a plane crash in South America after the successful fertilization of two ova in Australia. They were frozen and stored there. After the couple's deaths an Australian committee recommended that the embryos be destroyed, but the legislature passed a law suggesting the ova be implanted in another woman and if a child is born as a result, the child should be adopted. The California court, however, ruled that the children would not inherit from the deceased parents.[57]

Also, in a 1989 divorce proceeding, the owner-ship of a divorcing couple's seven frozen embryos was disputed.[58] Initially the zygotes were awarded to Mrs. Davis so that she could utilize them for implantation. The court also held that (1) human embryos are not property; (2) life begins at conception; (3) the state's *parens patriae* doctrine is applicable; and (4) it is in the best interest of the child(ren) *in vitro* to provide the mother with the opportunity for a successful pregnancy(ies).[59] After the court decision, the ex-wife stated she would then prefer to donate the embryos to a childless couple for their use, but would accept them in the alternative.[60] The ex-husband appealed the decision, arguing that the state could not force him to become a father. The Tennessee Appeals Court agreed with him, holding that the state could not force either one of them to use the embryos to be parents. Forcing the ex-husband to become a father against his will would violate his "constitutionally protected right not to beget a child where no pregnancy has taken place."[61]

On June 1, 1992, the Tennessee Supreme Court upheld the appeals court decision. In doing so, it held that when a divorcing couple is not able to agree on what is to be done with frozen embryos, the individual who does not want to be a parent should prevail, unless the party favoring parenthood has no other way of becoming a parent.[62] Furthermore, the court opinion clearly struck down the concept that the embryos were children; in other words, life does not begin at conception.[63] Last, the court held that the clinic storing the embryos was "free to follow its normal procedures in dealing with the unused 'pre-embryos' (the court's term) as long as that procedure is not in conflict with this opinion."[64]

The case, decided before the Pennsylvania abortion case, seems to favor parental rights over those of potential children. In addition, although both of the divorcing couple's viewpoints were considered, a balancing test was used to make a determination as to which position would prevail.[65]

Haunting legal questions remain concerning

what is to be done with fertilized zygotes. To begin with, there is a question in the *Davis* case whether the pre-embryos can be utilized for implantation, since they have been frozen for 3 years. Experts indicate that 2 years is the outer limit for freezing prior to implantation.[66] If not used for implantation, should they be destroyed? In what manner? Whose consent must be obtained to destroy them? Assuming their viability, can they be utilized by someone wanting to be a "surrogate mother"? Is the destruction of the fertilized cells covered in some way by state abortion statutes prohibiting destruction and experimentation with a fetus? And, as pro-life proponents suggest, do embryos need to be protected from destruction?[67]

Negligent destruction of the embryos creates additional concerns for health care providers. In a 1978 case, a university, hospital, and physician were found liable for the intentional destruction of a couple's cultured cells.[68] The plaintiffs sued under a theory of intentional infliction of emotional distress.

Nursing Implications

Many of the nursing implications discussed in the section *In Vitro* Fertilization are applicable to this form of reproductive technique. Some additional ramifications, however, include the nurse keeping up to date about information concerning existing state laws and the destruction of zygotes not used for implantation. The nurse will need to include in the written consent form any and all information concerning the use or destruction of cells not used for implantation. If the nurse assists the physician in the procedure, providing non-negligent care before, during, and after the procedure is essential.

Surrogate Motherhood

Surrogate motherhood is an arrangement whereby one woman (the "surrogate") conceives and bears a child under an agreement to surrender the child to another person or persons, who must then adopt the child as their own.[69] Several variations of this arrangement exist. One variation is an infertile couple agreeing to use the husband's sperm to artificially inseminate a woman who agrees to carry the child to term and then give up all parental rights. A second arrangement is when an infertile couple uses their respective ovum and sperm, fertilizing them in vitro and then having them implanted in a surrogate who carries the child to term and then gives up all parental rights. It has been estimated that since 1988, approximately 600 babies have been born by this method.[70]

Regardless of the method used, the agreement for this arrangement is regulated by state law. Some states, such as Nevada, Kentucky, and Arkansas, have passed specific legislation concerning surrogacy. Those that have not passed specific laws utilize existing state laws dealing with adoption; for example, the illegality of selling babies or acting as an "intermediary" or "broker" in the process. Thus, where surrogate motherhood is not prohibited, the arrangement with the surrogate may include the payment of medical and living expenses but not a fee for her consent to give up the child for adoption.[71]

When a surrogate mothering arrangement goes well, there is little controversy. However, when the surrogate mother decides not to give up the child at birth, a whole myriad of legal issues arises, including the respective rights of all involved in the arrangement. These issues can be best explored by reviewing the landmark case *In Re Baby M.*

Nursing Implications

The nurse's involvement with this type of reproductive technique most probably will be only in the provision of care to the surrogate mother, whether during regular checkups during the pregnancy, delivery, or postpartum period. Accurate and complete documentation concerning the care given will, of course, be necessary.

KEY CASE 11–2

In Re Baby M (1988)[72]

Surrogate mother contract entered into by husband and wife and surrogate mother

Contract provisions include payment of money to surrogate mother and surrender of child (and all parental rights to child) to husband and wife

Surrogate mother decides not to give up child or rights to child. Husband and wife sue to seek enforcement of contract

Contract found enforceable

New Jersey Supreme Court holds contract unenforceable as void against public policy and illegally allowed payment for a child

Court holds husband and wife should have custody of child, as this arrangement in child's best interest

FACTS: Plaintiff, diagnosed with multiple sclerosis, wanted children but did not want to have the disease passed on to her children. She and her husband decided to go through a surrogate mother service and use the husband's sperm to impregnate the surrogate mother. The surrogate mother selected by the service was married with two children and had tried to be a surrogate mother for another couple but was unsuccessful. The surrogate mother did become pregnant this time, however. The written contract entered into by the parties stipulated that the surrogate mother would become pregnant, carry and bear the child, deliver it to the couple, and do whatever was necessary to terminate her parental rights; the father would contest the child's paternity so there would not be a question under New Jersey law that his wife was the mother; and the father would pay the surrogate mother $10,000 upon delivery of the child to him plus the fertility services fees, which included the provision of adoption services. In the event of the father's death before completion of the contract, his wife was to be given custody of the child.

When the child, a girl, was born, the surrogate mother refused to give her to the husband and wife and terminate her rights. The couple sued (they were able to maintain the physical custody of the child during the suit), seeking enforcement of the contract and asking the court to find that placement with them was in the child's best interest.

TRIAL COURT DECISION: The New Jersey Superior Court found the contract enforceable. The husband and wife appealed directly to the New Jersey Supreme Court.

NEW JERSEY SUPREME COURT DECISION: The court reversed the superior court decision and remanded the case back to the superior court for a determination of the visitation rights of the surrogate mother. In doing so, it held that (1) the contract was unenforceable under New Jersey law because it provided payment for the adoption of a child (illegal), *not* fees for services; (2) the contract violated public policy and was therefore void and unenforceable, for it determined custody before birth (and was thus contrary to the best interest of the child); (3) it was contrary to the public policy of encouraging a child to be raised by its natural parents (in this case, the biological mother and father, not the father and his wife); and (4) it favored the rights of the natural father at the expense of the natural mother's rights. The court then determined the custody issues. Doing so by ignoring the surrogacy contract, it held that, based on the child's best interests, the father and his wife should have custody of the child. The surrogate mother was granted visitation rights because of her natural parent status. The case was remanded back to the trial court for a determination of her specific visitation rights.

KEY CASE 11–2   In Re Baby M (1988)[72] Continued

Surrogate mother granted liberal visitation rights

DECISION ON REMAND: The trial court granted the surrogate mother liberal visitation rights. The child's privacy was protected by the prohibition of selling "movie rights" without approval of court. The parties could also utilize services of court-appointed mental health professionals.

ANALYSIS: This state court decision does not end the controversy concerning surrogate mothering. In fact, in at least two cases decided since *Baby M*, different state courts have upheld surrogacy contracts as enforceable (one decision upholding the contract as not against public policy and the other upholding it to formalize the adoption agreed to).[73] Clearly, the right of privacy inherent in entering into a surrogate motherhood arrangement has yet to be determined by the highest court of the land. Until that decision occurs, the legal, ethical, and moral debate over this type of reproductive method will continue. It is also clear that a child born from a surrogacy arrangement also has privacy rights. The court was very concerned about protecting those rights and making a decision that was in the surrogate child's best interest.

No attempt should be made by the nurse to obtain information about the surrogacy relationship or participate in the decision concerning custody after the birth of the child.[74] If, however, the surrogate mother initiates a discussion about her role, or expresses concerns about it, the nurse should provide whatever support is possible. Any concerns, as well as any interventions initiated by the nurse, should be documented in the medical record.

Although there may be a well-intended interest on a nurse's part to try to connect those interested in being a surrogate mother with couples who are looking for someone to act in that role, it is best that the nurse not do so. This prohibition is applicable not only to the nurse employee, but also to the nurse who offers to do so outside of the employment setting. Involvement of this nature may clearly be in violation of state laws concerning surrogacy or adoption or both.

Nurses who work in labor and delivery services must be certain to discharge a newborn pursuant to the policy in effect in that institution. If an infant is released to the wrong party or agency, the nurse and institution will most certainly face a lawsuit. When a nurse is unclear to whom the infant should be released, contacting the nurse manager is essential.

DOCUMENTATION REMINDER 11–2
REPRODUCTIVE INNOVATIONS

▼ Patient questions/comments/concerns

▼ Consent forms complete and executed

▼ Coding of donor-identifying information to maintain confidentiality and privacy

▼ Any and all patient/family teaching concerning procedure, discharge instructions, follow-up care

▼ Complete donor sperm or ovum screening, results, and the like in chart, and information shared with female patient

▼ MD certification requirements mandated by state laws complete

- ▼ Storage of sperm, ovum, or zygotes and procedure documented
- ▼ Sperm, ovum, or zygote disposal recorded
- ▼ Refusal of any part of procedure, follow-up care, or discharge instructions

Genetic Counseling

Genetic counseling includes both the preconception determination of heritable disease and the prenatal diagnosis of fetal disease or abnormality.[75] Preconception counseling attempts to estimate the probability of recurrence of an identified genetic defect and aids prospective parents in deciding on a course of action.[76] If the female is already pregnant, specific diagnostic tests may be ordered, including amniocentesis, ultrasound, fetoscopy, and chorionic villus sampling.[77]

Clearly the timing of genetic screening is crucial. As soon as it is determined that there is a potential for a particular heritable disease or a fetal disease or abnormality, a referral to a geneticist must be made. This is particularly important for the nurse-midwife who determines that a particular client may not be one who can be expected to have a normal pregnancy or delivery.

If the prospective parents decide not to have children based on the information the geneticist provides them with, there is little else that can be done for the couple. They may consider adopting a child or children, however. If a fetal disease or abnormality is discovered, the care of the female during the pregnancy, should she decide to carry the fetus to term, must be carefully orchestrated.

Nursing Implications

The nurse working in a genetic counseling center or facility may take on any number of roles. For example, if an ultrasound examination is ordered, the nurse may function as an educator or coordinator of services.[78] If amniocentesis is required, the nurse may assist the physician. Any role requires that the nurse provide support to the female during the procedure, provide whatever patient teaching is necessary and consistent with the nursing role, monitor the patient's condition before, during, and after the procedure, and document the care given. If the nurse handles any specimens taken during the diagnostic test, careful labeling, management, and storage are also essential.

Alternative Family Structures

Adoption

Adoption has no historical basis in the common law and therefore is governed entirely by (state) statute.[79] The process involves termination of the legal relationship (and its rights and duties) between natural parents and their child and conferring the relationship upon adoptive parents and the child. The purpose of adoption is to promote the welfare of the child, especially when parents have died, or cannot, or do not, properly care for their child.

> *Adoption has no historical basis in the common law and therefore is governed entirely by (state) statute.*

The specifics concerning the adoption process are varied, because each state has its own particular law governing adoption. Even so, some common elements can be identified. Adoption can occur through an agency or through private placement. Consent for the adoption must be given by the natural parents—both the mother *and* father—unless there has been a determination of "unfitness" of the parents or a judicial termination of parental rights has already occurred (e.g., in the case of proven child abuse). The buying and selling of babies is considered illegal. Adoption records are generally sealed once the adoption is complete and cannot be opened unless "good cause" is shown.

Because an adoption is a result of state law that terminates rights and creates new ones, certain constitutional requirements must be followed. To begin with, due process protections are afforded all parties. Thus, the biological parent(s) and the child to be adopted must be given notice of the pending adoption, and the father must be given the right to consent to, or contest, the adoption. In addition, any involuntary termination of the biological parents' rights cannot occur unless the decision is supported by "clear and convincing" evidence.

The adoption itself takes place in open court, with specific orders entered into the court record so that other documentation, such as the birth certificate, can reflect the adoptive parent(s) as the natural parent(s). Adoption records are generally sealed, and thus protected from disclosure, unless good cause can be shown for their release.

Adoptive children enjoy all of the privileges of naturally born children, including the right of inheritance and recognition of the adoption in any state in which the family lives.

The Divorced Family

The process of divorce dissolves a marriage relationship.[80] As a result, the legal relationship between the former husband and wife is terminated, and thus, most, if not all, duties and obligations between the two are also terminated. If any duties or obligations survive the divorce, such as the payment of rehabilitative maintenance to the female or the continued payment of the mortgage on the home of the former couple, they would be included in the divorce decree.

If children were born during the marital relationship, their care, custody, and control would also be spelled out in the divorce decree. Although divorce terminates the duties and rights of the husband and wife, it does not terminate *parental* rights and responsibilities toward the children of that marriage. Rather, a divorce re-

quires that the parental obligations be spelled out carefully, including child support payments, consent for, and the payment for, medical care of the children, and custody arrangements.

Only when decisions concerning the custody of the children cannot be made by the divorcing couple does the court intervene to resolve the dispute. When confronted with custody battles, the court uses a "best-interest-of-the-child" test to make its determination; that is, based on such factors as the child's age, health, and desires (if able to be ascertained), what the best placement for the child or children would be.

As with adoption decrees, a custody decree is valid in all other states because of the passage of the Uniform Child Custody Jurisdiction Act.[81]

Single-Parent Families

Single-parent families, once unique, are fairly common in today's society. Recent statistics indicate, for example, that an estimated 62% of black children and 20% of white children are born without a legal father.[82] Millions more lose fathers—full or part time—to divorce.[83] In addition, the death of one parent or a single female or male adopting a child adds to the numbers of single-parent families.

Although at one time children born out of wedlock were considered illegitimate, today, children of single-parent families, whatever the cause, are legally no different from those of two-parent families. Specifically, they cannot be adopted without the consent of both biological parents, are entitled to full inheritance rights of both parents (when paternity is proven, when needed), and must be supported by the biological father (when paternity is proven, when needed).

Blended Families

The living arrangements possible for families in today's society are almost endless. A widowed man with children may marry a divorced woman with children, or a single mother may decide to live with another individual, or a divorced mother with one child may marry a previously unmarried man. The "blending" of these individuals into a family redefines the traditional notion of the "nuclear" or "primary" family of years past and adds new meaning to the term *stepfamily*.

Regardless of the manner in which the family comes together, traditional legal relationships remain unchanged. For example, unless any of the children in the aforementioned families are adopted by the respective spouse or live-in member, those spouses or live-in individuals have no legal obligation, rights, or duties in relation to the children. A subsequent marriage to another does not terminate the parental rights of the divorced couple. Likewise, marrying someone with children does not confer parental rights on the new spouse. Therefore, consent issues, custody concerns, and support obligations remain the duties, rights, and obligations of the biological parents until, and if, the biological parents' rights are severed.

Nursing Implications

A nurse will most probably provide nursing care to at least one person in an alternative family structure.

A nurse will most probably provide nursing care to at least one person in an alternative family structure.

When confronted with a patient who is pregnant but who would like to give the baby up for adoption, it is best that the nurse who is working in the community help the patient contact a reputable private or public adoption agency. It is very important that the nurse not accept money or other items of value for referring the expectant mother to a prospective adopting couple.

If the nurse is providing care to an adopted child, the adoptive parents have full parental rights and can therefore be involved in the patient's care and must be consulted for their consent for the care of their child. If the adoption has not yet been finalized, but the couple has custody of the child during the pendency of the adoption procedure, they usually are given the right to consent for treatment of the child. The nurse may want to verify that fact with the couple before treatment is given.

The nurse working with a child who is experiencing the divorce of his or her parents will need to be sensitive to the emotional trauma the minor is going through. Once the divorce is finalized, it will be important to ascertain the parent who has been given the right to consent for medical treatment. It may be possible that joint custody was agreed to or decided by the court. If that is the case, then the nurse must be certain that both parents give consent for the treatment needed by their child.

The nurse working with children in a blended family will need to assess who is the natural parent in that constellation. Generally only the natural parent can give consent for, or refusal for, treatment.

In addition to consent for treatment issues, the nurse, whether a school nurse or a nurse working in acute care, must be certain to release a child to the adult identified as being legally able to take possession of that minor. For example, the mother of a sick child may not be able to pick up the child from school. If, however, she contacts the school nurse and, consistent with the school's policy, she gives permission for her daughter to be picked up by her husband (who is not the child's father), then the school nurse can release the child to the designated person. The school nurse should document that permission in the child's school record.

SPECIAL CONSIDERATIONS IN REPRODUCTIVE AND FAMILY CONCERNS

Refusal of Treatment by Pregnant Woman

The right of the competent adult to refuse treatment, even life-sustaining treatment, has been firmly established as a protection under the Fourteenth Amendment's right of liberty (freedom from unwanted medical care) and privacy. That right becomes somewhat troublesome, however, when the competent adult is pregnant. No controlling decision declaring the fetus a person and therefore entitled to constitutional protections has been handed down by the United States Supreme Court. Even so, when the pregnant woman declines treatment, many legal issues arise in relation to the refusal's effect on the fetus.

The refusal of treatment by a pregnant woman has occurred with blood tests, diagnostic screening procedures, cesarean section, and blood transfusions.[84] To date, the cases dealing with this issue have been split; that is, some have issued court orders that the refused treatment should be given (cesarean section[85]) while others have upheld the right of refusal (blood transfusion[86]).

However, in a 1990 case, *In Re A.C.*,[87] the District of Columbia Court of Appeals held that when a terminally ill pregnant mother is near death, the question whether or not a cesarean section will be done to possibly save the life of the fetus is to be decided by the pregnant woman. If the patient cannot make that decision because of incompetency or some other reason, then the substituted judgment test must be used to make the decision.[88]

The *A.C.* case notwithstanding, what *is* often taken into consideration in the refusal situation is the age of the fetus. Prior to the *Casey* decision, some courts using the *Roe v. Wade* framework justified requiring treatment when the pregnancy was in its last trimester. At least one commentator has argued, however, that the *Roe* justification is not appropriate unless the mandated treatment is to prevent miscarriage.[89] Rather than see women as "fetal containers," she argues that constitutional protections dictate that the pregnant woman herself decide about medical treatment and her decision should control except in very limited instances.[90]

In view of the *Casey* decision, this argument and others concerning the role of women in selecting medical treatment when pregnant may well be moot. The *Casey* Court held that a state's "legitimate" interest in "fetal life" exists "throughout pregnancy."[91] If future decisions support this position, restrictions on a pregnant woman's choices concerning treatment or nontreatment may well be considered subservient to treatment options that serve the fetus's well-being. As one legal author feared, the "personhood" of pregnant women appears threatened.[92]

High-Risk Maternal Conduct during Pregnancy

The well-being of both the mother and the fetus during pregnancy is a concern of health care providers. It is also a concern to the state, especially when the mother's conduct may create a risk to the well-being or very survival of the fetus. A well-known example of the type of conduct that places the fetus at risk is the use of alcohol and drugs. Other types of behavior, such as heavy smoking and lack of prenatal care, have also been identified.

A state's interest in a pregnant woman's high-risk behavior has been demonstrated in two ways, both involving the criminal law. In a 1985 well-publicized case, the San Diego District Attorney charged Pamela Rae Monson Stewart with failing to furnish her yet-unborn child with "necessary medical care."

Specifically, Ms. Stewart was charged under the California Penal Code for disregarding her physician's advice during pregnancy. Because the pregnancy was a "problem pregnancy," her physician had advised Ms. Stewart to seek medical treatment at the first signs of any bleeding; refrain from sex with her husband; not take any amphetamines; and not be on her feet for long periods.

Ms. Stewart continued to take amphetamines and have sexual intercourse with her husband. In addition, when the bleeding did occur, she waited for 12 hours before going to the hospital for medical care.[93] A son was born, but because of severe brain damage, he died 6 weeks later.

The court dismissed the charges against Ms. Stewart, holding that the criminal statute was intended to make fathers and mothers responsible for the expenses of pregnancy and not as an obligation on females to obey a physician's orders.[94]

A second approach to halt high-risk maternal behavior has been the use of the state's child abuse statutes. This approach has not been consistently successful. For example, after the state of California was not able to prosecute Ms. Stewart under the penal code, it attempted to do so under the California child abuse law. But, in an earlier case, *Reyes v. Superior Court*[95] (pregnant woman would not stop using heroin), the court held that child abuse laws do not apply to fetal abuse. Thus the case against Ms. Stewart could not be sustained.

However, in some states, including Colorado, child abuse laws have been used to successfully prosecute pregnant women when their behavior creates a risk to the well-being of the fetus.[96]

It may be that in the future, again in view of the *Casey* decision, additional steps may be taken by the state when pregnant women engage in behavior that endangers the fetus. For example, would the protection of privacy guaranteed by the Fourteenth Amendment extend to a prohibition of a state to order a woman (or a man, for that matter) *not* to procreate when prior conduct has resulted in a finding of child abuse or neglect? In two cases, one in California and one in Kansas,[97] the courts have held that a prohibition of procreation as a condition of parole was an unpermissible intrusion of the right of privacy.

Use of Aborted Fetal Tissue for Transplantation or Research

The use of fetal remains for transplantation or research is a subject of great controversy, legally, ethically, and morally. The controversy stems mainly from the manner in which fetal tissue becomes available—through abortions.[98] Although the use of fetal tissue resulting from a spontaneous abortion or one induced to save the life of the mother may be less problematic to some, the use of an abortus from an elective abortion triggers objections from many individuals. Furthermore, the argument continues, the use of fetal tissue for experimentation and research, however noble, humane, and helpful that use may be, encourages abortion.[99]

The use of fetal tissue for research and transplantation is not new. It has occurred for some time pursuant to Department of Health and Human Service regulations, passed initially in 1975, and state laws such as the Uniform Anatomical Gift Act (UAGA), passed by all of the states between 1969 and 1973.[100] However, in March of 1988 during the Reagan administration, the Assistant Secretary declared a "temporary moratorium" on federally funded research that uses fetal tissue from induced (elective) abortions.[101]

Congress attempted to lift the ban on at least two occasions, but was unsuccessful.[102] President Bush established a tissue bank for fetal tissue resulting from miscarriages, stillbirths, or ectopic pregnancies in May of 1992, but critics stated that doing so was not enough. Such tissues are not easily available or suitable for transplant in many circumstances.[103]

On January 22, 1994 (2 days after his election), President Bill Clinton directed his newly appointed Secretary of Health and Human Services to lift the ban placed on federal funding for human fetal tissue transplantation research.[104]

Current regulations applicable to fetal tissue transplantation research include, among other provisions, definitions concerning when the death of a fetus occurs,[105] prohibitions against those using the fetal tissue from deciding the "timing, method and procedures used to terminate the pregnancy,"[106] and prohibiting the use of any inducements to influence the pregnant woman's decision to terminate her pregnancy.[107]

It is certain that the debate over the use of fetal tissue for research and transplantation will continue.

It is certain that the debate over the use of fetal tissue for research and transplantation will continue. Those who support fetal tissue use state that it holds potential promise for those with Parkinson's and Alzheimer's diseases, diabetes, and spinal cord injuries.[108] Additionally, the number of abortions performed every year—1.6 million—did not decrease after federal funding was withdrawn from fetal tissue research.[109] Opponents, however, continue to argue that support of fetal tissue use supports only "a demand for tissues from unborn babies."[110]

Fetal Research

Fetal research is defined in three ways by the federal government: in utero, ex utero, or when it is directed toward pregnant women.[111] The regulations mandate that limitations be placed on any of those types of research: (1) Preliminary studies on animals and nonpregnant subjects must take place before experimentation occurs on pregnant human subjects; (2) nontherapeutic research can pose no more than a minimal risk to the fetus; (3) no inducements may be made to terminate a pregnancy; (4) abortion procedures may pose no more than minimal risk to the fetus and pregnant woman; and (5) researchers cannot take part in any decision concerning the timing or method of abortion or the viability of the fetus when the pregnancy terminates.[112]

In addition to these requirements, specific regulations require that when research is done in utero, the informed consent of both the mother and father be obtained, the research pose minimal risk to the fetus and serve the fetus's health needs, and the information obtained is not available in other ways.[113]

If a nonviable, ex-utero fetus is utilized for research, federal regulations specifically require that vital functions will not be artificially maintained; the research will not terminate heartbeat or respiration; and the information gained through the procedure is not obtainable in another manner.[114]

Freedom of Access to Clinic Entrances Act of 1994

Because abortion and reproductive health services are such controversial issues, many instances of violence have accompanied these issues. The violence has taken many forms, including the murder of those who perform abortion services and blocking access to clinics providing abortion and other reproductive health care. In an attempt to prevent further violence from occurring, Congress passed the Freedom of Access to Clinic Entrances Act (Public Law 103-259).[115]

The Act provides civil and criminal remedies against those who block, assault, or commit other violent or threatening acts against women, their families, or health care providers at a facility providing reproductive services. The Act does permit peaceful picketing or other peaceful demonstrations protected by the First Amendment at such facilities.[116]

Nursing Implications

The nurse working with a patient in a situation in which any one of the special considerations arises will need to be certain that any informed consent or refusal documents are executed and in the patient's record. If a nurse or nurse-midwife is providing prenatal care to a pregnant woman and high-risk behavior is occurring, the nurse must adequately inform the patient of the ramifications of that behavior through patient teaching. In addition, proper documentation in the chart is essential. Furthermore, if the nurse practices in a state where such conduct is considered child abuse or neglect under the state's statute, he or she is required to report that conduct to the state agency enforcing the law.

It is important to remember that in any of the Special Considerations in Reproductive and Family Concerns situations, the medical record may be utilized in court, whether in a civil suit alleging negligence, a divorce action concerning the "best interests" of an embryo or child, or a criminal action alleging neglect or abuse on the part of a parent. Therefore, accurate, complete documentation is essential. If the nurse is subpoenaed to testify in court concerning the matter at issue, adequate preparation for that testimony is essential.

SUMMARY OF PRINCIPLES AND APPLICATIONS

Perhaps in no other area of the law are changes seen as rapidly and as frequently as in the area of family and reproductive concerns. Furthermore, new and different legal, ethical, and moral dilemmas that follow these changes will need to be resolved.

For example, the birth of a child to a woman well past menopause as a result of *in vitro* fertilization brings into question the traditional reproductive period for women that has existed prior to this birth. The ability of a mother to become the "surrogate mother" for her daughter and son-in-law by *in vitro* fertilization when the daughter cannot become pregnant also raises questions about established, traditional roles.

Moreover, the potential for abuse of reproductive innovations may well be a sign of things to come. The conviction of a physician utilizing his own sperm for *in vitro* transplantation of his patients without their consent is indeed troubling.

And, there is the ever-constant concern over research involving the ex utero reimplantation human embryo. Should such research be federally funded? Which embryos should be used for research? Will this technique be abused? The answers to these, and other, questions surrounding human embryo research will not be easily obtained.[117]

It is certain that additional developments will continue to occur in the area of reproductive health and the family. The nurse practicing in this area of nursing will need to continually update his or her knowledge base of legal developments *and* practice changes, especially as the effects of the *Casey* decision become clear. The nurse will need to be ever vigilant concerning the ethical and moral issues raised by advances in the area of family and reproductive care. This is important not only in relation to the provision of care to patients but also for the nurse's own level of comfort with innovations in this interesting area of nursing practice.

Thus, the nurse will need to:

▼ Continually update practice skills and knowledge base in this area of nursing care

▼ Explore his or her own thoughts and feelings concerning family and reproductive issues

▼ Carefully consider the constitutional protections of the right of privacy for all patients when providing care

▼ Remember that no right is absolute and that, in some instances, a right may be limited by the government if that limitation can pass the applicable constitutional test

▼ Understand the two basic tests for decision-making when an individual cannot do so himself or herself—the "substituted judgment" and "best-interest-of-the-person" tests

▼ Remember that, currently, neither the fetus nor an embryo is considered a person under the law

▼ Remember that informed consent for reproductive innovations is necessary, and in some instances, requires the biological father also to give his informed consent

▼ Remember that access to abortion and other reproductive health services are protected by federal law

▼ Understand that sterilization procedures are carefully scrutinized by the courts, and the procedure cannot be done without conformity with constitutional principles

▼ Document completely and accurately in this area of nursing practice

▼ Voice an inability to participate in any procedure that is offensive to religious beliefs, including abortion, and share those concerns with nurse managers and administration so that the nurse is not required to care for the patient

▼ Ensure that the role of "baby broker" in any private or agency adoption is not undertaken

▼ Conduct or participate in research in this area consistent with federal and state regulations

▼ Ensure that consent for treatment for minors is obtained from the proper person (e.g., parent, not stepparent)

TOPICS FOR FURTHER INQUIRY

1. Compare and contrast laws from selected states that govern involuntary sterilization to determine what protections are provided individuals who may be subject to involuntary sterilization.

2. Draft a model bill supporting or rejecting the right of a minor to obtain birth control services without parental consent.

3. Develop an interview guide for use with individuals who live in alternative family structures to measure experienced legal difficulties, if any, due to those alternative structures (e.g., discrimination, difficulty in obtaining loans).

4. Analyze selected cases reported in your state dealing with women who exhibited high-risk behaviors during pregnancy and what punishment, sanctions, or other limitations were imposed on the women by the court.

REFERENCES

1. Ralph Chandler, Richard Enslen, and Peter Renstrom. *Constitutional Law Deskbook: Individual Rights*, 2d Edi-

tion. Rochester, NY: The Lawyers Co-Operative Publishing Company, 1987, 386 (with Cumulative Supplement Issued May 1994).

2. *Olmstead v. United States*, 277 U.S. 438 (1928).

3. Chandler, Enslen, and Renstrom, *supra* note 1, at 384.

4. *Id*. at 387.

5. Henry Campbell Black. *Black's Law Dictionary*. 6th Edition. St. Paul, Minn.: West Publishing Company, 1991, 786.

6. Chandler, Enslen, and Renstrom, *supra* note 1, at 386, *citing* Justice Goldberg in *Griswold v. Connecticut* 381 U.S. 479 (1965).

7. Henry Campbell Black, *supra* note 5, at 769.

8. Daniel Griffith, "The Best Interest Standard: A Comparison of the State's Parens Patriae Authority and Judicial Oversights in Best Interest Determinations for Children and Incompetent Patients," 7(3) *Issues in Law & Medicine* (Winter 1991), 288, *citing Late Corporation of the Church of Jesus Christ of Latter Day Saints v. United States*, 136 U.S. 1, 57 (1890).

9. Griffith, *Id., citing* Dresser, "Life, Death and Incompetent Patients: Conceptual Infirmities and Hidden Values in the Law," 28 *Arizona Law Review* 373, 385 (1986).

10. *Id*. at 302–303, *citing* Quinn, "The Best Interests of Incompetent Patients: The Capacity for Interpersonal Relationships as a Standard for Decisionmaking," 76 *California Law Review* 897, 902–904 (1988).

11. *Id*. at 913.

12. Sarah Cohn. *Malpractice and Liability in Clinical Obstetrical Nursing*. Rockville, Md.: Aspen Publishers, Inc., 1990, 76, *citing* S.J. Gould. *The Flamingo's Smile—Reflections in Natural History*. New York: W.W. Norton Company, 1965, 306–318.

13. 274 U.S. 200 (1927).

14. 316 U.S. 535 (1942).

15. Robert D. Miller. *Problems in Hospital Law*. 6th Edition. Rockville, Md.: Aspen Publishers, Inc., 1990, 319.

16. *Id*. at 320.

17. Cohn, *supra* note 12, at 78–79.

18. Miller, *supra* note 15, at 318.

19. *Id*. at 318–319.

20. 381 U.S. 479 (1965).

21. 405 U.S. 438 (1972).

22. 325 ILCS 10/1 (1993).

23. *Taber's Cyclopedic Medical Dictionary*. 16th Edition Illustrated. Philadelphia: F.A. Davis Company, 1989, 7.

24. *Id*.

25. Miller, *supra* note 15, at 317.

26. Cohn, *supra* note 12, at 51, *citing* K. Niswander and M. Porto, "Abortion Practices in the United States: A Medical Viewpoint," *in Abortion, Medicine and the Law*. Edited by J.D. Butler and D. Walbert. New York: Facts on File Publications, 1986, 249; J. Raisler, "Abortion 1980: Battleground for Reproductive Rights," *Journal of Nurse Midwifery* 25 (March/April 1980), 28.

27. *Id., citing* H. David, "Abortion Policies," *in Abortion and Sterilization: Medical and Social Aspects*. Edited by J. Hodgson. New York: Grune & Stratton, 1985, 5.

28. *Id*. at 52, *citing* B.J. George, Jr, "The Evolving Law of Abortion," *Case Western Reserve Law Review* 23, 1972, 715–720.

29. 410 U.S. 113 (1973).
30. 448 U.S. 297 (1980).
31. 462 U.S. 416 (1983).
32. 429 U.S. 490 (1989).
33. 497 U.S. 417 (1990).
34. 497 U.S. 502 (1990).
35. 500 U.S. 173 (1991).
36. "Gag Rule Loosened, Satisfying No One," *AJN* (May 1992), 102 (NEWSCAPS).
37. The Associated Press, "US Court Blocks 'Gag Rule,'" *Newsday* 54(63), November 4, 1992, at 13.
38. 112 S. Ct. 2791 (1992).
39. Richard Carelli, "Court Hearing Abortion Case; Activists Say Rights Jeopardized," 138(76) *Chicago Daily Law Bulletin*, April 17, 1992, 1.
40. Henry J. Reske, "Is This the End of *Roe*? The Court Revisits Abortion," 78 *ABA Journal* (May 1992), 65.
41. *Id.*
42. R. Alta Charo, "Life After *Casey*: The View From Rehnquist's Potemkin Village," 21(1) *Hastings Center Report* (Spring 1993), 59.
43. 112 S. Ct. 2820 (1992).
44. Anne J. Davis and Mila Aroskar. *Ethical Dilemmas and Nursing Practice*. 3rd Edition. Norwalk, Conn.: Appleton and Lange, 1991, 136.
45. Cohn, *supra* note 12, at 98.
46. *Id.*
47. Theodore LeBlang, Eugene Basanta, Douglas Peters, and others. *The Law of Medical Malpractice in Illinois*. Rochester, NY: The Lawyers Cooperative Publishing Company, 1986 (with September 1993 Cumulative Supplement), 862, *citing* Frankel, "Reproductive Technologies: Artificial Insemination" 4 *Encyclopedia of Bioethics* 1444 (W. Rich ed. 1978).
48. *Taber's Cyclopedic Medical Dictionary*. 16th Edition. Philadelphia: F.A. Davis Company, 1989, 921.
49. George Pozgar. *Legal Aspects of Health Care Administration*. 6th Edition. Gaithersburg, Md.: Aspen Publishers, Inc., 1996, 444–445.
50. LeBlang, Basanta, Peters, et al., *supra* note 47, at 862.
51. American Medical Association. *Code of Medical Ethics: Current Opinions with Annotations of the Council on Ethical and Judicial Affairs*. Opinions 2.04 and 2.05 (1994), 7–9.
52. Cohn, *supra* note 12, at 101.
53. *Id.*
54. Cohn, *supra* note 12, at 103.
55. *Id., citing* P. Steptoe and R. Edwards, "Birth after Reimplantation of a Human Embryo," 2 *Lancet*, 1978, 366.
56. *Id.*
57. Miller, *supra* note 15, at 322, *citing New York Times*, June 23, 1984, at 9, column 1; October 24, 1984, at 9, column 1; December 5, 1987, at 11, column 5.
58. *Davis v. Davis*, No. E-14496, 1989 WL 140495 (Tenn. Cir. 1989).
59. *Id.*
60. Duncan Mansfield, "Court Rules for Ex-Husband in Frozen Embryo Case," 138 (107) *Chicago Daily Law Bulletin*, June 1, 1992, 1, 14.
61. *Id.* at 14.
62. *Davis v. Davis*, 842 S.W. 2d 588 (Tenn. 1992).

63. *Id.*
64. Mansfield, *supra* note 59 at 1.
65. CBS Nightly News, June 1, 1992.
66. "Groups Want to Save Frozen Embryos," *Chicago Tribune*, June 3, 1992, Section 1, 10.
67. *Id.*
68. *Del Zio v. Presbyterian Hospital*, 74 Civ. 3588 (S.D.N.Y. April 12, 1978).
69. Mark Hall and Ira Ellman. *Health Care Law and Ethics in a Nutshell*. St. Paul, Minn.: West Publishing Company, 1990, 341.
70. R.A. Charo, "Legislative Approaches to Surrogate Motherhood," 16 *Law, Medicine & Health Care* (1988), 96.
71. Hall and Ellman, *supra* note 69, at 344.
72. 525 A. 2d 1128 (N.J. Super. Ct. 1987), *cert. granted*, 526 A. 2d 203 (N.J. 1987), *affirmed in part and reversed in part*, 537 A. 2d 1227 (N.J. 1988), *on remand* 542 A. 2d 52 (N.J. Super Ct. 1988).
73. *Surrogate Parenting Associates, Inc. v. Commonwealth ex. rel. Armstrong*, 704 S.W. 2d 209 (Ky. 1986); *In Re Adoption of Baby Girl L.J.*, 505 N.Y.S. 2d 813 (N.Y. Sur. 1986).
74. Cohn, *supra* note 12, at 106.
75. LeBlang, Basanta, Peters, and others, *supra* note 47, at 867.
76. *Id., citing* J. Norma and F. Fraser. *Medical Genetics: Principles and Practice*. 2d Edition, 1981, 477–478.
77. American Medical Association. *Code of Medical Ethics: Current Opinions with Annotations of the Council on Ethical and Judicial Affairs*. Opinion 2.12 (1994), 20–21.
78. Cohn, *supra* note 12, at 120.
79. Black, *supra* note 5, at 32.
80. *Id.* at 333.
81. For a text of the Uniform Act, variations and annotations concerning jurisdictions that have adopted it, see *Uniform Laws Annotated*, Master Edition, Volume 9, Pt. I (1988).
82. Joan Beck, "Don't Dwell on the Messenger; Listen to Quayle's Message," *Chicago Tribune*, May 25, 1992, Section 1, page 9.
83. *Id.*
84. Cohn, *supra* note 12, at 175–190.
85. *In Re Ayesha Madyun*, 114 *Daily Washington Law Report* 2233 (D.C. Superior Court July 26, 1986). The decision was affirmed on appeal to the Court of Appeals of the District of Columbia in an unreported opinion. Martha Field, "Controlling the Woman to Protect the Fetus," 17 (2) *Law, Medicine & Health Care* (Summer 1989), 126.
86. *Mercy Hospital, Inc. v. Jackson*, 489 A. 2d 1130 (Md. App. 1985).
87. 573 A. 2d 1235 (D.C. App. 1990).
88. *Id.* at 1235.
89. Field, *supra* note 85, at 129.
90. *Id.* at 124.
91. Laurence Gostin, "*Planned Parenthood v. Casey*: The Impact of the New Undue Burden Standard on Reproductive Health Care." 269(17) *JAMA* (May 5, 1993), 2252.
92. George J. Annas, "The Impact of Medical Technology on the Pregnant Woman's Right of Privacy," XIII(2 & 3) *American Journal of Law & Medicine* (1987), 232.
93. Field, *supra* note 85, at 118.
94. *Id.*, Footnote 41, 127.

95. 141 Cal. Rptr. 912 (Cal. App. 4 Dist. 1977).

96. *Id.*, Footnote 43, *citing* Watson A. Bowes, Jr. and Brad Selgestad, "Fetal vs. Maternal Rights: Medical and Legal Perspectives," 58 *Obstetrics and Gynecology* (1981), 209–214.

97. See *People v. Pointer*, 199 Cal. Rptr. 357 (Cal. App. 1 Dist. 1984); *State v. Mosburg*, 768 P. 2d 313 (Kan. App. 1989).

98. Mary Mahowald, Jerry Silver, and Robert Ratcheson, "The Ethical Options In Transplanting Fetal Tissue," 17(1) *Hastings Center Report* (February 1987), 13.

99. Alan Fine, "The Ethics of Fetal Tissue Transplants," 18 (3) *Hastings Center Report* (June/July 1988), 6–7.

100. *Id.* at 10–11.

101. Nikki Constantine Bell, "Regulating Transfer and Use of Fetal Tissue in Transplantation Procedures: The Ethical Dimensions," XX (3) *American Journal of Law & Medicine* (1994), 278.

102. "House Votes to Lift Fetal–Tissue Ban—Margin Not Wide Enough to Override Promised Veto," *Chicago Tribune,* May 29, 1992, Section 1, 5.

103. *Id.*

104. Bell, *supra* note 101, at 281.

105. 45 C.F.R. Section 46.203(f) (1991). " 'Dead fetus' means a dead fetus *ex utero* which exhibits neither heartbeat, spontaneous respiratory activity, spontaneous movement of voluntary muscles, nor pulsation of the umbilical cord (if still attached)."

106. 45 C.F.R. Section 46.206 (a)(3).

107. 45 C.F.R. Section 46.206 (b).

108. *Chicago Tribune,* supra note 102.

109. Joan Beck, "Promising Fetal Tissue Research a Hostage to Politics," *Chicago Tribune,* June 1, 1992, Section 1, 13.

110. *Chicago Tribune,* supra note 109, *quoting* Rep. Barbara F. Vucanovich (R-Nev.).

111. LeBlang, Basanta, Peters, and others, *supra* note 47, at 947, *citing* 45 CFR Section 46.205 *et. seq.* (1985).

112. *Id., citing* 45 CFR Section 45.206 (1985).

113. *Id., citing* 45 CFR Sections 46.207, 46.208(a) and 46.209(a) (1985).

114. *Id., citing* 45 CFR Section 46.209 (b) (1985).

115. 108 Stat. 694 (1994).

116. 108 Stat. 696 (1994).

117. "Symposium: What Research? Which Embryos?" 25(1) *Hastings Center Report* (January-February 1995), 36–46.

12 Informed Consent and Refusal of Treatment

The legal doctrine of consent, informed consent, and refusal for treatment has been influenced by many disciplines, including ethics, moral philosophy, the behavioral sciences, and, of course, the law.[1] Legally, obtaining permission for treatment was initially derived from the common law and was the result of establishing its parameters and exceptions.[2] Furthermore, the early decisions were almost exclusively derived from the physician-patient relationship, as opposed to research, transplantation, and other clinical situations.[3]

The early decisions provided guidance for the health care provider, including the nurse, in terms of compliance with the doctrine of consent. Specifically, if the doctrine's parameters were not complied with, liability for assault and battery could occur. Although there were several earlier cases that illustrated liability when consent was not obtained from a patient for treatment, the most well known case, *Schloendorff v. Society of New York Hospitals*,[4] clearly established this right. Justice Cardozo, in establishing the right of "self-determination," said:

> Every human being of adult years and sound mind has a right to determine what will be done with his own body; and a surgeon who performs an operation without his patient's consent commits an assault, for which he is liable in damages. This is true, except in cases of emergency where the patient is unconscious, and where it is necessary to operate before consent can be obtained.[5]

The common law protection of the right of giving consent was later augmented by other cases that specifically required that the patient give *informed* consent for treatment; that is, that the health care provider had a duty to provide certain information to the patient before consent was obtained.[6] If the duty was breached, then liability under a negligence theory could also be alleged by the patient.

The best known of the *informed* consent cases, *Salgo v. Leland Stanford Jr. University Board of Trustees*,[7] held that a physician had a duty to disclose "any facts necessary to form the basis of an intelligent consent by the patient to proposed treatment."[8]

Every human being of adult years and sound mind has a right to determine what will be done with his own body . . .

In addition to the common law protections that developed in relation to consent and informed consent, statutory mandates evolved. Constitutional protections, based on violations of an individual's constitutional rights of privacy, liberty, and religious freedom (First Amendment), concerning informed consent and refusal of treatment were applied to various treatment situations, including the right to refuse life-sustaining treatment. The latter has evolved as the "right to die."

INFORMED CONSENT

A patient's right of informed consent includes knowing and understanding what health care treatment is being undertaken. Obtaining informed consent is also important for the health care provider, for without it, he or she may be subject to a lawsuit alleging assault, battery, negligence, or a combination of these causes of

---

KEY PRINCIPLES

Decision-Making Capacity

Patient Self-Determination Act

Advance Directive

Surrogate Decision-Maker/Proxy Decision-Maker

Ethics Committee

Informed Consent

Informed Refusal

action. Understanding the concept of informed consent, then, is important to protect both the patient's right to supply informed consent and avoid, insofar as is possible, health care providers' inclusion in a suit for allegedly not obtaining the patient's authorization.

Types of Consent

Generally there are two types of consent: express and implied. Express consent is manifested by an oral declaration concerning a particular treatment ("yes") or by a written document (a consent form) that the patient signs. In health care, the written consent form is most often used, especially in hospitals, ambulatory surgery centers, and clinics.

It is important to note that except in certain situations (e.g., research), written consent for health care is not a requirement. Rather, it helps the patient understand what it is he or she is consenting to.

A written document indicating consent for treatment is a more reliable piece of evidence to prove that consent was obtained if a suit is filed alleging consent was not obtained before treatment. However, the use of consent forms cannot prevent the patient from taking legal action altogether. A patient can still challenge a health care situation in which a consent form was used to obtain consent. Nor can forms take the place of going through the *process* of obtaining informed consent from the patient. Obtaining informed consent is not just having a

patient sign a consent form. Rather, it is the sharing of information whereby a dialogue takes place between the health care provider and the patient.

Implied consent is consent that is given by an individual's conduct rather than verbally or in writing. For example, when a nurse tells a patient that he or she is going to take the patient's blood pressure and the patient extends the arm, implied consent is given for that procedure. Likewise, when an individual stands in line, extends the arm and receives a vaccination without protest,[9] implied consent occurs.

Implied consent has also been held by the courts to exist: (1) when a true emergency exists and the individual cannot provide consent orally or in writing; (2) during a surgical procedure when additional surgery is indicated, so long as it is not substantially divergent from that originally consented to (the "extension doctrine"); and (3) when a patient continues to take treatments without objecting to them.

If an individual does object to the health care in any way, implied consent no longer exists. For example, if a patient in an emergency department refuses further treatment after being revived from an unconscious state, then no implied consent for treatment can be used to continue treatment. Also, as with oral consent, implied consent often raises difficulties in health care situations, one of which is proof of the reason for initiating treatment without the patient's express consent.

Elements of Consent

For consent to be valid, certain requisites need to be met. The first is decision-making capacity. Decision-making capacity is an essential element of giving informed consent or refusal for treatment. Without it, consent or refusal for treatment is invalid.[10] It is defined as the "ability to appreciate the nature, extent or probable consequences of the [health care provider's] conduct to which consent is given."[11]

In the early development of the theory of

informed consent and refusal this capacity was almost always called competency, and when not present, incompetency. However, the use of those terms led to much confusion for several reasons.

One reason is that several definitions of incompetency exist. A person may be declared incompetent by a court (*de jure* incompetency) or an individual may be unable to function as a result, for example, of advanced Alzheimer's disease. Even though not declared incompetent by a court, the person may be regarded as incompetent (*de facto* incompetence).

Second, someone who has been declared incompetent by a court may not always lack the capacity to consent to treatment. Similarly, an individual with a progressive disease that eventually impairs cognitive ability is not always unable to consent in the early stages of the disease's progression.

Third, in many situations, an individual's "incompetency" is situational or transitional; that is, it is temporary. Clinically managing the environment with consistency in surroundings and personnel or appropriately using medication and adequate hydration and food reduces cognitive impairment.

Because of the confusion in the meaning and use of the terms *incompetency* and *competency*, the Presidential Commission for the Study of Ethical Problems in Medicine and Biomedical and Behavioral Research suggested that the use of the term *decision-making capacity* or *incapacity* be used to describe decision-making ability in treatment situations.[12]

Generally there is a presumption of decision-making capacity for the adult. Therefore, someone who is mentally ill, elderly, "confused," mentally retarded, or involuntarily committed to a psychiatric facility for treatment does not, by law, automatically lose decision-making capacity. Rather, there must be a determination made as to the *effect*, if any, of the illness or condition on the ability to decide about treatment or nontreatment.[13]

> *Generally there is a presumption of decision-making capacity for the adult.*

If clinical evidence demonstrates that decision-making capacity is compromised because of an illness or condition, then resort to the courts for an adjudication of the *legal disability* (current term for "incompetency" in many states) and the appointment of a guardian is necessary. Or, in those states that have adopted surrogate decision-making procedures, the procedures can be followed to allow another to provide informed consent or refusal for the patient's treatment.

Some individuals are, by statute, presumed to lack decision-making capacity. For example, minors are not able to provide consent or refusal for treatment. Instead, the parent(s) or legal guardian is given the ability to consent for and refuse treatment. However, there are exceptions to this general principle.

A second requisite necessary for consent to be valid is that the individual must give consent voluntarily; that is, given freely, without duress, coercion, or undue influence.[14] Although each case would be evaluated individually and include such factors as age of the patient, relationship between the patient and the health care provider, and the patient's mental capacity,[15] physically forcing a patient to provide consent, or restricting his or her liberty until a form is signed, might invalidate the consent obtained.

A third factor necessary for consent to be valid is that it not be obtained under fraudulent circumstances. For example, asking a patient to sign what is described as a release of medical records that, in fact, is a consent form for a particular procedure, would invalidate the consent.

Whether consent is given orally or in writing, the information given to the patient must be in a language that the patient can understand. This requirement is composed of two elements. First, the use of "medicalese" should be kept at a minimum, as it stands as one of the "greatest impediments" to patient understanding.[16] Second, the information shared must be in the patient's native language. Discussing the ramifications of a particular procedure in English to a patient who speaks and understands only Russian is of little help in obtaining consent or informed consent.

Last, but by no means least, valid consent requires that the patient have knowledge and understanding about the proposed medical regimen. Whether or not this element of consent has been met is likely the most problematic for health care providers and patients alike. Some studies indicate that despite adequate and accurate information given to patients about their proposed medical care, few truly understand what they consented to.[17] Thus there is a duty to ascertain if the patient truly knows and understands what will be done. This can be evaluated without much difficulty. For example, simply asking if the patient has any questions, leaving adequate time for the patient to ponder information received and to make a decision, and providing written instructions concerning the treatment can clarify and assist in meeting this requisite of valid consent.

Knowledge and understanding become the foundation for a patient giving *informed* consent for treatment. Although all of the elements are vital for informed choice to be present, without adequate information concerning the proposed regimen and an understanding of it, no informed consent can occur.

Obtaining Informed Consent and Necessary Elements

Generally speaking, the physician is the one who has the duty to obtain the informed consent of the patient for medical care and treatment.[18] Hospitals and other health care delivery systems have not been held to share this duty, although in recent years, some court decisions have indicated that hospitals do have a duty to ensure that staff physicians obtain the informed consent of patients before providing treatment.[19] Other independent health care providers, such as nurse anesthetists or surgeons, are responsible for obtaining informed consent for their particular procedures. And, when providing nursing care, the nurse would be the appropriate provider to obtain informed consent for that *nursing* care.

The elements of informed consent have been established by courts across the country when faced with deciding whether or not adequate information concerning particular treatments was given to patients by their physicians. Although each particular situation may require additional or less information, generally speaking, the physician is to provide the following information to a patient:

1. The patient's diagnosis and name of the treatment, procedure, medication
2. An explanation of the treatment, procedure, medication, and intended purpose
3. The hoped-for benefits of the proposed regimen (with no guarantees as to outcome)
4. The material risks, if any, of the treatment, procedure, medication
5. Alternative treatments, if any
6. The prognosis if the recommended care, procedure, medication are refused.[20]

The Therapeutic Privilege Doctrine

Although these elements are excellent guidelines to follow when obtaining the informed consent from a patient, it is important to note that the law does not require this information be given in each and every circumstance. Rather, it has developed the doctrine of therapeutic privilege that "suspends the duty to disclose if disclosure would be harmful to the patient."[21]

However, the privilege not to disclose certain information to the patient was narrowly drawn in the *Canterbury v. Spence* case.[22] The basis of the therapeutic privilege, according to the court, is not to influence the patient to undertake a medical regimen the physician thinks necessary by withholding information. Rather, its purpose is to allow the physician latitude of judgment when the information shared with the patient might be so detrimental to the patient that it is medically "unfeasible" . . . or "contraindicated."[23]

A patient injured by the failure to share information can sue the health care provider for that injury, under the concept of negligence. In determining whether the physician breached his or her duty of providing the elements necessary for the patient to give informed consent, two standards currently exist. One is the "professional standard"; that is, determining what other physicians in the same or similar circumstances would have revealed. This approach would require the use of an expert witness to establish the standard of care.

The second standard, the "reasonable patient" standard, looks at what "material information" the patient needed in the particular situation.[24] No expert testimony is needed to establish this standard because its focus is on the patient, not the physician. However, an expert witness—a physician—may be necessary if there is a question whether information concerning risks and alternatives to treatment should have been given to the patient.[25]

Other Exceptions to the Informed Consent Requirement

In some health care situations the law waives the need to obtain consent. In these cases, the state may have an interest in providing treatment to a particular individual.[26] Thus, neither the individual's right to give informed consent, nor the state's right to provide treatment, is absolute. As with many other circumstances, these rights must be balanced. In relation to informed consent, the nature of the exception *and* the facts and circumstances of the specific situation must be evaluated.[27]

True Emergency

One exception that has been established, for instance, is the case of a true emergency. In a true emergency, the life or the well-being of the individual is threatened and consent cannot be obtained, or if sought, might result in undue delay in treatment. In such a situation, the health care provider is able to provide necessary care. Some legal commentators have also characterized the ability to provide care in such circumstances because consent for treatment is implied, as discussed above.

For this exception to apply, however, there can be no patient directions to the contrary (for example, an oral declaration of refusal or an advance directive refusing care). Furthermore, it is the patient's *condition* that serves as the touchstone of the emergent need for care. Also, the exception is not a blanket one. It may be, for example, that based on the patient's condition, *some* information can be provided to a patient to allow the patient to consent to the treatment to be rendered, even if less information is given than would occur if the patient's condition allowed fuller disclosure.

Patient Waiver

Patient waiver of the right of giving informed consent is another exception recognized by the law. Not all patients want to be given information concerning treatment for various reasons. When the patient expresses a desire not to be informed, that right should be honored. However, it is important to note that simply because an individual chooses not to be informed about treatment, it in no way affects his or her right to *decide* about the medical regimen recommended, unless that right is waived as well.[28]

Lack of Decision-Making Capacity

The last exception is made when decision-making capacity does not exist. Although a lack of decision-making capacity would not require a health care provider to discuss treatment information with the patient, it does not exempt the health care provider from sharing the information with a surrogate or proxy decision-maker or a guardian, for example. Thus, it is an "exception" only insofar as it means that the information is not shared with the patient but rather is shared with another who is legally recognized to provide or refuse authorization for treatment.

Documentation of Informed Consent

The documentation of the patient's informed consent for treatment in the medical record is important. Documentation guidelines exist in institutional policies, JCAHO accreditation standards, and state licensing laws for health care delivery systems.

The manner most often used to denote informed consent is the consent form. As was discussed earlier, its use should be "adjunctive" only;[29] that is, as a supplement to the dialogue required between the patient and the health care provider in obtaining informed consent. Most institutions and health care delivery systems develop their own specific forms for use in the facility. Their contents are based on applicable guidelines, including federal and state case and statutory law.

Three types of consent forms have been identified: blanket, battery, and treatment specific. Blanket forms, defined as a form that arguably gives a health care provider unbridled authority and discretion to provide whatever treatment is decided upon by the provider, are not recommended for specific treatments.[30] They can be used to cover situations in which general consent will suffice; for example, on admission to a facility and for *routine* care and procedures (e.g., blood pressure, initial laboratory tests, and assignment of health insurance benefits to the institution).

Consent forms that protect health care providers against allegations of battery include information specific to a particular procedure or treatment. They are different from treatment-specific forms, however, in that the latter include *very* detailed information concerning the medical care recommended.[31] For example, when one is conducting research or experimental treat-

ment, the consent form may contain more information than one used for more conventional treatment.

The use of written consent forms to document permission for treatment cannot avoid all legal problems. The patient can challenge the way in which his or her consent was obtained, what information was shared concerning the recommended treatment, or other aspects of the *process* of obtaining informed consent. Challenges can also be raised about the form itself. For instance, a patient may ask a court to render void any clauses that waive the patient's rights to sue or that limit damages if the patient is injured ("exculpatory clauses").

The use of written consent forms to document permission for treatment cannot avoid all legal problems.

Once informed consent is given and the form signed, the consent is valid unless or until it is retracted by the patient or a change in condition renders the informed consent invalid. Thus, generally speaking, there is no specific time limitation after which the given consent of the patient is no longer valid.

Some institutions or agencies have adopted their own policies concerning this issue. For example, it may be that consent that is more than 20 days old is not valid. However, a more reasonable approach is to consider each situation on a case-by-case basis that takes into account the patient's condition, the treatment consented to, and, of course, how long ago the consent was obtained.

Informed Consent for Adults and Minors

Adults are presumed to possess decision-making capacity, and therefore anyone 18 years of age or older is able to provide his or her own consent. Thus, unless decision-making capacity does not exist, informed consent must be obtained from the adult patient. When a decision cannot be made by the patient, legal mechanisms exist for another to be consulted and provide informed consent.

Minors—those under 18 years of age—generally are seen as lacking decision-making capacity. As a result, the parent(s) or the legal guardian of the minor is the one who provides informed consent for the minor patient. However, most states have passed laws that allow a minor to provide informed consent for treatment in certain circumstances. Although the laws may vary, the following minors may be able to provide their own consent for treatment:

▼ Married minors

▼ Pregnant minors (for themselves and the fetus. However, once the fetus is born, the minor mother usually retains the right to provide consent for the minor child but not herself *unless* she fits into one of the other exceptions)

▼ Minors over a specified age—for example, 12 years of age—for sexually transmitted diseases, HIV testing, AIDS treatment, and drug and alcohol treatment

▼ Emancipated and mature minors (usually specifically defined by state law)

▼ Minors seeking birth control services

▼ Minors seeking outpatient psychiatric services or inpatient voluntary admissions to a psychiatric facility (the latter often requires *notification*—not consent—of the parents)

The exceptions to obtaining informed consent presented earlier in the chapter also apply to the minor patient. Thus, if an emergency exists or a waiver occurs, for example, then obtaining informed consent is not required.

Nursing Implications

Regardless of the setting, the nurse who works with patients will be involved in some way with obtaining informed consent. As a staff nurse in a home health care agency, hospital, or ambulatory care setting, the nurse will need to be certain to obtain consent for any nursing care directly provided the patient. This most often will be on an informal basis; for example, telling the patient that a nursing procedure is going to be done, if agreeable to the patient. It may be more formalized, however, if the nurse is doing discharge planning or teaching. In either case, making sure the patient agrees with the care will be important. Documentation of that agreement is also important.

Likewise, advanced nurse practitioners, such as nurse anesthetists, nurse practitioners, and nurse-midwives, will need to obtain written informed consent from their clients concerning the care they will be delivering. Independent nurse practitioners can clearly be sued for not obtaining the informed consent of their patients.

In addition to obtaining permission for nursing care, the nurse may be involved in the process of obtaining informed consent for medical procedures by *witnessing* the patient's signature on the consent form in some way after the physician has completed the informed consent *process*. This role is different from obtaining consent, for the nurse is either obtaining the patient's signature (where the nurse becomes a witness to the signing only) or observing the patient sign the form in the presence of the physician.[32] There is no legal requirement that the witness be a nurse or, in fact, that a witness be used at all.[33] The use of a witness is a good risk-management tool, however, and the role can be performed by *any* competent adult, including a family member.[34]

Regardless of the nurse's role in the informed consent process, certain guidelines are critical to keep in mind. The patient should never be coerced, threatened, or hurried when his or her signature is sought. If questions concerning the procedure or treatment are raised by the patient, the nurse must evaluate if the patient is truly informed about that regimen. If there is any doubt, the nurse must ask the patient not to sign the form and contact the physician or independent nurse practitioner so that whatever additional clarification or information is needed is received by the patient. Notification by the nurse of his or her nurse manager is also necessary.

If the nurse questions the patient's decision-making capacity, notification of the physician or advanced nurse practitioner and nurse manager is vital so that an appropriate evaluation of the patient's ability to provide informed consent can occur. Likewise, if a change in the patient's condition takes place after informed consent has been obtained—an increase or decrease in blood pressure prior to surgery, for example—the appropriate health care provider and nurse manager must be informed.

If English is not the primary language of the patient or parent whose consent is needed, an interpreter will be necessary. When using an interpreter, the nurse or other health care provider is *not* certifying that the interpreter provided the information needed correctly. Rather, the health care provider is simply indicating that the duty to provide information in a language the patient understands was met. Again, *any* individual, including a minor family member, can fulfill this role.

Although information concerning the patient's age should be clear long before informed consent for treatment is obtained, the nurse may need to validate the patient's age in order that consent is obtained from the proper person. If the patient is a minor, any exceptions that might allow the minor to provide consent should be ascertained. If the minor's parents are divorced, it will be important to obtain informed consent from the parent awarded that right during the divorce.

Last, but not least, the nurse must be actively involved in developing and updating agency or institutional policies and procedures concerning informed consent and the nurse's role in the process. Clear policies and procedures that delineate the nurse's role can be helpful in ensuring their consistent application and can be help-

ful in resolving controversies that may arise in practice.

DOCUMENTATION REMINDER 12–1
INFORMED CONSENT

▼ If nurse present when process of informed consent was carried out, who was present (by name), condition of patient, questions asked by patient, and the like

▼ Signed consent form (done pursuant to policy) included in patient record

▼ Communication with physician, advanced nurse practitioner and/or nurse manager as to time, discussion, instructions, and changes of orders, patient response

▼ Presence of interpreter by name, address, time, others present in medical record and on consent form

▼ Any exceptions to the need for informed consent (detailed as to circumstance, attempts to obtain consent, knowing waiver)

▼ If consent withdrawn by patient, notification of appropriate health care provider, time called, patient statement, individuals present, other actions taken

---

INFORMED REFUSAL

The right of informed refusal for treatment is analogous to informed consent for treatment.[35] A refusal of treatment can take place at the initiation of treatment, or it can occur at any time after treatment is begun. Furthermore, a refusal is valid even after informed consent has been given.

In some instances, the right to refuse treatment may result in a compromise of the individual's overall health and well-being. In other circumstances, the refusal may result in the death of the patient who refuses medical intervention. The latter, known as the "right to die," is the ultimate outcome of the right to refuse treatment.

The right of informed refusal for treatment is analogous to informed consent for treatment.

Types of Refusal

There can be two types of refusal of treatment. One is, of course, an express refusal. Either through an oral declaration or written document, the patient articulates what he or she does not want done when medical care is contemplated. Most often, in health care settings a written form to document refusal is used. This may take the form of an advance directive or a refusal of treatment form developed by the institution that substantiates the refusal and becomes a part of the patient's medical record.

Refusal of treatment may also be implied; that is, the patient's conduct indicates unwillingness to undergo medical intervention. For example, if a nurse in the emergency department tells a patient that the physician has ordered an injection and asks the patient to extend the arm for the shot, and the patient holds the arms tightly to the body instead, the patient has refused that treatment. Likewise, if attempt is made to give oral medication, and the patient refuses to open his or her mouth, a refusal of that medication has occurred.

Elements of Refusal

The refusal of treatment requires that the patient possess decision-making capacity; the refusal must be voluntary, uncoerced, and not given under fraudulent circumstances; and the patient must refuse treatment with knowledge and understanding of the refusal.

Obtaining Informed Refusal and Necessary Elements

The obligation to obtain informed refusal for treatment rests with the independent health care provider who is providing care to the patient. Thus, for medical issues, the physician would be responsible for ensuring that the refusal of the patient is obtained and is informed. A nurse who functions in an advanced role would also be the responsible health care provider to procure this information.

A health care institution's potential liability in refusal of care situations is somewhat different than for informed consent situations. When a patient does refuse care, the institution is obligated to make sure that no institution staff perform the refused treatment.[36] Furthermore, along with the health care provider, the facility is obligated to continue to provide "the best medical care possible" within the parameters of the patient's refusal.[37] In other words, informed refusal does not imply consent for "mistreatment."[38]

The elements of informed refusal are, in essence, the same as those required when the patient gives informed consent for treatment. In other words, the patient must be given all information necessary under the circumstances, including treatment options, risks, benefits, and the prognosis if the treatment is not undertaken.[39] The reason(s) for refusal is immaterial. So long as the patient has decision-making capacity, the refusal must be honored.[40]

Exceptions to Honoring Informed Refusal by Patient

Although the right of informed refusal for health care has been articulated in a long line of cases, including the *Cruzan v. Harmon* decision[41] that was affirmed in the United States Supreme Court case *Cruzan v. Director*,[42] the right is not absolute. There are special populations and circumstances that require exceptions to the general principle that informed refusal must be honored. Those populations and circumstances will be discussed later in this chapter.

Documentation of Informed Refusal

When a patient refuses treatment, the informed refusal must be documented in the medical record. If the refusal is in a form other than an advance directive, then specific documentation must be done pursuant to the facility's policies and procedures.

Most health care delivery systems use an informed refusal form when a patient orally decides not to undergo treatment. The patient would be asked to sign the form, fashioned in a manner similar to informed consent forms, in the presence of a witness or witnesses. Areas that might be included in the form would be (1) an explanation of what treatment, surgery, or medication was recommended and refused; (2) the hoped-for benefits had the treatment been undertaken; (3) the ramifications of the refusal, and specifically the prognosis; and (4) any alternative treatment that was recommended and refused.

In addition, the institution may include a waiver of the right to sue the institution and the health care provider and/or a hold-harmless clause in the event the patient experiences injury or death due to the refusal of treatment. The validity of such clauses is questionable. In most instances, such clauses are not upheld by the courts because they are against public policy. This position is based on the fact that the patient does not have the same ability to bargain with the institution in such situations and therefore may feel there is no choice but to sign such an agreement.[43]

An example of a situation in which a form is often used to document refusal of care is when a patient decides to leave the institution against medical advice (AMA). When used, the form should include the fact that the patient was informed of the risks and consequences of leaving without continued treatment; who, if anyone the patient left with; and the fact that the patient can return for treatment if he or she changes his or her mind.[44]

Informed Refusal for Adults and Minors

Informed refusal for treatment is given by the adult with decision-making capacity. When decision-making capacity is absent, the use of an advance directive, if one exists, is acceptable, or a legally recognized substitute/proxy decision-maker can make the decision.

In situations in which minors are able to give informed consent for treatment, they are also usually given the right to provide informed refusal for treatment. When the minor does not possess that ability, it is the parent(s) or legal guardian who has the legal right to decide whether or not treatment will be refused.

However, the right to refuse treatment is not absolute, either for the adult or the minor patient. The limitations on the right to refuse treatment will be discussed later in this chapter.

Nursing Implications

Many of the same implications discussed under informed consent for treatment are applicable to the nurse when a patient refuses treatment. Those implications include not coercing an individual into refusing treatment, clarifying any concern over a patient's ability to provide informed refusal for treatment, and participating in the development of policies and procedures governing refusal of treatment.

One of the most important things for the nurse working with a patient who expresses a refusal of treatment is to make certain that the request is honored. Generally speaking, a refusal should alert the nurse not to initiate care, to contact the physician and nurse manager, and to document the refusal in the record. The nurse should not hold the patient down physically or otherwise force or coerce the individual to accept treatment. Unless there is a true emergency or a situation in which treatment is necessary because of a danger posed by patients to themselves or others (e.g., when a psychiatric patient is acting out by hitting others or self-mutilating), coercion or force could result in allegations of false imprisonment, battery, and a violation of the patient's constitutional rights.

If an adult patient announces an intent to leave the facility against medical advice (AMA), he or she should be requested to stay until the physician has the opportunity to speak with him or her. If the patient refuses to wait, then an against-medical-advice form should be offered to the patient for signing. If the patient refuses to sign the form, however, then the nurse should let the patient leave and document the incident in the patient's medical record. Notification of appropriate staff and the physician is also vital.

When a parent or a guardian of a minor refuses treatment for the minor child or ward, the physician and others in the facility must be notified according to institutional policies and procedures. The refusal may trigger mandatory reporting requirements (e.g., if the refusal results in the neglect of the minor). If so, the nurse will need to comply with those requirements and document his or her actions in the minor patient's medical record.

If required by institutional policy, an incident report should also be filed by the nurse and sent to the designated individuals in the facility.

The refusal of treatment may raise controversial issues for the nurse, especially if the refusal results in the death of the individual. Nursing staff should feel free to discuss these thoughts and feelings with other staff and nursing administration to obtain support and clarification of the potential conflict of values the refusal may raise.

DOCUMENTATION REMINDER 12–2
INFORMED REFUSAL

▼ If nurse present when treatment refused, who was present (by name), condition of patient, statement(s) made by patient

▼ Signed refusal form by patient, included as part of patient medical record and discussed in nursing notes

▼ If patient leaves against medical advice, complete and concise entry in nursing note concerning refusal and other information contained on form (e.g., time left, with whom left, risks and consequences of no further treatment, who will be notified)

▼ Incident report documentation should completely and accurately include the same information as in the nursing note

---

LEGAL MECHANISMS FOR CONSENT OR REFUSAL OF TREATMENT WHEN PATIENT LACKS DECISION-MAKING CAPACITY

When an adult patient or a minor who is legally able to provide consent or refusal for treatment is unable to personally express treatment decisions, the law has provided for several mechanisms for the individual's choices to be voiced. Many times the approach used is the advance directive. Three examples of advance directives most often seen are the living will, the durable power of attorney for health care, and the "medical directive."[45]

An advance directive is a written statement that directs health care providers concerning consent or refusal for treatment when the individual patient does not possess decision-making capacity. As such, they are anticipatory rather than contemporaneous documents.[46]

Advance directives are not cumulative or the exclusive manner in which an individual may direct decisions concerning treatment. Rather, they are but one way for the patient to express treatment choices in the event he or she cannot do so personally. They provide guidance for health care providers when decisions must be made and the patient cannot be consulted.[47]

When the directive provides for the appointment of a surrogate decision-maker or a proxy decision-maker, health care providers have the opportunity to work with that individual to provide care consistent with the patient's wishes.

An advance directive is a written statement that directs health care providers concerning consent or refusal for treatment when the individual patient does not possess decision-making capacity.

Living wills and durable powers of attorney are created by state statutes and are called natural death acts, medical treatment decisions acts, and substituted consent acts, for example. In some states, the statutes are paradigms of model legislation, while others have adopted portions of suggested legislation. For example, the Uniform Rights of the Terminally Ill Act[48] has been adopted by several jurisdictions, including Alaska, Maine, Montana, Missouri, and Oklahoma. Other states, such as Alabama, Illinois, Kansas, and New Hampshire have adopted legislation influenced by suggested, but not enacted, model laws (e.g., the Medical Treatment Decision Act, drafted by the Society for the Right to Die [now called Choice in Dying]).[49] In contrast, the medical directive is not developed by state statute but by two physician-PhDs. In any case, an advance directive may be instructive (stating care to be carried out, withdrawn, or withheld), may appoint a surrogate/proxy decision-maker, or do both.[50]

If an advance directive does not exist, then a second mechanism may be the use of a surrogate/proxy decision-maker. Established by state law, this mechanism may be specific to a particular situation, such as donating organs or body parts for transplantation or refusing life-sustaining treatment, or may be of a more general nature in *any* health care situations in which the principal lacks decision-making capacity.

A third manner in which decisions for another may be made is through the use of the state guardianship laws that have been in existence in most states for some time.

None of these mechanisms is exempt from challenges by family members or others who may not agree with an individual's choice or who may believe the decision concerning medical care was not freely given. As a result, contests can arise even with an advance care document or with surrogate/proxy decision-making. When they occur, a resort to the state probate court is the only way to resolve any questions concerning such issues as free choice, the presence or absence of decision-making ability, and whose decision concerning a particular patient should be given weight in treatment decisions.

Advance Directives

Living Will

A living will is a document that establishes a written mechanism for an individual to specify wishes concerning the withdrawing or forgoing of life-sustaining treatment (treatment that only prolongs or delays the process of dying). Typically the individual must be an adult or an emancipated minor (as defined by state law) to execute a living will. In addition, the presence of a terminal condition, persistent vegetative state, or permanent unconsciousness must exist before any instructions in the will are given effect.[51] Currently, 47 states and the District of Columbia have living will statutes.[52]

The instructions in a living will direct health care providers concerning types of treatments the individual does not want initiated, or wants withdrawn, when the patient's condition meets the requisite diagnosis. The diagnosis is certified to by at least one physician and documented in the patient's medical record. Orders are then written by the physician that are consistent with the patient's instructions. Specific treatments that can be withdrawn or withheld include, but are not necessarily limited to, surgery, blood transfusions, cardiopulmonary resuscitation, and artificial nutrition and hydration.

Living wills are required to be in writing and signed by the patient. The patient's signature either must be witnessed by specified individuals or notarized. Many states (e.g., Colorado, Hawaii, and West Virginia) prohibit from being a witness any employee, including a nurse, of a facility where the declarant is receiving care. The form the living will is to take is frequently included in the state statute, and an individual should use that form for his or her own will. State statutes also include how a living will can be revoked after it is executed. Some examples include oral revocation, destroying the will, or amending it in writing.

Living will legislation most often provides immunity from civil and criminal suits and disciplinary actions by state licensing agencies for health care providers who in good faith and consistent with good medical and nursing practice abide by a patient's wishes in the document. A sample living will form is shown in Figure 12–1.

Durable Power of Attorney for Health Care

A durable power of attorney for health care is a written, signed, and witnessed document that appoints an individual ("agent") to make health care decisions when the patient (the "principal") cannot do so himself or herself. As such, it is different from the living will in that the instructions are communicated to the agent who as a proxy or surrogate decision-maker works with the health care providers concerning the treatment decisions of the principal.

As with living wills, the person executing a durable power for health care decisions must be an adult or, in some instances, an emancipated minor. The agent or agents appointed (many statutes provide for successor agents to be listed in the event the first agent named cannot serve)

can generally be anyone the principal selects; in other words, it does not have to be a family member, although it may be. However, there are some restrictions on who can serve as an agent. One frequent restriction in many state statutes is the inability of a health care provider, including a nurse, to act as an agent when providing patient care to the principal.

The durable power of attorney for health care decisions is a much more flexible and broader-based document than the living will is. To begin with, it often allows the agent to make all health care decisions, including consent for *and* refusal of treatment. Those treatments include, but are not limited to, surgery, blood transfusions, dialysis, cardiopulmonary resuscitation, and artificial nutrition and hydration. Furthermore, it is not restricted to situations in which the principal is terminally ill but can be used for any treatment circumstance, such as elective or required surgery, in which decision-making capacity would not be present.

Health care durable power of attorney laws also provide for revocation, amendments, or alterations of the document. Similar to living will legislation, immunity from civil, criminal, and disciplinary actions for health care providers is provided in these statutes.

Currently, 48 states and the District of Columbia allow agents to make decisions concerning the withholding or termination of treatment consistent with the patient's listed wishes.[53]

Figure 12–2 illustrates a sample Durable Power of Attorney for Health Care Decisions form.

Medical Directive

The medical directive is a non–statute-based advance directive that is being suggested by its authors for use because it is designed as a "comprehensive" document; specifically, it can be used for various treatment and patient condition situations and also provides for the appointment of a proxy decision-maker[54] (Figure 12–3).

In states in which a particular form is not

SAMPLE*

Living will

DECLARATION

Declaration made this _____ day of
_____ 198 _____,
I, _____,
being of sound mind, willfully and voluntarily make known
my desires that my dying shall not be artificially prolonged
under the circumstances set forth below, and do declare:

If at any time I should have an incurable injury, disease,
or illness certified to be a terminal condition by two (2)
physicians who have personally examined me, one of whom
shall be my attending physician, and the physicians have
determined that my death will occur whether or not life-
sustaining procedures are utilized and where the application
of life-sustaining procedures would serve only to artificially
prolong the dying process, I direct that such procedures be
withheld or withdrawn, and that I be permitted to die naturally with only the administration of medication or the
performance of any medical procedure deemed necessary to
provide me with comfort, care or to alleviate pain.

In the absence of my ability to give directions regarding
the use of such life-sustaining procedures, it is my intention
that this declaration shall be honored by my family and
physician(s) as the final expression of my legal right to
refuse medical or surgical treatment and accept the consequences from such refusal.

I understand the full import of this declaration and I am
emotionally and mentally competent to make this declaration.

Signed _____
Address _____

I believe the declarant to be of sound mind. I did not
sign the declarant's signature above for or at the direction
of the declarant. I am at least 18 years of age and am
not related to the declarant by blood or marriage, entitled
to any portion of the estate of the declarant according to
the laws of intestate succession of the _____
or under any will of the declarant or codicil thereto, or
directly financially responsible for declarant's medical care.
I am not the declarant's attending physician, an employee
of the attending physician, or an employee of the health
facility in which the declarant is a patient.

Witness _____
Address _____

Witness _____
Address _____
ss.:

Before   me,   the   undersigned   authority,   on   this
_____ day of _____,
198 _____, personally appeared _____,
_____, and _____, known
to me to be the Declarant and the witnesses, respectively,
whose names are signed to the foregoing instrument, and
who, in the presence of each other, did subscribe their
names to the attached Declaration (Living Will) on this
date, and that said Declarant at the time of execution of
said Declaration was over the age of eighteen (18) years
and of sound mind.

[Seal]
My commission expires:

_____
                    Notary Public
*Check requirements of individual state statute.

FIGURE 12-1 Sample living will form. (Roy Hoopes, ''Turning Out the Light,'' 31(3) *Modern Maturity* (June-July 1988), 33.
Reprinted with permission. Copyright 1988, The American Association of Retired Persons.)

Durable power of attorney *SAMPLE**

FOR HEALTH CARE

I, _____

hereby appoint: _____

name _____

home address _____

home telephone number _____

work telephone number _____

as my agent to make health care decisions for me if and when I am unable to make my own health care decisions. This gives my agent the power to consent to giving, with-holding or stopping any health care, treatment, service, or diagnostic procedure. My agent also has the authority to talk with health care personnel, get information, and sign forms necessary to carry out those decisions.

If the person named as my agent is not available or is unable to act as my agent, then I appoint the following person(s) to serve in the order listed below:

1. name _____

   home address _____

   home telephone number_____

   work telephone number_____

2. name _____

   home address _____

   home telephone number_____

   work telephone number_____

By this document I intend to create a power of attorney for health care which shall take effect upon my incapacity to make my own health care decisions and shall continue during that incapacity.

My agent shall make health care decisions as I direct below or as I make known to him or her in some other way.

  (a) Statement of desires concerning life-prolonging care, treatment, services, and procedures:

_____

_____

_____

_____

  (b) Special provisions and limitations:

_____

_____

_____

_____

_____

_____

BY SIGNING HERE I INDICATE THAT I UNDERSTAND THE PURPOSE AND EFFECT OF THIS DOCUMENT.

I sign my name to this form on _____
                                             (date)

My current home address:

_____

_____

_____

(You sign here)

WITNESSES

I declare that the person who signed or acknowledged this document is personally known to me, that he/she signed or acknowledged this durable power of attorney in my presence, and that he/she appears to be of sound mind and under no duress, fraud, or undue influence. I am not the person appointed as agent by this document, nor am I the patient's health care provider, or an employee of the patient's health care provider.

First Witness

Signature: _____

Home Address: _____

Print Name: _____

Date: _____

Second Witness

Signature: _____

Home Address: _____

Print Name: _____

Date: _____

(At least one of the above witnesses must also sign the following declaration.)

I further declare that I am not related to the patient by blood, marriage, or adoption, and, to the best of my knowl-edge, I am not entitled to any part of his/her estate under a will now existing or by operation of law.

Signature: _____

Signature: _____

I further declare that I am not related to the patient by blood, marriage, or adoption, and, to the best of my knowl-edge, I am not entitled to any part of his/her estate under a will now existing or by operation of law.

Signature: _____

Signature: _____

*Check requirements of individual state statute.

FIGURE 12-2 Sample durable power of attorney form. (Roy Hoopes, "Turning Out the Light," 31(3) *Modern Maturity* (June-July 1988), 88. Reprinted with permission. Copyright 1988, The American Association of Retired Persons.)

MY MEDICAL DIRECTIVE
This Medical Directive expresses, and shall stand for, my wishes regarding medical treatments in the event that illness should make me unable to communicate them directly. I make this Directive, being 18 years or more of age, of sound mind and appreciating the consequences of my decisions.

SITUATION (A)
If I am in a coma or in a persistent vegetative state, and in the opinion of my physician and several consultants have no known hope of regaining awareness and higher mental functions no matter what is done, then my wishes regarding use of the following, if considered medically reasonable, would be:

	I WANT	I DO NOT WANT	I AM UNDECIDED	I WANT A TRIAL: IF NO CLEAR IMPROVEMENT STOP TREATMENT
1) CARDIOPULMONARY RESUSCITATION— if on the point of dying the use of drugs and electric shock to start the heart beating, and artificial breathing.				░
2) MECHANICAL BREATHING— breathing by a machine.				
3) ARTIFICIAL NUTRITION AND HYDRATION— nutrition and fluid given through a tube in the veins, nose, or stomach.				
4) MAJOR SURGERY— such as removing the gall bladder or part of the intestines.				░
5) KIDNEY DIALYSIS— cleaning the blood by machine or by fluid passed through the belly.				
6) CHEMOTHERAPY— drugs to fight cancer.				
7) MINOR SURGERY— such as removing some tissue from an infected toe.				░
8) INVASIVE DIAGNOSTIC TESTS— such as using a flexible tube to look into the stomach.				░
9) BLOOD OR BLOOD PRODUCTS—				
10) ANTIBIOTICS— drugs to fight infection.				
11) SIMPLE DIAGNOSTIC TESTS— such as blood tests or x-rays.				░
12) PAIN MEDICATIONS, EVEN IF THEY DULL CONSCIOUSNESS AND INDIRECTLY SHORTEN MY LIFE—				░

FIGURE 12-3 Sample medical directive form (portion). (Linda Emanuel and Ezekiel Emanuel, ''The Medical Directive: A New Comprehensive Advance Care Document,'' 261(22) *JAMA* (1989), 3288–3293. Reprinted with permission. Copyright 1989, American Medical Association.)

required or strongly suggested, the medical directive could be used as an instructive document as well as a mechanism to appoint a surrogate/ proxy decision-maker. Because it is not a state law, however, many of the protections afforded in advance directive legislation (e.g., immunity from suit and guidelines concerning witnesses and agents) may not be applicable when the medical directive is used. A portion of the Medical Directive is represented in Figure 12–3.

Surrogate/Proxy Decision-Maker (Other Than a Guardian)

In health care situations, the surrogate or proxy decision-maker is an individual who is an agent for the declarant or principal (the patient), representing and acting for the patient in making health care decisions.[55] The surrogate decision-maker can be designated either by a written document (e.g., advance directive) or by state statute.

If a written document has been executed by the principal or declarant, then the surrogate decision-maker or proxy appointed in that document would make decisions in conformity with the patient's wishes and governing state law. If the person making health care decisions on behalf of another is doing so by statute, he or she must make decisions utilizing the "substituted-judgment test" (if other evidence exists concerning the patient's wishes) or the "best-interest-of-the-patient test."

The surrogate/proxy laws are often included in living will or durable power of attorney for health care decisions legislation, although Illinois and Virginia have separate statutes for substituted decision-making.[56] Surrogate/proxy laws that are separate from other statutes list individuals, in decending order of priority, able to make decisions for a person without decision-making capacity or an advance directive, and who fit the legislatively identified conditions (e.g., terminal illness or chronic vegetative state). Decision-makers often include (in order of priority) a guardian of the person, spouse, adult children, adult parents, and adult siblings.

Immunity provisions for health care providers as well as ways to resolve a health care provider's objection to the carrying out of any decisions of the surrogate/proxy are also often included in this type of legislation. Moreover, provisions are included for disagreements among and between the listed individuals (e.g., petitioning for a guardianship); documentation requirements; and responsibilities of health care providers in identifying and following the directions of the surrogate/proxy decision-maker.

It is important to contrast a guardian's role with that of a surrogate or proxy decision-maker. Although a guardian is, technically, another who makes decisions on behalf of the ward (the person declared legally disabled), the guardian is appointed by the court after judicial determination of the nature and extent of the ward's disability. A surrogate or proxy decision-maker is one who exercises the role without appointment by a court.

Guardianship for Adults

Guardianship laws have been in existence for some time and are an example of the state's power to "act as a parent" (parens patriae) in protecting those who cannot make decisions for themselves because of lack of decision-making ability. Prior to the enactment of advance directive legislation and in states in which surrogate/proxy decision-making was not possible, the appointment of a guardian was one of the few, if only, legally recognized ways that health care decisions could be made for those who could not do so themselves. Guardianship is still used for treatment decisions today, although not as frequently, because of the advent of advance directive legislation and common law decisions developing alternate ways to establish decision-making abilities.

Despite guardianship laws serving a very useful and helpful mechanism for treatment decisions, the appointment of a guardian cannot be undertaken lightly. For example, when a guardian of the person is appointed, the individual (known as the ward) may lose other fundamental rights in addition to the ability to consent to treatment. If the patient's medical condition warrants it, the right to own property, vote, and obtain a divorce may also be removed from the ward.[57]

Many early state guardianship laws did not require the guardian to make decisions in accordance with the expressed desires of the ward.[58] Laws have been, in many instances, reformed, but even today a guardian is required to act in the best interests of the ward, which may or may not be consistent with the ward's desires.

As a result, in some states, like Illinois, when an agent has been appointed pursuant to a durable power of attorney, a guardian has no power to make health care decisions unless the probate court enters an order to that effect. Other states, including Arizona, have provisions in state medical treatment acts requiring a guardian to honor any declaration made by a ward pursuant to the act.

If a guardian is needed to make personal (in contrast to estate or financial) decisions for an individual, a personal guardian or guardian of the person is appointed. Generally the personal guardian has the responsibility to provide for the care, support, comfort, health, education, and maintenance of the ward. Additional powers may be specifically granted by the court, or limitations may be imposed on the guardian's powers depending on state law. Some of the limitations may include inability of the guardian to admit a nonconsenting ward to a mental health facility for treatment as a voluntary patient or providing consent for highly invasive medical treatment. Provisions usually exist in the state's probate law so that the guardian can seek permission for these procedures from the court after evidence is presented for the need to do so. If granted, an order is entered giving the guardian authority to act as was requested.

In some instances, a minor may have a personal guardian who makes decisions concerning health care rather than the parent(s) doing so if parental rights have been limited or rescinded. The personal guardian of a minor is granted specific rights depending on the circumstances for the appointment. Although education and custody of the minor may be given to the personal guardian, he or she may not have permission to consent for medical care for the minor ward. Therefore the order granting guardianship must be consulted to determine the specific powers of the personal guardian of the minor.

It is important to distinguish a guardian from a *guardian ad litem*. A *guardian ad litem* is a court-appointed position made during the course of the proceeding to protect the interests of the alleged disabled adult or minor.[59] The *guardian ad litem* has no control over the person or his or her estate. Rather, the *guardian ad litem* serves as the court's investigator; that is, providing information to the court as to what is in the best interest of the alleged disabled adult or minor concerning the appointment of a guardian. Once a guardian is appointed, the *guardian ad litem*'s role may end. If there are other judicial proceedings concerning the ward, the *guardian ad litem*'s role may continue, especially when the guardian appointed by the court is unwilling or unable to make decisions concerning the ward's personal or financial matters.

Not all states provide for the appointment of *guardian ad litems* in guardianship proceedings. In addition, their roles vary considerably even when they are used.[60]

Patient Self-Determination Act (PSDA)[61]

Because of the difficulty many people had in deciding about health care decisions, especially decisions about the termination of treatment, Congress passed the Patient Self-Determination Act. Passed as part of the federal Omnibus Budget Reconciliation Act (OBRA) of 1990 and effective December 1, 1991, the Patient Self-Determination Act requires hospitals, nursing homes, health maintenance organizations (HMOs), and home health care agencies receiving Medicare and Medicaid funds to (1) have written policies and procedures concerning adult patients and their ability to provide informed consent and refusal for treatment, and inform patients of those policies; (2) inform patients concerning their rights under state law, including the use of advance directives, to make decisions concerning treatment or nontreatment; (3) assess for the existence of any advance directives and document the same in the patient's medical record; (4) not condition the provision of care or otherwise discriminate against the patient who does or does not have an advance directive; (5) comply with state law concerning advance directives; and (6) provide educational programs to facility staff and the community on the law and on advance directives.[62]

The assessment of whether or not an advance directive exists, or of the patient's preference to execute one, must occur at the time of admission if the facility is a hospital or skilled care facility. For an HMO or other prepaid health care program, the information must be gathered at the time the individual enrolls in the health care plan. For home health care agencies and hospice programs, the requirement is "in advance" of providing care and "at the time of initial receipt" of hospice care.[63]

An advance directive is defined by the Patient Self-Determination Act as a *written* instruction, like a living will or durable power of attorney for health care, recognized under state law and which relates to the provision of care when the individual is incapacitated.[64]

Enforcement of the requirements of the Patient Self-Determination Act are carried out through the usual Medicare and Medicaid enforcement procedures by the Secretary of Health and Human Services and the Health Care Financing Administration (HCFA). These procedures include on-site surveys, withdrawal of funding under the applicable program, and failure to renew a provider agreement.[65]

The requirements of the Act do not apply to providers of outpatient services. Nor does the Act require a patient to execute an advance directive. The content and format of the written information to be given to the adult patient concerning advance directives are not dictated by the Department of Health and Human Services or the Health Care Financing Administration.[66] Also, health care providers are not required to carry out an advance directive if state law provides the ability of the health care provider to object to carrying out a patient's wishes on the basis of his or her conscience.[67]

Nursing Implications

With passage of the Patient Self-Determination Act, the chances that a nurse will provide care to patients who have advance directives has increased. Furthermore, the nurse may be the first person the patient discusses the advance directive with. Because the Patient Self-Determination Act required a health care facility, nursing home, and home health care agency to determine whether the patient has an advance directive, that responsibility may be assigned to the nurse. In fact, the American Nurses' Association (ANA) recommends that determining if an advance directive exists be a part of the nursing admission assessment.[68]

> *. . . the American Nurses' Association . . . recommends that determining if an advance directive exists be a part of the nursing admission assessment.*

Thus, when opening a new case, the home health care nurse will need to ascertain whether an advance care document exists. Likewise, the triage nurse in the emergency department will need to determine if any written documents for health care have been initiated by the patient.

Even if the responsibility for determining the existence of an advance directive is assigned to another health care provider or employee, it is the nurse's responsibility to ask about the advance directive when the patient is admitted to the unit or service. Because the advance directive must be made a part of the patient's medical record, the nurse should get the advance directive from the patient or family, place it in the record, document its existence in the nursing note or admission form, and notify the physician so that orders can be written consistent with the advance directive.

It is important for the nurse to remember that unless orders are given or written consistent with the advance directive, the nurse cannot institute care or withdraw or withhold care as directed by the patient in the directive. Although this prohibition may seem ethically contraindicated, legally the nurse is not able to prescribe medications or treatments (unless able to do so by the state nurse practice act). Furthermore, advance directive laws require certification of any prerequisite patient condition by a *physician*. Thus the nurse needs to obtain orders from the attending physician(s) that comply with the state advance directive laws in relation to certification and documentation requirements. Once obtained, care should be provided consistent with those orders.

If a patient does not have an advance directive on admission and wishes to execute one, the nurse should document this request and notify the appropriate department in the facility pursuant to policy. The nurse needs to remember not to be a witness to a living will or durable power of attorney. If asked, the nurse should refuse to act as an agent for the patient under a durable power of attorney for health care. Also, the nurse should not condition care on the existence or nonexistence of an advance directive or coerce, intimidate, or force a patient to initiate one.

If an advance directive is revoked, altered, or amended by the patient, the physician and the nurse manager should be notified consistent with facility policy. Care must be provided without regard to the instructions in the directive until new medical orders are provided by the physician.

When no advance directive exists and use of a surrogate/proxy decision-maker is necessary, the nurse should obtain information as to care decisions from the decision-maker and the physician only. The identity of the surrogate/proxy decision-maker needs to be clearly noted on the patient's chart.

If a guardian has been appointed for the patient, it is imperative that the *type* of guardian and *powers* be ascertained. This can be done best by asking for a copy of the order appointing the individual as guardian and making it a part of the patient's medical record. In addition, notify-

ing the physician and nursing administration is necessary.

If the nurse practices in the neonatal intensive care unit or with pediatric clients, a guardian for the minor may be making treatment decisions. As with the guardian for an adult, the nurse must ensure that the minor's guardian is legally able to provide consent or refusal for treatment.

The nurse must be active in developing clear, concise policies and procedures concerning the nurse's role and advance directives. This can be accomplished through membership on the policy and procedure committee or by communicating issues and concerns to those who serve on the committee. Important components to include in institutional policy are (1) who is to be contacted when a document exists; (2) who is to be notified when a revocation occurs; (3) the nurse's role in providing care when a revocation takes place; (4) definition of terms used in the policy (e.g., *DNR, assisted ventilation, artificial food and hydration*); (5) who is to verify the appropriate surrogate/proxy decision-maker; and (6) documentation requirements.

The nurse's active involvement on the facility ethics committee should also occur. Ethics committees were initiated primarily as a result of the *In Re Quinlan*[69] decision. In that case, the court, in holding that Karen Quinlan's father, who was her legal guardian, could remove her from the ventilator, stated that no criminal liability would occur so long as the hospital's ethics committee (really a *prognosis* committee at that point) review and confirm her prognosis.[70]

The functions of ethics committees vary. They include education, contributing to the development of institutional or agency policies and procedures, supporting those who are involved in treatment decisions, providing a forum for the airing of treatment issues and resolution of disputes, and providing a vehicle for analytic moral and legal inquiry.[71]

The American Nurses' Association's Committee on Ethics has published guidelines for nurses' participation and leadership on an ethics committee.[72] The guidelines include active participation in review processes, the importance of lay membership from the community, and reasoned decision-making concerning patient care decisions. Nursing has an invaluable contribution to make in resolving difficulties arising from refusal situations, especially when a conflict among family surrogate decision-makers or a difference of opinion among health care providers can obscure the intent of an advance directive's instructions.

Last, if the nurse is unable to carry out the instructions of a patient's advance directive or surrogate/proxy decision-maker, he or she should notify nursing administration and be assigned to another patient, as has been previously discussed.

DOCUMENTATION REMINDER 12–3
ADVANCE DIRECTIVES

▼ If advance directive made out by patient, include document in medical record

▼ Notification of physician, nurse manager, and others concerning patient's advance directive

▼ Name of surrogate/proxy decision-maker or guardian and if involved in decision-making

▼ Orders provided by physician

▼ If care transferred to another staff nurse, to whom, when, and summary notation in nursing notes

▼ If present when revocation or alteration occurs, specifics of revocation (what patient said, who was present, when and manner of revocation)

▼ Guardianship court papers included in medical record

▼ If present when care withdrawn, document clearly and concisely details (when, who present, who terminated care, patient response)

▼ Document other patient care provided that is not limited or rejected by patient

---

SPECIAL CONSIDERATIONS

Consent/Refusal for Organ and Tissue Transplantation

Organ and tissue donation is almost a common occurrence in health care today. With the many advances in medical science and the development of drugs to minimize or eliminate rejection, transplants of livers, kidneys, and hearts, for example, have been done with varying degrees of success.[73] Likewise, tissues such as bone marrow, skin, and corneas have also been transplanted.[74]

For the most part, cadavers are the primary source of donated organs.[75] Although consent or refusal for such a donation could occur orally or by a written document before the patient dies, often the decision to donate is made before the immediate situation arises in which donation is contemplated. As a result, the donation of organs or tissues is often done through a uniform law that has been passed in all states, The Uniform Anatomical Gift Act (UAGA).[76]

The Uniform Anatomical Gift Act allows an adult "of sound mind and body" to donate all or part of his or her body as a gift that takes effect upon his or her death. The gift can be made formally (e.g., in a will) or through another written and signed document, such as a donor card that is included on some state drivers' licenses, or an advance directive. In all situations, the signature of the donor is required to be certified by two witnesses. If no prior donation has occurred, the Act provides a list of individuals (in descending order of priority) who can consent for donation at the time of death.

Likewise, some states have passed other statutes granting the ability of the individual and/or the family to donate specific organs or tissues, such as corneas, when death occurs.

When an organ or tissue donation is made by a living person to another, different legal and ethical problems arise. When the donation occurs by an adult who possesses decision-making capacity, the main legal concern is that the donor is doing so after being fully informed of the procedure to be undertaken. When the donor is a minor or an adult who lacks decision-making abilities, however, the crucial question is whether or not the guardian, parent, or other surrogate decision-maker has the authority to provide consent for the procedure.

Some courts across the country have allowed donations by substituted consent to occur while other jurisdictions have not. Because of the uniqueness of every situation surrounding organ donation when an adult lacking decision-making ability or a minor is involved, the best option is to resort to the court for determination of the issue. Generally speaking, a court would most likely authorize a donation if one or more of the following criteria are met.[77]

▼ The individual would agree if he or she had decision-making capacity.

▼ The procedure poses only a minimal risk, and long-term risks of donation are remote.

▼ The donor is in good health.

▼ The potential donor is the only suitable donor.

▼ The donor would benefit emotionally and psychologically from the procedure and would not be likely to experience any psychological harm.

▼ The donee has a good likelihood of recovery with the donated organ or tissue.

▼ There is no other reasonable medical alternative for the donee.

▼ The parents or guardian of the donor consent to the procedure.

The National Organ Transplant Act[78] was passed by Congress to provide for a Task Force on Organ Procurement and Transplantation to oversee and report on issues in this area, including equitable access to organs and insurance reimbursement for transplantations. The Act also established Organ Procurement Organizations (OPOs), federally funded, nonprofit organizations established to coordinate organ dona-

tion and procurement in identified service areas.[79] Also, the Act prohibits the sale of human organs "for valuable consideration" as do many state laws.

Continued advances can be expected in organ and tissue transplantation in the years ahead. For example, animal-to-human transplantations have already occurred. In the first instance, "Baby Fae" received the heart of a baboon at Loma Linda University Medical Center in 1984 and lived for 10 days. In 1992, the use of a baboon liver for an adult male recipient at the University of Pittsburgh Hospital made the headlines. These and other developments to come raise new and different ethical and legal implications for nursing and other health care professionals.

Consent/Refusal for Human Subject Research

The American Nurses' Association has defined research as the "advancement of scientific knowledge toward achievement of improved nursing practice and better patient care."[80] Generally speaking, there are two types of medical research—therapeutic and nontherapeutic.[81] Therapeutic research is aimed toward aiding all humans, including the individual undergoing the care or treatment. In contrast, in nontherapeutic research, treatment is carried out on individuals who have no medical need for the treatment.[82] To carry out either type of research with humans as subjects, the law has established clear guidelines that must be followed to avoid, insofar as possible, abuse and misuse of the research process.

The first standards established to regulate research were the Code of Ethics in Medical Research,[83] promulgated by the Nuremberg Tribunal after World War II to avoid a duplication of the "research" done by Nazis in their concentration camps. This and subsequent codes, both national and international, led to the establishment of research guidelines by professional organizations as well as state and federal governments.

The current guidelines covering research are promulgated by the Department of Health and Human Services (HHS) and the Food and Drug Administration (FDA). The guidelines require the establishment of an Institutional Review Board (IRB) in any public or private entity engaged in research involving humans and funded totally or partially by Health and Human Services funds, or within the purview of the Food and Drug Administration.[84] The Institutional Review Board is to be composed of members (at least five) who can adequately and completely review research activities.[85] The obligations of an Institutional Review Board include: (1) initially reviewing and approving research protocols involving human subjects; (2) recommending modifications in the proposed research as needed; and (3) continually reviewing the research after its initiation.

Although other factors are evaluated by Institutional Review Boards, informed consent is one of the components analyzed before approval is given for a research design. Specifically, research subjects are to be provided with the following information:

▼ Knowledge that the study involves research

▼ Any reasonably foreseeable risks or discomforts

▼ Procedures that will be followed

▼ How long the individual will be participating

▼ Purposes of the research

▼ Reasonably expected benefits from the research

▼ Alternative treatments, if any

▼ Confidentiality of research records in relation to the individual's identity

▼ When more than a minimal risk is involved, if compensation and additional medical treatment are available and where further information can be obtained

▼ Identity of person to contact for additional questions concerning the research, the individual's rights, and if an injury occurs

▼ Statement that participation in the research is voluntary, and refusal to participate or withdrawal from study can occur without retaliation[86]

Depending on the type of research project, these minimum requirements for informed consent may be supplemented by additional requirements, including circumstances under which the individual subject's participation in the study may be terminated by the researcher without the participant's consent.[87]

The federal regulations, as well as ethical codes established by professional associations and most health care delivery systems, require the individual's informed consent to be in writing.[88]

Further federal guidelines have also been promulgated for research with special populations. For example, minors are afforded specific protections that include obtaining the minor's consent, where possible, in addition to that of *both* parents (except in certain situations).[89]

When research involves prisoners, the rules categorize research that is permissible. Permissible topics include the study of health problems affecting prisoners as a class (e.g., hepatitis, chemical use) so long as consultation with medical and ethical experts occurs.[90] An Institutional Review Board must be utilized to determine if the research proposal conforms with requirements already discussed for informed consent.[91]

Research participants who are mentally ill, especially those who are institutionalized, may not be able to exercise free choice in the same manner that noninstitutionalized individuals do. Although decision-making capacity is retained upon admission to a psychiatric facility, continued hospitalization may result in a weakening of the individual to make decisions freely. Therefore, strict compliance with federal and state guidelines concerning informed consent and research, and the use of an Institutional Review Board to oversee the study, is vital.

Consent/Refusal for HIV Testing

Obtaining informed consent when testing persons for the human immunodeficiency virus

(HIV) is important not only because of the reasons already presented in this chapter, but also because of the possible stigma of the testing itself. For example, many persons tested for HIV experience difficulty in obtaining health or life insurance.[92] As a result, many states have enacted informed consent requirements for HIV testing.

Although state statutes vary, most require that written, informed consent of the test subject be obtained before testing for HIV status. Particular information to be included in obtaining informed consent may include an explanation of the test procedure, policies concerning confidentiality of the test results, the requirement of counseling if the test is positive, and what a seropositive result means.

In some states, minors over a certain age can consent to their own HIV testing. For minors who are taken into temporary custody under the state's child abuse law, the state agency administering and enforcing the law may be given the power to consent for HIV testing so long as the consent conforms to the state HIV testing law(s).

In some states, minors over a certain age can consent to their own HIV testing.

The informed consent requirement for HIV testing is not required in all circumstances. When, for example, accidental blood or bodily fluid exposure occurs to a health care worker, some states allow testing of the individual without his or her consent. Particular requirements must be met in these cases, including a physician determining that the individual's blood or bodily fluid "may be of a nature to transmit HIV" or obtaining a court order mandating the test.

Informed refusal for HIV testing is possible, although it is not an absolute right. For example,

when a rape or another type of criminal sexual assault has allegedly occurred, in some states a victim can request that the offender be tested for HIV status.[93] If a court order is obtained by the state's attorney to compel testing, the accused can be tested over his or her objection.

Consent/Refusal and Law Enforcement

Nurses working in the emergency department (ED) of a health care facility, or staff nurses providing care for a patient under police guard, may be asked to perform procedures that are aimed at obtaining medical evidence to support a particular criminal charge against the individual. These procedures include drawing blood (for a blood alcohol or drug screen), removing stomach contents, physical examinations, and surgery (to remove a bullet or a swallowed object). Because they risk being charged with the commission of a crime, many, if not most, of the individuals refuse to provide consent for the requested procedure.

The refusal cannot be taken lightly by nursing staff, regardless of the circumstances under which the individual denies consent for treatment. Clear nursing implications exist when a refusal occurs, but it is important for the nurse to know that many states have implied consent statutes, especially in relation to driving under the influence (DUI) of chemical substances. In other words, by obtaining a driver's license, the individual provides implied consent to be tested for drugs or alcohol when suspected of being impaired when driving. When a law exists, and the individual refuses to consent for a blood test, it is likely that an action for assault and battery against the nurse or health care facility would be successful if the sample is taken over his or her objection.

Obtaining a blood sample is not as invasive a procedure as, for example, surgery to remove a bullet lodged in the patient's abdomen. The more invasive the procedure refused, the more likely an action for assault, battery, or a violation of the patient's constitutional rights (if the facility is a public facility) would be successful. Even so, a good rule of thumb is for the nurse not to participate in any refused procedure. The police have the ability to obtain a search warrant or a court order if the alleged offender refuses to provide consent for the desired medical intervention. If either of those are obtained, the protection of the nurse and health care facility against suit is almost certain.

Consent/Refusal and the Psychiatric Patient

Individuals receiving mental health services are presumed to possess decision-making capacity, regardless of whether their admission to a mental health facility is a voluntary or involuntary one (commitment). In fact, this presumption is often codified in state mental health statutes. In any case, the recipient of mental health services retains the right to provide informed consent or refusal for treatment, including, but not limited to electroconvulsive therapy, psychosurgery, dental and medical treatment, and medications. The only way in which this right can be limited in some way is through the appointment of a guardian or the use of advance directives.

Because of the far-reaching effects of some treatment methods in psychiatry, informed consent for treatment has been clearly defined in many state mental health statutes. For example, California, Florida, Georgia, Illinois, Michigan, Ohio, and Virginia provide for informed consent by the psychiatric client.[94]

The psychiatric patient's right of refusal is not absolute. In addition to the traditional exceptions to the mandate of obtaining informed consent for treatment, some additional ones exist for the psychiatric patient. One exception involves medications, particularly psychotropic medications. The right of refusing medications has been firmly established. Many cases, however, have limited that right to situations in which the patient is not a danger to himself or to others as a result of that refusal, including *Rennie v. Klein*[95]

(Thorazine and Prolixin) and *Rogers v. Orkin*[96] (several medications). These, and other, court challenges have been based on several legal theories, including the First Amendment (freedom of speech, freedom of association) and Fourteenth Amendment (privacy, due process) constitutional protections.

A second area in which refusal of treatment presents unique issues in psychiatry is when the individual refuses to be hospitalized for a psychiatric problem. Although this topic will be discussed at length in Chapter 17, it is necessary to point out here that a refusal for admission may not be honored if the individual fits the criteria in the state mental health code for an involuntary civil admission (commitment). In a far-reaching 1975 United States Supreme Court case, *O'Connor v. Donaldson*,[97] those criteria were defined as requiring a finding by the court that the individual is a danger to himself or others *as well as* being mentally ill. The decision was steadfastly based on the constitutional protections of liberty and due process guaranteed by the Fourteenth Amendment.

If a psychiatric client is determined to be in need of a guardian, the judicial procedure is a separate one from any other judicial determination. If a guardian is appointed, the guardian may be able to provide informed consent or refusal for treatment of the psychiatric ward consistent with provisions in the state mental health code. When the treatment contemplated is particularly invasive or experimental, many state statutes require the guardian to seek court approval before consent or refusal is given. For example, in Illinois, a court order must be obtained by the guardian for electroconvulsive therapy, psychosurgery, or other "highly invasive medical treatment."[98]

Other Parameters of Consent/Refusal

Other boundaries exist in relation to an individual consenting to, or refusing, treatment. Insofar as informed consent is concerned, four additional limitations on an individual's authority to consent for treatment have been identified. Those limitations include consent for (1) mayhem; (2) aiding suicide; (3) medical products and drugs prohibited by law; and (4) inappropriate treatment.[99]

Mayhem is defined as the intentional and knowing permanent disfigurement or dismemberment of a body part without justification.[100] In many states it is currently called aggravated assault or battery[101] and is a criminal violation. Consent from a patient to perform a procedure that would result in disfigurement or dismemberment does not protect the individual whose actions resulted in the bodily injury to another. For example, in a 1961 case, a physician was convicted of aiding and abetting mayhem as a result of his anesthetizing a patient's finger (at the patient's request) so it could later be removed by the patient's brother.[102]

Inducing, aiding, or forcing another to commit suicide is a crime in many states; that is, murder.[103] This is so even if the individual does so at the request of the person and with his or her consent. Moreover, a conviction for murder may result even when the request is to end suffering experienced in a serious or terminal illness.[104] This particular issue will be discussed at length in Chapter 13.

If a medical device or drug has not been approved by the Food and Drug Administration and is used in patient care situations other than those approved for testing, the practitioner using the device or drug may face several legal problems. To begin with, if there is injury to the patient, he or she may be able to sue the health care provider under a negligence theory. In addition, the practitioner would most probably face disciplinary action by the state licensing agency, by the institution where he or she practices, and by various professional associations. Again, the consent of the patient to use untested or unapproved devices or drugs would not protect the health care professional from these legal challenges.

Similarly, a health care provider is bound by ethical *and* legal mandates to provide appropriate care. A patient's expressed request and permission for the provider to do something illegal or contrary to standards of good medical or nursing practice is no justification to do so. Penalties for carrying out inappropriate or illegal care can include a suit alleging malpractice, licensing and other disciplinary actions, and even criminal charges.

Nursing Implications

The special considerations in informed consent and refusal for treatment raise additional nursing ramifications. For example, when working with patients or their families where organ or tissue donation is a possibility, adherence to established policies and procedures concerning donation can be helpful to the nurse. The nurse may have a pivotal role in approaching the patient or family concerning their decision to donate an organ, especially when the nurse works in a health care facility with a transplant unit or where a state has passed a required organ-donation request act.

Initially assessing whether the patient has executed some type of document, like a donor card, to donate a body part or parts, is also important because it may alleviate the need to determine this issue after death has occurred.

The nurse should be clear about the fact that procuring and selling body parts for donation is a crime in most states, unless done pursuant to established laws (e.g., the Uniform Anatomical Gift Act). If someone approaches the nurse concerning willingness to donate an organ or informs the nurse that a source is available, referral to an attorney, an organ procurement agency, or other advisor who can aid the person in donating the organ(s) legally is best.

Whatever the legal status of payment for organs will ultimately be, ethical dilemmas surrounding payment for organs will exist. One proposal, for example, provided a death benefit payment of $1000 to a family who consented to the donation of a deceased family member's organ(s).[105] The nurse must actively ensure that donations are carried out with dignity and respect for the donor and donee.[106]

The nurse must actively ensure that [organ] donations are carried out with dignity and respect for the donor and donee.

A nurse may be involved in research in a number of roles. If a participant in a clinical study, the nurse must be certain that the patient is fully informed concerning the research and that the written consent is present in the medical record. If questions are raised by the patient, the nurse can help the patient in obtaining whatever additional information is needed.[107] If the nurse researcher is the principal investigator, he or she will need to ensure that the patient's informed consent is obtained consistent with all applicable laws and the institution's Institutional Review Board.[108]

HIV testing requires that written, informed consent is obtained and in the medical record before testing occurs, unless an exception exists. If an exception occurs that excuses obtainment of informed consent, the nurse should carefully and completely document the facts surrounding that exception in the medical record.

If a patient is accompanied by a law enforcement officer and refuses care, the nurse should consult established policy and procedure in the facility concerning his or her role. Contacting the nurse manager is always a wise option if the nurse is unclear about what to do in the situation. If the patient consents to whatever treatment request the officer makes, the use of a facility consent form, which specifically covers consent for a procedure at the request of a law enforcement officer, is a good risk management approach. The form would become a part of the patient record as would any other consent form signed by a patient.

Psychiatric clients must be treated like all other clients in relation to informed consent and refusal for treatment; that is, they are able to grant or refuse permission for treatment. If an exception arises in which the decision cannot be honored (e.g., the patient is a danger to himself), then appropriate medical or nursing intervention should occur and those actions documented. This requires a thorough knowledge of the state mental health code's provisions on consent and refusal for treatment.

Many of the special considerations in informed consent/refusal require the nurse to exercise common sense. Yet, because the legal issues are unique, the nurse should seek guidance from his or her nurse manager and facility policies and procedures when necessary.

The ethical dilemmas raised by these situations may be more difficult to resolve than the legal concerns. Seeking out support, identifying one's own thoughts and feelings about these issues, and consistently reviewing theories of ethical decision-making and models of practice can help the nurse begin to formulate his or her own resolution to these complex patient care situations.

SUMMARY OF PRINCIPLES AND APPLICATIONS

The right of self-determination is an important one that should not be abridged by health care entities or health care providers. Whether founded upon constitutional underpinnings or couched in terms of power, autonomy, or respect, self-determination is important for consumers of health care, whether voluntarily or involuntarily. The nurse plays an essential role in aiding the patient to provide or withhold consent for treatment. Moreover, the nurse is a patient advocate. As such, he or she must protect the patient when the ability to provide continuing input into medical and nursing treatment is questioned or threatened. The nurse can fulfill those roles by:

▼ Being knowledgeable about informed consent and informed refusal state and federal laws

▼ Recognizing that the right of informed consent/refusal is based on many legal theories, including the constitutional rights of privacy, due process, liberty, and freedom of religion

▼ Protecting the patient's rights under the Patient Self-Determination Act

▼ Understanding the various advance directives, their use, and the nurse's roles when executed

▼ Volunteering to serve on the facility's ethics committee

▼ Documenting carefully, accurately, and completely in the medical record information concerning informed consent and refusal

▼ Understanding substituted consent/refusal mechanisms, especially with minors, guardians, and others

▼ Remembering that adults enjoy a presumption of possessing decision-making capacity

▼ Remembering that some minors can provide their own consent/refusal for treatment

▼ Remembering that living wills, durable powers of attorney, and medical directives are examples of advance directives

▼ Differentiating among a guardian of the person, a guardian of the estate, and a *guardian ad litem*

▼ Remembering that special circumstances in informed consent/refusal present additional nursing implications for the nurse

▼ Keeping in mind that the rights of informed consent and refusal for treatment are not absolute

TOPICS FOR FURTHER INQUIRY

1. Develop a study to compare the right of minors to consent to or refuse medical treatment in at least three states by reviewing all of the respective state statutes covering this topic.

2. Review institutional policies on informed consent/refusal for treatment in at least three health care facilities and evaluate their conformity with the Patient Self-Determination Act.

3. Design an advance directive form consistent with state law that can be used by patients to consent to or refuse treatment.

4. Compare the rights of nonpsychiatric patients to consent to/refuse treatment with those of psychiatric patients in at least two states and propose needed changes.

REFERENCES

1. Ruth Faden and Tom Beauchamp. *A History and Theory of Informed Consent.* New York: Oxford University Press, 1986, 23.
2. *Id.* at 25.
3. *Id.*
4. 105 N.E. 92 (1914).
5. *Id.* at 93.
6. Faden and Beauchamp, *supra* note 1, at 125.
7. 317 P.2d 170 (1957).
8. *Id.* at 181.
9. *O'Brian v. Cunard S.S.Co.*, 28 N.E. 266 (Mass. 1891).
10. Restatement (Second) of Torts Section 892A (2)(a)(1977).
11. *Id.* at 892(a) Comment b.
12. President's Commission for the Study of Ethical Problems in Medicine and Biomedical and Behavioral Research. *Making Health Care Decisions: The Ethical and Legal Implications of Informed Consent in the Patient-Practitioner Relationship.* Washington, D.C.: U.S. Government Printing Office, (1982) 169–175; *Deciding to Forego Life-Sustaining Treatment.* Washington, D.C.: U.S. Government Printing Office (1983), 119–126.
13. Alan Meisel. *The Right to Die.* New York: John Wiley & Sons, 1989, 174 (with 1994 Cumulative Supplement No. 2).
14. Meisel, *supra* note 13 at 30, *citing* President's Commission, *supra* note 12, Restatement of Torts Section 892, at 486 (1939), Restatement (Second) of Torts Section 892B(3)(1977), *In Re Jobes*, 529 A. 2d at 454, and *Rasmussen v. Fleming*, 741 P. 2d 674 (1987).
15. Restatement (Second) of Torts Section 892B(3)(1977).
16. Theodore LeBlang, W. Eugene Basanta, J. Douglas Peters, Keith Fineberg, and others. *The Law of Medical Practice in Illinois.* Rochester, NY: The Lawyers Co-Operative Publishing Company, 1986, 473 (with September 1993 Cumulative Supplement), *citing* Andrews, "Informed Consent Statutes and the Decision-Making Process," 5 *Journal of Legal Medicine* 164 (1984).
17. See, for example, Elizabeth Dixon and Rosemarie Park, "Do Patients Understand Written Health Information?", 38(6) *Nursing Outlook* (November/December 1990), 278–281.

18. LeBlang, Basanta, Peters, Fineberg, and others, *supra* note 16 at 472.

19. See, for example, *Tobias v. Winkler*, 509 N.E.2d 1050 (1987), *app. denied*, 517 N.E. 2d 1096 (1987).

20. Meisel, *supra* note 13 at 28–29; LeBlang, Basanta, Peters, Fineberg, and others, *supra* note 16 at 472–473.

21. Meisel, *supra* note 13 at 37.

22. 464 F.2d 772 (Washington D.C. 1972).

23. *Id*. at 789.

24. Robert Miller. *Problems In Hospital Law*. 6th edition. Rockville, Maryland: Aspen Publishers, Inc., 1990, 345–346.

25. *Id*. at 244.

26. Meisel, *supra* note 13 at 35.

27. *Id*.

28. Meisel, *supra* note 13 at 40.

29. Paul Applebaum, Charles Lidz, and Alan Meisel. *Informed Consent: Legal Theory and Clinical Practice*. New York: Oxford University Press, 1987, 182–283.

30. *Medicolegal Forms with Legal Analysis*. Chicago: American Medical Association, 1991, 130.

31. Miller, *supra* note 24, at 248.

32. Janine Fiesta. *20 Legal Pitfalls for Nurses to Avoid*. Albany, NY: Delmar Publishers, 1994, 78–79.

33. Michael Guthrie, "The Medical Staff and Risk Management," in *Handbook of Health Care Risk Management*. Glen Troyer and Steve Salman, Editors. Rockville, Md: Aspen Publishers, (1986) 358–359.

34. *Id*.

35. Meisel, *supra* note 13, at 47.

36. George J. Annas. *The Rights of Patients*. 2nd Edition. Totowa, NJ: Humana Press, 1992, 98.

37. *Id*.

38. *Id*.

39. Meisel, *supra* note 13 at 49.

40. *Id., citing St. Mary's Hospital v. Ramsey*, 465 So. 2d 666 (Florida App. 1985) (refusal of a blood transfusion regardless whether the decision is based on fear of an adverse reaction, religion, hesitation to undergo the process or cost); see also, *Normal Hospital v. Munoz*, 564 N.E.2d 1017 (1991).

41. 760 S.W. 2d 408 (Mo. 1988).

42. 110 S. Ct. 2841 (1990).

43. Annas, *supra* note 36, at 96.

44. *Nurse's Handbook of Law and Ethics*. Springhouse, Pa: Springhouse Corporation, 1992, 92–95.

45. Meisel, *supra* note 13, at 312.

46. *Id*. at 314.

47. Linda Emanuel and Ezekiel Emanuel, "The Medical Directive: A New Comprehensive Advance Care Document," 261(22) *JAMA* (1989), 3288–3293.

48. 98 U.L.A. 609 (1987).

49. Meisel, *supra* note 13, at 336.

50. Meisel, *supra* note 13, at 320.

51. Concern for Dying. *Refusal of Treatment Legislation: A State By State Compilation of Enacted and Model Statutes*. New York: Concern For Dying, 1991, Intro. 1 & 2 (with 1994 update).

52. *Id*.

53. Concern for Dying, *supra* note 51, at Intro. 2.

54. Linda Emanuel, Michael Barry, John Stoeckle, Lucy Ettelson, and Ezekiel Emanuel, "Advance Directives For Medical Care—A Case for Greater Use," *The New England Journal of Medicine* (March 28, 1991), 889.

55. Henry Campbell Black. *Black's Law Dictionary*. 6th Edition. St. Paul, Minn: West Publishing Company, 1991, 853.

56. *Id*. See 755 ILCS 40/1 *et seq*. (1991) (*Health Care Surrogate Act*); Va. Code, Sections 54.1–2981–2992 (1991) and Va. Code, Sections 37.1–134.4 (Supp. 1989) (*Natural Death Act and Substituted Consent Act*).

57. Penelope Hommel, Lu-in Wang, and James Bergman, "Trends in Guardianship Reform: Implications for the Medical and Legal Professions," 18(3) *Law, Medicine & Health Care* (Fall 1990), 214.

58. *Id., citing* Annina M. Mitchell, "Involuntary Guardianship for Incompetents: A Strategy for Legal Services Advocates," 12 *Clearinghouse Review* 451, 460 (1978).

59. Robert N. Brown and The Legal Counsel of the Elderly. *The Rights of Older Persons*. 2d Edition. Carbondale, Ill: Southern Illinois University Press, 1989, 344–345 (An American Civil Liberties Union Handbook).

60. *Id*.

61. Public Law 101–508 Sections 4206–4207; 4751–4752; *Omnibus Budget Reconciliation Act of 1990*, 42 U.S.C. 1395cc(f)(1) and 43 U.S.C. 1396a(a) (Supp. 1991).

62. *Id*.

63. *Id*. at 4206(a)(2), 42 U.S.C. Section 1395cc (f)(2) (A)–(E); 4751(a)(2), 43 U.S.C. 1396 a(w)(2) (A)–(E).

64. *Id*. at 4206 (3); 4751 (4).

65. *Federal Register* Vol. 57, No. 45, March 6, 1992, *Final Interim Rule*, 8194–8195.

66. *Id*. at 8196–8198.

67. *Id*. at 4206(c); 4751(a)(2); 42 U.S.C. 1396a(w)(3).

68. American Nurses' Association. *Position Statement on Nursing and the Patient Self-Determination Act*. Kansas City, Mo: ANA, November 18, 1991.

69. 355 A.2d 647, *cert. denied sub nom. Garger v. New Jersey*, 429 U.S. 922 (1976), *overruled in part*, In Re Conroy, 486 A. 2d 1209 (1965).

70. *Id*. at 672.

71. John A. Robertson, "Ethics Committees In Hospitals," 7(1) *Issues in Law and Medicine* (Summer 1991), 84.

72. American Nurses' Association Committee on Ethics. *Guidelines for Nurses' Participation and Leadership in Institutional Ethical Review Processes*. ANA: Kansas City, Kan (no date given).

73. LeBlang, Basanta, Peters, Fineberg, and Kroll, *supra* note 16, at 893.

74. *Id*.

75. *Id*.

76. *Uniform Laws Annotated, Master Edition*. Volume 8A (1989).

77. LeBlang and others, *supra* note 16, at 896, *citing* F. Rozovky. *Consent to Treatment: A Practical Guide*. 2nd Edition. (1990), 600.

78. P.L. 98–507, 42 U.S.C. Section 273 *et seq*. (1984).

79. LeBlang and others, *supra* note 16, at 900.

80. American Nurses' Association. *Human Rights Guidelines for Nurses in Clinical and Other Research*. ANA: Kansas City, Kan, 1985, 1.

81. LeBlang, Basanta, Peters, Fineberg, and others, *supra* note 16, at 928.

82. *Id.*
83. *Trials of War Criminals before the Nuremberg Military Tribunals under Control Council Law No. 10* (1949).
84. 45 C.F.R. Section 46.103 (a), (b), (1985).
85. 45 C.F.R. 46.107 (1985).
86. 45 C.F.R. Section 46.116(a) (1985).
87. *Id.*
88. 45 C.F.R. Section 46.117(b) (1985).
89. 45 C.F.R. Section 46.404 (1985).
90. 45 C.F.R. Section 46.306 (1985).
91. 45 C.F.R. Section 46.305 (1985).
92. Mark Scherzer, "Insurance," *in AIDS Law Today: A New Guide for The Public.* Harlon L. Dalton, Scott Burris, Judith Miller, and the Yale AIDS Project, Editors. New Haven: Yale University Press, 1993.
93. 720 ICLS 5/12-18(e) (1991) (Illinois).
94. Edward Beis. *Mental Health and the Law.* Rockville, Md: Aspen Publishers, Inc., 1984, Appendix G, 347–349.
95. 462 F. Supp. 1131 (N.J. 1978); 476 F. Supp. 1294 (D. N.J. 1979).
96. 478 F. Supp. 1342 (D. Mass. 1979); 634 F. 2d 650 (1st Cir. 1980).
97. 422 U.S. 563 (1975).
98. 405 ICLS 5/2–110 (1979).
99. Miller, *supra* note 24, at 255.
100. Henry Campbell Black. *Black's Law Dictionary.* 6th Edition. St. Paul, Minn: West Publishing Company, 1991, 676.
101. *Id.*
102. *State v. Bass*, 120 S.E. 2d 580 (1961).
103. Wayne R. LaFave and Austin W. Scott, Jr. *Criminal Law.* 2nd Edition. St. Paul, Minnesota: West Publishing Company, 1986, 650.
104. *Id.*
105. T. G. Peters, "Life or Death: The Issue of Payment in Cadaveric Organ Donation," *JAMA* 265 (March 13, 1991), 1302–1305.
106. See, for example, Sara Fry, "Are New Proposals to Increase Organ Donations Ethical?", 39(4) *Nursing Outlook* (July/August 1991), 192.
107. Nancy J. Brent, "Legal Issues in Research: Informed Consent," 22(3) *Journal of Neuroscience Nursing* (June 1990), 190.
108. *Id.*

13

Issues in Death and Dying

In Chapter 12, the concepts of informed consent and refusal for treatment were analyzed. Refusal for treatment may ultimately result in an individual's death, and the right to refuse treatment clearly includes the "right to die." The right to refuse life-sustaining treatment is not a new concept; rather, it is a by-product of the law of informed decision-making limited by the restrictions of the criminal law.[1]

Despite refusal of treatment that leads to one's death not being a novel concept, its acceptance has been fraught with controversy. The controversy has centered on the legal, ethical, and moral issues involved in the refusal of treatment; types of treatment refused; whether the patient refusing treatment was "terminally ill"; whether the patient possessed decision-making capacity; and, of course, health care professionals' obligations to provide treatment and concomitant liability issues if treatment was withheld or withdrawn.

Although all of the above factors are important, one author has identified the central problems in refusing treatment as the legitimacy of *forgoing* or *administering* treatment and the procedures used for those decisions.[2]

The previous chapter focused on the procedures for making treatment decisions. This chapter will center on the right to refuse life-sustaining treatment, including its legal development, specific cases involving that right, and

special considerations that arise when an individual exercises his or her right to die.

HISTORICAL DEVELOPMENT OF THE RIGHT TO DIE

Adults

The right to refuse life-sustaining treatment is a relatively new right. Life-sustaining (or death-delaying) treatments or procedures sustain, restore, or supplant a necessary function of an individual patient's life.[3] They primarily serve to prolong the moment of death; if they were not utilized, death would be imminent.[4] The determination concerning the procedures' or treatments' effect on the life of the patient is certified by the attending and consulting physician in the patient's medical record. Examples of life-sustaining treatment are listed and may include ventilator support, artificial nutrition and hydration, hemodialysis, surgery, the administration of medications, cardiopulmonary resuscitation, and blood transfusions.

KEY PRINCIPLES

Life-Sustaining Procedures/Death-Delaying Procedures

Suicide

Assisted Suicide

Euthanasia/Mercy Killing

Death

Decision-Making Standards for Withdrawal or Withholding Treatment

Lack of Decision-Making Capacity

The right to refuse life-sustaining treatment is a relatively new right.

The first reported case concerning this issue,

In Re Quinlan, was decided in 1976. The right has been shaped, reshaped, expanded, and clarified since the *Quinlan* decision. Refusing life-sustaining treatment has been exercised by various individuals, including patients, family members, guardians, and other substitute/proxy decision-makers. Moreover, its basis has found roots in many legal theories.

Many of the early cases, including *Quinlan*, were based on a constitutional right of personal privacy; that is, the ability to have control over what is done with one's body. The reader will recall that this rationale also formed the basis for reproductive rights discussed in Chapter 11. It was not until the United States Supreme Court decision in *Cruzan v. Director* in 1990, however, that the right was firmly couched in constitutional language.

It was not until the United States Supreme Court decision in Cruzan v. Director *in 1990, however, that the right [to refuse treatment] was firmly couched in constitutional language.*

A second legal theory supporting the right to refuse life-sustaining treatment was a common-law one. Its character was phrased in many ways, including the right to be free from unwanted bodily intrusion(s); the right to self-determination; and the right of bodily integrity.[5] Remedies for individuals who were not granted this right included suing for assault and battery, lack of informed consent/refusal, and, of course, alleging the intentional tort of invasion of privacy.

Other support for the right to die utilized state or federal legislation and concomitant regulations. For example, living wills were often successfully utilized in the early cases to support an individual's right to refuse life-sustaining treatment. However, some were not easily resolved because of the presence of advance directive legislation. For example, in one Illinois case, *In Re Estate of (Dorothy) Longeway*,[6] the Illinois Living Will Act's definition of terminal illness was used to determine if artificial food and fluid could be removed at the request of the guardian (the patient's daughter). Although Ms. Longeway had never executed a living will, the Illinois Supreme Court held that the guardian had a right to refuse the treatment, but only if the patient's condition met the Living Will Act's definition of terminal illness as well as other conditions set forth by the court.

Sustaining challenges by citing other state or federal legislation or policies and regulations of the particular health care facility was another viable legal theory. For example, in *In Re (Beverly) Requena*[7] and *Elbaum v. Grace Plaza of Great Neck*,[8] the respective institutional policies of not honoring a patient's refusal of life-sustaining treatment had to yield to the exercise of the rights of these two patients. In *Requena*, the institution did not inform the patient of the policy until after she had been hospitalized there for 15 months, and her deteriorating condition due to Lou Gehrig's disease (amyotrophic lateral sclerosis) resulted in her request not to institute administration of artificial food and fluid. Likewise, in *Elbaum* the nursing home did not inform the family that it would not honor a refusal of artificial feedings and antibiotic therapy until after it was requested by the family when subarachnoid bleeding resulted in Mrs. Elbaum's persistent vegetative state with no hope of recovery.

Last, it is important to note that another constitutional argument has been raised to support a right to refuse life-sustaining treatment—freedom of religion guaranteed by the First Amendment. Many of these cases were brought by Jehovah's Witnesses in an attempt to support their religious belief against blood transfusions. Generally the early cases mandated that the transfusions be given, especially if they were seen as life-saving and the patient was not terminally ill. That trend changed, however.

The change may be due in part to medical treatment advances that eliminate the need to seek court intervention. The use of autotransfusion (when possible) and the development of synthetic blood substitutes has begun to change the need for transfusing the blood of another. For example, perfluorocarbons (Fluosol-DA) and Perfluorocytlbromide (PFOB) showed promise when first used.[9] In 1984, Fluosol-DA was used in place of blood for a Jehovah's Witness who needed surgery for a trochanteric pressure sore.[10] Not used as a total blood replacement but rather as a transporter of oxygen and carbon dioxide, it allowed the surgery and outcome to be successful.[11] Transfusion medicine, the new name given to the development and use of blood substitutes, is currently seeking new synthetic blood substitutes, including stroma-free hemoglobin solutions.[12]

In addition, the change may also have been due to heightened emphasis on sustaining a treatment decision based on an individual's religious beliefs. For example, in *In Re Osborne*,[13] the court denied a hospital's motion for a court order to override a 34-year-old competent patient's refusal of a blood transfusion for internal bleeding. The court held that the patient's religious beliefs as a Jehovah's Witness and his interest in autonomy prevailed over any interest in preserving life and its sanctity.

Minors

Although reported cases testing the right of parents to make treatment decisions did not appear until the late 1800s,[14] parents since then have been testing and clarifying their rights in this regard. Clearly the legal issues involved in withdrawing and refusing life-sustaining treatment for a minor are somewhat more complex than those raised with adult individuals. The difficulty most probably stems from the fact that a minor, particularly if a newborn or very young, has never possessed decision-making capacity. As a result, it is impossible to determine what the minor would want in a particular situation.

Decision-making for such a minor is arguably no different than making a similar decision for an adult who has *never* possessed decision-making abilities (due to severe brain injury or retardation since birth, for example). Even so, the emotional issues involved in making treatment decisions for minors have raised additional legal concerns for health care providers. For example, specific legal protections are afforded neonates born with congenital anomalies when refusal or withholding of treatment is contemplated. This situation, as well as others affecting treatment decisions for minors, will be discussed in the Special Considerations section.

> *. . . the emotional issues involved in making treatment decisions for minors have raised additional legal concerns for health care providers.*

Despite some of the unique issues raised in refusing or withholding life-sustaining treatment for minors, the difficulties for determining what to do in a particular treatment situation for a minor are conceptually similar to those difficulties for adults.[15] Essentially the courts and federal regulatory laws concerning treatment and minors have taken a prognostic approach.[16] That is, if treatment is futile, it is not ordered. However, it should be noted that the cases cannot be cited for the proposition that only where treatment is futile will the courts uphold a refusal. Rather, as one author has suggested, this result is more reasonably related to the fact that the cases brought before the courts simply involve situations in which the minor is terminally ill.[17]

The reader will remember from Chapter 12 that parents are the natural guardians and provide informed consent or refusal for treatment for the child. As a result, most often court cases concerning treatment decisions for minors involve surrogate/proxy decision-making. The parents of minors, exercising their constitutional rights to privacy in family affairs,[18] religious freedom under the First Amendment,[19] and state statutes (e.g., Rhode Island, Arizona, and Minnesota) applicable to treatment decisions and children, have brought cases testing these rights, especially as they relate to life-sustaining treatments in state and federal courts. See Table 13–2 for summarization of some of these cases.

Despite the ability of the parents to make treatment decisions, the right is not absolute. Rather, it has been balanced with various countervailing state interests. The four state interests used by a court in evaluating a parent's right (or for that matter, any person's right) to refuse treatment include the preservation of life, prevention of suicide, protection of innocent third parties, and protection of the ethical integrity of health care professionals.[20] Moreover, parents exercising a treatment decision for a minor must also do so utilizing certain standards. Those standards include the best interest or substituted judgment standards.[21] The best interest (of the patient) standard has been also described as the "objective approach" to decision-making concerning treatment or nontreatment choices, because an "objective" evaluation as to what is "best" for the patient is made. In contrast, the substituted judgment standard has been looked at as a "subjective approach," meaning that a choice is made based upon what the patient or minor would have wanted if he or she could make the choice personally. Which guideline is used for a minor will depend upon the minor's age. For example, a young infant (seen as incompetent by the law) would never have explained his or her wishes to the parents. As a result, the best interest standard might be the most appropriate one to use. In contrast, an older minor who expressed treatment preferences to the parents may be better served by the use of the substituted judgment test.[22]

These tests are often supplemented with others. Other factors looked at when determining treatment decisions include whether the regimen in question (1) is a burden or a benefit to the patient; (2) will cause indignity, will relieve suffering, is intrusive, or has additional material risks; and (3) will affect the patient's quality of life.[23]

Some cases involving minors also tested refusal of treatment by the minor himself or herself rather than the parents doing so. These cases arose under varied circumstances. For example, in one 1941 case,[24] a 15-year-old won the ability to consent for a donation of skin to another who needed it for a skin graft operation. Other cases have involved situations in which, for example, the minor's wishes were different from those of the parents. At times the cases involved life-sustaining treatment, while in others the treatment at issue was not strictly life-sustaining.

Several Key Cases are presented involving the refusal of treatment for minors. In addition, in the Special Considerations section, additional cases concerning refusal of treatment for minors will be discussed in which allegations of child abuse or neglect (or other charges) are brought against the parents. A brief analysis of the law in relation to treatment decisions for newborns born with disabilities will also be highlighted. These types of cases raise unique and difficult legal issues.

KEY CASES INVOLVING ADULTS

Although all of the court cases in which individuals asserted their right to refuse treatment, either in their own behalf or through another, are important, two cases will be presented as key ones. The *Quinlan* and *Cruzan* cases are, literally, landmark decisions in relation to refusing life-sustaining treatment. *Quinlan* was the first to raise the country's awareness of the issue and initiated a plethora of subsequent cases. *Cruzan* was the first case decided by the United States Supreme Court concerning the right to die and under what circumstances this choice would be honored. In both cases, the individuals involved—Karen Quinlan and Nancy Cruzan—had lost their decision-making ability. Guardians—family members in both instances—exercised the right on behalf of their respective daughters.

KEY CASE 13–1   In Re Karen Quinlan (1976)[25]

A 21-year-old patient on ventilator after respiratory arrests

A diagnosis of persistent vegetative state (PVS) is made

Father petitions court to be appointed guardian to give permission to remove daughter from ventilator

Court denies father's petition for guardianship and denies power to remove Karen from ventilator

Appellate court certifies case to go to New Jersey Supreme Court

Supreme Court of New Jersey grants father's requests

FACTS: Karen Quinlan, a 21-year-old, suffered two respiratory arrests at a party after reportedly ingesting drugs and alcohol. She was given mouth-to-mouth resuscitation by friends and was taken to a New Jersey hospital. She arrived unresponsive and unconscious and was placed on a respirator and a nasogastric feeding tube was inserted. After receiving treatment and continued monitoring, it was determined that she was in a PVS and would not be able to survive without the respirator. After a careful and difficult period of decision-making, the family believed it best that Karen be removed from the respirator. Her physicians, however, refused to do so, stating that the removal would not conform to medical standards, practices, and traditions, especially because Karen was not brain dead and because the ventilator was not seen as "extraordinary," but rather "ordinary," treatment. The father then filed a petition in court asking that he be appointed the guardian of his daughter and that he be given the express power to provide consent to have Karen removed from the ventilator.

INITIAL COURT DECISION: The Chancery judge denied the father's petition to have him appointed as a personal guardian for Karen. Rather, a *guardian ad litem* was appointed for Karen and the father was granted guardianship over her financial affairs. Furthermore, a denial of the power to remove Karen from the respirator also occurred.

Mr. Quinlan appealed the decision to the Appeals Court and also asked for specific injunctive and declaratory relief.

APPELLATE COURT DECISION: The Appeals Court granted certification for the case to go directly to the New Jersey Supreme Court and did not hear the case.

NEW JERSEY SUPREME COURT DECISION: At this stage in the proceedings, a number of other parties had been added to the case because of the far-reaching impact the decision would have. The physicians, the hospital, and the prosecutor of the county where Karen lived were enjoined (through an injunction) from interfering with the carrying out of any court decision to allow removal if it was granted and from prosecuting anyone for a violation of the criminal laws, respectively. In addition, the Attorney General of New Jersey was joined in the case because of his obligation to represent the state in its interest in the preservation of life.

The New Jersey Supreme Court granted Joseph Quinlan's requests. Specifically, it held that (1) Mr. Quinlan would be appointed the personal and estate guardian of his daughter; (2) full power was granted Mr. Quinlan to make treatment decisions; (3) if the physicians

KEY CASE 13–1   In Re Karen Quinlan (1976)[25] Continued

agree that no hope of recovery exists for Karen, with the concurrence of the guardian and the family, she could be removed from the respirator; (4) an "ethics committee" or similar institutional body should affirm the decision to remove the ventilator; and (5) if all of the guidelines were met, no civil or criminal liability would be possible against the hospital, guardian, or physicians. The Court also held that its decision should not be interpreted as meaning that other treatment situations needed to obtain judicial review before implementing treatment choices.

ANALYSIS: The *Quinlan* Court based its decision on the constitutional right to privacy, both federal and state, and cited many United States Supreme Court cases that supported that right. Furthermore, the Court clearly upheld the power of a guardian to exercise that right on behalf of a ward. Also far-reaching was the Court's analysis of the ventilator as "extraordinary" treatment *in this situation*; that is, it was not curative or restorative but served only to forcibly "sustain" cardiorespiratory functions of an "irreversibly doomed patient." This ordinary/ extraordinary treatment distinction was used for subsequent cases for several years after *Quinlan*, albeit unsatisfactorily, especially in view of the advancement of medical technology that has made the "extraordinary" "ordinary." Because the distinction has been described as hazy (the *Quinlan* Court itself used this term), it is rarely used today. When it is, it is often called the benefit/burden approach. The benefit/ burden approach, however, has been supplemented by the best interest test and others.[26]

The *Quinlan* Court also illustrated the use of the balancing test required when competing interest of a state and individual exists. Although the Court clearly acknowledged New Jersey's interests in preserving life and ensuring that physicians practice medicine according to their best judgment without interference from others, the Court held that those state interests did not outweigh Karen Quinlan's right to be free from unwanted treatment. The Court's support of ethics committees also had far-reaching consequences. The input that was required by the Court was more of a "prognosis" confirmation than anything else, for the committee was to evaluate if Karen Quinlan's diagnosed condition would ever reverse itself.[27] Even so, ethics committees slowly began to develop and have flourished since 1980.[28]

Last, the Court's holding that no criminal or civil liability would result from the decision to remove Karen from the respirator was vitally important in giving some early guidance on culpability issues for health care facilities and practitioners. Despite this guidance, subsequent cases tested the liability waters in relation to such decisions.

Karen Quinlan's father did exercise his power as guardian and had his daughter removed from ventilator support. She continued to breathe on her own and was transferred to Morris View Nursing Home in New Jersey. The home had no respirator, so placing her back on respiratory support was not an issue. Its ethics committee (functioning in one author's viewpoint as a *true* ethics panel) confirmed the decision, in accordance with the court ruling, that she would not be resuscitated.[29]

Karen Quinlan survived for 10 years, sustained by nasogastric feedings and antibiotics. She died at the age of 31 from acute respiratory failure following pneumonia.[30]

It was not until 14 years after the *Quinlan* case was decided that the United States Supreme Court rendered its opinion in the *Cruzan* case. During that interim, many courts were confronting the right to refuse life-sustaining treatment with varying outcomes. Table 13–1 summarizes some of those court decisions.

KEY CASE 13–2   Cruzan v. Director, Missouri Department of Health (1990)[31]

Nancy Cruzan suffers cardiopulmonary arrest after a car accident

Cardiopulmonary functions restored, but coma occurs

Diagnosis made of persistent vegetative state

Gastrostomy tube inserted

Parents ask that food and fluid via tube be terminated, but hospital refused

Parents, as co-guardians, file petition asking for authority to remove gastrostomy tube

Trial court grants permission to co-guardians to remove gastrostomy tube

Decision is appealed to Missouri Supreme Court

FACTS: On January 11, 1983, Nancy Cruzan apparently lost control of her car. It overturned, and she was thrown into a ditch. When the paramedics arrived, she had no heart beat and was not breathing. Those functions were restored at the accident scene, and she was taken to the hospital in an unconscious state. The physicians at the hospital estimated she had not had cardiopulmonary functions for at least 12 to 14 minutes and diagnosed "probable cerebral contusions" compounded by the anoxia. Nancy remained in a coma for 3 weeks, when her condition was diagnosed as persistent vegetative state. Even though she could take some food and fluid orally, consent was given by her then-husband to implant a gastrostomy tube. When her condition did not improve and it became clear that it would never do so, Nancy's parents asked the hospital to terminate the artificial food and hydration. There was no doubt that the withdrawal of food and fluid would result in her death. The hospital refused to do so without a court order. The parents, appointed co-guardians of their daughter in 1984, filed a petition in 1988 asking for the power to authorize the removal of the feeding and hydration tube.

TRIAL COURT DECISION: The state court granted the parents as co-guardians the power to provide consent to withdraw the gastrostomy tube. It based its decision on the Missouri and federal Constitution's protection of the right to refuse "death-delaying procedures." In addition, the court held that Nancy Cruzan had expressed her wishes not to be kept alive unless she could "live at least halfway normally." The conversation with a friend suggested to the court that her present condition was one in which Nancy herself would not want artificial feedings and hydration to continue.

The decision was appealed to the Missouri Supreme Court by the state and the *guardian ad litem.*

KEY CASE 13–2

Cruzan v. Director, Missouri Department of Health (1990)[31]
Continued

Missouri Supreme Court reverses trial court decision

MISSOURI SUPREME COURT DECISION: In reversing the trial court, the Supreme Court of Missouri (1) recognized the right to refuse treatment that was supported by the common-law doctrine of informed consent, but was not certain that it applied in this case because of Ms. Cruzan's inability to speak for herself; (2) declined to read a broad right of privacy to refuse treatment in all circumstances into either the Missouri or federal Constitution; (3) read the Missouri Living Will statute as favoring the preservation of life, and therefore Ms. Cruzan's statement concerning her life and death were "unreliable" for determining her intent to have medical treatment withdrawn; (4) held that the co-guardians could not exercise substituted judgment on behalf of their daughter because no "clear and convincing" evidence existed nor had a living will been executed by Nancy; and (5) believed that issues bearing on life and death are better addressed by a legislative body than by the courts. The Cruzans appealed the decision to the United States Supreme Court, which granted *certiorari* to consider the issue whether Nancy Cruzan had a right under the federal Constitution to mandate removal of life-sustaining treatment "under these circumstances."

The Cruzans appeal the decision to the United States Supreme Court

The United States Supreme Court affirms the Missouri Supreme Court decision

UNITED STATES SUPREME COURT DECISION: The United States Supreme Court affirmed the Missouri Supreme Court's decision. It held that (1) Missouri's requirement of "clear and convincing evidence" was not forbidden under the federal Constitution; (2) a person has a *liberty* interest in refusing unwanted medical treatment, but that right must be balanced with the state's interest in preserving life, especially when a surrogate decision-maker is giving permission to withdraw food and fluid that will result in the person's death; (3) no clear and convincing evidence existed concerning Ms. Cruzan's wishes to withdraw food and fluid; and (4) that because there was no such evidence, the state was not required to honor the wishes of the parents.

ANALYSIS: The *Cruzan* decision has been scrutinized carefully since its publication.[32] Although other cases may test the guidelines set forth in *Cruzan*, some consensus exists as to what guidelines were established. They are: (1) because the right to refuse treatment for a competent adult was supported by a "liberty" interest rather than a right of "privacy," a state must show only a rationally related interest (e.g., preservation of or protection of life) to place restrictions on the right; (2) the "right to die" is not a fundamental right but an "interest"; (3) states would most probably have to abide by a health care surrogate's decision to terminate/withdraw treatment for another when that person expressed that in an advance directive; (4) a feeding tube is one of many life-sustaining treatments that an individual may refuse; and (5) those who

---

KEY CASE 13–2   **Cruzan v. Director, Missouri Department of Health (1990)**[31]
Continued

---

lack decision-making capacity and who have not expressed wishes concerning life-sustaining treatment with the clarity required by a state need protection from potential abuse and the "loss of life involuntarily" when others assert that right on their behalf.[33]

Ironically, after the Supreme Court decision, another hearing to present "new evidence" of Nancy Cruzan's treatment wishes was held before the same trial (probate) court that originally heard her case.[34] The state of Missouri did not contest the petition, and the court granted the co-guardians' request to withdraw the feeding tube. Nancy Cruzan died on December 26, 1990, 11 days after the court granted permission to withdraw the gastrostomy tube.[35]

Two Post-*Cruzan* Cases

Two interesting post-*Cruzan* cases bear mentioning because both of them raised additional issues the *Cruzan* court had only set the stage for.

In the case *In The Matter of Sue Ann Lawrance*,[36] the Indiana Supreme Court upheld the right of Ms. Lawrance's parents to consent to the removal of artificial food and fluid from their 42-year-old daughter, who had been injured in an accident at the age of 9 years that left her mentally retarded. A second injury resulted in another craniotomy, a diagnosis of persistent vegetative state, and no hope of recovery. Despite Sue Ann Lawrance's death due to natural causes during the appeal of the case to the Indiana Supreme Court, both sides desired to have a ruling on the issues presented by her situation.

In upholding the parents' treatment decision to withdraw food and fluid, the Court cited Indiana's Health Care Consent Act (HCCA) that specifically spelled out the procedures for a competent patient or an incompetent patient's

family member to follow. In addition, the Court continued, the removal of food and fluid was permissible under the Act.[37] The Court also held that a court proceeding was not required for situations similar to this case in which the Indiana Health Care Consent Act's procedures were met; specifically, that the family was authorized to make necessary decisions, was willing to make a treatment decision, and the family and physician concurred in the decision.

The *Lawrance* case is noteworthy for several reasons. To begin with, it was the first case to be decided after *Cruzan* concerning a person in a persistent vegetative state and in a state with no prior case law on the right to die.[38] Yet, the Indiana court never mentioned the *Cruzan* decision in its opinion. Moreover, the case dealt with surrogate/proxy decision-making allowed by a state statute rather than through the use of an advance directive. Therefore, it may also stand as an example for other states to follow in which treatment decisions must be made by others and the patient has never expressed his or her wishes because decision-making capacity never existed. Also, contrary to the *Cruzan* Court's opinion, the *Lawrance* decision may well stand for the axiom that others can make such choices without meeting a "substituted judgment" rationale.[39] There is no doubt that Sue Ann Lawrance's parents had no other "good-faith" guidance for their decision but what might be called the "best interest" of their never-competent daughter.

It is also important to point out how haunt-

TABLE 13-1

Selected Court Decisions after *Quinlan* and before *Cruzan* Concerning Right to Refuse Life-Sustaining Treatment

CASE NAME/YEAR/STATE	DIAGNOSIS	TREATMENT(S) AT ISSUE	GUARDIAN, FAMILY, OTHER	DECISION	STANDARD(S) USED	COMMENTS
Superintendent of Belchertown State School vs Saikewicz (1977) (Massachusetts)[1]	Leukemia	O (Chemotherapy)	GAL	Ct. upheld no treatment	C (Privacy) S	Ct. held state's interests must give way to privacy; patient 67-yr.-old profoundly retarded male; treatment futile
Tune v. Walter Reed Army Medical Hospital (1985) (District of Columbia)[2]	Malignancy of pericardium; question of lung tumor	V (Removal)	Pt.	Ct. upheld removal	Q	First Fed. Ct. ruling on patient's right in military hospital to refuse life-sustaining treatment
Matter of Conroy (1985) (New Jersey)[3]	Arteriosclerotic heart disease, hypertension, diabetes, gangrenous leg	ANTH (Nasogastric tube)	GF (Nephew) and GAL appointed by court	Ct. upheld right to remove life-sustaining treatment from nursing home residents expected to die within 1 yr. even with treatment using 3 tests (1) subjective; (2) limited objective, (3) pure-objective. Ct. also set up specific court procedures and documentation requirements, before removing/withholding treatment	B & B (self-determination) CL B S	84-year-old nursing home resident; Ms. Conroy died during court battle; decision narrow in that only applied to nursing home residents; court supported use of living wills as a way for patient to express treatment wishes; feeding tube similar to other artificial sustaining measures
Brophy v. New England Sinai Hospital (1986) (Massachusetts)	Brain aneurysm; PVS	ANTH (Gastrostomy tube)	GF (wife)	Ct. upheld removal of G-tube	C (Privacy) S CL (Privacy)	Ct. held state's interests must give way to privacy rights even though pt. not terminally ill; no legal distinction between withholding/withdrawing treatment; unwanted, painless feeding tube can be "intrusive" and "extraordinary"
Delio v. Westchester County Medical Center (1987) (New York)[5]	PVS after cardiac arrest	ANTH (Gastrostomy and jejunostomy tube)	CF (wife) and GAL appointed by court	Ct. upheld removal	CL (Self-determination)	First NY case to support withdrawal, especially with young (33), nonterminal patient; ct. held no legal distinction between withholding and withdrawing treatment
Matter of Farrell (1987) (New Jersey)[6]	Amyotrophic lateral sclerosis (Lou Gehrig's disease)	V	GF (husband) and GAL appointed by court for children	Ct. upheld removal with guidelines; pt. is competent and two nonattending MDs confirm decision-making ability and that informed consent/refusal has occurred	CL (Privacy) C (Privacy)	Ms. Farrell died during ct. battle; first case dealing with removal of treatment *at home*; gave support to family (not courts) to make decisions; re-emphasized no civil or criminal liability for "good faith actions" in removing/withdrawing treatment; two other cases, *In Re Jones* and *In Re Peter*, also decided on same day with essentially same outcomes

Case	Diagnosis	Treatment	Decision-maker	Holding	Basis	Comments
Rasmussen v. Fleming (1987) (Arizona)[7]	Progressive neurological disorder (Multiple Sclerosis?; PVS or Chronic Vegetative State (CVS)	Do-not-resuscitate and do not hospitalize (DNR and DNH orders)	G and GAL approved by court	Ct. upheld ability of guardian to refuse treatment	SJ B CL (Bodily Integrity) C Q B & B	Ms. Rasmussen died during court battle. Initial concern about nasogastric tube mooted when patient able to swallow, so case went forward on other medical treatment issues; one of first court decisions to hold no material difference between irreversible coma and PVS; ct. also emphasizes when agreement exists as to course of treatment, no need for court intervention
Gray v. Romeo (1988) (Federal District Court, Rhode Island)[8]	Cerebral hemorrhage PVS	ANTH (Gastrostomy tube) and further life support	G (Husband) and GAL appointed by court	Ct. upheld right of guardian to refuse treatment	C (Privacy) SJ	First federal decision (1) dealing with refusal of life-sustaining treatment (nonmilitary hospital); (2) based on Federal Constitutional Right to Privacy; (3) brought under Section 1983 because hospital refused to honor request and was state facility; (4) held state's interests must give way to individual choice, especially when family agrees

V = ventilator
ANTH = Artificial nutrition, hydration
M = Medication
CPR = Cardiopulmonary resuscitation
O = Other
CF = Family member
C = Conservator

PT = Patient with diminished capacity
GAL = *Guardian ad litem*
G = Guardian
GF = Guardian/family member
LW = Living will
DPAHC = Durable Power of Attorney for Health Care
S = Statute

CL = Common law
SJ = Substituted judgment
B&B = Benefits burden
Q = Quality of life
B = Best interest
C = Const. basis
IS = Interpretation of statute

CASE CITATIONS
1. 370 N.E. 2d 417 (Mass. 1977)
2. 602 F. Supp. 1452 (D.O. 1985)
3. 457 A. 2d 1232 (N.J. Super. Ch. 1983), *rev'd.* 464 A. 2d 303 (N.J. Sup. A.D. 1983), *cert. granted*, 470 A. 2d 418 (N.J. 1983), *rev'd* 486 A. 2d 1209 (N.J. 1985)
4. 497 N.E. 2d 626 (Mass. 1986)
5. 510 N.Y.S. 2d 415 (N.J. Sup. 1986), *rev'd* 516 N.Y.S. 2d 677 (N.Y. A.D. 2 Dept. 1987)
6. 529 A. 2d 404 (N.J. 1987)
7. 741 P. 2d 674 (Ariz. 1987)
8. 697 F. Supp. 580 (D.R.I. 1988)

ingly similar the *Lawrance* decision was to the *Quinlan* opinion: (1) both dealt with individuals in a persistent vegetative state; (2) neither New Jersey nor Indiana had any prior case law interpreting state law or statutes in relation to the removal or withdrawal of medical treatment; (3) both cases involved parents asserting rights on behalf of their daughter, albeit in different roles (guardian vs. surrogate decision-makers by statute); (4) both courts resoundingly held that with consensus among those who are legally involved in the decision-making process, no resort to the courts is necessary; (5) each court ruled that ventilator support and artificial fluid and nutrition respectively were "medical treatments" that could be refused or withdrawn; and (6) both courts held that no liability would result for those involved in the decision and the carrying out of that decision if the respective guidelines set forth in the opinions were followed. Perhaps these similarities simply support the opinion that the *Lawrance* court reaffirmed most of the post-*Quinlan* decisions and that the Cruzan decision was a clear departure from earlier decisions.[40]

A second case, *In Re Busalacchi*,[41] illustrates other potential ramifications of the *Cruzan* decision. Because *Cruzan* supports the ability of the respective states to set their own standards concerning the removal of death-delaying medical treatment, a "patchwork" effect may occur. Thus, one state may authorize those decisions in a manner quite different—and perhaps less restrictively—than a neighboring state.

In the *Busalacchi* case, which paradoxically was also decided in Missouri, the father of Christine Busalacchi was appointed guardian of his daughter, who had suffered severe head injuries as the result of a car accident. A persistent vegetative state was diagnosed and a gastrostomy tube implanted. After it was clear that rehabilitation was not possible, a recommendation was made that Christine be placed in a skilled nursing facility. The father was unable to get her admitted into any in Missouri or California, and then began to look at other states, including Minnesota.

When admission into a Minnesota home seemed likely, the rehabilitation agency changed Christine's diagnosis to one less serious than persistent vegetative state, and filed a petition for a temporary restraining order (TRO) and a permanent injunction prohibiting Mr. Busalacchi from removing Christine from the state and alleging that he was doing so to remove the gastrostomy tube. The trial court denied the state's motion for a permanent injunction and dissolved the temporary restraining order.

The decision was appealed to the Missouri Court of Appeals, which reversed the lower court decision and remanded the case back to that court. The court opined that the issue to be decided was not whether the feeding tube should be removed, but rather whether the guardian was acting in the ward's best interest by removing her to another jurisdiction where allegedly the feeding tube could be removed more easily than in Missouri.[42] Furthermore, the court held that the state had the burden of proving that Christine Busalacchi's needs are being adequately met in Missouri. If the state meets its burden, then the guardian must prove that a move to another state is in her best interests.

The decision of the Missouri Court of Appeals was appealed to the Missouri Supreme Court, then back to the lower court for additional information on Ms. Busalacchi's diagnosis of persistent vegetative state. The lower court, after reconsidering the evidence, upheld the decision to transfer, but that decision was also appealed by the state of Missouri. Several days after, the Supreme Court of Missouri dismissed the case on the motion of the state. In an interesting twist, a "right to life" advocate then filed a petition requesting a temporary restraining order, which was granted by a St. Louis court.[43]

Christine Busalacchi died on March 7, 1993, after her feeding tube was removed, almost 6 years after the accident that left her in a persistent vegetative state.[44]

These, and other cases, will continue to test the parameters of the *Cruzan* decision. What standard will be applied when others make removal/withholding medical treatment decisions? Will an advance directive be required? If an advance directive is required in a particular state, will it suffice as "evidence" as to an individual's specific treatment preferences? Will a surrogate/proxy decision-making statute withstand legal challenge?

Despite the less-than-bright parameters of *Cruzan*, it can be said with certainty that there is legal support for the right to die, although the nature of that right may be called by other names (e.g., right to refuse treatment). Even so, *Cruzan* appears to have raised more questions than it answered. The decision also seems to clearly underscore the fact that the law has not progressed as far as many would like to believe it has in resolving issues surrounding the withholding or withdrawing of medical treatment that results in death.

> *Despite the less-than-bright parameters of* Cruzan, *it can be said with certainty that there is legal support for the right to die . . .*

Nursing Implications

There is no doubt that nurses providing health care in almost any delivery system will work with a patient who is dying. In many of those situations, the issue of withdrawing or removing medical treatment will arise. To provide compassionate and caring nursing care, the nurse must be clear about his or her personal feelings concerning dying, death, and the withholding or withdrawing of treatment. The nurse can utilize many resources to help with clarification of those feelings, including, but not limited to, ethics texts and chapters, professional organization position statements, professional journal articles, and formal and informal support groups.

Whatever the nurse's feelings, they must not interfere with a patient's decision concerning treatment. The nurse can, and should, exercise the right to not participate in whatever treatment or nontreatment he or she has an objection to. Notifying the nurse manager and asking for another assignment is certainly permissible both legally and ethically.

If the nurse decides to care for the individual for whom treatment is withdrawn or withheld, it is important to do so by continuing whatever treatment is *not* refused. Furthermore, the comfort of the patient and any relief of pain, if it exists, is vital. The American Nurses' Association's 1991 Position Statement on this topic fully supports the need for the proper management of pain in the dying patient and the utilization of full and effective doses of pain medication consistent with the patient's wishes, even at the expense of the patient's life.[45]

The nurse should also take advantage of the institution's ethics committee, grand rounds, or other vehicles to resolve complex care situations in which treatment is withheld or refused. A 1991 study indicated that registered nurses are much less likely to utilize ethics committees than are physicians.[46] Many reasons are proposed why this may be so. One troubling analysis is that the structure of the nursing hierarchy in a facility may not provide an easy mechanism for a nurse to freely bring patient care concerns to a non-nursing arena.[47] If that commentary is correct, nurse managers must establish a mechanism that facilitates nursing staff to obtain input and guidance from ethics forums for complex patient care situations. Concomitantly, all nursing staff should take advantage of the opportunity to seek guidance and input from multidisciplinary bodies in complex care situations.

Nurses will also need to be knowledgeable about state legislative developments and case law that is decided concerning refusal of life-sustaining treatment. Participating in legislative hearings, writing legislators, and educating the public are examples of how nurses can be proactive and possibly aid in the development of law in this area.

Last, but by no means least, the nurse must push for clear policies and procedures to be developed and implemented in the institution or agency concerning refusal of life-sustaining treatment. Those policies should include, but not be limited to, the patient's right to refuse treatment and any limitations on that right; the documentation of refusal; pain control; definitions of terms (such as cardiopulmonary resuscitation); management of patient comfort; and the nurse's role in the care of the patient whose treatment has been withdrawn or withheld according to his or her wishes.

DOCUMENTATION REMINDER 13–1 REFUSAL/WITHDRAWAL OF TREATMENT

▼ Accurate, complete description of actual withdrawal of treatment (e.g., who present, time, patient response)

▼ Results of continued care/monitoring of patient

▼ Consistent notations as to patient condition

▼ Patient comments, complaints

▼ Notification of other health care providers when condition changes or additional orders needed

▼ Family presence, requests, concerns

KEY CASES INVOLVING MINORS

Many of the well-known cases involving minors and the refusal of life-sustaining treatment center around criminal charges or termination of parental rights proceedings being brought against the parents. However, many other cases have been decided when those types of allegations are not the issue. Rather, the issues involved are similar to those decided by cases with adult individuals; that is, establishing the legal parameters of the family's or the minor's right to refuse life-sustaining treatment.

KEY CASE 13–3   In Re L.H.R. (1984)[48]

A 15-day-old newborn suffers medical problem

Diagnosis made of persistent vegetative state and newborn placed on respirator

Parents and others file petition to remove ventilator support

Trial court grants relief and suggests appeal to state supreme court

Georgia Supreme Court upholds trial court decision

FACTS: Fifteen days after a normal birth, a medical problem (unspecified) left L.H.R. in a persistent vegetative state with an "absence of cognitive function." There was no hope of recovery. The infant had been placed on a respirator shortly after the medical crisis arose. The physician and the parents agreed that the respirator should be withdrawn. The hospital's Infant Care Review Committee (ICRC) agreed with that decision. After obtaining an agreement with the Georgia Attorney General and the local district attorney, the parents, physician, and hospital filed a declaratory judgment action in the local state court seeking authorization to carry out withdrawal of the ventilator.

TRIAL COURT DECISION: The De Kalb County Superior Court granted the relief requested by the petitioners. It also ordered the Attorney General to file an appeal to the Georgia Supreme Court so that guidelines would be established for future cases.

GEORGIA SUPREME COURT DECISION: The Georgia Supreme Court upheld the decision of the trial court and set specific guidelines for both adults and minors in a persistent vegetative state with no chance of

KEY CASE 13–3   In Re L.H.R. (1984)[48] Continued

and sets guidelines for removal of ventilator

recovery. They were: (1) the termination of treatment in the situation can be authorized by family or a legal guardian; (2) the diagnosis and prognosis must be made by the treating physician and two other physicians who agree; (3) no prior court approval is needed nor does the decision need to be reviewed or affirmed by a hospital committee.

ANALYSIS: The Court's decision was based on the constitutional right of privacy to refuse treatment when a "terminal" condition exists. In addition, the Court supported this right regardless of whether the patient lost decision-making capacity or was young. Furthermore, the Court's decision clearly underscores the fact that it is the family or legal guardian who are the most appropriate persons to make the decision. The decision was the first to diminish the role of ethics or infant care review (ICR) committees in decisions concerning the withdrawal or withholding of life-sustaining treatment. This was a curious development, especially in view of the growth of institutional ethics bodies, during the period in which *L.H.R.* was decided (See Special Considerations section). It is also important to note that there was no disagreement in this case concerning the diagnosis or recommended course of treatment. Had L.H.R.'s condition not been terminal or if no consensus had been reached by the physician, parents, and legal community, the progress and the outcome of this case may have been very different indeed.

KEY CASE 13–4   In Re Chad Eric Swan (1990)[49]

A 17-year-old is in a car accident that leaves him in a persistent vegetative state

Gastrostomy tube inserted

Petition filed by parents asking for gastrostomy tube to be withdrawn

Complications arise with gastrostomy tube

Gastrostomy tube "closes" and infection present

FACTS: Seventeen-year-old Chad Swan was in a car accident that left him in a persistent vegetative state without ever regaining consciousness. A gastrostomy tube was inserted. Because there was no hope of recovery, his parents and older brother agreed that the feeding tube should be removed. They decided to file a petition for declaratory judgment, asking that no civil or criminal liability would be incurred by the family, the physician, or the medical center if the feeding tube were removed. The petition was supported by affidavits from Chad's brother and mother that Chad told them he would not want to be kept alive by artificial means. Shortly after the petition was filed, an infection was discovered around the entry point of the feeding tube. A consultation with a gastrointestinal specialist determined that Chad's body had "rejected" the tube and the tube and opening were sealed. As a result, no food or hydration was able to be administered. Further complicating the matter was the fact that until the infection cleared, no reinsertion

KEY CASE 13–4   In Re Chad Eric Swan (1990)[49] Continued

Neither gastrostomy tube nor nasogastric tube can be inserted

Central venous line inserted pending court decision

Trial court orders central venous line to be removed, but stays order until appeal taken

Appellate court unanimously upholds trial court decision

could take place. And, because of Chad's severe facial injuries sustained in the accident, a nasogastric tube was not feasible. The physician suggested that another tube not be inserted. The family agreed with this decision.

Prior to the hearing on the declaratory judgment petition, the medical center asked for directions while awaiting a hearing on the petition. The court ordered a central venous line be inserted to provide Chad with fluid until a decision was made.

TRIAL COURT DECISION: With all interested parties but the district attorney supporting the petition, the court entered an order allowing the central venous line to be removed. The court further opined that this kind of decision was best made by the parents in conjunction with the physician. The district attorney and the *guardian ad litem* asked that the line be continued until an appeal was taken. Because the court was concerned that Chad could die before the appeal was completed, it stayed the order removing the line until the appeals court rendered its decision.

APPELLATE COURT DECISION: In a unanimous decision, the appeals court upheld the lower court's decision. Chad's age was only "one factor" in determining if he had "clearly and convincingly" stated his treatment preferences. The court held that capacity exists for a minor when he or she has the ability of the average person to understand and weigh risks and benefits. In Chad's case, he had discussed treatment choices on two separate occasions, one time 8 days before the accident. In both instances, he clearly indicated his preference not to be kept alive if there was no hope for recovery. The court also held it made no difference that the gastrostomy tube was "rejected," thus making the issue "reinsertion" rather than "withdrawal." Citing another Maine case, *In Re Gardner*,[50] the court said that the distinction did not decrease *Gardner's* binding authority.

ANALYSIS: This case is a noteworthy one in supporting the removal of life-sustaining treatment, and specifically food and fluid, for a minor. By citing the *Gardner* case, which dealt with a 22-year-old adult's expressed wishes concerning treatment, the *Swan* court gave credence to an oral advance directive by a minor.[51] Furthermore, by stating that Chad Swan's oral advance directives were "clear and convincing," the substituted judgment test often used when a surrogate/proxy decision-maker is involved was seemingly not important.

It is ironic to note that during one of the two conversations that Chad Swan had concerning his treatment preferences, he referred to the *Gardner* case. Swan was talking with his mother about the case because of its wide publicity and also because Joseph Gardner was the

---

KEY CASE 13–4	In Re Chad Eric Swan (1990)[49] Continued

stepgrandson of a close friend of Chad's grandmother.[52] Then 16 years old, he told his mother that he could not understand why they would not let Gardner die. After discussing Gardner's condition (persistent vegetative state) Swan stated: "If I can't be myself . . . no way . . . let me go to sleep."[53]

Subsequent decisions involving minors, especially after *Quinlan* and *Cruzan*, have shaped the right of the minor or the minor's parents to make decisions concerning the withholding or withdrawing of life-sustaining treatment. Some of those decisions are summarized in Table 13–2.

The treatment issues surrounding the removal of life-sustaining treatment with minors will continue to be molded and shaped by additional court decisions. It may well be that support of a mature minor's choice to refuse life-sustaining treatment will continue to be the touchstone of those decisions. It may also be that the underscoring of the family's authority to assert the right on behalf of a minor child will not weaken. It will take a United States Supreme Court decision, however, to begin to resolve the multifarious legal issues with more certainty.

Nursing Implications

Many of the nursing implications discussed in the section on cases involving adults and the removal or withholding of life-sustaining treatment are applicable here. What is unique about working with minors, however, is clearly the role the parents have in relation to decision making that must occur when treatment issues need to be decided. The nurse must be cognizant of the fact that the parents are experiencing a great deal of emotional distress during the entire situation. As a result, they will need emotional support, clarification of information concerning the treatment issues germane to their child's situation, and time to make whatever decisions are made.

In addition, whether the minor is 7 years old or 17, young family members and friends of the patient may also be present in the hospital setting. A knowledge of child and adolescent behavior and their reactions to death and dying will help the nurse interact with them as they struggle to understand what is happening to their family member or friend.

If the nurse is able to obtain membership on an ethics committee or institutional review committee (IRC), he or she can be a valuable contributing member.

If the nurse is able to obtain membership on an ethics committee or institutional review committee (IRC), he or she can be a valuable contributing member. In fact, nursing membership is recommended.[54] If, however, that option is not open to the nurse, membership on a *nursing* ethics or institutional review committee is a consideration. This type of forum provides many benefits to nursing staff, not the least of which is a resource group in which ethical issues can be shared and analyzed and a model for decision-making adopted.[55]

TABLE 13–2

Selected Court Decisions after *Quinlan* Concerning Right to Refuse Life-Sustaining Treatment Involving Minors

CASE NAME/YEAR/ STATE	DIAGNOSIS	TREATMENT(S) AT ISSUE	GUARDIAN, FAMILY, OTHER	DECISION	STANDARD(S) USED	COMMENTS
In Re Guardianship of Barry (1984) (Florida)[1]	PVS	V; O (all life-sustaining)	CF	Ct. upholds right of parents to reject treatment	SJ	Ct. decision similar to *In Re L.H.R.* in text; minor was an infant
Newmark v. Williams (1991) (Delaware)[2]	Burkit's lymphoma	O (Chemotherapy)	CF (parents)	Ct. upheld no treatment	B, B&B	Parents refused treatment based on religious grounds; child was 3 years old; court clearly stated treatment very risky, invasive, and painful; no neglect on parents' part for refusing treatment
Rosebush v. Oakland County Prosecutor (1992) (Michigan)[3]	PVS	V	CF (parents)	Ct. upheld removal of life support	S	Minor was 16 years old; when 10½, she made oral statement about her treatment wishes; when parents tried to remove daughter from state rehabilitation center to hospital, prosecutor attempted to stop transfer
In the Matter of Baby K (1994) (Virginia)[4]	Anencephaly, but with functioning brain stem; minor permanently unconscious	V; CPR; O	GAL and S (federal and state); hospital requested interpretation of laws if it did not ventilate without mother's consent	Ct. upholds mother's right to require ventilation; holds hospital would violate one specific federal law if treatment not given	IS	Although District Ct. held not treating Baby K would violate Section 504 of the Rehabilitation Act, the Americans with Disabilities Act, the Child Abuse Act, and the Emergency Medical Treatment and Active Labor Act, Appeals Court held that because it found a violation of the EMTALA, it would not rule on others; raises question again as to futility of care concerns, as in *Wanglie*

V = Ventilator
ANTH = Artificial nutrition, hydration
M = Medication
CPR = Cardiopulmonary res.
O = Other
CF = Family member
C = Conservator

PT = Patient with diminished capacity
GAL = *Guardian ad litem*
G = Guardian
GF = Guardian/family member
LW = Living will
DPAHC = Durable Power of Attorney for Health Care
S = Statute

CL = Common law
SJ = Substituted judgment
B&B = Benefits burden
Q = Quality of life
B = Best interest
C = Const. basis
IS = Interpretation of statute

CASE CITATIONS
1. 445 So. 2d 365 (Fla. Dist. Ct. App. 1984)
2. 588 A. 2d 1108 (Del. 1991)
3. 491 N.W. 2d 6331 (Mich. Ct. App. 1992)
4. 832 F. Supp. 1022 (E.D. Va. 1993), *aff'd.*, 16 F. 3d 590 (4th Cir. 1994), *cert. denied*, 115 S. Ct. 91 (1994)

SPECIAL CONSIDERATIONS

Defining Death

Originally, death was defined medically and by the common law as the cessation of spontaneous function of the cardiac and respiratory system ("heart death"), using accepted medical criteria when making such a determination.[56] As advances in medical technology occurred, however, this definition was difficult to adhere to because these systems could be maintained for long periods by such devices as the ventilator and other life-sustaining medical equipment. As a result, an alternative definition was proposed. That definition was the brain death standard: that is, death occurs when all vital functions of the brain, brain stem, and spinal reflexes are irreversibly nonexistent, again determined by accepted medical standards.[57]

The brain death standard was initially used for donor-donee situations and, in fact, had been incorporated into the Uniform Anatomical Gift Act (UAGA) discussed in Chapter 12. The criteria proposed to determine if brain death occurred were developed by the Harvard Medical School's Ad Hoc Committee to Examine the Definition of Death, chaired by Dr. Henry K. Beecher.[58] Briefly, the initial criteria to determine if an "irreversible coma" was present were (1) absence of reflexes; (2) no spontaneous respirations or muscular movements; and (3) no response to normally painful stimuli.[59] These clinical signs were to be confirmed by a flat EEG (two readings at least 24 hours apart), computerized tomography (CAT SCAN), and other diagnostic measures. Furthermore, ensuring that no drug intoxication or hypothermia was present was also important.[60]

These guidelines were expanded upon after they were developed by various groups, including the President's Commission for the Study of Ethical Problems in Medicine and Biomedical and Behavioral Research.[61] In 1980, the Harvard criteria were adopted into the Uniform Determination of Death Act (UDDA),[62] along with the common law "heart death" standard.[63] Only a few states have adopted the Uniform Determination of Death Act (e.g., Colorado, Delaware, Idaho, Maryland, Pennsylvania, and Nevada). However, all 50 states and the District of Columbia have adopted brain death as a legal definition of death, whether by case law, amendments to current statutes, or regulatory means.[64]

If brain death is diagnosed in an individual, there is no legal duty to provide continuing treatment because that person is clinically dead. Therefore, treatment can be discontinued without criminal or civil liability. In fact, continuing to treat a dead individual can be a basis for liability if the surrogate/proxy decision-maker does not consent to additional treatment.[65]

Brain death is different from a persistent vegetative state in which substantial losses of function in the cerebral cortex occur, but autonomous functions continue because there is no damage to the brain stem. Although a diagnosis of brain death does not ensure the absence of legal issues when there is withholding or terminating of treatment, a diagnosis of persistent vegetative state raises very different legal, and other, issues, when such a decision is being made.[66] In fact, cases challenging the right to refuse life-sustaining treatment, including the two key cases in this chapter and many of those in Tables 13–1 and 13–2, involved individuals in a persistent vegetative state.

Refusal of Cardiopulmonary Resuscitation

The type of life-sustaining treatment refused or withdrawn has been as controversial, both legally and ethically, as has been the right to refuse treatment. The specific types of treatments focused on have, of course, changed. For example, the early cases involved ventilator support. Later cases involved artificial nutrition and hydration. One particular treatment that needs specific discussion is the refusal or withholding of cardiopulmonary resuscitation (CPR). It was one of the first specific treatments tested in the judicial system after the *Quinlan* case.

The type of life-sustaining treatment refused or withdrawn has been as controversial, both legally and ethically, as has been the right to refuse treatment.

The historical development of CPR has a great deal to do with its course in the right to refuse life-sustaining-treatment arena. It has a long-standing chronology of use, one of the earliest accounts of which appears in the Old Testament.[67] It was not until the 1960s, however, that research demonstrated that circulation could be maintained by external cardiac massage.[68] External cardiac massage was adopted quickly in hospitals and over the next 15 years became a routine procedure.[69] In fact, it was used for virtually *every* patient who experienced cardiopulmonary arrest.

It became clear to both the medical community and the consumer of health care that perhaps CPR was not indicated for every patient. However, there was concern about the liability of not initiating CPR. As a result, many "slow codes," "no-codes," and the use of removable purple dots on charts were used formally and informally when a decision was made not to initiate CPR with certain patients.

In 1974, The National Conference on Standards for CPR and Emergency Cardiac Care issued a statement that (1) the purpose of CPR is to prevent unexpected death; (2) it is not indicated in certain situations, such as terminal irreversible illness; and (3) when CPR is not indicated, it should be noted in the patient's medical record (progress notes and order sheet).[70] After that statement, many institutions developed policies and began to utilize do-not-resuscitate (DNR) orders. It was not until a 1978 Massachusetts case, however, that the legal status of do-not-resuscitate orders was clarified.

KEY CASE 13–5   In Re Shirley Dinnerstein (1978)[71]

A 67-year-old woman with Alzheimer's disease suffers stroke

Nasogastric tube and catheter inserted

Physician suggests do-not-resuscitate order be written, for condition would never improve

FACTS: Shirley Dinnerstein was a 67-year-old woman in whom Alzheimer's disease had been diagnosed in 1975, although she may have had the disease as early as 1972. She had been placed in a nursing home in 1975 when her family could no longer care for her at home. Her condition at that time was considered to be similar to a persistent vegetative state.

In 1978, Ms. Dinnerstein suffered a massive stroke that left her paralyzed on the left side. A nasogastric tube and catheter were inserted by the hospital to which she was admitted after the stroke. The physician's opinion was that Ms. Dinnerstein would never recover and that her condition was terminal, although a prediction as to the length of her life could not be made. What was clear, however, was that if she suffered a cardiopulmonary arrest, she would die. Thus, the physician's opinion was that she should not be resuscitated should an arrest occur. The patient's son (a physician) and daughter agreed with the physician. The hospital, physician, and family filed a declaratory judgment action in the probate court asking the court to guide them in making this type of decision (that is, writing a do-not-resuscitate order) or, if need be, have the court authorize such a medical order.

KEY CASE 13–5   In Re Shirley Dinnerstein (1978)[71] Continued

Family and others file case asking for guidance with do-not-resuscitate order

Trial court sends case to Appeals court

Appeals court remands case back to trial court for an order granting the do-not-resuscitate order be written by M.D.

TRIAL COURT DECISION: The trial court did not make a decision in the case. Rather, it appointed a temporary guardian to protect Ms. Dinnerstein's interests, appointed a *guardian ad litem* (who opposed the do-not-resuscitate order), and made an extensive factual report for the Appeals Court to consider.

APPEALS COURT DECISION: The Appellate court remanded the case back to the trial court for an order granting the relief requested in the case. Specifically, the court held that the law would clearly allow a course of medical treatment that included a do-not-resuscitate order. In addition, the court opined that when there is full agreement by all those involved, no court order is necessary prior to the initiation of such medical treatment. Only if there is disagreement, or a physician's decision to initiate a do-not-resuscitate order is inconsistent with acceptable medical practice, should a court order be sought.

ANALYSIS: The *Dinnerstein* decision was a far-reaching one for it clarified an earlier Massachusetts decision, *Saikewicz* (see Table 13–1). There had been some speculation after that decision that a court order would be necessary for any withholding or removal of life-sustaining treatment. The *Dinnerstein* court specifically held that "life-sustaining treatment" meant medical care in which a temporary or permanent cure would result. In both cases, the medical regimen to be withheld or withdrawn was not curative. Thus, court orders were not needed. The case again supports the right of a patient without decision-making capacity to decide against treatment, albeit through another, whether that other be a court, guardian, and/or family member.

Since *Dinnerstein*, do-not-resuscitate orders have had a circuitous development. Even though somewhat legitimized after the court opinion, the liability concerns associated with such an order continued to abound. This was not helped when, for example, in 1982 a criminal investigation was initiated against a hospital in Queens because of reported do-not-resuscitate orders being written for elderly, incompetent patients.[72]

Despite these concerns, most hospitals and other health care delivery systems began to develop policies to cover do-not-resuscitate orders and essentially treat them as any other medical order. Thus, for example, the policies require that (1) the order be written in the patient's medical record like other medical orders; (2) the order is reviewed and/or renewed on a specific basis; (3) a telephone do-not-resuscitate order is valid only under limited circumstances and must be witnessed by two registered nurses and documented as such in the patient's record; (4) if no do-not-resuscitate order exists, a patient must be resuscitated; (5) the patient or the legally recognized decision-maker must be informed and provide consent for the treatment;

and (6) do-not-resuscitate and CPR be clearly defined so that other treatment not refused can be continued.[73]

Several states, including New York, Georgia, and Montana were so concerned about liability and do-not-resuscitate orders that the state legislatures passed specific acts or authorized state agencies to promulgate rules and regulations to deal with such orders.[74] Many other states followed suit, with "do-not-resuscitate legislation" passed by state legislatures in the form of "freestanding" statutes or including provisions for do-not-resuscitate in other state legislation, such as advance directive laws.[75]

The development of clear do-not-resuscitate policies in health care facilities, and perhaps a decrease in some of the liability concerns, was augmented by the Joint Commission on Accreditation of Health Care Organizations (JCAHO) requirement in 1988 that all hospitals have policies on resuscitation services to be accredited.[76]

The requirement of the Joint Commission on Accreditation of Health Care Organizations did not end the controversy surrounding do-not-resuscitate orders, however. Adding to the controversy are recent studies indicating that not all patients truly benefit from CPR. For example, in one study of 2643 patients in general and intensive care units, factors that correlated with decreased survival rates included age over 70 years, having cancer, and impaired renal function.[77] In contrast, those with a diagnosis of myocardial infarction were more likely to survive, with all other things being equal.[78]

Furthermore, a new issue with do-not-resuscitate orders is surfacing, an issue particularly ironic in view of the solid development of the right of the patient to have input into treatment decisions. Although not yet definitively litigated, the propriety of a physician writing a do-not-resuscitate order without informed consent from the patient or surrogate/proxy decision-maker, or writing one when no consent has occurred, may well be the next legal frontier with this type of life-sustaining treatment.[79]

When Treatment Decisions Conflict with Medical Treatment Recommendations

The right to refuse treatment is not absolute and may need to be balanced against other interests, including the maintenance of the ethical integrity of the health care profession. Situations raising a threat to the ethical integrity of medicine or nursing are manifold. However, two general categories in which those situations arise can be identified: first, when treatment is refused that a physician or nurse believes should be provided, and second, when treatment is seen as necessary by the patient or family but is not medically indicated.

The right to refuse treatment is not absolute and may need to be balanced against other interests, including the maintenance of the ethical integrity of the health care profession.

The first category has been raised in almost all of the cases dealing with the right to refuse life-sustaining treatment, including but not limited to *Saikewicz, Brophy,* and *Gray* (see Table 13–1). Generally the case decisions have clearly held that the state's interest, if it exists, must give way to the right of the patient to refuse life-sustaining treatment.

The second category has been the issue in some reported cases in which surrogate/proxy decision-makers have refused to allow the termination of life-sustaining treatment with brain-dead patients.[80] In 1991, another case received attention. In that case, the propriety of continuing ventilator support at the insistence of a surrogate/proxy decision-maker when it was not medically recommended was decided.

KEY CASE 13–6   In Re Helga Wanglie (1991)[81]

An 86-year-old breaks hip

In nursing home, Mrs. Wanglie develops respiratory failure and is placed on ventilator

Attempts to wean patient from ventilator result in cardiopulmonary arrest

Revival occurs, but diagnosis of persistent vegetative state made

M.D. recommends removal of ventilator

Husband, as guardian, and family will not consent to removal

Do-not-resuscitate status was OK'd by husband

Hospital files petition to replace Mr. Wanglie as guardian

Trial court denies hospital's request

FACTS: Helga Wanglie broke her hip at the age of 86 years when she slipped on a rug in her home. After successful repair of the hip fracture, she was sent to a nursing home. She was readmitted to the hospital that repaired her hip after she developed respiratory failure due to emphysema. She was placed on a respirator. Several attempts to wean her from the respirator were unsuccessful. She was then transferred to another medical facility that specialized in the care of ventilator-dependent patients.[82]

Additional attempts at weaning occurred, one of which resulted in cardiopulmonary arrest. She was resuscitated and admitted to another hospital. Because of severe and irreversible brain damage due to the arrest, a persistent vegetative state and hopeless condition were diagnosed. The facility ethics committee and physicians recommended that the ventilator be removed and further life-sustaining treatment be withheld. The husband, as her guardian, and the family would not agree because Mrs. Wanglie would want treatment. She was then transferred back to the hospital where her hip had been repaired.[83]

The physicians there also recommended that the respirator should be removed, but the family and husband/guardian refused to agree. They did agree to a do-not-resuscitate order, however, because of the fact that recovery from an arrest would be unlikely. Despite the facility's ethics committee also recommending the withdrawal of the ventilator, the family would not waver from its decision. The basis for their position was an expressed desire by Mrs. Wanglie that her life not be prematurely "shortened or taken" if anything happened to her and she could not care for herself.[84]

After many attempts to resolve the situation with the family, the hospital filed a petition seeking the replacement of Mr. Wanglie as the guardian of his wife.

TRIAL COURT DECISION: The Probate Court refused to replace Mr. Wanglie as guardian (conservator) of his wife, holding that he was "dedicated to promoting his wife's welfare" and was competent to continue in his role.[85]

ANALYSIS: The decision resulted in a floodgate of reactions. Some of the responses included: (1) the decision was appropriate, especially in view of her wishes and the fact that the patient's private medical insurance would pay for the continued care;[86] and (2) how a determination is made about "medically necessary" as opposed to "medically futile" treatment.[87]

The impact of the case will continue to be seen in future cases. The court clearly held that a competent family member is the more suitable surrogate/proxy decision-maker than a stranger in the same role. In

KEY CASE 13–6   In Re Helga Wanglie (1991)[81] Continued

addition, the court's decision also stands for the principle that treatment decisions to withhold or withdraw treatment must be followed by health care practitioners. Mrs. Wanglie was not brain dead, a situation in which the appropriateness of continuing ventilator support would be highly questionable, to say the least. Rather, she was in a persistent vegetative state, and her guardian refused to give permission to have the ventilator removed.

Despite the controversy concerning the ethical and medical position of the health care providers in this case, the decision offers little guidance for other, future cases in which the questions surrounding futile care will have to be decided.[88]

Helga Wanglie was kept on the ventilator in accordance with the court order. She died 4 days after the decision.[89]

Hospice Care

The purpose of hospice care is to provide services to the terminally ill and their families so that during the course of the illness the patient and family can live life as fully and comfortably as possible.[90] An interdisciplinary team provides medical, nursing, psychological, and other support. The main goals are to control pain, maintain independence, and minimize the stress and trauma of death.[91]

Hospice care originated in Canada and England. Its acceptance in the United States was controversial. However, currently hospice care has gained recognition as an alternative to hospital care for the terminally ill. It is cost effective and provides needed services for many patients, including the elderly with cancer and those suffering from AIDS.[92]

One of the goals of hospice care—pain management—can be a disputatious issue when adequate amounts of medication are not pro-

vided to the patient or are unavailable to nursing staff to administer. In August of 1991, charges were brought against six hospice nurses (the "Hospice Six") of the Hospice of St. Peter's Hospital in Montana. Specifically, their conduct of keeping a "stash" of narcotics (including morphine) in a locked drawer for use when patients' conditions deteriorated, or when obtaining a new order or a change in medication was not possible (when the pharmacy was closed or the physician was not available), was challenged by an official body, the Montana Department of Commerce, Professional and Occupational Licensing Bureau.

After a hearing, the Montana Board of Nursing held that the six nurses committed unprofessional conduct by (1) altering and/or manipulating drug supplies, narcotics, or patients' records; (2) appropriating medications of patients; and (3) violating state or federal laws relative to drugs.[93] The Board also held that the nurses (1) dispensed, or possessed with intent to dispense, morphine and other controlled substances without authority to do so; (2) did not keep records of the drugs received, dispensed, or possessed; (3) functioned as a medical doctor or pharmacist rather than as a nurse; (4) transferred controlled substances among and between patients contrary to federal and state laws on controlled substances; and (5) violated Montana criminal statutes regarding dangerous drugs.[94]

The Board instituted probationary status on the licenses of the nurses for 3 to 5 years. The conditions of probation included barring the nurses from holding supervisory positions, making them obtain the Board's approval before taking a new position, and making them submit quarterly reports to the Board.[95]

Since the Board decision, only two of the nurses remained on staff at the hospice. Two others have taken a leave, one has resigned, and another has taken a non-nursing position in the hospital.[96]

An appeal was filed by the nurses asking for judicial review of the Board's final order. They alleged the Board had rejected the Hearing Officer's recommendations and ordered different discipline, which was an abuse of its discretion. The court reversed the findings, conclusions of law, and final order of the Board, and adopted the Hearing Officer's recommendations. The Board then appealed that decision. The Supreme Court of Montana upheld the Hearing Officer's findings, conclusion, and order. The Hearing Officer's findings and order were that (1) charges against the nurses for "unprofessional conduct" were not proven and should be dismissed; (2) letters of reprimand be placed in the files of the nurses for 3 years; and (3) all charges against one nurse, Verna Van-Duynhoven, be dismissed.[97]

The case centered on the legalistics of the practice of nursing, dispensing v. administering medications, and the role of the nurse (as opposed to the physician or pharmacist) in prescribing controlled substances. However, the "real issue" of the case was the social and medical ethic of how to let dying people die.[98]

Montana's living will statute did not authorize health care providers to "hasten death."[99] Because the hospice's living will form stated that medications "can and should" be adminis-

tered to alleviate suffering, even though death could be hastened as a result, the nurses, according to the allegations of the attorney for the state agency, overstepped the legal limits of their practice.[100]

When Withdrawal or Withholding of Medical Care for a Minor Results in Alleged Child Abuse or Neglect, Criminal Conduct, or Juvenile Proceedings

The cases dealing with this issue with newborns and minors can be categorized into two general classifications: minors with varying medical conditions and "seriously ill newborns" (a term coined by the President's Commission in its 1983 study), including those with congenital anomalies. The legal responses to these two categories have differed.

Minors with Varying Medical Conditions

In this group, allegations of criminal behavior or child abuse and neglect are brought against the parents. Charges result after a report is made to the state agency responsible for enforcing the state child abuse and neglect reporting statutes or when a petition is filed in the state juvenile court system.

When criminal conduct is alleged, the case is filed against the parents in the state criminal court. Specific causes of action when death of the minor occurs include involuntary manslaughter and murder.

Two cases alleging neglect in state juvenile court systems, one of the first such cases and one decided more recently, are presented as Key Cases. Selected other cases, including those involving criminal charges against the parents, are presented in Table 13–2.

KEY CASE 13–7   In Re Green (1972)[101]

Ricky Green's M.D. recommends a spinal fusion

Jehovah's Witness mother OK's surgery but refuses consent for blood transfusion

Hospital files petition to have 16-year-old declared "neglected child" and to have guardian appointed

Trial court denies request

Appeals court unanimously reverses decision

Pennsylvania Supreme Court reverses appeals court and remands case back to trial court with specific guidelines

FACTS: Sixteen-year-old Ricky Green suffered two attacks of polio that resulted in obesity and paralytic scoliosis (94% curvature of the spine). As a result, he is wheelchair bound. His physicians recommended a "spinal fusion," which would require taking bone from his pelvis and placing it in his spine. Ricky's mother, a Jehovah's Witness, agreed to the operation provided that no blood transfusion occur. The orthopedic specialist informed Mrs. Green that the operation is "not without risk."

Because Mrs. Green would not consent to blood transfusions, the State Hospital For Crippled Children filed a petition to initiate juvenile proceedings to declare Ricky a "neglected child" under Pennsylvania's Juvenile Court Law. The hospital also asked for a guardian to be appointed for Ricky (Ricky lives with his mother, who is separated from his father).

TRIAL COURT DECISION: After an evidentiary hearing, the trial court dismissed the petition. An appeal was filed by the hospital.

APPEALS COURT DECISION: The Appeals Court unanimously reversed and remanded the case back to the trial court for the appointment of a guardian. That decision was granted review by the Pennsylvania Supreme Court.

PENNSYLVANIA SUPREME COURT DECISION: The Pennsylvania Supreme Court reversed the appeals court decision and remanded the case back to the trial court for additional proceedings. In so doing, the Supreme Court instructed the trial court to evaluate the following issues: (1) the charge of neglect is based on a religious belief; therefore, the exercise of religious freedom is an important constitutional right; (2) any state impingement of religious freedom must be justified; (3) the treatment in the case is not life-sustaining; (4) Ricky's wishes must be determined; and (5) whose religious beliefs will prevail if there is a parental-child conflict concerning the treatment.

ANALYSIS: This case essentially stands for the principle that unless the life of a child is at stake, the state does not have an interest strong enough to override a parent's right to refuse treatment based on a religious belief. In addition, the case supported the trend of allowing input from the minor (especially the "mature minor") concerning treatment preferences. This is especially important when the child's religious preferences or beliefs may be different from those of the parent(s) and when the treatment is not life-saving.

Ricky testified about his preferences of treatment in a hearing conducted pursuant to the Pennsylvania Supreme Court decision. It was clear he did not want the operation. The case worked its way up to the Pennsylvania Supreme Court again,[102] and the Court upheld his wishes.

KEY CASE 13–8   In Re E.G., A Minor (1989)[103]

Jehovah's Witness mother and patient refuse blood transfusions

FACTS: E.G., 17 years old, contracted leukemia and required blood transfusions. Her mother and E.G., both Jehovah's Witnesses, refused the treatment based on their religious beliefs. All other treatment was consented to by E.G.'s mother.

Illinois files "neglect" petition

The State of Illinois filed a neglect petition in the Illinois juvenile court.

Trial court holds 17-year-old a "neglected minor" and appoints guardian

TRIAL COURT DECISION: The trial court found E.G. to be medically neglected and appointed a guardian over the person to make medical decisions. The court stated that the appointment was in the child's best interest, despite describing her as a "mature 17-year-old." Even with E.G. being clear about her wishes and that death was "assured absent treatment," the court held that the state's interest in the preservation of life outweighed that of E.G. and her mother.

The decision was appealed.

Appeals court vacates trial court order in part and modifies it in part

APPEALS COURT DECISION: The appeals court vacated the trial court order in part and modified it in part. Citing an Illinois case that upheld a Jehovah's Witness's First Amendment right to refuse transfusions, the court extended that right to "mature minors" based on the long line of United States Supreme Court decisions allowing minors to consent to abortions (without parental consent). That right, the court opined, was based on the constitutional right of privacy and that extended to the right to refuse medical treatment. Somewhat surprisingly, however, the court upheld the neglect finding against the mother.

The decision was appealed to the Illinois Supreme Court.

Illinois Supreme Court upholds refusal

ILLINOIS SUPREME COURT DECISION: The Illinois Supreme Court made its decision despite E.G.'s turning 18 years old—the age of majority in Illinois—prior to its decision. In so doing, the court held that the issues in the case, although technically moot, were of "substantial public interest" and therefore should be decided. The court held that (1) a mature minor has a right to give consent or refusal for treatment; (2) the right is based not only on constitutional protections but state law as well; (3) state interests exist that must be balanced against the rights afforded the mature minor; (4) if the treatment refused is life-threatening, the state's interest may be greater than the mature minor's; (5) the mother and E.G. agreed in this case, but in those in which others—family, adult siblings, for example—disagree, their opposition to the mature minor's refusing treatment "would weigh heavily against the minor's right to refuse;" and (6) the neglect finding against the mother must be expunged.

ANALYSIS: This case is an interesting one in supporting the common-law right of a minor to refuse treatment. Even though the court discussed many of the constitutional arguments for allowing the refusal of treatment by a minor, it declined to rule on the constitutional issue because it could

KEY CASE 13–8   In Re E.G., A Minor (1989)[103] Continued

rest its decision on other precedent. The decision's impact may not be as far-reaching as it seems upon a first reading, however. The Illinois Supreme Court points out in its opinion that if E.G. had refused the transfusions and her mother had consented to them, E.G.'s wishes may have had to give way to her mother's request. Perhaps, then, the right of the mature minor to refuse treatment in Illinois is conditioned on the parental support of that choice. Also it is important to point out, although not a basis of the decision, the court's reliance on the abortion decisions granting a minor the right to seek those services without parental consent. Obviously the decision was reached prior to the United States Supreme Court decision in *Casey v. Planned Parenthood* discussed in Chapter 11. Whether that opinion will impact, directly or indirectly, on a minor's right to refuse medical treatment will remain to be seen.

Seriously Ill Newborns, Including Those with Congenital Anomalies

When withdrawal or withholding treatment decisions involve this category, newborns with such conditions as prematurity and its concurrent developmental problems, spina bifida cystica and anencephaly for example, the legal and ethical issues surrounding those decisions are volatile.[104] Two early examples of these situations illustrate the emotional nature of those decisions.

In 1970, a film produced by the Joseph P. Kennedy Foundation entitled "Who Should Survive?" depicted an actual case at John Hopkins University.[105] The parents of a 2-day-old infant with multiple anomalies, including Down's syndrome and duodenal atresia, asked that no surgical intervention take place. The physicians agreed, and the infant was given nothing by mouth and intravenous therapy was discontinued; 15 days later, the child died.

In 1973, a study done by two physicians at Yale–New Haven Hospital reported practices at that particular institution concerning treatment decisions for newborns with birth defects.[106] In a 2 1/2-year period of study in the special care nursery, 299 deaths occurred. Of those 299 deaths, 14% transpired because of a decision to

withhold or withdraw treatment.[107] The conditions of the infants who died included spina bifida, trisomies, and multiple anomalies.[108]

It was not until 1982, however, that situations concerning the nontreatment of infants with congenital anomalies received national attention as they worked their way into the judicial system. Although a few earlier cases had been decided in other jurisdictions, including Florida and New York, one particular decision set the stage for far-reaching changes in federal and state law concerning newborns and treatment decisions. The case, *In Re Treatment and Care of Infant Doe*, is discussed as Key Case 13–9 on the next page.

Baby Doe died within 6 days of the decision of his parents to refuse treatment, surrounded by the legal frenzy to obtain treatment for him.

As a result of the Baby Doe case, the Reagan administration began to respond to the issue of withholding and withdrawing treatment from newborns with disabilities. The Director of the Office of Civil Rights of the United States Department of Health and Human Services (DHHS), directed by then-President Reagan, issued a notice to 7000 hospitals receiving federal funding.[112] The notice specifically stated:

KEY CASE 13–9   In Re Treatment and Care of Infant Doe (1982)[109]

Baby John Doe born with multiple anomalies

Parents refuse surgery and intravenous therapy discontinued

Hospital files petition to reverse parents' decision

Court upholds parents' decision

Appointed guardian ad litem does not appeal decision

"Neglected child" petition denied. Appeal to United States Supreme Court denied

FACTS: Baby John Doe was born with trisomy 21, a tracheoesophageal fistula, and esophageal atresia. The parents (the father was a teacher and had worked with Down's syndrome students "occasionally") believed that their son would not have "minimally acceptable quality of life" and that it was in his best interest, as well as in the best interests of the rest of the family (two other children) that surgical repair of the anomalies not take place. Since the infant could not be fed orally, intravenous therapy was discontinued. The hospital filed an emergency petition asking that the parents' decision be overriden.

TRIAL COURT DECISION: After hearing testimony from several medical experts, including Baby Doe's pediatrician and a pediatric expert, the court held that the parents were fully informed of the treatment options available to their child and a decision concerning treatment in those circumstances was theirs to make. The court also appointed local child welfare authorities as a *guardian ad litem* in the event an appeal was to occur.

The *guardian ad litem* decided against an appeal.

JUVENILE COURT PETITION AND DECISION: The district attorney then petitioned the Indiana Juvenile Court asking for determination whether Baby Doe was a "neglected" child under Indiana law. The petition was denied.

Further attempts to have the case heard, including an appeal to the United States Supreme Court, were denied.

ANALYSIS: The case received nationwide publicity and was very controversial. According to one author, those responses are very curious, particularly because limited palliative therapy for seriously compromised handicapped infants was fairly common at the time.[110] It is also the author's speculation that the controversial issue in the case was the presence of Down's syndrome, a handicap not particularly serious when compared with other congenital anomalies.[111]

Under Section 504 (of the Rehabilitation Act of 1973) it is unlawful for a recipient of federal financial assistance to withhold from a handicapped infant nutritional sustenance or medical or surgical treatment to correct a life-threatening condition if: (1) the withholding is based on the fact that the infant is handicapped; and (2) the handicap does not render the treatment or nutritional sustenance medically contradicted.[113]

Furthermore, the Department of Health and Hu-

man Services stated that Down's syndrome was a handicap covered under the Act and threatened to terminate financial assistance to any hospital that engaged in discriminatory conduct against handicapped newborns or "facilitated" such conduct by parents of handicapped newborns.

The initial notice was followed by an interim final rule.[114] Again citing Section 504 of the Rehabilitation Act, the Department of Health and

Human Services required health care facilities to post notices in a conspicuous place in pediatric wards, newborn nurseries, and special care units to alert staff that "discriminatory failure to feed and care for a handicapped infant" was prohibited by federal law.[115] In addition, a hotline number was listed with instructions for anyone with information concerning discrimination against a handicapped infant to report that conduct anonymously.[116] Last, the notice clearly stated that retaliation or intimidation of any person who did report conduct was prohibited and that the non-care and non-feeding of infants may also violate state civil and criminal law.

If any calls were received through the hotline, the Office of Civil Rights was prepared to initiate an immediate on-site investigation concerning the conduct. The investigators were nicknamed the "Baby Doe squads." They had the authority to question all health care providers and/or family members and had access to health care records and facilities.

The interim final rule was challenged by the American Academy of Pediatrics. The rule was invalidated 3 weeks after its effective date because of noncompliance with rule-making requirements of the federal Administrative Procedure Act (APA).[117]

As a result of the invalidation of its rule, the Department of Health and Human Services proposed another rule and allowed for public comment under the Administrative Procedure Act. It elicited 17,000 responses.[118] The final rule, which was to take effect in February of 1984, contained the following provisions: (1) smaller notices similar to the earlier ones were to be posted, but not in public places; (2) the information reported would be kept confidential; (3) a list of illustrative conditions requiring treatment; (4) a recommendation that hospitals establish Infant Care Review Committees (ICRCs); and (5) state child protective agencies receiving federal funds must establish procedures to receive and investigate allegations of medical neglect of newborns.[119]

Interestingly, the final rule was declared in-

valid by the United States Supreme Court in 1986 in the *Bowen v. American Hospital* case.[120] That case had a long, circuitous route to the Supreme Court.

The *Bowen* case began when a New York Court upheld a decision by the parents of "Baby Jane Doe," who suffered from spina bifida, microcephaly, and hydrocephalus, to refuse surgical intervention but to agree to other medical care and nourishment.[121] Shortly after New York's highest court decision, the United States Department of Justice initiated a suit in federal court seeking to have the hospital that cared for Baby Jane Doe produce its treatment records.[122] The Department wanted the records so that the Department of Health and Human Services could review whether Baby Jane Doe had been discriminated against in violation of federal law and its rules concerning discrimination against handicapped infants.

The federal court denied the request, holding that the parents' decision was a reasonable one and that the hospital had not discriminated against the infant. Rather, the court opined, it simply followed the parents' refusal to grant consent for treatment.[123] The Federal Appeals Court affirmed the lower court's decision.[124] An appeal to the United States Supreme Court followed.

In declaring the final rule not authorized by Section 504 of the Rehabilitation Act and upholding the decisions of the lower federal courts, the United States Supreme Court was clear in its analysis of the Rehabilitation Act. It held that (1) when parents refuse treatment for their newborn, no discrimination by a health care facility takes place; (2) the final rule was not based on evidence that any facility had failed to report instances of discrimination under Section 504; and (3) the Department of Health and Human Services had no authority to require state agencies to investigate allegations of medical neglect.

Despite the Supreme Court's decision, the matter concerning the withholding and withdrawal of treatment for newborns with handicaps was already put to rest. During the legal course of these cases in the lower federal courts,

Congress passed the Child Abuse Amendments of 1984 (CAA),[125] altering the Child Abuse Prevention and Treatment and Adoption Reform Act originally passed in 1974.[126]

The Child Abuse Amendments, although controversial, were much more far reaching than a court decision testing the final interim rules would have been. Had a favorable decision for the Department of Health and Human Services been reached, compliance with the court order would have been required only of health care facilities receiving federal funds—Medicare specifically. The Amendments, in contrast, required state child protective agencies receiving federal grants to: (1) change the definition of child abuse and neglect to include the "withholding of medically indicated treatment"; and (2) establish programs in their systems to ensure that reports of medical neglect were investigated and, if appropriate, take necessary action.

Thus, those health care providers mandated to report child abuse and neglect under their respective state laws were required to report instances of "medical neglect" when "medically indicated treatment" was withheld, including nutrition, hydration, and medication. Several exceptions to the requirement of reporting instances of withholding treatment include when (1) an infant is chronically and permanently comatose; or (2) treatment would only prolong dying, not correct an infant's life-threatening condition, and/or was futile; or (3) the treatment would be futile and may in fact be inhumane.[127]

In the end, then, the Reagan administration achieved its goal of upholding its position that the nonprovision of "medically indicated treatment" for newborns with congenital handicaps was illegal. It is simplistic, however, for anyone to think that the issue has been laid to rest. The emotional and legal issues surrounding the decision not to provide treatment to a seriously ill newborn continue to remain controversial and unsettled.[128]

Euthanasia/Mercy Killing

In the United States, both of these terms mean mercifully putting to death people who suffer from painful, incurable, and distressing diseases.[129] The word *euthanasia*, meaning "good death" in Greek, is further defined in terms of active or passive and voluntary, involuntary, or nonvoluntary. It has also been contrasted with assisted suicide by focusing on the role of the health care provider: with assisted suicide, the health care provider only provides the means with which the patient ultimately acts "last" to end his or her life. In contrast, in euthanasia, the health care provider acts "last" by performing the act that results in the death of the patient.[130]

> *In the United States, [euthanasia, mercy killing] . . . mean mercifully putting to death people who suffer from painful, incurable, and distressing diseases.*

The health care provider's actions would, of course, be seen as an example of active euthanasia. Moreover, it would most likely result in criminal liability for the health care provider. In addition to the potential legal ramifications, such conduct on the part of health care practitioners also raises complex ethical issues.[131] Despite these complex ethical issues, attempts have been made by state legislatures and professional groups to pass legislation allowing for active euthanasia under certain limited circumstances. This development will be discussed in the Assisted Suicide section.

Passive euthanasia is, in fact, the "right to die" as it has been developed to date by the courts and legislative process.[132] However, it is still fraught with some confusion, mainly because of the inability of society to differentiate between the conduct of the health care provider in withholding or withdrawing specific treatment (acts of "commission" or "omission") and the underlying medical condition that ultimately causes the death of the patient.[133] Even so, most court decisions wrestling with this issue have held that it is the *underlying condition* that causes the death of the individual and not the withholding or withdrawing of the treatment, whether the treatment be artifical food and fluid[134] or other forms of medical care.[135]

Voluntary euthanasia usually denotes a situation in which the patient is actively involved in the decision of withdrawing or withholding of treatment by providing informed refusal for treatment, whether by an oral declaration or an advance directive. In contrast, involuntary euthanasia is defined as withholding or withdrawing treatment without the individual's informed consent to do so.[136] Nonvoluntary euthanasia takes place when the individual without decision-making capacity has not expressed his or her desires, and a decision is made without any real or presumed understanding of what the patient would have wanted.[137]

Suicide

Suicide is the deliberate termination of one's life by one's own hand.[138] Although suicide was a felony under the English law (forfeiture of the estate and burial in the highway as punishment), penalties in American jurisdictions are no longer imposed for successful suicide.[139] However, attempted suicide is sometimes categorized as illegal or unlawful in some states. If so, the jurisdiction may require a psychiatric hospitalization for the individual. The rationale for this position is that the state has an interest in the preservation of life.

In relation to the refusal of life-sustaining treatment, the courts have been careful not to equate suicide with refusal of treatment.[140] The basis for not equating the two is one of two theories: causation and intent. The causation approach rests upon the premise that it is the underlying condition, and not self-destruction, that causes the death.[141] Likewise, the intent theory is based on the fact that the individual intends only to forgo life-sustaining treatment—treatment that is seen as futile, painful, and/or

burdensome—and does not intend death.[142] In fact, in one case, *Satz v. Perlmutter*,[143] which involved a competent patient suffering from Lou Gehrig's disease (amyotrophic lateral sclerosis), the court squarely rested its decision on both theories in upholding Mr. Perlmutter's request to be removed from the ventilator.

In relation to the refusal of life-sustaining treatment, the courts have been careful not to equate suicide with refusal of treatment.

In another important case, *Bouvia v. Superior Court (Glenchur)*,[144] the California Court of Appeals distinguished suicide from the patient's refusal to accept artificial food and hydration and forced spoon feeding as her resignation to accept an earlier death rather than accept forced feeding.[145] Ms. Bouvia was a patient whose disease—cerebral palsy—did not affect her decision-making capacity. The court upheld her refusal, stating that the right to terminate one's life is based on the right of privacy.[146] It is important to note that, unlike Mr. Perlmutter and many others involved in the right-to-die cases, she was not terminally ill.

In addition to courts distinguishing between suicide and the right to refuse life-sustaining treatment, most state legislatures have made this demarcation clear. Advance directive legislation in most states contains a provision clearly stating that the refusal of any treatment, including life-sustaining treatment, is not considered suicide. Furthermore, the legislation often contains a clear disclaimer that the state does not condone or support suicide.

Assisted Suicide

Assisted suicide is the inducing, aiding, or forcing of another to commit suicide.[147] In all American jurisdictions, if an individual forcefully or under conditions of duress causes another to kill himself or herself, a charge of murder would be brought against the individual.[148] Moreover, even if the deceased asked a person for help in achieving death for any reason, including a desire to end suffering from an illness or injury, a charge of murder would most probably be brought against that individual.[149]

In the health care arena, if one accepts the premise that refusing life-sustaining treatment is not suicide, then it follows that if a health care provider adheres to a patient's oral or written request to refuse treatment or have certain treatment withdrawn, there can be no liability for assisted suicide, so long as the provider does not overstep the patient's requests. This conclusion was not initially clear, however, and many of the initial right-to-die cases focused on the liability issues for physicians, nurses, and health care institutions if care was withdrawn or withheld.[150] The end result of the early decisions clearly articulated the principle that health care providers, institutions, and ethics committees would not be liable for assisting suicide.[151]

That principle was again affirmed in the *Bouvia* case discussed above. The court clearly held that a health care provider's presence (when a patient exercises his or her constitutional right of refusing life-sustaining treatment) is not the same as "affirmative assertive, proximate, direct conduct such as providing a gun, poison or . . . another instrumentality" that the person uses to "inflict injury upon himself."[152]

Most advance directive legislation also protects health care providers who "in good faith" abide by a patient's advance directive. The protection lies in immunity from criminal, civil, or disciplinary actions brought by others challenging the decision or actions of the health care practitioner or institution.

Health Care Provider–Assisted Suicide

In rare situations, the protection against liability for assisted suicide may not be present for actions of a health care provider. If a health care provider oversteps his or her role when a patient exercises the constitutional right to refuse life-sustaining treatment, liability may be a reality. This is especially so when the health care provider's conduct receives national attention.

The issue of health care provider–assisted suicide is not new, at least in the world arena. In the Netherlands and Germany, for example, assisted suicide by physicians is firmly planted in the respective countries' cultures.[153] It was not until recently, however, that this issue was openly dealt with in the United States.

> *It was not until recently, however, that [assisted suicide] was openly dealt with in the United States.*

Commentaries on the topic of assisted suicide existed prior to 1988.[154] It was not until 1988 that consistent media coverage began on the issue when the article "It's Over, Debbie"[155] appeared in the Journal of the American Medical Association. In March of 1990, another article, by Dr. Timothy Quill, openly discussed how he aided a young cancer patient die by prescribing a lethal dose of barbiturates at her request, so she could take them and end her suffering.[156]

Shortly thereafter, on June 4, 1990, Dr. Jack Kevorkian shocked the medical and lay community by aiding a woman to kill herself with his homemade "suicide machine." The 54-year-old woman, Janet Adkins, sought Dr. Kevorkian's help when she decided that she did not want to suffer any more from Alzheimer's disease, which had been diagnosed. She traveled to Royal Oak, Michigan, from her home in Portland, Oregon, with her husband and several friends to effectuate her death. Before her death, she reportedly wrote a suicide note stating that the decision was freely entered into because she did not want her disease to progress any further.[157]

She ended her life in Dr. Kevorkian's van in a private parking lot by pushing buttons on the machine that delivered thiopental and potassium chloride into her body.[158] She died in 5 minutes.

Kevorkian contacted the police and informed them of what happened. His van was impounded. Three days later, he was barred by a court-ordered injunction from using the machine again. On December 3, Kevorkian was charged with first-degree murder for her death and jailed in lieu of $150,000.00 bond.[159] He was released when the bond money was raised by his lawyers.

On December 13, the judge dismissed the first-degree murder charges against Kevorkian, stating that prosecutors had failed to prove that he had planned and carried out Mrs. Adkins' death.[160] Rather, the judge held, Mrs. Adkins had caused her death. Furthermore, the judge based his decision on the fact that Michigan had no law prohibiting assisted suicide at the time. The earlier order barring Dr. Kevorkian from using his suicide machine, however, continued to exist.

In October of 1991, Dr. Kevorkian again made the headlines after he assisted two other women with their deaths in Pontiac, Michigan. Ms. Majorie Wantz, 58 years old, and Ms. Sherry Miller, 43, died after using another suicide device assembled by Kevorkian. Both suffered from chronic illnesses (chronic pelvic disease and multiple sclerosis), but neither was terminally ill.

Kevorkian was indicted on murder charges for the deaths after the coroner amended the women's respective death certificates to indicate that the deaths were homicides. The prosecutor also sought a contempt-of-court order against Kevorkian for violating the 1990 order banning him from using a suicide machine and participating in any further deaths. On July 21, 1992, the judge dismissed the murder charges, ruling that although Kevorkian was present during the two deaths, he did not initiate them. The ban on the use of the suicide machine was upheld, however.

After his third involvement in the assisted suicides, the Michigan Board of Medicine suspended Kevorkian's license to practice medicine.[161] Thereafter, Kevorkian participated in other deaths by providing carbon monoxide. In an attempt to stop any further "assisted suicides" by Kevorkian, the State of Michigan passed a temporary statute criminalizing assisted suicide.[162] The statute was effective for 6 months only to allow a state commission to decide what Michigan's policy on such conduct would be.

Undaunted, Kevorkian continued to participate in aiding others to die. Three of those deaths resulted in two respective suits against Kevorkian. In the first trial, Kevorkian was acquitted by the jury.[163] In the second, which was brought under the temporary statute criminalizing assisted suicide (even though the statute had expired), Kevorkian was also acquitted.[164] The jury reportedly stated that the expired law banning assisted suicide was confusing. They also decided that if, according to his testimony at trial, Kevorkian's main intent was to relieve pain and not cause death, then he could not be guilty of violating the statute.[165]

Kevorkian was also cleared of civil charges in two other deaths under Michigan common law, which prohibits helping others commit suicide. Despite the criminal and civil trials he faced, Kevorkian has participated in at least 34 deaths since 1990.[166]

Interestingly, during the Kevorkian cases, the disputatious book *Final Exit: The Practicalities of Self-Deliverance and Assisted Suicide for the Dying* by Derek Humphry[167] was published. It sold enough copies to reach the New York Times Best Seller List. Part 2, consisting of five chapters, discusses the role of physicians and nurses in euthanasia.

Legislative Support for Health Care Provider–Assisted Suicide

One of the ways in which the debate over assisted suicide may be resolved is through the passage of legislation supporting a health care provider's participation in the death of those who decide to exercise this option. In two states, Washington and Oregon, this process is under way.

The first physician-assisted suicide case was decided *en banc* by the Ninth Circuit Court of Appeals in *Compassion in Dying v. Washington State*.[168] The court held that Washington's ban on assisted suicide is unconstitutional as applied to terminally ill, competent patients who ask physicians for help in ending their lives with dignity.[169] The court rested its decision on the constitutional liberty interest those patients have in determining the time and manner of their own death.[170] The court also held that some state regulation of assisted suicide might be constitutional, especially where state interests outweigh the exercise of the right (e.g., avoiding undue influence).

In Oregon, also included in the Ninth Circuit, the same court lifted the injunction that had been placed by a lower Oregon district court banning the implementation of a voter-approved law that would allow physicians to prescribe medications for use by patients wanting to end their lives.[171] The court held that the lower court's ruling that the statute unconstitutionally deprived terminally ill persons of the benefit of state law criminalizing physician-assisted suicide was in conflict with the constitutional right of competent, terminally ill patients to die.[172] Like the Washington case, this case may be far from completion. Even so, its decision is an interesting development on legislation supporting the right to assisted suicide.

Last, in a case involving a criminal statute that banned assisted suicide, the Second Circuit Court of Appeals held that the lower district court erred in upholding the New York law.[173] Banning the right of physicians to assist a mentally competent, terminally ill patient with death is unconstitutional according to the court.[174]

The United States Supreme Court has decided to review both the Washington and New York appellate court decisions. Both cases raise several due process and equal protection questions surrounding physician-assisted suicide.

The legal and ethical debate and controversy over health practitioner–assisted suicide will continue, as perhaps it should, openly and analytically.[175] Despite the discomfort of such debate and controversy, many believe it is better to deal with the issue openly rather than in a clandestine manner, which had been the case prior to 1988.

Family-Initiated Death of an Adult or Minor within a Health Care Facility

In rare circumstances, health care providers may be involved in situations in which a family member decides that no further treatment or care should be given to a member of his or her family in a health care facility. The family member then takes immediate personal action to carry out that decision in the facility. For example, in 1986, Mr. Edward Baker forced a nurse at gunpoint to remove his father, suffering from cancer, from the ventilator.[176] During the same year, a Phoenix, Arizona, man, armed with a shotgun, held physicians at bay for 2 hours after he disconnected his father who was suffering from cancer from a respirator.[177]

In 1988, a similar situation in Chicago, Illinois, involved a minor, Samuel Linares. When he was 6 months old, Samuel aspirated a balloon at a birthday party. When his father found him, he was in cardiorespiratory arrest due to asphyxiation.[178] His father immediately initiated CPR. When paramedics arrived, they removed the aspirated balloon and continued CPR until a "normal cardiac rhythm and output" was established in the ED of a suburban hospital. The estimated time from the discovery of the obstructed airway until cardiac functioning was restored was approximately 20 minutes.[179] Samuel was placed on a ventilator and after his condition stabilized, he was transported to another hospital in Chicago.

Samuel was admitted in a comatose state, but

he was not brain dead. Initially he was not expected to survive the incident, but he did so. However, it became clear that Samuel would never regain consciousness, and a diagnosis of persistent vegatative state was made. Attempts to wean him from the ventilator were not successful, and it was clear that without it, he would die. His family was informed of his condition and this prognosis. The family, especially the father, Mr. Rudolf Linares, asked that Samuel be removed from the ventilator. The request was considered by the hospital, but it was decided that it could not comply with the request.[180] However, a do-not-resuscitate status with no heroic measures was agreed to.

In December of 1988, while visiting, Mr. Linares took his son from the respirator. Security guards wrestled him to the ground, and Samuel was reconnected to the respirator.[181]

In 1989, it was decided that Samuel would need to be transferred to a nursing home. The family consented, but they were clearly concerned about Samuel's continued existence in his current medical state. Furthermore, the family's welfare payments were being terminated.

On April 25, 1989, Mr. and Mrs. Linares went to the hospital to visit their son. Hospital security guards met them as they entered because the hospital had received a call from a neighbor stating that Mr. Linares was quite upset before he left for the hospital.[182] However, they were allowed to visit Samuel in the pediatric intensive care unit.

Mrs. Linares was told to leave the unit by her husband after they were there for a short time. Mr. Linares pulled out a handgun, disconnected Samuel from the respirator, and kept staff at bay with the gun. He allowed the staff to remove the other infants from the unit and said, "I'm not here to hurt anyone."[183] Thirty minutes later, Samuel Linares died in his father's arms.

Linares surrendered to police, telling them that he did what he did because he loved his son and his wife, and because he wanted his son "to be at rest." Linares was charged with

first-degree murder on April 26, 1989.[184] The Cook County State's Attorney's Office presented the case to a grand jury, which decided not to indict Mr. Linares for murder.[185] Linares did, however, plead guilty to a weapons charge and was placed on probation.[186]

The Linares case was a tragic and drastic situation that was unfortunate for many reasons. It was clearly complicated by the legal and ethical issues involved in it, including, but not limited to, (1) the definition of death in Illinois (brain death); (2) the concern of the institution for liability, both criminal and civil; (3) the Federal Child Abuse Amendments discussed earlier; and (4) the complex ethical issues involved in the case.[187]

The case did, however, have a positive outcome. It provided the impetus for open discussion about such situations and was the thrust behind the passage of the Illinois Health Care Surrogate Act.[188] The Act establishes surrogate/proxy decision-making mechanisms without the need for court intervention for minors and adults who cannot make treatment decisions for themselves.

Pronouncement of Death

Traditionally the determination of death has been by the patient's physician, or, in cases of a death occurring outside of a hospital situation or under suspicious circumstances, a coroner. Recently, however, nurses have begun to take over this task, albeit in limited circumstances.

Governed by state law, nurses in long-term care, in a home health care agency, a hospice, and, in some instances, a hospital are given the authority to pronounce an individual dead. Most often that pronouncement must be certified by a physician within specified time frames.[189] Currently, New Jersey, Connecticut, New Hampshire, Massachusetts, Hawaii, and Alaska have authorized nurses in long-term care to declare specific patients dead.

As this ability of the nurse continues to develop, especially in relation to nurses who function in more independent, advanced practice roles, this role may become more commonplace than it currently is. For example, South Dakota specifically grants this power to nurse practitioners.

Nursing Implications

The nurse working with patients who are dying must do so by taking into account all of the legal and ethical ramifications associated with their care. When, for example, a patient has a do-not-resuscitate order, it is important that the order be obtained consistent with the institution or agency policy. Under no circumstances should a nurse accept and carry out a do-not-resuscitate order that is not consistent with policy. Rather, the nurse should contact and inform the nurse manager of the request to do so inconsistent with the policy. Also, the nurse must be clear that, unless a contradictory order exists, the do-not-resuscitate patient must be given all other nursing care that is not refused. Studies have shown that nurses believe all other care should be provided and provide that care consistent with the patient's or surrogate/proxy decision-maker's decisions.[190] Family members and others should be reassured by the nurse that other care will not be neglected for the do-not-resuscitate patient.

The nurse working with patients who are dying must do so by taking into account all of the legal and ethical ramifications associated with their care.

The nurse should be ever vigilant about ensuring that any decision to withhold or withdraw treatment is made with the patient's, or the legally recognized surrogate/proxy's, informed refusal. If the nurse determines that in-

formed refusal has not been obtained, the nurse should contact the nurse manager. Furthermore, the situation may be one that needs to be brought before the institution's ethics committee or nursing ethics committee.

When patient care disagreements surrounding pain management arise, whether the nurse works in a hospice or an acute care setting, he or she should raise the disagreement through the established institutional avenues.[191] Under no circumstance should the nurse decide to "take matters into his or her own hands" and alter medication doses or orders or initiate the administration of new medications. In addition, the personal storage of medications, especially controlled substances, in violation of the agency or facility policy, is not recommended.

If the nurse is working with minors, additional concerns are present, especially if the older or mature minor refuses treatment that has been consented to by the parent(s). The physician and nurse manager should be contacted immediately. Furthermore, if a conflict exists between the minor's treatment wishes and what treatment the parent is consenting to or refusing, notification of the physician and nursing administration is again necessary.

The nurse may be subpoenaed to testify in court if a treatment situation involving a minor or other patient has not been resolved through other routes. The nurse should contact the risk management department of the facility and also seek legal advice (from the institution's attorney and/or his or her own attorney) before responding to the subpoena in any way.

If the nurse in the neonatal intensive care unit is faced with refusal of treatment because of the presence of a disability, and none of the exceptions discussed in the Federal Child Abuse Amendments apply, the nurse should seek legal advice concerning her responsibilities in that situation. At issue, of course, is whether the nurse would be required to report that situation under the state's child abuse laws. Another way of handling the situation would be to bring the issue before the institutional review committee or other ethics group, if possible.

Insofar as assisted suicide is concerned, the nurse would need to carefully evaluate his or her participation in those situations. A complete understanding of state criminal and civil law is vital, as are the ethical and professional issues assisted suicide raises.[192] It is important, however, that the nurse be active in raising the issue generally in nursing ethics committees, team meetings, and with other nurse colleagues to establish open channels of communication concerning the matter.[193] Keeping abreast of the latest legislative developments in his or her own state, and other states, is also important.

If the nurse is faced with a *Linares*-type situation, it will be important not to become actively involved in the removal of the family member from whatever life-sustaining treatment is being provided, if at all possible. Patients nearby should be kept from harm. Talking calmly with the family member who is carrying out the removal can occur, but in no instance should the nurse attempt to stop the individual from his or her self-imposed mission. Rather, that should be left to security personnel if it is to occur at all.

There is no doubt that the nurse in such a situation is in a legal and ethical nightmare: His or her inaction may cause the death of the family member. Yet, actively attempting to stop the conduct may also cause the patient's death and endanger the nurse's personal safety and the safety of other patients in the vicinity. As one noted nurse ethicist said about the nurses in the *Linares* situation, a nurse involved in such a situation becomes a "character in a play, driven by internal and external forces, speaking . . . lines in context, and subject to a host of interpretations by the audience."[194]

If the nurse practices in a state where he or she can pronounce patients dead, the nurse should do so consistent with the state law granting that authority. The notification of required individuals should also occur.

Last, but by no means least, nurses need to have systematic support as they work with patients like Nancy Cruzan, Samuel Linares, and

Baby Doe.[195] The emotional impact of any such case on the nurse is overwhelming to say the least. Providing support for nurses is just as important as providing it for others.

DOCUMENTATION REMINDER 13–2 SPECIAL CONSIDERATIONS

▼ Document completely and accurately any and all medical orders for withdrawing or withholding treatment, including do-not-resuscitate orders, doing so consistent with facility policy

▼ If do-not-resuscitate order given inconsistent with facility policy, document who notified and file incident report

▼ Utilize proper forms when requesting any and all medical supplies, including medications and controlled substances

▼ If controlled substances or other medications not obtained from pharmacy, contact nursing administration and file incident report

▼ Any and all telephone or other requests for changes in medications

▼ Any and all orders given for changes in medications, especially controlled substances

▼ Any and all contacts, discussions, and the like with pharmacy, physician, nursing management

▼ Utilize required reporting forms when reporting child abuse/neglect pursuant to state law

▼ Accurate and complete entry concerning mandated report; incidents with family or others concerning withdrawal or withholding of treatment; results of reporting; presentation before ethics committee

▼ Accurate and complete entry concerning pronouncement of death following state law mandates

---

SUMMARY OF PRINCIPLES
AND APPLICATIONS

The issues surrounding death and dying will probably never be fully resolved. Just as one particular issue is met with perhaps some "comfort," another begins to create discomfort, discord, and introspection. As uncomfortable as those feelings may be, health care and its practitioners, including nurses, cannot shy away from meeting the innumerable issues that will continue to be raised by the refusal of life-sustaining treatment. Credit should be given to those individuals who, in their role as patients, demanded that health care and society as a whole wrestle with those issues head on.

Nurses, then, can continue to grapple with issues in death and dying by:

▼ Understanding the various legal and clinical terms associated with death and dying, including, but not limited to, brain death, suicide, and euthanasia.

▼ Comparing and contrasting the many ethical and legal issues surrounding decisions to withhold or withdraw life-sustaining medical care

▼ Keeping abreast of the legislative and case law development concerning refusal of treatment

▼ Comparing and contrasting the issues involved with an adult's right to refuse life-sustaining treatment with that of a minor (or the parents of a minor)

▼ Carefully evaluating the differences, if any, between refusal of life-sustaining treatment and health care practitioner–assisted suicide

▼ Firmly identifying and articulating one's own values and beliefs concerning refusal of life-sustaining treatment

▼ Protecting those who cannot protect themselves—the disabled newborn, minor, or "incompetent" adult—when the need exists (lack of informed input into treatment decisions, conflict surrounding treatment decisions, for example) by notifying appropriate individuals and organizations

▼ Aiding patients and families in obtaining necessary information to make reasoned, informed decisions concerning medical treatment

▼ Complying with the law when a treatment situa-

tion requires it (mandatory reporting, testifying at a trial or hearing)

▼ Actively participating on institutional committees that explore issues in death and dying (institutional review, ethics, or nursing ethics committees)

▼ Testifying at hearings when legislative changes are proposed concerning issues impacting on the right to refuse life-sustaining treatment

▼ Understanding that the right to refuse life-sustaining treatment is not absolute but may be balanced against particular state interests

▼ Striving to keep open lines of communication between and among nursing and other medical colleagues, the family, and the patient

TOPICS FOR FURTHER INQUIRY

1. Compare and contrast the nursing profession's positions on assisted suicide with those of other health care professions, including medicine and social work. Identify and analyze any similarities and differences. Suggest reasons for any similarities and differences, including an evaluation of the historical development of the profession.

2. Develop a model institutional policy for use in a particular health care delivery system concerning a nursing ethics committee. Include its purpose, composition, and how the committee will function, especially if another ethics committee already exists.

3. Research your state law on the reporting of abuse or neglect cases of minors involving the parents' refusal of treatment or the withdrawal of treatment that is considered lifesaving. Determine how many cases were successful, how many were dismissed, and how many went to a hearing or trial. Suggest ways in which the system for reporting such alleged situations can be improved or changed.

4. Develop a questionnaire interview tool to evaluate nurses' attitudes about refusal of life-sustaining treatment or assisted suicide. Include questions such as how the nurse would react in a given situation and the basis for his or her actions; when the belief or beliefs about the topic were formed by the nurse; and how the nurse sees nursing roles in the topic under investigation. After the data are analyzed, present the findings at a nursing meeting or publish the results in a nursing journal.

REFERENCES

1. Alan Meisel. *The Right to Die*. 2nd Edition. New York: John Wiley & Sons, 1995, Volume 1, 16.
2. *Id*. at 5.
3. Henry Campbell Black. *Black's Law Dictionary*. 6th Edition. St. Paul, Minn: West Publishing Company, 1991, 637.
4. *Id*.
5. Meisel, *supra* note 1, Volume 1 at 56–61.
6. 549 N.E. 2d 292 (Ill. 1989).
7. 517 A.2d 886 (N.J. Super. 1986), *aff'd*, 517 A.2d 869 (N.J. Super. A.D. 1986).
8. 544 N.Y.S. 2d 840 (N.Y. App. Div. 1989).
9. Theodore R. LeBlang, W. Eugene Basanta, J. Douglas Peters, Keith Fineberg, and Donald Kroll. *The Law of Medical Practice in Illinois*. Rochester, NY: The Lawyers Co-Operative Publishing Company, 1986, 925 (with Cumulative Supplements).
10. *Id*., *citing* Brown, "Fluosol-DA, A Perfluorochemical Oxygen-Transport Fluid for the Management of a Trochanteric Pressure Sore in a Jehovah's Witness", 12 *Annals of Plastic Surgery* 449 (1984).
11. *Id*.
12. Andrew Skolnick, "As the Blood Supply Gets Safer, Experts Still Call for Ways to Reduce the Need for Transfusions," 268 *JAMA* (August 12, 1992), 698–700.
13. 294 A. 2d 372 (D.C. App. 1972).
14. Meisel, *supra* note 1, Volume 2, at 285, *citing Heinemann's Appeal*, 96 Pa 112 (1880). In this case, the father's custody of his children was terminated and the children given to the grandmother because he had refused to call a physician for needed medical care. *Id*.
15. Meisel, *supra* note 1, Volume 2 at 290–291.
16. *Id*. at 292.
17. *Id*. at 290–291.
18. *Id*. at 283–284, *citing Parham v. J.R.*, 442 U.S. 584 (1979).
19. *Wisconsin v. Yoder*, 406 U.S. 205 (1972).
20. Meisel, *supra* note 1, Volume 1, at 69.
21. For an interesting analysis of these standards and the state's interest in termination of treatment decisions involving minors, see Daniel B. Griffith, "The Best Interests Standard: A Comparison of the State's Parens Patriae Authority and Judicial Oversight in Best Inter-

ests Determinations for Children and Incompetent Patients," 7(3) *Issues in Law and Medicine* (Winter 1991), 283–338.
22. See, for example, *In Re Phillip B*, 156 Cal. Rptr. 48, 51 (Ct. App. 1979) (State should examine expressed treatment wishes of a mentally retarded child); Key Case 13–4.
23. Meisel, *supra* note 1, Volume 1, at 341–464.
24. *Bonner v. Moran*, 126 F.2d 121 (App. D.C. 1941).
25. 348 A.2d 801 (N.J. Super. Ch. 1975), *cert. granted*, 354 A.2d 326 (N.J. 1975), *modified*, 355 A.2d 647 (N.J. 1976), *cert. denied sub nom., Garger v. New Jersey*, 429 U.S. 922 (1976).
26. Meisel, *supra* note 1, Volume 1, at 343–347.
27. *In Re Quinlan*, 355 A.2d 647, 671–72 (N.J. 1976).
28. Meisel, *supra* note 1, Volume 1, at 265.
29. Bowen Husford. *Bioethics Committees: The Health Care Provider's Guide*. Rockville, Md: Aspen Publishers, Inc., 1986, 70.
30. *Id*. at 71.
31. 497 U.S. 261 (1990).
32. See, for example, "*Cruzan*: Clear and Convincing?", 20 (5) *Hastings Center Report* (September/October 1990), 5–12 (A series of articles dealing with the decision); Alexander Capron, Guest Editor, "Medical Decision-Making and the 'Right-to-Die' After *Cruzan*", 19 (1–2) *Law, Medicine & Health Care* (Spring, Summer 1991) (the entire edition includes reactions to the Supreme Court decision); Mila Ann Aroskar, "The Aftermath of the Cruzan Decision: Dying in a Twilight Zone", 38(6) *Nursing Outlook* (November/December 1990), 256–257; Mary Hansen, "Comparison of Quinlan and Cruzan Decisions", 23(4) *Nursing Management* (April 1992), 40–41.
33. James Bopp and Thomas Marzen, "*Cruzan*: Facing the Inevitable," 19 (1–2) *Law, Medicine & Health Care* (Spring, Summer 1991), 37–51; Larry Gostin, "Life and Death Choices after *Cruzan*," *Id*., 9–12; William Colby, "Missouri Stands Alone", 20(5) *Hasting Center Report* (September/October 1990), 5–6; Charles Baron, "On Taking Substituted Judgment Seriously," *Id*., 7–8.
34. *Cruzan v. Mouton*, Estate No. CV 384–9P (Cir. Ct. Jasper County, Mo. December 14, 1990).
35. *New York Times*, December 27, 1990, A9 (National Edition).
36. 579 N.E. 2d 32 (Ind. 1991).
37. *Id*. at 38–41.
38. *Id*. at 41 (footnote 8).
39. Meisel, *supra* note 1, Volume 1, at 393–394.
40. *Id*. at 394.
41. *In Re Busalacchi*, No. 59582, 1991 WL 26851, 1991 Mo. App. LEXIS 315 (March 5, 1991), *reh'g and/or transfer denied* (Mo. App. March 26, 1991), *cause ordered transferred* to Mo. Sup. Ct. (Mo. Ct. App. April 15, 1991), *appealed and remanded sub nom. Busalacchi v. Busalacchi*, No. 73677, 1991 Mo. LEXIS 107 (October 16, 1991), *appeal dismissed*, No. 73677, 1993 WESTLAW 32356 (Mo. January 26, 1993).
42. *Meisil*, *supra* note 1, Volume 1, at 132, *citing In re Busalacchi*, No. 59582, slip. op. at 3 (Mo. Ct. App. March 5, 1991).
43. "Father Regains Control in Right-to-Die Case," *Chicago Tribune*, February 20, 1993, Section 1, at 2.

44. Meisel, *supra* note 1, Volume 1, at 134, *citing* "Comatose Woman, Focus of Court Battle, Dies," *New York Times*, March 8, 1993, at A7 (National Edition).

45. American Nurses' Association. *Position Statement on Promotion of Comfort and Relief of Pain in Dying Patients*. Kansas City, Mo: September 5, 1991.

46. Diane Hoffmann, "Does Legislating Hospital Ethics Committees Make a Difference? A Study of Hospital Ethics Committees in Maryland, The District of Columbia, and Virginia," 19(1–2) *Law, Medicine & Health Care* (Spring, Summer 1991), 118–119.

47. *Id*.

48. 321 S.E. 2d 716 (Ga. 1984).

49. 569 A.2d 1202 (Me. 1990).

50. 534 A. 2d 947 (Me. 1987).

51. Meisel, *supra* note 1, Volume 2 at 39.

52. *In Re Chad Eric Swan*, *supra* note 49, at 1205.

53. *Id*.

54. Meisel, *supra* note 1, Volume 1, at 297–298.

55. Sheryl Buchanan and Liz Cook, "Nursing Ethics Committees: The Time Is Now", 23(8) *Nursing Management* (August 1992), 40–41.

56. LeBlang, Basanta, Peters, Fineberg and Kroll, *supra* note 9, at 925.

57. *Taber's Cyclopedic Medical Dictionary*. 16th Edition. Philadelphia: F.A. Davis, 1989, 457–458.

58. Ad Hoc Committee, "A Definition of Irreversible Coma," 205 *JAMA* 337 (1968).

59. *Id*.

60. *Id*.

61. President's Commission. *Defining Death: Medical, Legal and Ethical Issues in the Determination of Death*. Washington, D.C.: U.S. Government Printing Office, 1981.

62. 12 Uniform Laws Annotated (U.L.A.) 412, 412 (Supp. 1994).

63. Meisel, *supra* note 1, Volume 1, at 625.

64. *Id*. at 631.

65. *Id*. at 631, *citing Strachan v. John F. Kennedy Memorial Hospital*, 538 A. 2d 346 (N.J. 1988).

66. For interesting commentaries on this issue, see, for example, M. Angell, "After *Quinlan*: The Dilemma of the Persistent Vegetative State," 330 *New England Journal of Medicine* (1994), 1524; R. Crandford, "The Persistent Vegetative State: The Medical Reality (Getting the Facts Straight), 18 *Hastings Center Report* (February–March 1988), 27; K. Andres "Recovery of Patients after Four Months in the Persistent Vegetative State," 306 *British Medical Journal* 1597, 1992.

67. President's Commission for The Study of Ethical Problems in Medicine and Biomedical and Behavioral Research, "Resuscitation Decisions for Hospitalized Patients", *in Deciding to Forgo Life-Sustaining Treatment: Ethical, Medical and Legal Issues In Treatment Decisions*. Washington, D.C.: U.S. Government Printing Office, 1983, 231, *citing* 2 Kings 4:31–7 (New English).

68. *Id*. at 233, *citing* W.B. Kouwenhoven, J.R. Jude, and G.G. Knickerbocker, "Closed-Chest Cardiac Massage," 173 *JAMA* 1064 (1960).

69. *Id*. at 234.

70. National Conference on Standards for Cardiopulmonary Resuscitation and Emergency Cardiac Care, "Standards for Cardiopulmonary Resuscitation (CPR) and Emergency Cardiac Care (EEC)," 227 *JAMA* 837, 864 (1974).

71. 380 N.E.2d 134 (Mass. App. 1978)

72. President's Commission, *Deciding to Forgo Life-Sustaining Treatment, supra* note 67, at 238, *citing* David Margolick, "Hospital Is Investigated on Life Support Policy." *New York Times*, June 20, 1982 at A/34.

73. *Id*. at 248–252; See also: The Hastings Center. *Guidelines on the Termination of Life-Sustaining Treatment and the Care of the Dying*. Briarcliff Manor, NY: The Hastings Center, 1987, Part Two, Section B (Guidelines on Emergency Interventions-CPR and Treatment for Life-Threatening Bleeding), 43–52; American Nurses' Association. *Position Paper on Nursing Care and Do Not Resuscitate Decisions*. Washington, D.C.: ANA, 1992.

74. N.Y. Public Health Law, Article 29-B, Section 2960 *et seq.* (1988); Ga. Code Ann. Sections 31–39–1 to –9(1991); Mont. Code Ann. Sections 50–10–101 to –106 (1991); Tenn. Code Ann. Section 66–11–224 (1990).

75. Meisel, *supra* note 1, Volume 1, at 559.

76. Joint Commission on Accreditation of Hospitals. *Accreditation Manual For Hospitals*. Chicago, Ill, 1988, Section MA 1.4.11, 90; Joint Commission on Accreditation of Healthcare Organizations. *Accreditation Manual for Hospitals*. Oak Brook Terrace, Ill, 1992, Section MA 1.3.7., 44.

77. "When Is CPR Futile?", *AJN* (August 1992), 14, *citing* a study done by Mark Ebell, MD of Athens, Georgia Regional Medical Center (CLINICAL NEWS COLUMN).

78. *Id*.

79. Meisel, *supra* note 1, Volume 1, at 554–555.

80. Meisel, *supra* note 1, Volume 2, at 532–533, *citing Dority v. Superior Court*, 193 Cal. Rptr. 288 (1983); *Alvarado v. New York City Health and Hospitals Corp.*, 547 N.Y.S.2d 190 (1989), *vacated and dismissed sub nom. Alvarado v. City of New York*, 550 N.Y.S.2d 353 (1990).

81. No. PX–91–283 (4th Dist. Ct. Hennepin County, Minn. July 1, 1991).

82. Ronald E. Cranford, "Helga Wanglie's Ventilator," 21(4) *Hastings Center Report* (July–August 1991), 23.

83. *Id*.

84. *Id*.

85. *Wanglie, supra* note 81, slip. op. at 5 (finding of fact #4), *reprinted in* 2 *Biolaw* U:2161 (August–September 1991).

86. Felicia Ackerman, "The Significance of a Wish," 21(4) *Hastings Center Report* (July–August 1991), 27.

87. Daniel Callahan, "Medical Futility, Medical Necessity: The Problem without a Name," 21(4) *Hastings Center Report* (July–August 1991), 30–35.

88. Meisel, *supra* note 1, Volume 2, at 534.

89. *New York Times*, July 6, 1991, 8 col. 1 (National Edition)

90. Hila Richardson, "Long Term Care," *Health Care Delivery in the United States*. Anthony Kovner, Editor. 4th Edition. New York: Springer Publishing Company, 1990, 187.

91. *Id*.

92. See, for example, "Home Care Services for Persons with AIDS," Parts 1 and 2. *Journal of Home Health Care Practice*. Edited by Jo Ann Parzick and Helen Triebsch. Volume 3, Numbers 2 and 3 (February and May 1991).

93. *In the Matter of the Proposed Disciplinary Treatment of the*

Licenses of Mary Brackman, RN, Mary Mouat, RN, Debbie Ruggles, RN, Ruth Sasser, RN, Verna VanDuynhoven, RN, and Lynn Zavalney, RN, Docket No.'s cc-90-68-RN, cc-90-66 RN, cc-90-69 RN, cc-90-70-RN, cc-90-71-RN, cc-90-67, RN. *Finding of Facts, Conclusions of Law and Final Order*, 20–24, June 28, 1992.

94. *Id*. at 24–31.
95. *Id*. at 34–37.
96. "Montana's Hospice Six Raise Issue of 'Compassion'" *AJN* (August 1991), 65, 71 (NEWS SECTION).
97. *Brackman v. Board of Nursing*, 820 P. 2d 1314 (Mon. 1991); 851 P. 2d 1055 (Mon. 1993), *rehearing denied* May 20, 1993.
98. *AJN, supra* note 96, *citing The Independent Record*, A Montana newspaper.
99. *Id*. at 65, *citing* Steven Shapiro, attorney for the Montana Department of Commerce, Professional and Occupational Licensing Bureau.
100. *Id*.
101. 292 A. 2d 387 (PA. 1972).
102. 307 A.2d 279 (PA. 1973).
103. 549 N.E. 2d 322 (Ill. 1989).
104. See, for example, *Symposium*: "Pediatrics Decision Making", 23(1) *Journal of Law, Medicine & Ethics* (Spring 1995), 5–46; Margaret Mahon, "The Nurse's Role in Treatment Decision Making for the Child with Disabilities," 6(3) *Issues in Law & Medicine* (Winter 1990), 247–268; *In Re Baby K*, 832 F. Supp. 1022 (E.D. Va. 1993), *aff'd*, 16 F. 3d 590 (4th Circ. 1994), *cert. denied*, 115 S. Ct. 91 (1994).
105. Joseph P. Kennedy, Jr. Foundation, West Hartford, Connecticut, 1971.
106. Raymond Duff and A.G.M. Campbell, "Moral and Ethical Dilemmas in the Special Care Nursery," 289 *New England Journal of Medicine*, 890 (1973).
107. *Id*.
108. *Id*.
109. No. GU 8204–00 (Ind. Cir. Ct. Monroe County April 12, 1982), *petition for writ of mandamus and prohibition denied, sub nom State of Indiana ex rel. Infant Doe v. Baker*, No. 482 S 140 (Ind. May 27, 1982), *cert. denied*, 464 U.S. 96 (1983).
110. Meisel, *supra* note 1, at 308.
111. *Id*. at 309.
112. *Discrimination against the Handicapped by Withholding Treatment or Nourishment: Notice of (sic) Health Care Providers*, 47 Fed. Reg. 26027 (1982).
113. *Id*.
114. "Non-Discrimination on the Basis of Handicap," 48 Fed. Reg. 9630 (March 7, 1983).
115. *Id*. at 9631.
116. *Id*. at 9631–9632.
117. *American Academy of Pediatrics v. Heckler*, 561 F. Supp. 395 (D.D.C. 1983).
118. Margaret M. Mahon, "The Nurse's Role in Treatment Decisionmaking for the Child with Disabilities," 6(3) *Issues In Law & Medicine* (Winter 1990), 247, 254, *citing* 48 Fed. Reg. 30846 (1983).
119. "Procedures Relating to Health Care for Handicapped Infants," 45 C.F.R. Section 84.55 *et seq*. (1989).
120. *American Hospital Ass'n v. Heckler*, 585 F. Supp. 541 (S.D.N.Y.), *aff'd*, 794 F. 2d 676 (2d Cir. 1984), *aff'd sub*

nom. *Bowen v. American Hospital Association*, 476 U.S. 610 (1986).
121. *Weber v. Stony Brook Hospital*, 467 N.Y.S. 2d 685, *aff'd per curiam*, 456 N.E.2d 1186, *cert. denied*, 464 U.S. 1026 (1983).
122. *United States v. University Hospital*, 575 F. Supp. 607 (E.D.N.Y. 1983).
123. *Id*. at 514–615.
124. 729 F. 2d 144 (2d Cir. 1984).
125. Pub. L. No. 98–457, 98 Stat. 1749, 42 U.S.C. Sections 5101–5107 (October 4, 1984).
126. Pub. Law No. 93–247, 88 Stat. 4, (1974).
127. 42 U.S.C. Section 5102(3); 42 C.F.R. Section 1340.15(b)(2) (1985). See, generally, 42 C.F.R. Section 1340 *et seq*. (1985) for additional definitions, objectives, and interpretive guidelines.
128. See, for example, footnote 104.
129. Black, *supra* note 3, at 384; *Taber's Cyclopedic Medical Dictionary supra* note 57, at 629.
130. Dan Brock, "Voluntary Active Euthanasia," 22(2) *Hastings Center Report* (March/April 1992), 10.
131. See, for example, Daniel Callahan. *What Kind of Life: The Limits of Medical Progress*. New York: Simon & Schuster, Inc., 1990; Anne J. Davis and Mila Aroskar. *Ethical Dilemmas and Nursing Practice*. 3rd Edition. Norwalk, Conn: Appleton & Lange, 1991; Mary Johnson, "Voluntary Active Euthanasia: The Next Frontier?" 81(3) *Issues In Law and Medicine* (Winter 1992), 343–359; Chapter 10.
132. Meisel, *supra* note 1, at 452, 472.
133. See, for example, Daniel Callahan, "When Self-Determination Runs Amok," 22(2) *Hastings Center Report* (March/April 1992), 53; Meisel, *supra* note 1, at 63–64.
134. See, for example, *In Re Estate of Greenspan*, 558 N.E. 2d 1194 (1990); *L.W. v L.E. Phillips Career Dev. Ctr.*, 482 N.W. 2d 60, 71 (Wis. 1992).
135. *Barber v. Superior Court of the State of California for Los Angeles County*, 195 Cal. Rptr. 484 (Cal. App. 2nd Dist 1983). This case is also discussed in Chapter 8, Criminal Law.
136. Callahan, *supra* note 133, at 238, *citing* Roger Evans, "Health Care Technology and the Inevitability of Resource Allocation and Rationing Decisions," 249 *JAMA* (April 22/29, 1983), 2212 (Part 2).
137. Meisel, *supra* note 1, at 515.
138. *Black, supra* note 3, at 1000.
139. Wayne LaFave and Austin Scott. *Criminal Law*. 2nd Edition. St. Paul, Minn: West Publishing Company (1986), 649 (with 1995 Pocket Part).
140. See, for example, *In Re Farrell*, 529 A. 2d 404 (1987); *Matter of Conroy*, 457 A. 2d 1232 (N.J. Super. Ch. 1983), *rev'd* 464 A. 2d 303 (N.J. Super. 1983), *cert. granted*, 470 A.2d 418 (N.J. 1983), *rev'd* 486 A. 2d 1209 (N.J. 1983).
141. Meisel, *supra* note 1, at 458, *citing Gray v. Romero*, 697 F. Supp. 580 (D.R.I. 1988); *Donaldson v. Van de Kamp*, 4 Cal. Rptr. 2d 59 62 (Ct. App. 1992).
142. See, for example, *Fosmire v. Nicoleau*, 551 N.E. 2d 77, 82 (N.Y. 1990); *Thor v. Superior Court*, 885 P.2d 375, 386 (Cal. 1994).
143. 362 So. 2d 160 (Fla. App. 4 Dist. 1978), *aff'd* 379 So. 2d 359 (Fla. 1980).
144. 225 Cal. Rptr. 297 (Ct. App. 2nd Dist. 1986), *review denied* (June 5, 1986).

145. 225 Cal. Rptr. 297.

146. *Id.*

147. LaFave and Scott, *supra* note 139, at 650.

148. *Id.*

149. *Id.*

150. See, as examples *Satz v. Perlmutter, supra* note 143; *Application of Eichner* (Storar), 423 N.Y.S.2d 580 (N.Y. Sup. 1979), *modified,* 426 N.Y.S.2d 517 (N.Y. 1980); *modified,* 420 N.E.2d 64 (N.Y. 1981), *cert. denied,* 454 U.S. 858 (1981); *In Re Dinnerstein,* 380 N.E.2d 134 (Mass. App. Ct. 1978); other cases in Table 13–1.

151. Meisel, *supra* note 1, at 455–457.

152. *Bouvia, supra* note 144, at 297.

153. Margaret Battin, "Assisted Suicide: Can We Learn from Germany?" 22(2) *Hastings Center Report* (March–April 1992), 44–51; Maurice A.M. deWachter, "Euthanasia in the Netherlands," *Id.,* 23–30; I. van der Sluis, "The Practice of Euthanasia in the Netherlands", 4(4) *Issues in Law & Medicine* (Spring 1989), 455–465; Patrick Derr, "Hadamar, Hippocrates, and the Future of Medicine: Reflections on Euthanasia and the History of German Medicine," *Id.,* 487–495.

154. See, for example, Derek Humphry. *Jean's Way.* Eugene, Ore: Hemlock Society (1978); Brian Clark. *Whose Life Is It Anyway?* New York: Avon Books, 1980; Bonnie Steinbock, Editor. *Killing and Allowing to Die.* Englewood Cliffs, NJ: Prentice-Hall, 1980; Christian Bernard. *Good Life, Good Death: A Doctor's Case for Euthanasia and Suicide.* (1981).

155. Anonymous 259 *JAMA* 272 (1988).

156. Timothy Quill, "Death and Dignity: A Case of Individualized Decision-Making," 324 *New England Journal of Medicine* 691 (1991).

157. "Kevorkian Murder Charge Dropped but not Forgotten," *Hospital Ethics* (January/February 1991), 6.

158. "Temporary Ban Asked against 'Dr. Death'," *Chicago Tribune,* June 7, 1990, Section 1, 8.

159. "Kevorkian Murder Charged Dropped . . ." *supra* note 157.

160. *Id.*

161. Meisel, *supra* note 1, at 476.

162. *Id.*

163. "Kevorkian Acquitted of Assisted Suicide: Prosecutors Plan to File Other Charges," 5(11) *BNA Health Law Reporter* (March 14, 1996), 396.

164. *Id.*

165. *Id.*

166. "Kevorkian Helps In 34th Suicide," 22 *Chicago Tribune* August 8, 1996, Section 1, 21.

167. Eugene, Ore: The Hemlock Society, 1991.

168. 79 F.3d 790 (9th Cir. 1996).

169. "Ninth Circuit Holds Unconstitutional Ban Against Physician-Assisted Suicide," 5(11) *BNA Health Law Reporter* (March 14, 1996), 369.

170. *Id.*

171. NBC Evening News, March 24, 1996.

172. "Oregon Asks Ninth Circuit Court To Lift Injunction On Suicide Measure," 5(11) *BNA Health Law Reporter* (March 14, 1996), 395.

173. "Ninth Circuit Holds Unconstitutional Ban Against Physician-Assisted Suicide," *supra* note 169, 369.

174. NBC Evening News, April 2, 1996. The New York case is *Quill v. Vacco,* 80 F.3d 716 (2d Cir. 1996).

175. See, for example, David Price and Patricia Murphy, "Assisted Suicide: New ANA Policy Reflects Difficulty of Issue," 2(2) *Journal of Nursing Law* (1996), 53–62; Nancy Osgood, "Assisted Suicide and Older People—A Deadly Combination: Ethical Problems in Permitting Assisted Suicide," 10(4) *Issues In Law & Medicine* (Spring 1995), 415–435; Maria CeloCruz, "Aid-In-Dying: Should We Decriminalize Physician-Assisted Suicide and Physician-Committed Euthanasia," XVIII(4) *American Journal Of Law & Medicine* (1992), 369–394.

176. John D. Lantos, Steven H. Miles, Christine K. Cassell, "The Linares Affair," 14(4) *Law, Medicine & Health Care* (Winter 1989), 308, *citing* Lawrence Nelson and Les Rothenberg.

177. *Id.*

178. Gilbert Goldman, Karen Stratton, Max Douglas Brown, "What Actually Happened: An Informed Review Of The Linares Incident." 17(4) *Law, Medicine & Health Care* (Winter 1989), 298.

179. *Id.*

180. *Id.*

181. Lantos, Miles and Cassel, *supra* note 176, at 309.

182. *Id.*

183. *Id.*

184. Goldman, Stratton and Brown, *supra* note 178, at 303.

185. *Report of the Cook County State's Attorney's Task Force on the Foregoing of Life-Sustaining Treatment.* Chicago, IL: Cook County State's Attorney's Office (March 1990), 1.

186. *Id.*

187. For an interesting compilation of these, and other issues in the Linares case, see *Family Privacy and PVS: A Symposium on the Linares Case.* Larry Gostin, Editor. 17(4) *Law, Medicine & Health Care* (Winter 1989), 295–339.

188. 755 ILCS 40/1 *et seq.* (1989).

189. Robert D. Miller. *Problems In Health Care Law.* 7th Edition. Gaithersburg, MD: Aspen Publishers, Inc. (1996), 508.

190. See, for example, Patricia Wager, "Effect of DNR Orders on Level of Care," 4(6) *Research Review: Studies for Nursing Practice* (May/June 1988), 2 ("Science Update" Section); Kathleen Kaiser, Q. Scott Ringenberg, Thelma Moore and Ann Rosenow, "Care Decisions for No-Code Patients," 1(4) *Nursing Connections* (Winter 1988), 25–35. See also, American Nurses' Association. *Position Statement on Nursing Care and Do-Not-Resuscitate Decisions.* Washington, D.C.: ANA (1992), 2.

191. See also, American Nurses' Association. *Position Statement on Promotion of Comfort and Relief of Pain in Dying Patients.* Washington, DC: ANA, 1991.

192. See, for example, Price and Murphy, *supra* note 175; American Nurses' Association. *Position Statement on Assisted Suicide.* Washington, DC: ANA, 1994; American Nurses' Association. *Position Statement On Active Euthanasia.* Washington, DC: ANA, 1994; Chapter 10.

193. David Price, "Ethics Committees And Nurses," 2(1) *Journal of Nursing Law* (1995), 62.

194. Christine Mitchell, "On The Heroes and Villains in the Linares Drama," 17(4) *Law, Medicine & Health Care* (Winter 1989), 339, 345.

195. "Nurses Seek a Voice in Right-to-Die Cases," 120(3) *AJN* (March 1991), 26 (CONTROVERSIES IN CARE COLUMN).

14

Issues Related to Violence

Violence, abuse, neglect, and exploitation are widespread in the United States. Murder is ranked as the 11th cause of death in the United States.[1] Injuries from assault totaled 2.2 million each year from 1979 through 1986.[2] Abuse, neglect, and/or exploitation of the elderly are so frequent that 1 in 25 Americans over 65 years of age is a victim of such conduct.[3]

"Intrafamilial violence" or "domestic violence" is also alarmingly prevalent and takes many forms. In 1986, for example, an estimated 1.6 million children nationwide experienced some type of abuse or neglect.[4] Each year, 1.8 million wives are beaten by their husbands.[5] Sadly, most domestic homicides are preceded by acts of violence.[6]

Sexual abuse or exploitation, including criminal sexual assault and incest, is another common form of violent behavior. Sexual violence occurs within families and in extrafamilial relationships; no one is immune. Physical violence and sexual injury often occur together.[7]

Because nurses are involved in all aspects of health care and practice in all health care delivery settings, they can actively participate in reducing the continuing spiral of violence. Whether in the role of a school nurse, a home health care nurse, or a nurse psychotherapist, the nurse can play an important role in assessment, intervention, and prevention of violence.

The nurse's legal obligations include mandatory reporting of certain instances of violence. The nurse also needs to be aware of the potential

RELATED TOPICS	
Chapter 8	Criminal Law
Chapter 11	Reproductive and Family Concerns
Chapter 13	Issues in Death and Dying

for violence against patients by health care providers and violence and the potential for abuse against health care practitioners.

THE NURSE AS MANDATORY REPORTER

Both federal and state laws require certain individuals to report particular instances of violence, abuse, and/or neglect to governmental agencies. For example, the Federal Child Abuse Prevention and Treatment Act requires alleged instances of medical neglect to be reported to state agencies empowered to enforce child protective services.

Because health care practitioners, including nurses, are often in a unique position to identify and assess cases of violence against others, they are almost always included as *mandated reporters*; that is, when an identified instance of injury appears to be present and the result of abuse, neglect, or exploitation, the mandated reporter must report the situation to the proper authorities. Thus, mandatory reporting laws include two specific types: those for child abuse and neglect and those for injury to the elderly.

Because health care practitioners, including nurses, are often in a unique position to identify and assess cases of violence against others, they are almost always included as mandated reporters [in federal and state reporting laws].

KEY PRINCIPLES

Violence

Abuse

Neglect

Exploitation

Mandatory Reporting Statutes

Rape/Criminal Sexual Assault

Laws that require mandated reporting specifically provide certain protections for the reporter. They include (1) not requiring "hard evidence" of the abuse or neglect in order to report, but rather a "good faith belief" or a "reasonable suspicion" that the injury is the result of abuse or neglect; (2) immunity from civil and criminal liability and licensing actions for reporting "in good faith" or with a "reasonable suspicion" that the conduct required to be reported has occurred; (3) presumed "good faith" of the reporter so that good faith must be rebutted by anyone challenging it; (4) specifically nullifying any confidentiality, privacy, and privilege mandates the health care professional would otherwise be required to adhere to because of the health care provider–patient relationship; and (5) providing confidentiality to any report made under the particular law.

For a health care provider who is a mandated reporter and does not fulfill his or her duties under the law(s), various penalties exist. They include (1) criminal prosecution (for a misdemeanor, for example); (2) proceedings under the applicable state licensing law for a violation of the particular licensing act (nursing or medical practice act in which a duty to report is included); and (3) proceedings to cancel any certifications granted by the state (a school nurse certificate, for example).[8]

Table 14–1 lists the more common mandatory reporting requirements for nurses and other health care providers in all health care delivery settings.

SETTINGS AND TYPES OF VIOLENCE

Regardless of the specific setting in which violence occurs, violence has a definition that transcends those sites. Violence is the unjust and unwarranted exercise of force, often physical (but also psychological) and accompanied by outrage, fury, or vehemence.[9] The use of violence is a deliberate act(s) that can result in abuse, injury, or damage.[10]

TABLE 14–1
Mandatory Reporting Statutes for Nurses Relating to Violence

CONDUCT/INJURY	WHERE REPORT MUST BE MADE
Child abuse and neglect	State child protective agency and/or police
Elder abuse and neglect	State department on aging and/or police
Suspicious or unnatural deaths	Medical examiner or coroner and/or police
Injuries due to lethal weapons (gun, knife)	Medical examiner or coroner and/or police
Injuries due to criminal conduct (criminal sexual assault, battery, assault)	Medical examiner or coroner and/or police

Domestic/Intrafamilial Violence

The home is no stranger to violence. Domestic violence is insidiously brutal because it can go undetected for long periods, if not forever. Domestic violence is conduct of a family member or a member of a household toward another family or household member so that the result is physical, psychological, or developmental injury or damage. Domestic violence is a broad category. It typically encompasses abuse, neglect, and/or exploitation. A direct act of domestic violence occurs when a spouse is physically beaten. A more indirect act of violence occurs when a spouse is psychologically terrorized by a partner. The nurse who observes belongings smashed and broken in a patient's home may be seeing evidence of violence.

In some types of domestic disorder, such as child abuse or neglect, the nurse can intervene more easily because of mandated reporting for health care providers. Thus, when a school nurse discovers unexplained bruises on a student's body or an emergency department (ED) physician is suspicious about an injury manifested by an infant, an evaluation of the injury and the family can begin when the reporting occurs.

Not all types of domestic violence, however,

mandate reporting to governmental agencies. Spousal beating and, in some states, elder abuse in the home or community do not require reporting. Protection in these states can be sought only after consent of the victim is obtained or after the abused individual seeks aid using other judicial remedies.

One remedy is the protection afforded under a state's domestic violence law. Most laws broadly define violence covered under the act. Those instances include, for example, intimidation, interference with the personal liberty of another, and neglect (failure to provide food, medical care, and health and safety protections for a disabled or dependent individual).[11] In addition, they provide judicial relief (orders of protection) and police protection (e.g., arrest of offender, transportation of victim and family to a medical facility or shelter) to victims of domestic violence. Those covered under the state statutes include spouses, parents, adults with disabilities, family members, and household members.

The domestic violence statutes are civil and are not the only choice a person has to obtain relief from domestic terror. Other civil remedies that can be pursued by the victim, either alone or in combination with the laws governing domestic violence, include divorce (if applicable) and criminal actions. For example, the charge of aggravated criminal assault may be used, and victims may obtain a cease and desist or restraining order.

Child Abuse and Neglect

Abuse (mental or physical maltreatment)[12] or neglect (the failure or omission to do something one could do or is required to do),[13] can occur in any setting. The abuse or neglect of a minor—someone 17 years of age or younger—is no exception. Abuse or neglect often occurs in the home but can also occur in school, in a neighbor's home, or in a relative's residence. The most prevalent type of abuse or neglect against minors is physical; psychological and sexual violence are second and third.[14]

> *The most prevalent type of abuse or neglect against minors is physical; psychological and sexual violence are second and third.*

Abuse can be evident in affirmative acts, such as striking an individual or verbally intimidating someone to force compliance. Abuse can also occur more indirectly when, for example, a child is not given the attention needed to become a healthy adult. Abuse can be sexual in nature as in intercourse and exhibitionism; incest may also occur.

Neglect also includes absence of care or attention in a particular situation.[15] When, for example, a minor child is not fed or is kept isolated and ignored in the home, psychological as well as physical neglect occurs.

As with abuse, neglect is specifically defined in child and elder abuse and neglect statutes passed by state legislatures.

All states and the District of Columbia have laws protecting abused and neglected minors,[16] through mandated reporting for individuals specified. All laws require that the reporter have a "good faith" or "reasonable belief" that abuse or neglect is occurring or has occurred. Although the laws vary widely from state to state, most mandate reporting for *any* serious injury inflicted on a minor through other than accidental means by someone responsible for the minor's care.[17] Specific definitions of abuse and neglect, however, are included in each state's law. Some definitions for abuse include physical injury (burns, internal abdominal injuries), psychological injury (scapegoating, repeated name calling), sexual abuse (including genital injuries), and cruel punishment. Neglect is often described as the deprivation of necessities, medical neglect, malnutrition, and even moral neglect (specifically in Arizona, Idaho, and Missouri).[18]

Child abuse and neglect laws also contain

unique provisions concerning the role of nurses and others when abuse or neglect is suspected. For example, statutes allow a physician or police officer to take a minor into temporary "protective" custody without the parents' consent. This action can occur when returning the child to the parents may, in the judgment of the physician or police, result in the child's continued endangerment or death, and there is no time to obtain a court order for the temporary custody.[19]

When protective custody is possible, statutory provisions provide for the immediate care of the imperiled child. For example, notification of the child protective agency must occur; the child must be admitted to a health care facility for any needed medical treatment; and the child must be placed in a foster or other home until a hearing on the parental custody issue is held.[20]

Child abuse and neglect statutes also give physicians and facilities authority to take photographic and radiographic films of the minor (if indicated) and to conduct other medical tests without parental consent if these measures will help confirm that abuse or neglect has occurred. Spiral fractures or a subdural hematoma evidenced by medical tests, for example, can help a health care provider decide about reporting the incident and/or taking the child into protective custody.

Nurses and other mandated reporters are usually informed in writing of the investigation done and the disposition of any case reported to the child protective agency. The records compiled by the state agency, including the identity of the reporter, are confidential, however, and can be disclosed only pursuant to the child abuse and neglect statute.

To date, there have been no reported cases against nurses for reporting abuse or neglect or not fulfilling required duties under those acts, although other mandated reporters have been used. For example, in *Landeros v. Flood*,[21] an ED physician was sued by a minor's *guardian ad litem* when the physician failed to report abuse by the 11-month-old's parents. The abuse included a comminuted spiral fracture of the right

tibia and fibula, bruises over the entire body, and a healing, nondepressed linear fracture. The court held that the physician was negligent for not reporting the injuries. Had the physician reported the abuses, the court could have intervened and additional injuries would have been avoided that the minor suffered after the physician let the child go home with her parents. Therefore, it opined, a negligence case could be filed against the physician in the civil court.

Also, in *State v. Hurd*,[22] the court sustained the conviction of a teacher who failed to report abuse in a situation in which a prudent person would have had reasonable cause to suspect that abuse was occurring. Under the Wisconsin child abuse law, a teacher is mandated to report abuse when a "reasonable cause to believe" abuse is present.

Comparable suits have been brought against social workers and child welfare agencies when reporting of suspected abuse and neglect did not occur.[23]

Elder Abuse and Neglect

The problems of elder abuse and neglect are in their infancy.[24] Concern about elders is relatively new, mainly because abuse and neglect of the elderly have remained a hidden and shameful problem until very recently.[25] In addition, with an estimated 23% increase in the number of persons between ages 65 and 75 years by the year 2000,[26] the problem can only continue to expand.

Because of the reluctance on the part of the elderly to report it, the actual incidence of elder abuse and neglect is most probably underestimated and certainly not well documented.[27] This is so especially when abuse and neglect occur at the hands of family members or caretakers. Furthermore, health care providers often unintentionaly overlook elder abuse and neglect, explaining a fracture or loss of weight as expected consequences of the aging process (e.g., loss of balance, decrease in appetite). In other situations, health care providers, including home health care nurses, are reluctant to report elder abuse or neglect because of a lack of cooperation by the family, lack of cooperation by the patient, or doubt about whether the abuse or neglect really occurred.[28] Consequently, only one in six instances of elder abuse and neglect are reported to elder protective services or other authorities.[29]

. . . health care providers often unintentionally overlook instances of elder abuse and neglect, explaining a fracture or loss of weight as expected consequences of the aging process . . .

Laws protecting the elderly from abuse and neglect exist in almost every state. Unfortunately, the mistreatment of the elderly can occur in the community, including the home, or in health care facilities, including nursing homes or long-term care entities. Although anyone *could* report elder abuse or neglect to the state protective agency (a department on aging, for example), only 42 states have enacted some form of mandatory reporting of elder abuse or neglect.[30] Most often, these mandatory reporting statutes resemble child abuse and neglect laws. Unlike the child abuse and neglect legislation, however, many require mandatory reporting only when elder abuse or neglect occurs in health facilities.

For example, Illinois, Michigan, New Jersey, and California have mandatory reporting statutes for the mistreatment of the elderly in long-term care or nursing home facilities.[31] Definitions of abuse and neglect include instances of physical or mental injury by other than accidental means, sexual abuse, and lack of adequate medical or personal care or maintenance. Mandatory reporters include nurses, nursing home administrators, and podiatrists.

Clearly, these statutes must also be read with other state and federal laws that protect the elderly in health care facilities. Illinois and New Mexico, for example, have criminal laws often making it a felony to abuse or neglect an elderly person in a long-term care facility.[32] State and federal laws also govern the use of chemical and physical restraints with elderly residents of health care facilities. Recent proposed amendments to the Medicare and Medicaid programs, for example, affirmatively prohibit the misuse of medications and physical restraints in long-term care facilities. Guidelines for their appropriate use and the documentation of that use are also defined.[33]

While elderly residents in health care facilities should now be protected by mandatory reporting laws, however, elderly individuals who live in their own homes, with their families, or in boarding homes are not protected. Statistics reveal most of the abusers of elderly individuals in the community are relatives; 40% are spouses of elderly victims, and 50% are children or grandchildren.[34]

Furthermore, the types of abuse and neglect that can occur in a domestic situation are much more elusive and insidious. Financial abuse (unusual checkbook activity, forcing the elder person to sign over property), improper medication administration, and environmental control (room or home not warm enough or cool enough, locking the elderly person in a room) are just a few examples.

Only a few states have passed mandatory reporting of elder abuse or neglect in the community. Alabama, California, Wisconsin, Massachusetts, and Florida are among them.[35] However, the laws vary widely in terms of their scope of coverage and in the actions mandated by required reporters.[36] Other states have passed protective laws for the elderly in the community, but they include permissive rather than mandated reporting so that the nurse must obtain permission before making a report. For example, Illinois's Elder Abuse and Neglect Act[37] requires the consent of the elder person or guardian before a report can be made to the Illinois Department on Aging.[38] If an emergency exists in which the elderly person lacks the ability to consent, an order under the state's domestic violence law is possible.[39]

In addition to the reporting laws concerning elder abuse or neglect, other state regulations protect the elderly in the community when no mandated reporting laws exist. For example, state criminal laws have been passed to punish the neglect of an elderly person or the financial exploitation of an aged citizen. The reporting of such conduct to the police can cut further abuse by as much as 40% to 60%.[40]

In states in which no specific laws have been promulgated, use of already existing criminal laws, such as those prohibiting assault and battery, can also protect the elderly in the community. In fact, many states (including Florida, Louisiana, and Colorado) have made assault or battery against an elderly person an "aggravation" of the crime.[41] If convicted, the defendant can then be sentenced to additional prison time.

Abuse and Neglect of Disabled Individuals

Although a disability can be defined in many ways, here it is defined as a physical or mental condition, distinct from illness or disease, that limits one's ability to function.[42] Disabilities include amputations, paralysis, mental retardation, and mental illness. Disability knows no specific age limitations. Estimates indicate that 34 to 43 million individuals in the United States have chronic, significant disabilities.[43]

The protection afforded the disabled against abuse and neglect is supported, in many instances, by other laws. For example, a disabled person in a nursing home has the same protections the elderly resident would have under the state's mandatory reporting of *any* abuse or neglect of a facility resident. A nursing home resident who does not receive proper and necessary care for a broken hip, for example, is experiencing criminal neglect. In the same way, the abuse or neglect of a disabled minor would be reportable under the state child abuse and neglect law.

In addition, if an individual's disability requires hospitalization or institutionalization in a developmental disability or mental health facility, state codes, such as those in Illinois and Texas, regulating care include penalties for the abuse or neglect.[44]

When the disabled person lives in the community, however, less stringent reporting requirements apply. Both permissive and mandatory reporting statutes protect a disabled person who is abused, neglected, or exploited.[45] When not mandated to report instances of violence against the disabled, however, health care providers often face difficult choices concerning whether or not (1) the patient will consent to the reporting; (2) alternative living arrangements are possible; and (3) verification (insofar as possible) of the abuse, neglect, or exploitation can occur.

As with elder abuse and neglect in the community, a state's criminal code can be used to punish those who inflict abuse and neglect on the disabled. For example, "criminal neglect of an elderly or disabled person" makes it a felony to (among other things) endanger or cause to deteriorate a pre-existing mental or physical condition of a disabled or elderly person. Such a law most often applies to "caregivers" in the community and broadly defines that role.[46]

Rape/Criminal Sexual Assault

At one time, rape was defined as the use of threat or violence to force a woman to engage in sexual activity against her will.[47] Now, to be more gender-neutral and reflect the unfortunate expansion of this type of violence among men and women alike, its name has changed. For example, in Illinois[48] rape is now called criminal sexual assault and abuse.

The definitions of force and sexual activity have also changed, although the changes vary from state to state. Common ones include (1) an expansion to include specific acts that are gender-neutral, including "sexual penetration" and "sexual conduct"; (2) the elimination of the need to prove consent for the conduct in question; (3)

augmenting the definition of "force or threat of force" by the aggressor; and (4) abandoning the need to show evidence of the emission of semen to prove that sexual penetration took place.[49]

One of the early categories of sexual assault was that of statutory rape. It covered situations in which a young female of a specified age (e.g., 12 to 16) was involved in a sexual encounter with a male. The protection afforded the minor female was based on her inability to provide valid consent to sexual intercourse.[50] Currently, in those states with changed statutes, *any* minor under a specified age is a victim of sexual assault if the other requirements in the criminal statute are met.

Marital rape is a category of sexual violence against women, but surprisingly has only recently been made a crime. Oregon, Iowa, and the District of Columbia are among those with criminal statutes covering marital rape. Some states, however, including Kansas, South Dakota, Texas, and West Virginia, provide immunity from suit for husbands who force sexual activity on their wives.[51] Moreover, in other states in which a conviction is possible—Missouri, Nevada, and New Mexico—it can be successful only if the husband and wife are not living together because of a court order or are legally separated.

In addition, some states make a distinction between sexual assault between married couples and between nonmarried couples. Thus, if two people are not married but are living together, the woman cannot allege marital rape or sexual assault. In other states, including New York, New Jersey, California, and Wisconsin, however, marriage is not required to pursue a criminal action against a cohabitant.

Sexual Abuse and Exploitation

Sexual abuse and exploitation (taking unjust advantage of another for one's own benefit or gain[52]) know no favorites. They can occur with adults, minors, the elderly, the disabled, within families, and outside families. In fact, their prevalence is so widespread that all mandatory reporting protective statutes include sexual abuse and exploitation. It is important to note that violence, abuse, neglect, and exploitation are not mutually exclusive. Any particular situation may result in all four types of conduct against an individual or individuals.

Sexual abuse and exploitation . . . know no favorites. They can occur with adults, minors, the elderly, the disabled, within families, and outside families.

Although common, sexual abuse and exploitation are sometimes difficult to identify because they can be manifested in many ways. Evidence may appear as a change in appetite in a minor child or as unexplained depression that a school nurse sees in an adolescent. More direct evidence might include a diagnosis of a sexually transmitted disease or genital/perineal trauma in a minor or in an elderly nursing home resident. A minor adolescent female may be sexually exploited if she is forced to provide sexual favors in return for a place to stay. Or an elderly female may be forced into giving a monthly social security check to the male boarding house owner who does not use it for the elderly boarder's living expenses.

Perpetrators of sexual abuse and exploitation are as diverse as the forms this violence takes. Those who commit acts of sexual abuse and exploitation can be family members (spouses, parents, step-parents, siblings), caretakers, health care providers (facility staff, psychotherapists), teachers, clergy, strangers, pedophiles, males or females. When sexual abuse or exploitation is suspected, specific interventions must occur, and they will depend not only on the age of the suspected victim but also on the type of injury.

Because of the embarrassment, shame, fear, and stigma often felt by victims of sexual violence and exploitation, many states have enacted protective laws to minimize, insofar as possible, any unnecessary publicity. For example, mandatory reports concerning child abuse and neglect are considered confidential and can be released only under certain circumstances (to law enforcement officers or during a trial). In addition, if the suspected or documented victim is a child who receives treatment, any and all records are usually made confidential so that release occurs only in specified circumstances (to law enforcement agencies, for example).[53] In addition, when a school nurse or other school personnel reports suspected child abuse or neglect, a copy of the report is usually not placed in the student record because the report is not considered to be a school record.[54]

If an individual is a victim of a rape or criminal sexual assault and seeks counseling for that violence, in some states any and all communications between the victim and the "rape counseling staff" are confidential and cannot be released without the consent of the victim.[55] This prohibition includes release at the trial. If the latter is necessary, an *in camera* (in the judge's chambers) review is allowed to determine if the information should be released. If the information is needed in the case against the accused, the judge can order it to be released.[56]

In addition to concerns over confidentiality, victims of sexual abuse and exploitation are at risk for contracting sexually transmitted diseases, including AIDS. As a result, most state statutes requiring the mandatory reporting of child abuse contain provisions for testing the victim so that care and counseling can begin immediately if necessary.[57]

Adult victims can ask that testing for HIV of the individual accused of rape or other criminal sexual assault be done to effectuate the same results. This ability is usually provided under the state's criminal laws and also protects the subject being tested.[58]

Nursing Implications in Cases of Abuse and Neglect

Working with victims of abuse, neglect, and exploitation demands patience, empathy, and a thorough knowledge of the law. Because acts of violence can be inflicted on anyone, all nurses must be aware of the possibility of violent behavior with all patients.

Working with victims of abuse, neglect, and exploitation demands patience, empathy, and a thorough knowledge of the law.

Thus, policies and procedures concerning the nurse's role in abuse, neglect, or exploitation cases are essential. The guidelines must be specific for both adults and minors. The policies should include who is to be notified when suspected or documented abuse or neglect is present; documentation guidelines; and treatment issues and protocols.

Second, the nurse who encounters suspected or documented violence against a patient must follow state law and facility guidelines in reporting to the proper agency. Because the nurse is almost always identified as a mandatory reporter in statutes requiring compulsory reporting, there is no room for the nurse's discretion in reporting the incident. The only leeway the nurse has is whether or not the injury(ies) are believed "in good faith" or "reasonably" to be the result of abuse, neglect, or exploitation. The nurse should also keep in mind that many of the required reporting statutes prohibit anyone else in the facility or organization from hindering or obstructing a report.

The nurse can help in the intervention of violent behavior by obtaining as much information from the victim as possible. This will require good interpersonal communication skills, especially if the patient is young or is fearful of sharing information. A very young victim may not be able to discuss the incident directly, so careful listening of what is said—and not said—will be vital. In addition, particular methods—role playing or story telling—may help the minor share the incident.

Similarly, observing and noting any unusual behavior may indicate that abuse or neglect has occurred. For example, does the home health care nurse notice that the 10-year-old in the family seen for another health problem is suddenly truant from school? Does an elderly client being seen postoperatively suddenly seem lethargic and inattentive?

If the particular state in which the nurse practices protects the identity of victims of assault and abuse, the nurse should maintain that confidentiality by following the law's mandate. If a blood test of the victim is obtained, conforming with state statutes concerning confidentiality for HIV and AIDS is essential.

When the victim of violence is a child and protective custody is necessary, the nurse should be clear about the nurse's role in that situation. Most often it is the *physician* who is given the authority to place a child in protective custody. The nurse who is not authorized to perform this function can indirectly help with such an emergency by ensuring that the child does not leave the facility with the abuser. For example, the nurse may need to call security to help with the removal of the family or abuser or contact the facility administration about the problem.

If photographs are to be taken of the victim, especially a minor, the nurse should be clear about who is given the authority to do so. The nurse who is not granted that power can help as a witness by being present in the room with the victim or by fulfilling the mandate for reporting the situation to the proper agency.

The nurse in the community—whether as a visiting nurse, in home health care, or in a senior citizen center—must be attentive to abuse, neglect, and exploitation. If the state does not mandate reporting, the nurse can try to convince the elderly person to seek help through the state agencies set up to provide protection from the abuser. If persuasion does not work, providing support services for the abuser, including respite time, is another option.

Nurses may be involved in gathering evidence to document sexual abuse or neglect. Although this request can occur in any health care delivery setting, it will most often occur in the ED. Evidence often includes the results of a physical examination. The ED nurse should have an exhaustive orientation in the collection of evidence. Whether assisting its collection, or collecting evidence personally, the nurse must exert great care to ensure that the evidence is collected properly and that any laboratory work, including a pregnancy and HIV test, is not overlooked. Any specimens taken, including vaginal aspiration, mouth and rectum swabs or foreign pubic hair, should be immediately and accurately labeled and sent to the laboratory for analysis. Of particular importance is the establishment of a "chain of custody" to ensure that the specimen is not lost, destroyed, or mishandled, making it inadmissible in subsequent trial or other proceeding. Documentation Reminder 14-1 lists areas to remember when documenting violence.

DOCUMENTATION REMINDER 14–1
VIOLENCE

▼ Completion of all required forms for the reporting of abuse, neglect, exploitation (e.g., name and address, age of victim, type of injury, name and occupation of person who files report, actions taken)

▼ Condition of patient, who accompanied patient, quotes by patient, tests and care provided, who was notified, mandatory reporting completed

▼ Clothing, photographs, and so on, given to police, identity of officer by name, time, badge or star number, police station and district

▼ Patient refusal of treatment or consent to report incident (where applicable)

▼ Protective custody decisions, who was involved, who contacted, where minor taken (inpatient at facility or custody of state agency)

▼ Obtaining and handling of evidence

▼ Referrals to other social service agencies, including therapy for victim, home care or respite services, discussion in student care conference, legal services

▼ Informed consent for treatment and tests when obtained and given

▼ Discussion of problem with family, caregiver(s), their reponse, or actions taken

▼ Any follow-up care suggested or recommended, whether or not care was provided at time of discovery of abuse, neglect, or exploitation

---

The nurse must also promote awareness of sexual abuse, neglect, and exploitation for both colleagues and the public. For other nurses, continuing education or in-service programs can address these topics. These issues can also be included in undergraduate nursing curriculums.[59] Furthermore, exploring personally held values about women, aging, the disabled, and male-female relationships can help colleagues to clarify their feelings concerning violence against others.

Educating the public may be more difficult to achieve, but the prevention of violence, including sexual abuse and neglect, is a goal worth pursuing both formally and informally. The school nurse meeting with a student's parents and helping them identify better ways to cope with the stress caused by their school-age child may be preventing future violence.

The nursing association or school of nursing that sponsors a seminar on abuse and neglect may also serve the public. The participation of others who work with victims of violence—including social workers, mental health professionals, and those who have successfully overcome the problems of abuse and neglect—can be very effective.

The nurse should also be involved in legislative efforts to protect those who experience abuse, neglect, and exploitation. Exercising the right to vote, especially for those who support

protective laws, is essential. So too is attempting to influence the legislative process through testifying at public hearings on proposed legislative changes and fund-raising efforts. Without financial support or legislative appropriations for protective laws, new statutes become nothing but hollow victories.

The nurse who is involved in testifying at any judicial proceeding concerning abuse, neglect, or exploitation should seek counsel from the facility attorney and/or an attorney of the nurse's choice *before* responding to a subpoena or any other request to provide testimony. To protect the nurse during that process, it is imperative that representation continue throughout the proceeding. For example, the nurse may not be aware of the need to assert the confidentiality of the information requested or to request an *in camera* review of documents before they are released.

Obtaining adequate counsel not only protects the patient but also shields the nurse against allegations of a breach of the patient's rights. For example, many state licensing laws prohibit a nurse from breaching nurse–patient confidentiality except in certain situations. Conformity with the technicalities of a nurse practice act or other state laws is critical for the nurse who must not only facilitate the patient's case but also meet personal and professional obligations.

SPECIAL SITUATIONS INVOLVING VIOLENCE

Violence Against Patients and Residents by Health Care Providers

Violence by health care practitioners against patients in health care settings occurs in varying ways. Violence may take place when an overworked and overtired surgeon is unduly rough when removing a patient's postoperative stitches or abuse can happen when a nurse responds harshly to a patient who asks a seemingly innocent question. Abuse and neglect of vulnerable inpatients and residents of health care facilities—disabled, mentally retarded, and elderly persons—by health care providers occur frequently. The excuses offered for the maltreatment of patients and resident populations are numerous. They include overworked medical and nursing staff; vulnerable residents' inability to complain; frequent understaffing; large patient care assignments that result in staff frustration; and, in some instances, inadequate preparation of both professional and ancillary staff who work with the populations they care for.

> *The excuses offered for the maltreatment of patient and resident populations by health care personnel are numerous.*

Forms of Patient Abuse and Neglect

Maltreatment or injury to a patient is often obvious. In one case, a nurse assistant allegedly verbally harassed a 97-year-old nursing home resident and forcibly dragged her by her arthritic arm.[60] In another, a nurse assistant allegedly hit and rubbed soap in the eyes of a 70-year-old double amputee after the patient had soiled his bath water.[61] Misconduct by health care providers may, however, be more subtle. In one instance, a nurse assistant refused to provide a bedpan to a resident more than once per night so that the resident urinated in her bed and had to wait until morning to be bathed and have her bedding changed.[62] Also, abuse may occur when baths, shaving, and feeding are not carried out on a regular basis or are done in a substandard manner.[63] Forcibly providing medical care without consent, such as CPR or feeding tubes, is yet another subtle type of abuse. Verbal abuse can occur when a patient is called a name or when belittling or derogatory remarks are made.[64] In one reported case involv-

ing an ED nurse, a patient with spinal meningitis whose behavior was difficult to control was called names and told to leave the hospital if he didn't like the way it was run.[65]

Abuse and neglect sometimes involve the misuse of methods of treatment. A patient may be subjected to medical procedures without required sedation or extubated too early. Medications or physical restraints may be used as punishment or as a convenience to the nursing staff. For example, a nurse in a long-term care facility may not have adequate staff to monitor residents who need observation. As a result, an unruly or fragile resident may be administered medication more frequently than necessary or be placed in a Posey belt or other restraint to reduce the need for frequent monitoring.

Neglect or exploitation by health care providers can also be obvious, as when a bedridden patient suffers from numerous infected bedsores. So too is severe weight loss in a resident who also complains of hunger and reduced portions at erratic mealtimes.[66] The unlawful taking of a patient's money, social security check, or other personal property is a form of exploitation that may go undetected for some time.

Nursing Implications in Cases of Violence by Health Care Providers

Regardless of the type of violence and regardless of its being inflicted by a colleague or staff member, the nurse who knows of a problem must report it. To whom the situation must be reported will depend on the type of health care facility.

In an acute-care setting, the nurse should share concerns with the nurse manager and nurse executive. In addition, an occurrence report and any other required internal documents should be initiated. In a long-term care facility, the situation must also be reported to the appropriate state agency if mandatory reporting is required. Depending on the state law covering abuse in the community, the nurse may or may not be required to report the maltreatment of vulnerable community residents to identified authorities. If reporting is not mandatory, the nurse may work with the victim in obtaining consent to intervene in whatever manner is necessary to avoid further mistreatment.

When a patient or resident appears to have been abused or neglected, proper nursing and medical care must take place immediately. The nurse will need to notify the attending physician of the necessity for orders for diagnostic work and additional medical treatment.

The nurse who witnesses verbal or psychological abuse against a patient or resident should report the incident to the nurse manager and also initiate any required supporting facility or agency documents. Early intervention into inappropriate conduct by nursing and other staff is vital to help staff learn healthier ways of working with patients.

The nurse must also use medication and physical restraints judiciously and consistently with good nursing practice, institutional or agency policy, and state and federal law. If inadequate staffing is inhibiting the proper monitoring of patients, the nurse must inform nursing administration so that additional help can be obtained.

In addition, the nurse manager will need to carefully supervise and evaluate nursing staff and nurse assistants. If a performance problem arises in which residents are not treated properly, the employee must be informed and his or her conduct improved. If abuse or neglect occurs after the employee has been informed, the employee should be dealt with pursuant to facility guidelines for discipline, suspension, or termination.

Violence Against Health Care Providers

Perhaps the most common illustrations of violence against health care providers are injuries and maltreatment inflicted by patients against facility staff. Although no area of a facility or type of health care provider is immune from abuse or injury by patients, certain areas and

practitioners have experienced greater incidence of injury than others.

Risks for Violence Against Nurses

The ED and mental health care units (including those providing substance abuse treatment and treatment for the developmentally disabled) are two areas with a high proportion of violence by patients. Increased violence in these areas may be due to many factors. For example, EDs function 24 hours a day, are unlocked, have minimal security, and are often in high-crime urban areas.[67] Mental health care units and facilities are often understaffed and have inadequate security. Even so, they provide services to populations that, because of their emotional difficulties, may "act out" against facility staff.[68]

Violence experienced at the hands of patients can be physical or verbal. Kicking, beating, stabbing, and the throwing of objects are just a few samples of the physical violence that a patient may inflict. Verbal abuse or harassment may include name calling and shouting. Interestingly, among 264 nurses studied in 1989, verbal abuse by patients and by their families made up the first and second most common sources of violence.[69]

A second type of abuse experienced by health care providers is inflicted by colleagues. Although a long-standing problem, such violence has only recently been documented.[70] It occurs against all types of health care providers, including nurses, medical students, social workers, respiratory therapists, and radiographers.[71] A study of nurse-physician relationships indicated that nurses are often subjected to temper tantrums, scapegoating, condescending attitudes, and public humiliation by physicians.[72] Likewise, physical abuse, including assault and battery, has also been imposed upon nurses by physicians.

Several lawsuits have been won by nurses against physicians who have inflicted violence against them. In one reported case, a nurse sued a physician for striking her on the forearm during provision of care to a patient who had a severe nosebleed.[73] Although no physical injury was experienced by the nurse, she won an award of $10,001 in punitive damages against the physician.

A study of nurse-physician relationships indicated that nurses are often subjected to temper tantrums, scapegoating, condescending attitudes, and public humiliation by physicians.

Nursing Implications in Cases of Violence Against Health Care Providers

No nurse can stand by and let abuse occur without taking action. One most obvious response is to prevent the abuse, insofar as that is humanly possible. Therefore, nurses practicing in the ED and mental health units must be educated in the techniques and strategies to control abusive behavior, whether physical or verbal. These techniques and strategies include team work; careful assessment of prior violence by the patient, when possible; astute observation of current behavior; early intervention into potentially abusive situations (including, but not limited to, interpersonal approaches and medication); and adequate security and staff whenever abusive situations may arise.[74] In addition, nursing staff members must push for "architectural security" of the unit in which they practice,[75] including adequate room size, safety features (e.g., safety glass and alarm systems to call for help), and camera monitoring. Standing orders and written protocols for the use of medication and restraint, when clinically necessary, can also help the nurse when a decision must be made quickly to intervene in an explosive situation.

The nurse in the community must also be careful to avoid situations in which a patient may initiate violence. The nurse who is uncomfortable about seeing a patient alone should request that another nurse or agency staff member be present during the visit. The community nurse should always keep the agency informed of the planned route and should check in frequently with the agency.[76]

Although prevention is the best approach to avoiding violence in health care, it does not always work. Therefore the nurse who experiences violence by a patient should seek help and adequate protection, especially if the threat is physical. Obtaining help, retreating after isolating the violent patient, and protecting other patients and staff are all necessary.

Likewise, if a patient begins to seem out of control during a home visit, the nurse should attempt to calm the patient. If success does not occur quickly, however, the nurse should leave the situation and contact the agency, family, or other appropriate persons (e.g., police).

When a nurse is abused by another health care provider, the nurse should assertively request that the violence stop and not happen again. If that approach does not work, the nurse must report the incident(s) to the nurse manager and others in nursing administration. If appropriate intervention is not forthcoming, the nurse may need to report the circumstances to outside authorities, including the state licensing agency. In addition, the nurse should obtain legal advice about filing civil or criminal action against the abuser.

Last, but by no means least, the formal education of health care practitioners should include at least one ethics course so all students are "sensitized" to violence in health care. Including these issues can raise student awareness of the problem and offer a framework within which to resolve it. In turn, the graduate practitioner will be better able to treat others in a caring, rather than a violent, manner.[77]

SUMMARY OF PRINCIPLES AND APPLICATIONS

Violence is a way of life, a common occurrence, in today's society. Acquiescence is not the answer, however, for the effects of violence are far reaching, permanent, and self-perpetuating. Child abuse experts, for example, clearly support the theory that those who abuse children and others are repeating patterns of their own rearing.[78] The cost of violence against women, although probably underestimated, reached $80 billion in 1990 for hospitalization costs alone.[79] Abusive teachers who act as mentors to students during their education experience may also transmit such conduct to students, thereby perpetuating the cycle in a new generation of practitioners.[80]

Recent studies of verbal abuse experienced by nurses accounted for resignations, compromised patient care, decreased morale, and reduction in productivity.[81] These, together with other facts and figures, clearly support the need to intervene in the spiral of violence. The Department of Health and Human Services has set as two of its goals the reduction of homicides and assault injuries by 15% and 10% respectively by the year 2000.[82] In addition, The American College of Obstetricians and Gynecologists, the Surgeon General, and the Centers for Disease Control have suggested that all women be routinely screened for physical abuse.[83] Those who work with the elderly envision the use of multidisciplinary teams to evaluate and treat elder abuse.[84]

The nurse can play an active and important role in preventing violence in health care by:

▼ Attending continuing education programs and seminars on abuse, neglect, and exploitation

▼ Assessing for the possibility of abuse, neglect, or exploitation with all patients

▼ Intervening consistently with legal and ethical duties when violence occurs against patients

▼ Educating patients and the public about the existence of abuse

▼ Protecting victims' confidentiality and privacy as mandated by law

▼ Testifying truthfully if called as a witness in any proceedings related to a patient who is the victim of violence

▼ Participating in the development of agency or facility policies and procedures dealing with patients who are victims of violence

▼ Reporting in good faith any concerns or beliefs that colleagues may be abusers of a patient or patients

▼ Eliminating abuse of staff by colleagues by reporting instances to appropriate agency or staff authorities

▼ Supervising staff carefully to intervene quickly in any staff-induced violence against patients

▼ Practicing nursing with an ever-vigilant eye toward personal safety when caring for potentially violent patients and/or families

▼ Documenting accurately and completely in any records concerned with instances of abuse, neglect, or exploitation

▼ Voting for elected officials who support laws deterring violence in the home, community, and health care

▼ Educating patients and their families about violence and self-protection, especially if mandatory reporting laws do not apply

▼ Encouraging state and federal legislatures to provide needed financial support for continued programs for victims of violence (e.g., therapy, shelters, health care)

TOPICS FOR FURTHER INQUIRY

1. Design a study to determine if protective orders or other judicially developed mechanisms to prohibit violence against victims do, in fact, reduce or eliminate further injury.

2. Develop an interview tool to use with nurses and other health care providers (e.g., physicians, social workers, physical therapists) to identify respective experiences of violence by colleagues in health care settings.

3. Evaluate how many nurses have been involved in reporting instances of child abuse and/or neglect to state agencies with the use

of an interview tool or questionnaire. Select particular practice areas (e.g., nursing, home health care nurses, nurses in child care clinics) and compare and contrast them.

4. Design a tool to evaluate nursing home facilities' established policies for dealing with abuse of residents by nursing and other staff.

REFERENCES

1. "Priorities for Health Promotion and Disease Prevention—Violent and Abusive Behavior," U.S. Department of Health and Human Services; Public Health Service. *Healthy People 2000—National Health Promotion and Disease Prevention Objectives.* Washington, D.C.: U.S. Government Printing Office, 1990, 61 (DHHS Pub. No. (PHS) 91–50213), *citing* National Center for Health Statistics. *Health, United States, 1989 and Prevention Profile.* Washington, D.C.: U.S. Department of Health and Human Services, 1990 (DHHS Pub. No. (PHS) 90–1232).

2. *Id., citing* C.W. Harlow. *Injuries from Crime.* Washington, D.C.: U.S. Department of Justice, 1989.

3. *Elder Abuse: An Assessment of the Federal Response: Hearings before the Subcommittee on Human Services of the Select Committee on Aging* (1989).

4. *Id., citing* Westat, Inc. *Study of the National Incidence of Child Abuse and Neglect.* Washington, D.C.: U.S. Department of Health and Human Services, 1988.

5. American Nurses' Association. *Position Statement on Physical Violence against Women.* Washington, D.C.: ANA, September 6, 1991; Senate Judiciary Committee Report (October 2, 1992), *reported in Chicago Daily Law Bulletin* (October 4, 1992), 3.

6. *Healthy People 2000, supra* note 1, 61, *citing National Family Violence Survey 1985.* National Institute of Mental Health, Alcohol, Drug Abuse, and Mental Health Administration, Public Health Service, U.S. Department of Public Health and Human Services, Rockville, Md.

7. Rose Odum, "Family Violence," in *Family Centered Nursing in the Community.* Barbara Logan and Cecillia Dawkins, Editors. Menlo Park, Calif: Addison-Wesley Publishing Company, 1986, 729.

8. Allen Schwartz, "Child Abuse—Despite the Law It's Not Reported," *CBA Record* (March 1991), 24–28.

9. Henry Campbell Black. *Black's Law Dictionary.* 6th Edition. St. Paul, Minn: West Publishing Company, 1991, 1085.

10. *Id.*

11. See Illinois Domestic Act of 1986, 750 ICLS 60/101 *et seq.* (1992).

12. Black, *supra* note 9, at 5.

13. *Id.* at 716.

14. *Healthy People 2000, supra* note 1, at 61.

15. Black, *supra* note 9, at 716.

16. George D. Pozgar. *Legal Aspects of Health Care Administration.* 4th Edition. Gaithersburg, Md: Aspen Publishers, Inc., 1990, 140.

17. Marcia O'Kelly, Jesse Trentadue, Diane Geraghty, William Walker, and others, "Family Law," *in You and the Law.* Lincolnwood, Ill: Publications International, Ltd., 1990, 123 (An American Bar Association Consumer Guide Book).

18. Pozgar, *supra* note 16, at 140.

19. See, 325 ICLS 5/5 (1992); Ill. Admin. Code tit. 89, Section 300.120 (1991).

20. *Id.*

21. 551 P. 2d 389 (Cal. 1976).

22. 400 N.W. 2d 42 (Wis. 1986).

23. See, for example, American Bar Association. *Criminal and Civil Liability in Child Abuse Welfare Work: The Growing Trend.* Washington, D.C.: ABA, 1983; *Mannov v. Arizona, reported in* 24 *American Trial Lawyers' Association Reporter* 76 (1981).

24. Tammy Zeitchick Movsas and Benjamin Movsas, "Abuse versus Neglect: A Model to Understand the Causes and Treatment Strategies for Mistreatment of Older Persons," 6(2) *Issues In Law & Medicine* (Fall 1990), 164.

25. *Id.* at 163, *citing* House Select Committee On Aging. *Elder Abuse: An Examination of a Hidden Problem.* H.R. Report No. 277, 97th Congress, 1st Session, at XIII (1981).

26. Movsas and Movsas, *supra* note 24, at 164, *citing* Taler and Ansello, "Elder Abuse," *American Family Physician* (August 1985), 107, 108.

27. Movsas and Movsas, *supra* note 24, at 164; See also, Madelyn Iris and Flora Johnson Skelly, "The Rights of Older Americans," *in You And The Law, supra* note 17, 539–543.

28. Carolyn Clark-Daniels, Steven Daniels, and Lorin Baumhover, "The Dilemma of Elder Abuse," 8(6) *Home Healthcare Nurse* (November/December 1990), 7–12.

29. House Select Committee on Aging, *supra* note 25, at XIV.

30. Daniels, Daniels, and Baumhover, *supra* note 28, at 8, *citing* C. Culhane, "Federal, State Effort in Order to Prevent Elder Abuse," *American Medical News* (July 21, 1989), 18–19.

31. 210 ICLS 3011 *et seq.* (1992), [Welfare and Institutions], *as amended;* Michigan Compiled Laws Annotated, Section 400.11a (1993), *as amended;* New Jersey Statutes Annotated, 720 ICLS 5/12–5/19 (1992), Section 52: 27G-7.1 (West 1993) *as amended;* California Code, Section 15630 (West 1991), *as amended.*

32. Abuse and Gross Neglect of a Long Term Care Facility Resident Law, 720 ICLS 5/12–5/19 (1992), *as amended* (Illinois); New Mexico Statutes Chapter 30 Article 47 Section 30–47–4 (1978), *as amended.*

33. "Medicare and Medicaid Programs: Omnibus Nursing Home Requirements" (Proposed Rule), *Federal Register,* Vol. 57 No. 24, February 5, 1992, 4516–4520.

34. Movsas and Movsas, *supra* note 24, *citing* Taler and Ansello (same footnote) at 108, 109.

35. Nancy J. Brent, "Elder Abuse: The Next Step," 6(6) *Home Healthcare Nurse* (November/December 1988), 4–5.

36. *Id.*

37. 320 ICLS 20/1 *et seq.* (1992).

38. 320 ICLS 20/9(a) (1992).

39. 320 ICLS 20/9(d) (1992).

40. Lee Beneze and Ann Neighbors, "Elder Abuse and Ne-

glect Cases: An Attorney's Guide," 79(8) *Illinois Bar Journal* (August 1991), 391, *citing* Illinois Coalition on Domestic Violence. *Illinois Domestic Violence Act of 1986: Implementation Manual* (1987), 1–4.

41. Florida Stat. Ann. Section 784.08 (West 1989), *as amended*; Louisiana Stat. Ann. Volume 9 Section 50.1 (West 1986), *as amended*; Colorado Revised Statutes Section 18-3-209 (1993).

42. *Healthy People 2000, supra* note 1, at 39.

43. *Id.* at 40.

44. 405 ICLS 5/6-102 (1992), *as amended*; Texas [Human Resources] Code Annotated 48.036 (1990), *as amended*.

45. Illinois' *Domestic Abuse of Disabled Adults Intervention Act*, 20 ICLS 2435/1 *et seq.* (1993), (permissive reporting with consent of individual); Washington's *Abuse of Children and Adult Dependent or Developmentally Disabled Act*, Wash. Revised Code Annotated Section 26.44.010 *et seq.* (West 1993) (mandatory reporting).

46. 720 ICLS 5/12–21 (1992).

47. Susan Ross, Isabelle Pinzler, Deborah Ellis, and Kary Moss. *The Rights of Women: The Basic ACLU Guide to Women's Rights.* 3rd Edition. Carbondale, Ill: Southern Illinois University Press, 1993, 221–222.

48. 720 ICLS 5/12–12 to 5/12–18 (1992), as amended.

49. *Id.*; see also, *The Rights of Women, supra* note 47, 221–233.

50. NOW Legal Defense and Education Fund and Dr. Renee Chero-O'Leary. *The State-by-State Guide to Women's Legal Rights.* New York: McGraw-Hill, 1987, 81.

51. *Id.* at 81.

52. Black, *supra* note 9, at 401.

53. 325 ICLS 15/5 (1992), *as amended* (Illinois' *Child Sexual Abuse Prevention Act*).

54. Schwartz, *supra* note 8, at 28.

55. See 735 ICLS 5/802.1–802.2 (1992).

56. 735 ICLS 5/802.1–802.2 (1992).

57. See 325 ICLS 5/4 (1992), *Abused and Neglected Child Reporting Act*.

58. 720 ICLS 5/12–18 (1992) (Illinois).

59. ANA *Position Statement, supra* note 5.

60. *Americana Health Care Corp. (of Ohio)*, 252 N.L.R.B. 380 (1980).

61. *Ambassador Convalescent Center, Inc.*, 83 Lab. Arb. (BNA) 44 (1984).

62. *IDAK Convalescent Center of Fall River, Inc. (Crawford House)*, 238 N.L.R.B. 410 (1978).

63. *Id.*

64. See *Hall v. Bio-Medical Application, Inc.*, 671 F. 2d 300 (8th Cir. 1982).

65. *Baptist Memorial Hospital v. Bowen*, 591 So. 2d 74 (Ala. 1991).

66. *State v. Serebin*, 350 N.W. 2d 65 (Wis. 1984).

67. Lenore H. Kurlowicz, "Violence in the Emergency Department," *AJN* (September 1990), 35.

68. See, for example, Pam Towne, "Safety Surveys Reveal Alarming Abuse of RNs on Understaffed Units," 89(6) *Chart for Nurses* (July/August 1992), 4 (the official publication of the Illinois Nurses' Association).

69. Kathryn Braun, Donna Christle, Duane Walker, and Gail Tiwanak, "Verbal Abuse of Nurses and Non-Nurses," 22(3) *Nursing Management* (March 1991), 73–74.

70. Jacquelyn Slomka, "Violence in the Hospital," 268 *JAMA* (August 26, 1992), 984–985 (Letter to the Editor).

71. Braun, Christile, Walker, and Tiwanak, *supra* note 69, at 72.

72. Braun, Christile, Walker, and Tiwanak, *supra* note 69, at 72, *citing* F.B. Friedmann, "A Nurse's Guide to the Care and Handling of MDs," *RN* (March 1982), 38–42.

73. *Peete v. Blackwell*, 504 So. 2d 222 (Ala. 1986), *rehearing denied, March 20, 1987.*

74. Michael Hannigan, "Emergency Department Violence," 23(9) *Nursing Management* (September 1992), 150–151, *in* Notes from the Field.

75. *Id.*, at 150.

76. For additional safety tips, see Jaqueline Nadwairski, "Inner City Safety for Home Care Providers," 22(9) *JONA* (September 1992) 42–47.

77. Slomka, *supra* note 70, at 985.

78. B. Steele, "Psychodynamic Factors in Child Abuse," *in The Battered Child.* C. Kempe and R. Heifer, Editors. Chicago: The University of Chicago Press (1980), 49–85; Movsas and Movsas, *supra* note 24, at 165, *citing* Mildenberger and Wessman, "Abuse and Neglect of Elderly Persons by Family Members: A Special Communication," 66 *Physical Therapy* 557, 538 (1986).

79. American Nurses' Association, *Position Statement, supra* note 5.

80. Anita Glicken, "In Reply," 268(8) *JAMA* (August 26, 1992), 985 (reply to Slomka, *supra*, note 70), *citing* D. Rosenberg, H. Silver, "Medical Student Abuse: An Unnecessary and Preventable Cause of Stress," 251 *JAMA* (1984), 739–743, and H. Silver, "Medical Students and Medical School," 247 *JAMA* (1982), 309–310.

81. Helen Cox, "Verbal Abuse Nationwide, Part II: Impact and Modifications," 22(3) *Nursing Management* (March 1991), 66–69.

82. *Healthy People 2000, supra* note 1, at 61.

83. *Id.*

84. Movsas and Movsas, *supra* note 24, *citing* T. Fulmer and T. O'Malley. *Inadequate Care of the Elderly: A Health Care Perspective on Abuse and Neglect* (1987).

3

part three

Legal Concerns of Nurses in Diverse Roles and Settings

15

Licensure and Nursing Practice

contents

Nurses, like other licensed professionals, are regulated by various state laws. One vitally important state law that directly affects the practice of nursing is the state nursing practice act. The ability of the state to govern nursing, other health care providers, and health care delivery systems is based in the state's constitution, which grants the state "police power" to ensure that its citizens' health, welfare, and safety are protected, and the federal Constitution's Tenth Amendment, which allows the respective states to establish and enforce any laws not prohibited or pre-empted by federal law.[1] Thus, so long as the state laws are reasonable and further the overall objective of protecting its citizens, they stand as legitimate regulations on those individuals who seek to practice a profession or establish a health care entity.

Although the concept of state power is an important one, the ability of each state to regulate nursing and nursing practice has resulted in a wide variety of regulatory laws that are not consistent from state to state, and that have resulted in confusion among nurses and the public alike in relation to scope of practice, educational issues, and specialties in nursing. Furthermore, this diversity has led to wide variations of state licensing boards or agencies regulating nursing practice, not only in terms of their structure, but also in terms of their respective powers. For example, a 1985 study of boards of nursing conducted by the American Nurses' Association's Center for Research cited five structure models for occupational licensing bodies.[2] They include boards with complete autonomy (the ability to hire staff, discipline licensees, and set standards of practice, for example) to a "regulatory system" run by an agency director, commission, or council, in which the board or identified nursing group (e.g., a committee) functions as an advisory body to the agency head.[3]

Despite the multifarious laws governing nursing practice from state to state, any nurse graduate seeking licensure for the first time, or any licensed nurse, must be familiar with the agency or board administering the act, its rules and regulations adopted to do so, and his or her rights *and* responsibilities granted by the act. This chapter will provide such an overview that can form the basis for a more in-depth analysis of the nurse's own state practice act and state occupational licensing body (e.g., board of nursing or bureau of professional regulation).

NURSE PRACTICE ACTS

History

It is no secret that in the United States occupational licensure was first controlled by physicians. The American Medical Association, established in 1847, was very active in the political process, especially in relation to lobbying for state regulation of health care providers through licensure.[4] With the United States Supreme Court deciding in 1888 that occupational licensure was within the legitimate "political power" of the state, the licensing of physicians was well established,[5] and physician licensure was rapidly adopted throughout the states.

KEY PRINCIPLES

Due Process Rights
Right Against Self-Incrimination
Property Rights
Administrative Law
Adminstrative Procedure Act

It is no secret that in the United States occupational licensure was first controlled by physicians.

This initial control over licensure by physicians clearly impacted on other health care professions later regulated by the states, including nursing. Because medicine was the first to define its practice, other professions had to be described by the states not only in very different terms, but also by excluding any functions or responsibilities that were clearly included in the already established definition of medical practice.

This impact can clearly be seen in the development of nursing practice acts across the country. One well-known author on the history of nursing has organized that development into three specific phases: (1) The Early Nurse Registration Acts (1903–1938); (2) The Scope of Practice Definition Era (1938–1970); and (3) The Era of Expanding Functions for Registered Nurses (1971–present).[6]

Early Nurse Registration Acts Era

This phase was dominated by the predecessor to the American Nurses' Association, the Nurses' Associated Alumnae of the United States and Canada, attempting to obtain legislative recognition of nurses and the nursing profession. Established in 1896, the Association had to overcome great odds in doing so, but in 1903 convinced the North Carolina legislature to pass the first registration act.[7] Other states soon followed North Carolina's example, and by 1923, all of the states then in existence had nurse practice acts. These acts were *permissive* acts, however, which meant that although one could register with the state agency or board to practice nursing, one did not *have* to do so. If an individual did not register with the state, that individual could continue to provide nursing care to patients, but could not utilize the initials

"RN" after his or her name. Furthermore, until the first *mandatory* act was passed, the permissive acts did not include any definition of the scope of nursing practice or had few prerequisites the individual seeking registration had to comply with.[8] In addition, and perhaps most telling, few, if any, nurses sat on the boards of nursing established by the acts. Rather, physicians composed the membership of the early boards.

Scope of Practice Definition Era

In 1938, New York State passed the first *mandatory* nurse practice act. The New York legislation was remarkably different from the prior acts because it required individuals practicing nursing to be licensed to do so. Thus, no longer could an individual provide nursing care *or* use the initials "RN" after his or her name without being licensed. Moreover, the New York Act included a definition of nursing practice in it, and established a new nursing level, that of the licensed practical nurse. The licensed practical nurse role was also defined in terms of scope of practice and qualifications.[9] Also, vitally important for the development of nursing as an autonomous profession controlled by *nurses* rather than *physicians*, registered nurses and licensed practical nurses began to compose the membership on nursing boards.

In 1938, New York State passed the first mandatory *nurse practice act.*

By this time, the Nurses' Associated Alumnae Organization had become the American Nurses' Association, and continued to be active in supporting the regulation of nursing practice. In the early 1940s, it prepared a statement on provisions that should be included in nurse practice acts.[10] In 1955, the Association attempted to develop a "model definition" of professional nursing practice that unfortunately included a restrictive sentence stating that the practice of professional nursing "shall not be deemed to include any acts of diagnosis or prescription of therapeutic or corrective measures."[11] This language was necessary, so the thinking went, because of the need for mandatory acts to include a definition of nursing reflecting a distinction from medical practice that was already defined and carefully protected by the medical community.

The 1955 statement was followed in 1980 by another document, which was intended to serve as a policy guide for "nurses, state nursing associations, state boards of nursing, and state officials" in amending nurse practice acts. The publication's purposes were to (1) reflect changes in the profession; (2) protect the public from unsafe practitioners; (3) ensure that the acts contained only those restrictions on licensure necessary to the regulation of safe practice; and (4) provide the minimal legal foundations in the acts for practice in the state, with control over the scope and definition of nursing practice remaining within the professional organization.[12]

Although the definition of professional nursing in this document did not include the restrictive language seen in the 1955 statement concerning what was the practice of nursing and what was to be reserved for physicians only, the 1955 language saw its way into many nursing practice acts, both before the 1980 position was adopted and afterward. In 1983, the American Nurses' Association's own study indicated that nine states still had language similar or identical to the 1955 definition of nursing.[13]

Era of Expanding Functions for Registered Nurses

Although this period is more fully developed in Chapter 21, The Nurse in Advanced Practice, it is important to note in this chapter that beginning in 1971, nurse practice acts were modified not only to provide a legal foundation for specialty areas of nursing practice, such as nurse practitioners, nurse-midwives, and nurse anes-

thetists, but also to eliminate the restrictive language established in the previous period. Again, New York became the first state, in 1972, to alter that restriction on practice.[14] In addition, terms like "nursing diagnosis," "expanded role," and "joint practice" (between nurses and physicians) were touchstones of this era.

The American Nurses' Association also developed a new position statement (*Suggested State Legislation: Nurse Practice Act, Disciplinary Division Act and Prescriptive Authority Act*) concerning nurse practice acts, which reflected the many changes in nursing practice and health care delivery.[15] Insofar as the nursing practice acts are concerned, the document is important, not only for its support of advanced practice and its definitions of *delegation* and *supervision*, but also for its attention to boards of nursing. Boards, according to this publication, are to be given clear powers and duties rather than simply inferring them.[16] Furthermore, the document clearly provides guidelines for the retention of responsibilities for boards that are not autonomous units, but rather function within a department or other state agency. They include but are not limited to (1) evaluating and approving requirements for licensure and renewal of that license; (2) disciplining professional nurses and licensed practical nurses who are not fit to practice in accordance with due process principles; and (3) establishing and applying competency requirements to continue or re-enter practice after a disciplinary action has been taken.[17]

Current Status

Clearly, outside forces as well as state legislatures were responsible for molding nurse practice acts into various models. As a result, there is wide variation among state acts. Even with these variations, certain similarities exist, and consistency results more from concepts and principles of administrative law than from a consensus in nursing or the general public as to what should be included in these acts. Even so, nurse practice acts continue to be an important aspect of the regulation of nursing practice, nursing education, and the protection of the public from unsafe and unlicensed practice.

BOARDS OF NURSING OR OTHER REGULATORY UNITS

Composition and General Powers

The board of nursing or similiar body is a creature of state law. The state nurse practice act contains provisions concerning the board's or other unit's composition, power, and authority. Membership on a board or committee occurs through appointment by the state governor, and most state boards or other units have between 3 and 20 members.[18] Because the state legislature grants to the board of nursing or a less autonomous unit (such as a committee on nursing) certain powers clearly specified in the nurse practice act, the board or committee can carry out only those powers or those that can reasonably flow from them. Thus, boards of nursing are considered to be of "limited jurisdiction." This limited jurisdiction may be further limited by the number of powers given to it by the legislature. Common powers given to boards of nursing may include rule-making, licensing ability, and the authority to conduct and participate in cases involving the discipline of nurses licensed under the act. Despite the wide variations in power and the kinds of power that may be given to the board or less autonomous unit, these regulatory bodies are involved in administering and enforcing the state nurse practice act.

Disciplinary Process and Procedure

Grounds for Disciplinary Actions

Through the state nurse practice act section on discipline, specific grounds are listed upon which the board or regulatory unit can take disciplinary action against the nurse and his or her license. The American Nurses' Association, in a 1986 publication, suggested numerous grounds that should be included in state nurse practice acts to protect the public from unsafe or ineligible practitioners.[19] Those grounds include:

▼ Violation of any provision of the nursing practice act

▼ Addiction to or dependency on alcohol or other habit-forming drugs

▼ Habitual use of narcotics or other drugs that have the same effect as narcotics

▼ Falsification of patient records or failure to record essential information in the patient's record

▼ Unprofessional conduct likely to deceive, defraud, or harm the public

▼ Conviction of a felony or a crime involving moral turpitude, or pleading *nolo contendere* (no contest) to either

▼ Negligent or willful violation of nursing practice standards

▼ "Unlawful" acts, including, but not limited to, practicing nursing without a license, fraudulently obtaining or furnishing any nursing license or diploma, or aiding and abetting another in such acts.

Common powers given to boards of nursing may include rule-making, licensing ability, and the authority to conduct and participate in cases involving the discipline of nurses licensed under the act.

As a result of these, and other, suggestions, most state nurse practice acts have adopted eight categories of disciplinary actions that can be taken against nurses. They are fraud and deceit; criminal activity; negligence, risk to clients, and physical and mental incapacity; violations of the nursing practice act or rules; disciplinary action by another board; incompetency; unethical conduct; and drug and/or alcohol use.[20]

> *Most state nurse practice acts have adopted eight categories of disciplinary actions that can be taken against nurses.*

Fraud and Deceit

Although the specific conduct that might violate this general category of grounds for disciplinary actions can vary and can be involved in other violations, such as criminal activity or drug or alcohol abuse, many times the deceit and fraud occur when the individual attempts to secure a nursing license, as seen in Key Case 15–1.

Criminal Activity

Generally, two main provisions are included in most nurse practice acts concerning criminal activity. They are: (1) when the registered or licensed practical nurse has been convicted of a felony; and (2) when the nurse is found guilty of a crime involving "moral turpitude" or "gross immorality."

Although there are wide variations in the kinds of crimes that might be included under the latter two categories, generally they involve those that have dishonesty as a central element, such as theft, fraud, misrepresentation, and embezzlement.[22]

Felonies, on the other hand, are those violations enumerated in the federal or state criminal statutes, and because of their serious nature, usually require more than 1 year in jail and a fine above a certain amount. Some examples include possession of a controlled substance, forgery, and deception.

Regardless of the type of criminal activity that may be alleged against the nurse, criminal alle-gations raise additional implications for the nurse. Specifically, the issue of self-incrimination must be carefully evaluated. The right against self-incrimination is based in the Fifth Amendment of the United States Constitution and similar state constitutional provisions. It protects an individual from being "compelled" to be a witness against himself or herself in a criminal case and requires the government to prove its case against the accused.

The right against self-incrimination is applicable in agency or boards of nursing actions when the nurse or licensed practical nurse is accused of conduct that not only allegedly violates the nurse practice act, but that also may violate state or federal criminal laws. If the conduct in question may violate state criminal law (e.g., diverting controlled substances from the employer or falsifying narcotics or medical records to cover the diversion), an admission by the nurse to investigators, either by an oral or written declaration or by any other act (and especially after being given a *Miranda* warning by those investigators), allows the state to bring criminal charges against the nurse. Of course, *any* admission, with or without a *Miranda* warning, can be used against the nurse in the disciplinary proceeding itself.

Despite the trend toward including the above categories in nurse practice acts, in 1986 eight states did not list any kind of criminal activity ("felony" or "crime") as grounds for discipline; five contained no language concerning "criminal activity, felony, or moral turpitude"; and 16 simply stated that a conviction of "a crime" constituted grounds for disciplinary action.[23]

Negligence, Risk to Clients, and Physical or Mental Incapacity

This overall category clearly reflects the board of nursing's concern about protecting the public from unsafe or incompetent practitioners. Although some states simply indicate "negligence" in the delivery of nursing care as a ground for discipline, many state statutes require "gross negligence" to occur, or require more than one

KEY CASE 15-1   Nicholson v. Ambach (1981)[21]

Hearing panel recommends revocation of license

Review court upholds hearing panel's decision because it was based on "substantial evidence"

FACTS: The petitioner, Rudolph Nicholson, was a licensed practical nurse who was charged by the Commissioner of Education with practicing practical nursing fraudulently and with unprofessional conduct. It was alleged that when he applied for a New York nurse license and admission to Long Island University, he submitted a New Jersey registered nurse license at the University when not licensed, corresponded with the University's nursing department by holding himself out to be a registered nurse when not licensed, submitted false New Jersey nursing board results when he applied for licensure in New York, and, to obtain a school nurse teacher's certificate, did so with a false and fraudulent transcript from Long Island University.

HEARING PANEL: After being charged with the above violations in accordance with New York State's Education Law, Mr. Nicholson was found guilty of the conduct alleged by the Hearing Panel, and the Panel recommended that his practical nurse license be revoked. Those findings and recommendations were accepted by the Commissioner of Education.

COURT REVIEW OF FINDINGS: Upon review of the Hearing Panel's record, the New York Supreme Court, Appellate Division, held that the decisions of the Panel were supported by "substantial evidence" and would not be changed, and that the revocation of the practical nurse license was fair and would be sustained.

ANALYSIS: This case illustrates the ability of the licensing authority to discipline a licensed professional when that person's license has not been obtained honestly. In addition, unprofessional conduct can be evaluated, as it was here, so that the board or regulatory agency has several grounds upon which to proceed. So long as the proceedings are fair, and the decision supported by evidence, it will not be disturbed.

---

incident to have taken place before taking action against the nurse. Likewise, the risks to clients that are grounds for actions against professional or licensed practical nurses are, most often, significant risks to the health, safety, or physical or mental well-being of the patient and may also include actual injury to the patient.

A nurse's physical or mental incapacity, whether due to disease or injury, must relate to the nurse's *current* ability to practice and deliver health care safely, as seen in Key Case 15-2.

Violations of the Nursing Practice Act or Rules

Almost all of the state nurse practice acts have included language allowing discipline against a nurse for a violation of the act, with 24 acts also including any violation of the related administrative rules as valid grounds for taking action against the nurse or licensed practical nurse.[25]

Rules and regulations further define a particular statute by giving more details and guidelines concerning the administration and enforcement

KEY CASE 15–2   State Board of Nursing v. Crickenberger (1988)[24]

FACTS: Colleen Crickenberger, an RN, was employed as a staff nurse. She had been drinking excessively prior to the Fall of 1984. Her drinking caused her to be physically ill and absent from work, even though she was never intoxicated or under the influence of alcohol while at work. Realizing she had a problem, Crickenberger entered into treatment for her alcoholism and attended group meetings established to help those who had alcohol problems. She also informed her Director of Nursing that she was undertaking treatment. On November 20, 1984, Crickenberger called the Director and told her she was ill and would not be reporting for work that day. The Nursing Director, certain that her illness and absence were the result of a relapse of treatment, terminated her, and filed a complaint with the Colorado Board of Nursing.

Board of Nursing imposes discipline, despite no alcohol problem at time of hearing

BOARD OF NURSING: Although the hearing officer for the Board found that Crickenberger had not "had any alcoholic beverages since October of 1984," that the illness and absence in November of 1984 could therefore *not* have been the result of alcohol use, and ordered the case dismissed, the Board imposed discipline because the alcohol problem existed at the time of the employer's complaint to the Board, whether or not it was "active." Crickenberger asked the Colorado Court of Appeals to review the decision.

COURT REVIEW OF FINDINGS: The Colorado Court of Appeals carefully analyzed the language in Colorado's Nurse Practice Act concerning disciplinary actions and held that the "plain language" of the Act required that any addiction or dependency be proven to exist at the time of the hearing for any disciplinary action to be upheld. Thus, the Court ruled, the final order imposing discipline must be "set aside."

Review court sets aside Board decision because no alcohol dependency existed at the hearing stage

ANALYSIS: This case is an important one in ensuring that a Board or other regulatory unit not exceed its authority when evaluating conduct alleged to be in violation of the nurse practice act. If a nurse is unable to care for patients safely and competently because of any of the conditions in this category *at the time a complaint is filed*, and that inability is proven, then the nurse may not practice until and unless the disability is removed. To discipline a nurse when there is no *current* threat to the public's safety is to ignore constitutional and other protections afforded an individual in his or her due process and property rights.

of the act. The administrative rules and regulations for nurse practice acts are as divergent as the acts themselves, but some areas of coverage include standards of conduct for professional and licensed practical nurses (e.g., Illinois and Wisconsin); definitions of terms used in the act (e.g., "unprofessional conduct," negligence, and mental incompetency); and scope of practice statements, tasks allowed, and required supervision for those states' licensing specialty areas of practice (e.g., nurse-midwifery or nurse practitioners).

With the establishment of the National Bank and the National Council of State Boards of Nursing Disciplinary Data Bank in 1980, tracking prior disciplinary actions against nurses will be easier for nursing boards.

Disciplinary Action by Another Jurisdiction

Prior to the enactment of the Health Care Quality Improvement Act of 1986 and the Medicare and Medicaid Patient and Program Protection Act of 1987[26] that require mandatory reporting to a national data bank of disciplinary actions taken by hospitals, licensing boards, professional associations, peer review committees, and insurers, the ability of nurses and other health care providers to move from one state to another without any tracking of prior disciplinary problems was relatively easy. As a result, actions taken by another state against a nurse as a ground for filing an action against the nurse or licensed practical nurse in that current state were often not utilized unless an inadvertent discovery of that information occurred. However, with the establishment of the National Bank and the National Council of State Boards

of Nursing Disciplinary Data Bank in 1980,[27] tracking prior disciplinary actions against nurses will be easier for nursing boards. Thus, it is certain that this provision will continue to be included in nurse practice acts as a basis for disciplinary action against the nurse.

Incompetence

This general category as a basis for disciplinary action against nurses has not been specifically recommended by the American Nurses' Association for inclusion in nurse practice acts.[29] Even so, this ground does appear, again in varying forms, in 23 acts.[30] The various forms include mental disability that would interfere with safe patient care (many times phrased as an involuntary admission to a psychiatric facility); negligence; and failure to meet generally accepted standards of nursing practice.

In a reported study of 100 files of nurses brought before one board of nursing, 40 of those nurses were disciplined for incompetency.[31] The types of conduct that constituted incompetent conduct were medication errors, including IVs, blood, and "repeated errors" (19 cases); lack of technique and knowledge of procedures, including drug calculations, cardiopulmonary resuscitation, and sterile technique (7 cases); and failure to maintain adequate records, including failing to transcribe physician orders correctly and failing to record patient assessments and changes in the patient's condition.[32]

Unethical Conduct

Unethical conduct can include many types of behavior, including some of the actions of nurses already presented in the Key Cases. In addition to those situations, many nurse practice acts or their rules and regulations contain specific provisions concerning unethical behavior, including breach of nurse-patient confidentiality, refusal to care for someone of a certain race, creed, color, or national origin, fraud in obtaining reimbursement, and violation of the ethical code for nurses.

KEY CASE 15–3   Shoenhair v. Commonwealth of Pennsylvania et al (1983)[28]

FACTS: Dona Jean Shoenhair, a registered nurse, was licensed in the State of Florida and Pennsylvania. On March 29, 1978, the Florida Board of Nursing issued a complaint against her, alleging unprofessional conduct because she failed to properly chart drugs she administered, took a telephone order from a physician for a controlled substance for which the physician never co-signed, and slept on duty. Because of a lack of money to hire an attorney and no means of transportation from her home (Daytona) to Miami, where the hearing was to take place, Ms. Shoenhair waived her right to a hearing on the allegations. At the Board's next meeting, the Board found her "guilty" of the charges and ordered that her license be revoked. Shoenhair never contested the decision, nor did she petition the Board for the reinstatement of her license. Thinking that the action taken by the Florida Board would not have any effect on her Pennsylvania license, Shoenhair returned to Pennsylvania in 1980 and began working at a nursing home as its night supervisor. In December of the same year, she received a citation and notice of a hearing from the Pennsylvania Board to determine if her license should be suspended or revoked because of the revocation by the Florida Board.

BOARD OF NURSING: The Pennsylvania Board found that the Florida revocation had, in fact, taken place, and that despite the fact that Ms. Shoenhair was now behaving in a professional and responsible manner, it could not overlook the "misconduct" that caused the revocation. Thus the Board revoked her Pennsylvania license. Shoenhair petitioned the court for a review of that decision, alleging that she involuntarily and unintelligently waived her right to a hearing in Florida, and thus the Pennsylvania Board decision was a violation of her due process rights since it was dependent solely on the faulty Florida action.

Pennsylvania Board of Nursing revoked nurse license because of revocation by Florida Board

COURT REVIEW OF FINDINGS: Citing Pennsylvania case law that clearly supported the right of the Board to take action against a nurse simply on the *fact* of disciplinary action in another state rather than on the underlying events leading to the decision to take action, the Pennsylvania court upheld the Board's revocation. The court stated that Shoenhair did not challenge the Florida decision, and therefore trying to do so in Pennsylvania is not possible. Furthermore, the court held, because there was no challenge to the Florida Board's decision in Florida, it is entitled to the presumption of validity and reliability. Nor did an abuse of discretion occur, because, as with the Board decision in Pennsylvania, due process protections were afforded the nurse prior to the decisions made.

Review court upholds Pennsylvania Board decision because failure to contest Florida Board's decision prohibits nurse from contesting Pennsylvania Board decision

Key Case continued on following page

KEY CASE 15–3

Shoenhair v. Commonwealth of Pennsylvania et al (1983)[28]
Continued

ANALYSIS: *Shoenhair* clearly supports the ability of a Board to take action against a nurse exclusively on the basis of a previous action by another Board. It is important to note here that this is a case in which Ms. Shoenhair already had licensure in Pennsylvania when the Board in Florida made its decision to revoke her license. It is *not* a case in which, after a revocation in one state, one applies for licensure in another state and reveals the prior disciplinary action to the state board where licensure is now sought, and the board there refuses to issue the license. A property interest already obtained (in the professional license) may be revoked.

This case also illustrates the importance of challenging any type of disciplinary action, even if not successfully. The fact that Ms. Shoenhair did nothing to question or dispute the Florida Board's action was a pivotal issue in the Pennsylvania Court's eye. Not only is this "common sense," it is also an important legal point, for the Pennsylvania Court could not give credence to the "collateral attack" on the Florida action (the purpose of which is to overturn the decision) when the petitioner did not do so when she could have.

Drug and Alcohol Use

The number of disciplinary actions against nurses utilizing this ground in nurse practice acts is disturbing and is on the rise. In 1985 alone, there were 1520 documented cases of disciplinary actions taken by state boards of nursing against nurses for drug and alcohol impairment or use that affected the nurse's practice.[33] In addition to impairment or use, other problems that often concurrently arise with drug or alcohol use are diversion of an addicted-to drug (often controlled substances) from the employer, selling diverted drugs or drug paraphernalia (syringes, IV tubing) to others, and falsification of patient and other records.

Although it was once fairly common for state boards or other regulatory units to be punitive in nature when nurses had addiction problems, whatever the reason and however it manifested itself, a shift has occurred from that posture to one of acknowledging the addiction as an illness that requires treatment. Viewing addiction as an illness has not changed any board of nursing's responsibility to protect the public by removing the impaired nurse's license when that need is present, but it has resulted in a vision of treatment and rehabilitation for the impaired nurse so that continued recovery can be obtained and maintained. With the help of professional organizations such as the National Nurses' Society for Addictions, the Drug and Alcohol Nurses' Associations, and the American Organization of Nurse Executives, treatment and educational programs, as well as input into legislative changes in nurse practice acts, have been established to help impaired nurses and, at the same time, protect the public from unsafe practitioners.

Two interesting results have taken place because of the efforts of these organizations. First, many nurse practice acts contain mandatory reporting provisions requiring certain nurses, such as nurse administrators or owners of nurse registries, to report impairment that affects the nurse's practice, and report diversion of controlled substances to the board of nursing or regulatory unit. Doing so creates many problems for the nurse who is reported. However, in an attempt to be more rehabilitative, some of the practice acts provide an exception to reporting when the nurse seeks treatment, is monitored by the facility, and stays employed there. The difficulties with this approach are varied. One is that many times, there simply are not adequate treatment options available for the nurse in his or her community. A second problem lies with the act itself: If the nurse is fired, for example, for theft or forgery pursuant to the employer's disciplinary policy, the nurse must then be reported to the state agency because one of the key provisions of nonreporting—employment—cannot be met.

The second, that of developing alternative approaches to disciplinary actions against the nurse, is perhaps more flexible, and serves to protect the public *and* provide needed treatment and rehabilitation to the impaired nurse. The alternative approaches have been established in several states, including Florida and California. The California model, which is a community-based one, and the Florida approach, which allows the impaired nurse to enter an approved treatment facility and be shielded from disciplinary action so long as treatment is successful, and to return to work with monitoring by the board, are innovative.[34]

Because of the professional organizations' efforts, and because of better understanding by the public of the problem of addiction, several model acts have been proposed for state legislatures to follow in developing alternatives to disciplinary actions against nurses abusing drugs or alcohol.[35] Until *all* jurisdictions adopt such an approach to the impaired nurse, however, more traditional actions, including disciplinary actions, will continue against the nurse or licensed practical nurse whose chemical addiction affects his or her professional practice.

Actions Possible by Board or Regulatory Agency

The ability of the board of nursing or regulatory agency to take action against the registered or licensed practical nurse rests with the statutory authority given the licensing authority by the state legislature. The American Nurses' Association clearly supports the position that the licensing authority be given broad powers to discipline nurses. Those powers include denying an application for licensure; revoking a license or other authorization to practice; requiring a licensee to submit to "care, counseling, or treatment" for initial, continued, or renewed licensure; and administering a public or private reprimand.[36]

. . . the licensing authority [should] be given broad powers to discipline nurses. Those powers include denying an application for licensure; revoking a license or other authorization to practice; requiring a licensee to submit to "care, counseling or treatment" for initial, continued, or renewed licensure; and administering a public or private reprimand.

Regardless of the possible actions against a registered or licensed practical nurse, the regulatory agency or board is also usually given wide latitude in combining the actions possible. For example, in a situation in which drug use is found to exist, the registered nurse's license may be placed on probation (e.g., periodic, random drug screens and employer reports to be submitted to the agency) in addition to requiring the nurse to successfully complete treatment for the drug problem.

If the registered or licensed practical nurse's license is suspended or revoked and the conditions specified in the case are met, the nurse may usually petition the board or regulatory agency for reinstatment of the license. The burden of proof of showing that the reinstatement is warranted rests with the nurse. If that burden is met, then reinstatement can occur, with or without additional reporting mechanisms to the licensing authority (e.g., additional employer reports). However, if the burden of proof is not met, the individual may be denied reinstatement of his or her license at that time.

Actions taken by the board or regulatory agency are often challenged by individuals seeking initial licensure when their application is denied;[37] by registered and licensed practical nurses when a revocation occurs;[38] and when the action is alleged to be a violation of certain due process rights of the licensee.[39] Unless the licensing authority's decision is beyond its scope of power, unconstitutional, or arbitrary, however, the decisions are not overturned by the reviewing court.

Procedural and Substantive Due Process Rights of Licensees

The registered or licensed practical nurse possesses clear protections against any arbitrary and unfair actions by the state licensing authority. A nursing board or regulatory agency licensing nurses is a governmental agency and therefore must abide by both *substantive* and *procedural* due process principles. Procedural and substantive due process rights are based in the United States and respective state Constitutions, as well as in the federal and state's administrative procedure act. The minimum protections afforded the nurse licensee are therefore fairly universal in practice acts and include:

▼ Notice of time and place of any proceeding

▼ A clear statement of the charge(s)

▼ Representation by counsel

▼ Cross-examination of adverse witnesses

▼ Presentation of own witnesses

▼ Hearing before a proper and authorized group, with the group making its decision in a fair manner based on the evidence presented

▼ Record/transcript of the proceedings

▼ Judicial review of the decision

A nursing board or regulatory agency licensing nurses is a governmental agency and therefore must abide by both substantive *and* procedural *due process principles.*

Allegations of violations of these rights often serve as the basis for a challenge of the board or licensing authority's decisions concerning actions against the nurse, as seen in Key Case 15–4.

Burden of Proof and Evidence in Hearings

Any decision of a board of nursing or regulatory agency must be based on the facts introduced into evidence during the hearing. Generally the rules governing administrative hearings and evidence are not as rigid as when a civil or criminal hearing or trial takes place. Furthermore, because administrative hearings take place before a hearing officer who may or may not be a lawyer, the rules and regulations concerning evidence are relaxed somewhat. For example, in administrative hearings, hearsay (an out-of-court/hearing statement offered to support the truth of something at issue in the court or hearing) may be admitted into evidence more easily.

Although the more relaxed rules may be bene-

KEY CASE 15–4

Rafferty v. Commonwealth of Pennsylvania and State Board of Nurse Examiners (1986)[40]

FACTS: Anne Marie Rafferty, a neurosurgical nurse in the ICU at Thomas Jefferson University Hospital, was to bathe a comatose patient who was on a respirator. She decided to disconnect the respirator during the bath to check for spontaneous respirations, because the patient began experiencing premature ventricular contractions (PVCs). After testing his breathing without the respirator (no spontaneous breathing occurred), she reconnected the ventilator. She resumed the bath, but noticed "significant changes" in the patient's blood pressure and PVCs. Nurse Rafferty did not call a code, despite being instructed to do so by several other ICU nurses who realized that the patient was experiencing cardiac arrest. The patient died. Ms. Rafferty was reported to the Board by the hospital and was charged with "willfully or repeatedly" violating several of the regulations of the Pennsylvania Nursing Act dealing with assessing human responses to nursing care, external cardiac resuscitation, and artificial respiration. The regulations also stated that the Board could discipline a nurse when there were "willful or repeated" violations of the (nurse practice) act or regulations. There were never any allegations by the Board that Ms. Rafferty caused the patient's death, nor were there any findings to that effect.

Pennsylvania Board revokes the license due to the nurse's conduct deviating from accepted standards of care

BOARD OF NURSING: After a hearing, the Pennsylvania Board of Nursing revoked Ms. Rafferty's license, because she violated several of the regulations of the Act, and her conduct deviated from accepted nursing practice. She appealed that decision to the Commonwealth Court of Pennsylvania.

The initial Court of Review reversed the Board's decision due to insufficient evidence

COURT REVIEW OF FINDINGS: The initial court of review reversed the findings of the Board, holding that there were no repeated violations, just the one incident; there was no evidence of any "willful" violation of the regulations; Ms. Rafferty's record prior to this incident was "unblemished"; and although Ms. Rafferty's conduct was in error and subject to "severe criticism," the Board erred in finding substantial evidence on which to base the revocation. The Board of Nursing appealed the decision to the Pennsylvania Supreme Court.

Key Case continued on following page

KEY CASE 15–4

Rafferty v. Commonwealth of Pennsylvania and State Board of Nurse Examiners (1986)[40] Continued

The Pennsylvania Supreme Court reversed the initial Review Court decision, holding there was "ample evidence" in the record for its decision

The Pennsylvania Supreme Court also remanded several issues back to the Commonwealth Court for its decision

The Commonwealth Court held that the decision would stand because the issues it reviewed did not require a reversal of the Board's decision

PA. SUPREME COURT REVIEW OF FINDINGS: The Pennsylvania Supreme Court reversed the lower court decision and remanded the case back to the Commonwealth Court. The Supreme Court held that the Board was not required to prove specific intent when looking at "willful" conduct, because doing so would negate the Board's charge of insuring "safe nursing services for the *citizens* of the Commonwealth." The Court also upheld the Board's decisions that Ms. Rafferty's conduct in removing the patient from the respirator to check for spontaneous respirations rather than to do so by other means, and that her other conduct was "willful," were based upon ample evidence in the record. However, the Court remanded several issues back to the Commonwealth Court for its decision because they were raised during the appeal. They were whether or not the Board regulations were constitutional; whether the presence of the hospital's attorney at the board hearing denied her a fair hearing; and whether the board's refusal to reopen the record for additional testimony of the treating physician was proper.

COURT DETERMINATION OF ISSUES ON REMAND: The Commonwealth Court affirmed the decision of the Pennsylvania Board of Nursing to revoke Ms. Rafferty's license, holding that the additional issues raised did not merit overturning that decision. In so doing, the court stated that (1) the rules were not vague as to *her* conduct (and therefore were constitutional); (2) the presence of the hospital attorney in no way prejudiced her or the Board's decision; and (3) not reopening the record was proper since, according to Pennsylvania's Code of Procedure, there was no new evidence requiring the Board to do so.

ANALYSIS: The *Rafferty* case is an example of how alleged due process rights violations are handled by the courts. Clearly, Ms. Rafferty was concerned with her rights to a fair hearing, to a decision based on the evidence by an appropriate body, to present and cross-examine witnesses, and, of course, to judicial review. Although one may not agree about the ultimate outcome of this, or any other, case concerning licensing actions, it clearly illustrates that the process of review and the rights of the licensee are carefully protected.

ficial to the nurse who faces a disciplinary hearing, the inability to utilize the strict rules of evidence may also be harmful to the nurse. For example, if heresay were allowed in a particular board hearing, and a witness *adverse* to the nurse facing disciplinary action testified about something she said she heard another person say about the nurse whose license was at issue, and that other person could not be found to support or refute the statement, the licensee may not be able to defend herself as she more fully could if the rules of evidence were more strictly applied.

The burden of proof in administrative hearings varies from state to state and is based on statutory and case law. In addition, it may vary based on who initiates the hearing or proceeding. For example, in Illinois, if a nurse petitions the Department (of Professional Regulation) for reinstatement of his or her license after it has been suspended, the nurse must show, by a preponderance of the evidence, that the license should be reinstated.[41] If, however, the Department initiates a disciplinary action against a professional or licensed practical nurse, the burden of proof the Department must meet in proving the allegations is one of clear and convincing evidence.[42]

Although the clear and convincing evidence standard is a common one in administrative hearings, other evidentiary standards required for the board or regulatory agency to prove the allegations against the licensee include doing so by "substantial evidence," by a preponderance of the evidence, by a clear preponderance, and by satisfactory proof.[43]

When a board or regulatory agency does not meet its burden of proof, the nurse licensee can challenge the decision rendered, as seen in Key Case 15–5.

Judicial Review of Board or Agency Decisions

The ability of the licensee to have a decision reviewed by the appropriate court is an important one, but it cannot be used unless certain prerequisites are met by the nurse. As with many of the topics discussed thus far, the ability to seek judicial review varies from state to state, although it is clear that every nurse who decides to question a decision of a board or regulatory agency has the right to do so.

One of the requirements that must usually be met before judicial review can occur is exhaustion of any and all remedies afforded for review of the administrative decision *within* the administrative agency or body itself. For example, if a nurse were in disagreement with a decision, a request for a rehearing before the same administrative officer or body might be required before any judicial review could occur.

When judicial review does take place, the reviewing court's role is dictated by state case and statutory law, including the state administrative procedure act. The reviewing court's main role is to ensure that the administrative hearing that did take place was a fair one and that the applicable law was interpreted and applied accurately. As a result, the reviewing court will most often uphold the decision of the board or regulatory agency unless one or more of the situations presented in Table 15–1 occur.

> *When judicial review does take place, . . . the reviewing court's main role is to ensure that the administrative hearing that did take place was a fair one and that the applicable law was interpreted and applied accurately.*

Challenges to Powers or Actions of Boards or Regulatory Agencies

Although many of the cases discussed thus far in this chapter have, in one form or another, challenged board or agency decisions, a licensed

KEY CASE 15–5   Hogan v. Mississippi Board of Nursing (1984)[44]

Board of Nursing revokes Ms. Hogan's license due to the nurse "misappropriating" Demerol

Reviewing court upholds Board decision

The Mississippi Supreme Court reverses the Chancery Court decision, holding that the correct test for proving the allegations was "clear and convincing" evidence

The Court also holds that the Nurse Practice Act does not allow a revocation simply for failing to account for the missing narcotics

FACTS: Patricia Hogan, a certified registered nurse anesthetist, was employed by Lawrence County Hospital until a 1981 audit indicated that many of the controlled narcotics signed out by Ms. Hogan could not be accounted for. Specifically, the wasted narcotics could not be reasonably accounted for by Ms. Hogan.

BOARD OF NURSING: The Board of Nursing filed a 17-count complaint against Ms. Hogan, and during the hearing, the Board itself dismissed 11 of the counts, leaving 5 against her, all of them alleging the *misappropriation* of Demerol. The Board found Ms. Hogan guilty of each of the five charges, and her license to practice nursing was revoked.

COURT REVIEW OF FINDINGS: Ms. Hogan appealed the Board's decision to the Chancery Court, which affirmed the Board's decision. Ms. Hogan then appealed to the Mississippi Supreme Court.

MISS. SUPREME COURT REVIEW OF FINDINGS: The Mississippi Supreme Court reversed the Chancery Court's decision, holding that the correct test for proving a charge of misappropriation of narcotics, which could clearly result in a license revocation if proven, was the clear and convincing standard. Simply proving that Ms. Hogan did not "reasonably account" for the missing narcotics did not meet the required standard. Furthermore, the Court said, failing to account for the narcotics is not grounds for revoking the license, and based its position on the applicable statutory law. The Court remanded the case back to the Board of Nursing with directions that the Board restore Ms. Hogan's license.

ANALYSIS: The Mississippi Supreme Court's opinion focuses on the nature of an administrative hearing when a license revocation is possible under state law. Characterizing the possibility of a license revocation as penal in nature, the Court stated that an administrative hearing under these circumstances becomes quasi-criminal in nature. As such, the higher "clear and convincing" standard of proof is required. This higher standard of proof is especially important when the government is involved in taking legal action against an individual.

---

practical or registered nurse also has the ability to raise this general objection specifically against the board taking any disciplinary action against the licensee.

One type of specific challenge to the board or agency's filing of disciplinary actions against the nurse is when the agency has not done so in a timely manner. For example, in *Harper v. Louisiana State Board of Nursing*,[45] the Board did not bring a complaint against the nurse for more than 2 years after it was aware that Ms. Harper had "improperly handled" narcotics. In upholding the Board's suspension of Ms. Harper's license, the court held that no specific time frames

TABLE 15–1

Board or Agency Actions Not Upheld on
Judicial Review

BOARD OR AGENCY	CASE EXAMPLES
Acted arbitrarily, capriciously, or in an unreasonable manner	*Scott v. Nebraska Board of Nursing*[46]
Abused its discretion	*State of Florida v. McTigue*[47]
Violated constitutionally protected right(s) of licensee	*Woods v. DC Nurses' Examining Board*[48]
Made an error of law	*Hoyte v. Board of Regents of the University of the State of New York*[49]
Based its decision on insufficient evidence	*Hogan v. Mississippi; Arkansas State Board of Nursing v. Long*[50]

for bringing a case against a licensee were present in the Louisiana Nurse Practice Act and also held that because such cases do not become "stale," there is no need to file them within a certain time.

A different result would most probably occur, however, if a particular state nurse practice act *did* contain a specific period within which a complaint must be filed against the nurse licensee. Illinois' Nurse Practice Act, for example, requires that any action against a registered nurse or licensed practical nurse must take place within 3 years from the commission of the conduct allegedly violating the Act or from a final conviction order.[51] This time limitation can be extended by 1 year when a professional negligence case, or a settlement of such a case, is pending against the licensee for the alleged conduct.[52]

A second challenge to board or agency power can rest on the jurisdiction of the entity to bring its complaint; that is, to its authority to exercise its powers. This challenge can take many forms, such as alleging that the board or agency exceeded its authority granted by the legislature in revoking a license based on intoxication while on duty;[53] alleging that the entity cannot take action against *lay* midwives as opposed to *licensed nurse-midwives*;[54] or alleging that no regu-

lations existed to guide the board or agency in taking action against the nurse, as seen in Key Case 15–6.

Other Specific Duties

In addition to participating in disciplinary proceedings, a state board of nursing usually has additional responsibilities and duties delegated to it by the legislature. Common additional responsibilities of most boards or regulatory units include approval of educational programs, licensing powers, and rule-making authority.[56]

Education Responsibilities

The board of nursing or agency responsible for nursing practice in the state has, as one of its main goals, the setting of educational standards for nursing programs throughout the state, whether they be 2-, 3-, or 4-year basic programs, graduate programs, or continuing education and refresher courses. Although there may not be total agreement on the actual powers to be given to state nursing boards, the American Nurses' Association's position is that they be given the general authority to evaluate and *approve* (not *accredit*) nursing *programs* (not *schools*).[57] Accreditation of nursing programs is best handled by private accrediting bodies, such as the National League for Nursing.

The approval process for proposed nursing educational programs can be quite involved and prolonged, but the procedure must be completed before any program can begin operating. The board or regulatory agency is usually given the ability to develop standards and rules for the curriculum, faculty, students, and facilities.

In addition to approving nursing education programs, many state boards of nursing are given the power to deny or withdraw approval after a hearing or other due process protections are afforded the program.

Licensing Powers

Regulatory units governing nursing practice have the ability to grant nursing licenses to

Tuma v. Board of Nursing (1979)[55]

FACTS: Jolene Tuma was a registered nurse employed as a clinical instructor of nursing at the College of South Idaho. While performing those duties, she met a patient with myelogenous leukemia, whose only hope of survival was chemotherapy. Ms. Tuma asked to administer the chemotherapy to the patient. During initiation of treatment, the patient brought up the subject of Laetrile and asked Ms. Tuma about it as an alternate form of therapy. After several discussions with Ms. Tuma about Laetrile, the patient withdrew her consent for the chemotherapy. A family member of the patient then contacted the doctor. The physician discontinued the chemotherapy, and the patient died about 2 weeks later. Although the death did not result from Ms. Tuma's actions "in any way," she was reported to the Board of Nursing by the physician for "interfering with the physician-patient relationship."

The Idaho Board of Nursing suspends Ms. Tuma's license for "unprofessional conduct"

BOARD OF NURSING: After a hearing, Ms. Tuma was found to have engaged in "unprofessional conduct" under the Idaho Nursing Act and her license was suspended for 6 months.

The initial Review court upholds the Board's decision

COURT REVIEW OF FINDINGS: The District Court affirmed the 6-month suspension, and Ms. Tuma then appealed to the Supreme Court of Idaho on the grounds that her due process rights were violated. Specifically, Ms. Tuma alleged that the term *unprofessional conduct* was unconstitutionally vague and therefore did not give *her* notice that speaking with a patient about alternative treatment—Laetrile—would be a violation of the Act.

The Idaho Supreme Court reverses the District Court, holding that any disciplinary action must be done pursuant to notice of the misconduct to the licensee and pursuant to established rules and regulations

IDAHO SUPREME COURT REVIEW OF FINDINGS: The Idaho Supreme Court reversed the District Court's decision, holding that the Board had not exercised its ability to expand the initial legislative definition of nursing prior to the *Tuma* case. Therefore it could not suspend the license of *this* person without a clear warning to Ms. Tuma that the conduct she engaged in—talking with a patient about alternative treatments—was "unprofessional conduct." Furthermore, the Court held that in addition to giving adequate notice to Ms. Tuma of any prohibited conduct, developing specific rules and regulations was also necessary to guide the Board in making judgments concerning any licensee who comes before it for alleged misconduct.

ANALYSIS: The *Tuma* case is an example of many of the points discussed throughout this chapter, including, but not limited to, the importance of protecting the due process rights of nurses in disciplinary actions (notice and adequacy of the hearing) and requiring clear, defined prohibitions of conduct when an adverse outcome—suspension or revocation of a license—may take place. The case also illustrates the interplay between the legislature and the entities it creates. It is not enough to be given the power to do something; rather, the agency, board, or other entity created must do so within the powers given *and* in a nonarbitrary manner.

those individuals who meet certain require-ments so that those individuals can legally prac-tice nursing.[58] The board or agency establishes the requirements through its statutory authority (the nurse practice act itself) as well as through developed standards, rules, and regulations. The requirements for initial licensure application usually include completion of or graduation from an approved nursing program; obtaining a passing score on the licensing examination; and proof of good character, age, and citizenship. If the applicant does not meet one or more of the requirements, the board or agency can, of course, deny the applicant the professional reg-istered nurse license or the practical nurse li-cense. Adverse decisions have been the subject of many cases by those denied a license. How-ever, unless the unfavorable agency decision falls into one of the categories listed in Table 15–1, it will be upheld upon judicial review.

In addition to applications for *initial* licensure, the board or regulatory agency also has juris-diction to make licensure decisions for those professional and licensed practical nurses who seek licensure in that state after a license was granted in another state or foreign country. Al-though the manner in which the state grants an individual a license may vary, the four options available to the state agency are endorsement, reciprocity, waiver (or "grandfathering"), and examination.[59]

Although the manner in which the state grants an individual a license may vary, the four options available to the state agency are endorsement, reciprocity, waiver (or "grandfathering"), and examination.

Endorsement and reciprocity differ. *Endorse-ment* refers to the process of granting a license after an evaluation of whether the individual already granted a license in another state, and *those* requirements, satisfy the requirements in the state where the application is pending.[60] *Re-ciprocity*, on the other hand, is the process of granting a license when two states have exactly the same licensing requirements. There are no such actual agreements in reality,[61] however, and therefore the overall manner in which most, if not all, nurses receive a license in another state after initial licensure is by way of endorsement.

Licensing powers of boards of nursing or reg-ulatory agencies also may include the ability to grant temporary licenses, place a license on inactive status, and renew licenses during estab-lished renewal periods.[62] Clearly, these powers, when granted to the board, also include the ability to establish rules and regulations to carry out these responsibilities.

The licensing of foreign nurses in the United States has been the subject of much controversy and litigation. The debate has centered on quali-fications and the need for the foreign nurse to be proficient in English. As a result of these concerns, most state nursing practice acts re-quire a certificate by the Commission on Gradu-ates of Foreign Nursing Schools (CGFNS) evi-dencing proficiency in English and satisfactory educational preparation before a license in that state will be issued.[63]

Rule-Making

The board of nursing or regulatory agency's ability to promulgate rules and regulations is usually founded in the state's administrative procedure act and respective administrative law decisions. This aspect of board power is vital, for without the option of establishing rules and regulations to carry out the nursing practice act, the board or agency's power would indeed be a hollow one.

To promulgate rules, the governmental agency is required to adopt them in a constitutional manner; that is, with notice to the public, with a hearing for the purpose of allowing for public testimony in support of or against the proposed rules and regulations, and with publication of the final version of the adopted directives in the required reporter.[64]

As has been illustrated in many of the cases reviewed in this chapter, the rules and regulations adopted by the regulatory agency can be challenged, but will withstand such a test unless the action taken, or the rule or regulation, is invalidated by the reviewing court.

Regulation of Advanced Practice

The ability of the state board of nursing or regulatory agency to regulate advanced nursing practice—the practice of clinical nurse specialists, nurse-midwives, nurse practitioners, and nurse anesthetists—has been the subject of much debate, not only within the nursing profession, but also between the nursing profession and other professional groups.[65] The American Nurses' Association has been involved in this debate, not only in relation to supporting the ability of prepared nurses to practice in expanded roles, but also in relation to how specific nursing practice acts should be in regulating expanded roles.

Specifically the American Nurses' Association's position is that the state nurse practice act should give authority to the board or regulatory agency only to "prescribe the manner in which specialists and other nurses desiring to restrict their practice to a particular area of nursing announce their practice to the public."[66] Certification, adopting rules for the practice of advanced nurse practitioners, and establishing categories of advanced nurse practitioners should rest with the professional associations, and doing so in a nurse practice act is seen as restricting the nursing practice of advanced and nonadvanced practitioners.[67] Even so, many state nurse practice acts establish categories of advanced practitioners, certify them, adopt rules for their practice, and/or define education and other qualifications for specialty practice.[68]

SUMMARY OF PRINCIPLES AND APPLICATIONS

Most nurses are familiar with liability principles related to professional negligence and attempt to practice their profession with those principles in mind. Equally important, however, is the value of the nurse's nursing license and potential liability the nurse faces if there is an alleged violation of the nursing practice act.

A registered nurse or licensed practical nurse possesses a "property interest" in his or her license, meaning that it has value in terms of ownership, utilization, and possession.[69] The federal or state government cannot deprive an individual of life, liberty, or property without due process of law.[70] Therefore the government cannot limit or take that interest away without clear due process protections being afforded the owner of the property interest. When a nurse is accused of conduct that may result in his or her license being disciplined, fairness and justice must surround the proceedings to protect the nurse's clear "property interest" in that license from being transgressed.

If there are allegations that the nurse has violated one or more of the act's provisions, and those allegations are proven, it is clear that the professional or licensed practical nurse will be disciplined in some way. Because the nurse's very livelihood is at stake when a disciplinary action is pending, the nurse should avoid, insofar as humanly possible, any potential violation of the state nurse practice act by:

▼ Understanding the history and purpose of nurse practice acts generally

▼ Knowing the state nurse practice act, and its rules and regulations, in the state(s) in which she or he is licensed

▼ Obtaining legal counsel if an action by the state board of nursing or state regulatory agency is taken against the nurse

▼ Obtaining updates on cases decided by state courts and/or regulatory agencies concerning nursing practice and the nurse practice act

▼ Taking an active role in the professional associations of the nurse's choice, especially in relation to nursing practice issues

▼ Taking an active role in the legislative process, especially in relation to nursing practice issues, by writing legislators and providing testimony about pending bills or amendments to current statutory law

▼ Attending nursing board or committee meetings on a regular basis

▼ Considering applying for a position on the state board of nursing or committee and, if appointed, serving as a member of the board or committee, or suggesting names of nurse colleagues to serve on the nursing board or committee

TOPICS FOR FURTHER INQUIRY

1. Design a study to compare the following state practice acts in terms of similar provisions covering scope of practice, delegation and supervision, promulgated rules and regulations, and grounds for discipline: nursing practice act, pharmacy practice act, medical practice act, and social work practice act.

2. Interview a nurse or practical nurse who has been disciplined by the state regulatory agency for his or her impressions of the due process protections present during the process.

3. Obtain minutes of the meetings of the state nursing board or regulatory agency through the state Freedom of Information Act and analyze actions taken by the board or agency.

4. Interview a state legislator supportive of nursing practice and identify the various successes and failures experienced by the legislator in attempting to change the act through the legislative process.

REFERENCES

1. U.S.C.A. Const. Amend. 10: "The powers not delegated to the United States by the Constitution, nor prohibited by it to the States, are reserved to the States respectively, or to the people."
2. Clare LeBar. *Boards of Nursing: Composition, Member Qualifications and Statutory Authority.* Kansas City: American Nurses' Association Center for Research, 1985, 2, *citing* Council of State Governments. *Occupational Licensing: Centralizing State Licensing Functions.* Lexington, Ky: The Council, 1980, 1.
3. *Id.*
4. Bonnie Bullough, "Introduction—Nursing Practice Law," in *Nursing Issues and Nursing Strategies for the Eighties.* Edited by Bonnie Bullough, Vern Bullough, and Mary Claire Soukup. New York: Springer Publishing Company, 1983, 279.
5. *Id.*
6. Bonnie Bullough, Editor. *The Law and the Expanding Nursing Role.* 2nd Edition. New York: Appleton-Century-Crofts, 1980, 47–50; see also Elizabeth Hadley, "Nurses and Prescriptive Authority: A Legal and Economic Analysis," XV Numbers 2 & 3, *American Journal of Law & Medicine* (1989), 245–299.
7. Bullough, *supra* note 6, at 47.
8. Hadley, *supra* note 6, at 249.
9. "Levels of Nursing Practice," *Nurses Handbook of Law and Ethics.* Springhouse, Pa: Springhouse Corporation, 1992, 3.
10. American Nurses' Association. *Suggestions for Major Provisions to be Included in a Nursing Practice Act.* Kansas City, Mo: ANA, 1943.
11. American Nurses' Association. *Educational Preparation for Nurse Practitioners and Assistants to Nurses.* Kansas City, Mo: ANA, 1955.
12. American Nurses' Association. *The Nursing Practice Act: Suggested State Legislation.* Kansas City, Mo: ANA, 1981.
13. Clare LaBar. *Statutory Definitions of Nursing Practice and Their Conformity to Certain ANA Principles.* Kansas City, Mo: ANA, 1983, 51.
14. Bullough, *supra* note 4, at 283.
15. American Nurses' Association. *Suggested State Legislation: Nursing Practice Act, Nursing Disciplinary Diversion Act, and Prescriptive Authority Act.* Kansas City, Mo: ANA, 1990.
16. *Id.* at 13.
17. *Id.*
18. Karen Hawley Henry, "Nursing Licensure, Requirements and Standards of Practice", in *Nursing Administration and Law Manual.* Edited by Patricia Younger and Cynthia Conner. Rockville, Md: Aspen Publishers, Inc., 1987, 6:8.
19. Clare LeBar. *Enforcement of the Nursing Practice Act.* Kansas City, Mo: ANA, 1986, 2.
20. See also Randolph Reaves. *The Law of Professional Licensing and Certification.* 2d Edition. Montgomery, Ala, 1993, 160.
21. 436 N.Y.S. 2d 465, *appeal dismissed,* 446 N.Y.S. 2d 1024 (1981).
22. ANA, *Suggested State Legislation: Nursing Practice Act,*

Nursing Disciplinary Diversion Act, Prescriptive Authority Act, supra note 15, at 24.

23. LeBar, *Enforcement of the Nursing Practice Act, supra* note 19, at 3.

24. 757 P. 2d 1167 (Colo. Ct. App. 1988).

25. LaBar, *Enforcement Of The Nursing Practice Act, supra* note 19, at 3.

26. Public Law 99–660, 42 U.S.C.A. Section 11101 *et seq.* (1986); Public Law 100–93, 42 U.S.C.A. Section 132-a–5 *et seq.* (1987).

27. Telephone interview with Ms. Vicki Sheets, RN, JD, Director of Public Policy, Nursing Practice and Education, National Council of State Boards of Nursing, Inc. (March 18, 1991).

28. 459 A.2d 877 (Pa. Cmwlth. 1983).

29. LaBar, *Enforcement of the Nursing Practice Act, supra* note 19, at 3.

30. *Id.* at Table 5.

31. Connie Connell and Juanita Murphy, "New Dimensions of Regulating the Practice of Professional Nursing," 18(8) *Nursing Management* (August 1987), 62–64.

32. *Id.* at 63.

33. Eleanor Sullivan, LeClair Bissell, and Etta Williams. *Chemical Dependency in Nursing: The Deadly Diversion.* Menlo Park, Calif: Addison-Wesley Publishing Company (1988), 173–174. See also, Elanor Sullivan, "Chemical Dependency in the Nursing Profession," 39(10) *AAOHN Journal* (1991), 474–477.

34. Marty Jessup and Jean Sullivan, "Community-Based Programs: Two California Models for Intervention," and Jean Penny, Anne Catanzarite, and Judie Ritter, "Florida's Alternative to Disciplinary Action," *in Addiction in the Nursing Profession.* Edited by Mary R. Haack and Tonda Hughes. New York: Springer Publishing Company, 1989, 35–49, 50–63.

35. See American Nurses' Association, *Suggested State Legislation: Nurse Practice Act, Nurse Disciplinary Diversion Act, Prescriptive Authority Act, supra* note 15, at 29–34; National Nurses' Society on Addictions, *Statement on Model Diversion Legislation for Chemically Impaired Nurses.* Evanston, Ill: NNSA, 1991.

36. LaBar, *supra* note 19, at 13.

37. *Richardson v. Brunelle*, 398 A. 2d 838 (1979).

38. *Stevens v. Blake*, 456 So. 2d 793 (Ala. Civ. App. 1984).

39. *Woods v. District of Columbia Nurses' Examining Board*, 436 A. 2d 369 (D.C. App. 1981).

40. 471 A. 2d 1339 (Pa. Comm. 1984), *rev'd. in part, remanded in part*, 499 A. 2d 289 (Pa. 1985), *on remand*, 505 A. 2d 357 (Pa. Comwlth. 1986).

41. 68 *Illinois Administrative Code*, Chapter I, Subchapter a, Part 110 (Rules of Practice in Administrative Hearings), Section 110.190 (1983).

42. *Id.*

43. Geoffrey Hazard and Cameron Beard, "A Lawyer's Privilege against Self-Incrimination in Disciplinary Proceedings," *The Yale Law Journal*, 1060, 1061 (1987).

44. 457 So. 2d 931 (Miss. 1984).

45. 484 So. 2d 857 (La. App. 1986).

46. 244 N.W. 2d 683 (Neb. 1976).

47. 387 So. 2d 454 (Fl. 1980).

48. 436 A. 2d 369 (D.C. App. 1981).

49. 304 N.Y.S. 2d 693 (1969).

50. 651 S.W. 2d 109 (Ark. 1983).

51. 225 ILCS 65/26 (1988).

52. *Id.*

53. *Alabama Board of Nursing v. Herrick*, 454 So. 2d 1041 (Ala. Civ. App. 1984).

54. *Leggett v. Tennessee Board of Nursing*, 612 S.W. 2d 476 (Tenn. App. 1981); *Leigh v. Board of Registration*, 481 N.E. 2d 1347 (Mass. 1985).

55. 593 P. 2d 711 (Idaho 1979).

56. LeBar, *Boards of Nursing, supra* note 2, at 33.

57. *Id.* at 44; American Nurses' Association, *Suggested State Legislation, supra* note 15, at 19–20.

58. Henry, *supra* note 18, at 6:2.

59. American Nurses' Association, *Suggested State Legislation, supra* note 15, at 15–18.

60. *Id.*

61. *Id.* at 16.

62. LeBar, *Boards of Nursing, supra* note 2, at 50–59.

63. LeBar, *supra* note 2, at 16.

64. Ernest Gellhorn and Ronald Levin. *Administrative Law and Process in a Nutshell.* 3rd Edition. St. Paul, Minn: West Publishing Company, 1990.

65. Sharon A. Brown and Deanna Grimes. Nurse Practitioners and Certified Nurse-Midwives: A Meta-Analysis of Studies on Nurses in Primary Care Roles. Washington, DC: American Nurses' Association, 1993; see, for example, Charles A. Sargent, *Nurse Practitioners and Physician Assistants in the North Central Region: Their Status and Role in Rural Primary Health Care*. Lafayette, Ind: Purdue University, January 1987; *Nurse Practitioners, Physician Assistants and Certified Nurse-Midwives: A Policy Analysis*. Washington, DC: Office of Technology Assessment, December 1986.

66. LeBar, *Boards of Nursing, supra* note 2, at 60.

67. *Id.*

68. *Id.* at 61. Some of those states include Alaska, Wisconsin, California, Florida, Iowa, South Dakota, Tennessee, and Vermont. See also "Annual Update of How Each State Stands on Legislative Issues Affecting Advanced Nursing Practice" in the January issue of *The Nurse Practitioner*, appearing yearly.

69. Henry Campbell Black. *Black's Law Dictionary.* 6th Edition. St. Paul, Minn: West Publishing Company, 1991, 845–846.

70. U.S.C.A. Const. Amend. 5 and U.S.C.A. Const. Amend. 14 respectively.

16

The Nurse As Employee

According to recent figures, there are approximately 1.8 million licensed registered professional nurses in the United States who are employed.[1] The work settings of the nurses are varied: the majority work in hospitals, 7% in nursing homes, and the remainder in community health, ambulatory care, and in other health care delivery settings.[2] A breakdown of 1990 figures revealed that 68% of nurses held staff positions, 12% occupied first and middle level nurse manager positions, and 5% functioned as nurse executives.[3]

The figures clearly indicate that most nurses are employees; that is, one who (1) works for another under a contract of hire, whether express, implied, written, or oral; (2) is paid a salary or wages; and (3) is under the power or control of the employer insofar as the details and means of how the work to be done is accomplished.[4]

Being employed implies that the work performed occurs within an employer-employee relationship. That relationship is affected and influenced by many factors, not the least of which is the law. Countless federal and state statutes, rules and regulations, case law, and common law shape the employment relationship in such areas as "terms and conditions of employment," employee privacy, wages and salaries, and safety in the workplace.

This chapter will explore the employment relationship and its legal components, including employment status, fair employment practices, employee benefits, and labor relations. In addition, special considerations such as the right to refuse an assignment and employee access to personnel records will be reviewed.

EMPLOYMENT STATUS

A health care delivery system delivers patient care through its employees. Nurses comprise a large segment of employees in any health care

KEY PRINCIPLES
At-Will Employment
Wrongful/Retaliatory Discharge
Equal Employment Opportunity Laws
Occupational Health and Safety
Labor Relations
Termination of Employment
Employee Compensation and Benefits
Employee Privacy and Confidentiality
Human Resource/Personnel Records

system. Generally speaking, those nurses are one of two types of employees—an at-will or contractual employee.

The number of nurse employees who have a contract of employment with an employing entity is low. This is due to the fact that customarily only nurse executives (the chief nurse officer), advanced nurse practitioners (a nurse anesthetist or nurse-midwife), and nurse faculty, as examples, may have contracts of employment. The rationale for nurse executives, advanced nurse practitioners, and nurse faculty entering into an employment contract is due, in part, to the different roles and responsibilities of these groups.

Nurse executives, for example, may find an employment contract helpful in fulfilling responsibilities in a changing work environment without fear of losing their job.[5] Factors such as health care competition, physician discomfort, and risk taking may stifle health care executives without some assurance that their position is more secure than without the employment con-

RELATED TOPICS	
Chapter 6	Other Torts and Civil Rights
Chapter 9	Contract Law
Part 3	Legal Concerns of Nurses in Diverse Roles and Settings

tract.[6] Likewise, advanced nurse practitioners, who function in a more independent role than their staff nurse colleagues, also need to be able to exercise their decision-making without unnecessary fear of losing their job. Similarly, nurse faculty (particularly those without tenure) are often hired on a year-to-year basis (or for some other limited time frame). This type of arrangement is beneficial to the academic institution in being able to rely on the nurse faculty's services for a particular academic time period.

In contrast, staff nurses, nurse managers, and nurses in other health care organizations rarely, if ever, are given the opportunity to negotiate a contract of employment. That is not to say that their responsibilities are less important than those who do have employment contracts. Rather, the common law has generally treated employees as at-will workers, and most nurses are no exception to this general rule.

At-Will Employment Doctrine

This doctrine originated in England and was adopted by the American legal system as early as 1908.[7] Briefly stated, it protects both the employer and the employee's right to terminate their relationship at any time for any reason.[8] Because the relationship is one of indefinite duration (assuming, of course, no agreement to the contrary), it can be ended "at the will" of either party for a good reason, a bad reason, or for no reason.[9] When the termination occurs pursuant to this doctrine, no legal liability will occur.[10]

Under this doctrine, then, a nurse could be terminated by the employer, and the nurse would not be able to successfully challenge the loss of the job. This would be true regardless of the (1) length of time the nurse had been an employee in the institution; (2) quality of work performed; and (3) lack of notice. The doctrine also allows a nurse to leave a position without being *legally* required to provide a requested period of notice to the employer. Although the nurse employee may want to do so because it is professional and responsible to do so, he or she is not under a legal obligation to do so.

[The at-will employment doctrine] protects both the employer and the employee's right to terminate their relationship at any time for any reason.

The at-will employment doctrine is not absolute, however. Several exceptions exist. They are important because, if present, the nurse or the employer can challenge the discontinuation of the employment relationship. The challenge to the termination of employment is brought under various names, including wrongful discharge and retaliatory discharge.

The exceptions to the at-will employment doctrine include federal or state statutes that invalidate the doctrine; the "public policy" exception; the existence of an implied contract of employment; and a lack of "good faith and fair dealing" by the employer.[11]

Exceptions to the at-will employment doctrine include a contract of employment when the discharge is in violation of a public policy or when the termination is discriminatory (e.g., based on gender or religion).

Federal or State Statutes That Invalidate the Doctrine

This category of exceptions includes many federal and state laws that will be discussed in detail in the following sections of this chapter. Therefore they are listed only briefly in Table 16–1.

TABLE 16–1

Federal and State Statutes Nullifying At-Will Employment Doctrine

LAW	STATE OR FEDERAL	PROTECTION AFFORDED
Labor Relations Management Act (includes National Labor Relations Act of 1935 and Taft-Hartley Amendents of 1947)[12]	Federal	Union employees cannot be discharged in violation of union contract; no employee can be terminated if exercising rights of mutual aid and protection of working conditions
Whistle-blowing acts	Federal & state	Public and private employees cannot be terminated for reporting certain employer conduct (e.g., illegal activity) to identified agencies
Equal employment opportunity laws	Federal & state	Prohibits termination if employee is a member of protected class and termination based on that characteristic; examples include age, gender, religion, disability
Laws requiring termination only for ''just cause''	State	Termination can occur only for reasons listed in law (e.g., failure to do job or theft of employer's property)

Data from: Kenneth Sovereign. *Personnel Law.* 3rd Edition. Englewood Cliffs, NJ: Prentice-Hall, 1994, 171–185; Robert Miller. *Problems in Health Care Law.* 7th Edition. Rockville, Md: Aspen Publishers, Inc., 1996, 234–251.

Public Policy Exception

This exception states that an employer does not have a right to terminate an employee who refuses to participate in illegal activity at the request of the employer or who exercises a protected right (e.g., filing a worker's compensation claim). This limitation on the employer's ability to terminate an employee "at will" is narrowly drawn by most courts, however. For a nurse employee to successfully use this challenge, the nurse must show that (1) the protected conduct is rooted in law and not the result of the nurse's definition of the "public good"; (2) a "clear mandate" of public policy exists; and (3) the concern motivating the nurse's particular conduct must be within the "public interest," not just a "private" concern.[13]

Examples of court cases illustrating these three requisites are numerous and depict varying outcomes:

▼ A New Jersey court upheld the firing of a nurse who worked in the dialysis unit when she refused to dialyze a patient she believed might die if the procedure was done. The nurse argued that the American Nurses' Association *Code of Ethics* supported her refusal to perform the treatment because of its requirement to provide care with respect for human dignity and the nature of the health problem (Principle 1). The court held the *Code*, although possibly rising to a "public policy" protection, generally serves to protect the interests of the *profession*, not the public. As such, the *Code* could not be relied on to protect the public. This was especially true in this case, the court held, in which neither the patient nor his family objected to the dialysis (*Warthen v. Toms River Community Memorial Hospital*).[14]

▼ A North Carolina court ruled that the firing of a nurse anesthetist was a wrongful termination because she refused to provide false testimony at a deposition when instructed to do so by her employer. The nurse anesthetist had witnessed the cardiopulmonary arrest and death of a young boy in the OR. The parents alleged negligence on the part of the anesthesiologist. When the nurse testified truthfully at the deposition, she was fired. The court opined that a firing for refusing to do something unlawful was against public policy (*Sides v. Duke University Medical Center*).[15]

▼ A psychiatric nurse in Illinois, concerned

about the care received by patients at a psychiatric hospital, reported her concerns to a state agency responsible for monitoring the care of the mentally ill and those with guardians. She was terminated from her position. She filed a wrongful discharge suit alleging that her firing was due to the report and cited the public policy section of the Illinois statute that protected reporters from retaliation when they communicated concerns to the state agency. The employer argued that her termination was due to the mistreatment of patients, insubordination, and other misconduct. The court held the nurse was wrongfully discharged as a result of the sharing of information with the state agency and sent the case back to the trial court. Despite this favorable ruling, the trial court did not reinstate the nurse to her former position. Because the nurse's services were of a *personal* nature (and not for *goods* or *products*), the court refused to require an employer-employee relationship to be reinstated.

Furthermore, the court held, reinstatement to a position was not a specific remedy in the reporting sections in the Illinois law relied on by the nurse. In addition, the court held that since the trial court entered a finding of fact that the nurse's conduct as alleged by the employer was true, requiring reinstatement of the nurse to her position and awarding damages to her was not supportable *(Witt v. Forest Hospital).*[16]

Additional examples of wrongful discharge include terminating the nurse's employment when the nurse serves as a juror, files a worker's compensation claim, or reports information to law enforcement authorities.

Implied Contract of Employment

This exception is one that is used with increasing frequency in recent years to destroy the presumption of an employment relationship for an indefinite period. An employer's conduct, communications, and documents can be used by an employee to support his or her understanding that the employee was hired for a *definite* period of time. If the nurse employee is able to show sufficient evidence of a definite period of employment, the court can hold that an implied contract of employment exists. If an implied contract is found to exist, then dismissal can occur only pursuant to the terms of that implied contract.

An implied contract can be formed orally, through written documents, or through established employment practices. For example, during the job interview, a nurse may be told that if the job is done correctly, the nurse will have the position for life.[17] Or, a nurse may be assured that the position accepted would last until the nurse reaches retirement.[18] Likewise, oral assurances of promotions, bonuses, employee benefits, and a course of employer conduct over a long period of time have also been found to support terms of an implied employment contract.[19]

Written communications to employees can also be helpful in deciding if an implied contract of employment exists. In several reported cases, an internal memorandum, a letter to the employee concerning a bonus, and policies and procedures depicting standard operating procedures within the organization have been successfully used by employees to establish implied contract terms in the employment relationship.[20]

Perhaps the most widely known written document used to establish an implied contract of employment is the employee handbook or manual. Since the 1970s, courts have consistently evaluated employee handbooks for clear language of enforceable promises within the employment relationship.[21]

Although not a guarantee of a successful challenge to an at-will termination, nurse employees have used employee handbook language to file suits alleging violation of promises contained in them:

▼ The Illinois Supreme Court held that a nurse was terminated in violation of the protections afforded in the employee handbook. The nurse was fired without "prior written notice" (including three warnings) or an investigation that was required for all nonprobationary employees. The Court stated that the handbook created a contract because it contained clear language offering something to the nurse employee, that she was aware of the offer, and that she accepted the offer by continuing to work as a nurse employee under those conditions *(Duldulao v. St. Mary of Nazareth Hospital).*[22]

▼ An Arizona appellate court ordered that a case involving a director of nursing go back to the trial court for a trial on the issue of, among other things, whether the employee handbook created an employment contract. The director of nursing alleged that her termination was wrongful because the employer discharged her after she requested to be placed in her former supervisory position. The trial court had entered a summary judgment (no material issue of fact) in favor of the employer and the nurse appealed *(Liekvold v. Valley View Community Hospital).*[23]

▼ An LPN in Nebraska sued her employer alleging a violation of the employee handbook's provisions concerning discharge and asking for reinstatement. Those provisions mandated certain policies and procedures to be followed in the event of termination and in the event the employee grieved that decision. According to the evidence presented, the LPN had been terminated for dishonesty because she did not renew her LPN license but falsely told the employer she had done so. Even so, the Nebraska Supreme Court held that the terms of the handbook did not guarantee the LPN continued employment. The court did hold, however, that the terms did rise to the status of an implied contract governing grievances and discharge procedures *(Jeffers v. Bishop Clarkson Memorial Hospital).*[24]

It is important to note that this exception to the at-will employment doctrine has been lim-

ited in recent years. When an employee handbook or manual contains a disclaimer, prominently displayed, stating that (1) the handbook is not intended to, nor should it be interpreted as, creating an express or implied contract of employment; (2) the information contained therein is "advisory only"; (3) the employer reserves the right to change or alter the terms in the handbook without notice and for any reason; and (4) the employer reserves the right to fire employees for any or no reason, courts usually rule that there is no violation of the at-will employment doctrine.[25]

Of course, when a disclaimer exists, the particular facts and circumstances of each situation are taken into account by the court. For example, in an Illinois case, the disclaimer contained in the employee handbook effectively eliminated any contract of employment between a nurse and her employer. The employer was free to discharge the nurse "automatically" when she left work without proper authorization to do so.[26]

In contrast, another court held that the one-sentence disclaimer contained in the handbook at issue in the case was not sufficient to support the ability of the hospital to discharge a nurse at will. In *Jones v. Central Peninsula General Hospital,*[27] the employer revised the handbook to include the fact that there was no employment contract established. The earlier manual did not include this disclaimer. Furthermore, the revised manual contained 85 detailed pages of policies and procedures. The court held that because the manual contained many provisions relating to employee rights, the disclaimer was inadequate.[28]

Other Exceptions

A few additional exceptions to the at-will employment doctrine exist although they are not as common as the ones already discussed. One is the "constructive discharge" exception. When this occurs, the employee seemingly has voluntarily resigned from his or her position when, in actuality, a firing took place. For this exception to apply, however, the employer must make working conditions so "intolerable" that the employee really has no choice but to resign.[29]

For example, a nurse employee exposed to constant ridicule, unreasonable assignments, or harassment may resign from the position rather than continue to be subjected to that treatment. If the nurse is able to prove that the employer intentionally made working conditions such that there was no choice but to resign, the nurse may successfully win a suit alleging constructive discharge. The nurse would be entitled to damages and other remedies available to an employee who was, in fact, discharged.[30]

A similar exception to the at-will employment doctrine is the intentional infliction of emotional distress exemption, based on tort theory. The essence of this allegation is that the employer's conduct exceeds all limitations of acceptable behavior and would offend any reasonable person.[31] Most often, these cases arise because of the conduct of a supervisor, manager, or another who has immediate control over the employee and who makes decisions concerning employment conditions.

Insults, disagreements, uncooperativeness, or termination of employment itself has been found *not* to constitute the conduct this exception seeks to prohibit.[32] In contrast, examples of conduct that would most likely result in a verdict in favor of a nurse employee against an employer include racial and sexual harassment[33] and describing an employee's spouse's behavior as "adulterous."[34]

Implications of the At-Will Employment Doctrine for Nurse Employees

At-will employment can result in loss of employment when the employee least expects it. Because the doctrine allows for loss of a job without notice in many, if not most, instances, preparation for that possibility by the nurse employee is vital. This requires knowledge of the at-will employment law in the state where the nurse practices. In addition, it is vital that the nurse employee carefully read the employee handbook and possess a clear understanding of the conditions of the employer-employee relationship. If something is unclear, or if the nurse does not agree with a particular stipulation of employment, the nurse must inform the employer. It is best to do so in writing.

If the nurse believes termination of employment took place in violation of the at-will employment doctrine, the nurse can try to grieve the termination through the employer's internal grievance procedures. If not successful, or the nurse believes a grievance is not the course of action he or she should take, seeking legal advice for an opinion concerning the termination is wise. The nurse will need to bring any documents available for the attorney to review (e.g., the employee handbook) and present the facts of the termination clearly and completely.

It is also important for the nurse to be clear about the fact that if possible, any concerns about patient care or employment practices should attempt to be resolved within the employer-employee relationship. Although "whistle blowing" and patient advocacy are valuable processes, indeed necessary in some instances, the possible outcome—the loss of a job—is not always what the former employee anticipated.

EMPLOYEE COMPENSATION AND BENEFIT PROGRAMS

Employee benefit packages and the wages or salary paid to the nurse employee can vary widely from employer to employer. There is little variation, however, in the overall management of both benefits and compensation because these areas are covered by federal and state laws. The employer must comply with the mandates established by federal and state statutes and their rules and regulations. If adherence by the employer does not occur, the employee can use various legal proceedings to obtain his or her rightful benefits under these laws.

Fair Labor Standards Act[35]

This federal law, the Fair Labor Standards Act (FLSA), passed in 1938, established minimum wages, overtime pay (one and one-half of regular pay rate) and maximum hours of employment. The normal work week was defined as 40 hours in 7 days, and based on an 8-hour work day. Non-profit and for-profit employers, including state and local governments, are required to conform to the Act's mandates.[36] Employees who are considered professional, administrative, or "bona fide executives," paid no less than $250/week, and who meet statutory job responsibilities, are exempted from the minimum wage, overtime, and maximum hours of employment requirements.

In addition, the requirement of paying overtime rates to those employees who work in excess of 40 hours a week was altered for health care facility employees providing care to the ill, aged, infirm, or mentally retarded when those patients are staying on the facility's premise. The Act provides for the ability of institutions to enter into agreements with its employees whereby a 14-day work week is the basis for calculating overtime wages. If agreed to, the employer must pay overtime rates to those employees who work in excess of 80 hours in the 14-day period.[37] However, the employer is required to pay overtime rates to the employee for hours worked in excess of 8 hours in any *one* day. This agreement has been called the "8–80" rule or plan.

On-call duty, in which the employee (other than those exempted above) is required to be available, either at the work site or nearby, so that reporting to work is swift when the employee is needed, is also governed by the Fair Labor Standards Act and its rules and regulations. For example, if a perioperative nurse is on call under these circumstances, he or she is usually deemed to be working while on call and is therefore paid for that time, although not at the usual hourly rate of pay.[38] In contrast, if perioperative nurses simply leave word at work where they can be reached and do not have to be immediately required to get to work, payment for work on call is not required.[39]

Section 6 of the Fair Labor Standards Act was amended in 1963. The amendment, called the Equal Pay Act (EPA),[40] added the requirement that no employer could discriminate in the payment of wages on the basis of gender/sex when equal work of equal skill, equal effort, and equal responsibility was done under similar working conditions. The only exceptions to the requirement of equal pay for equal work listed in the Act are seniority, a bona fide merit system, an incentive pay system, or a difference in wage based on a factor other than gender/sex.

The Equal Pay Act has been interpreted through many court decisions. For example, the equal-pay-for-equal-work standard has been interpreted to mean that the jobs being evaluated do not have to be equal, just substantially so.[41] If men are paid a different wage because they perform "extra duties," that difference is discriminatory unless women are offered the chance to perform the same jobs.[42] Also, paying men a different rate than women employees because the men worked the night shift and the women worked days—all doing the same work—was a violation of the Act.[43]

It is important for the reader to remember also that (1) the Fair Labor Standards Act may be supplemented or exceeded by state law mandates; (2) if employees are unionized, the union contract may provide additional protections; (3) no employee is excluded from coverage under the Equal Pay Act whereas some—"bona fide executives," for example—are not covered under the Fair Labor Standards Act.[44]

Enforcement of the Fair Labor Standards Act is done by the Wage and Hour Division of the Division of Labor Standards. The agency can investigate complaints, conduct employer audits, and interview employees.[45] The Division can also bring suit on behalf of the employee, or the employee can do so. Remedies include obtaining unpaid compensation due the employee and reasonable attorney's fees and costs for the suit. If an employer "willfully" violates the federal law, fines and a prison sentence can occur.[46]

A nurse employee may select to pursue a complaint under the state's labor department, especially if the state law provides more protection than the federal statute.

Comparable Pay for Comparable Worth

In recent years, this theory has been promoted as a way to provide further protection to those employees who may not be able to meet the requisites necessary under the Fair Labor Standards Act and the Equal Pay Act, but whose work is of "equal value" to the employer. The comparable worth theory rejects the notion of "equal work" and instead supports equal wages for jobs that are equally important or worthy to the employer. Under this theory, a nurse would receive as much pay as the environmental services department head, for example, because both jobs are of equal importance to the successful functioning of the institution.

The comparable worth concept has been in existence since 1942.[47] It was not fully tested until recently, however, when the number of women in the work force doubled from 1960 to 1983 without concomitant increases in salaries and wages under the current wage and hour laws.[48] The lack of increases in compensation for female workers, supporters argued, was due to the fact that women could not climb up the wage or salary ladder quickly because they had not been in the work force long enough to work in jobs equal to male workers, who had been in the work force for years. Thus, proponents argued, male workers would always be paid more than females because they could not obtain an equal or substantially equal position.

Despite the potential attractiveness of this theory, it has not been supported by the courts, including the United States Supreme Court. Generally the claim of a female worker not receiving the same pay as a male worker has not been successful unless additional proof of the employer's intent to discriminate between male and female workers can also be shown.[49] This position is based on another federal law, Title VII and its Bennett Amendment, which will be discussed later in this chapter.

Deductions from Paycheck

Any deductions taken from an employee's paycheck must be authorized by the employee, usually through written consent. Deductions for health care insurance, a retirement plan, or a savings plan are examples of common deductions.

One deduction that can occur without the employee's consent is a wage garnishment; that is, when a court enters an order to an employer to pay a portion of the employee's (debtor's) paycheck to a creditor until the debt is paid.[50] Many federal and state laws, including The Federal Wage Garnishment Law,[51] control how those deductions take place, their amount, and notice to the employee, and they prohibit the employee from retaliating against the employer for its required compliance with the court order.

Examples of the kinds of wage garnishment that may affect a nurse employee include the nonpayment of child support and the satisfaction of a monetary award to an injured plaintiff (patient) after a professional negligence trial in which the nurse was found to be negligent.

Several other deductions that occur without the employee's consent because they are part of a compulsory program of social insurance for the benefit of older workers, retired workers, disabled workers and their dependents and survivors are due to the Social Security Act of 1935, as amended, and the Federal Insurance Contributions Act (FICA).[52] Covered employers and employees each pay a certain portion of the required amount from payroll taxes. The amount is regulated by Congress, and the employee's contribution is reflected as deductions on the employee's paycheck stub.

Eligibility for particular benefits under the Social Security Program is based on specific prerequisites being met. Whether or not the prerequisites are met for a particular employee is "tracked" by using the employee's social security number. Therefore, the nurse employee needs to ensure the correct social security number is used for each covered employment position.

Health Insurance

Many employers offer the benefit of health/medical insurance to employees. Some employers will pay the entire cost of the employee's coverage, while others require a co-payment from the employee. The benefit may include both a basic medical plan and a major medical option. Coverage for dependents or spouses is not always provided, or if it is, at an additional cost to the employee. Even so, health insurance is a very important employee benefit for many reasons, one of which is its "current" rather than "future" value, such as a retirement benefit package.[53]

There are usually two general types of health plans that may be offered to employees: (1) a prepaid plan, often through a health maintenance organization (HMO) or a preferred provider organization (PPO); or (2) a postpaid plan, in which there is a fee for service.[54] Either may require that a certain amount, a deductible, be met by the employee before the plan begins to pay for health care, as well as require co-insurance payments. Co-insurance payments mean that the plan covers up to a certain percentage of costs—e.g., 80%—with the remainder covered by the employee.[55]

Regardless of the plan provided by the employer, a federal law, The Consolidated Omnibus Budget Reconciliation Act (COBRA),[56] requires employers with 20 or more employees to continue health care benefits to employees who are terminated; laid off, or have a reduction in their work hours; divorced or separated; retire; or who trigger other qualifying events. If an employee is discharged for misconduct (e.g., di-

verting controlled substances from the employer for the nurse employee's own use), or the employer terminates health insurance benefits for all employees, The Consolidated Omnibus Budget Reconciliation Act's continued coverage is not required.[57]

A federal law, The Consolidated Omnibus Budget Reconciliation Act (COBRA), requires employers with 20 or more employees to continue health care benefits to [certain] employees [after termination of their employment status].

The employer must provide notice to the terminated or otherwise qualified employee or beneficiaries concerning their ability to continue to carry health insurance coverage. The employee must pay for the coverage, and continued benefits can occur for the employee for 18 months. Spouses and other dependents can obtain coverage for up to 36 months.[58]

An employee may have more protections under parallel state laws concerning the continuation of health insurance. If state laws provide less protection, however, then The Consolidated Omnibus Budget Reconciliation law controls the continuation of health insurance plans.[59]

Violations of The Consolidated Omnibus Budget Reconciliation Act can result in fines against plan administrators. Various federal agencies, including the Department of Labor and the Internal Revenue Service, are authorized to issue regulations concerning the administration of the Act.[60]

Retirement Plans

Although the Social Security Program is a retirement program, it is not intended to replace a retired employee's entire salary.[61] Thus, supplemental programs, both private and employer sponsored, exist. When a program is employer sponsored, it must comply with the Employee Retirement Income Security Act of 1974 (ERISA).[62]

The Employee Retirement Income Security Act mandates that most employers, with the exception of governmental employers and some church-sponsored plans, comply with its requirements, including nondiscrimination, the provision of a summary plan description (SPD) to employees, the vesting of benefits, and plan terminations.[63]

The Employee Retirement Income Security Act sets minimum protections in the area of pension plans.[64] An employer's program may provide more protections, as may some state laws governing insurance and employment benefits. It also controls other employee benefit plans, including disability, health and medical, and death benefit programs.[65]

The Employee Retirement Income Security Act is an important protection for employees, including nurse employees. It would prohibit, for example, the firing of a nurse immediately before the nurse would vest in an established pension program, if the firing were solely for that purpose. It also requires that the employer transfer vested benefits for the nurse employee from the current plan to the new employer plan.

The Employee Retirement Income Security Act does not, however, necessarily mandate that certain coverage, either in terms of amounts or kinds of coverage, take place, at least in relation to health insurance coverage. In a 1992 case, *Greenberg v. H & H Music Company,*[66] the United States Supreme Court refused to review the 5th Circuit Appeals Court ruling that the employer could change, with proper notice, coverage in its health plan for AIDS from $1 million to $5000 per benefit year.

The Appeals court carefully evaluated The Employee Retirement Income Security Act's legislative intent and its language. The Act never guaranteed particular benefits or coverage, the court opined. In this particular case, the court

continued, no discrimination against the employee or employees with AIDS or a violation of other requirements occurred.[67] Therefore, the employer is free to alter benefits as it sees fit. The Employee Retirement Income Security Act is enforced by the United States Department of Labor, the Internal Revenue Service, and the Pension Benefit Guaranty Corporation.

Workers' Compensation

Workers' compensation laws have been in existence in the United States since the late nineteenth and twentieth centuries.[68] At that time, the rapid growth of businesses and industry during the Industrial Revolution gave rise to safety concerns in the workplace. Many believed that caring for employees injured at work was a duty of the respective states.[69]

Workers' compensation [and unemployment compensation] laws have been in existence in the United States since the late nineteenth and twentieth centuries.

Employers, however, did not agree with this viewpoint, because they would have to contribute monies into a fund to cover workers' injuries. Several states attempted to pass workers' compensation laws in the early 1900s, but they were struck down as being a violation of the employer's due process rights. Wisconsin's law, passed in 1911, withstood constitutional challenge,[70] however, and set the stage for other states to pass similar protections for workers.[71]

Currently, all states have some form of workers' compensation laws, covering all *employees* (those who are independent contractors and domestic workers are usually excluded). Federal civilian employees are covered by the Federal Employees Compensation Act,[72] and another federal law is applicable to maritime workers.

In either case, their purpose is to provide a means for employees who are injured during their job to obtain compensation for those injuries. Costs for coverage, whether by self-insurance or private insurance, are borne entirely by the employer. Compensation can include claims for the cost of medical care, rehabilitation, monies for the "partial" or "total disability" the worker suffers (thus rendering the employee unable to work for a particular time or unable to return to work at all), and death benefits.

Workers' compensation laws are relatively untouched by federal law. As such, they vary widely. Even so, some generalities can be made about them. One generality is the purpose of such laws, presented in Table 16–2.

Second, the types of injuries or illnesses covered by state workers' compensation laws are fairly uniform. Customarily, accidental injuries "arising out of and during the course of employment" are compensable under workers' compensation laws.[73] These requirements have understandably been the subject of much controversy in the state workers' compensation systems. Examples of injuries and illnesses seen as meeting that standard include:

▼ Injuries sustained by a nurse who was attacked by a patient at Florida State Hospital prior to the beginning of her shift while waiting to pick up a key for her ward[74]

▼ Death benefits to the spouse of a nurse who died after suffering a heart attack at work that was the result of a stressful job[75]

▼ Stab wounds sustained by a nurse in a Louisiana hospital elevator on her way to work the night shift[76]

▼ Ankle fracture suffered by an LPN in an automobile accident on her way to an assigned patient's home for care[77]

Illnesses sustained under the same conditions would also be covered under workers' compensation laws. Such illnesses would include psy-

---

TABLE 16–2

Purposes of Workers' Compensation Laws

1. Provide payment and other benefits without regard to the respective fault of the employer or employee
2. Provide payment and other benefits without regard to the financial circumstances of the employer
3. Reduce lengthy litigation, litigation costs, and attorneys fees by avoiding blame for the injury or illness
4. Reduce the economic drain on governments by having the employer pay for work-related injuries and illnesses
5. Encourage employers to continually improve working conditions to avoid paying for work-related injuries or illnesses
6. Promote honest evaluation(s) of work-related illnesses and injuries so continual improvement of working conditions occurs
7. Limit the employer's liability under the laws to injuries or illnesses that arise out of and during the course of employment
8. Require employees to give up right to sue employer for any covered work-related injury (but allows judicial review of decisions)
9. Mandate employee claims be handled through a state agency (industrial commission or workers' compensation board) rather than through the courts
10. Allow the employee to file suit against defendants other than the employer who might be responsible for the injury or illness (e.g., the manufacturer of patient equipment alleged to be the cause of the injury)

Data from: Kenneth Sovereign. *Personnel Law.* 3rd Edition. Englewood Cliffs, NJ: Prentice-Hall, 1994, 232–233; Jeffrey Nackley. *Primer on Workers' Compensation.* 2nd Edition. Washington, DC: Bureau of National Affairs, 1989, 1–9.

---

chiatric or mental diseases. They would also include the contracting of illnesses or diseases, including contagious diseases such as AIDS, hepatitis, or tuberculosis, as a result of caring for patients.

Pre-existing medical injuries are also usually covered when those conditions are "aggravated" or "exacerbated." The distinction is important for the employee. An aggravation of a pre-existing injury most often results in an acknowledgment of the entire medical problem. In contrast, an exacerbation of a pre-existing injury is seen as compensable to the worker during its flare-up.[78]

Exclusions of injuries or illnesses under the state workers' compensation laws can include (1) those not arising out of and during the course of employment (for example, a nurse leaves the facility at lunch to go to the bank to cash a personal check and is injured); (2) self-inflicted injuries or illnesses (a nurse attempts suicide at his or her place of employment); (3) an injury or illness sustained under the influence of drugs or alcohol; and (4) willful misconduct or violation of a safety rule (a psychiatric nurse intentionally goes into a seclusion patient's room alone—in violation of an established unit policy—and is attacked by the patient).[79]

Unemployment Compensation

Unemployment compensation had its origins in trade union benefit plans; the earliest plan was founded in 1831 by a New York local trade union.[80] However, by the early 1900s attempts were made to require state governments to provide benefits for a limited amount of time to those employees who were out of work through no fault of their own.

In 1932, Wisconsin passed the first compulsory unemployment compensation plan. Shortly thereafter, when the federal government included unemployment compensation in the Social Security Act and stated it would set minimum standards for the programs unless states did so, all states passed laws governing their state's program.[81]

Federal involvement still exists in state unemployment compensation programs, however, mainly in the form of contributions to the state programs. Generally, the Internal Revenue Service (IRS) assesses a special payroll tax on wages paid by employers to employees, as does the state. In this framework, which exists in all but three states, money paid into the unemployment compensation system is entirely funded with *no* contributions from employees. In two states, Alaska and New Jersey, employees *also* contribute to the fund.[82]

It is important to note that the system, although clearly established to benefit employees who are temporarily out of work, has a built-in adversarial component between employer and employee. The employer's payroll tax rate is increased by the regulatory agency or agencies as more unemployment benefits are paid out to former employees. In contrast, if an employer has few, if any, benefits paid out to former employees, the payroll tax rate remains the same. Thus, a common approach by employers is to contest unemployment compensation claims.

Like workers' compensation laws, unemployment compensation laws vary widely from state to state. Some similarities do exist, however, and they are listed in Table 16–3.

Each state unemployment compensation law also delineates those employees who are not eligible for unemployment compensation benefits. They include:

- Employees who leave work voluntarily without good reason
- Employees who are terminated for misconduct at work
- Employees who refuse to accept suitable work without good cause
- Employees who are on strike

The ineligibility categories are understandably the focus of employer–employee contests when a former employee files for unemployment compensation. After applying for benefits at the state agency (e.g., bureau of employment security or department of labor and employment), the employer receives notice of the filing and the initial determination of the agency. If the employer wishes to contest a granting of benefits, or the employee decides to contest a denial of benefits, a hearing is held with both parties present. After that determination is made, most states usually provide for additional appeals within the agency or department.

Nurse employees have been involved in unemployment compensation cases. In one case, refusing to accept suitable work without good cause was successfully argued by the former employer of a nurse who quit her job because she refused to take a position on the night shift.[83]

In *Taylor v. Burley Care Center*,[84] the charge

TABLE 16–3

Components of Many Unemployment Compensation Laws

- Employees covered include: part-time and full-time; private, federal, state, and local government; executives, officers, and "rank-and-file"
- Workers not covered: independent contractors; children who work for their parents; individuals who work for their children or spouse; self-employed
- Employee must be out of work through no fault of own; be able to work; be willing to work; and satisfy "base period" specified in state law
- Employee cannot receive unemployment compensation until other received benefits (e.g., vacation and severance pay) no longer paid
- Benefits exist for specified period only (e.g., 32 weeks) and include a certain percentage of employee's pay
- Waiting period for benefits, if employee is eligible, must also be satisfied (e.g., 1 week after application)
- Employee must apply for benefits at local agency office; employer *does not* do so for employee
- Judicial review of final decision by agency

Data from: James W. Hunt. *The Law of the Workplace: Rights of Employers and Employees.* 3rd Edition. Washington, DC: The Bureau of National Affairs, 1994, 98–105; William F. McHugh, "Law and the Workplace," in *You And The Law.* Lincolnwood, Ill: Publications International, Inc., 1990, 430–435 (An American Bar Association Consumer Guide Book).

nurse, Helen Taylor, was denied unemployment benefits because of misconduct while at work. Her employer submitted proof that Ms. Taylor refused to meet with her superiors to discuss her "poor work performance and attitude" without her sister's presence. The sister was a nurse at another facility and the Director of Nursing's position was that confidentiality would be breached if discussions about patients took place in front of the sister.

The Director of Nursing attempted to alleviate Ms. Taylor's fears of discussing her work performance with her alone by scheduling a meeting with the administrator also present. Ms. Taylor refused to meet with anyone other than her sister and the Director of Nursing. She was terminated and applied for benefits; they were denied.

When Ms. Taylor asked the Supreme Court of Idaho to review the denial of benefits by the state agency, the court upheld the decision. The

test for misconduct in Idaho, the court held, was whether the employee's conduct fell below the standard expected by the employer and if the employer's standard was a reasonable one. In this case, both tests were met.

And, in *Clarke v. North Detroit General Hospital*,[85] two nurses who were terminated from their positions because they failed to pass the nursing board examinations were granted unemployment compensation benefits. The employer argued that they left work voluntarily without good reason attributable to the employer. The nurses argued that they did not leave voluntarily.

The Michigan Supreme Court agreed with the nurses, holding that they did not fail the examinations purposefully. In addition, it rebuffed the hospital's claims that it could not allow the nurses to continue working because only *licensed* nurses could be hired pursuant to various Michigan laws, including the Michigan nurse practice act. Although the latter was true, the court continued, that fact was not the test for denying unemployment benefits.

Implications of Employee Benefits for the Nurse Employee

Most employees do not have ready access to their respective rights and responsibilities in relation to employee benefits. Obtaining information about those concerns, however, can be achieved by contacting the human resource department at the workplace. The nurse can also contact the state or federal agency responsible for enforcing the particular employee benefit. The agency is listed in the telephone book, usually in the state (or federal) government section.

In addition to obtaining information when needed, the nurse employee should also review any and all documents given to employees by the employer concerning benefits. Any questions about coverage or exclusions can be directed to the human resource or employee benefits department of the institution.

If questions arise concerning wage and hour

issues, or overtime pay, for example, those queries should be directed to the nurse's supervisor. If they are unresolved, additional information can be sought by contacting the employer's payroll department.

When the nurse is injured while working, he or she should be certain to seek treatment for the injury and to comply with any employer-required procedures (e.g., filling out specific forms, seeking additional opinions or treatments). If partially or totally disabled, the nurse should file a compensation claim. Legal counsel can be retained by the nurse if the nurse decides advice or representation is necessary (e.g., the claim is not processed in a timely manner or the nurse is pressured to accept a settlement).

If unemployment occurs, the nurse can file for unemployment compensation and obtain an agency determination concerning his or her eligibility for those benefits. It is important that the nurse supply the state agency with whatever accurate and factual information is available concerning the termination. If the case goes to a hearing, the nurse should be present and be prepared to present any additional information that supports his or her position. This would include witnesses and additional documents (e.g., a copy of the particular employee policy at issue).

EMPLOYEE PERFORMANCE AND DISCIPLINE

The employer has a right to expect that employees will conduct themselves according to certain guidelines when at work and performing their duties. Likewise, employees have a right to know what the parameters of their conduct are and any consequences of not meeting established guidelines. When expectations are not met, discipline of the employee can occur.

Usually the expectations and rights of the employer and employee are spelled out in writing in the employee discipline policy. In addition, the written employee grievance policy affords the employee instruction as to how to contest a disciplinary action and the roles of both in that process.

In some instances the written parameters of an employer-employee disciplinary policy can alter the at-will employment doctrine. That is, the methods for discipline may make it possible for the employer to terminate an employee only for "just cause" rather than for "any" or "no cause." In just cause terminations, then, the employee's conduct must violate the rules of conduct established by the employer in order to be terminated from his or her position. The employee's argument is based on the express or implied contract of employment theory discussed earlier in the chapter.

One consistent way to evaluate employee performance and compliance with expected behaviors, and avoid successful challenges to a termination decision by the employer, is through the use of performance appraisals or employee evaluations.

In some instances, the written parameters of an employer-employee disciplinary policy can alter the at-will employment doctrine.

Performance Appraisals

In the clinical setting, performance evaluations are a way to ensure quality patient care.[86] They also provide valuable data in making decisions concerning nurse employee retention, promotion, and salary.[87] For both uses, however, employee evaluation must be fair and objective.

The forms of performance appraisals are varied. They include, but are not limited to, rating scales, checklists, narrative evaluations, or some combination of these formats. Regardless of their form, the instruments must (1) establish clear, measurable clinical standards; (2) be in writing; (3) provide documentation of representative performance of the staff member; (4) evaluate criteria related to the particular job the nurse is performing in the facility; and (5) provide notification of areas of needed improvement and the consequences if improvement is not seen.[88]

When the nurse employee does not measure up to established standards for clinical performance, or if improvement is not noted, corrective action may be taken against the nurse. Any action taken would be pursuant to the employer disciplinary policy and procedure and could include termination.

Disciplinary Policy and Procedure

Despite the fact that an employer is generally free to terminate an employee at will, many employers have elected to provide a means whereby an employee is given an opportunity to improve his or her conduct before termination takes place. The philosophy behind this approach is to aid in correcting the behavior rather than punish the employee for conduct not consistent with established requirements.[89] The policies are called various names, including corrective action or disciplinary policies. Regardless of the term used, the foundation for the framework consists of a series of steps that lead to termination if improvement is not seen.

A progressive or incremental employee discipline policy provides an employee with one or more warnings concerning unacceptable conduct.[90] The system "progresses" through a series of warnings, each more serious than the former, and informs the employee that unless compliance occurs, the risk of termination is pending.[91]

Although progressive disciplinary policies vary greatly, they are usually comprised of (1) notice of the unacceptable conduct subject to the corrective policy (e.g., sleeping on the job, repeated absenteeism,); (2) the various steps in the policy (e.g., verbal warning, written warnings I and II); (3) the ability to suspend an em-

ployee, with or without pay, pending an investigation into any alleged conduct violative of the policy; (4) any required meetings or conferences with the employee; and (5) how prior, resolved discipline will be used in future actions against the employee (e.g., no use if a period of 1 year is completed without additional violations).

In addition, the policy often specifies when an immediate termination (also called summary termination) can take place for egregious conduct. Examples of behavior that could form the basis for immediate termination include falsification of any record used in patient care, insubordination, theft of facility property (including drugs), and a breach of patient confidentiality.

If a nurse employee believes any disciplinary action taken against him or her is unfair, unfounded, or not consistent with the employer's policies, the nurse can grieve the decision through the grievance procedure.

Grievance Policy and Procedure

A grievance procedure is any process by which an employee may question or appeal a superior's decision affecting job security.[92] The process can be informal or formal and is referred to by many names, including resolution procedures and information exchanges.[93]

Informal systems usually consist of a policy statement in an employee handbook supporting the resolution of differences by encouraging those who are in disagreement to try to resolve their points of view. Sometimes individuals in administration are listed in ascending order for the employee to discuss his or her concerns with. In reality, these types of complaint procedures offer the employee little, if any, potential for resolution of their concerns. As a result, they are often not used by employees.[94]

A formal employee grievance system is more common in the workplace and is composed of a series of steps the employee and employer must progress through in an attempt to resolve their respective differences. Highlights of a formal grievance system include (1) a definition of what is grievable (e.g., *any* employment decision or any decision other than termination); (2) which employees can utilize the system (e.g., probationary employees vs. nonprobationary employees); (3) the steps that must be followed by both parties and any time constraints on the initiation of those steps; (4) whether the grievance must be submitted in writing and, if so, in what manner (human resource form, other requirements); (5) employee rights (e.g., accompaniment of other employee or attorney, presentation of witnesses); and (6) whether the decision in the final step in the procedure (e.g., by outside arbitration, panel of peers randomly selected, board of directors, CEO) is binding.

If the employer-established grievance procedure is fair, provides whatever due process protections should be afforded to the employee in the situation, and is not violative of other employee rights (including fair employment protections), the decision will not be reversed by a court. *Khalifa v. Henry Ford Hospital*[95] illustrates this general approach by the courts.

In *Khalifa*, an employee challenged the hospital's grievance procedure by alleging that the procedure was unfair. Specifically, he took the position that the decision of the grievance council (composed of nonsupervisory employees), which was the last step in the procedure, should not be "final and binding."

The court upheld the procedure and the council's determination, holding that the procedure was fair, that the employee was given many "due process" protections (adequate notice, a right to present witnesses and adequate time to prepare) and he was therefore bound by the council's decision.

Implications of Performance Appraisals and Grievances for Nurse Employees

Performance appraisals that establish unacceptable performance and adverse disciplinary actions are not enjoyable experiences for any nurse employee. Therefore, the best approach for the nurse employee is to avoid being involved in either situation. This can be attempted by knowing the employer's expectations by reviewing the employee handbook, performance requirements, and performance appraisal forms. When a work problem arises, the nurse employee should attempt to resolve the difficulty through established channels as soon as possible. Allowing a problem to escalate, whether it be a concern about nursing competency or a breakdown in the communication channels among the nursing staff, may prove fatal to the nurse employee's employment status.

If a poor performance appraisal occurs, or the nurse employee believes he or she has been disciplined unfairly, an immediate review of the employer policies and procedures governing the situation is vital. Adherence to the policies, especially in relation to required time frames and to whom a grievance should be addressed, is important. If a particular form is required for a grievance, the nurse employee should utilize that form. Most often, it can be obtained from the human resource department.

Many times a nurse employee may think that a grievance is a waste of time because the decision will not be overturned. Even if the result of the grievance does not change the original decision, making a record of why the nurse believed the original employment decision was unfair is important. Because a disciplinary action, and any grievance filed as a result, including the final disposition, is often kept in the employee's personnel file, the grievance is a way for the nurse employee to provide his or her side of the event for the record.

When formulating his or her position, the nurse employee should utilize facts to support why the corrective action is not warranted. Facts include actual happenings or events, the policy and procedure applicable to the situation and whether or not they were followed, and details left out by the employer. This approach can be utilized for *any* employment decision covered in the grievance policy, including termination or an "unfair" performance appraisal.

If a grievance procedure allows the nurse to be accompanied at any time during the process, the nurse should take advantage of that option. The person attending the procedure with the nurse employee can have various roles, depending on the employer policy. They range from acting as an advocate to functioning in a supportive capacity.

If this option is not available to the nurse, he or she may want to consider consulting with an attorney to strategize the best way in which to proceed with the grievance. This is important, not only in the grievance procedure itself, but also if the nurse employee decides to file a case against the employer for possible violations of state or federal laws that can only be resolved in the courts or other proceedings. Not raising the arguments in the grievance procedure may create problems for the nurse when seeking redress in those other forums.

If the nurse is a member of a union, the collective bargaining contract should be consulted and the union representative contacted so that whatever protections are afforded under the union contracted are utilized.

If available, the nurse employee grieving an employment decision should obtain credible evidence concerning other employees who were not disciplined in the same manner for the same reason. Although no two situations are exactly alike, and there must be room for employer judgment and individualized discipline, deviations that arguably affect fairness may prove successful to the nurse employee if challenged.[96]

> [The Occupational Safety and Health Act of 1970] *was passed by Congress to ensure a healthy and safe workplace for workers.*

The nurse employee can also challenge a performance appraisal or other employment decision if principles of fairness or due process were not provided or adhered to. For example, if the nurse was not placed on probation (as policy required) for poor clinical performance prior to a written warning or termination, a successful grievance of those corrective actions might occur.

LAWS GOVERNING THE EMPLOYER-EMPLOYEE RELATIONSHIP

Occupational Safety and Health Act of 1970[97]

This federal law was passed by Congress to ensure a healthy and safe workplace for workers.[98] The Act covers five million work sites and 75 million employees in every state, the District of Columbia, Puerto Rico, and all of the American territories.[99] Although state and federal employees are not directly covered by the Act, those employees are covered by state or other federal statutes affecting healthy and safe workplaces.

The federal law imposes two duties on covered employers to (1) provide a workplace free from recognized hazards that are causing or likely to cause death or serious physical harm to employees (also called the employer's "general duty"); and (2) comply with regulations promulgated by the Occupational Safety and Health Administration (OSHA) of the Labor Department.[100]

Enforcement of the Act is the responsibility of OSHA and the Secretary of Labor. OSHA has the power to receive complaints, inspect work sites (with or without prior notice), interview employees during an inspection tour, and issue citations for violations of the Act. If the employer does not rectify the harmful workplace violations, fines can be imposed. Those fines range from $1.00 to $7000 for serious violations and from $5000 to $70,000 for willful violations.[101] Criminal penalties for willful violations that result in death of one or more employees are also possible. Employers are granted certain due process rights in relation to alleged violations, including the right to (1) be present during an inspection tour; (2) written notice of any violations; (3) contest any alleged violations; and (3) appeal an adverse decision of the agency.

The Act also complements other federal employment laws protecting employees. For example, if a "good faith" strike or refusal to work occurs by employees because of safety or health concerns, the United States Supreme Court has ruled that the employees cannot be disciplined by the employer.[102] Also, in *International Union UAW v. Johnson Controls, Inc.*,[103] the United States Supreme Court held that under Title VII, an employer could not use one of the statutory exemptions—bona fide occupational qualification (BFOQ)—to discriminate against female employees.

In *Johnson*, the employer had excluded only women who were of childbearing age from lead-exposed positions in the workplace under its fetal protection policy. Males who were also exposed to lead were not excluded. This exclusion was found to be direct, dissimilar treatment of female workers that could not be supported by the bona fide occupational qualification defense raised by the employer.

Gender or pregnancy *may* support dissimilar treatment of females, the Court opined, but only when pregnancy or gender "actually interferes with the employee's ability to perform the job."[104] Although reproductive hazards in the workplace must be protected against, protection can occur only when it does not discriminate on the basis of gender or is necessitated by one of the employer defenses allowed by Title VII.

Clearly, the Act's protections for a healthful and safe workplace are applied to health care employees. The Act and its standards have been utilized to communicate dangers to employees handling hazardous chemicals (e.g., chemotherapeutic agents)[105] and to provide closed systems for the retrieval of patient anesthesia gases in the OR, for example. Perhaps the Act's most far-reaching effect on health care employees, how-

ever, has been in the area of universal protections against blood-borne pathogens, including hepatitis and HIV.

Bloodborne Pathogen Standard[106]

The 1991 rules were promulgated in response to recommendations from the Centers for Disease Control and Prevention (CDC) for health care workers to follow to avoid undue exposure to bloodborne contagious diseases. Called "universal precautions," the guidelines included (1) treating all human blood and certain bodily fluids as if positive for HIV, HBV, and other bloodborne pathogens; (2) using gloves, masks, gowns, and eyewear whenever there was a possibility of exposure to blood or bodily fluids; and (3) following good handwashing techniques in addition to using the other suggestions.

Although many health care employers voluntarily adopted the recommendations, it was not until they became *requirements* under the Act that *all* employers covered began to utilize the standard. The requirements of the standard, along with employer and employee requisites, are listed in Table 16–4.

The standard has been met with controversy, and many employers were not happy with its mandates, especially because of the costs of providing the vaccine, gloves, and other personal protective equipment (PPE).[107] In addition, the American Dental Association (ADA) and Home Health Services and Staffing Association, Inc., filed a suit against the Secretary of Labor, OSHA, and the Department of Labor challenging the standard's application to dentists and home health care agencies.[108]

The Court of Appeals for the 7th Circuit upheld the standard's application in the dental profession despite arguments by the ADA that its provisions were too costly and too cumbersome (e.g., keeping employee records for 30 years, laundering gowns at a separate facility).

The court vacated the regulation's standard to home health care and temporary medical personnel employers in which the employer does

TABLE 16–4
Summary of Bloodborne Pathogen Standard

EMPLOYER REQUIREMENTS	EMPLOYEE RESPONSIBILITIES
• Offer hepatitis vaccine to new employees within 10 days at employer's cost; keep records or written consent/refusal	Written acceptance/refusal of vaccine; ability to change mind if initially refused
• Require, in written policy, use of universal precautions	Follow universal precautions per policy
• Written list of which employees, which jobs classes, and which tasks have occupational exposure to bloodborne pathogens	
• Ensure handwashing, proper separation of food storage, smoking, and the like from areas where potential exposure; no recapping, shearing, breaking, or removal of contaminated sharps unless a mechanical or one-handed technique used by instituting work practice controls and work environment changes (e.g., sinks for handwashing, areas for eating)	Follow established policies
• Sharps, blood, and other infectious matter must be disposed of in leak-proof and properly labeled containers with sharps in puncture-resistant, "easily accessible . . . maintained upright and routinely replaced" containers	Follow established policies
• Require and supply the use of PPE, including gloves, masks, and gowns	Use PPE per policy
• Establish requirements for housekeeping re: decontamination of surfaces, protective coverage of "overtly contaminated" areas	Follow established policies
• Establish requirements for proper handling of laundry (e.g., "minimum of agitation," proper labeling of contaminated laundry, use of leakproof bags/containers)	Follow established policies
• Provide employee with confidential post-exposure medical care, blood test, counseling, and follow-up;	Seek immediate medical treatment if exposed to blood or bodily fluid; can refuse, however
• Use of BIOHAZARD label	Be alert for label and follow required handling requirements
• Provide in-service training on regulations on annual basis with content specified in regulations; keep written records of attendance and content	Attend in-service programs and keep abreast of latest developments

PPE = Personal protective equipment.
Data from: Bloodborne Pathogen Standard, 29 C.F.R. 1910.1030 (1991); William Buss, William Dornette, Laura Gasarch, and others. *AIDS and the Law.* 2nd Edition. New York, John Wiley & Sons, Inc., 1992 (With 1996 Cumulative Supplement No. 1), 239–247, Appendix N (Suppl.).

not control the work site, however. The rationale was based on a long history of decisions wherein OSHA allowed employers to use the "multi-employer work site" defense. This defense states that employers are not cited for hazards that cannot be controlled (e.g., placement of a sink for handwashing) so long as reasonable precautionary steps were taken to protect the worker.[109]

Obviously a patient's home cannot be controlled by the employer in the same way a hospital or clinic can be. Thus the court held, when work sites cannot be controlled by the employer, hospital, nursing home, or other entity specifically subject to the rule, it is not applicable to those work sites. The court did, however, uphold the "main rule."[110]

How this decision will ultimately affect home care and temporary agency employers and employees will remain to be seen. It is more likely than not that additional challenges to the bloodborne pathogen standard will occur. That *some type* of mandated guidelines for employee protection is needed is clear. Perhaps the best support for this need are recent statistics concerning workplace exposure to contagious diseases.

Workplace Exposure Statistics

Work-related exposure to HIV, HBV, and TB results in increasing infection rates in health care workers annually. As of September 30, 1992, the Centers for Disease Control and Prevention (CDC) received reports of 32 United States health care workers with documented work-related HIV infection and 69 workers with possible work-related HIV contamination.[111] As of July 1993, the CDC reported 37 documented cases of health care worker occupational HIV exposure and 78 cases of possible health care worker occupational transmission.[112]

Work-related exposure to HIV, HBV, and TB results in increasing infection rates in health care workers annually.

One of the first three reported transmissions involving health care workers was a nurse from the University of Iowa Hospital, Barbara Fassbinder.[113] Her exposure occurred in the ED where a cut on her hand from gardening became contaminated after she applied pressure to a removed IV catheter site to stop bleeding. The patient died, and it was determined he had AIDS. Universal precautions were not "generally observed" at the time of her exposure.[114]

Among the 32 documented cases in 1992, most of which involved nurses and laboratory technicians, exposure included percutaneous (27 or 84%) and mucocutaneous (4 or 13%) incidents. Seven (22%) have developed AIDS.[115] Of the 69 workers in 1992 who may have been occupationally exposed to HIV, 14 are nurses;[116] 54 (78%) of the 69 have developed AIDS.[117]

Infection with HBV affects 75 to 120 of every 1000 workers who are exposed. Of the 12,000 health care employees who are infected annually with the virus, 200 to 300 die every year.[118]

Active multi-drug–resistant tuberculosis is also a contagion problem for health care workers. At least 17 health care workers, 5 of whom have died, have been reported to the CDC. Four

of the five who died were also infected with HIV.[119]

Implications of the Occupational Safety and Health Act for Nurse Employees

The American Nurses' Association has supported the use of CDC guidelines, the importance of postexposure policies and practices in the event of workplace exposure to bloodborne pathogens, and the need for personnel policies concerning HIV in the workplace.[120] The nurse employee must be familiar with these statements and the responsibilities incorporated in them, including attending training programs, adherence to postexposure plans when the potential for transmission occurs, and, of course, following CDC guidelines. Because needle stick injury is the most common cause of occupationally related HIV infection,[121] the nurse must religiously follow employer policy concerning the handling of used needles.

In addition, compliance with any and all other employer-developed policies protecting the nurse employee must be adhered to. These policies may include such protections as regular monitoring of equipment for proper functioning, wearing certain types of shoes in particular areas of the facility (e.g., rubber soles rather than leather or plastic), and not wearing certain kinds of jewelry around patient care equipment.

A healthful and safe workplace also requires the nurse employee to participate on facility committees that develop policies for employee protection in the workplace. Reviewing any citations from OSHA, if they occur (the employer is required to post them for employees to see) and utilizing that information to update and change policies can be helpful.

If the nurse is concerned about an unhealthy or unsafe situation in the workplace, discussing the condition immediately with the nurse manager is important. If no change in the condition occurs, the nurse should seek out the nurse executive in the facility. If continued discussions do not remedy the problem, the nurse may need to factually and truthfully report concerns to the nearest OSHA office. Asking that the report remain confidential is an option the nurse has when speaking with an OSHA official.

If an OSHA site inspection occurs, the nurse may be the only person in charge if it occurs on a weekend or holiday. It is best for the nurse to let the inspector know that he or she must contact the nurse executive, CEO, or other designated administration official and ask the inspector to wait on the premises until that person provides further instructions. Once the inspection begins, truthfully answering any questions the inspector may pose to the nurse concerning the work site hazard is important.

Equal Employment Opportunity Laws

Equal employment opportunity laws (also called antidiscrimination laws) prohibit employment policies and practices that result in different treatment of, or a disparate impact on, any protected class of applicants or employees.[122] Both state and federal laws have been passed that affect all phases of the employment process.[123]

Equal employment opportunity laws prohibit discriminatory policies and practices in the workplace.

The agency empowered to enforce most of the federal antidiscrimination laws is the Equal Employment Opportunity Commission (EEOC). Its roles also include promulgating regulations and monitoring the statutes it enforces.

If illegal discrimination is found to exist, remedies to the aggrieved individual can include reinstatement, back pay, equitable relief (an injunction to prohibit further conduct, for example), attorneys fees, and compensatory damages.

Because of the wide variances in state law, federal law will be focused upon. The more familiar federal antidiscrimination laws are presented in Table 16–5.

Affirmative Action Plans

An affirmative action plan is a program established to overcome the effects of past discrimination against groups protected by antidiscrimination laws.[130] If a health care delivery system does business with, or receives funds from, the government, affirmative action is required.[131] Two Executive Orders, No. 11246 and No. 11375, were passed to ensure that the requirement was met. If it is violated, the Office of Federal Contract Compliance Program (OFCCP) of the Department of Labor can enforce the Executive Orders. The Office of Federal Contract Compliance Program can also share information with the Equal Employment Opportunity Commission when Title VII action is also possible.

An affirmative action program may also be required as part of a settlement or judgment in a discrimination suit filed with the EEOC or in federal court. In addition, a policy supporting affirmative action may be voluntarily adopted by an employer.

The Equal Employment Opportunity Commission regulations spell out the requirements of an affirmative action plan: (1) a policy specifying equal employment opportunity; (2) strategies for internal and external distribution of the policy; (3) identification of whose responsibility it is to implement the policy; (4) analysis of all job titles and descriptions; (5) a plan of action; and (6) an internal audit and reporting system of compliance with the program.[132]

Although affirmative action is agreed to, at least in theory, by most employers and society in general, its implementation is sometimes difficult. In addition, the issue of reverse discrimination—members of groups not initially protected by antidiscrimination laws feeling discriminated against because of an affirmative action plan—is also controversial. Throughout the years, the courts have not been clear about a particular approach to the reverse discrimination issue. Rather, it appears that the courts decide each situation on a case-by-case basis.[133]

TABLE 16–5

Summary of Common Federal Equal Employment Opportunity Laws

LAW	CONDUCT PROHIBITED	COMMENTS
Civil Rights Act of 1866 and Amendments[124]	Actions occurring under "color of state law" (includes any local, state, or federal government unit)	Makes employer or employee who acts on employer's behalf personally liable; commonly referred to as Section 1981 and Section 1983 cases
Title VII of the Civil Rights Act of 1964[125]	Refusal to hire, to discharge, or otherwise discriminate against any person on basis of sex, race, color, religion, national origin; employer cannot make any other employment decision, including pay, benefits, promotions, job assignments based on those classes	Amendments include protections for abortion, pregnancy, sexual harassment. Exceptions/defenses to prohibitions are (1) bona fide occupational qualification (BFOQ); (2) business necessity; (3) nondiscriminatory reason for decisions. Applies to employers, labor organizations, state and local governments with 15 or more employees
Rehabilitation Act of 1973[126]	Discrimination against qualified handicapped person who can, with reasonable accommodation, perform essential job functions	Section 503 governs government contractors; Section 504 applies to *any* entity receiving federal financial assistance. Exceptions/defenses to prohibited conduct are (1) person *not* qualified; (2) accommodation required *not* reasonable and is undue hardship for employer or substantially increases cost for employer; (3) person *not* handicapped; (4) safety is a concern despite person being able to perform job essentials (BFOQ)
Age Discrimination in Employment Act[127]	Discrimination against individuals 40 years of age and older for all employment-related decisions	Applies to employers with 20 or more employees, including public employers, labor organizations, and employment agencies. Mandatory retirement also prohibited unless certain exceptions apply (e.g., not doing job or an executive in policy-making role). Exceptions/defenses include (1) if age a BFOQ; (2) decisions made on reasonable factor other than age; (3) decisions based on bona-fide seniority system; (4) decisions for just cause (e.g., not performing job). Voluntary early retirement OK under Act so long as requirements under amendment to Act (Older Workers Benefit Protection Act) met
Civil Rights Act of 1991[128]	Further supports antidiscrimination laws already in existence	Provides additional relief of (1) availability of jury trial; (2) damages for intentional discrimination on basis of sex, disability, and religion (before only for race, national origin, and ethnicity); and other procedural protections for employees
Americans with Disabilities Act[129]	Discrimination on the basis of a disability if person qualified to perform "essential" job functions, with or without reasonable accommodation (Title I)	Applies to *all* employers with 15 or more employees. Exceptions/defenses inlcude (1) individual *not* qualified; (2) individual a "direct threat" to health and safety of others; (3) no reasonable accommodation possible; (4) "undue" hardship on employer's part to accommodate; (5) person cannot perform essential job functions. Act also prohibits pre-employment physicals, but allows them after offer of employment and if required of *all* applicants. Drug testing of applicants OK, but no discrimination against recovering alcoholics or drug addicts allowed. No questions about disability possible during pre-employment interview, but prospective employer can ask if essential job functions can be performed

Data from: Kenneth Sovereign. *Personnel Law.* 3rd Edition. Englewood Cliffs, NJ: Prentice-Hall, 1994; Henry Perritt. *Americans with Disabilities Act Handbook. Second Edition.* New York: John Wiley & Sons, Inc., 1991 (With 1996 Cumulative Supplement No. 1); Henry Perritt. *Civil Rights Act of 1991: Special Report.* New York: John Wiley & Sons, 1992.

Selected Cases Dealing with Equal Employment Opportunity

Many cases involving antidiscrimination laws have been decided throughout the years. Some have involved nurses as plaintiffs.

▼ In *Wallace v. Veterans Administration*,[134] Dorothy Wallace, an RN, won her suit against the VA Medical Center in Wichita, Kansas, after it unlawfully refused to hire her because of a restriction on her ability to administer narcotics after her successful, but continuing recovery from chemical addiction. Ms. Wallace successfully argued that her addiction was a handicap covered by the Rehabilitation Act of 1973 and that she was a handicapped individual otherwise qualified for the position she applied for. The refusal of the VA to hire her because she could not pass narcotics was a violation of its duty to reasonably accommodate her.

▼ In *Waters v. Churchill*,[135] the firing of an RN from her position at an Illinois public hospital for speaking out against the reduced quality of nursing care in the obstetrics department because of a "cross-training program" (nurses transferring to other departments than those they were trained in and usually assigned) was held to be a possible violation of the nurse's First Amendment right of free speech and Section 1983 of the Civil Rights Act of 1866. The District Court's summary judgment decision and its dismissal of the case was vacated by the United States Supreme Court, and the case was remanded back to the trial court for further proceedings consistent with its decision.

▼ In *Meritor Savings Bank v. Vinson*,[136] the United States Supreme Court held that a female bank employee was sexually harassed in violation of Title VII when her supervisor created a "hostile (work) environment." The Court's decision is an important one for many reasons, but especially because of its inclusion of the hostile work environment (e.g., offensive re-marks, offensive pictures) as equally violative of Title VII as the "other type" of sexual harassment—*quid pro quo harassment*; that is, unwanted sexual advances and employment decisions based on the employee's "cooperation" with, or refusal of, those advances.[137]

▼ In *Buckley v. Hospital Corporation of America*,[138] the federal court reversed the trial court's summary judgment against a 62-year-old nurse supervisor who had been terminated from her position and remanded the case back to the federal trial court for trial. The appeals court held that sufficient evidence existed for a trial on whether or not Ms. Buckley had been discharged because of her age in violation of the Age Discrimination in Employment Act (ADEA). Comments from the administrator that: "new blood" was needed; younger doctors and nurses were going to be hired; and Ms. Buckley's "advanced age" was causing her anxiety and stress at work required a trial on the merits.

▼ In *School Board of Nassua County, Florida v. Arline*,[139] a lawsuit was filed by a teacher who was discharged from her position because she had recurring tuberculosis. She alleged she was a handicapped person under the Rehabilitation Act of 1973. The United States Supreme Court agreed, holding that a contagious disease is a handicap under the Act. Furthermore, the Court opined that any contagious disease must be evaluated by factual and medical evidence before a nondiscriminatory decision concerning employment can be made. The evaluation includes careful analysis of the severity of the risk to others due to the disease and the method of transmission.

▼ An HIV-infected pharmacist was successful in challenging a hospital's refusal to hire him because of his HIV+ status in *In re Westchester County Medical Center*.[140] Finding a violation of the Rehabilitation Act of 1973, the administrative law judge ruled that the pharmacist was not a direct threat to the health and safety of others. In addition, his HIV+ status did not prevent him from performing the duties of his position.

Implications of Antidiscrimination Laws for Nurse Employees

Equal employment laws benefit both employers and employees, and, in most instances, compliance by employers is the norm. The nurse employee should be knowledgeable about state and federal antidiscrimination laws, however, in the event there is a question about a potentially discriminatory employment decision. Furthermore, seeking a legal opinion about his or her concerns as soon as possible will help the nurse employee determine what, if any, action is best to pursue under the circumstances.

Knowing and utilizing the employer's policies and procedures for the handling of any potential discriminatory employment practice is also important. If a nurse believes he or she is a victim of sexual harassment, for example, following the policy adopted by the employer as to whom is to be notified can hopefully stop the offender's conduct. Also, directing a request for reasonable accommodation (e.g., job restructuring, scheduling days off to accommodate tests or doctor visits or changes in the physical structure of the workplace) after a disability exists to the appropriate administrator or employee representative can result in a nonadversarial resolution to the situation.

If the nurse employee experiences disinterest or nonintervention by the employer with complaints brought to its attention, the nurse employee can always seek input from the local Equal Employment Opportunity Commission office. If the Commission believes there is sufficient data to support a charge of employment discrimination, it will accept the employee's charge of discrimination and investigate the claim on behalf of the employee.

A nurse who applies for a position in a health care delivery system will need to be alert for any practice that is potentially discriminatory, especially when the job is not offered to the nurse. Asking questions about the nurse's marital status, age, number of children, plans for childbearing, disabilities, and religious affiliation, as examples, are prohibited by the fair employment practice laws unless they are protected by the laws' exceptions. Similarly, indirect comments about younger nurses, older nurses, and a gender preference for a particular position are not acceptable applicant inquiries.

If a nurse employee is part of a lay-off, early retirement plan, or is asked to leave his or her position, and is 40 years of age or older, information about the protections under the Age Discrimination in Employment Act (ADEA) should be obtained. One specific concern is the content of the written agreement governing the plan or termination and any waivers (giving up the right to pursue legal remedies as a condition of accepting the plan or any benefits of termination) that may be included.

It is too early to predict what additional protections the Americans with Disabilities Act (ADA) may provide employees, including nurse employees, against discrimination on the basis of a disability. Approximately 1000 charges per month have been filed with the EEOC since the Act's initial effective date.[141] The leading employer conduct being complained of from August to October of 1992 was discharge on the basis of handicap. Failure to make reasonable accommodations, discriminatory hiring practices, and disciplinary actions based on one's disability were additional complaints alleged by employees or former employees. Types of disabilities claimed included back problems, mental illness, and diabetes.[142]

Despite the number of cases filed with the EEOC, no precedent-setting decision from the United States Supreme Court has occurred to date. Most commentators agree, however, that the Act and court decisions interpreting it will, at the very least, provide similar protections to those that have been decided under the Rehabilitation Act of 1973.[143]

National Labor Relations Act[144]

Employees have always been concerned about job security, wages, and other aspects of working conditions, and nurse employees are no exception. Employers have been troubled by increasing costs in running their businesses, and health care delivery systems have been no exception either. One way in which these respective concerns can be aired and resolutions obtained is through unionization and collective bargaining.

The National Labor Relations Act (NLRA), also known as the *Wagner Act*, was passed by Congress to regulate private employers and employees in relation to collective bargaining and unionization; to protect the public from interruptions in commerce that might occur due to unfair labor practices and strikes; and to encourage free private collective bargaining.[145] The Act established the National Labor Relations Board (NLRB) to administer and enforce the National Labor Relations Act in terms of the election process for unionization and the unfair labor practice sections of the Act.[146]

Later amendments to the Act, the *Taft-Hartley Act of 1947* and the *Landrum-Griffin Act of 1959*, altered the original Act from a heavily pro-labor document to a more "equitably balanced" control of employers and unions.[147] In addition, the Taft-Hartley amendments also (1) brought private, nonprofit health care delivery systems and their employees under the Act's protection (for-profit health care systems had been covered since 1935); (2) required unions to give a 10-day notice to the health care system before a strike, picketing, or other concerted activity takes place; (3) required unions to notify a health care facility 90 days in advance of their intention to modify or terminate an existing collective bargaining agreement; and (4) required mandatory mediation by the Federal Mediation and Conciliation Service (FMCS) on issues in dispute during bargaining contract negotiations.[148]

Two other laws, the (federal) *Civil Service Reform Act of 1978*[149] and respective state laws governing public employment, regulate rights and responsibilities concerning collective bargaining and unionization for those two groups of employers and employees (e.g., Veterans Adminis-

tration Hospitals and state and local governmental facilities).

This discussion will focus on the National Labor Relations Act, which covers any employer (and its employees) whose business affects interstate commerce. However, it is important to note that many of the same or similar protections and duties in the NLRA are also afforded by the other two laws.

Sections 7 and 8 of the National Labor Relations Act *(NLRA) specify employee, employer, and union rights, responsibilities, and expected conduct when collective bargaining is contemplated or undertaken in the workplace.*

Basic Provisions of the National Labor Relations Act

The Act identifies the respective rights and responsibilities of employers, employees, and unions. Those rights and responsibilities are summarized in Table 16–6.

After a union has been elected, a bargaining agreement or contract is negotiated between the employer and the union. The contract governs the employer–employee relationship. Provisions of such contract agreements include both mandatory subjects (those required under the National Labor Relations Act) and voluntary areas (whatever the employer and union agree is important to include). Common examples of subjects included in a bargaining agreement consist of: (1) the union is the exclusive bargaining unit for those employees in the unit; (2) member benefits; (3) grievance and disciplinary procedures; (4) hours of work and pay raises; (5) "union security" provisions (e.g., the work site is a "union shop" (all new employees must join

TABLE 16–6

Employer, Employee, and Union Rights and Responsibilities Under the NLRA

SECTION	RIGHTS/RESPONSIBILITIES	COMMENTS
7	Employees can (1) self-organize; (2) join, form, or assist labor organizations; (3) bargain collectively through representative of own choice; (4) engage in other concerted activities for purpose of collective bargaining or other mutual aid; and (5) refrain from any and all such activities	Protects all employees, not just union employees; "concerted activity" defined as employees acting together for their mutual assistance and protection concerning areas covered by Act
8	Employers cannot (1) interfere with, restrain, or coerce employees in exercise of their rights; (2) dominate or interfere with forming or administration of labor organization or contribute money or other support to it; (3) discriminate against employees in any term or condition of employment to encourage or discourage union membership or because of filing of charges or testifying under the Act; (4) refuse to bargain in good faith with employee representatives on matters subject to Act	This is the Unfair Labor Practice (ULP) Section. Examples of conduct prohibited include banning wearing union insignia in facility at all times; asking employees their thoughts about union; asking applicants if they are union members; telling an employee a pay raise will take place if he or she opposes union
	Unions cannot (1) restrain or coerce employees in the exercise of rights or restrain or coerce employer in selection of representatives for purpose of collective bargaining or adjustment of grievance; (2) require employer to discriminate against an employee; (3) discriminate against any employee when membership denied or terminated on a ground other than failure to pay dues and initiation fees required by all employees; (4) refusal to bargain in good faith with employer; (5) engage in, induce, or encourage employees to participate in a strike for the purpose of union recognition	Examples of prohibited conduct include asking employer to fire employee for not joining union; physical or verbal threats or actual instances of violence; charging excessive or discriminatory fees
9	Sets up union recognition rules: *voluntary recognition* by employer; *NLRB election*; and *Gissel Bargaining Order* from NLRB	Employer and union bound by rules; voluntary recognition not usual way union recognized; NLRB election is, with petition filed; determination that union is one employees want (through union authorization cards); election held; union wins or loses
2(11)	Employer supervisors cannot be members of union if individual has authority to grant wage increases, hire, fire, settle grievances, assign work or make recommendations concerning any of these issues	This section's application to nursing supervisors problematic; decisions made by NLRB on basis of responsibilities of nurse supervisor, not on title; nurse executive cannot be union member

Data from: "Union Organizing, Collective Bargaining, and Strikes," Maynard Sautter, in *Employment in Illinois: A Guide to Employment Laws, Regulations and Practices*. 2nd Edition. Issue 5. Carlsbad, Calif: Butterworth Legal Publications, 1994; Patricia Younger and Cynthia Conner, Editors. *Nursing Administration and Law Manual*. Volume 2. Rockville, Md: Aspen Publishers, Inc., 1985 (with updates).

the union within a specified time) or an "agency shop" (joining the union is not mandated, but all employees must pay union dues or a portion of the dues to the union); and (6) a strike or no strike clause.

Which employees are included in a particular bargaining unit is also governed by the bargaining contract. The National Labor Relations Board uses a "community of interest" test in determining the composition of any collective bargaining unit; that is, the members must have similarity in job functions, common supervision, and operational integration.[150] Professional employees, such as nurses, and nonprofessional employees (those whose jobs do not require independent judgment for performance and do not require study in an institution of higher learning) cannot be in the same bargaining unit unless a majority of the professional employees vote for inclusion in that unit.

Until recently there was a question whether registered nurses should be in their own bargaining unit when they decided to unionize. The controversy surrounding this issue stemmed from the long-standing concern (voiced by employers, their professional organizations, and Congress) that the "proliferation" of bargaining units in health care would create undue difficulty for health care delivery systems trying to satisfy so many different "community of interests."

Even so, eight units identified by rule by the NLRB in 1987 as acceptable for acute care hospitals were: (1) RNs; (2) doctors; (3) other professionals (not doctors or RNs); (4) technical employees; (5) skilled maintenance employees; (6) security personnel; (7) business and clerical employees; and (8) all other nonprofessional employees.

In 1987 the American Hospital Association filed suit challenging the decision of the National Labor Relations Board. In *American Hospital Association v. NLRB*,[151] the Association alleged that (1) the Board was required under the National Labor Relations Act to define acceptable units "in each case" so the promulgation of a general rule was invalid; (2) the rule was a violation of Congress's warning not to proliferate bargaining units in health care; and (3) the rule was arbitrary and capricious. The United States Supreme Court unanimously upheld the rule, however.

It was thought that the Court's decision would result in a flurry of union activity in hospitals. Although union activity has steadily increased, unionization has not reached its predicted levels. Facts indicate that about 291 new representation petitions for acute care hospitals were filed from April 23, 1991 until December 31, 1992, with 212 going to election.[152] For 5 years prior to the rule going into effect, new representation petitions in all health care facilities ranged from 236 to 354.[153] It is interesting to note that of the 212 petitions that resulted in elections, more than half occurred in RN (48) and skilled maintenance units (65).[154] Of the 48

RN elections, unions lost 25 and won 23 of the elections.[155] For RNs, the union most frequently selected for election petitions was the American Nurses' Association (ANA) (28), followed by the Service Employees International Union (SEIU) (7), and the American Federation of State, County and Municipal Employees (AFSCME) (3).[156]

One of the most powerful provisions of the NLRA's concerted activity protections and any union bargaining contract is the power to exercise "economic action" against the employer. Economic pressure, of course, includes a strike; that is, a work stoppage, slow-down, or other concerted interruption of operations by employees to enforce compliance with work demands.[157] Strikes by workers in health care have been controversial, and work interruptions by registered nurses are no exception. In fact, it was not until 1968 that the American Nurses' Association rescinded its previous 18-year-old no-strike policy.[158] Since then, many nurses have participated in strikes throughout the country to obtain better working conditions.

Implications of the National Labor Relations Act for the Nurse Employee

The National Labor Relations Act and the National Labor Relations Board exist to set parameters and guidelines for employers and employees to resolve differences concerning terms and conditions of the workplace. Neither, however, are guarantees that agreement will always be reached. Therefore, one of the first things the nurse employee should be familiar with is the NLRA and any state laws that might alter his or her collective bargaining rights. For example, the nurse may practice in a "right-to-work" state (e.g., Alabama, Georgia, North Dakota, Utah, and Virginia) that prohibits union bargaining contracts from containing union or agency shop contract provisions.

Second, all employees, whether nurse managers or nurse employees, should be familiar with acceptable and unacceptable behaviors before, during, and after a union election process. Inadvertent participation in an alleged unfair labor practice can result in an undesired decision or one that is not in the best interest of all involved.

If the nurse who is a member of a union decides to vote for, and participate in, a strike, it is important that he or she understand what the ramifications of that decision might be on job status. For example, generally speaking, an employer can hire temporary employees to replace striking workers. The employer may hire those temporary employees as permanent employees if the strike is an "economic" one (over anything other than an unfair labor practice [ULP] on the employer's part) or if the strike is "unprotected" (e.g., in violation of a no-strike clause in the union contract). In contrast, if the strike is a result of an employer ULP (e.g., simply refusing to reinstate striking workers), it cannot hire the temporary employees in the striking employee's place.[159]

If a nurse is a member of a union, he or she should be very familiar with the union contract, for it governs the nurse's relationship with the employer in a different way than those who are nonunionized. For example, if the nurse faces a disciplinary action, the union representative and the contract should be consulted. The nurse's rights will be carefully spelled out in these situations, including the right to have a union representative present if requested when an investigatory interview takes place.

This rule of representative, called the *Weingarten* rule,[160] has also been applied to nonunion employees by the courts in several cases. However, after initially applying it to nonunion employees as well, the National Labor Relations Board reversed its position in 1985 and has refused to allow its protection to nonunionized employees since that date.

Nurse employees who are nonunionized should keep in mind that the National Labor Relations Act does apply to them in terms of its basic provisions. Therefore, nurses who are unable to effect change in their working conditions may want to consider joining together to have protection under the National Labor Relations Act. For example, bringing employee concerns about wages to the employer by a representative selected by the employees is a good way to obtain protection under the Act.

It is interesting to note that another way nonunion employees joined together to obtain better working conditions is through participation on employee committees. The character and composition of these committees have to be carefully evaluated, however, because if they fit the definition of a labor organization and are employer dominated or controlled, the employer may be found to have committed an unfair labor practice.

In a recent NLRB case, *Electromation, Inc. and International Brotherhood of Teamsters, Local No. 1049, AFL-CIO and "Action Committees,"*[161] the National Labor Relations Board held that the Action Committees at issue in that case were employer established, administered, and dominated, thus resulting in "unilateral" bargaining by the employer with nonunionized employees in violation of the Act.

The *Electromation* decision was appealed to the 7th Circuit Court of Appeals.[162] The Appellate Court affirmed the NLRB's decision, holding that the Board had limited its decision only to committees that were employer dominated *and* had as their purpose the improvement of working conditions. The court clearly opined that "legitimate employee participation" committees that do not represent employees but rather focus on increasing company productivity, efficiency, and quality control are not prohibited by the Act.

The full impact of the *Electromation* decision will not be clearly seen for some time. It is certain that additional challenges to the court's decision will occur. Even so, nurse employees should keep in mind that any employee committee that has as its purpose the improvement of working conditions, wages, and/or hours of work when the employer is involved may result in a violation of the National Labor Relations Act. Committees that can make decisions on their own, establish short-term or task-specific goals and allow for all staff to participate should be able to function without a violation of the Act.[163]

Nurse employees (excluding nurse executives and other nursing administration members) who function as "supervisors" and were covered by the Act prior to 1994 may no longer be included in its protections. In *NLRB v. Health Care & Retirement Corp. of America*,[164] the United States Supreme Court rejected the Board's test for determining whether a nurse was a supervisor. Prior to the Supreme Court decision, the Board used a "patient care analysis" in making its decision.

Briefly, that analysis allowed the Board to evaluate a nurse's direction of other employees on the basis of whether the direction was "incidental to the treatment" of patients. If so, then the judgment and authority exercised by that nurse would not exclude the nurse from the protection of the National Labor Relations Act because it was authority not exercised in the interest of the employer.[165] If, however, the nurse's direction and decision-making were "independent" in an area other than how to care for a patient, then the nurse would be considered a supervisor and excluded from the Act's protection (see Table 16–6).

In *NLRB*, however, the United States Supreme Court held that since patient care is the health care employer's business, making decisions about patient care is making decisions in the interest of the employer. Thus, any nurse who makes such decisions is a supervisor and cannot enjoy the protections of the Act.

As is the case with the *Electromation* decision, the full impact of the *NLRB* decision remains to be seen. Many concerns have been raised, including its effect on union organizing, its effect on unions already in existence insofar as bargaining units including "supervisors" (based on the earlier analysis) as members are concerned, and how this decision may be used to further alter nursing's role in health care delivery in light of health care reform.[166] Many hope that rather than take a blanket approach to

nurses who function as supervisors, the National Labor Relations Board—and any subsequent court decisions—will evaluate each situation on a case-by-case basis.

Although nurse employees who are truly supervisors, however that term is ultimately defined, do not have protections under the National Labor Relations Act, there are certain circumstances in which they do have protection under Section 7 of the Act. If the employer discharges the nurse manager for any of the following reasons, the discharge is an unfair labor practice: (1) refusal to commit an ULP; (2) refusal to testify for the employer in an NLRB hearing involving union activity; (3) giving adverse testimony about the employer in a NLRB hearing; or (4) failure to prevent a union from organizing employees.[167]

SPECIAL NURSE EMPLOYEE CONSIDERATIONS

Review of Personnel Records

Fourteen states, including Illinois, New Hampshire, Utah, and Vermont, have passed laws delineating the rights of the employee and obligations of the employer in reviewing personnel records. The right of review is not absolute, however. Certain materials, such as reference letters and personal information about another employee, may not be included as reviewable in the state laws. Other provisions, including the right of the employee to protest certain information in the file and the number of times the employee can review the file, are also included in the state statutes.

In addition to these protections, the nurse who is a member of a union may have additional rights to review an employment file if those rights are included in the union contract.

If a nurse works in a state in which no law or union mandates review of personnel records, the nurse must rely on any employer policy concerning examination of employment records or must utilize legal avenues (e.g., subpoena) to gain access to his or her records.

Refusing an Assignment, Including Floating Assignments

Understaffing, unsafe assignments (due to either inadequate numbers of RNs or inadequately skilled RNs) and lack of adequate training to care for a particular patient have been long-standing professional concerns for nurse employees. The concerns have been accompanied by confusion as to how to object to and rectify the particular issue impacting safe patient care.

One way in which these concerns have been translated into concrete direction for nurses is through unionization. Patient care assignments, numbers of staff per shift, other terms and conditions of work, and approaches to rectifying these problems are often carefully spelled out in the union contract. In addition, in 1987 the American Nurses' Association's then-Cabinet on Economic and General Welfare recommended that state nurses' associations (SNAs) develop a position statement identifying mechanisms to support a nurse's ability to exercise his or her right to accept or reject an assignment.[168] Many state nurses' associations, including Massachusetts, North Carolina, and New York, did so.[169]

Nonunion employees have less clear solutions, however. As far back as 1983 only three options were identified: (1) accept the "objectionable" assignment; (2) accept the "objectionable" assignment and file a grievance or appeal; and (3) reject the "objectionable" assignment.[170]

Each of these options had consequences, including being sued for professional negligence and/or facing a disciplinary action by the state licensing agency if the patient was injured, and/or being disciplined for "insubordination," "abandonment of (the) patient," or other violations of the employer's disciplinary code.[171]

Other alternatives nurses have to object to professionally unacceptable assignments are grounded in state or federal laws. For example,

some states have "right of conscience" acts that protect a nurse's objection to a particular assignment when based on a religious or moral belief of an established, recognized religion.[172] In addition, other state statutes provide for refusal in certain care situations, such as abortion or the withholding or withdrawing of food and/or fluid.

Federal laws have been cited by nurse employees who find an assignment objectionable because of safety issues in the workplace. They include The Occupational Safety and Health Act and The Toxic and Hazardous Substances Hazard Communication Standard.[173]

Federal and state accrediting and licensing standards, such as those promulgated by the Social Security Administration (Medicare and Medicaid) and a state's public health department are also cited by the nurse employee to support an objection to a particular care assignment, especially when the protest concerns staffing and expertise of staff issues. Joint Commission on the Accreditation of Health Care Organizations (JCAHO) standards are relied on as well. Furthermore, in a 1993 Wisconsin case, *Winkelman v. Beliot Memorial Hospital*,[174] the Wisconsin Supreme Court affirmed the trial court's decision in favor of a nurse who utilized the Wisconsin Board of Nursing's rules and regulations when contesting her firing due to her refusal to float to a patient care area in which she was untrained and unskilled.

Despite nurses utilizing these various supports for their objections for some time, all have some limitations and drawbacks. For example, in *Francis v. Memorial General Hospital*,[175] a nurse's termination due to his refusal to float from the ICU to the orthopedic floor was upheld by the New Mexico Supreme Court. The court opined that since Francis refused the offer by the hospital to orient him to any and all units he would be requested to float to, he could not claim that the employer refused to acknowledge that concern. In addition, Francis' claims of breach of contract (there was a policy on floating, of which he was aware) and wrongful discharge were also rejected.

Employee Testing

Alcohol and Drug Screens

Alcohol and drug use by health care providers, including nurses, is greater than that of the general population.[176] It is estimated that 40,000 to 75,000 chemically impaired nurses are currently working.[177] To protect patients who may be harmed if a nurse is working while impaired and to limit their own liability, many health care employers have established drug- and alcohol-testing policies and procedures.

Employer rules for testing employees in the workplace must conform to state and federal laws. For example, the federal Drug Free Workplace Act of 1988[178] requires employers who receive grants from the federal government to, among other things, publish their drug policy and provide the policy to each employee. Seventeen states, including Connecticut, Utah, Mississippi, and Vermont, have laws concerning drug testing of employees.[179]

Employer rules for testing employees [for drug or alcohol impairment] in the workplace must conform to state and federal laws.

Also, the federal and respective state constitutions, and case law interpreting those charters, provide guidelines under the Fourth Amendment's prohibition against unreasonable searches and seizures for governmental employees and private employees whose testing is required or allowed by governmental regulations.[180]

The nurse employee should be familiar with employer-adopted policies and procedures concerning substance abuse in the workplace and testing for chemicals. Good employer policies will include the following information for its employees: (1) definitions of terms such as *abuse, use,* and *impaired*; (2) conduct that is prohibited (e.g., conversion or diversion of controlled substances, falsification of patient care records); (3) the employer's response to a positive test or when a test is refused by the employee; (4) maintaining the confidentiality of test results; and (5) under what circumstances testing will occur (e.g., "reasonable suspicion").[181]

If the nurse is asked to submit to a drug or alcohol test and refuses, most often the refusal will result in termination. If, on the other hand, the test is agreed to and is positive, unless the nurse can document the positive drug as legally and therapeutically prescribed, termination may also occur. In addition, depending on the state nurse practice act, he or she may also be reported to the state board of nursing or other regulatory agency.

The nurse employee who has a positive test may want to challenge the results of the test on several grounds through the employer's grievance procedure, if possible. An important point to raise is whether or not the testing procedure was flawed in any way. For example, regardless of whether the sample was blood, urine, or other body chemicals, the testing should be a two-stage process; that is, the first test should be used only as a "screening" test. If positive, a second, or "confirmatory" test should be done by Gas Chromatography/Mass Spectrometry (GC/MS) or a similarly reliable method.[182]

A second concern surrounding the testing procedure is if the "chain of custody" was strictly adhered to. Without question, the sample must be accounted for *at all times* from its collection to the reporting of its result. Any break in the chain can cast doubt on the integrity of the entire process and testing results.

It is important for the nurse employee to remember that under the Americans with Disabilities Act of 1990, there is no prohibition for the testing of employees for "illegal" chemical use. Rather, the Act has been characterized as "neutral" on the issue of drug testing.[183] It does allow an employer to establish drug and alcohol policies that prohibit chemical use in the workplace, take disciplinary actions against employees who violate the policies, and test recovering employees to ensure they are not engaged in illegal drug or alcohol use or abuse.[184]

If the nurse employee is addicted to alcohol or illegal drugs (whether they be controlled substances, marijuana, or cocaine), it is important that the nurse seek treatment and continue in recovery after the initial regimen is concluded. This is important for two reasons. The nurse applicant or employee who is in a treatment program or has successfully completed one is protected under the Americans with Disabilities Act as an individual with a disability.

Therefore, if "otherwise qualified" and able to perform the "essential functions of the job," with or without reasonable accommodation, no discrimination can take place by the employer in relation to employment. For example, if the recovering nurse would need to have time off to attend AA or NA meetings, or not administer narcotic medications to patients for a period of time after treatment, the employer would have to adjust the nurse's work schedule and assignments.

The most important consideration for undergoing treatment, however, is the fact that chemical use and abuse is self-destructive and can lead to death if intervention does not occur.[185] Many employers and nurse administrators possess positive and supportive attitudes toward chemical addiction and recovery.[186] The nurse employee can, and must, utilize those attitudes to break his or her cycle of self-devastation and re-establish himself or herself as a contributing and healthy member of society and of the nursing profession.

Polygraph/Lie Detector Tests

Employer use of the polygraph machine to detect dishonesty has been available for some time.[187] Few, if any, laws regulated its use, however, until 1988 when the *Employee Polygraph*

Protection Act was passed by Congress.[188] The Act broadly prohibits the use of a "lie detector" (any mechanical or electrical device) to determine an opinion about an individual's honesty or dishonesty.[189]

The Act prohibits private employers from certain conduct, including (1) suggesting or requiring job applicants or employees to take a polygraph test; (2) asking about or using a past polygraph result; (3) refusing to hire a prospective employee who refuses to take a polygraph test; and (4) discharging or disciplining any employee who refuses to take a lie detector test, or otherwise taking action against an employee solely on the basis of the polygraph test.

The Act does contain certain exceptions to the general prohibitions against polygraph tests in the workplace. Two important ones are drug testing and public employers. Others include employer investigations in which there is economic loss or injury and when the employer is authorized to manufacture, distribute, or dispense controlled substances.[190] For hospitals and other health care delivery systems, then, the employer can administer a test to a prospective employee "having direct access" to controlled substances. It can also conduct a test on a current employee who has direct access to controlled substances as part of an ongoing investigation of "criminal or other misconduct" involving controlled substances.[191]

Even with the exceptions listed in the Act, the employer has additional restrictions. The test must be administered in accordance with the mandates in the Act, including specific information to be given the employee *before* the test is administered and his or her rights under the Act. In addition, private employers can use only polygraph machines, whereas governmental employers can use other honesty-detecting devices, such as a voice stress analyzer.[192]

The Act is enforced by the Secretary of Labor of the Department of Labor. An aggrieved employee or applicant can file a suit against the employer for violations and seek reinstatement, a promotion, and back payment of lost wages and benefits. The Act also provides for civil penalties of up to $10,000. Generally, the employee's rights under the Act cannot be waived unless a written agreement is signed by all parties involved.[193]

If a nurse employee is asked to take a polygraph test, he or she should consult with an attorney as soon as possible before responding to the request. If the federal law is not followed, and an adverse employment decision occurs, the nurse and the attorney can evaluate whether or not a suit will be undertaken. Furthermore, any state law violations or union contract protecting the nurse employee will also need to be considered.

HIV Testing or Disclosure of HIV Status

HIV+ status and AIDS in the workplace have become a controversial and complex issue for both employers and employees. Much of the controversy stems from ignorance concerning the disease itself and its possible transmission to others; in this case, health care consumers.[194] Statistics from the Centers for Disease Control and Prevention estimate that the risk of transmission from an HIV-infected health care provider is "small" and can be decreased with the appropriate use of infection-control procedures.[195] Even so, the apparent transmission of HIV to six patients by a Florida dentist—the *only* possible documented HIV health care-provider–to-patient transmissions to date—have continued to create public concern and anxiety, especially in view of the inability to identify *how* the transmissions occurred.[196]

As a result, some employers have instituted what they see as safeguards to protect health care consumers and those who work with HIV+ co-workers or those with AIDS. These precautions include HIV screening and/or asking a health care professional to voluntarily disclose his or her HIV status or the diagnosis of AIDS to the employer.

These precautions, however well intended, are questionable under various legal challenges. To begin with, because a contagious disease is considered a handicap (under the Rehabilitation Act of 1973) and a disability under the Americans with Disabilities Act, testing for HIV status or AIDS, or asking about this information, would have to be done *carefully,* if permitted at all. Likewise, under state and local laws prohibiting discrimination, the same procedures would be questionable.

As a result of the questionable status of such employer practices, many professional associations, including the American Nurses' Association, support *voluntary* anonymous or confidential testing for HIV and the voluntary disclosure of HIV+ status, when necessary, by infected health care providers.[197] In addition, a voluntary avoidance of participation in any invasive procedures that might place a patient at risk for transmission is also recommended.[198]

Many professional associations, including the American Nurses' Association, support voluntary *anonymous or confidential testing for HIV and the voluntary disclosure of HIV+ status, when necessary, by infected health care providers.*

The courts are beginning to deal with the issues raised by HIV testing, HIV+ status, and AIDS in the health care industry. In 1990, a male LPN whose roommate had AIDS was required to reveal the results of his HIV test. When he refused, he was fired. The federal district court upheld the firing, holding that the hospital had a "substantial interest" in maintaining the integrity of its infection control procedures. The termination was based on the LPN's refusal to reveal a possible infectious condition, which was a violation of its infection control policy, not on whether the test was negative or positive, according to the court.[199]

Because of the refusal, the court continued, the employer did not discriminate against the LPN on the basis of a "handicap" or a "disability." Furthermore, the hospital could not determine if the LPN "was otherwise qualified" and therefore precluded it from evaluating whether or not it could make the necessary accommodations to protect him and his patients.

In contrast, in another case decided prior to court action, a hospital in Kansas City, Missouri, agreed to reinstate a male RN to his clinical care position after he was removed from it and placed in a position with no direct patient contact when he tested positive for HIV. The Department of Health and Human Services also worked out an agreement with the hospital whereby its policies would be revised to conform to its recommendations on exposure-prone procedures and HIV+ employees.[200]

Also, in a 1993 case, *Faya v. Almaraz*,[201] the Maryland Court of Appeals held that physicians who are HIV+ have a legal duty (under an informed consent theory) to inform patients of their HIV status before operating on them.

The nurse employee who is asked to take an HIV test and reveal its results or is asked about a diagnosis of AIDS should seek the advice of an attorney as soon as possible. Hopefully, the guidance the attorney can give the nurse employee can result in a resolution of the situation in a manner protective of all the parties' respective legal rights and legal and ethical responsibilities.

Family and Medical Leave Act of 1993[202]

The Family and Medical Leave Act (FMLA), effective August 5, 1993, requires employers with 50 or more employees to grant up to 12 weeks of unpaid leave annually "for the birth or adoption of a child, to care for a spouse or

immediate family member with a serious health condition, or when unable to work because of a serious health condition."[203] The employer is required to maintain any pre-existing health coverage during the leave, and when the worker is ready to return to work, reinstate the employee to the same or an equivalent job.[204]

The Act also requires the employee to provide the employer with 30 days' notice concerning the leave, if possible. In addition, to be eligible for the leave, the employee must have worked at least 12 months for the employer and have worked at least 1250 hours in the year *prior* to the leave.

Because the Act is new, some confusion will most likely be present until it has been in force for some time and the Department of Labor regulations clarified, if that need occurs. The nurse employee should review the employer's policy and procedures concerning the Family and Medical Leave Act and raise any questions with its human resource department. If a leave is necessary, as much notice as possible should be given to the employer.

It is important for the nurse to know that the employer may request "certification" of the need for the leave from the employee's health care provider. Generally, employees taking a leave under the Act must be restored to their position or equivalent position when they return to work. If the nurse employee does not return to work after the leave time is utilized, however, the employer can recoup from the employee the money paid for health benefits during the leave.[205]

Refusal of Nurse to Care for a Particular Patient as a Result of Diagnosis, Race, or Other Discriminatory Reason

Health care delivery systems cannot discriminate against any individual on the basis of such protected classes as race, color, religion, national origin, or disability. Nor can nurse employees engage in such conduct. This prohibition is grounded in ethics as well as in the law.

As an employee, a nurse's conduct can result in the health care employer also being sued if discriminatory conduct by the nurse is alleged. For example, under the Americans with Disabilities Act's public accommodation requirements (Title III), a refusal to care for a patient because of the presence of a disability (e.g., AIDS) could result in an alleged violation by both the nurse and the institution. Title III of the Act requires, among other things, that those with a disability not be denied the "full and equal enjoyment" of goods, services, facilities, privileges, advantages, or accommodations of any place of public accommodation.[206] In short, those with disabilities must be given an equal opportunity to obtain the same results as nondisabled people.[207]

To date, no precedent-setting decision by the United States Supreme Court concerning refusal of care by health care workers or employers under Title III of the Americans with Disabilities Act has taken place.[208] However, cases have been decided relating to a nurse's or other health care worker's refusal to provide services in the employment setting under other theories.

For example, in *Armstrong v. Flowers Hospital, Inc.*,[209] the 11th Circuit Court of Appeals ruled against a pregnant nurse who refused to care for an AIDS patient and sought relief under Title VII of the Civil Rights Act when she was fired from her position.

Ms. Armstrong, a home health care nurse in the hospital's home care department, based her refusal on the fact that she was in the first trimester of her pregnancy, suffered from gestational diabetes, and was worried about the opportunistic infections common in AIDS patients.[210] The employer's policy was to fire any employee who refused to care for patients with AIDS. When Ms. Armstrong refused to change her mind, she was fired according to the policy. Armstrong then filed a complaint with the Equal Employment Opportunity Commission alleging discrimination on the basis of gender (pregnancy).

The appeals court upheld the federal trial court's opinion that the employer had no duty to provide special or preferential treatment to every pregnant nurse under Title VII. Furthermore, the court continued, the employer's policy applied equally to pregnant and nonpregnant employees.[211]

In another case involving a laboratory staff technician,[212] Dorothy Stepp refused to work on laboratory specimens that had biohazard warning labels on them, despite the employer's clear compliance with the Centers for Disease Control and Prevention guidelines. Her refusal was based on her belief that AIDS was a plague from God.[213] Ms. Stepp was suspended for 3 days because the refusal was seen as insubordination.

Upon return from the suspension, Ms. Stepp continued to refuse to work with contaminated specimens and was discharged. She sought unemployment compensation and was denied payments because she was fired for "just cause." The decision of the unemployment compensation board was affirmed by all levels of its review procedures.

Ms. Stepp then filed suit for a review of those decisions by the Indiana judicial system. Her allegations were based on OSHA regulations that allowed a refusal if based on a "reasonable apprehension" of death or serious injury due to an unsafe workplace.

The Indiana court upheld the decision of the unemployment compensation department. It rejected Ms. Stepp's argument concerning the justification of the refusal and the unsafe workplace. Rather, it held, the refusal was based on her religious beliefs. Furthermore, the court continued, she had been adequately and properly warned about the consequences of her refusal. Therefore, the employer was justified in firing her based on her refusal to do a "required task."

It is important to note that despite these decisions, the employer cannot ignore an employee's concerns about infectious diseases. In *Doe v. State of New York*,[214] a nurse employed by the state correctional facility successfully sued her employer when she attempted to restrain an HIV+ inmate who suffered a seizure. Correctional officers did not respond to the nurse's requests for help, and during the struggle, she accidently stuck herself with an IV needle she was trying to reattach when it became dislodged during the struggle. Ms. Doe tested positive for HIV 1 year after the needle stick.

The court ruled that the guards were negligent in not intervening to help the nurse and awarded her nearly $5 million.

The nurse employee who is concerned about an individual's contagious disease status or any other characteristic that is protected against discrimination should seriously evaluate his or her position if a refusal to provide care is contemplated. Generally such a refusal will not be protected. As a result, the nurse employee will probably not be successful in challenging a host of repercussions that will take place after the refusal, including, but not limited to, termination, refusal of unemployment compensation, and possible disciplinary action by the state licensing authority.

If the refusal of care is seen as necessary by the nurse, he or she will need to base that denial on solid legal ground (e.g., unsafe workplace or lack of personal protective equipment). Regardless of the legal foundation upon which such a refusal may rest, however, there are ethical ramifications to the decision as well.

The American Nurses' Association supports an ethical model for refusal by asking the nurse to differentiate when the benefit to the patient is a moral duty and when it becomes a moral option.[215] The equation for decision-making includes the step of evaluating the risk to the nurse, if any, in providing care to a particular patient.[216] Other ethical theories, including virtue ethics and the ethics of care, require careful inquiry into any contemplated or actual refusal to administer treatment to another.[217]

new laws are passed and new social issues emerge, the relationship will continue to be shaped by those events. The nurse employee cannot ignore the many changes that will continue to occur in his or her relationship with employers. Therefore, it is important for the nurse employee to:

▼ Keep abreast of changes in the laws of the workplace

▼ Understand the at-will employment doctrine and its exceptions

▼ Be familiar with employee benefits and the nurse's obligations under them

▼ Regularly examine his or her personnel file

▼ Regularly review the employee handbook

▼ Utilize employee protection laws, whether state or federal in origin, to ensure a safe workplace

▼ Adhere to universal precautions when providing care to patients

▼ Adhere to all Centers for Disease Control and Prevention standards/guidelines and employer policies concerning a safe and healthful workplace

▼ Understand antidiscrimination laws as they apply to both the nurse and the consumer of health care

▼ Compare and contrast the benefits and drawbacks of union vs. nonunion membership

▼ Consult with an attorney when a questionable workplace issue arises (e.g., HIV testing)

▼ Understand that refusing to care for any patient places the nurse at legal risk (unless the refusal is justified) and compromises the ethical duty to care for patients

SUMMARY OF PRINCIPLES AND APPLICATIONS

The employer–employee relationship is constantly evolving, despite its long-standing existence. As

TOPICS FOR FURTHER INQUIRY

1. Design a study to evaluate nurses' attitudes toward unionization.

2. Interview nurses in particular specialty areas

of nursing (e.g., coronary care units, mental health units) concerning their respective attitudes toward caring for patients with contagious diseases.

3. Design a study to evaluate the effectiveness of employee handbooks in informing nurse employees about their rights and responsibilities in the workplace.

4. Compare and contrast several health care providers' experiences (including nurses') when applying for workers' compensation claims for patient care–related injuries.

REFERENCES

1. Institute of Medicine. *Nursing Staff in Hospitals and Nursing Homes: Is it Adequate?* Goolco Wunderlich, Frank Sloan and Carolyne Davis, Editors. Washington, DC: National Academy Press, 1996, 4.
2. *Id*. at 4–76, 79–85.
3. Christine Kovner, "Nursing" in *Health Care Delivery in the United States*. 4th Edition. Edited by Anthony Kovner. New York: Springer Publishing Company, 1990, 96.
4. Henry Campbell Black. *Black's Law Dictionary*. 6th Edition. St. Paul, Minn: West Publishing Company, 1993, 363.
5. American College of Healthcare Executives. *Contracts for Healthcare Executives*. Chicago: The Foundation of the American College of Healthcare Executives, 1987, 7–10.
6. *Id*.
7. *Adair v. United States*, 208 U.S. 161 (1908).
8. Henry Campbell Black, *supra* note 4, at 363.
9. Kenneth Sovereign. *Personnel Law*. 3rd Edition. Englewood Cliffs, NJ: Prentice Hall, 1994, 171.
10. *Id*.
11. Sovereign, *supra* note 9, 171–178. See also Alfred G. Feliu. *Primer on Individual Employee Rights*. Washington, DC: The Bureau of National Affairs, Inc., 1992, 167–208.
12. 29 U.S.C.A. Sections 141–187 (1973, 1992 Supp.); Act of July 5, 1935, ch. 372, 49 Stat. 449; Act of June 23, 1947, ch. 120, 61 Stat. 136.
13. Feliu, *supra* note 11, at 169.
14. 488 A. 2d 229 (N.J. App. Div.), *cert. denied*, 501 A. 2d 926 (1985).
15. 328 S.E. 2d 818 (N.C. App.), *rev. denied*, 333 S.E. 2d 490, and *rev. denied*, 335 S.E. 2d 13 (1985).
16. 450 N.E. 2d 811 (Ill. Ct. App. 1st Dist. 1983).
17. For a case example where this kind of communication was held to support an implied contract of employment, see *Varis v. Arnot-Ogden Memorial Hospital* 891 F. 2d 51 (2d Cir. 1989).
18. See, for example, *Eales v. Tanana Valley Medical-Surgical Group*, 663 P. 2d 985 (Alaska 1983).
19. Feliu, *supra* note 11, at 47–50.
20. *Id*. at 39–43.
21. *Id*. at 40.
22. 505 N.E. 2d 314 (Ill. 1987).
23. 688 P. 2d 201 (Ariz. App. 1983), *vacated*, 688 P 2d 170 (1985).
24. 387 N.W. 2d 692 (Neb. 1986).
25. Feliu, *supra* note 11, at 21.
26. *Daymon v. Hardin County General Hospital*, 569 N.E. 2d 316 (Ct. App.), *appeal denied*, 580 N.E. 2d 111 (1991).
27. 779 P.2d 783 (Alaska 1989).
28. *Id*.
29. Sovereign, *supra* note 9, at 185.
30. *Id*., at 185.
31. Feliu, *supra* note 11, at 195–196.
32. *Id*.
33. *Id*., *citing Agarwal v. Johnson*, 25 Cal. 3d 932 (1979) and *Shrout v. Black Clawson Co.*, 689 F. Supp. 774 (S.D. Ohio 1988).
34. *Id*., *citing Keehr v. Consolidated Freightways Of Delaware, Inc.*, 825 F. 2d 133 (7th Cir. 1987).
35. 29 U.S.C. Sections 201–219.
36. Robert D. Miller. *Problems in Health Care Law*. 7th Edition. Rockville, Md: Aspen Publishers, Inc., 1996, 251.
37. *Id*. at 157.
38. Maynard G. Sautter. *Employment in Illinois: A Guide To Employment Laws, Regulations and Practices*. 2nd Edition. Issue 5. Carlsbad, CA: Butterworth Legal Publishers, 1994, 100. *citing* 29 C.F.R. Section 778.115.
39. *Id*.
40. 29 U.S.C. 206 *et seq*.
41. *Schultz v. Wheaton Glass Co.*, 421 F. 2d 259 (3rd Cir.), *cert. denied*, 398 U.S. 905, *on remand to*, 319 F. Supp. 229 (D.N.J. 1970), *aff'd in part, vacated in part, remanded by*, 446 F. 2d 527 (3rd Cir. 1971).
42. *Id*.
43. *Corning Glass Works v. Brennan*, 417 U.S. 188 (1974).
44. Patricia Younger and Cynthia Conner, Editors. *Nursing Administration and Law Manual*. Volume 2. Rockville, Md: Aspen Publishers, Inc., 1989, 12:54f(3).
45. 29 U.S.C. Section 211.
46. 29 U.S.C. Section 216(a).
47. Sovereign, *supra* note 9, at 103.
48. *Id*.
49. Sautter, *supra* note 38, at 240–241.
50. Black's Law Dictionary, *supra* note 4, at 469.
51. 15 U.S.C.A. Sections 201–219.
52. 42 U.S.C. Sections 301–1397(e).
53. Employee Benefit Research Institute. *Fundamentals of Employee Benefit Programs*. 3rd Edition. Washington, DC: EBRI, 1987, 175.
54. *Id*.
55. *Id*. at 178–179.
56. P.L. 99–509 Title X (1986), 29 U.S.C. Section 601–608.
57. Sovereign, *supra* note 9, at 139.
58. *Id*.
59. *Id*.
60. *Id*.
61. James W. Hunt. *The Law of the Workplace: Rights Of*

Employers and Employees. 3rd Edition. Washington, DC: The Bureau of National Affairs, 1994, 202.

62. 29 U.S.C. *1001 et seq.*; C.F.R. 2509–2677.

63. Miller, *supra* note 36, at 157; *Fundamentals of Employee Benefit Programs, supra* note 53, at 28.

64. William F. McHugh, "Law and the Workplace," *in You And The Law.* Lincolnwood, Ill: Publications International, Ltd., 1990, 442 (An American Bar Association Consumer Guide).

65. Miller, *supra* note 36, at 157.

66. *McGann v. H & H Music Co.,* 742 F. Supp. 392 (S.D. Tex. 1990), *aff'd,* 946 F. 2d 401 (5th Cir., 1991), *cert. denied sub nom. Greenberg v. H & H Music Co.,* 113 S.Ct. 482 (1992).

67. 946 F. 2d 401, 407–408.

68. Jeffrey V. Nackley. *Primer on Workers' Compensation.* 2nd Edition. Washington, DC: The Bureau of National Affairs, 1989, 1.

69. Sovereign, *supra* note 9, at 232.

70. *Id., citing White v. New York Central Railroad,* 243 U.S. 188 (1917).

71. *Id.* at 232.

72. 5 U.S.C. Section 8101 *et seq.* (1988 and Supp. IV 1992).

73. Nackley, *supra* note 68, at 12.

74. *Johns v. State, Dept. of Health & Rehab.,* 485 So. 2d 857 (Fla. Dist. Ct. App.), *rev. denied,* 492 So. 2d 1333 (1986).

75. *Herman v. Miners' Hospital,* 807 P. 2d 734 (1991).

76. *Mundy v. Dept. of Health & Human Resources,* 580 So. 2d 493 (La. Ct. App.), *writ granted,* 586 So. 2d 519 (1991), *rev'd,* 593 So. 2d 346, *remanded to,* 609 So. 2d 909 (La. Ct. App. 1992), *writ granted,* 613 So. 2d 960, *aff'd.* 620 So. 2d 811 (1993).

77. *Peterson v. W.C.A.B. (PRN Nursing),* 597 A. 2d 1116 (1991).

78. Nackley, *supra* note 68, at 24.

79. Nackley, *supra* note 68, at 11–25.

80. Sovereign, *supra* note 9, at 219.

81. *Id.*

82. Hunt, *supra* note 61, at 98.

83. *Baptist Medical Center v. Stolte,* 475 So. 2d 959 (Fla. Dist. Ct. App. 1985), *rev. denied sub nom., Unemployment Appeals Comm'n v. Baptist Medical Center,* 486 So. 2d 598 (1986).

84. 828 P. 2d 821 (1991).

85. 470 N.W. 2d 393 (1991).

86. Dolores Bower, Linda Linc, and Doreen Denega. *Evaluation Instruments in Nursing.* New York: National League for Nursing, 1988, 135 (Publication Number 15–2178).

87. *Id.*

88. *Id.* at 41.

89. Sautter, *supra* note 38, at 288.

90. James Redeker. *Employee Discipline: Policies and Practices.* Washington, D.C.: The Bureau of National Affairs, 1989, 51.

91. *Id.*

92. Redeker, *supra* note 90, at 107.

93. *Id.*

94. *Id.*

95. 401 N.W. 2d 884 (Mich. App. 1987).

96. Redeker, *supra* note 90, at 68–69.

97. P. L. 91–596, 84 Stat. 1590, 29 U.S.C. Sections 651–78, *as amended.*

98. Mark Rothstein. *Occupational Health And Safety Law.* 3rd Edition. St. Paul, Minn: West Publishing Company, 1990, 5 (with 1996 Pocket Part).

99. *Id.* at 7.

100. *OSHA, supra* note 97, at 29 U.S.C. Section 654.

101. Omnibus Budget Reconciliation Act of 1990, P.L. 101–508, 104 Stat. 1388 (November 5, 1990).

102. *NLRB v. Washington Aluminum Company,* 370 U.S. 9 (1962).

103. 111 S. Ct. 1196 (1991), *on remand to,* 935 F. 2d 272 (7th Cir. 1991), *appeal sub nom., Local 322, Allied Indus. Workers of America, AFL-CIO v. Johnson Controls,* 969 F. 2d 290 (7th Cir. 1992).

104. *Id.* at 1206.

105. 42 U.S.C. Sections 11001–11050; 29 C.F.R. Section 1910.1200 (1987).

106. 29 C.F.R. Section 1910.1030; 56 Fed. Reg. 64004, 57 Fed. Reg. 29206 (1991).

107. "OSHA Stiffens Bloodborne Rules, Decrees Free Hepatitis B Vaccine," *AJN* (January 1992), 82–84.

108. *American Dental Association v. Martin, et al,* 984 F. 2d 823 (7th Cir.), *cert. denied,* 114 S. Ct. 172 (1993).

109. "OSHA Rule Upheld for Dentists, Partly Vacated for Home Health Industry," 2(5) *BNA's Health Law Reporter* (February 4, 1993), 132.

110. *ADA v. Martin, supra* note 108.

111. "Surveillance for Occupationally Acquired HIV Infection—United States 1981–1992," 266 *JAMA* (December 16, 1992), 3294.

112. CDC, *HIV/AIDS Surveillance Report* (Table 11) (2d quarter ed. (1993).

113. "Nurse Infected with HIV Virus Urges Others To Take Care," *AJN* (December 1990), 86.

114. *Id.*

115. *Id.*

116. American Nurses' Association. *HIV, Hepatitis-B, Hepatitis-C, Blood-Borne Diseases: Nurses' Risks, Rights, and Responsibilities.* Washington, DC: ANA, 1992 (WORKPLACE INFORMATION SERIES BROCHURE-WP-2).

117. *Id.*

118. "OSHA Backs Employer-Paid Hepatitis B Vaccine," *AJN* (March 1989), 416–417, *citing* then-Secretary of Labor Ann McLaughlin. See also *ADA v. OSHA, supra* note 108, at 3.

119. *AJN* (April 1993), 9 (Headlines Section). The CDC has published guidelines for the prevention of transmission of tuberculosis. See 59 Fed. Reg. 54242 (October 28, 1994).

120. See, for example, *Position Statement on Personnel Policies and HIV in the Workplace* (1991); *Position Statement on Post-Exposure Programs in the Event of Occupational Exposure to HIV/HBV* (1991); *Position Statement on Availability of Equipment and Safety Procedures to Prevent Transmission of Bloodborne Diseases* (1991), *in* American Nurses' Association *Compendium of HIV/AIDS Positions, Policies and Documents.* Washington, DC: ANA, 1992.

121. American Nurses' Association. *HIV, Hepatitis-B, Hepatitis-C, Blood-Borne Diseases: Nurses' Risks, Rights, and Responsibilities, supra* note 116. See also, Angela Kopfer, and Patricia McGovern, "Transmission of HIV Via A Needlestick Injury: Practice Recommendations and Re-

search Implications," 41(8) *AAOHN Journal* (August 1993), 374–381.

122. Sovereign, *supra* note 9, at 26–27.

123. *Id.*

124. 42 U.S.C. Sections 1981, 1983.

125. 42 U.S.C. Sections 2000e-4 through e9.

126. 29 U.S.C.A. Sections 701–794 (1993 Supplement).

127. 29 U.S.C.A. Sections 621–634, 663(a) (1993 Supplement).

128. Pub. Law No. 102–166, 105. Stat. 1071 (1991).

129. 42 U.S.C. Sections 12101–12214 (1990).

130. Sautter, *supra* note 38, at 256.

131. Affirmative Action Guidelines, EEOC, *Federal Register,* Volume 44 (January 19, 1979).

132. 41 C.F.R. 60–2.13(a) and 60–2.20; 60–2.13(b) and 60–2.21; 60–2.13(c) and 60–2.22; S 60–2.11(a); 60–2.13(f) and 60–2.24; S 60–2.13(g) and 60–2.25.

133. Sovereign, *supra* note 9, at 107–112.

134. 683 F. Supp. 758 (D. Kan. 1988).

135. 114 S. Ct. 1878 (1994).

136. 106 S.Ct. 2399 (1986), *remanded to,* 801 F. 2d 1436 (D.C. Cir. 1986).

137. Susan Ross, Isabelle Pinzler, Deborah Ellis, and Kary Moss. *The Rights of Women: The Basic ACLU Guide to Women's Rights.* 3rd Edition. Carbondale, Ill: Southern Illinois University Press, 1993, 32.

138. 758 F.2d 1525 (11th Cir. 1985).

139. 480 U.S. 273 (1987), *rehearing denied,* 481 U.S. 1024 (1987), *on remand to,* 692 F. Supp. 1286 (M.D. Fla. 1988).

140. No. 91–504–2, Decision No. CR 191 (Department of Health and Human Services, Departmental Appeals Board, Civil Remedies Division, April 20, 1992); decision upheld, No. 91–504–2, DAB Decision No. 1357 (Department of Health and Human Services Civil Rights Reviewing Authority, September 25, 1992).

141. "More Disability Charges Filed Than Estimated, EEOC Counsel Says," 2(5) *BNA's Health Law Reporter* (February 4, 1993), 135–136.

142. Beatrice Yorker, "Update on the Americans With Disabilities Act For Occupational Health Nurses," 41(5) *AAOHN Journal* (May, 1993), 250–257.

143. Henry Perrit. *Americans with Disabilities Act Handbook.* 2nd Edition. New York: John Wiley & Sons, Inc., 1991, 29 (with 1996 Cumulative Supplement No. 1).

144. 29 U.S.C. Section 141–187 (1935), *as amended.*

145. Sautter, *supra* note 38 at 337, *citing Arena v. Lincoln Lutheran of Racine,* 437 N.W. 2d 538 (Wis. 1989); *U.S. Steel Corp. v. United Mine Workers,* 519 F. 2d 1236 (5th Cir. Ala. 1975); *Barbour v. General Serv. Employment Union,* 453 F. Supp. 694 (N.D. Ill 1978).

146. 29 U.S.C. Sections 153, 158, 159, 160, 161.

147. Sautter, *supra* note 38, at 334.

148. 29 U.S.C. Sections 158(g), 158(d) and 183.

149. 5 U.S.C. Sections 7101–7135.

150. Black, *supra* note 4, at 192.

151. 499 U.S. 606 (1991).

152. "NLRB Health Care Bargaining Unit Rule Having Little Effect on Union Activity," 2(21) *BNA's Health Law Reporter* (May 27, 1993), 695 (SPECIAL REPORT).

153. *Id.*

154. *Id.* at 696.

155. *Id.*

156. *Id.* at 700.

157. Henry Campbell Black, *supra* note 4, at 992.

157. *ANA's Economic & General Welfare Program: A Historical Perspective.* Kansas City, MO: ANA, 1981, 5.

159. See, for example, *Waterbury Hospital v. NLRB,* 950 F. 2d 849 (CT 1991).

160. *NLRB v. J. Weingarten, Inc.,* 420 U.S. 251 (1975), *on remand to,* 511 F. 2d 1163 (5th Cir. 1975).

161. 309 *NLRB* No. 163, Case No. 25-CA-19818 (December 16, 1992).

162. *Electromation, Incorporated v. National Labor Relations Board,* Nos: 92–4129 and 93–1169 (7th Cir. 1994).

163. Jill Sherer, "Controversial Committees," *Hospital and Health Networks* (May 20, 1994), 66–67.

164. 114 S. Ct. 1778 (1994).

165. *Newton-Wellesley Hospital,* NLRB 699, 700 (1975).

166. "Full Impact of High Court Ruling on Status of Nurses Still Unclear," 3(35) *BNA's Health Law Reporter* (September 1, 1994), 1225–1226 (LEAD REPORT).

167. Sovereign, *supra* note 9, at 273, *citing NLRB v. Talladega Cotton Factory, Inc.,* 213 F. 2d 209 (5th Cir. 1954); *NLRB v. Miami Coca-Cola Bottling Co.,* 702 F. 2d 1 (1st Cir. 1983).

168. American Nurses' Association. Report to the Board of Directors from the Cabinet on Economic and General Welfare. *Right to Accept or Reject an Assignment.* ANA (1987).

169. Massachusetts Nurses' Association. *Mechanisms to Support Nurses' Abilities to Exercise Their Right to Accept or Reject an Assignment: Position Statement* (November 9, 1982); North Carolina Nurses' Association. *Guidelines for the Registered Nurse in Giving, Accepting, or Rejecting a Work Assignment* (1986); New York State Nurses' Association. *Protesting of Assignment-Documentation of Practice Situation* (May 1985).

170. Alan MacDonald, "Commentary on Nurses' Right to Accept or Reject Assignment," *The Massachusetts Nurse* (February 1983).

171. *Id.* See also, Nancy J. Brent, "Avoiding 'Abandonment of Patient' Allegations," 2(15) *The Nursing Spectrum* (July 24, 1989), 12–13.

172. See, for example, 745/Illinois Complied Statutes Annotated (ILCS) 70/1 *et seq.* (1977), *as amended.*

173. OSHA Hazard Communication Standard, 29 C.F.R. Section 1910.1200 (1993).

174. 483 N.W. 2d 211 (1992).

175. 726 P. 2d 852 (NM 1986).

176. Beverly Wheeler, "Addressing Substance Abuse within Nursing," 22(9) *JONA* (September 1992), 8.

177. George Byron Smith, "Attitudes of Nurse Managers and Assistant Nurse Managers toward Chemically Impaired Colleagues," 24(4) *Image: Journal of Nursing Scholarship* (Winter 1992), 295, *citing* P. O'Conner and R. S. Robinson, "Managing Impaired Nurses," (9)2 *Nursing Administration Quarterly* (1985), 1–9.

178. 41 U.S.C. Sections 707–707.

179. Kevin B. Zeese. *Drug Testing Legal Manual and Practice: AIDS.* Deerfield, Ill: Clark, Boardman, Callaghan, 1994, Vol. 2, Appendix C-1-1 to C-1-2.

180. See Chapter 5, "Public Employees," *in* Zeese, *supra* note 179. See also, *Skinner v. Railway Labor Executives Association,* 109 S.Ct. 1402 (1989); *National Treasury Em-*

ployees Union v. Von Raab, 489 U.S. 656 (1989); *Kemp v. Claiborne County Hospital*, 763 F. Supp. 1362 (S.D. Miss. 1991).

181. Kurt Decker and H. Thomas Felix. *Drafting and Revising Employment Handbooks*. New York: John Wiley & Sons, 1991, 194–195 (with 1995 Cumulative Supplement).

182. Zeese, *supra* note 179, at 2–28.2.

183. 42 U.S.C. 12114(d)(2).

184. 42 U.S.C. Section 12114(c)(5); 12114 (a) & (b).

185. See, for example, Sally Hutchinson, "Chemically Dependent Nurses: The Trajectory toward Self-Annihilation," 35(4) *Nursing Research* (July/August 1986), 196–201.

186. George B. Smith, "Attitudes of Nurse Managers and Assistant Nurse Managers towards Chemically Impaired Colleagues," 24(4) *Image: Journal of Nursing Scholarship* (1992), 295–300; J. Lloyd Lachicotte and Judith Alexander, "Management Attitudes And Nurse Impairment," 21(9) *Nursing Management* (September 1990), 102–110; Nancy J. Brent, "The Impaired Nurse: Assisting Treatment to Achieve Continued Employment," 24(4) *Journal Of Health And Hospital Law* (April 1991), 112–118.

187. Sovereign, *supra* note 9, at 154.

188. 29 U.S.C. 2001 *et seq.*

189. *Id.*

190. 29 U.S.C. 2006(f)(1)&(2).

191. *Id.*

192. Sautter, *supra* note 38, at 208.

193. 29 U.S.C. Section 2005.

194. Sovereign, *supra* note 9, at 78.

195. Centers For Disease Control and Prevention, "Update: Investigations Of Persons Treated By HIV-Infected Health-Care Workers—United States," 269(20) *JAMA* (May 26, 1993), 2622–2623.

196. *Id., citing* C. Ciesielski, D. Marianos, CY Ou, and others, "Transmission of Human Immunodeficiency Virus in a Dental Practice," 116 *Ann Intern Med* (1992), 798–805. See also, Schaffner and Others, "A Surgeon with AIDS: Lack of Evidence of Transmission to Patients," (264) *JAMA* 467 (1990) (753 patients treated by surgeon with no transmission); Parker and Others, "Management Of Patients Treated by a Surgeon with HIV Infection," 113 *Lancet* (January 13, 1990) (76 out of 339 patients who asked for HIV testing were HIV negative); David Webber. *AIDS And The Law*. 2nd Edition. New York, John Wiley & Sons, Inc., 1992 (with 1996 Cumulative Supplement No. 1), 95.

197. American Nurses' Association. *Position Statement on HIV Testing*. Washington, DC: ANA, September 6, 1991. See also, American Dental Association. *Interim Policy on HIV-Infected Dentists*. Chicago: ADA, January 16,

1991; John Hammel, "A Cure That Fails: Mandatory HIV Testing of Health Care Providers," *Positively Aware* (September 1991), 29–30; "CDC's HIV-Testing Guidelines Get Mixed Reviews," 27(29) *AHA News*, July 22, 1991, 1 (guidelines recommend health care workers involved in "exposure prone" procedures be voluntarily tested and voluntarily inform patients when HIV test is positive).

198. "Position Statements Explore HIV Issues," *The American Nurse* (March 1993), 12.

199. *Leckelt v. Board of Commissioners*, 909 F. 2d 820 (5th Cir. 1990), *affirmed*, 909 F. 2d 820 (5th Cir. 1990), *aff'q.*, 714 F. Supp. 1377 (E.D. LA. 1989).

200. "Hospital to Reinstate HIV-Positive Nurse to a Clinical Care Position," 1(1) *BNA's Health Law Reporter* (December 21, 1992), 411 (News and Developments Department).

201. 620 A. 2d 327 (Md. 1993).

202. Pub. Law 103–3 (February 3, 1993), 107 Stat. 6.

203. Barbara Presley Noble, "Interpreting Family Leave Act" *Chicago Daily Law Bulletin* (August 2, 1993), 6, *quoting* the Labor Department.

204. *Id.*

205. *Id.*

206. 42 U.S.C. Section 12102(a); 28 C.F.R. Section 36.201(a).

207. Micheal Dowell, "The Americans with Disabilities Act: The Responsibilities of Health Care Providers, Insurers and Managed Care Organizations," 25(10) *Journal of Health and Hospital Law* (October 1992), 297.

208. See, for example, Jane Friedman, "Duties under the Americans with Disabilities Act: Is a Surgeon Required to Perform Elective Surgery On An HIV+ Patient?" 25(10) *Journal of Health and Hospital Law* (October 1992), 307–312.

209. 812 F. Supp. 1183 (M.D. Ala. 1993), Call No. 93–6502 (October 3, 1994).

210. "Court Dismisses Complaint of Pregnant Nurse Who Refused to Treat AIDS Patient," 2(20) *BNA's Health Law Reporter* (May 20, 1993), 641.

211. "Home Care Nurse Who Refused to Treat HIV Patient Fails in Pregnancy Bias Claim," 3(40) *BNA's Health Law Reporter* (October 13, 1994), 1445.

212. *Stepp v. Review Board of the Indiana Employment Security Division*, 521 N.E. 2d 350 (Ind. App. Ct. 1988).

213. Winifred Carson, "AIDS and the Nurse—A Legal Update," *The American Nurse* (March 1993), 18.

214. 588 N.Y.S. 2d 698 (Ct. Cl. 1992), 595 N.Y.S. 2d 592 (N.Y. App. Div. 1993), *rev'g in part*, 588 N.Y.S. 2d 698 (Ct. Cl. 1992).

215. ANA. *Position Statement Regarding Risk v. Responsibility in Providing Nursing Care*. ANA: Kansas City, MO, 1986.

216. *Id.*

217. See Chapter 10.

17

The Nurse in the Acute Care Setting

contents

A t one time, hospitals were the most familiar type of health care delivery system in the United States. In fact, until the 1980s, the growth of hospitals and hospital services thrived.[1] Since then, however, hospitals have seen a decline in their occupancy rates[2] and increasing competition from alternative delivery systems (ADS) such as health maintenance organizations (HMOs) and preferred provider organizations (PPOs).[3] Even so, hospitals still provide a wide array of services to those who have a need for their services, including emergency care, surgery, specialty care (ICU/CCU), and labor and delivery services. Moreover, hospitals are the major employers of nursing personnel.[4]

Recent statistics indicate that hospitals employ 958,000 registered nurses and 175,000 licensed practical nurses.[5] This chapter will explore only a few of the many legal issues of interest to the staff nurse working in acute care in the following practice areas: emergency nursing, perioperative nursing, and adult psychiatric/mental health nursing.

NURSING IN THE EMERGENCY DEPARTMENT

Emergency department (ED) nursing is a highly challenging, complex, and rapid-paced nursing practice. It is also a high area of liability.[6] In one study analyzing adverse events in the emergency department, 70% were due to negligence.[7]

In one study analyzing adverse events in the emergency department, 70% were due to negligence.

Many reasons account for the potential for malpractice claims in the ED. To begin with,

large numbers of individuals utilize the emergency department as a primary health clinic or in lieu of a physician's office. Because there is little, if any, continuity of care, follow-up is often nonexistent. The lack of follow-up care can result in further injury or death to the patient.[8]

Second, EDs often treat individuals with severe trauma, including gunshot wounds and multiple injuries due to vehicular accidents.

Trauma injuries are not always easily identified, at least initially. An expected or unexpected change in the patient's condition requires prompt intervention by the ED team. When the intervention does not work, and a patient allegedly suffers further injury or death as a result, a malpractice or wrongful death suit often follows.

These more traditional areas of liability for the ED, as well as recent case and statutory law, have resulted in ED nurses' involvement in lawsuits.

Duty to Provide Care

The duty of a hospital to provide emergency care is a long-standing one established by case law and federal and state statutory law and respective rules and regulations. The earliest federal law passed by Congress establishing the duty was the Hill-Burton Act of 1946.[9] Among other obligations, it mandated that hospitals receiving money for construction and modernization of their facilities could not refuse to provide emergency care to those who could not pay for those services or whenever the hospital had an "uncompensated care obligation."[10]

Many states also passed statutes requiring hospitals to provide emergency care, including Illinois, Florida, Tennessee, and Wyoming. Illinois' act was passed in 1927 and has been used as a model for subsequent state laws. Even so, the particulars of the acts vary considerably.

One of the early cases ensconcing the duty to provide emergency care was *Wilmington General Hospital v. Manlove*,[11] decided in 1961. When Mr. and Mrs. Manlove brought their child to the ED with diarrhea and an elevated temperature, the nurse on duty in the ED informed the Manloves that, pursuant to hospital policy, no care could be provided by physicians at the hospital until the attending doctor was consulted. The ED nurse attempted to contact the pediatrician, but could not reach him. As a result, no care was given to the infant and the Manloves were sent home with instructions to return to the pediatric clinic in the morning. The Manloves did make

an appointment for their son to see the pediatrician that evening, but that afternoon, Darien Manlove died of bronchial pneumonia.

The parents brought suit against the hospital. The trial court denied the request by the hospital for a summary judgment. That decision was appealed, and the Delaware Supreme Court affirmed the trial court decision and sent the case back to the trial court for further proceedings to determine if the hospital had been negligent in not responding to the emergency condition of the infant. The Court's theory in underscoring its decision was that if a hospital has an ED, there is a duty to provide care and treatment to all those who need services *when an emergency exists*.

One of the problems in the *Manlove* case was the lack of an assessment of the infant's condition. According to the nurse involved in the case, despite the parents' voiced concerns, the child did not appear in any apparent distress. Even so, the child died.

Thus, one of the other rules of law in relation to the duty to treat that has emerged from the *Manlove* case is the duty to evaluate the patient to determine if a true emergency exists. That evaluation involves a decision whether the nontreatment of the patient may result in a threat to the patient's well-being or life. If the answer is affirmative, treatment must occur. If a delay will not result in harm to the patient, then an "emergency" does not exist, and there is no obligation to provide care. In short, the rule clearly focuses on the individual's *condition* at the time he or she arrives in the ED.

In 1986, Congress passed another law further expanding and defining the duty to provide emergency care. The Emergency Medical Treatment and Active Labor Act (EMTALA)[12] prohibited facilities receiving Medicare and Medicaid funds from "dumping" patients out of their emergency rooms when they could not pay. The Act requires hospitals to (1) medically screen a patient for the existence of an emergency medical condition, and (2) stabilize the patient's condition; if transfer of the patient is required, the transfer can occur only after stabilization of the condition, after the patient or the patient's legal representative gives informed consent for the transfer, there is a facility to accept the transfer, and the physician documents and certifies certain factors (e.g., the benefits of transfer outweigh the risks of transfer).[13]

The Emergency Medical Treatment and Active Labor Act also defines an emergency medical condition and active labor. An emergency medical condition is one with acute symptoms of such severity that the absence of medical care "could reasonably be expected" to result in (1) placing the health of the patient (including the woman and unborn child) in serious jeopardy; (2) serious impairment of bodily functions; (3) serious dysfunction of any bodily part or organ; or (4) with a woman in active labor, sufficient time to effect a safe transfer before delivery is not possible, or the transfer may pose a threat to the health and safety of both the woman and fetus.[14]

Violations of the Emergency Medical Treatment and Active Labor Act can result in termination of the facility's participation in the Medicare and Medicaid programs. In addition, the Act provides for civil penalties against the offender facility. Also, the injured party may sue for any "personal injury" under the laws of the state in which the hospital exists and may seek "equitable relief" (e.g., an injunction) as well.[15]

In fact, several cases have been filed alleging violations of the Emergency Medical Treatment and Active Labor Act.[16] In one case, *Stevison by Collins v. Enid Health Systems, Inc.*,[17] Mrs. Stevison brought her 13-year-old daughter to the ED at Enid Hospital for abdominal pain. According to Mrs. Stevison, the ED nurse told her that her daughter could not be seen unless a $50.00 payment was made. Because Mrs. Stevison was on welfare, she could not pay the required fee. The nurse testified that she told Mrs. Stevison that welfare did not cover ED visits, and she would be billed for any care and treatment for her daughter.

Despite conflicting stories, it was undisputed that Mrs. Stevison and the daughter left without receiving treatment. The next day, the daughter suffered a ruptured appendix, had the appendix removed at another hospital owned by the defendant hospital, and her postoperative recovery was prolonged and more painful than normal. In addition, due to the rupture, the daughter's ability to have children was probably compromised.

Mrs. Stevison filed suit in federal court alleging that no screening of her daughter's condition took place as required by the EMTALA. The jury returned a verdict in favor of the hospital, and Mrs. Stevison appealed. The Court of Appeals for the Tenth Circuit reversed the lower court decision. The Court held that the hospital had the burden of proof of supporting its contention that Mrs. Stevison "withdrew" her request for treatment after being told of the $50.00 payment. Although the EMTALA does provide that no violation of the Act occurs if a patient refuses screening and treatment after it is offered, the ED must establish this fact by a preponderance of the evidence. The Court based its rationale on the intent of the Act; that is, to deter "patient-dumping" of indigent patients who do not have health insurance or cannot pay for ED services.

Also, in *Johnson v. University of Chicago Hospitals*,[18] the Seventh Circuit Court of Appeals held that the EMTALA does not apply to situations in which the patient does not physically enter the ED for treatment and telemetry services alone are used to divert the patient to another facility. According to the three-judge panel, a hospital-operated telemetry system is distinct from the same hospital's ED.[19]

In the *Johnson* case, a 1-month-old infant stopped breathing and was transported by ambulance to the University of Chicago Hospital. The ambulance personnel were in touch with the hospital's telemetry nurse. When the ambulance was within five blocks of the ED, the nurse informed the ambulance that the pediatric unit was full, they were on "by-pass" status, and the child would have to be taken to another hospital. The child was taken to St. Bernard Hospital's

ED, but had to be transported again to Cook County Hospital because St. Bernard had no pediatric ICU. The child died after being transferred to Cook County Hospital.

Although the Appeals Court held that several causes of action could be brought against the University of Chicago Hospital under Illinois laws, none could be brought under the Emergency Medical Treatment and Active Labor Act.

Triage

Triage is the screening and classification of ED patients to determine their priority of treatment.[20] Many times this process is done by ED nurses with the help of physician-based standing orders and written protocols. Triage is important for many reasons, including providing an immediate response to a patient's needs and in controlling patient flow throughout the ED.

Triage is the screening and classification of ED patients to determine their priority of treatment.

The manner in which triage occurs is varied. It can occur on the telephone, in the ED waiting room, or when several patients arrive at the ED via ambulance. Regardless of its form, triage decisions can result in potential liability for the nurse making treatment priority choices.

In some instances, the ED nurse's liability results from a failure to carry out triage on the patient at all, as in the *Manlove* case discussed earlier. In other situations, the nurse performs triage, but does so negligently. In *Ramsey v. Physician's Memorial Hospital*,[21] for example, the ED nurse evaluated two young boys who were brought to the ED by their mother. Both had symptoms of high fever and a rash. The mother told the ED nurse that she had removed two ticks from one of her sons. The ED nurse failed to inform the physician of this fact and told him only of her physical findings. As a result, the physician diagnosed measles. Unfortunately, one of the children had Rocky Mountain spotted fever and died.

Other cases involving negligent triage by ED nurses include *Lunsford v. Board of Nurse Examiners for State of Texas*[22] (nurse failed to properly assess patient's heart condition; told patient to drive himself to another hospital and he died en route) and *Thomas v. Corso*[23] (nurse failed to report vital signs of automobile accident victim to physician and underestimated injuries and patient's voiced complaints, resulting in his death).

Duty to Report Certain Patient Conditions

To protect the public health and safety, states have passed laws that require the reporting of certain events to an identified state agency. EDs and ED personnel, including nurses, are almost always included as mandated reporters in these laws. Although the respective state laws can vary widely as to what situations must be reported, some of the more common events include:

▼ Child abuse and neglect
▼ Communicable diseases (e.g., tuberculosis, AIDS, sexually transmitted diseases)
▼ Person dead on arrival in the ED
▼ Gunshot wounds, stab wounds, or other injuries due to violence
▼ Sexual assaults
▼ Food poisoning
▼ Industrial accidents[24]

Staffing/Administration of Emergency Department

Adequate staffing of the ED is essential. Adequate staffing is essential not only because of the high-paced, unpredictable nature of ED nursing, but also because of the level of stress associated with practicing in this specialty area and its potential effect on the care provided. A 1992 study of 69 ED nurses identified sources of stress in the ED and ways in which to address them.[25] Stressors seen as inhibiting the provision of quality care included inadequate staffing and untrained relief staff.[26]

Because of the complex cases and patient conditions treated in the ED, it is important that staff be qualified, competent, and adequately trained as well. Although EDs may be classified at different levels (I, II, and III), it is recommended that all EDs be staffed as a Level I center.[27] Specifically, all ED physicians, including the physician director, should be board certified in emergency medicine. At a minimum, all staff physicians should have experience and training in a specialty relevant to emergency care.[28] All ED nurses and physicians should be certified in Advanced Cardiac Life Support (ACLS). Likewise, ED nurses should be certified in emergency nursing and continually update their nursing knowledge base through continuing education and in-service programs.[29]

The non-RN caregivers who are used [in the ED] include emergency medical technicians, . . . paramedics, emergency department technicians, and physician assistants.

In response to increased health care costs and a shortage of nursing resources in some areas, EDs are using non-RN caregivers to meet patient care needs in the ED.[30] The non-RN caregivers who are used include emergency medical technicians (EMTs), paramedics, emergency department technicians, and physician assistants.[31] Although the use of the non-RN staff member may, at least superficially, provide more staff numbers

in the ED, their use can contribute to "a fragmented approach to patient care and infringement on nursing's scope of practice" as well as compromise quality patient care.[32]

Implications for Emergency Department Nurses

The ED nurse must help the ED establish and maintain clear and complete policies and procedures concerning the nurse's role in the assessment and treatment of patients who come to the ED for care. The policies must reflect the ED's duty to provide care when a true emergency exists. Furthermore, it should be established hospital policy that no patient is refused care based on his or her inability to pay. If the ED nurse believes a patient is refused care on the basis of this factor, the ED nurse should discuss this with the ED physician and contact the ED nursing supervisor immediately, and an incident report should be filed with the hospital risk manager.

Likewise, a patient should not be refused care or transferred to another facility in violation of the EMTALA. The ED nurse will need to ensure this does not happen by discussing the Act with the ED physician when refusal or transfer is being contemplated[33] and notify the nursing supervisor immediately.

When a decision is made to transfer a patient consistent with the Emergency Medical Treatment and Active Labor Act, the ED record should also reflect any treatment given to stabilize the patient and the patient's condition upon transfer.

Any decision concerning non-care of a patient in the ED must be carefully documented. If the patient refuses care, or leaves against medical advice (AMA), a complete and factual entry should be made by the ED nurse in the ED record. Some EDs have developed AMA forms for the patient to sign that state that the patient has refused care and releases the ED, ED staff, and hospital from any liability due to his or her decision to leave.

The teaching of the patient/family in the ED must be carefully done and documented fully in the ED record. When teaching is not documented, whether they were given instructions can be the basis of a suit, particularly when an injury or death occurs. For example, in one reported case, *Crawford v. Earl Long Hospital*,[34] a deceased man's mother filed a suit against the hospital alleging that no patient care instructions were given to her after her adult son was treated in the ED when hit on the head with a baseball bat and stabbed in a fight. The patient was not admitted to the hospital, and therefore, according to hospital policy, a responsible adult— the mother of the patient, with whom he was living—was called to come to the ED to get oral discharge instructions. At the time the case arose, it was not the accepted standard of care to provide either the patient or the family written discharge instructions.

Although the nurse testified at trial that she had specifically called the mother to come into the ED and had given her instructions about the care to give to her son after discharge (e.g., check pupil size and orientation of son), the nurse did not document the instructions in the ED record. The jury returned a verdict in favor of the hospital because it believed the nurse's testimony. The appellate court upheld the verdict for the hospital. If the nurse had only documented the instructions given, the mother could not have alleged the teaching was not done.

To help ED nurses with discharge instructions, many EDs have developed teaching forms that provide a ready way in which to include and document needed instructions given to the patient and/or family. Whether the ED nurse uses a teaching form for documenting the teaching done, or whether the teaching is documented narratively, the nurse will also want to be certain to discuss with the patient and/or family the ramifications on the health and well-being of the patient if the instructions are not followed. In *LeBlanc v. Northern Colfax County Hospital*,[35] the death of a patient after being seen in the ED was alleged to have been caused by the ED

nurse's inadequate instructions concerning the pain the patient was experiencing after being kicked in the stomach. Because the patient did not have any medical knowledge, the ED nurse's instructions to the patient to "come back to the ED if the pain persists" may not have been clear enough for the patient to act upon. The patient delayed going back to the ED for 6 days despite his continued pain. The pain resulted from a lacerated liver and gastrointestinal bleeding due to a ruptured ulcer, which, combined with no food, the ingestion of unprescribed Darvon, and only small amounts of liquid, caused his death.

To help ED nurses with discharge instructions, many EDs have developed teaching forms . . .

The appellate court reversed the trial court's summary judgment for the hospital (based on its finding that the patient's death was due to his delay in seeking treatment and not on the nurse's instructions) and sent the case back to the trial court for a trial. Although the case settled out of court, it may well be an indication that discussing and documenting implications if treatment recommendations are not followed is a good risk management approach for the ED nurse.

Many times the ED will receive a telephone call from an individual requesting medical advice over the phone. The call may be from an individual never seen in the ED before, or it may be from a patient who was treated in the ED but sent home because admission was not necessary. The ED nurse must be very careful about giving telephone advice in this manner. It is more prudent to encourage the individual to come into the ED or see his or her physician as soon as possible.[36] Similarly, if a person asks whether or not a visit to the ED is necessary, the ED nurse should err on the side of encouraging the individual to be seen in the ED.

Policies and procedures for proper reporting of required events in the ED are also important. The development of forms to help the ED nurse with his or her responsibilities in this regard can also be very helpful.

If the ED nurse works in a setting where EMTs, paramedics, or other non-RN care providers work, the nurse will need to be very clear about the state nurse practice act requirements concerning working with non-RN staff. The ED nurse should carefully review any delegation, supervision, and other requirements in order to be in compliance with the practice act.

If the nurse is working with a physician assistant, the scope of practice of the physician assistant and the nurse's responsibilities under the nurse practice act when working with a physician assistant will need to be reviewed. For example, if the ED nurse can carry out orders (whether standing or otherwise) only from a physician, then an order from a physician assistant could not be legally carried out by the ED nurse. If, on the other hand, the state nurse practice act allows orders to be carried out by anyone who is authorized by state law to prescribe orders or treatments, then the ED nurse has the legal basis upon which to carry out the orders of the physician assistant.

PERIOPERATIVE NURSING

There are more than 80,000 perioperative nurses in the United States.[37] The perioperative nurse fulfills various roles in the perioperative department, including that of circulating nurse, monitoring and caring for the patient in the postanesthesia area, and that of the RN first assistant (RNFA). Perioperative nursing is, by its very nature, complex and demanding. Because a patient's condition can change rapidly during or after surgery, adverse patient outcomes are always a possibility. Often the adverse outcomes result from a breakdown in the patient's continuity of care during the surgical process.[38]

There are more than 80,000 perioperative nurses in the United States.

Adverse Patient Outcomes in Perioperative Nursing

Many of the allegations of professional negligence in the perioperative area involve the administration of anesthesia or the negligent monitoring of patients who are under anesthesia[39] or who are recovering from anesthesia in the postanesthesia care unit (PACU). Several malpractice cases involving the certified registered nurse anesthetist are discussed in Chapter 21. Examples of other cases against perioperative nurses are presented in Table 17–1.

The RN First Assistant

The RN first assistant (RNFA) in the perioperative setting possesses an expanded role. Although the RN first assistant's role may be prescribed by the state nurse practice act, it is also often molded by the health care facility's policies and procedures.[40] The American Association of Operating Room Nurses (AORN) official statement on the RN first assistant[41] provides a consistent definition of what the first assistant does and defines the Association's qualifications for the nurse in this role.

The RN first assistant collaborates with the surgeon and practices under his or her supervision when performing the first assistant role. . . .

The RN first assistant collaborates with the surgeon and practices under his or her supervi-

TABLE 17–1
Malpractice Cases Involving Perioperative Nurses

CASE NAME	ALLEGATION	DECISION
Goldsby v. Evangelical Deaconess Hospital (1978)[1]	Failure to follow nursing monitoring procedures postop caused patient death	Judgment against hospital due to postanesthesia nurse's negligence
Laidlow v. Lion Gate Hospital (1969)[2]	Failure of postanesthesia nurses and supervisor to provide adequate supervision and nurses caused patient arrest, resulting in permanent brain damage to patient	Judgment against hospital due to nurses' and supervisor's conduct
Evoma v. Falco (1991)[3]	Failure of postanesthesia nurse to ask what drug patient was given during surgery, to ensure patient would be monitored when leaving PACU, and failing to recognize patient was not breathing, resulting in initial comatose state and then death of patient over a year later	PACU nurse's conduct 100% responsible for patient injury; court verdict for patient's estate
Robinson v. N. E. Alabama Regional Medical Center (1989)[4]	Nurse in OR counted sponges incorrectly after vaginal hysterectomy, resulting in patient's pain, nausea, vomiting, inability to sleep, and dizziness for 5 months postop	Verdict for patient and against hospital in amount of $250,000

[1]74-004-754 (N.M. 1978)
[2]70 W.W.R. 727 (1969)
[3]589 A. 2d 653 (N.J. 1991)
[4]548 So. 2d 439 (Ala. 1989)

sion when performing the first assistant role in the intraoperative phase of the patient's perioperative experience.[42] The RN first assistant's scope of practice is firmly grounded in perioperative nursing practice, but is a "refinement" of that nursing specialty.[43] Responsibilities of the RN first assistant include obtaining informed consent for surgical procedures (where allowed by state law and institutional procedures),[44] handling tissue, suturing, and hemostasis.[45]

The American Association of Operating Room Nurses recommends that the RN first assistant be certified in operating room nursing (CNOR) and possess scrub and circulating proficiency. In addition, the first assistant should complete a formal education program that includes didactic and supervised clinical experience and learning.[46] The formal programs must include all content from the *Core Curriculum for the RN First Assistant*[47] and take place in academic institutions accredited by the Associations of Colleges and Schools.[48] Obviously the ultimate goal is

certification (certified RN first assistant; CRNFA) or a degree as an RN first assistant.

Staffing/Administration of Perioperative Department

Surgery scheduling is essential to the efficient and effective provision of services in perioperative care.[49] So, too, is the scheduling of qualified staff. In the operating room (OR) itself, for example, the basic requirement is that at least one RN will function as circulating nurse in each OR.[50] Moreover, the RN is an essential staff member in the OR.[51]

Other factors that must be taken into consideration when scheduling staff include the number of patients that will be moving through the perioperative area on a given day, the number of OR suites, the types of procedures that will be performed, whether registry/outside contract personnel will be necessary, and the method of staffing used (e.g., fixed or variable).[52]

The use of ancillary personnel, such as OR materiels services technicians and perioperative nursing assistants, can help staffing concerns by their respective provision of assistive and support services to the perioperative nursing staff. They cannot, however, be a substitute for the perioperative nurse or perform perioperative nursing functions. For example, in some instances, surgical technologists (STs) want to perform as first assistants or have circulating responsibilities.[53] This trend, at least in one author's view, threatens the essence of perioperative nursing and raises patient care concerns.[54]

Implications for Perioperative Nurses

All perioperative nurses must be certain to provide non-negligent care consistent with established standards of care for this specialty practice.[55] Although assessment, observation, and evaluation are important responsibilities for all perioperative nurses, they are very important in the PACU. As the court stated in the *Laidlow* case presented in Table 17–1:

> The patient in this room requires the greatest attention because it is fraught with the greatest potential dangers to the patient. This hazard carries with it . . . a high degree of duty owed by the hospital to the patient. . . . There should be no relaxing of vigilance if one is to comply with the standard of care required in this room. . . .[56]

That standard of care includes not leaving the postanesthesia patient alone with no monitoring as well as monitoring the patient effectively.

Monitoring the patient well, in addition to performing all of the other responsibilities in perioperative nursing, requires adequate numbers of personnel in the perioperative areas as well as adequately trained staff. The Association of Operating Room Nurses recommends a 1:1 perioperative RN to patient ratio during operative and other invasive procedures.[57] Yet, in a 1995 study by the Association surveying 2000 hospitals, results indicated that there was a major decrease (40% to 29%) in 1:1 staffing ratios

from a similar 1988 study.[58] More encouraging in terms of staffing implications was the finding that there seemed to be a slight increase since the 1988 survey in RN/non-RN ratios.[59] The perioperative nurse will need to voice any and all concerns about inadequate staffing to the nurse manager in the perioperative suite. Using Association of Operating Room Nurses' guidelines, as well as licensing requirements and accreditation suggestions, may help rectify any staffing issues.

The documentation of the care given to the perioperative patient must be complete, factual, and timely. Utilizing well-developed documentation forms can enhance the effectiveness of required documentation. Likewise, well-formulated and accessible policies and procedures are invaluable.[60] Specific areas that need to be focused on by the perioperative nurse include when and how the patient was monitored, the identification of persons who provided perioperative care to the patient, the continual assessment of the patient's condition preoperatively, intraoperatively, and postoperatively, any significant or unusual occurrences, the interventions taken during the patient's stay in the perioperative area, notification of the patient's surgeon or others if a change in the patient's condition occurred, and, of course, the patient's condition and status upon leaving the perioperative suite.[61]

If the perioperative nurse is functioning as an RN first assistant, it is important that that be the only role of the nurse at that time. For example, the RN first assistant should not also function as the scrub nurse while first assisting.[62] Current certification in both OR nursing and as a first assistant is essential. It is also important that the RN first assistant comply with any policies and procedures required of the institution concerning the role of the first assistant.

RN first assistants will also need to work to change nursing practice acts in states in which the RN first assistant is not recognized. Moreover, if the hospital in which the RN first assistant works provides a mechanism for the RN first assistant to obtain clinical privileges, that procedure should be used so that the RN first assistant can function effectively in the role and consistent with his or her education and clinical background.

Assistive workers in the perioperative area can be utilized to aid the nurse consistent with the assistive worker's job description, the state nurse practice act, and other regulatory requirements. The perioperative nurse will need to be clear about what the nursing profession, the professional associations, and the law allow the nurse to delegate to the assistive worker. The nurse can then use that information to delegate certain patient care tasks to the competent assistive worker without violating those guidelines. For example, the Association of Operating Room Nurses clearly states that assessment, diagnosis, identification, planning, and evaluation of the patient—all "core activities" of perioperative nursing—cannot be delegated to assistive workers.[63] In deciding what perioperative patient care might be delegated to the unlicensed assistive worker in the perioperative area, the amount of supervision the RN will be able to provide, the competency of the worker, the complexity of the patient's condition, and the ratio of RNs to assistive workers based on patient need are some of the factors that must be evaluated.[64]

All perioperative nurses will need to be ever vigilant in guarding against any intrusion into their practice. Reorganization or restructuring of the hospital or perioperative area, the use of surgical technicians to replace RN first assistants, the laying-off of qualified perioperative nurses and replacing them with assistive workers, and requiring more professional responsibilities of the nurse without hiring adequate numbers of qualified staff to carry out those responsibilities are all examples of ways in which perioperative nursing practice can be, and is being, threatened. For example, in the 1995 Association of Operating Room Nurses' study, restructuring affected staffing ratios in 18% of the hospitals in the sample.[65] The effects included some RNs being replaced with assistive workers and a decrease in RN positions in 25% of the sample.[66]

The perioperative nurse will also need to be involved in research concerning the role of the nurse in providing quality care to patients. Documented research findings are helpful, not only in stemming the tide against intrusion by others into perioperative nursing practice, but also for convincing legislators to provide, or continue to provide, the legal basis for perioperative nursing practice.

PSYCHIATRIC/MENTAL HEALTH NURSING

The nurse who works in psychiatric/mental health nursing must not only be knowledgeable about general legal issues in the provision of care to patients (e.g., informed consent/refusal for treatment, documentation) but must also be mindful of the application of those general legal issues to this specialty area of practice. Many of the applications faced by the nurse when caring for the client who has psychiatric difficulties are relatively new in comparison to the length of time general legal rights and issues have been in existence. It was not until the 1960s that legal rights of the mentally ill were finally recognized by the courts and state and federal governments.[67] With those established rights came concomitant responsibilities for health care providers, including psychiatric/mental health nurses.

It was not until the 1960s that legal rights of the mentally ill were finally recognized by the courts and state and federal governments.

The legal responsibilities of nurses in psychiatric nursing are further compounded by the fact that the law has in many instances provided more legal protections for those with psychiatric problems because of the very nature of the illness and the treatment required. For example, the very fact that someone requires admission to a psychiatric unit for care can stigmatize that person. Moreover, if the individual does not consent to admission and an involuntary admission is necessary, many constitutional issues must be carefully handled, not the least of which are numerous constitutional due process protections.[68]

Table 17–2 lists the types of admissions possible and the constitutional issues raised by those admissions.

Duty to Protect the Patient from Harm

Once admitted to a hospital psychiatric unit, the recipient of mental health care requires a thorough assessment, careful monitoring, and the establishment of a sound plan of care throughout his or her stay in the unit. This is especially so for the psychiatric patient who may be suicidal. The psychiatric nurse must ensure the patient's safety in accordance with established standards of care.[69] When the assessment, monitoring, or plan of care does not meet established standards of care and a patient is injured or dies, liability for the nurse may occur.

For example, in *Johnson v. Grant Hospital*,[70] a woman patient in the psychiatric unit told several staff members about her suicidal thoughts one evening. The nurse supervisor informed the patient's psychiatrist of the patient's conversations with staff. The psychiatrist ordered the patient secluded for the remainder of the evening. The next day, the day nurse, unaware of the patient's suicidal thoughts, assigned the pa-

---

TABLE 17–2
Types of Psychiatric Admissions

NAME	REQUIREMENTS FOR USE	WHEN DISCHARGE POSSIBLE	CONSTITUTIONAL ISSUES
Informal	Patient identifies need and signs informal admission form	Whenever patient chooses to leave, unless involuntary admission procedures initiated by hospital or mental health care provider	None if patient is admitted and discharged without difficulties
Voluntary	Patient, or legal representative, consents to admission	Whenever patient chooses to leave *after* time specified in mental health code (e.g., 5 days), unless involuntary admission procedures initiated by hospital or mental health care provider	14th Amendment (due process, liberty, privacy (right to refuse treatment))
Involuntary A. Emergency certificate B. Judicial commitment C. Other	Most states require that individual be a danger to self or others and be mentally ill; other criteria might include inability to care for own basic needs	Whenever patient no longer mentally ill or danger to self or others or can care for own basic needs. Determined by hospital, physician, or other mental health care provider or court, depending on how patient was involuntarily committed	14th Amendment (due process, liberty, privacy (right to refuse treatment)); 8th Amendment (cruel and unusual punishment, especially if certain treatment required); 14th Amendment (equal protection). Courts have called treatment issues, especially confinement against one's consent, as right to least restrictive alternative placement (LRA). LRA also has been extended to type of treatment; that is, treatment that is effective but that does not overly inhibit personal liberties

Data from Rose Eva Baba Constantino, "Legal Issues in Psychiatric-Mental Health Nursing," *Psychiatric Nursing: A Comprehensive Reference*. Suzanne Lego, Editor. Philadelphia: J. B. Lippincott, 1996, 551–561; Ralph Chandler, Richard Enslen, and Peter Renstrom. *Constitutional Law Deskbook: Individual Rights*. 2nd Edition. Rochester, NY: Lawyers Cooperative Publishing, 1993 (with April 1995 Supplement).

tient to a newly hired staff member. After leaving the seclusion room with the new staff member, the patient was left alone for a few moments. She was able to jump to her death through a nearby window of the unit. The court returned a verdict against the hospital, holding that it was the staff's duty to protect the patient from potential harm.

The duty to protect a recipient of mental health services from harm also extends to the use of seclusion and restraints. The purpose of seclusion and restraints is to manage aggressive or self-destructive behavior when other measures (e.g., the therapeutic relationship or medication) do not work.[71] Notwithstanding the necessity of both methods in certain situations, utilizing them negligently, or failing to utilize them when needed, can result in injury or death to a patient.

In *Pisel v. Stamford Hospital*,[72] a patient in a seclusion room on a steel-frame bed suffered brain damage after being left in the seclusion room without proper monitoring. The patient was able to wedge her neck between one raised side rail and the mattress, which decreased blood flow to her head. In entering a judgment against the hospital, the court held that, among other things, the staff and hospital had been negligent in (1) secluding the patient with the bed frame in the seclusion room; (2) failing to monitor the patient properly; and (3) improperly designing and locating the seclusion room, which could not be clearly seen from the nursing station.[73]

Duty to Maintain Patient Confidentiality

All nurses have a legal and ethical responsibility to protect patient confidentiality and privacy. The responsibility for psychiatric patients is even more encompassing. Specific state and federal statutes[74] govern the release of patient information to others when that takes place other than with the patient's consent. The state statute may be called a "confidentiality act," or the pro-

tections may be included in a general statute dealing with mental health care. Although the contents of the state statutes vary, most include:

▼ Written consent from patient or legal representative required for release of records or information

▼ Provisions when written consent from patient or legal representative not possible (e.g., upon death of patient)

▼ Information necessary for written consent to be honored

▼ Guidelines for patient access to and review of own records

▼ Situations in which information or records can be released without patient's written consent (e.g., when the patient must be involuntarily committed for psychiatric care, when child abuse or neglect is suspected)[75]

When the guidelines for protecting patient confidentiality are not followed, liability can result for breaching the patient's confidentiality. The reverse is also true; that is, when there is a requirement to release information and it does not happen, a breach of the psychiatric/mental health nurse's duty can also occur.

In *Tarasoff v. Regents of the University of California*,[76] a graduate student who was being seen in the school mental health clinic told his psychologist-therapist that he intended to kill a woman student. The psychologist, concerned about what his patient had told him, especially in light of his duty to maintain confidentiality, shared his concerns with others on the clinic staff. It was decided that because of the nature of the communication, the psychologist needed to inform the police about the threat. The police brought the graduate student to the police station and questioned him, but did not detain him because they did not think he was irrational.

No one attempted to notify the woman student or her family. Nor did anyone initiate commitment proceedings against the male patient. The patient did stab Tanya Tarasoff to death several days later.

The parents of Ms. Tarasoff brought a suit against the mental health professionals and the university alleging negligence in their handling of the situation. The California Supreme Court returned a verdict against the university and its clinic staff and opined:

> Once a therapist does in fact determine, or under applicable professional standards should have determined, that a patient poses a serious danger of violence to others, he bears a duty to exercise reasonable care to protect the foreseeable victim of that danger. While the discharge of this duty of due care will necessarily vary with the facts of each case, in each instance the adequacy of the therapist's conduct must be measured against the traditional standard of reasonable care under the circumstances.[77]

The Court's requirement that a mental health professional protect a foreseeable victim based on the circumstances of the situation has been characterized as the "duty to warn third parties" of potential injury or death. This characterization is probably inaccurate, because the duty established in the opinion is much broader. In some instances, for example, the duty of the health care provider may indeed be to warn the intended victim. In other instances, it may be more appropriate to initiate involuntary admission proceedings against the person threatening another. Or, a combination of these two actions may be necessary. Therefore the duty is more accurately characterized as the "duty to inform third parties."

The *Tarasoff* decision was adopted by many other jurisdictions through case decisions and through amendments to state mental health codes/laws. Its adoption provides a legal basis for the mental health professional, including the psychiatric/mental health nurse, to share patient information when confronted with this type of situation without incurring liability for a breach of confidentiality.

Privilege

In addition to the protection of confidentiality of mental health information and treatment, psychiatric patients are also given protection against the release of any information obtained during the relationship between the patient and the mental health professional without the patient's consent within the context of judicial proceedings. Unlike the duty to maintain confidentiality, which is clearly borne by the mental health professional, the protection of privilege is owned by the patient.[78] Therefore, it is the patient who determines when the privilege can be waived.

The . . . requirement that a mental health professional protect a foreseeable victim based on the circumstances of the situation has been characterized as the "duty to warn third parties" . . .

Privilege is established in respective state statutes. It can be found, for example, in specific mental health "confidentiality statutes" or in other provisions of state law. In Illinois, for example, the Mental Health and Developmental Disabilities Confidentiality Act contains specific provisions concerning when mental health providers, including nurses, can refuse to testify in judicial and administrative proceedings by asserting this privilege on their own, or on behalf of the recipient of mental health services.[79] Other states protect the patient's privilege in civil practice rules concerning testimony or in licensing acts.

The protection of privilege, like the protection of confidentiality, is not absolute. Exceptions to the right of the patient to refuse to allow the nurse to testify in judicial or administrative proceedings include many of the same exceptions concerning the confidentiality of mental health records. They include (1) when child abuse or neglect is reasonably suspected; (2) when a person needs to be involuntarily admitted to a psychiatric facility; (3) when a patient introduces his or her own mental condition into any court or administrative proceeding; and (4) during investigations and trials for homicide or murder.[80]

Presumption of Competency of the Psychiatric Patient

When an individual is admitted to a psychiatric facility, the patient retains any and all abilities to make decisions on his or her own behalf, including treatment decisions. In other words, there is a presumption of competency of the psychiatric patient. This presumption extends to both voluntary and involuntary patients. The presumption of competency is usually codified in the state mental health code or it may be established as a result of case law. In either situation, the psychiatric client retains the right to make decisions and carry out other responsibilities that non-psychiatric patients possess (e.g., enter into a contract, obtain a divorce, sell stock).

In some instances, a patient receiving mental health services may not be able to enjoy the protections of this presumption. The diagnosed illness may impair his or her ability to make appropriate decisions. If the patient's competency is a concern for mental health professionals working with the patient, then a guardianship proceeding may need to be initiated to judicially appoint another to make decisions for the patient. This is especially so when no other legal mechanism exists to appoint a surrogate decision maker (e.g., durable power of attorney).

State guardianship statutes define the requirements necessary for a guardian to be appointed for the person alleged to be legally incompetent (the ward). For example, many require the presence of a physical or emotional illness that seriously affects the person's ability to make decisions.[81] Evidence is heard by a judge concerning the person's inability to make decisions. Such evidence includes testimony from family members as well as treating mental health professionals.

If a guardian is appointed, the role of the guardian and his or her powers will be carefully spelled out by the court. For example, the guardian may be a "personal" guardian or an "estate" guardian. The powers of the guardian may be "limited" or "plenary."

Insofar as treatment issues are concerned, the guardian must have powers of a personal guardian; that is, to give informed consent for treatment/nontreatment and make decisions surrounding other life choices. In contrast, "estate" guardians are responsible for making financial decisions concerning the ward (e.g., selling property, paying bills). In either case, the guardian must always act consistent with the state guardianship statute and the best interest of the ward.

A guardianship is not necessarily permanent. State statutes provide for judicial oversight of the guardianship to ensure that it meets the needs of the ward. The court can remove a guardian at any time. Likewise, a petition for restoration of competency can be filed by the ward.[82] The ward must prove he or she is able to handle his or her own affairs by competent (relevant and material) evidence.

Implications for Psychiatric/ Mental Health Nurses

The type of psychiatric unit in which the psychiatric/mental health nurse practices will affect some of the practice decisions that will need to be made to comply with the legal obligations protecting the psychiatric client. When a patient is admitted to the unit, it will be necessary for the nurse to ensure that all necessary documentation is in the patient's record concerning the type of admission for that patient. For example, if the patient is a voluntary patient, the form for that admission should be complete and signed by the patient. Whether a voluntary or involuntary patient, the patient should receive a written list of his or her rights consistent with the state's mental health code.

Immediately upon admission, but also throughout the patient's stay in the unit, careful, complete and adequate monitoring of the patient's condition will be necessary. Because safety of the patient and others on the unit is paramount, any acting-out behavior, violent behavior, or expressions of suicidal thinking must be immediately handled. Doing so will require thorough knowledge of the state mental health laws in this area and the institution's policies concerning medication administration, seclusion, restraint, and suicidal precautions. The psychiatric/mental health nurse will need to carefully document any behavior observed and notify the psychiatrist and others on the mental health team as soon as possible.

When intervening with violent behavior or suicidal ideation, the nurse will need to obtain orders from the psychiatrist or other mental health team member for the institution of seclusion, restraint, or medication. However, if there is an emergency that requires immediate intervention, the psychiatric/mental health nurse can initiate whatever care is needed so long as that initiation is consistent with his or her institution's policies and procedures and state law. For example, it may be possible for the nurse to place a patient in restraints without an order beforehand if an emergency exists in which the patient is physically harmful to himself or herself or is physically abusing others.[83] In such an event, any proper notification to other mental health team members, including the psychiatrist, will need to occur.

Because the procedure for placing a patient in restraints can be potentially injurious to both the patient and staff, many facilities require that only staff trained in restraint application be permitted to place patients in restraints.[84] In-service training is also often required on a continual basis for this procedure and for placing a patient in seclusion.

The psychiatric/mental health nurse will need to constantly monitor the patient who is in restraints or seclusion and document carefully the time and manner of monitoring. The use of a form or checklist that contains the required monitoring times and other information for use by the nursing staff can help the mental health team comply with this duty.

Proper and complete documentation of the need for restraint and seclusion is also important in the event the patient decides to charge the nurse and others with false imprisonment. Several successful cases alleging this intentional tort have been filed.[85]

When the psychiatric/mental health nurse is faced with releasing information about the patient as a recipient of mental health services, his or her treatment, or any other information surrounding the provision of mental health services, the nurse must consult applicable state and federal laws and institutional policies. If the nurse has a clinical concern that a threat by a patient against another may occur, notification of the psychiatrist or other health care provider is vital so that a determination can be made as to how to handle the situation. Whatever the decision, complete documentation in the patient's record as to the course of action taken is necessary.

If asked to testify in any judicial or administrative proceeding, the psychiatric/mental health nurse will want to obtain the advice of the institution's attorney and/or an attorney of his or her own to ascertain the best approach to take concerning the testimony. Under no circumstance should the nurse simply agree to testify, show up at the trial or hearing, or respond to a subpoena requesting treatment records without first obtaining advice from an attorney.

Consent for psychiatric/mental health treatment should be obtained from the patient unless a guardian has been appointed to perform this role or some other legally recognized surrogate decision maker exists for that purpose. If there is a question of a patient's competency (or decision-making ability) to provide consent or refusal for treatment, the psychiatric/mental health nurse should notify the psychiatrist, nurse manager, and others on the team to decide how to proceed. If a guardianship petition is filed, the nurse may well be asked to testify at the guardianship hearing concerning the patient's conduct and behavior while in the psychiatric unit. Again, it is essential for the nurse to obtain legal advice before testifying concerning the patient and his or her conduct while in treatment.

SUMMARY OF PRINCIPLES AND APPLICATIONS

Practicing in the acute care setting is varied, challenging, and exciting. Regardless of the changes in health care delivery, hospitals are here to stay. There is no doubt that as hospitals continue to exist, nurses in hospitals will continue to exist because nursing and nursing services are central to the provision of hospital care.[86] Even so, the character of nursing in acute care settings will probably continue to change. With that change will come increasing concerns for the provision of quality care, nursing staff satisfaction, and liability concerns. The nurse in the acute care setting may be able to resolve some of these concerns in the three nursing practice areas presented by:

▼ Keeping up to date about the many laws and regulations that affect the nurse's specific area of practice

▼ Providing care in accordance with standards of care established by the profession, professional associations, and the law

▼ Advocating for safe nursing staffing patterns, in terms of both numbers of staff and competency of staff

▼ Resisting encroachment of nursing practice

▼ Delegating to and supervising unlicensed assistive workers in accordance with state laws, regulatory guidelines, and professional nursing association mandates

▼ Guarding the patient's right to confidentiality and the patient's right of testimonial privilege

▼ Continuing to attend in-service training, continuing education programs, and formal nursing educational programs to achieve additional knowledge in his or her area of practice

▼ Utilizing appropriate resources, including legal resources, for guidance when a difficult practice issue arises

TOPICS FOR FURTHER INQUIRY

1. Conduct a survey of emergency or perioperative departments in at least two hospitals in your community. Evaluate the use of assistive workers in those units. The survey can include interviews of staff—including nursing management—job descriptions, or other indicia concerning use of non-RN caregivers. Suggest how improvements in the use of RNs in the units could occur. Suggest how the assistive worker could be used in a better manner to assist the RN.

2. Compare and contrast at least five nurse practice acts for their respective support of RN first assistants. Determine how the act defines the role; what rules, if any, have been promulgated to further define the role; and other provisions unique to this role.

3. Identify case decisions in your state concerning the duty of mental health care providers to warn third parties of potential injury by a psychiatric patient. Determine if any psychiatric/mental health nurses were involved in any of the cases, and if so, under what circumstances. Identify any themes the cases might show (e.g., types of violence involved, how a communication was handled), and from them, draft a "model" statute concerning the duty to warn third parties.

4. Interview a nurse in a hospital ED for his or her opinion concerning triage in the facility. Areas for consideration might include what factors the nurse uses when doing triage, how the triage system was developed, and what limitations exist when the nurse carries out triage (e.g., scope of practice concerns). Then develop a policy and procedure for triage based on the information obtained from the interview.

REFERENCES

1. Anthony Kovner, "Hospitals," *Health Care Delivery in the United States*. 4th Edition. Anthony Kovner, Editor. New York: Springer Publishing Company, 1990, 141–144.
2. *Id.*
3. Dulcelina Stahl, "The Pulse of Managed Care in 1996 and Beyond," 27(4) *Nursing Management* (April 1996), 16–17.
4. Institute of Medicine. *Nursing Staff in Hospitals and Nursing Homes: Is It Adequate?* Washington, DC: National Academy Press, 1996, 4.
5. "Who's on Staff at Nation's Hospitals?" *Nursing News*, September 1995, 1 (diagram depicting numbers from 1993 data from the American Hospital Association).
6. Paul A. Craig, "Risk Management Issues in the Emergency Department," *The Risk Manager's Desk Reference*. Edited by Barbara J. Youngberg. Gaithersburg, Md: Aspen Publishers, Inc., 1994, 484.
7. Robert Wood Johnson Foundation, "Negligent Medical Care: What Is It, Where Is It, and How Widespread Is It?" *Abridge* (Spring 1991), 7.
8. *Id.*
9. Hospital Survey and Construction Act of 1946, 60 Stat. 1040, codified at various sections of 24 U.S.C., 33 U.S.C., 41 U.S.C., 46 U.S.C. and 49 U.S.C.
10. Robert Miller. *Problems in Health Care Law*. 7th Edition. Gaithersburg, Md: Aspen Publishers, Inc., 1996, 360.
11. 174 A. 2d 135 (1961).
12. 42 U.S.C. Section 1395dd(a) *et seq.*
13. 42 U.S.C. Sections 1395dd(3)(A), 1395dd(c)(1), and 1395dd(b)(2).
14. 42 U.S.C. Section 1395dd(e)(1).
15. 42 U.S.C. Section 1395dd(d)(2)(A).
16. For an interesting summary of cases brought under the EMTALA, see Donald Wilcox and Hugh Barton, "Overview of the Emergency Medical Treatment Act," *1992 Health Law Handbook*. Alice G. Gosfield, Editor. Deerfield, Ill: Clark Boardman Callaghan, 1992, 83–107.
17. 920 F. 2d 710 (Oklahoma 1990).
18. 982 F. 2d 230 (7th Cir. 1992); see also, "Seventh Circuit Reverses Controversial Ruling on Hospital Telemetry Services," 2(1) *BNA's Health Law Reporter* (January 7, 1993), 5.
19. *Id.*
20. Craig, *supra* note 6, at 473, *citing* S. Frye-Revere, "Emergency Rooms: The Triage Metaphor Error," 24(30) *Journal of Health and Hospital Law* (December 1991), 370–372.
21. 373 A. 2d 26 (Md. App. 1977).
22. 648 S.W. 2d 391 (Ct. App. Texas 1983).
23. 288 A. 2d 379 (Md. 1972).
24. William Roach, Jr., and The Aspen Health Law Center, "Access to Medical Records Information," *Medical Records and the Law*. 2nd Edition. Gaithersburg, Md: Aspen Publishers, Inc., 1994, 127–135.
25. Bonnie Rogers, "Nursing Injury, Stress, and Nursing Care," Institute of Medicine. *Nursing Staff in Hospitals and Nursing Homes: Is It Adequate?, supra* note 4, at 517, *citing* M. P. Hawley, "Sources of Stress for Emergency Nurses in Four Urban Canadian Emergency Depart-

ments," 18(3) *Journal of Emergency Nursing* (1992), 211–216.
26. *Id.*
27. Craig, *supra* note 6, at 471–472.
28. *Id.*
29. *Id.*
30. Emergency Nurses' Association. *Position Statement—The Use of Non-Registered Nurse (Non-RN) Caregivers in Emergency Care*. Chicago: ENA, 1993, 1.
31. *Id.*
32. *Id.*
33. See, for example, *Burditt v. US DHHS*, 934 F.2d 1362 (5th Cir. 1991), which affirmed a $20,000 penalty against the emergency department physician for, among other things, transferring a patient in active labor in violation of the Act. A nurse in the ED at the time of the incident attempted to inform Dr. Burditt that his intention to transfer the patient would be in violation of the Act, and gave him a copy of it, but he did not read it. See also, Wilcox and Barton, *supra* note 16, at 103.
34. 431 So. 2d 40 (La. 1983).
35. 672 P. 2d 667 (1983).
36. John Dronsfield, "Emergency Services," *Risk Management Handbook for Health Care Facilities*. Linda Harpster and Margaret Veach, Editors. Chicago: American Hospital Association, 1990, 155.
37. Mark Phippen and Maryann Papanier Wells. *Perioperative Nursing Practice*. Philadelphia: W.B. Saunders Company, 1994, xi.
38. John Dronsfield, "Surgery, Anesthesia, and Recovery," *Risk Management Handbook for Health Care Facilities, supra* note 36, at 161.
39. Barbara J. Youngberg, "Risk Management Issues Associated with Anesthesia," *The Risk Manager's Desk Reference, supra* note 6, at 456.
40. Lori Ominsky and Mark Phippen, "Preparing the Patient for Surgery," Phippen and Wells, *supra* note 37, at 303.
41. *AORN Official Statement on RN First Assistants*, March 3, 1993.
42. *Id.*
43. Association of Operating Room Nurses, Inc. *Core Curriculum for the RN First Assistant*. Denver: AORN, Inc., 1990.
44. Phippen and Wells, *supra* note 37, at 313.
45. AORN, *Official Statement, supra* note 41, at 1.
46. AORN, *Core Curriculum, supra* note 43.
47. AORN, *Core Curriculum, supra* note 43.
48. AORN, *Official Statement, supra* note 41, 2.
49. Inez Tenzer, "Staffing and Scheduling," Phippen and Wells, *supra* note 37, at 902.
50. *Id.* at 909.
51. AORN. *Resolution on the Necessity for the Registered Nurse in the Operating Room*. March 22, 1973.
52. *Id.* at 910.
53. Suzanne Ward, "Encroachment of Practice: Implications for the Perioperative Nurse," Phippen and Wells, *supra* note 37, at 1014; see also, Association of Surgical Technologists. *Standards of Practice*. Littleton, Colo: AST (1989).
54. *Id.*
55. See, for example, Association of Operating Room Nurses. *Standards and Recommended Practices for Perioperative Nursing*. Denver, 1992.

56. "Negligence in the Recovery Room," 66(26) *Canadian Nurse* (July 1970), 4.

57. AORN, *Statement on Mandate for the Registered Nurse as Circulator in the Operating Room.* (1994).

58. AORN. *1995–96 Nursing Research Committee Staffing Study.* (1996), 1.

59. *Id.*

60. AORN. *Recommended Practices for Documentation of Perioperative Nursing Care,* 1995, 2.

61. *Id.*

62. AORN, *Official Statement, supra* note 41.

63. AORN. *AORN Official Statement on Unlicensed Assistive Personnel,* March 9, 1995, 1.

64. *Id.*

65. AORN, *1995–96 Staffing Study, supra* note 58, at 3.

66. *Id.*

67. Nancy J. Brent, "Legal Issues in Adult Psychiatric Nursing," *Adult Psychiatric Nursing.* 3rd Edition. Jeanette Lancaster, Editor. New York: Medical Examination Company (1988), 620.

68. See, for example, Rose Eva Bana Constantino, "Legal Issues in Psychiatric-Mental Health Nursing," *Psychiatric Nursing: A Comprehensive Reference.* 2nd Edition. Suzanne Lego, Editor. Philadelphia: J. B. Lippincott, 1996; *O'Connor v. Donaldson,* 422 U.S. 563 (1975); *Wyatt v. Stickney,* now *Wyatt v. Alderholt,* 325 F. Supp. 781 (M.D. Ala. 1971), 344 F. Supp. 373 (M.D. Ala. 1971), 334 F. Supp. 1341 (M.D. Ala. 1972), *aff'd in part, modified in part,* 503 F. 2d 1305 (5th Cir. 1974).

69. See, for example, American Nurses' Association. *Statement on Psychiatric-Mental Health Clinical Nursing Practice and Standards of Care of Psychiatric-Mental Health Nursing Practice.* Washington, DC: ANA, 1994.

70. 286 N.E. 2d 308 (1972).

71. Fatima Ramos, "Use of Seclusion and Restraints," in *Psychiatric Nursing, supra* note 68, at 469.

72. 430 A. 2d 1 (1980).

73. *Id.*

74. The federal statute is the Mental Health Systems Act of 1980, Pub. L. 96-398, 94 Stat. 1564 (October 7, 1980).

75. See, for example, 740 ILCS 110/1 *et seq.* (1979), *as amended,* for Illinois' protections. The Act is called The Illinois Mental Health Confidentiality Act.

76. 529 P. 2d 553 (Cal. 1974), *vac., reheard en bank and aff'd.,* 551 P. 2d 334 (1976).

77. *Id.* at 345.

78. Joseph T. Smith. *Medical Malpractice: Psychiatric Care.* Colorado Springs, Colo: Shepard's/McGraw-Hill, Inc., 1986, 54 (with Cumulative Supplement May 1, 1995).

79. 740 ICLS 110/10 (1979), *as amended.*

80. See, for example, Rose Eva Bana Constantino, *supra* note 68, at 561; Illinois Mental Health and Developmental Disabilities Confidentiality Act, 740 ILCS 110/1 *et seq.* (1979), *as amended.*

81. Madelyn Iris and Flora Kelly, "Guardianship," *You and the Law.* Lincolnwood, Ill: American Bar Association and Publications International, 1990, 536.

82. *Id.* at 538.

83. See, for example, Illinois' Mental Health Code, 405 ICLS 5/2–107.1 (1979), *as amended.*

84. Claudia Teich, "Risk Management in the Psychiatric Setting," *The Risk Manager's Desk Reference, supra* note 6, at 446–447.

85. W. Page Keeton, Editor. *Prosser and Keaton on Torts.* 5th Edition. St. Paul, Minn: West Publishing Company, 1984, 47–54 (with 1988 Pocket Part).

86. *Nursing Staff in Hospitals and Nursing Homes, supra* note 4, at 5.

18

The Nurse As Administrator

contents

An administrator is a person who manages affairs of any kind.[1] Administration and management involve many functions, some of which include directing, regulating, governing, and supervising.

In the mid 1880s, Florence Nightingale defined the major role of the nurse administrator as that of educating others in the care of the sick and ill.[2] Since that first definition, the role was further expanded to include 10 major roles identified for any executive by Mintzberg.[3] Categorized into three major areas—interpersonal, informational, and decisional—the roles are figurehead, leader, liaison, monitor, disseminator, spokesperson, entrepreneur, disturbance handler, resource allocator, and negotiator.[4]

In the mid 1880s, Florence Nightingale defined the major role of the nurse administrator as that of educating others in the care of the sick and ill.

The nurse administrator performs these various roles in many health care delivery settings, including hospitals, home health care agencies, and psychiatric/mental health facilities. Moreover, the nurse administrator may perform the roles at various levels within the health care delivery system. For example, the nurse administrator may hold an executive position as part of senior administration. Most often, the nurse administrator's title in that role is that of chief nurse executive (CNE) or chief nurse officer (CNO) and the position is described as, for example, Vice-President of Nursing Services.

In contrast, the nurse administrator may hold a position as a nurse manager, either at a first- or middle-level position, whose responsibilities include patient care concerns (e.g., staff schedul-

---

KEY PRINCIPLES

Liability
Professional Negligence
Negligent Supervision
Board of Directors
Employment Contract
Severance Agreement/Benefit

---

ing and coordinating nursing activities) and who reports to the nurse executive.[5] Titles of nurse managers include head nurse, nursing supervisor, and clinical nurse manager.[6]

Moreover, nurse administrators perform their various roles in nursing departments that are organized differently. A nurse administrator may be employed in a decentralized agency or one that is more bureaucratic.[7] Shared governance or a participative management framework, described by Stevens and Kerfoot as authority structures, also affect the nurse administrator's role.[8]

Regardless of which role a nurse has in administration and which organizational structure is present, both the nurse executive's role and that of the nurse manager are in a state of flux.[9] Factors that have affected nursing administra-

---

tion practice include increased governmental involvement in the nursing services provided to patients, work redesign, managed care, and the use of computers in nursing administration.[10] This chapter will briefly focus on some of the many legal issues affecting nurse administrators in this time of change.

THE NURSE MANAGER

Nurse managers in decentralized facilities are involved in three major activities as part of their role: hiring, staffing, and budgeting.[11] Statistics reveal that nurse managers manage budgets in excess of $1 million and often are responsible for 25 to 50 full-time equivalent nursing staff employees.[12] There is no doubt that these responsibilities may result in liability for the nurse manager.

Selection of Nursing Staff

A major responsibility of nurse managers is the hiring of nursing staff. This role requires excellent interpersonal skills during the interviewing of prospective employees. It also requies awareness of employment and other laws affecting this aspect of a potential employment relationship. The nurse manager cannot ask about or attempt to obtain information from the applicant that may violate state or federal antidiscrimination and employment laws.

For example, asking a female applicant about her marital status or plans for having children is a violation of Title VII when the answers are used to make employment decisions, as discussed in Chapter 16. Similarly, asking an applicant about disability-related issues prior to the applicant being given a conditional job offer is a violation of the Americans With Disabilities Act, also discussed in Chapter 16.

Guidelines are available to the nurse manager for review and for use when interviewing prospective staff. The guidelines include rules and regulations promulgated by the Equal Employment Opportunity Commission (EEOC) and other agencies published in the Code of Federal Regulations (C.F.R.), EEOC and other agency enforcement guidance documents, textbooks dealing with antidiscrimination and personnel law, and nursing journal articles that highlight this type of information for their readers (e.g., *American Association of Occupational Health Nursing Journal*).

Negligent Supervision

One of the important roles—indeed duties—the nurse manager has is the provision of adequate supervision of staff nurses for whom he or she is responsible.[13] When adequate supervision does not occur and a patient is injured, the patient may allege that the nurse manager's supervision of the nurse providing the direct patient care in the situation was negligent. Liability for negligent supervision may be based upon several types of conduct of the nurse manager. For example, if the nurse manager delegates patient care to a nurse who is unable to perform the care, and/or if the nurse manager fails to personally supervise the nurse providing care when the manager knew, or should have known, that supervision was necessary, liability may be imposed on the nurse manager.[14] Liability may also be found by a court when the nurse manager does not take the necessary steps to avoid patient injury when he or she was present and able to intervene. And, if the nurse manager does not properly allocate the time of available staff and an injury occurs, the nurse manager may be responsible for his or her own negligent judgment in the nurse manager role.[15]

Liability for negligent supervision may be based upon several types of conduct of the nurse manager.

The liability of the nurse manager for negligent supervision does not arise under the *respon-*

deat superior theory discussed in Chapter 3. The nurse manager is not the employer of the nursing staff that he or she manages and supervises. Rather, the liability is based on the nurse manager's breach of his or her own duties as a nurse manager. As a result, when negligent supervision is alleged, the standard of care that will be used to measure the nurse manager's conduct will be that of other ordinary, reasonable, and prudent nurse managers in the same or similar circumstances.

Because the nurse manager is an employee of a particular facility, the nurse manager's alleged negligent supervision can, of course, allow the patient to also name the employer as a defendant under *respondeat superior*. Table 18–1 lists several cases against nurse managers.

Managing Employee Issues

Because the nurse manager is responsible for the supervision of the nursing staff, he or she must be well versed in the many employment, and other, laws that affect the manager–staff nurse relationship. These laws were presented in earlier chapters. It is clear that nurse managers are often involved in suits alleging violations of these laws.

For example, in *Watson v. Idaho Falls Consolidated Hospitals*,[16] a nurse's aide alleged that the head nurse on her unit had intentionally interfered with the aide's employment relationship, had inflicted emotional distress, and that the reasons given for her termination were slanderous. The Court dismissed the allegations of slander against the head nurse.[17]

Moreover, the nurse manager will be faced with the possibility of increasing involvement in such lawsuits for additional causes of action alleged by staff, including sexual harassment under Title VII,[18] invasions of workplace privacy,[19] and "English-only" work rules.[20]

Implications for Nurse Managers

The nurse manager can maintain some control over involvement in lawsuits alleging negligent supervision or a violation of staff rights by insti-

TABLE 18–1
Cases Involving Nurse Managers

CASE NAME	TYPE OF FACILITY	ALLEGATIONS	COMMENTS
Moon Lake Convalescent Ctr. v. Margolis (1989)[1]	Nursing home	DON breached duty to maintain policy concerning bathing of residents and for not having policy for excessive bath temperatures	Decision for resident; DON helped with bathing of resident but did not follow policy for safe bathing; resident injured and burned; court also found DON and home liable because no policy established for safe temperatures when bathing residents
Bowers v. Olch (1953)[2]	Hospital OR	Supervising nurse in OR responsible, along with hospital and surgeon, for leaving needle in patient's abdomen during surgery	Supervising nurse not responsible for injury; she had properly assigned two competent nurses to assist surgeon during surgery; supervisor not present during surgery so could not intervene
State v. Washington Sanitarium and Hospital (1960)[3]	Psychiatric hospital	Supervising nurse and hospital negligent in not preventing patient's suicide when they allowed him to wander on unit rather than keep hydrotherapy appointment	No liability on part of nurse or hospital; patient gave no indication that he was suicidal; psychiatrist had no orders for suicide precautions

1. 535 N.E. 2d 956 (1989).
2. 260 P. 2d 997 (1953).
3. 165 A. 2d 764 (1960).

tuting a sound management style that has a proactive risk management focus.[21] When hiring new staff, for example, careful attention to the questions asked during the interviewing process is essential. Information that may be seen as discriminatory or an intrusion into the applicant's privacy cannot be requested by the nurse manager. Rather, the information obtained, and the decision to hire or not hire an applicant, must be based on a careful analysis of the applicant's skill, experience, and ability to work within the demands of the unit or agency milieu.

Adequate orientation of new staff is essential. The orientation plan may be a formalized program or a less formal preceptor-type plan.[22] In-service programs are also essential to provide ongoing improvement and enhancement of the nursing staff's capabilities.[23]

The nurse manager can maintain some control over involvement in lawsuits alleging negligent supervision or a violation of staff rights by instituting a sound management style that has a proactive risk management focus.

The supervision of nursing staff by the nurse manager must be consistent and in accordance with standards of care. When a problem is identified, whether it be concerning the quality of the care provided by the nursing staff member or with the interpersonal relationships on the unit or in the agency, prompt intervention by the nurse manager is essential. Not only will prompt intervention hopefully rectify the problem, it may also avoid additional problems for the nurse manager. In *Ethridge v. Arizona State Board of Nursing*,[24] a nurse manager was held accountable and was disciplined by the board of nursing for her failure to respond to the nursing staff's concerns about, among other things, pos-

sible drug diversion and falsification of records at the hospital. The Arizona State Board of Nursing held that the nurse manager's failure to intervene in the staff concerns, and especially her failure to report a staff nurse's diversion of Valium to the board, was unprofessional conduct under the Arizona Nurse Practice Act. Ms. Ethridge was censured, and her professional nurse license was placed on 12 months' probation.

The nurse manager must also develop effective policies and procedures for the staff working in the facility or on his or her unit. They must reflect current practice and be reviewed and updated as needed.[25]

When a patient or family member expresses unhappiness with patient care, the nurse manager should respond to those concerns immediately and in a caring manner.[26] Research has indicated that doing so may avoid a suit from being filed, even when an injury to the patient has occurred.[27]

The nurse manager's communication with staff is also an important preventive measure.[28] Open lines of communication at all times can aid in resolution of potential difficulties before they become a legal risk within the health care delivery system or influence the quality of care provided by nursing staff.[29] In addition, communication patterns that stress feedback, participation, tolerance for new ways of providing patient care, and solving problems when they arise contribute to a "satisfied" nursing staff.[30]

Open lines of communication and nurse manager support during any restructuring of the facility will also help avoid patient care problems and enhance staff morale. Nurse manager support includes allowing staff to help in the planning of any changes necessary due to the restructuring, a safe environment in which to express anxieties and concerns, providing time for any new training or changes that must be "learned," and mentoring those who are implementing the restructuring.[31]

THE CHIEF NURSE EXECUTIVE

The chief nurse executive has always possessed a very important role within the health care delivery system. Whether planning strategy, evaluating the overall quality of nursing care within an entity, or allocating human and fiscal resources, the chief nurse executive's role in the organization, the community, and the profession cannot be underestimated.[32] Even so, the role of the chief nurse executive is evolving from a focus on nursing services in traditional settings to an even broader accountability for patient care services in community-based practice.[33] Termed the *continuum of care concept,* it will require the chief nurse executive to expand his or her expertise in this area.[34]

> *The chief nurse executive has always possessed a very important role within the health care delivery system.*

As the chief nurse executive develops skills and expertise in the continuum of care, the traditional skills and expertise of the chief nurse executive will continue to be needed. Moreover, both the traditional and new responsibilities and roles will create legal concerns for the nurse executive.

Board of Director Membership

Most often a health care facility's organizational structure is that of a corporation. Incorporated pursuant to state law, the corporation may be a for-profit or not-for-profit entity. A corporation must be managed by a governing body, referred to as a board of directors or a board of trustees.[35] The board has three major functions: oversight, direction, and evaluation.[36] Through these functions the board manages and fulfills the obligations of the organization and is legally accountable for its decisions.

Board membership may vary from organization to organization. Even so, it is recommended that the membership be composed of representa-

tives from the entity itself and the community it serves.[37] Often the chief nurse executive is a member of the board. In fact, a 1992 American Organization of Nurse Executives membership survey[38] indicated that of 1520 nurse executives surveyed (not all were chief nurse executives), 52% (786) sat on their hospital's governing board.[39]

With board membership comes the potential for liability if the board breaches any of its duties. Boards of health care facilities have many duties. One is, of course, to ensure that the health care delivered by the corporation's employees is non-negligent. If this duty is breached, the board and its members may be sued under the doctrine of *respondeat superior* and/or *corporate negligence.* This duty includes (1) selecting a capable and competent administrator; (2) complying with any applicable statutes, rules, and regulations pertaining to the delivery of health care; (3) providing adequate and capable health care delivery staff; and (4) providing adequate facilities.[40] Additional board member management responsibilities include the establishment of institutional goals, policies, and procedures; the appointment of the chief operating officer (COO); and the preservation of assets of the corporation.[41]

When an alleged breach of any of these duties and responsibilities occurs, the chief nurse executive member may be named in the suit, particularly if the nurse executive had voting privileges on the board. Suits have been filed against boards of directors. The landmark case establishing the doctrine of corporate negligence was *Darling v. Charleston Community Hospital*[42] discussed in Chapter 3. Other selected cases appear in Table 18–2.

Implications for the Chief Nurse Executive

Sitting on the board of one's health care facility is an important and positive step for the nurse executive.[43] However, it is also a responsibility, and the nurse executive will need to be

TABLE 18–2

Selected Cases of Corporate Negligence

CASE NAME	ALLEGATIONS	DECISION	COMMENTS
Montgomery Health Care Facility v. Ballard (1990)[1]	Understaffing caused death of resident due to infected bedsores	Court decided for estate of deceased resident; upheld $2 million punitive award against parent corporation that owned nursing home	Three nurses were witnesses and testified about short-staffing; one nurse testified that she told supervisor more staff was needed, but none was provided
Johnson v. Misericordia Hospital (1981)[2]	Permanent paralysis of right thigh due to surgeon severing right femoral artery	Decision for injured 18-year-old and against hospital based on failure of hospital to carefully screen surgeon prior to admission to medical staff	Plaintiff had settled case against surgeon, so hospital was only defendant
Czubinsky v. Doctors Hospital (1983)[3]	Postanesthesia patient's cardiac arrest results in permanent brain injury due to postanesthesia nurse leaving area when monitoring should have been ongoing	Judgment for patient based on failure of hospital to provide adequate staff to monitor post-operative patients	Court reversed verdict of jury in favor of hospital, ruling that injuries were directly related to lack of adequate staff

1. 565 So. 2d 221 (1990).
2. 301 N.W. 2d 156 (1981).
3. 188 Cal. Rptr. 685 (1983).

knowledgeable about liability issues inherent in the role. In addition, familiarity with the organization's by-laws and articles of incorporation is essential.[44] Being an active participant on the board is also required.

> *Sitting on the board of one's health care facility is an important and positive step for the nurse executive.*

If the chief nurse executive has voting privileges as a board member, he or she will need to carefully review each decision that is to be made before casting the vote. This will be especially important with any patient care issues. Because the nurse executive has a unique perspective in relation to patient care concerns, he or she will be seen by other board members as an expert in this area.[45] As a result, the nurse executive's contribution to the decision-making process can have a long-lasting effect on the character of the corporation.[46]

The chief nurse executive will also want to determine if liability insurance coverage for board members (called directors and officers or D & O liability insurance) is provided by the health care facility. D & O liability insurance coverage is an important protection for board members. A survey of almost 8000 corporate and not-for-profit entities, 350 of which were hospital chief executive officers, indicated that 12% of the respondents' board members had been involved in lawsuits related to director and officer liability issues.[47] Of the hospital respondents, 86% were covered by entity-purchased liability insurance.[48]

The D & O liability insurance provided should include indemnification of the board member for all liabilities and expenses, including attorney fees, fines and penalties, and any funds paid to satisfy judgments.[49] Most often, coverage will occur only if the board member acted in good faith and reasonably believed his or her action was lawful and in the best interests of the corporation.[50]

If the nurse executive is not provided with liability insurance from the health care facility, it can be purchased personally. However, it is expensive, and a careful and thorough comparison of rates will be necessary. In the 350 hospital response group discussed above, for example, the 13% without any D & O liability insurance stated that they could not purchase the insurance at an affordable cost.[51]

The nurse executive will also want to talk with other nurse colleagues who sit on governing boards to gain as much insight into that experience as possible.[52] Even though it is a vicarious way in which to begin to examine the role, it provides an excellent opportunity to begin to understand and develop the role of the chief nurse executive as a board member.

Employment Concerns of the Chief Nurse Executive

One of the many responsibilities the chief nurse executive has is the management of organized nursing services within the health care facility or agency. This includes defining the qualifications of staff and developing policies and programs to attract and retain competent nursing staff.[53] This process requires a thorough knowledge of employment and labor law, including the many nuances of the at-will employment doctrine.

The nurse executive has, however, unfortunately failed in many instances to use this knowledge to develop a realistic plan to maintain his or her own employment in the health care delivery system in which he or she works. Despite holding a senior administrative position, few chief nurse executives may have employment contracts.[54] As a result, they, too, are employees at-will and can face termination at any time during their employment in the health care delivery system.

Statistics support just how often chief nurse executives face unwanted termination from employment. In one study of university or university-affiliated hospitals, 40% of 257 directors of nursing were terminated or asked to leave within the previous 10 years, according to sam-

pled chief executive officers and the current directors of nursing.[55] As a result of the turbulent nature of health care today—mergers, work redesign, and managed care, to name a few—the trend of unwanted terminations will probably continue to be experienced by chief nurse executives.[56]

Despite holding a senior administrative position, few chief nurse executives may have employment contracts.

If the nurse executive is terminated as an at-will employee, there may be little legal recourse for the nurse. Several cases involving an attempt by nurse administrators and executives to challenge the terminations have been reported in recent years. In *Frank v. South Suburban Hospital Foundation*,[57] the nursing supervisor of the oncology unit filed a suit against her employer after being terminated for not carrying out a physician's order she believed to be harmful to a patient and for performing carotid massage on the unmonitored patient. Ms. Frank alleged the hospital wrongfully terminated her. The appellate court, however, upheld the summary judgment for the hospital and held that Ms. Frank was an at-will employee with no guarantee of continued employment. Moreover, the court opined, the employee handbook created no contract of employment for Ms. Frank.

It is important to note that whether or not Ms. Frank's actions helped or hindered the patient had no bearing on the decision of the court.[58] Because at-will employees can be terminated for "a good reason, a bad reason or no reason at all,"[59] the issue was not relevant to the termination.

Likewise, in *Bourgeous v. Horizon Healthcare Corporation*,[60] the Director of Nursing at one of

Horizon Healthcare's nursing centers was terminated from her employment during the 90-day probationary period required of all at-will employees. During her initial tenure at the center, Ms. Bourgeous maintained that she was orally told that she would be groomed for a medical consultant role and the Director of Nursing position was a prerequisite for that role. However, shortly after assuming the Director of Nursing position, Ms. Bourgeous felt she was not given adequate training for her role, complained that the facility was understaffed, and discovered that unlicensed personnel were providing physical therapy to residents. After meeting with officials from the center, she was asked to resign. Ms. Bourgeous refused and was terminated from the Director of Nursing position.

Ms. Bourgeous filed a suit against the center and alleged wrongful termination. The court entered a directed verdict in favor of the center and the Supreme Court of New Mexico affirmed that decision. In addition to illustrating the at-will employment doctrine, this decision also supports the important principle that, generally, relying on oral representations concerning continued employment is legally risky.[61]

If the chief nurse executive is terminated for an unlawful reason, however, he or she may be able to successfully challenge the unwanted termination. Unlawful reasons include a discriminatory motive, such as making the decision on the basis of a disability, age, or gender as presented in Chapter 16.

Implications for the Chief Nurse Executive

There is no doubt that the chief nurse executive should obtain a contract of employment for any senior administrative position. The contract should contain provisions concerning the position to be filled, the term (length) of the contract, salary (including any bonuses and how those will be determined), vacation, benefits (e.g., health insurance, computers, paid professional association dues), and sick pay.[62] The proposed contract should be reviewed by the nurse executive's attorney. It may be necessary for the nurse executive's attorney and the attorney for the health care facility to amend, change, or add provisions in the proposed contract.

In addition to the general provisions in the employment contract, the attorney for the nurse executive will want to review the contract for specific paragraphs. One will be the existence of any restrictive covenants. Restrictive covenants prohibit the employee from working for a competing employer or starting a competing business either during or after employment with the current employer.[63] To be legally enforceable, they must be reasonable (e.g., length of time, geographic area covered), protect a legitimate employer interest, be supported by valid consideration (e.g., the salary and other benefits the nurse executive is contracting for in the position), not against public policy or harmful to the public, and be part of the employment contract.[64]

A second provision of concern for the nurse executive will be the conditions of termination of the employment contract before the term of employment is completed. The best protection for the nurse executive will be language that requires a "for-cause" or "just-cause" termination, with some requirement of notice when the employer decides to exercise its ability to end the employment contract. Examples of for-cause or just-cause terminations include negligence, failure to perform job responsibilities, addiction to drugs or alcohol, and conviction of a crime.[65]

Obviously the requirement of a documented reason for terminating the nurse executive's employment provides job security. Moreover, if the employer does not abide by the contract terms and terminates the nurse executive in violation of those terms, the nurse can sue the employer for breach of the employment contract.

Another important provision in the nurse executive's employment contract should be one governing severance benefits in the event the employment contract is not renewed at the end of its term, or if the nurse executive's employment is terminated prior to the end of the contract's duration. Although severance benefits are not always mandated by state law, if validly contracted for, they are legally enforceable. However, a recent survey of 586 hospitals indicated that only half had formal severance policies, and just half of those policies are located in an "employee manual."[66]

Although severance benefits are not always mandated by state law, if validly contracted for, they are legally enforceable.

The purpose of a severance arrangement is to provide financial support for the former employee until he or she finds another position.[67] Therefore, the nurse executive will want to obtain the best severance benefit package possible at the time of hiring. Some elements of a good severance arrangement include a severance payment, outplacement services, and a positive reference from the former employer.[68]

If the nurse executive is not able to negotiate an employment contract that includes a severance arrangement, and an unwanted termination does occur, the nurse executive should attempt to negotiate a severance agreement with the employer at that time.[69] A negotiated exit may be seen by the employer as advantageous in terms of controlling future litigation,[70] particularly if a broad waiver of any right to sue the employer is agreed to by the nurse executive and included in the severance agreement. However, without an obligation to provide severance benefits, a negotiated severance agreement may be seen as unnecessary by the employer, especially if it believes there was no discrimination or other unlawful conduct on its part.

If the chief nurse executive is concerned that his or her involuntary job loss may be due to some discriminatory motive, a consultation with an attorney should be obtained. Although discrimination suits are costly and are not quickly resolved, it may be the only recourse the chief nurse executive has for a violation of his or her rights. The chief nurse executive will want to consider this option even when her unwanted termination is not the only one within an organization. For example, in a recent case filed under Title VII involving allegations of race discrimination as the motive for a large number of job terminations (not involving a nurse executive), the federal court evaluated such factors as how the hospital determined which positions would be eliminated, the process by which the terminations were effectuated, and the transferability of duties.[71] These factors must be carefully evaluated by the chief nurse executive who is part of a large reduction in force, especially in view of the fact that many nurse executives are women and over 40 years of age.[72]

SUMMARY OF PRINCIPLES AND APPLICATIONS

Nurse administrators are in a time of transition, not only in terms of the health care systems within which they are employed, but also in terms of their own roles and responsibilities. As if those changes were not enough to contend with, nurse administrators must also help the staff they govern prepare for the same changes.[73] Because nurse administrators balance many roles in diverse settings at various levels, these, as well as other, requirements can be met. However, they must be met proactively and innovatively.[74] The nurse administrator can do so by:

▼ Performing the nurse administrator role—whether as a nurse manager or chief nurse executive—consistent with applicable professional standards

▼ Continuing to develop skills and expertise in the many roles required by the nurse administrator

▼ Remaining sensitive to the many concerns staff nurses and other nurse colleagues have concerning the many changes faced by them in their nursing practice

▼ Evaluating carefully the role of a board member before accepting the responsibilities inherent in that role

▼ Obtaining advanced educational preparation for the role of nurse manager or chief nurse executive

▼ Keeping abreast of the latest developments in the law that impact upon the nurse administrator's practice

▼ Negotiating a contract of employment, either in the nurse executive's current position or before a new position is accepted

▼ Reviewing carefully any contract of employment or severance agreement before signing

▼ Obtaining legal advice when necessary to make informed decisions concerning employment and any involuntary separations

▼ Participating in research to identify trends and continuing issues faced by nurse administrators in their various roles in health care delivery

TOPICS FOR FURTHER INQUIRY

1. Develop a research tool to measure one of the major roles of the nurse executive identified by Mintzberg. Limit the use of the tool to a select group of nurse executive functions. Compare and contrast the findings.

2. Using available public records from the state regulatory agency, identify disciplinary actions against nurse administrators. Determine the frequency of the types of actions in the sample studied. Identify ways in which the nurse administrators could have avoided the disciplinary action taken against them.

3. Develop a questionnaire for use with chief nurse executives to explore their role on a health care facility board. Design the questionnaire to evaluate a particular aspect of the role of board member. Analyze the results for similarities and differences.

4. Investigate how many discrimination suits have been filed by nurse administrators against former employers in a given period since 1990. Identify how many of the nurse administrators included in the study were offered severance benefits that contained a waiver of their right to sue the employer if they accepted the benefits. Determine how many of the suits filed were decided in favor of the nurse administrator.

REFERENCES

1. *The Random House College Dictionary.* Revised Edition. New York: Random House, Inc., 1991, 18.
2. Barbara Volk Tebbitt, "Nurse Administrators: Who Are They, What Do They Do, And What Challenges Do They Face?" *Current Issues in Nursing.* Joanne McCloskey and Helen Grace, Editors. 4th Edition. St. Louis: C.V. Mosby, 1994, 26.
3. Henry Mintzberg. *The Nature Of Managerial Work.* New York: Harper and Row, 1973.
4. *Id.* at 92–93.
5. Eunice Turner. *Scope And Standards for Nurse Administrators.* Washington, D.C.: American Nurses Publishing, 1996.
6. Maureen Sullivan and Judy Carlson-Catalano. *Nursing Leadership and Management: A Study and Learning Tool.* Springhouse, Pa: Springhouse Corporation, 1990, 96.
7. "Governance Structures," Barbara Stevens Barnum and Karlene Kerfoot. *The Nurse As Executive.* 4th Edition. Gaithersburg, Md: Aspen Publishers, Inc., 1995, 59–63.
8. *Id.* at 61–62.
9. Paula Jaco, Sylvia Price, and Alice Davidson, "The Nurse Executive in the Public Sector," 24(3) *JONA* (March 1994), 61.
10. See Peter Buerhaus, Joyce Clifford, Mary Fay, and others, "Executive Nurse Leadership: The Harvard Nursing Research Institute's Conference Summary," 26(3) *JONA* (March 1996), 21–29; Virginia Saba, Joyce Johnson, and Roy Simpson. *Computers in Nursing Management.* Washington, D.C.: American Nurses Publishing, 1994, 2–3.
11. Barbara Mark, "The Emerging Role of the Nurse Manager: Implications for Educational Preparation," 24(1) *JONA* (January 1994), 51; See also American Organization Of Nurse Executives. *Role and Functions of Nurse Managers.* Chicago: American Hospital Association, 1992.
12. *Id.,* citing B. Mark and H. Smith. *Essentials of Finance for Nurses.* Germantown, Md: Aspen Publishers, Inc., 1987.
13. *Nursing-Legal Survival: A Risk Management Guide for Nurses.* Oak Brook, Ill: University Hospital Consortium, 1992, 111.

14. *Id.* at 112.

15. Robert D. Miller. *Problems in Hospital Law*. 7th Edition. Gaithersburg, Md: Aspen Publishers, Inc., 1996, 332–333.

16. 720 P. 2d 632 (1986).

17. *Id.*

18. See, for example, Christine Godsil Cooper, "Sexual Harassment: Preventive Steps for the Healthcare Practitioner," 2 *Annals of Health Law* (1993), 1–33.

19. See, for example, Kim Kirn, "Workplace Privacy in Illinois: A Review," 83(9) *Illinois Bar Journal*, September 1995, 454–461.

20. See, for example, Debra Novack, "English-Only Rules in the Workplace—The Need to Prove Disparate Impact," 83(9) *Illinois Bar Journal*, September 1995, 474–480.

21. *Nursing-Legal Survival, supra* note 13, 111–117.

22. Nancy J. Brent, "Risk Management in Home Health Care: Focus on Patient Care Liabilities," 20(3) *Loyola University of Chicago Law Journal* (Spring 1989), 775–795.

23. Nancy J. Brent, "Risk Management and Legal Issues in Home Care: The Utilization of Nursing Staff," 23(8) *JOGNN* (October 1994), 663.

24. 796 P. 2d 899 (1990).

25. *Nursing-Legal Survival, supra* note 13, at 115.

26. *Id.*

27. "Listening and Talking to Patients: A Remedy for Malpractice Suits?" 270 *JAMA* (July 28, 1993), 437, *citing* Gregory W. Lester and Susan G. Smith, "Listening and Talking to Patients: A Remedy for Malpractice Suits?" 158 *Western Journal of Medicine (1993),* 268–272 (Domestic Abstracts column).

28. *Nursing-Legal Survival, supra* note 13, at 91, *citing* Walter Killan, "Communication Is Risk Management Tool for RN's," *The American Nurse* (January 1991), 33.

29. Brent, "Risk Management in Home Health Care," *supra* note 22, at 795.

30. Mika Kivimaki and Mark Elovainio, "Coaching Practices of First-Line Nurse Managers in Hospital Wards with Highly Satisfied Personnel," 25(11) *JONA*, November 1995, 6,14 (CONSIDER THIS . . . column).

31. Michelle Dumpe, "Making a Change: The Importance of Administrative Support," 27(5) *Nursing Management* (May 1996), 60; Judy Worthington, "Successful Restructuring," 27(5) *Nursing Management* (May 1996), 63–64.

32. Saba, Johnson, and Simpson, *Computers in Nursing Management, supra* note 10, at 3.

33. American Organization Of Nurse Executives. *The Role and Function of Nurses in Executive Practice.* Chicago: AONE, 1995.

34. Majorie Beyers, "Is the Nurse Executive Role Expanding or Contracting?" 24(11) *JONA* (November 1994), 8–9.

35. George Pozgar, "Corporate Liability," *Legal Aspects of Health Care Administration.* 6th Edition. Gaithersburg, Md: Aspen Publishers, Inc., 1996, 198.

36. Tim Porter-O'Grady, "A Nurse on the Board,", 21(1) *JONA* (January 1991), 41–42.

37. Pozgar, "Corporate Liability," *supra* note 35, at 201–202.

38. American Organization of Nurse Executives. *Results of Membership Survey.* Chicago: AONE, 1992.

39. Ann Scott Blouin and Nancy J. Brent, "The Chief Nurse Office as a Board Member: Representation and Compensation," 23 (7/8) *JONA* (July/August 1993), 17, *citing* AONE study, *supra* note 38.

40. Pozgar, "Corporate Liability," *supra* note 35, at 212–228.

41. Robert Miller, "The Legal Basis and Governance of Health Care Organizations," *Problems in Hospital Law.* 7th Edition. Gaithersburg, Md: Aspen Publishers, Inc., 1996, 17–39.

42. 211 N.E. 2d 253 (1965), *cert. denied*, 383 U.S. 946 (1966).

43. Ann Scott Blouin and Nancy J. Brent, "The Chief Nurse Officer as a Board Member: Membership Duties," 23(5) *JONA* (May 1993), 6.

44. *Id.*

45. Tim Porter-O'Grady, "A Nurse on The Board," *supra* note 36, at 40.

46. Ann Scott Blouin and Nancy J. Brent, "The Chief Nurse Officer as a Board Member: An Overview," 23(3) *JONA* (March 1993), 14–15.

47. Robert E. Shimmel, "Directors and Officers Liability: A Crisis in the Making," 41(7) *Healthcare Financial Management* (July 1987), 33.

48. *Id.*

49. George Pozgar, "Malpractice Insurance," *Legal Aspects of Health Care Administration, supra* note 35, at 553.

50. Robert Miller, "The Legal Basis and Governance of Health Care Organizations," *Problems in Hospital Law, supra* note 41, at 30.

51. Schimmel, *supra* note 47, at 33.

52. See, for example, Ann Scott Blouin and Nancy J. Brent, "The Chief Nurse Officer as a Board Member: Insights and Experiences," 24(2) *JONA* (February 1994), 9–10, 48; Karen Gardner, "Nurses: Conscience of The Board," 45(11) *Trustee* (November 1992), 26.

53. Barbara Volk Tebbitt, "Nurse Administrators: Who Are They . . . .," *supra* note 2, at 28. See also, Turner, *Scope and Standards for Nurse Administrators, supra* note 5.

54. For example, in one small sample of 11 chief nurse executives who left their positions involuntarily, none had an explicit contract of employment. Three did have an implied employment contract in their letter of offer or letter of hire. Ann Scott Blouin and Nancy J. Brent, "Nurse Administrators in Job Transition: Stories from the Front," 22(12) *JONA* (December 1992), 13–14, 27.

55. Diana Luskin Biordi and Deborah Gardiner, "The Handwriting on the Wall: Warning Signs of Impending Job Loss," 22(11) *JONA* (November 1992), 15, *citing* C. Freund, "The Tenure of Directors of Nursing," 15(2) (1985), 11–15.

56. *Id.*

57. 628 N.E. 2d 943 (1993).

58. A. David Tammelleo, "Nurse Supervisor Challenges Doctor's Orders: Termination," 34(11) *The Regan Report on Nursing Law* (April 1994), 2.

59. Henry Perritt. *Employee Dismissal Law and Practice.* 3rd Edition. Volume I. New York: John Wiley & Sons, 1992, 3 (with 1996 Cumulative Supplement).

60. 872 P. 2d 852 (1994).

61. Perritt, "Contract Theories," *Employee Dismissal Law and Practice, supra* note 59, at 259–428.

62. See Kurt Decker and Thomas Fleix. *Drafting and Revising Employment Contracts.* New York: John Wiley & Sons, 1991 (with periodic updates); American College of

Healthcare Executives. *Contracts for Healthcare Executives.* Chicago: American College of Healthcare Executives, 1987.

63. Decker and Felix, *supra* note 62, at 105.
64. *Id.* at 105. See also Anne Whalen Gill, "Covenants Not to Compete," *1992 Wiley Employment Law Update.* Henry Perritt, Editor. New York: John Wiley & Sons, 1992, 156–179.
65. *Id.* at 135–141.
66. Kelly Shriver, "Hospitals Lack Severance Plans," *Modern Healthcare* (June 19, 1995), 58.
67. Kenneth Sovereign. *Personnel Law.* 3rd Edition. Englewood Cliffs, NJ: Prentice-Hall, 1994, 126.
68. Ann Scott Blouin and Nancy J. Brent, "Nurse Administrators In Job Transition: Negotiated Resignations and Severance Agreements," 22(7/8) *JONA* (July/August 1992), 16–17.
69. *Id.*
70. *Id.*
71. Mark Rothstein, "Labor And Employment Law Issues in Hospital Closures and Downsizing," 28(6) *Journal Of Health And Hospital Law* (1995), 340. The case discussed is *Khouri v. Frank Cuneo Hospital,* 929 F. 2d 703 (7th Cir. 1991).
72. See Bimal Patel and Brian Kleiner, "New Developments in Age Discrimination," 14(6) *Equal Opportunities International* (1995), 69–79.
73. See Institute of Medicine. *Nursing Staff in Hospitals and Nursing Homes: Is It Adequate?* Washington, D.C.: National Academy Press, 1996; Susan Odegaard Turner, "Is Your Nursing Staff Ready for The Healthcare Evolution?," 26(2) *JONA* (February 1996), 5–6 (CONSIDER THIS . . . column).
74. Barbara Volk Tebbitt, *supra* note 2, at 29.

19

The Nurse in the Community

Penny S. Brooke, R.N., M.S., J.D.

contents

Community, home health, and occupational health nurses must be aware of basic legal issues relevant to nursing practice in general, and to community health legal issues specifically. The sources and purposes of public health law must be understood in addition to other statutory, administrative, and common law principles that apply to all nurses. The legal responsibilities of community health nurses vary somewhat from those of nurses working in hospitals.

Community health nursing practice may impose greater legal obligations because of the autonomy enjoyed by persons who are practicing "in the field," where independent judgments must be made. Professional autonomy and accountability demand special attention to legal and ethical dilemmas faced by persons who must establish a professional nurse-patient relationship in community settings. Additionally, the community-based nurse must be aware of the employing agencies' policies and procedures and the differing expectations of public versus private agencies. Qualified legal immunities may exist for nurses working in public agencies because of the legal principle of sovereign immunity. The nurse in a public agency is the agent of the people, and when the nurse is sued, public funds may be used to settle the claim. Public policy for qualified immunities exists to preserve the public funds. If the nurse is grossly negligent or intentionally causes harm to the client, the nurse does not qualify for this immunity protection.

Community health nurses' legal responsibili-

ties evolve as society identifies patient needs and rights that must be protected. Many advocacy groups have developed to educate the public, including health care providers, about the needs of community-based clients. The public media are also an unlikely, yet ongoing source of information related to problems with the public's health.

LEGAL RESPONSIBILITIES OF THE NURSE IN THE COMMUNITY

Sources of Law

Chapter 15

State and Federal Statutes, Administrative Rules and Regulations, Case Precedents

Community health nurses must be aware of state and federal statutory laws as well as legal case decisions that pertain to the public's health. Numerous administrative rules and regulations, enacted by state boards of nursing, for example, also relate directly to community health practice.

Legislation and regulations to protect the public's health are primarily enacted by state governments. However, some federal guidelines exist and are issued through agencies such as the Centers for Disease Control and Prevention (CDC) and the Occupational Safety and Health

KEY PRINCIPLES

Duty
Confidentiality
Advocacy
Scope of Practice

Administration (OSHA). Data collection, analysis, surveillance of programs, and issuance of guidelines are mainly the role of the federal Congress or administrative bodies, including the Public Health Service and the CDC. OSHA requirements relate mainly to providing a safe and healthy working environment for employees.

The occupational health nurse may have the legal responsibility to inform employees of their rights under these regulations as well as the responsibility for instituting prevention and screening programs to protect workers' health and safety. An understanding of workers' compensation claims is necessary to provide comprehensive care to workers. An analysis of these claims will also assist the occupational health nurse in preparing a safer environment. Past employee injuries often serve as indicators that safety rules are not being followed or the work environment needs to be evaluated.

Community health nurses have the responsibility to become familiar with health codes at both the local and state levels. Orientation to the laws specific to community health nursing should be discussed at the nurse's orientation to employment. If this service is not provided, the nurse must consult with his or her supervisor, local health officer, or the legal counsel for the agency to become familiar with these legal responsibilities. Continuing education programs may be another source for becoming aware of the community health nurse's specific legal obligations. Additionally, common law or case precedence discusses legal issues in the community. These case decisions can also guide the community health nurse's development of an awareness of specific legal obligations.

It is estimated that more than 50 million Americans will be over age 65 by the year 2000.[1] According to the US census, 12% of all Americans are now over 65 years of age, and approximately 1 of every 25 elderly persons is victimized annually.[2] More elderly persons are being cared for by community health agencies, and nurses must serve as advocates for the elderly. The trend toward home health care following short-stay hospitalizations has also increased the risks of injury to clients because of the complex procedures that are now conducted by nurses in patients' homes.

The nurse working in a public health setting who has questions regarding the legality of procedures that are included in a job description or the scope of nursing within the state would be wise to request that his or her supervisor verify the nurse's role with the attorney general of the state. In many states the attorney general is the official legal counsel for public agencies. If the legal issues are of such concern that the nurse believes his or her liability risks are great, a written formal opinion may be requested from the attorney general's office. It is recommended that the nurse work through the correct channels of communication in the agency to make such a request.

Contracts

A formal, written contractual agreement may be necessary in some community health nursing situations. If the nurse works for an agency that is agreeing to provide services to another agency, it is wise to have the understanding in writing. A contract is evidence of what the parties are mutually agreeing to do. Before the nurse signs an employment contract, it is important to read the contract carefully. If the employment agreement requires the nurse to perform duties beyond the legal scope of nursing practice in his or her state, the nurse should not agree to provide these services.

Most nurses are hired without a formal written contract. The nurse is therefore advised to become aware of the agency's policies and procedures that describe the duties and responsibilities of the nurse, as these written documents are "incorporated by reference" to become the nurse's and the agency's legally binding employment agreement. If an employee handbook is available, this document also becomes important in setting the parameters of the nurse's employment.

It is advisable to learn what the expectations of the employer are at the onset of employment. It is more difficult to refuse to comply with the employer's request later, as possible charges of insubordination or abandonment may be brought by the employer if the nurse refuses to perform the work expected by the employer. If a nurse questions whether he or she should be performing some of the skills requested, it is advised to bring these concerns to the attention of the supervisor and request, if necessary, a formal legal opinion. The law as written will overrule any conflicting agency policies or procedures. The fact that an employer may request the nurse to perform certain procedures will not protect the nurse as an individual if the practice is found to be outside the scope of nursing. Agencies' policies and procedures should be reassessed every 2 years to ensure that the nurse's responsibilities are clearly stated and within the legal scope of nursing in the state, and to set a reasonable standard of care for patients.

Confidentiality and Release of Information

Many states have not enacted a legal statutory privilege that protects the confidentiality of nurse-patient communications. For the nurse to establish an effective therapeutic relationship, the patient must trust that the nurse will protect the patient's privacy. If the patient does not trust the nurse, important information may be withheld from the nurse. A therapeutic relationship must be established on a foundation of trust for all necessary information to be learned by the health care provider.

However, if a nurse becomes aware of information that is required by law to be reported (e.g., child abuse or criminal conduct), the nurse will most likely be responsible for reporting the conduct to the proper agency. Additionally, the community-based nurse must communicate pertinent information to other members of the health care team. If transfers of information regarding a patient are requested, the community

health nurse must obtain a signed release form from the patient prior to releasing information to sources outside of the agency. Release forms should identify exactly what information is to be released, to whom, and the duration of the period for which the release is granted.

The 1991 case of *New York Society of Surgeons v. Axelrod*[3] held that AIDS could not be classified as a sexually transmitted disease, which would have enabled physicians to have this information without consent from the patient. This case demonstrates not only the privacy protections in existence for AIDS patients but also the importance the law places on the patient's privacy rights and the importance of protecting confidential information. Statutes that allow disclosure of confidential information under a court order utilize a balancing test to determine whose rights demand protection. For example, in the case of *Rassmussen v. South Florida Blood Bank*,[4] the public's interest in maintaining the confidentiality of blood donors, so as to encourage donations in order to maintain a supply of blood, outweighed the need for a plaintiff to know whose blood was used when he received a transfusion.

> *[The* Axelrod*] case demonstrates not only the privacy protections in existence for AIDS patients but also the importance the law places on the patient's privacy rights and the importance of protecting confidential information.*

However, in the case of *Tarrant County Hospital District v. Hughes*,[5] the plaintiff was allowed to contact donors with the court's approval. This court did not believe that blood bank donors are protected under a physician-patient privilege. Whether the plaintiff can discover information

necessary to proceed with a case is also a deciding factor in whether the courts will allow the
names of blood donors to be disclosed *(Belle
Bonfils Memorial Blood Center v. District Court*[6]).

Physicians were obligated to disclose the fact
that they were HIV positive in the cases of *Faya
v. Almaraz*[7] and *Kerins v. Hartley.*[8] The American
Nurses' Association is opposed to mandatory
testing of nurses as a means of preventing the
transmission of HIV.[9] The Association does support voluntary anonymous or confidential testing with the informed consent of the individual
tested.[10]

Duty to Provide Safe Care and a Safe Environment

The nurse's duty to protect the patient is being
discussed more commonly in court cases. Home
health and occupational health nurses must ensure a safe environment for patients and employees. Agencies that agree to provide care for
patients have a contractual duty to provide a
safe environment. There are both criminal and
civil statutes enacted for the protection of the
public's health and individual patient's safety.

In *Shepherd v. Mielke,*[11] a nursing home patient
was sexually assaulted by a visitor to her room.
The court stated that the nursing home and staff
had a duty to protect the patient by providing
a safe environment and by taking reasonable
precautions to protect those who are unable to
protect themselves. The patient in this case
could not lock her door, screen visitors, or generally provide for her own safety. She was in a
nursing care facility precisely because she was
unable to perform these tasks for herself.

[The nurse] must ensure a
safe environment. . . .

In the 1993 case of *Jackson v. Pleasant Grove
Health Care Center,*[12] a confused patient wan-
dered off in January and died from exposure.

The nursing home was found guilty of neglecting its responsibility to protect the patient. In
the case of *Brown v. St. Paul Mercury Insurance
Company,*[13] an alcohol treatment center and its
insurer also were found responsible for the
death of a patient who was allowed to walk out
of an unlocked door onto the roof of a treatment
center and plunge to his death.

Duty to Report

In addition to the ongoing responsibility of
nurses to practice within the scope of the law,
the nurse in the community has the duty to
protect the public by enforcement of the reporting laws. The benefits derived from reporting laws may be for the protection of the
public's health or for the individual's specific
needs for survival. Patients must be referred for
treatment needed to protect the public's health.
For example, by reporting suspected abuse, or
infectious diseases, and referring these patients
to services through programs that protect members of communities, the nurse is benefiting the
patient and others who are at risk because of
the patient's behavior or illness.

The nurse who works in the community as a
school nurse, or a community health nurse with
school nurse responsibilities, must especially be
alert for contagious childhood diseases that can
spread very quickly through classroom populations. Many states have statutory requirements
for immunizations of school-age children. The
nurse may be the person who is legally responsible for determining if these immunization laws
are being followed. If the school population is
not compliant, the nurse must take action to
report the problem. Communicable disease reporting acts mandate that infectious diseases be
reported to local and state health departments.
The nurses must follow the employing agency's
procedures for reporting infectious diseases.

The duty to report communicable diseases is
clearly defined through state health codes. With
many variations of these laws throughout the
states, it is wise for the nurse to become familiar

with the reporting laws in the state where he or she practices. For example, the duty to report suspected or confirmed cases of HIV or AIDS is mandatory in some states, permissive in others, and not discussed in some jurisdictions' statutory health codes.

Most states require that contagious diseases, including AIDS, be reported to the CDC. Additionally, many states also require reporting to the local department of health. Disclosure to anyone but these reporting agencies is usually specifically identified by state regulations as only those persons who have a "need to know." Differing state statutes identify spouses, medical or emergency personnel, or other persons who are at risk of acquiring the disease without this knowledge as persons who have a need to know.

The duty to report is an important responsibility of community-based nurses and extends beyond communicable disease reporting. In 1994, California passed Proposition 187, which mandates that nurses and other health care providers report undocumented aliens in California. Also, because of the prevalence of abuse and neglect in today's society, health care providers are also required by state law to report abuse to identified agencies. According to the American Medical Association between 1.5 and 2 million adults over 60 years of age are victims of abuse.[14] Elder abuse occurs only slightly less frequently than child abuse.[15] In many jurisdictions, immunity from legal action is afforded to the health care provider who in good faith reports suspected abuse. Legislation that requires reporting also indicates the penalties associated with failure to report known or suspected abuse cases.

There are also reporting laws related to dangerous products. Nurses, in their duty to protect their patients, have a responsibility to ensure that equipment and products that can harm patients are identified and made safe. Nurses must understand that the duty to report suspected violations of the law is not a permissive activity in many cases, but a legal responsibility that must be complied with.

Duty to Inform

Community health nurses must be familiar with the programs that benefit their patients (e.g., Social Security, Medicaid, and Medicare) to be able to help them obtain their rights under these programs. The rules for Medicaid and Medicare claims must be carefully followed. As an example, patients must be screened for financial eligibility and their signatures must be witnessed after the legal contracts for service provided by these programs are explained.

One legal case involving a person in need of a liver transplant discussed the expectation that health care providers will inform patients of the means available for financing such extreme and expensive operations. However, in the 1993 case of *Mraz v. Taft*,[16] a husband sued a nursing home and hospital from which his spouse was transferred, seeking damages because of their failure to advise him that she qualified for Medicaid. The court held that there was no duty to advise the family regarding eligibility without a specific request for this information. This case alerts nurses to be knowledgeable about patients' rights to benefits under these programs. As suggested by the Mraz case, if a patient requests information regarding eligibility for benefits, the nurse should help the patient obtain information concerning Medicaid benefits. There does not, however, appear to be a duty in Ohio to bring this information to the attention of the patient or family if it is not requested.

> *. . . if a patient requests information regarding eligibility for benefits, the nurse should help the patient obtain information concerning Medicaid benefits.*

Community health nurses must be familiar with the Social Security laws under which Medicare and Medicaid are found. The Social Security Act was enacted in 1935 to assist states in furnishing financial assistance to needy, aged individuals. Medicare was an amendment made to the Social Security Act in 1965.[17] This amendment established hospital insurance benefits for persons over the age of 65 years. Medicaid was established to provide assistance to disabled persons and families with dependent children who do not have sufficient resources to meet the costs of necessary medical care. Medicaid is also utilized to provide long-term care for the aged who cannot afford these needed services.

Nurses also need to be aware of the Federal Omnibus Budget Reconciliation Acts.[18] These acts continue to be updated as social needs arise. The purpose of this block grant program is to consolidate federal assistance to the states for social services in an attempt to fight the causes of poverty. The Early and Periodic Screening, Diagnosis and Treatment Program (EPSDT), a federally funded program that provides preventive health care to children in low-income families, should also be understood by the nurse working in the community.

Duty to Teach Patients

The community health nurse's duty to inform extends to the duty to teach. Nurses must be prepared to teach patients about a great variety of topics related to human growth, development, wellness, and diseases. It is never wise to attempt to appear to have all of the answers if one is not sure of the correct response. The nurse should advise the patient that an attempt to find the answer will be made and then should return with the information in a timely manner. This approach assists the patient in recognizing the importance of accurate information.

Not only must the nurse be able to inform the client about preventive measures and the benefits of programs, but the nurse must also have a working knowledge of communicable diseases and other health-related information. It is very important that correct information is

given to persons who rely upon the accuracy of the nurse's knowledge. Rather than assuming that all the facts can be recalled, it is advisable, for example, to keep a communicable disease reference book handy and read the specific information needed to inform the patient. This behavior also demonstrates to the patient the importance of accurate information and how to access resources. Periods of contagiousness and the need for isolation must be communicated to patients. Some communicable disease regulations require that the nurse restrict an infected person's exposure to the public. For example, a patient with hepatitis should not be allowed to continue to work in a restaurant.

Although the law has recognized the duty to teach and inform patients throughout the practice of nursing, this becomes an especially important role for the community health nurse who may be the patient's only health care provider and the one person who is in contact with the patient in need of health-related education and information. Community-based teaching may include both preventive and self-care information, much like discharge teaching in a hospital setting. It is important to know if the patient is able to understand what is being taught. If the patient speaks a foreign language or is deaf, the assistance of an interpreter must be sought. If the nurse is not sure that the patient is able to understand the instructions, it is wise to involve family members or other caregivers who will be providing ongoing health care to the client. Parents should always be involved in learning how to care for their child. The nurse should document what was taught and to whom.

Duty to Refer in a Timely Manner

School nurses also have the duty to protect the safety of the children. In the case of *Schlussler v. Independent School District No. 200 (et al.)*,[19] a school nurse was found to be negligent in failing to properly assess the seriousness of a school child's asthma attack. The school nurse also fell below the required standard of care by allowing the sick student to use another student's asthma inhaler. The court found that the school nurse had a higher duty of care than a hospital nurse to assess the need for emergency medical services. Nurses in schools must refer injured and sick children for appropriate care in a timely manner. The court did not expect the nurse to provide the needed medical care, but rather to determine the need for referral for emergency care. The court found that the failure of the nurse to provide the needed care in a timely fashion was directly related to the child's death. The school's policy had also not been followed, as the nurse did not contact the student's parents.

Nurses in schools must refer injured and sick children for appropriate care in a timely manner.

It is very important that the community health nurse appropriately refer patients to other health care professionals if further care is needed. As an example, nurses may not stockpile medications to be given to patients without a proper prescription, as a means of avoiding a referral.

. . . nurses may not stockpile medications to be given to patients without a proper prescription. . . .

The 1993 case of *Brackman v. Board of Nursing*[20] resulted when it was discovered that nurses working in a hospice program were stockpiling pain medications, not for their personal use but for patient use, when they believed it would take too long to get new prescriptions filled for hospice patients "in need." This conduct was in violation of law. The Montana State Board of Nursing attempted to place the nurses' licenses

on probation for terms ranging from 3 to 5 years. The courts, however, found that the charges of unprofessional conduct were not proven and dismissed these charges, recommending that letters of reprimand be placed in the files of the nurses. Nurses who do not have prescriptive authority licenses cannot take these responsibilities into their own hands.

LEGAL ISSUES

Documentation

Prompt and specific documentation of what is done for patients in the community is essential to maintain an accurate record. It is difficult to remember everything that has been done for patients without timely documentation. The nurse's employing agency's policies and procedures for documentation should be followed. Because the nurse represents the agency as its legal agent, both will be held responsible for the care provided to patients by the nurse. The community agency's ability to be reimbursed for the care received by the nurse also depends upon documentation of the care provided.

The home health care nurse may be the only person in actual physical contact with the patient. Nursing judgments such as assessment of the patient's condition, and documentation of the signs and symptoms leading to nursing assessments, can be crucial in home health nursing. The skill with which the nurse describes adverse reactions, and the patient's response to treatment, will make a great difference in how other members of the health care team respond to the patient. Therefore, nursing assessments, as well as timely documentation and communication of these assessments to other members of the health care team who have a need to know, are essential. The elements of timeliness and accuracy of these communications have been tested in many cases involving nurses both in the community and in institutional settings.

If the situation arises in which it is appropriate to file an incident report, the community health nurse must ethically report the actual or potential harm to the patient, following the policies and procedures of the nurse's agency. It is important that the statements made in incident reports describe the occurrence in nonaccusatory and nonopinionated, but rather factual terms. As with all documentation, it is important to truthfully report information in a timely manner.

Antidiscrimination, AIDS, and the Americans with Disabilities Act

The Americans with Disabilities Act (ADA)[21] imposes an obligation upon the nurse to protect the rights of disabled persons in our society. The *Arline*[22] case established infectious diseases as a handicap under the *Rehabilitation Act of 1973* that deserves the protections of the law. The *Arline* case decision is incorporated in the ADA. Occupational nurses need to know that employers may not discriminate against employees on the basis of an infectious disease, either at the time of hiring or when considering promotions. If an employee is disabled, the employer has the legal obligation to "reasonably accommodate" the employee's needs so that the employee is able to perform his or her work with the disability.

A 1993 case, *Buckingham v. United States of America*,[23] discussed the reasonable accommodations required when a disability such as AIDS exists. In this case, the employer was obligated to reasonably accommodate the HIV-positive employee by transferring the employee to another city where better medical care could be obtained.

Nurses must follow their agency's policies regarding work with HIV-positive persons. Coworkers who refuse to work with HIV-positive people or nurses who refuse to care for HIV-positive persons may be open to charges of discrimination or insubordination. If a nurse refuses to care for an HIV/AIDS patient, the possibility of charges of abandonment also exists.

In the 1993 case of *Armstrong v. Flowers Hospi-*

tal,[24] a home health care nurse, in her first trimester of pregnancy, was fired when she refused to care for an AIDS patient. The nurse refused to care for the patient because she feared that she would contract opportunistic infections from the patient. Her employer, however, had a policy that provided no exceptions for refusing patient care assignments. The policy stated that if a nurse refused to care for a patient, the employee would be terminated. The nurse claimed that she was being discriminated against on the basis of gender because of her pregnancy, but the court did not agree.

> *Nurses may be required to care for all patients if employer policies provide no exceptions, or face termination.*

ADVOCACY AND PROFESSIONAL INVOLVEMENT

Vulnerable Populations

In addition to the legal responsibilities discussed, the community health nurse must be an advocate for the public's health as well as a protector of consumer's rights. An advocate is a person who identifies issues and educates the decision-makers regarding the health needs of a community. Patients of a community health nurse may belong to vulnerable populations in need of the nurse's advocacy skills. Helping a patient to maneuver through the bureaucracy of benefit systems is an appropriate role for the community health nurse.

The nurse also serves as an advocate when applying the OSHA regulations. Employees who feel vulnerable that their job security will be jeopardized if they complain about unsafe work environments need to rely upon the nurse's legal obligation to report potential problems and unsafe working conditions.

At-risk populations require the advocacy of community health nurses. Maternal and child health, mentally challenged persons, low-income and other vulnerable populations are the patients of the community health nurse. Initial research into the utilization of health care has shown that persons from low socioeconomic and limited educational backgrounds are less likely to receive the health care they need or the benefits available to them. Community health nurse advocates can assist these groups to receive the benefits of the services available.

Patients have the right to be treated equally and without discrimination. The community health nurse must be careful to provide resources on a fair and unbiased basis. Determination of who receives resources should not be based on race, gender, age, or any other determination that would treat one group of persons or individuals in society with fewer rights than others. Community health patients deserve equal protection and equal privileges under the law to receive care available through public agencies. Private agencies must also avoid abridging the civil rights of patients.

Competency and Consent Issues

Case law involving community health nurses may revolve around the necessary involvement of the nurse in acquiring informed consent from patients before procedures are performed in the home or agency. In institutional settings, implied consent is often adequate; however, when the community, home health, or occupational health nurse is involved in initiating more intrusive procedures or procedures with potentially serious outcomes, it is wise for the nurse to receive written informed consent from the patient. If the procedure to be performed is a medical procedure, it would not be appropriate for the nurse either to receive the informed consent or to conduct the procedure. Community health nurses must avoid the temptation to practice beyond the scope of nursing. If the procedure to be completed is a medical procedure, it is necessary for the physician to explain the significant risks, benefits, and potential alternatives of treatment. Nurses are not educated as physicians and should not be obtaining informed consent for medical procedures.

Federal guidelines require that patients give their informed consent prior to the use of chemical or physical restraints. Care facilities that receive federal funds from Medicare and Medicaid must comply with these laws. Only in emergency situations in which, for example, the patient is posing a serious danger to himself or herself or others, may restraints be applied without the patient's consent. Even in an emergency situation, the restraint applied should be closely monitored to protect the patient's safety. The least restrictive restraint applied for the shortest time is the safest rule. Restraints should never be applied for the mere convenience of the staff.

Community health nurses may also find themselves serving as the advocate of psychiatric patients. It is important to be familiar with the involuntary and emergency psychiatric admission procedures in the state in which the nurse practices. A person may not be deemed incompetent automatically; there must first be a judicial hearing to determine the patient's competence. Procedures may be instituted on a patient's behalf without consent only in true emergency situations. An emergency situation exists when action must be taken to prevent serious harm or the potential death of a person. Even psychiatric patients are deemed to be competent until legally determined incompetent by a court of law.

Commitment and competency hearing procedures are defined by state statutes. The patient can be legally detained for a limited time, as defined by the particular state statute, to facilitate a legal hearing. If a person is found by the court to be incompetent, a guardian or conservator is appointed by the court to act on behalf of the patient who cannot make sound decisions. A guardian or conservator has authority to handle decisions on the patient's behalf, as granted by the court.

The patient's right to autonomy is well recognized in our society. If a nurse proceeds to provide services without consent, charges of assault and battery are valid. Assault is the action that puts the patient in fear that he or she will be harmed, and battery is actual touching, or performing the act threatened. These legal principles apply in all nursing practice settings, including community-based care.

The right to refuse treatment is seen as a corollary of the doctrine of informed consent in that a patient always has the right not to consent to treatment *(Rodriguez v. Pino.)*[25] The community health nurse would be wise to understand advance directive statutes. Community health patients may turn to the nurse for direction and information regarding special directives, durable medical powers of attorney, and other documents that delegate decision-making to a surrogate decision-maker such as a guardian. If the nurse is unaware that the patient has created a living will, a durable medical power of attorney, or a special directive that specifically states that certain procedures are not desired, the community health nurse may act without the patient's consent.

Growing case law has substantiated the patient's right to refuse treatment and to exercise autonomy in deciding what care he or she will receive. The autonomy of patients is highly protected in the United States legal system when the patient is making the decision to refuse treatment. A prisoner was allowed to refuse all care, including food, in the 1993 California case of *Thor v. Superior.*[26] A nursing home patient was also granted the right to terminate feedings and to be allowed to die in the case of *In Re Requena.*[27] In 1994, a nursing home resident who had refused treatment was involuntarily discharged. The court held that the nursing care facility had not demonstrated that the patient was a danger to other residents, and thus they had no grounds for this discharge *(Matter of Involuntary Discharge or Transfer of J.S.).*[28]

Assisted Suicide

Assisted suicide has been widely debated in both the courts and in state legislatures. While refusing medical treatment simply permits life to run its course, suicide and assisted suicide involve an affirmative act to end life. Nurses in the community setting may have contact with patients who are considering suicide and ask the nurse for help in doing so. The majority of states treat assisted suicide as a crime separate from murder, with less onerous penalties, either through the state's common law or by statute.

The 1994 *People v. Kevorkian*[29] case described assisted suicide in Michigan as involving active misconduct or intentionally and artificially curtailing life. California discussed its assisted suicide statute in the case *People v. Cleaves.*[30] In this case, the patient was dying of AIDS and requested assistance in his own strangulation. The court believed that the decedent remained in sole control of his death by virtue of how tight the sash was around his neck. However, in the 1994 case, *State v. Sexton,*[31] the defendant was convicted of second-degree murder for participating in a suicide agreement in which the defendant held a rifle in position while the decedent pulled the trigger. The New Mexico assisted-suicide statute addressed in *Sexton* did not intend to allow active participation in the act that results in death.

The community-based nurse should be cautious about becoming involved in such controversial patient decisions without carefully evaluating the legal and ethical issues involved, as discussed in Chapters 10 and 13.

In 1994, Oregon voters approved the first physician-assisted suicide law. The Oregon Death with Dignity Act applies only to adult patients who are residents of the state, who have a terminal condition with less than 6 months to live, and who meet other qualifying preconditions. This law allows physicians to prescribe the lethal dose of drugs to end life, but does not allow the physician to administer them to the patient. Interestingly, the state's law against assisted suicide is not repealed by the Death with Dignity Act, but allows physicians to proceed according to narrowly defined standards. If the guidelines are followed, the physician is granted immunity from prosecution.[32]

The Oregon Death with Dignity Act was initially enjoined from taking effect until a full hearing on the constitutionality concerns of the law could be carefully considered.[33] The plaintiffs, which include two physicians and four terminally ill or potentially terminally ill patients, have raised Due Process and Equal Protection Violations in addition to several other violations.[34] The injunction was lifted by the Ninth Circuit Court of Appeals in March of 1996, but additional court proceedings on the Act are pending.

Family Planning Matters

Very private family matters often are shared with community health nurses. When the nurse is practicing in the patient's own home, school, or work environment, the patient may be more inclined to discuss issues such as abortion, distribution of contraceptives, and family violence. The Hyde Amendment to the Public Health Services Act states that federal funds will not support abortion when it is a method of family planning, but Medicaid funding of medically necessary abortions upon fetuses conceived by acts of rape or incest is allowed. Birth control is a sensitive matter, but nurses must be prepared to educate patients regarding their legal options. The 1993 case of *Ignacia Alfonso v. Joseph A. Fernandez*[35] held that schools may not dispense condoms to unemancipated minor students without parental or guardian permission, as distribution of condoms would be considered a health service rather than a health education issue. If the nurse anticipates that these difficult and sometimes ethical conversations will occur, then proper preparation for counseling that will abide by the law will be possible.

Anatomic Gifts

Required request laws have arisen because of the shortage of suitable organs for transplantation. The National Organ Transplant Act[36] addresses many problems of organ donation and should be understood by the community health nurse. The nurse may be asked to advise a patient regarding the procedure for indicating wishes regarding organ donations.

PROFESSIONAL LIABILITY AND PERSONAL PROTECTION ISSUES

Use of an Expert Witness at Trial

If a case of negligence or malpractice is brought against a community health nurse, it is important to make sure that the expert witness called in the case is truly familiar with the practice of community health, home health, or occupational health nursing. The community health nurse who is being sued deserves to have the nursing care he or she provided analyzed by an experienced community health nurse in a comparable setting. The expert witness should also have comparable educational credentials and experience that allows the expert witness to understand what a reasonably prudent nurse would have done in this community-setting situation. The standards of care in community, home health, and occupational health nursing must meet this same reasonableness test of other nursing standards, yet these practices may not be common knowledge to nurses not working in the community. As an example, in the 1994 case of *Thurman v. Pruitt Corporation*,[37] the court agreed that a nurse employed by a visiting nurse service was an appropriate expert witness in a case regarding the standard of care provided by a nursing home through its nursing staff.

Standing Orders

Standing orders for procedures and medications are commonly written for nurses working in home health and community settings. The nurse must have a standing order for any procedure, including ordering medications from a pharmacy. The nurse needs to ensure that standing orders are regularly reviewed and updated. It is also important to be sure that the physician signs a standing order that is acted upon by the nurse. Verbal orders as well as standing orders need to be cautiously clarified. The dangers of miscommunication are greatly heightened when communicating verbally. If a client is injured when the nurse follows a verbal order, there is no written evidence of what the physician ordered, and the nurse may become responsible for information that was miscommunicated or misunderstood that results in harm to a client.

Supervising Others

Supervisory liability is also of concern to community health nurses. A 1994 case, *National Labor Relations Board v. Health Care and Retirement Cooperative of America*,[38] raised new issues regarding the nurse's role as a supervisor. In this case, licensed practical nurses working in a long-term care facility were deemed by the Supreme Court to be employees who were working for the benefit of the owner. Their role was judged to be that of a supervisor because they were seen as ranking employees who were on duty most of the time to ensure adequate staffing; to make daily work assignments; and to monitor and evaluate the work of the nurses' aides in order to report to management. The result of this court finding may place nurses acting in the capacity of supervisors outside the protections of the National Labor Relations Act. Supervisors are considered to be loyal to the employer. The rationale for this belief includes the fact that supervisors are privy to information not ordinarily shared with every employee. Community health nurses who are "supervisors," as defined by the United States Supreme Court in this case, would not be able to belong to a union representing other nurses in the facility or agency.

Liability related to supervising other health

care personnel is possible through vicarious liability, or being responsible for another's actions. If a supervisor knowingly assigns work to another health care provider without regard for the person's ability to safely provide the care, the supervisor may be held vicariously responsible along with the employee who performed the acts that caused injury to the client. The nurse employee should also be careful to bring to the supervisor's attention the need for help in safely performing tasks delegated to him or her. Nurses in the community must be especially aware of their own limited abilities and not proceed to provide care for which they are unprepared, or care that may be outside the legal scope of nursing as defined by the nurse practice act in their state. Additionally, the risk of harm to the patient is greater when support staff are not readily available to rectify nursing errors made in community health settings.

Risks Outside the Scope of Employment

Travel is an issue for community health nurses that does not exist for most practicing nurses. While there may be a temptation to transport patients in the nurse's private automobile, it is not a wise practice for the nurse to chauffeur patients. Nurses may be covered by their employer's insurance during travel between visits to patients, but this protection does not extend to patients in the nurse's automobile. Because the nurse is transporting the patient in the capacity of an employed professional, the risk of liability is increased if an accident occurs and the patient is injured. The usual protections afforded under the Good Samaritan laws for persons offering gratuitous transportation diminish when the relationship is professional. Transporting patients usually is not included in the nurse's job description. If the employer urges the nurse to "help out" clients with their transportation needs, the nurse must clarify these insurance and liability issues or be personally vulnerable.

Any activity outside the scope of the nurse's employment description would not be protected by the employer's liability coverage of the nurse. For example, the protections afforded by the employer's professional liability policy coverage would not extend to the nurse's participation in health screening and immunization clinics sponsored by an agency other than the nurse's employer.

Risks to Patients and Professional Liability

The community health nurse can identify the major risks for liability through utilizing the elements of the community health assessment. Table 19–1 identifies key elements that should alert the nurse to potential risks to the patient. These factors define reasonable expectations of the responsibilities and duties the nurse should assume to protect the patient and to reduce the risks of injury to the patient. The community health nurse needs to know more than just what problems exist; he or she also must know what resources are available to solve them. Appropriate referrals to battered women's shelters, detoxification centers, and community mental health centers will reduce further risk of harm to patients. The nurse working in the community must be aware of the experts with whom he or she can consult when a patient problem is identified. The community health nurse has a responsibility as well as a legal duty to be informed regarding community resources as well as the foreseeable risks that exist in the specific community.

Violence in the Community Setting

Violence is of growing concern throughout our society. Family violence, often referred to as domestic violence, as well as street violence, are of concern to nurses in community settings. Not only are nurses called upon to identify and report dangerous situations, they must also be very aware of their own safety needs. Nurses, like all persons in our society, have the right to be protected from violent actions. Community-based nurses should be cautious to avoid placing themselves in situations that can lead to their becoming victims of violence.

Injury resulting from violence is not the responsibility of the employer. The nurse assumes the risk of normal community health practice. An employee in California sued his employer for damages resulting from the emotional distress he suffered from an armed robbery at his workplace. The court ruled that the worker could not bypass workers' compensation and sue the employer. Only when an injury is caused by the employer's intentional acts that expose the employee to greater than normal risks can the employer be held responsible. Even though the employer in the case had not taken adequate security measures to prevent violence in the workplace, the court believed that, like street crime, workplace violence can occur, and employers cannot always be held responsible (*Arendell v. Auto Parts Club, Inc.*).[39]

Injury resulting from violence is not the responsibility of the employer. The nurse assumes the risk of normal community health practice.

When an employee's injury arises from ordinary or even reckless conduct of an employer, the employee must turn to workers' compensation in California. Only when an employer deliberately intends to inflict injury may the employee sue the employer (*Fermino v. Fedco, Inc.*).[40] Nurses working in the community in California may therefore assume the risk for becoming victims of violence in their role as employees. All nurses are advised to become aware of the status of these laws in their own states.

TABLE 19–1

Key Elements of Census Data for a Community Health Assessment

1. AGE

The single best demographic predictor of health is age, because disease conditions differ so drastically from one age group to the next.

- **Infants:** The most prevalent problems stem from premature births, injuries, and infectious diseases: birth defects, pneumonia, sudden infant death syndrome, poisonings, burns, and falls.
- **Children:** The most prevalent problems are caused by injuries, infectious diseases, and abuse: poisonings, burns, falls, propelled vehicle-related crashes, influenza, ear, nose and throat (ENT) infections, bone fractures, and skin abrasions.
- **Adolescents:** The most prevalent problems result from risk-taking behaviors, injuries, infectious diseases and sexual behaviors: burns, bone fractures, spinal injuries, poisonings, firearm and automobile-related trauma, abuse of chemicals, consumption of tobacco products, sexually transmitted diseases, ENT infections, influenza, and unplanned pregnancies.
- **Adults 20–44:** The most prevalent problems stem from risk-taking behaviors, injuries, and infectious diseases: bone fractures, lacerations, spinal injuries, firearm-related trauma, abuse of chemicals, consumption of tobacco products, influenza, and asthma.
- **Adults 45–64:** The most prevalent problems are caused by chronic diseases and risk-taking behaviors: cancer, heart disease, hypertensive disease, dental diseases, arthritis, consumption of tobacco products, abuse of chemicals, and improper dietary practices.
- **Adults 65 and older:** The most prevalent problems are linked to acute diseases, injuries, and chronic diseases: influenza and pneumonia, falls, burns, suicides, cancer, heart disease, and cerebrovascular disease.

2. GENDER

Disease conditions or injuries can affect one gender more dramatically than the other (for example, breast cancer among women) and can even affect one gender exclusively (prostate cancer among men). In addition, average life expectancy in some states can be up to five years longer for women.

3. RACE AND ETHNICITY

Racial or ethnic disparities in health status often relate more to differences in income, education and occupations than to race. Nonetheless, it can be extremely helpful to note these kinds of distinctions when developing your plans. In Minnesota, for example, death due to injury in Native American and black children is three to four times that of Asian and white children.

4. RESIDENCE/LOCATION

Where people live can influence their health status in many ways. There are differences between emergency medical response times in rural versus urban areas. Some areas pose environmental threats to people living nearby, while others are noted for relatively clean air and water but relatively high levels of Lyme disease.

5. HOUSEHOLD INCOME AND EDUCATIONAL LEVEL OF HEAD OF HOUSEHOLD

These two demographic variables share a common type of association with health status because higher household income and educational level (to a point) are generally associated with higher levels of health status. For instance, low income and educational levels are the biggest risk factors for chronic diseases due to their association with tobacco use, poor eating habits, and lack of physical activity.

6. FAMILY SIZE

The correlation between family size and health status is complex and varies according to population group. In general, lower health status is associated with larger families.

7. OCCUPATION OF HEAD OF HOUSEHOLD

There is an observed tendency for blue-collar workers to have a lower health status than white-collar workers. Much of this association is related to risk-taking behaviors: alcohol misuse/abuse, poor eating habits, and failure to use seat belts.—J.A.R.

Reprinted with permission from *Community Health Assessment: The First Step in Community Health Planning.* Hospital Technology Series. Vol. 12, No. 13. Copyright 1993 American Hospital Association.

SUMMARY OF PRINCIPLES
AND APPLICATIONS

The role of the community health nurse interfaces with public health laws as well as other legal standards applicable to all nursing roles. Laws are constantly being enacted and revised, and it is therefore impossible to discuss all of the potential laws that a community health nurse must be aware of to enforce and abide by in his or her jurisdiction. Nurses must consistently and constantly update their knowledge of their legal responsibilities. It is difficult to separate and isolate the legal responsibilities of community health nurses because of the natural interrelatedness of the responsibilities to inform patients of their rights to benefits and teach wellness and preventive measures, while recognizing and referring actual or potential problems.

Even laws related to housing and the rights of renters are important to understand. The community health nurse may be faced with the problem of patient-family being evicted from their home or apartment. The impact of this legal action is a legitimate concern for the community health nurse. Laws related to environmental hazards are also being legislated and may be managed under state health departments through sanitation departments, but enforced by nurses. Preventive teaching related to laws requiring the use of seat belts and infant car seats also should be offered. Food preparation and food handler laws are also applicable to public health nursing practice. Nurses can help their patients avoid unsuspected problems by informing them of the legal responsibilities applicable to all people in our society. However, the nurse is not expected, or recommended, to give legal advice to community patients. Ignorance of the law will not protect either the consumer or the nurse from legal liability.

Because the law is constantly changing as our society identifies whose rights need to be protected, the community health nurse must:

▼ Keep current regarding the legal standards that govern all nursing practice as well as the regu-

lations and laws specifically enacted to protect the public's health.

▼ Protect the confidentiality of the information gained by virtue of the therapeutic relationship. Be prepared to disclose information that must legally be reported.

▼ Share private information regarding patients only with those who need to know, and have the patient's consent in writing for release of information to anyone outside the agency.

▼ Contracts are evidence of mutually agreed upon terms that should be put in written form to clarify the parties' understanding and serve as evidence of the agreement.

▼ Community health nurses have both contractual duties and professional responsibilities to maintain the standards of care within the scope of nursing practice as defined by their state's nurse practice act.

▼ Commonly recognized legal duties include the responsibility to maintain a safe working environment and protect the individual safety of patients; teach, inform, and refer patients; communicate in a timely and accurate manner with members of the health care team; enforce the reporting laws; and be knowledgeable of the laws and programs designed to benefit patients.

▼ It is unwise for community health nurses to transport patients in their personal vehicles.

▼ Infectious diseases are considered a disability, and therefore persons with HIV/AIDS are legally protected from discriminatory treatment by the Americans with Disabilities Act.

▼ Dangerous products and equipment must be identified by the nurse to reduce the risk of patient injuries.

▼ The Occupational Safety and Health Administration and the Centers for Disease Control and Prevention are administrative bodies that enact rules and regulations of importance to nurses who work in the community.

▼ The community health nurse has the responsibility to be familiar with the programs and procedures for accessing these programs, such as Medicare, Medicaid, Early and Periodic Screening, Diagnosis and Treatment Program and Workers' Compensation, for the benefit of their patients.

▼ Advocacy and professional involvement are appropriate roles for community health nurses who represent vulnerable patients and groups.

▼ Patients, including psychiatric patients, must be considered to be competent until legally judged by a court of law to be incompetent.

▼ The nurse as an advocate must protect the patient's autonomy and legal right to refuse treatment.

▼ The Hyde amendment to the Public Health Services Act provides that abortion will not be paid for with federal funds unless the fetus was conceived by acts of rape or incest.

▼ Patient-assisted suicide is a developing legal issue nurses must regard cautiously.

▼ An expert witness in a legal case involving a community health nurse should have experience in the specific area of practice of the defendant as well as comparable educational credentials.

▼ An employer's expectations of community health nurses must not conflict with the legal scope of nursing practice.

▼ Standing orders must be reviewed and updated regularly and signed by the physician in a timely manner when acted upon by the nurse.

▼ Verbal orders are more likely to be misunderstood, and therefore increase the risk of harm to the patient and liability for the nurse. Verbal orders should be avoided and must be followed up with a signature.

▼ Timely, written documentation of the nurse's actions and the patient's response is necessary evidence of the care provided in the community.

▼ Supervisory liability may occur when care is delegated to providers who, the supervisor should know, are not prepared to safely perform the task or skills and the patient is harmed.

▼ Violence is of major concern to nurses who work independently in clinics, homes, schools, and industry, as these environments are impacted by crime that exists in our society.

TOPICS FOR FURTHER INQUIRY

1. Design a study to evaluate your community's attitudes and knowledge regarding communicable diseases and immunizations.

2. Interview nurses who work in home health care agencies regarding how the process of informed consent for treatment is handled in their agency for intrusive treatments.

3. Research your state's statutes for the status of guidance on advance directives, the right to refuse treatment, and assisted suicide in your practice jurisdiction.

4. Interview occupational nurses and school nurses to assess their scope of practice in relation to the state nurse practice act.

REFERENCES

1. California Attorney General's Office, Crime Prevention Center, Daniel Lundgren, Attorney General (1992). Lifeline . . . Preventing Elder Abuse. 1–18.
2. O. Fuller. Elder Abuse. *Journal of Elder Abuse,* (1991), 36–45.
3. *New York Society of Surgeons v. Axelrod,* 569 N.Y.S. 2d 922 (1991).
4. *Rassmussen v. South Florida Blood Bank,* 500 So. 2d 533, (1987).
5. *Tarrant County Hospital District v. Hughes,* 734 S.W. 2d 675, (1987).
6. *Belle Bonfils Memorial Blood Center v. District Court,* 763 P. 2d 1003 (1988).
7. *Faya v. Almaraz,* 620 A. 2d 327, (1993).
8. *Kerins v. Hartley,* 93 Daily Journal, D.A. 9850 (July 30, 1993).
9. American Nurses' Association. *Position Statement on HIV Testing.* Washington, DC: American Nurses' Association (September 6, 1991).
10. *Id.*
11. *Shepherd v. Mielke,* 887 P. 2d 220, (Wash. App. Div. 3, 1994).

12. *Jackson v. Pleasant Grove Health Care Center*, 980 F. 2d 692 (11th Cir. 1993).
13. *Brown v. St. Paul Mercury Insurance Company*, 732 S.W. 2d 130, 1987.
14. American Medical Association. Diagnostic and Treatment Guidelines on Elder Abuse and Neglect (1992), 1–42.
15. B.J. Marshall. Elder Abuse, Neglect and Exploitation. *AARP Materials* (1990), 1–13.
16. *Mraz v. Taft*, 619 N.E. 2d 483 (Ohio App. 8 Dist. 1993).
17. U.S. Code, Congressional and Administrative News. (1935, 1937, 1944, 1963, 1965, 1975, 1977, 1981). St. Paul, Minn: West Publishing.
18. *Id.*
19. *Schlussler v. Independent School District No. 200 (et al),* Case Number MM89 14V Minnesota Case Reports (1989).
20. *Brackman v. Board of Nursing*, 851 P. 2d 1055 (1993).
21. Americans with Disabilities Act, 42 U.S.C. s 12101 (1990) *et seq.*, Public Law No. 101-336, 140 Stat. 327.
22. *School Board of Nassau County v. Arline*, 480 U.S. 273 (1987).
23. *Buckingham v. United States of America*, 93 Daily Journal D.A.R. 8976 (July 13, 1993).
24. *Armstrong v. Flowers Hospital, Inc.*, 33 F. 3d 1308 (11th Cir. 1994).
25. *Rodriguez v. Pino*, 634 So. 2d 681 (1994).
26. *Thor v. Superior*, 21 Cal. Rptr. 2d 3576 (1993).
27. *In Re Requena*, 517 A. 2d 869 (1986).
28. *Matter of Involuntary Discharge or Transfer of J.S.*, 512 N.W. 2d 604 (Minn. App. 1994).
29. *People v. Kevorkian*, 527 N.W. 2d 714 (Mich. 1994), cert. denied sub nom. *Kevorkian v. Michigan*, 115 S. Ct. 1795 (1995).
30. *People v. Cleaves*, 280 Cal. Rptr. 146 (1991).
31. *State v. Sexton*, 869 P. 2d 301 (N.M. App 1994).
32. Staff, "A Wake Up Call for Medicine? Oregon Voters Approve Physician-Assisted Suicide," *Medical Ethics Advisor* (Dec. 1994), 158.
33. *Lee v. State*, 869 F. Supp. 1491 (D. Or. 1994).
34. Alan Meisel. *The Right To Die.* 2nd Edition. New York: John Wiley & Sons, Inc., 1995, 509 (Volume II).
35. *In the Matter of Ignacia Alfonso v. Joseph Fernandez*, 606 N.Y.S. 2d 259, (1993).
36. National Organ Transplant Act, Public Law 98-507, Oct. 19, 1984.
37. *Thurman v. Pruitt Corporation*, 442 S.E. 2d 849 (Ga. App. 1994).
38. *National Labor Relations Board v. Health Care and Retirement Cooperative of America*, 114 S. Ct. 1778, 128 L.Ed.2d 586 (1994).
39. *Arendell v. Auto Parts Club, Inc.*, 35 Cal. Rptr. 2d 83 (Cal. Ct. App. 1994).
40. *Fermino v. Fedco, Inc.*, 872 P. 2d 559 (Cal 1994).

20 The Nurse in the Academic Setting

Nurses find themselves in the academic setting in one of two roles—that of the student and that of the faculty member. Both students and faculty have specific rights and responsibilities supported by law. Regardless of which role the nurse holds, those rights and responsibilities are important to adhere to.

This chapter will explore the selected areas of both roles, and applicable laws will be examined. The chapter will begin with the student, whether the student be in a 2- or 4-year collegiate program, a 3-year diploma program, or a graduate degree program (MS or terminal degree). Likewise, the faculty member's rights and responsibilities will be analyzed from general principles of law that apply to any type of educational program the nurse may be teaching in.

HISTORICAL DEVELOPMENT OF STUDENT RIGHTS AND FACULTY RESPONSIBILITIES

At one time, students in post-secondary educational settings had few, if any, enforceable legal rights in relation to the academic institution and its administration and faculty. The reasons for this lack of rights were rooted in a number of theories espoused by society and the judicial system concerning the student's relationship with the academic institution. Most often the

RELATED TOPICS	
Chapter 1	The Government and the Law
Chapter 2	The Nurse and the Judicial System
Chapter 3	Concepts of Negligence and Liability
Chapter 6	Other Torts and Civil Rights
Chapter 8	Criminal Law
Chapter 9	Contract Law

inability of the student to challenge any action by the academic institution focused on the institution's decisions about suspending or terminating the student from a program or from the school because of disciplinary and academic actions taken against the student.

At one time, students in post-secondary educational settings had few, if any, enforceable legal rights in relation to the academic institution and its administration and faculty.

One theory that was utilized in keeping the student from having any enforceable legal rights against the institution was the *beneficiary theory.* The student, a benefactor of the knowledge and wisdom imparted by the faculty, was not given the ability to challenge any action because the student should not question what was being given to him or her as a gift. Similarly, the *privilege theory* utilized the same reasoning: The student was privileged to be in the academic setting and therefore should not be armed with the legal ability to challenge any decision made that was adverse to him.

Perhaps the most successful theory utilized by the academic institution to support its decisions was the *in loco parentis doctrine,* which means "in

KEY PRINCIPLES

Due Process

Public Academic Institution

Private Academic Institution

Constitutional Protections

Disciplinary Dismissal

Academic Dismissal

Academic Freedom of Faculty

Tenure

the place of the parent."[1] In the academic setting, the academic institution acted as the parent(s) in disciplining the student, an action that might result in suspension or termination, or in dismissing a student from the school or program for academic reasons. Because the student could not challenge a parent's action against him or her, the academic institution's decision could not be questioned because it stood in the place of the parent.[2]

The *in loco parentis* doctrine was very helpful in shielding any challenges to an educational institution's decisions concerning dismissals or suspensions for disciplinary reasons (e.g., a breach of rules of conduct or dormitory rules). It was not helpful, however, when the decision to terminate or dismiss a student was based on an academic reason, for parents have never had the responsibility to grade their children in an academic setting. Thus the school could not really state that it had taken over a function of the parent(s). This, and other developments in society, set the stage for slow but dramatic changes in a student's right to question the educational institution's actions against him or her.

The Due Process Cases

The United States Constitution includes the Fourteenth Amendment that protects certain individual rights from being restricted by state government. The Fourteenth Amendment states that, among other things, no state can deprive a person of life, liberty, or property without due process of law.[3] This portion of the Amendment has been at the center of a multitude of lawsuits that have attempted to define both what due process is and what life, liberty, and property include. In defining due process, the courts generally define it as what is *fair* under the circumstances. In addition, rather than enumerate each and every situation that might arise in which due process is applicable and what would be *fair* in each and every instance, the courts customarily look at the right that might be limited or eliminated by the state government and then

ask the question: What process is due to ensure that fairness will prevail? As a result, the individual charged with a crime that carries with it the possibility of incarceration would receive more due process protections that would a student who is threatened with expulsion from an academic institution. However, in either case, the due process protections are mandated only when the state (government) is involved in possibly restriction of an individual's rights guaranteed by the Fourteenth Amendment. This application is often referred to as "state action" or an action "under the color of state law."[4]

In defining due process, the courts generally define it as what is fair *under the circumstances.*

What is and what is not state action is not always easily resolved. This is also true with the status of an academic institution and whether or not the institution is a public (state) or a private school.

Generally a public academic institution is one that is most often affiliated with a state government; in other words, a state school. As such, the school is supported by state revenues. In contrast, a private school is one that is *not* supported by state revenues, but rather receives its financial support from private funding.

If a school is a public one, the power of the state and federal government over faculty and students and their constitutional rights is limited by the Constitution. Private academic institutions do not have the same requirement of abiding by constitutional limitations on their actions, but cannot act in a manner that is arbitrary, capricious, or discriminatory when making decisions about students and faculty.

It is possible, though, that an academic institution, even if private, does receive state funds in some manner. If that is the case, it may be that the school must abide by the due process requirements of the Fourteenth Amendment required of public schools in dismissing students for misconduct.

The Dixon Case

One of the most important initial cases to delineate the due process rights of students in their relationship with the academic institution was *Dixon v. Alabama State Board of Education.*[5] In *Dixon*, six students at the Alabama State College for Negroes in Montgomery, Alabama were expelled from the College without notice and without a hearing for "misconduct." Although never clearly specified, it was believed that the misconduct engaged in by the six students was their participation in several off-campus civil rights demonstrations.[6] The students, after receiving a letter from the College President indicating the Board of Education's unanimous decision to expel them, filed a case asking the federal district court to grant them a preliminary and permanent injunction restraining the Board of Education and other college officials from prohibiting them from attending college. The district court upheld the dismissals and denied the students' requested relief. On appeal, the United States Court of Appeals for the 5th Circuit reversed the district court and remanded the case back to the circuit court for further proceedings consistent with its opinion.

The appeals court, in reversing the trial court's decision, held that the due process protections guaranteed in the Fourteenth Amendment of the United States Constitution required a state academic institution to give notice to students concerning their possible expulsion and a hearing prior to the expulsion. In so holding, the court also listed the following standards that should be followed when providing that notice and hearing: (1) the notice should be specific as to the allegations and basis for the potential expulsion; and (2) the nature of the hearing, which is adversarial in nature, should be dependent on the circumstances of each situation, but should allow an opportunity for both sides to present in detail their respective positions.[7]

The *Dixon* court also held that the students must be given the names of witnesses against them and what each witness would be testifying to, an opportunity to present their own defenses to the allegations, and, if the hearing was not to be held before the Board of Education, a written copy of its findings and decision in the case.[8]

Dixon, then, paved the way for students in post-secondary public academic institutions to possess clear due process protections when threatened with expulsion for misconduct or, stated in another way, when a disciplinary action was being taken against them. When an academic institution initiates a disciplinary dismissal against a student, it is a serious matter because the school is doing so as a result of the student's behavior that results in a violation of a code of conduct or rules and regulations. Because the behavior complained of allegedly violates standards of conduct, a disciplinary dismissal has the potential for a long-lasting effect on the student's reputation. *Dixon*, however, was clearly limited to those two prerequisites. Other case law decisions established additional protections and further defined their limitations.

The Goss Case

Although the *Dixon* case was a landmark one in terms of protecting public students' rights of due process vis-à-vis the institution and its faculty, *Goss v. Lopez*[9] firmly solidified them. Decided by the United States Supreme Court, the *Goss* decision required *all* public academic institutions, whether they be grade schools, highs schools, or colleges and universities, to provide due process protections to their students.

In *Goss*, nine public high school students filed a class action against the Columbus Board of Education and many administrators alleging that they were all suspended from their respective schools for "misconduct" for up to 10 days without a hearing. Although their respective suspensions were possible under an Ohio statute, the students alleged that the statute was unconstitutional in that it allowed a school principal and other public school administrators to suspend a student without a hearing prior to the suspension.[10] Alleging that this lack of a hearing was a violation of their procedural due process rights guaranteed by the Fourteenth Amendment to the United States Constitution, they also sought to enjoin the public school administrators from suspending more students and asked the court to require the schools to remove any reference concerning their suspensions from their respective files.

At the federal district court trial, a three-judge court held that (1) the students were denied due process; (2) the Ohio statute permitting a suspension to occur without a prior hearing, or within a reasonable time period after the suspensions, was unconstitutional; and (3) ordered that any and all references to the students' suspensions be removed from their school files.

The court also listed what was minimally necessary for a school to do before a suspension took place in an emergency situation that might require suspension before a hearing could be held. Those minimum requirements were notice of the suspension proceedings sent to the parents of the student within 24 hours of the decision to hold them; a hearing within 72 hours of the suspension, with the student present; and the right of the student to make a statement in his or her defense, to have statements of the charges against him or her, and that the school need not permit an attorney to be present.[11] In all nonemergency situations, however, the three-judge court held that notice and a hearing prior to suspension were required.

On a direct appeal by the defendants to the United States Supreme Court, the Court affirmed the three-judge court's holding. In doing so, the Court held that the property right created by Ohio in its statutes for a free public education to all residents between the ages of 5 and 21 years of age and the state's requirement of compulsory attendance in school for a certain period of time was one that could not be taken away in violation of the Fourteenth Amendment's requirement of due process.

The Court also discussed the issue a person's interest in liberty, as guaranteed by the Fourteenth Amendment. Because a suspension may result in a student's reputation or good name being damaged throughout his or her school career and beyond, therefore affecting his or her ability to freely choose future life options, the Constitution demanded that due process protections be adhered to, regardless of the length of the suspension.[12]

Last, but not least, the Court, in determining what process is due under these circumstances, held that some kind of notice and hearing is necessary before a suspension takes place. These requirements are essential to protect the student's due process rights and, in the words of the Court, "provide a meaningful hedge against erroneous action."[13]

Both the Dixon *and* Goss *courts . . . limited their decisions to disciplinary actions.*

Both the *Dixon* and *Goss* courts, in addition to limiting the respective decisions to public institutions, limited their decisions to disciplinary actions. What rights, if any, did a student have when an academic decision was made that resulted in dismissal from a program, course of study, or academic institution? Although difficult to define clearly, an academic dismissal by faculty is based on poor academic performance by a student. In other words, the student does not meet established criteria to successfully pass a course or clinical placement, or does not meet established criteria to enable the student to successfully continue in the course or program of study. An example of an academic dismissal would be when a student fails to maintain a C average in a nursing program pursuant to the program's requirements and is dismissed from it.

Until the United States Supreme Court decided the *Board of Curators of the University of Missouri v. Horowitz*[14] case in 1978, student rights when faced with an academic dismissal were unclear, whether enrolled in a public or private post-secondary institution.

The Horowitz Case

In *Horowitz*, the respondent, Charlotte Horowitz, was admitted to the University of Missouri's Medical School—a public institution—with advanced standing. Her academic record was impressive: a Bachelor of Science degree from Barnard College, a Master of Science degree in psychology from Columbia University, a year of study in Pharmacology at Duke University, a year's attendance at the Women's Medical College of Pennsylvania (withdrawing in good standing after 1 year because of illness), and more than 5 years of research in psychopharmacology at the National Institute of Mental Health.[15] After her first year in medical school, however, she was informed by the dean in writing that she was being placed on probation because of dissatisfaction by several faculty members over her clinical performance during her pediatrics rotation. The probationary status was based on several deficiencies, including poor relationships with others, erratic attendance during the clinical rotation, and poor personal hygiene (inadequate handwashing and poor grooming). Ms. Horowitz was informed that she needed to improve in these areas, but that, with the Council on Evaluation's recommendation, she would be allowed to advance to the next "rotational unit" in the curriculum.

Ms. Horowitz continued in the medical school program on probation during her second and third year, but the faculty was still "dissatisfied" with her performance. As a result, in January of 1973, the Council on Evaluation recommended that she not graduate in May of 1973. Ms. Horowitz was informed in writing of this decision and was also informed that, if she did not agree with it, she could take a set of oral and practical examinations with seven physicians who had no

prior contact with her in order to have them evaluate her academic performance and make recommendations as to her continuing as a student in the program. The oral and practical examinations were taken, and two of the physicians voted to have her graduate on schedule, two said she should be dismissed immediately, and the remaining physicians said she should not graduate in June but continue on probation until further evaluations concerning her clinical progress could be carried out and reviewed.[16] Based on the physicians' evaluations, the Council voted not to allow her to graduate in June, and informed her of this decision.

When the Council met again in May of 1973, it deliberated about whether or not Ms. Horowitz should be allowed to continue in the program beyond June of 1973. Because of the lack of major improvements in her performance, the Council voted to dismiss her from the school. When another negative evaluation of Ms. Horowitz's performance in the emergency rotation was received, the Council unanimously recommended that she be dropped from school. The recommendation was approved by the Coordinating Committee and the Dean, and the Dean notified the student in writing on July 6, 1973 that she was dismissed from the school. Ms. Horowitz appealed the decision in writing to the University Provost for Health Sciences, but the decision was upheld.

Ms. Horowitz then filed a case in the United States District Court for the Western District of Missouri and alleged that her civil rights were violated, citing 42 U.S.C. Section 1983.[17] The complaint also alleged that she was not afforded procedural due process rights prior to her dismissal from the school. After a full trial, the district court held that Ms. Horowitz had been given all the rights guaranteed to her by the Fourteenth Amendment and dismissed the complaint. The decision was appealed by the student, and the 8th Circuit Court of Appeals held that a dismissal from a medical school can have serious consequences for the student's ability to obtain a job in medicine, and therefore a hearing was required prior to dismissal. The court based this rationale on the Fourteenth Amendment's protection of "liberty"; in other words, the ability of this student to be free to obtain and change employment freely and the infringement of that right by the university (a public institution) in dismissing her from their program.[18]

The University appealed the 8th Circuit's decision, and the United States Supreme Court granted certiorari. By accepting the case for review, the Supreme Court would decide for the first time what procedure(s) must be given to a student at a state educational institution whose dismissal may constitute a deprivation of "liberty" or "property" within the meaning of the Fourteenth Amendment.[19]

The United States Supreme Court unanimously reversed the judgment of the appeals court. To begin with, it held that the action taken by the University was an *academic* one. As such, no hearing was required prior to the dismissal. The Court supported this holding by discussing the difference between disciplinary decisions, which require objective fact-finding and a subsequent decision based on those facts, and academic decisions, which are based more on a subjective determination of a student's abilities and which are based on a "continuing relationship between faculty and students."[20] Furthermore, the Court held that, because that relationship is not an adversarial one, is based on the expert evaluation of the faculty member who decides about student progress that is cumulative in nature, and historically such decisions have not been judicially scrutinized unless they are arbitrary or capricious, courts are generally "ill equipped" to evaluate academic performance and therefore will not, as a rule, intrude into academic decision-making.

In addition to its holding concerning the University's action being an academic one, the Court also held that there was no need to determine if there was a violation of Ms. Horowitz's "property" or "liberty" interests under the Fourteenth Amendment, because she had not alleged a violation of any "property" right in the courts below. The "liberty" interest allegation was not founded, the Court held, because the dismissal was not communicated publicly but to her alone, and because, assuming for the sake of argument it did exist, Ms. Horowitz had been given as much due process as the Fourteenth Amendment would require.[21]

Horowitz, then, set clear parameters for all academic institutions—whether public or private—to abide by when making decisions concerning the academic performance of students: No hearing is *required* prior to dismissal for academic reasons (although it can be afforded if the school selects to do so); adequate notice must be given to the student concerning his or her academic performance, what must be improved upon and under what time guidelines, and the impact on continuation in the program if the suggestions are not met; the decision to dismiss the student must not be disseminated publicly; and only careful and deliberate decisions by faculty concerning academic dismissals will be protected by the "hands-off" policy of the courts.

What remains unclear after Horowitz, *however, is what constitutes an academic, as opposed to a disciplinary, action or decision by the faculty . . .*

What remains unclear after *Horowitz*, however, is what constitutes an academic, as opposed to a disciplinary, action or decision by the faculty of the academic institution. This lack of clarity has not been corrected in subsequent cases, and, as a result, faculty and students must struggle with this issue on a regular basis. One way in which this concern is often resolved is by applying the due process principles discussed by the courts in *Dixon* and *Goss* whenever there is doubt about whether a decision is disciplinary or academic. The rationale for such an application is based on the idea that a court cannot fault an institution for providing more protections than are necessary in a certain situation.

The Contract Theory

The cases and theory presented thus far have dealt with dismissals from public academic institutions and have been based on constitutional protections afforded students. Other safeguards, however, were being concomitantly developed, especially for students in private institutions, and one very important theory was the contract theory; that is, the application of traditional contract law to the relationship between the student and the academic institution. Briefly, this theory supports an express or implied contract between the student and academic entity based on written documents (e.g., the student catalog) or oral representations or promises given (an academic advisor stating that a particular course could be taken as a substitution for another course, for example). If either party breaches the contract terms, then the student, for example, could be dismissed from the school for not maintaining the required grade point average, or conversely, the student could sue the school for dismissal in violation of the express or implied grade point average "provisions" of the contract.

Although the contract theory can be used by students in both private and public institutions, it is most often utilized by students in private academic settings because, as has been discussed, constitutional protections are not as readily available to those students. Furthermore, as stated by the *Dixon* court, the law has followed the "well-settled rule that the relations between a student and a private university are a matter of contract."[22] The contract theory has been applied in various situations and has proved to be flexible for both student and the academic institution,[23] not only with dismissals, but in all aspects of the student-institution relationship, as will be developed more fully in this chapter.

SPECIFIC STUDENT RIGHTS AND FACULTY RESPONSIBILITIES

Admission and Readmission

Whether public or private, academic institutions must abide by guidelines unique to the character of the institution when deciding about student admissions to the school and/or a specific program of study. Public academic institutions must abide by state and federal constitutional mandates. Private schools must adhere to express or implied requirements set forth in school publications or by faculty and staff. In addition, both public and private schools receiving state or federal funding or covered by state or federal statutory law prohibiting discrimination, bias, or other conduct in their decisions concerning admission to the academic institution must comply with those requirements. If not, the institution may not only face a lawsuit by the student allegedly aggrieved by the decision, but also loss of funding and other sanctions if the allegations are substantiated.

Nondiscrimination is one tenet that must be adhered to by academic institutions in admission and readmission decisions. This requirement stems not only from statutory (state and/or federal) laws, but also from case law. Table 20–1 summarizes selected cases dealing with discrimination issues litigated by students in relation to admission and readmission.

Implications for Nursing Students and Faculty

The decisions included in Table 20–1 can be helpful to nursing students and faculty when admission and readmission decisions are made. For example, the *Bakke* decision stands for the prohibition of utilizing race as one of the only factors in deciding admissions to academic institutions. It also stands for the importance of admission programs being as individualized as possible, whatever their format.

Like race discrimination, sex/gender discrimination will be carefully scrutinized by the

TABLE 20–1

Selected Cases on Discrimination in Admission and Readmission in Education

CASE NAME/DATE	DISCRIMINATION ALLEGED	BASIS OF SUIT	DECISION AND COMMENT
Brown v. Board of Education (1954)[1]	Race	14th Amendment Equal Protection clause	Decision for plaintiff, who was black, attempting to get into an all-white public school. Public schools cannot discriminate against an individual when making admission decisions on basis of race unless state has a "compelling state interest" in doing so. Here, no interest found. First case to set precedent for all public schools even though decision based on grades 1–12. Federally supported in Title VII of the Civil Rights Act of 1964, Title IX of the Education Amendments of 1972, and 42 USC Section 1981.
Regents of the University of California v. Bakke (1978)[2]	Race	University Affirmative Action Programs (specifically designed by the University to provide a separate admission system for minority students); 14th Amendment Equal Protection clause; California Constitution; Civil Rights Act of 1964	USS Ct. invalidates special admission programs and decided in favor of Bakke; Ct. held programs were a "racial quota"; Bakke ordered to be admitted to medical program and enjoined school from considering race in its admission programs; case called the "reverse discrimination" case because Bakke was white and minorities admitted were nonwhite.
Mississippi University for Women v. Hogan (1982)[3]	Sex/Gender	14th Amendment Equal Protection clause; Title IX of the Education Amendments of 1972; University's female-only admission policy	Decision for Hogan; applied to School of Nursing's B.S. Program but was denied admission because he was male; USS Ct. held that University's policy did not serve important "governmental objectives" required when single-sex policies challenged under 14th Amendment; Hogan decision dealt with public university; public and private universities must also not discriminate on the basis of gender/sex under Title IX of the Education Amendments of 1972 (includes marital status, family status, and pregnancy).
Southeast Community College v. Davis (1979)[4]	Handicap (bilateral sensorineural hearing loss)	Section 504 of Rehabilitation Act of 1973; 14th Amendment (Due Process and Equal Protection)	USS Ct. decision in favor of College; Ct. held that although Rehabilitation Act prohibits discrimination when school receives federal funding if student is "otherwise qualified" and can be "reasonably accommodated," student here not "otherwise qualified" and accommodation required was too extensive, especially considering clinical component of school program; to require school to admit this student would be costly and might compromise the quality of the program.
University of Texas Health Sciences Center at Houston v. Babb (1982)[5]	Change in School of Nursing catalog discriminated against student; required withdrawal and reapplication to program under "new" catalog that contained adverse requirements for student in comparison to initial catalog	Contract theory	Decision for student; appeals court held school catalog a written contract between student and school; because student only requested her cumulative grade point average be determined by initial catalog, ruling based on that request.

1. 347 U.S. 483 (1954)
2. 438 U.S. 265 (1978)
3. 458 U.S. 718 (1982)
4. 442 U.S. 397 (1979)
5. 646 S.W. 2d 502 (1982)

judicial system. State academic institutions must be able to conclusively show that any admission policy that favors members of one gender over another can pass the constitutional tests enumerated in *Hogan.*

The *Davis* decision is also an important case for students and faculty, but one that must be relied on cautiously. To begin with, it was based on the applicant's desire to enter a professional school that consisted of classroom *and* clinical components. The outcome may have been different if the program applied to was composed only of classroom requirements. Any requirements that are set by the academic institution must be essential ones for participation in that program. Additionally, *Davis* does not stand for the principle that a court would not require less burdensome accommodations to be made by an academic institution for a handicapped student so that he or she could participate in an academic program. Likewise, "auxiliary aids" (e.g., hearing aids or interpreters) and "support services" may be required in certain instances. Last, but by no means least, although there may be no *legal* obligation of a program accommodating an otherwise qualified applicant, there is no prohibition for a college or university from doing so voluntarily. However, if deciding to do so, the academic institution would have to establish clear-cut policies and procedures to ensure even-handed decision making in regard to every qualified handicapped student who was considered.

It is important to note that with the passage of the Americans with Disabilities Act (ADA),[24] the ADA may be used along with the Rehabilitation Act, or perhaps alone, in challenging decisions by academic institutions because Title III of the ADA clearly prohibits places of "public accommodation" (privately owned establishments that make goods, services, or programs available to the public)[25] from discriminating against individuals with disabilities. Likewise, Title II, which governs governmental entities, prohibits the same conduct.[26] Therefore, academic institutions may violate either of these two provisions with discriminatory admission or readmission policies and decisions.

> *. . . with the passage of the Americans with Disabilities Act (ADA), the ADA may be used along with the Rehabilitation Act, or perhaps alone, in challenging decisions by academic institutions . . .*

Although not presented in Table 20–1, nondiscrimination on the basis of age is another important canon that must be adhered to by the academic institution when deciding about applicants. Generally, as with the other protected categories already discussed, age cannot be used to deny admission to a college or university program. In addition to state laws protecting discrimination on the basis of age, the federal Age Discrimination Act of 1975[27] forbids discrimination on the basis of age for those public and private programs or activities receiving federal funds. Exceptions include when an age requirement is vital to the "normal operation" of the program receiving the funds, or when the age requirement conforms with a statutory purpose for which the program or activity is receiving the funds. Those exceptions are carefully monitored by the courts, and it is safe to say that any decision based solely on age will be carefully questioned by the courts if challenged.

Perhaps the best way an academic institution can avoid any unnecessary liability for discriminatory decision-making concerning admission is to have well-drafted policies concerning the admissions process. A statement that the postsecondary institution does not discriminate and adheres to all applicable state and federal laws concerning nondiscrimination is helpful. It is also important that any and all policies concerning the process, including, but not limited to admission classifications, advanced standing, tuition and fees, and withdrawal from the school or program be nondiscriminatory.

The general position statement and the academic policies statement should appear in any and all school academic catalogues and in department or specific program handbooks as well. Not only does this approach make clear the school's position in relation to nondiscrimination, it also provides notice to the potential applicant of the requirements necessary for admission to the college or program. As a result, whether a public or private institution, the school has met its legal and ethical obligations to inform the potential applicant of the rules that will be adhered to during the admission decision-making phase. Likewise, the student is equipped with information necessary to make choices concerning applying for admission, making up deficiencies before doing so, or deciding to forgo applying to that particular school.

Clear-cut statements and policies concerning readmissions to an academic institution or program are also important to include in the various documents given to applicants or students.

In addition to the requirement of nondiscrimination, decisions concerning readmissions must unquestionably follow catalog and other documents delineating the process. If the institution fails to follow these written guidelines, the student may allege a breach of the language in the document(s) and proceed to court on the contract theory, as was seen in the *Babb* case.

Although courts will look at whether an educational institution's conduct is arbitrary or capricious when that is alleged by a litigant, in *Babb* that was not an issue. Rather, as the court said, the issue was one of contract law and whether the nursing program breached the contract provisions. Carefully drafted catalogs, and other written documents governing students and their relationship with the academic institution, are essential. The written material must be clear, unambiguous, and state what is intended by the academic institution. Achieving clarity aids both the student and the academic institution, as either can be easily held to those mandates by the courts.

Carefully drafted catalogs, and other written documents governing students and their relationship with the academic institution, are essential.

Many academic institutions, concerned about decisions based on contract theory, often place disclaimers in school catalogs and other written documents stating, in effect, that the document does not create an express or implied contract, and that the institution reserves the right to make changes in curriculum, course content, fees, and in other areas at any time those changes are necessary or desirable. Although there is no guarantee that such a disclaimer would result in a judgment in favor of the postsecondary school, its inclusion in catalogs and other documents would be one issue a court would take into consideration when allegations of breach of contract against the academic entity are raised.

Advancement in the School or Program

Once a student has been admitted into a school and/or specific program, successful completion of all program and school requirements in a timely manner so that graduation, sitting for and passing nursing boards, and beginning one's professional life as a nurse can occur is the main goal for the student. However, that goal can be fraught with obstacles as students progress through their academic career, for their success is dependent upon evaluation in the form of grades, both in the classroom and clinical setting. Generally speaking, as was discussed in the *Horowitz* case, the court will not interfere or second-guess academic decision-making by faculty, for the court is not experienced in evaluating success or failure in the academic setting. Despite that general posture, the court will scrutinize decisions by faculty or administration if they are (1) arbitrary, malicious, capricious, not in accordance with adopted policies or procedures; (2) in bad faith; or (3) violate a student's constitutional or other rights.

Academic and Clinical Grading

In *Clements v. The County of Nassau*,[28] Helen Clements, age 51, enrolled in the state-supported Nassau County Community College's Licensed Practical Nursing program. A former laboratory technician and active member of many health-related community groups, Ms. Clements was not new to health care delivery. Her first year of the 2-year program went academically well, although there seemed to be a clash between Ms. Clements' alleged attitude of her "thinking she knew more than she actually did" and faculty allegedly "resenting (her) from the beginning" because of her knowledge and experience in aspects of health care.

During the second year of the program, Ms. Clements contaminated the newborn nursery during her pediatric rotation. Although she was told of the error and acknowledged it, Ms. Clements was allowed to continue in the rotation and program. However, several months later, she failed her clinical evaluation because she did not "maintain cleanliness." The F in her clinical evaluation resulted in an F for the entire course.[29]

Clements appealed her grade to the Dean of Health Sciences, and despite a school policy allowing only two chances to obtain a passing grade, the Dean provided Ms. Clements with another chance to rectify her grade and pass the course. This included being assigned to another instructor and successfully completing an additional clinical test in addition to the one she failed earlier. Clements passed the course with a B.

During the final clinical course, however, she again failed to maintain the sterile procedure required when changing a dressing, did not realize her mistake, and therefore did not correct it. The instructor made the judgment that Clements did not "understand sterile technique," and the student was allowed to withdraw with a W grade rather than receive an F for the course. The instructor also recommended that Clements "take time off" from school to improve her clinical skills and return to retake the course in a year. Although Clements did not disagree with the instructor's judgment, she was very unhappy about the recommendation that she leave the program for a year. When she approached the Dean again concerning this latest recommendation, the Dean refused to take any corrective action and agreed that she should drop out of school for the year. Ms. Clements then went to the Vice-President for Academic Affairs, who intervened on her behalf and allowed her to enroll in the Fall Semester.[30]

In addition to seeing the Vice-President for Academic Affairs, Ms. Clements had seen other administrators at the college since her difficulties began, had also written the New York State Education Department, and contacted her senator. Her complaints to these various individuals and organizations were, among other things, that she was being harassed.

Ms. Clements began the Fall 1983 term in clinical. Unfortunately, while giving a soapsuds enema to a patient, she did not provide for the patient's "safety needs," and was given an F in the course. Because this was the second failure for the student, she was unable to continue in it. Ms. Clements grieved the grade on the grounds that it was "unfair" to fail her on the second day of the course and because of the faculty's "inaccurate anecdotal records" about her. The first three steps of the grievance process were concluded, but the final step did not take place until April of 1985. The hearing, conducted by an ad hoc committee of the college academic standing committee, decided in favor of Ms. Clements and recommended that she be allowed to repeat the final course. Because the college's policy concerning grades is vested in the faculty, the nursing faculty member giving Ms. Clements the F refused to change it.

Ms. Clements then filed suit in the United States District Court of the Eastern District of New York and alleged that, under The Civil Rights Act of 1871 (42 U.S.C. Section 1983), the College and faculty violated her civil rights by not making judgments about her performance but rather on the basis of "personal animus and ill will" and "acted in concert" to force her out of the college's licensed practical nursing program. Thus, she alleged, her Fourteenth Amendment Due Process and Equal Protection rights were breached. She also alleged other causes of action, including, but not limited to contract and tort violations. The district court entered a summary judgment motion in favor of the college, and Clements appealed.

On appeal, the appeals court upheld the entry of the summary judgment for the college. Citing *Horowitz* and a subsequent case supporting that decision, the court stated that courts will not overturn academic decisions unless there is a clear departure from "accepted academic norms so as to demonstrate that the person or committee responsible did not actually exercise professional judgment."[31] Furthermore, the court said, the faculty and college were more than "sympathetic" to her situation and gave her many opportunities to rectify her behavior, which simply did not occur. In addition, no Due Process or Equal Protection violations took place, for the college's grievance process was more than adequate, and Ms. Clements was not subjected to academic standards that were additional to those similarly situated. Last, the anecdotal records kept by the faculty were not used in grading nor were they disseminated to the public. Thus, no liberty interest deprivation was present.

The *Clements* case is an important one because it continues to support a faculty's right to make

judgments concerning grades, both in the classroom and in the clinical area. However, any such judgment will be measured by current academic norms. Thus, for both the student and faculty, well-developed evaluation forms concerning student progress that constitute the basis of the student's clinical grade are vital. They must be criterion based, and contain behavioral objectives that can be measured. The student must be given a copy of the evaluation tool on the first day of class so that he or she has notice about what will be the basis of the grade. The evaluation process must be an ongoing one throughout the student's clinical rotation. If the student is not meeting clinical objectives, then he or she must be warned, told how to improve his or her difficulties, given any time constraints within which that improvement must occur, and be informed about what will take place if the required improvement does not occur (for example, suspension, request for withdrawal, receiving an F grade). Any policies requiring a written form to be sent to a specific college or program dean or department concerning the poor clinical performance should be complied with and a copy given to the student. Anecdotal records can, and should, be kept by faculty. However, they do not substitute for the utilization of the evaluation form and other documents and procedures set by the academic program concerning evaluation. Also, as the *Clements* court cautioned, they cannot be untrue or abused.

Academic evaluation of students also consists of the faculty member's judgment concerning the student's classroom performance. As with clinical evaluations, the decision concerning grading must be in accordance with acceptable standards utilized by faculty generally. Moreover, the decision-making process must be as fair and equitable as possible. Thus the student should be informed of what is to be expected of him or her at the initiation of the course. This is best accomplished by utilizing a syllabus that spells out the respective responsibilities of *both* the student and faculty member. Information to include in the syllabus for any course includes, but is not limited to (1) name of the course; (2) credit hours earned; (3) method of grading; (4) grading scale; and (5) topics to be covered, dates of coverage, and required preparation for each class. Objectives that form the basis of the grade, and that the student is required to fulfill, must be included in the syllabus. Likewise, if the course requires projects, papers, and/or examination, the dates those required projects are due are an essential feature to include in the syllabus.

The faculty member should go over the syllabus with the students on the first day of class to ensure that they are clear about its contents. In addition, the student should be given an opportunity to ask any questions or clarify any requirements that are unclear. The opportunity to continue to raise questions or seek clarification should continue throughout the course, however, and the faculty member should inform students of his or her office hours during the semester or quarter, either orally or placing that information in the syllabus.

It is important that the faculty member adhere to the syllabus. If it needs to be altered or corrected, these changes must be discussed with the students as soon as possible. Changes that might adversely affect the student will be ones that will require special care and consideration. Most often, changes in grading criteria, or changes in the evaluation of the student in terms of his or her grade, will be the kinds of changes most often seen as adversely affecting the student, especially from the student's perspective. The syllabus clearly becomes a "contract" between the student and the faculty member, and therefore can be used to challenge any deviations from its provisions. Moreover, the student can also allege that even if the terms of the syllabus were adhered to, they were applied in an arbitrary or capricious manner.[32]

In *Lyons v. Salve Regina College*,[33] for example, a senior nursing student who had received mostly A's and B's was absent for several days from a course that included a clinical component. As a result of her absences, which occurred not because of her own illness but rather so she could be with a friend who was hospitalized, the faculty member teaching the class and clinical course assured Ms. Lyons that she would receive an "Incomplete" rather than an F for the course.[34] The student continued in the course, finished all other course requirements, and took the final examination. When she received her grades, however, she had been given an "F" for the course.

Ms. Lyons appealed the grade through the school's grievance procedure listed in various documents of the College, including its catalog. These documents clearly stated that once the grievance was submitted to the appeals committee, its recommendation would be submitted to the Dean. During the time the committee was deliberating her situation, Ms. Lyons received a letter from the Dean informing her she could conditionally register for other classes, but that registration would be rescinded if the committee's recommendation was not in her favor.

The three-faculty-member committee recommended two to one in favor of Ms. Lyons; that is, that she receive an Incomplete and be allowed to make up the course deficiencies due to her absences. The third member voted to let the F stand, but to allow Ms. Lyons to apply for reinstatement. The Dean dismissed the student from the program, and Ms. Lyons filed suit in the Federal District Court in Rhode Island and asked the court to interpret the language in the school documents concerning the Dean's and the committee's role in the grievance procedure.

The trial court held that the school catalog, the appeal committee hearing procedures, and the letter from the Dean did constitute a contract between Ms. Lyons and the school.[35] Furthermore, the court held that based on those documents being a contract, the committee, not the Dean, was empowered to make the final decision in this matter. The school appealed the decision, and the appellate court reversed the trial court, stating that the lower court had applied contract law too strictly. Because the relationship of the student and academic institution is unique, a rigid application of contract law cannot occur. In this instance, the court continued, the Dean had the final say in whether or not a student continued in the nursing program. Even so, the court cautioned that a school catalog and other documents can be viewed as evidence of a contract between the school and student.

In *McIntosh v. Borough of Manhattan Community College*,[36] the New York Court of Appeals considered a student's allegation that the faculty's refusal to round off her 69.713 failing grade to a 70.000 passing grade was arbitrary and capricious. Citing *Horowitz*, the court stated that since the faculty member had not acted as the student alleged, no judicial review of the decision concerning the grade would occur.

Disciplinary Actions

A second obstacle that may occur for a student as he or she progresses through the academic program is conduct that is considered by the academic program to be a violation of its established code of acceptable behavior. Often formalized in "codes of conduct" or expected behaviors listed in school catalogs and other school documents, the prohibited behaviors cover, as examples, cheating and/or plagiarism, the use of alcoholic beverages on campus, participation in criminal activity, and in professional programs, unethical conduct not consistent with the profession's standards.

Dismissals for disciplinary reasons are subject to different rules of judicial review than are academic dismissals. The *Dixon* and *Goss* decisions are still "good law," and their continued applicability can be seen in subsequent case decisions.

Jones v. The Board of Governors of the University of North Carolina[37] is one such case illustrating the courts' continued application of those decisions. Nancy Jones, a nursing student in the University's program, was allegedly involved in cheating on an examination by obtaining answers to two of the questions from the faculty member teaching the course and changing a paper before turning it in. Five days after the

alleged incidents took place, Jones was informed by the Dean of the School of Nursing that she had been accused of cheating and could either take an F for the course or have a hearing before the University Student Court, which was composed of three students. Ms. Jones asked for, and had, a hearing before the Student Court, which found her guilty of "academic dishonesty."[38]

Consistent with university procedures, Jones appealed the decision to the University Chancellor and asked for a new hearing before the Chancellor's Hearing Panel, which was composed of three university faculty members. The Chancellor and the Panel decided that the hearing conducted by the Student Court was not a fair one and required a new hearing to be conducted by the Panel in which both sides could present evidence on the alleged conduct of Ms. Jones. After the hearing occurred, the Panel made its recommendation of "not guilty" and shared its decision with the Chancellor. The University's legal counsel filed an objection to this determination with the Chancellor. The Chancellor asked the Vice-Chancellor of Academic Affairs to review the hearing transcript and the objection of the University attorney. He did so, and decided that Ms. Jones was guilty of the alleged misconduct. He then upheld the Student Court's recommendation: that Ms. Jones receive an F in the course and be placed on disciplinary probation for a semester. Because she did not receive a passing grade in the course, Ms. Jones' registration was cancelled for the next semester because every student in the nursing program was required to pass all previous courses before being allowed to register and continue with subsequent courses.[39]

Nancy Jones filed suit in the United States Federal District Court for the Western District of North Carolina, alleging that, under 42 U.S.C. 1983, the University had violated her procedural due process rights. She also asked for an injunction to reinstate her as a student in good standing until the suit was resolved on its merits. The district court granted this latter request, and the University appealed the decision to issue an injunction, alleging that doing so was an abuse of the court's discretion.

In addition to discussing its role in issuing injunctions, the court again outlines its role in evaluating decisions by faculty and administration. Although "great deference" must be given to educational institutions, the court, citing *Goss*, stated that it must continue to ensure that "rudimentary precautions against unfair or mistaken findings of misconduct and arbitrary exclusion from school does not occur."[40] In this instance, the court continued, Ms. Jones will suffer "irreparable injury" by having to wait out a decision by the University—her education would be interrupted, she would be deprived of the opportunity to graduate with her classmates, and her goal of becoming a nurse will be delayed. In contrast, the University would not be harmed by having the student reinstated pending resolution of the case. In fact, the court pointed out, the confused and arguably irregular proceedings that took place, which were in stark divergence from established procedures, clearly deprived Ms. Jones of her due process rights as supported in *Goss*.

Although the *Jones* case was not decided on its merits at the appeals level, the opinion is an important one in supporting the right of the student to obtain a fair hearing on the facts surrounding his or her particular case. For Ms. Jones, that meant upholding the decision to allow her to be reinstated pending a full and fair hearing concerning the alleged misconduct and whether dismissal for disciplinary reasons would be warranted.

In another interesting case, *Slaughter v. Brigham Young University*,[41] a private university's actions were evaluated by a federal district court. The University dismissed a doctoral student after a hearing for using his professor's name as a coauthor of articles the student had written before being admitted as a student in the program. Prior to using the faculty member's name as a coauthor, the student could not get the papers published. The University cited its rules of conduct, which stated that the student should observe "high principles of honor, integrity and morality," and be honest in all behavior, as the basis for its dismissal.

The federal court held that the University's rules of conduct were reasonable, clear and well defined. Furthermore, the court held that all of the student's due process protections were afforded to him and therefore upheld the decision of the university.[42]

Physical or Mental Incapacity

A third obstacle that may stand in the way of a student's main goal in the academic environment is when physical or mental incapacity prohibits the student from successfully completing the program of study. Earlier in this chapter, a discussion of the general prohibition against making admission and readmission decisions solely on the basis of the presence of a handicap was summarized, and the general limitations on such decisions were presented. Likewise, limitations also exist for subsequent decisions based on a health problem that hinders the student's academic and clinical performance. These limitations do not mean that a faculty member cannot make a decision based on the existence of a mental or physical problem. Rather, they mean that the decisions made must be careful, deliberate, and clearly conform to existing state and federal laws protecting any student who may fall under their respective protections.[43]

Curriculum/Catalog Changes

Another obstacle facing students as they progress through their academic experience may be when a change in the curriculum affects that progression. Generally speaking, when changes in the curriculum do take place, they must be done in a timely manner and give students adequate notice of the change and how it will affect them. This notice is especially important if the effect is an adverse one; that is, not graduating as planned or requiring additional coursework that requires more cost to the student. Moreover, viable options must be provided for the student to comply with the "new requirements" without detriment.[44] When such conditions are allegedly not met by the educational entity and are challenged by students, the court must define how the institution's need for change can be balanced with fairness vis-à-vis the student body.

Another obstacle facing students as they progress through their academic experience may be when a change in the curriculum affects that progression.

In *Atkinson v. Traetta,*[45] six nursing students at Queensborough Community College who were unable to progress to additional nursing courses because of a change in the requirement of a C− grade, rather than a D− grade, as a prerequisite for subsequent course enrollment, filed a suit asking for an injunction mandating them to be allowed to continue in the nursing program. The students alleged that the change constituted a change in the curriculum *after* they had enrolled, and the change was therefore unfair. The trial court returned a verdict in favor of the students, granted the injunction, and the College appealed.

The New York Appellate Division Court reversed the trial court, holding that the change that did occur was not a "curriculum change" but rather a "grading change." The court stated that even if it were a curriculum change, the faculty had an obligation to uphold academic standards, particularly when those standards involved clinical practice and the public's safety.[46] Furthermore, the court continued, the changes were communicated to the student body well in advance of the change's effective date.

Likewise, in *Crabtree v. California University of Pennsylvania,*[47] the Pennsylvania Commonwealth Court upheld the University's requirement of an additional 1000-hour internship in a post-Masters' certificate program for Mary Ann Crabtree. Ms. Crabtree had graduated from the School's psychology program in 1988 and then enrolled in the certificate program. The 1985–1987 catalog clearly stated that the certificate required 450 hours of an internship. The catalog also contained a statement that the university retained the right to alter statements or procedures in the catalog. In addition, the catalog contained a statement that it was the student's responsibility to keep up with changes that might occur in requirements.

The student alleged that since she entered the university's program in 1986, the 1985–1987 catalog should control the number of hours she had to take to complete the certificate program.

The court, in supporting the University's decision, discussed the fact that the disclaimer in the catalog concerning changes in the requirements for the certificate allowed the University to make changes as it saw fit. Moreover, Ms. Crabtree was given adequate notice of the change by the University in announcements and a bulletin sent to all students enrolled in the program.[48]

Graduation

Academic institutions must also make careful decisions concerning the graduation of students, and the same principles discussed in the *Admission and Readmission* and *Advancement Through the School or Program* Sections apply to these decisions as well. Catalog and specific school or program documents must contain clear language and directives concerning graduation requirements, including any time limitations under which the student must operate, grade-point average required for graduation, semester or quarter hours needed for graduation, any application process that the student must initiate *prior* to graduation, and any fees necessary. If a student feels aggrieved by an adverse decision concerning graduation, the student can challenge it under the various legal mechanisms discussed earlier in this chapter; for example, a breach of an express or implied contract term, a violation of due process rights (if a public school and the decision not to graduate the student rests upon some disciplinary action by the school), or the school's decision was arbitrary or capricious.

In *Eiland v. Wolf*,[49] for example, the Court of Appeals for the 1st District (Houston) reviewed several allegations made by a medical student, Philip Wolf, concerning the decision of the University of Texas Medical Branch at Galveston not to graduate him from the Medical School. At the trial level, the court granted declaratory relief and a permanent injunction against the School for Wolf's "wrongful dismissal" from the School after he failed his final course in the program. In essence, the trial court ordered that Wolf graduate and receive the degree of Doctor of Medicine. The School appealed the decision.

The appeals court, in reversing the trial court's holding, cited *Horowitz* in upholding the School's decision to dismiss Wolf and not graduate him. Characterizing the decision as an *academic* one, no hearing was required—as was alleged by Wolf—and the process that did take place concerning the decision to dismiss the student was fair. Furthermore, the court continued, there was evidence in the trial record that the decision to dismiss Wolf was based on professional (faculty) judgment, and therefore could not be overturned absent a void of academic decision-making by faculty.[50]

Wolf's claim that the University, a public institution, violated his equal protection rights under the Fourteenth Amendment, was also held not to be a valid claim. Citing a United States Supreme Court case, *Regents of the University of Michigan v. Ewing*,[51] the court again reiterated that generally academic decisions are not subject to rigorous judicial review. Therefore, absent evidence to support an allegation that the decision made was "beyond the pale of reasoned academic decision-making," that decision must be upheld.[52]

Wolf's last count, a breach of contract claim, was based on the School catalog's language concerning graduation and its requirements. Distin-

guishing this case from the *Babb* case discussed earlier in this chapter, the court held that in this case, the catalog contained a disclaimer reserving the right of the school to change its contents and negating the establishment of a contract with any student. In addition, the University's catalog expressly stated that the School of Medicine had the "authority" to drop any student from enrollment . . . "if circumstances of a legal, moral, health, social or academic nature justify such a request."[53] Thus, no enforceable contract existed between Wolf and the University. Even if a contract did exist, the court concluded, the School and University adhered to the terms of the catalog (contract) without question.

Privacy

The student enrolled in a post-secondary academic institution has a right to privacy. That right has its basis in several legal arenas—state and federal constitutions and statutory law. The state and federal constitutional protections are firmly rooted in the Fourteenth Amendment to the United States Constitution. State protections of privacy are usually located in a parallel amendment, section, or article. The respective constitutions protect against violations of privacy by the state and federal government, and a student does not lose those protections when enrolled in primary, secondary, or post-secondary educational programs. Public entities have different obligations in maintaining the privacy of citizens, including students, than do private organizations, and educational institutions are no exception.

The student enrolled in a post-secondary academic institution has a right to privacy.

A student's constitutional right of privacy may be violated in several ways by the academic institution. One way in which it could be jeopardized is by seeking out information from a student that is invasive and of a private nature. "Overstepping" by academic faculty into areas not justified may be challenged. Therefore, information sought by an academic institution or program must be germane to the reason for the initial inquiry.

A second way in which a student's right to privacy may be violated is when there is a search of the student's room, locker, or person for whatever reason. When this occurs, the United States Constitution's Fourth Amendment protection against unreasonable searches and seizures and parallel state constitutional protections come into play. This student right will be discussed further in the section *Other Constitutional Rights.*

A student also has an interest in protecting the privacy of his or her student records. Although a state may protect releases of post-secondary student records by statute and/or case law, the Federal Family Educational Rights and Privacy Act of 1974 was amended by the Buckley Amendment[54] and is the controlling law in this area.

The Buckley Amendment was passed to ensure a consistent approach to the release of a student's school record. Prior to its enactment, only a few states had any laws regulating the release of information in the student's school file. In addition, it was often difficult for the student or student's parents to obtain information contained in the school file for their own review. Thus, Congress tied access and release of student files to the receipt of federal funds from any applicable federal program administered by the Department of Education and applied the act to both public and private "educational agencies."[55]

Briefly, the Buckley Amendment allows students 18 years of age and older the right of access to their records, the right to be informed of the school policy concerning that access, and the right to give consent for the release of information from their educational file, which includes, but is not limited to, "records, files, documents and other materials which contain information directly related to a student and are maintained by an educational agency or institution or a person acting for such agency or institution."[56] In addition, if there is anything in the educational record that the student objects to, procedures are spelled out in the act that must be adopted by the educational agency to allow the student to challenge that information.

The Buckley Amendment was passed to ensure a consistent approach to the release of a student's school record.

Exceptions exist in the Act concerning the need for consent to be obtained prior to the release of information under certain circumstances and also for certain materials being exempt from access or review by the student. For example, consent need not be obtained from the student to release file information when the release is to other school officials, including teachers, within the school who have been determined by the institution to have a legitimate educational interest in that information; when the release is pursuant to a judicial order or lawful subpoena (although notification prior to release is required); when the release is to appropriate individuals who need the information in an emergency to protect the health or safety of the student or other persons; and in connection with a student's application for, or receipt of, financial aid.[57] Student "directory information," which includes name, address, major field of study, dates of attendance, and degree awarded may also be released without consent, unless a refusal is given by the student.[58] A student does not have access to teachers' and administrators' personal notes solely within the teachers' or administrators' possession; the student's parents do not have access to the student's medical, psychiatric, or other professional treatment records; and, if the student has signed a waiver of access, the student cannot review letters or statements of recommendation if used solely for the purpose for which they were intended. If the student requested notification of those individuals who gave such letters of recommendation, the school must notify the student when the letters are received.[59]

Academic institutions and their respective schools or departments must ensure adherence to the Buckley Amendment's mandates concerning the privacy and accessibility of student records. Not only may a student be harmed by unauthorized release of information or by not being able to review that which he or she is entitled to examine, but the academic institution may have funding terminated if noncompliance is proven. The development of policies and procedures consistent with those mandates by nursing programs can aid with conformity. In addition, the careful storing of student records, evaluation, and other materials concerning the student by the nursing program is also essential. Student information in faculty offices should also be carefully stored, with access to that information limited to the faculty member or his or her secretary.

Other Constitutional Rights

Searches and Seizures/Privacy

A student's interest in maintaining privacy also rests in the federal and a state's constitutional protections against invasions of privacy under the prohibition against unreasonable searches and seizures by the government. The Fourth Amendment of the United States Constitution, and parallel state provisions, does not prohibit any and all searches and seizures. Rather, the ban extends only to unreasonable searches and, in some instances, to warrantless searches.[60]

Although it is clear that the constitutional protection against tyrannical governmental intrusion into privacy extends to students, how it applies has not always been clear. Initially, many of the cases concerning this right dealt with the student and his or her expectation of privacy in university- or college-sponsored student housing, whether in a residence hall or another type of dwelling. In those cases, courts have held that students do have an expectation of privacy in college- or university-sponsored housing, their possessions, and their person.[61] The expectation cannot be abrogated by the academic institution's reliance on the *in loco parentis* doctrine or its position as a "landlord" of the student. In other words, the institution cannot give consent to university or other police to conduct a search of the student's living quarters.[62]

There are exceptions to these limitations on an educational institution's ability to breach the privacy of students, however. One is when the student gives consent for a warrantless search under certain conditions. For example, the residence contract might contain a provision dealing with the ability of the university to enter and search a student's dwelling under very limited circumstances.[63] Or the student may verbally consent to a search at the instant it is asked for by university or college officials. However, as with any provision in a housing contract, the search consented to would have to be clearly requested, narrowly drawn, and *not* include the personal belongings of a roommate.[64]

A second exception to the requirement of a warrant prior to a search is when an emergency exists and protection of the health and safety of other students is at issue, or when necessary to maintain "order and discipline." For this exception to apply, however, there must be a true emergency; that is, when the life or well-being of the student(s) is of concern, such as a fire or when police are needed to provide assistance or help individuals in distress,[65] or when an incident is disrupting the functioning of the entity as an educational institution.[66] It is clear that if the university is simply conducting what has been termed an "administrative search," there is no emergency or disruption of the academic milieu. Moreover, when there is time to obtain a search warrant, the courts will usually require that one be obtained, unless consent for such searches has been obtained through the housing contract or from the student personally.[67]

A third exception concerning the need for a warrant before searching a student's residence is when an item is in the "plain view" of the school official. The plain-view doctrine has specific applicability to criminal law. It is also applied to student searches as well. Thus, when a school official or the police are lawfully in a student's room or home, and incriminating evidence is present in plain view of that officer or school official, it can be seized and used in a school disciplinary hearing, for example, or in a criminal trial. Of course, the question whether or not the evidence was seized pursuant to this doctrine is always subject to challenge and would occur under the "exclusionary rule" doctrine analyzed in Chapter 8. Generally speaking, however, because the rule has been interpreted by the United States Supreme Court as applying only to *criminal* defendants, its use in the academic setting is limited.

It is important to remember that the application of the rules covering unreasonable searches and seizures and student residences apply particularly to public academic institutions. Private institutions are less constrained by these constitutional protections. Yet, if local, state, or federal officials are involved in any search or seizure by a private academic agency, then the court would require adherence to those protections. In addition, the character of funding received by a private academic institution—from state or local taxes, for example—may color the institution more similar to a public, rather than strictly private, entity, and therefore necessitate adherence to privacy protections.

Drug and Alcohol Testing/Privacy

In recent years the character of the allegations of invasion of privacy actions of students has changed. Though privacy issues concerning a

student's living quarters and belongings are still important, the issue of drugs, drug testing, and any subsequent actions taken by the academic institution against the student based on the test results has become the focus of this constitutionally based right.

It would be inaccurate to say that none of the early cases dealing with student privacy dealt with drugs, drug testing, or disciplinary actions against students. However, it has not been until recently that this focus has taken on monumental proportions.

The issue of a student's constitutional rights in relation to searches and drug testing had its birth in the public school arena. In the first United States Supreme Court case, *New Jersey v. T.L.O.*,[68] the search of a 14-year-old freshman's purse for cigarettes after the student was found smoking in violation of the school's rule was upheld by the Court, even when the search turned up marijuana and paraphernalia used to make and smoke the marijuana. In so holding, the Court said that although public students do have an expectation of privacy when in school, the test for such a search is whether or not it was reasonable, taking into consideration all the circumstances surrounding the search. When there is a question of the student's conduct breaking the law or the rules of the school, that search will be justified under "ordinary circumstances," so long as the search is within reasonable parameters and scope to fulfil the objectives of the search, and is not "excessively" intrusive given the student's age, sex, and nature of the alleged offense.[69]

In addition, the Court held that if the above criteria are met, there is no need for a search warrant *prior* to the search, so long as the student is under the school's authority. Even so, the Court also held that the Fourth Amendment's protection against unreasonable searches and seizures does apply to public school officials because they are representatives of the state, and must therefore conduct themselves within the mandates also applicable to law enforcement officers.[70]

The issue of a student's constitutional rights in relation to searches and drug testing had its birth in the public school arena.

After the *New Jersey* decision, cases shifted from searches of property to searches of individuals, mainly through drug testing programs, by using blood or urine analysis to determine whether drugs are present in the student's system at the time of the test. Generally, the courts have been hesitant to uphold such programs in public high schools because they are viewed as invasive; the tests show only the presence of drugs in the system at the time of the test, not whether its presence resulted in the student being impaired during school time; and the concern that many of the programs were not based on suspicion of drug use or impairment but were overly broad in their application to all students.[71]

In 1995, however, the ability of high schools to test student athletes for drugs was supported by the United States Supreme Court in *Vernonia School District v. Acton*.[72] The Court upheld the Vernonia School District's initial testing (with the parents' consent) of all students when applying for any interscholastic sports team and then random testing thereafter. If consent was not obtained for the initial testing, the student could not be considered for the particular team. Likewise, if the student subsequently tested positive during random testing, several penalties were imposed, up to and including suspension from the team.[73]

James Acton did not feel it was fair to be tested for drugs since he never had a drug problem and was an excellent student. His parents agreed and sued the school board alleging that the policy violated the student's Fourth Amendment Rights.

The United States Supreme Court held that no Fourth Amendment violation occurred because the school was "reasonable under the circumstances," especially in view of the documented drug problem facing students and student athletes generally in Vernonia.[74] The policy was reasonable, the Court opined, because a student's legitimate expectation of privacy is lessened as a result of his or her constant supervision by school officials under the *in loco parentis* doctrine. Moreover, the Vernonia policy carefully fashioned an unobtrusive search (e.g., no direct observation of student giving specimen).[75] Last, the Court held that the policy was reasonable because there was a dire need for the testing to identify students who may be using drugs in order to help them overcome the problem and provide a safe interscholastic sports program.[76]

Implications for Nursing Students and Faculty

Nursing students who provide care to patients while under the influence of any drug that would impair their ability to provide safe care are problematic from a liability perspective for both the school and for the student. The school or program may have a clear interest, indeed may possess a clear duty, to evaluate those nursing students who are functioning in an impaired manner. How that interest or duty is carried out, however, will determine whether or not any testing program passes judicial scrutiny if challenged. Therefore, nursing programs considering testing nursing students for drug or alcohol use will need to do so very carefully.

To begin with, programs in public post-secondary institutions will need to conform strictly to constitutional protections as discussed so far. In addition, the utilization of a voluntary, as opposed to a mandatory, drug-testing program needs to be carefully evaluated. What standard will be applied when deciding to test a student must also be addressed. For example, in the *New Jersey* case, one of the issues discussed was the fact that the "reasonable suspicion" of drug presence standard applicable to high school students would probably not apply to college students.[77] The appropriate standard for students in colleges or universities would probably be a "probable cause" one, thus eliminating any random testing under either approach.

Secondly, if a nursing school or program does decide to do any testing of student nurses, compliance with the *Drug-Free Schools and Communities Act of 1986* and its 1989 amendments[78] will be helpful. Although there is no specific discussion or requirements concerning drug testing, the Act does require that any institution of higher education receiving federal funds or any other form of financial assistance under any federal program adopt and implement a drug and alcohol abuse policy.[79] The Act requires several components to any adopted program, including standards of conduct prohibiting unlawful possession, use, or distribution of drugs and alcohol on campus, what sanctions will be imposed by the institution if the code of conduct is violated, and continual evaluation of the program once implemented.[80]

Schools of nursing have already published articles concerning their established policies on drug and alcohol abuse.[81] Interestingly, as a way around the random testing issue, some policies require the nursing student to provide consent ("A Witness Contract") to be tested for drugs and alcohol and enter into treatment if any suspicious behavior is identified by faculty during their clinical or classroom experiences.[82]

The nursing student who is believed to be impaired while providing care to patients during clinical assignments will need to be ensured that his or her privacy is maintained concerning the conduct displayed, the testing itself, the procedure for gathering any blood or urine specimen, the test results, and any disciplinary actions taken as a consequence of a positive test result. Along this line, it is vital that clear due process protections are afforded the student who may be dismissed or otherwise disciplined by the program for a positive result.

Nursing school administrators and faculty must also be certain that they are not discriminating against the student who may have an alcohol or drug use problem in violation of state and Federal antidiscrimination laws (e.g., ADA). For example, for a first offense, it may be wise to counsel the student to take a leave of absence to obtain treatment rather than suspend or dismiss the student. Then, after successful completion of treatment, the student may reapply pursuant to the school's leave of absence policy, and, if criteria are met, be able to resume active status in the program.

The policy and procedures concerning any testing of the nursing student must also carefully analyze the confirming test that is used and be cognizant of the fact that there are many viable criticisms of the accuracy of such tests. In addition, strict procedures that ensure that, from the collection of the specimen to its ultimate acceptance by the testing site, a "chain of custody" exists is vital.[83] If there is any lapse in this chain, the student could successfully challenge that a particular specimen does not belong to him or her.

Until the legal issues surrounding drug testing are resolved with more clarity, it may be prudent for nursing programs to develop other ways of dealing with the impaired student in the clinical area. Including drug use that impairs a student's ability to safely provide patient care as one of the grounds upon which disciplinary action may be taken against a student would be important to include in the school's and program's catalog. Including information and research about chemical substance abuse in the school's curriculum would also be important in aiding students to increase their knowledge about chemical abuse. In addition, continuing education programs concerning drug use and treatment may also help the student identify the problem he or she is experiencing and therefore seek help voluntarily, thus eliminating further progression of the problem.

Open lines of communication between faculty and students may also be a valuable alternative for the student who needs treatment for chemical abuse. Faculty and administrators must be willing to confront students with evidence of impairment. In addition, suggesting ways the student can obtain the help he or she needs can be useful in aiding the student to complete educational and professional goals.

First Amendment Freedoms

First Amendment freedoms are important ones for any individual, and the student is no exception. The First Amendment guarantees freedom of peaceful assembly, speech, the establishment and exercise of religion, press, and petitioning the government for the remedy of grievances.[84] Early cases centering on student discharges violated these, and Fourteenth Amendment, rights when students were dismissed from post-secondary academic institutions for "conduct" that was not seen as conforming with a particular school's expectations of students. Unfortunately, allegations against academic institutions for breaching students' First Amendment protections still abound, and the judicial system continues to balance the academic entity's rights with those of the student body.

First Amendment freedoms are important ones for any individual, and the student is no exception.

The classic case setting forth students' free speech and assembly rights in an academic setting was *Tinker v. Des Moines Independent Community School District*.[85] Three public school students were suspended from school after protesting the government's involvement in the Vietnam war by wearing black armbands during school hours. The case was dismissed at the federal district court level, and affirmed by the appeals court *en banc*. Because both court decisions were based on the prinicple that it was within the school board's power to dismiss the students, even without any evidence of disruption of school activities by the students, the

United States Supreme Court reversed and remanded the case. In doing so, the Court held that the demonstration engaged in was peaceful and not disruptive and therefore was protected by the First and Fourteenth Amendments; that both students *and* teachers possess First Amendment rights, subject to the "special characteristics of the school environment"; and that the term *free speech* includes certain "symbolic acts" that express views.[86]

Tinker's holding was applied again by the United States Supreme Court in a case involving post-secondary students' First Amendment rights. In *Healy v. James*,[87] decided in 1972, a federal district court evaluated a situation that arose at Central Connecticut State College, where students' request for recognition of a local chapter of Students for a Democratic Society (SDS) was approved by the Student Affairs Committee. The College president denied the recognition on the basis that the organization's philosophy was contrary to the College's support of academic freedom and would be a disruptive force on campus. The denial had the effect of prohibiting the organization from utilizing school meeting rooms, bulletin boards, and newspapers.

The Supreme Court reversed and remanded the case back to the trial court for a determination by the court if the organization would abide by campus rules and regulations applicable to any organization on campus. If so, then the College would be required to approve the SDS pursuant to those rules and regulations. Citing *Tinker*, the Court held that although First Amendment freedoms in the school setting must be balanced with the right of school officials to constitutionally "prescribe and control" conduct there, college classrooms are the "marketplace of ideas," and academic freedom must continue to be protected from unconstitutional infringement.[88]

There is a plethora of First Amendment cases decided by the United States Supreme Court and respective federal courts since these two important cases.[89] Generally, they uphold the exercise of a student's First Amendment rights in the academic milieu. However, the student's exercise of those rights may be limited if materially and substantially disruptive to others and the operation of the school, if damage or injury to property or person occurs, if done for the purpose of producing lawless action, or if faculty or administrators are threatened.

Likewise, a student's freedom to exercise his or her religious beliefs has also generally been supported by the courts. This right, like those already discussed, may present itself in combination with the exercise of other First Amendment freedoms. For example, a nursing student, dressing a certain way because of religious beliefs, may not feel that he or she can wear the nursing student uniform in clinical settings because it is against the dress requirements of his or her religion. Or a religious group may request recognition from college or nursing program officials to establish a chapter of that organization on campus.

Nursing faculty and administrators, whether in public or private institutions, would be wise to carefully study the latest case law in this area before developing any formal or informal policies concerning the handling of First Amendment freedoms. Certainly, consultation with legal counsel for the academic institution would be vital, not only in exploring the issues, but also when a specific case or situation developed. In addition to developing a specific stance concerning First Amendment freedoms, school officials must ensure that any positions developed are applied in a just and equitable manner, that any restriction or limitation on First Amendment rights is factually based, and that if a restriction is to occur, the group is given the chance to comply with reasonable school requirements that may avoid the restriction or limitation. Last, but not least, faculty must keep up with the latest case law developments concerning First Amendment rights.

Equal Protection of the Law

Equal protection of the law as a constitutional requirement means that no one person or per-

sons shall be denied the protections of the law given other persons or individuals in like or similar circumstances.[90] Insofar as public post-secondary academic entities are concerned, it is important that faculty or administrative decisions not be unduly supportive of one student or a group of students to the exclusion or expense of another individual student or group.

Generally the cases alleging a denial of equal protection have been decided in favor of the college or university, mainly because the students involved in the cases were not in like or similar circumstances, or the alleged differences were permissible. However, some examples in which a violation of the equal protection clause was raised include not enforcing a cheating policy in the same manner against students, and placing restrictions on the use of the student activity fund by a particular school organization.[91]

ADDITIONAL STUDENT CONCERNS

Professional Negligence/ Negligence

Students in post-secondary academic institutions may have additional concerns that accompany them as they progress through their academic careers. One such concern for the student is that of liability for alleged *negligent care* that is given by the student during the educational program. Professional negligence occurs when there is an allegation that a standard of care was breached, causing injury to a patient. The overall conduct standard for the professional nurse would be what ordinary, prudent, and reasonable professional nurses would have done in the same or similar circumstances. When professional negligence is alleged against a student nurse, the standard of the graduate professional nurse in the same or similar situation applies.[92] Thus the student must ensure that he or she is well prepared for any patient care assignments being undertaken, must ask for supervision or additional instruction when unsure of the care to be provided, and must ask for a change in assignment if not able to carry the patient treatment out in a safe manner. Furthermore, the nursing student should carry professional liability insurance to ensure some financial protection against the costs of legal representation. A professional liability policy would also provide a financial base from which a judgment can be paid should a verdict be entered against the student nurse.

> *When professional negligence is alleged against a student nurse, the standard of the graduate professional nurse in the same or similar situation applies.*

Similarly, nursing students may be held responsible for their own non-nursing negligence, even when it takes place during school-related activities. For example, in *Central Security Mutual Insurance Company v. DePinto*,[93] a nursing student who was driving herself and other nursing students to a clinical placement in a college van was involved in an accident in which the driver of the other car was killed. At issue in the case was whether Ms. DePinto's father's automobile insurance excluded the van from being covered under the policy because the van was insured for "regular use." The court allowed the case to stand and held that the van was not being "used regularly," but was strictly limited to going and returning to the clinical placement via a specified route. It is important to note here that the school was not sued directly in this case, but was involved as an intervenor. Thus the case was allowed to go forward against the nursing student who was driving at the time of the accident.

Conformity with State Nurse Practice Act

Conformity with the state nurse practice act is another concern for the nursing student, both while progressing through the program and while awaiting licensure based upon successful passage of the state nursing boards. It is important for the student nurse to comply with all requirements concerning the provision of care while a student. For example, while a student, nurse practice acts require that patient care can only be given pursuant to a recognized nursing education program that meets faculty and clinical supervision requirements. The nursing student must also be aware of what restrictions are placed on his or her role when working as a nurse's aide or in other assistive roles. The student nurse must be careful not to perform responsibilities while in an assistive role that only a *licensed* nurse can perform pursuant to the nurse practice act. If that occurs, the student could be alleged to be practicing nursing without a license. Therefore, familiarity with the nursing practice act, and the rules and regulations to enforce it, is important, not only upon completion of the nursing program but during the time the student nurse is advancing toward graduation.

FACULTY RIGHTS AND CONCERNS

Although most of the chapter has thus far been devoted to student rights and concomitant faculty responsibilities, it is also important to highlight faculty rights and specific concerns that faculty may have when teaching. There are many rights that faculty possess when teaching in a post-secondary institution, including evaluation/grading rights and employment protections. Likewise, liability concerns exist in relation to suits initiated by students alleging negligent teaching, defamation, and invasion of privacy, to name a few. Some of those concerns and rights will be briefly presented.

Liability Concerns

The potential liability a faculty member and the academic institution face for an alleged violation of a student's due process rights or failure to progress through a particular program has been presented earlier in this chapter. In fact, a study of 24 cases filed against nursing education programs between 1961 and September of 1989 indicated that, among other findings, nursing students, particularly in baccalaureate programs, are more prone to sue schools of nursing and nursing faculty than other students in post-secondary institutions.[94] Of the 24 cases included in the study, 10 of the 11 filed by nursing students involved allegations concerning dismissals from, or denial of admissions to, nursing education programs.[95]

Educational Malpractice Suits

Admission and dismissal suits are not the only types of suits that faculty may be involved in. One additional allegation against faculty that may arise is that of educational malpractice. In this type of suit, the student alleges that graduation or successful passing of the state board did not occur because the nursing faculty member breached his or her duty to teach effectively. As a direct and proximate result of this failure to teach properly, the student was not able to graduate or successfully pass state boards. The student may seek an injunction and ask the court to require the nursing program to graduate him or her, or the student may seek compensation for the failure to graduate and/or pass state boards.

Educational malpractice suits against any faculty, including nurse faculty, have not been successful to date. As early as 1979, courts have not supported this cause of action against *public* school teachers, reasoning that (1) identifying why a student did not learn would be difficult to ascertain; (2) recognizing this type of cause of action would "open the floodgates" of litigation against teachers; and (3) allowing a suit for negligent teaching would also be a blatant interfer-

ence by the judicial system into the administration of public schools.[96] Subsequent decisions involving faculty in post-secondary institutions have reached similar conclusions.[97]

> *Educational malpractice suits against . . . faculty, including nurse faculty, have not been successful to date.*

Despite this protection, nurse faculty will want to continue to teach in a manner consistent with sound educational principles and in accordance with applicable standards. There is no question that nursing faculty have a basic duty to instruct students properly.[98] When, and if, a successful challenge alleging a breach of that duty will occur remains to be seen.

Being Named as a Defendant in a Suit

Nursing faculty may be named as a defendant in a suit filed by a student in one of two ways. Because the faculty member is an employee of the school or college, he or she may be sued as a named defendant, along with the school or college. So long as the student's allegations involve the faculty member's duties that are within the scope of his or her employment as a faculty member, then the faculty member can be named in the suit.

Nursing faculty may also be individually named in a suit by a student under the theory of personal liability. The student may sue the faculty member "individually" and as a faculty member if the student is unclear whether the conduct alleged against the faculty member was within the scope of the faculty's employment responsibilities, or if the conduct was "willful," or "intentional."[99]

Nursing faculty in public academic institutions may enjoy the benefit of sovereign or charitable immunity against tort actions given to the college or university where employed, depending on the particular state statute that affords the protection. If the immunity is absolute, the faculty member could not be sued successfully by a student when allegations concerning his or her employment duties were the basis of the suit. However, not all immunity protections are absolute, if they exist at all. Moreover, if the faculty member is sued individually, there may be no immunity protection. The faculty member will need to be knowledgeable about what protections, if any, are afforded to the institution and its faculty.

Grading and Evaluation of Students

Because of the emphasis on student rights in relation to evaluation and grading, faculty often think they do not possess any rights when making decisions about student competency in the clinical and academic area. However, nothing could be further from the truth. The *Horowitz* case presented earlier in this chapter provides support for faculty rights when professional judgments are made concerning the caliber of a student's abilities.

In its unanimous opinion, the United States Supreme Court relied on a long-standing precedent of lower court rulings holding that academic decisions (e.g., what is a passing grade, evaluations of students) are within the realm of the academic community alone.[100] Additionally, the Court stated courts were not equipped with the expertise that is needed for such determinations.[101] Since the Supreme Court has not overruled its own opinion concerning this issue, the decision, and the principles it supports, can still be relied on.

Even so, faculty cannot make academic decisions arbitrarily, capriciously, or in a discriminatory manner. Rather, faculty judgments must be deliberate and careful, as the Court found existed in the *Horowitz* and *Clements* cases. In this regard, anecdotal notes specific to difficulties encountered by the student in both the class-

room and clinical area are essential. Moreover, the faculty must inform the nursing student of the difficulties he or she is having in the program as well as the consequences if improvement does not occur (e.g., probation or dismissal). This will require the faculty to meet with the nursing student experiencing academic problems as required in the school of nursing policy.[102] If faculty also use *Horowitz* and *Clements* as a guide, it appears that the more notice given the student, the better the chance of compliance by faculty with any due process obligations that might exist for the student.

Any written materials given to nursing students during the time they are enrolled in the nursing school or program that govern their responsibilities, grading, and progression through the program should be carefully developed. School of nursing catalogs, syllabi, and descriptions of special projects need to include precise information informing the student of his or her responsibilities and how grading will occur. Objectives for each course and clinical rotation should be behaviorally defined.

Evaluation tools used by faculty must also be carefully developed. Because any evaluation is somewhat subjective, the tool should be as objective as possible and used in a consistent manner by the school of nursing faculty.[103]

Nursing faculty in private and public academic institutions clearly *do not* need to provide a hearing for a student prior to dismissing the student from the program or school for academic reasons. However, if the faculty member is in doubt about the character of dismissal that is going to occur, it is best to provide the student with whatever protections are afforded students who are being dismissed for disciplinary reasons. A court will not fault a faculty member or institution for providing *more* protections to a student than was necessary, but a court may impose liability if required faculty and institution responsibilities were not met.

Employment

Nursing faculty teach at both private and public academic institutions. The faculty member may have a contract of employment for a definite period of time (e.g., 1 year) in either type of institution, or the faculty member may be tenured; that is, possess a property right of continued employment unless discharged "for cause."[104] A tenured position, although not a guarantee of lifetime employment,[105] is more secure for a number of reasons. First, it provides procedural protections for the faculty member when there is an allegation that "adequate cause" exists to terminate the faculty member's employment (e.g., incompetency, neglect of duties). Second, it limits the ability of the institution to terminate the faculty to for-cause situations, thus protecting the faculty member's academic freedom.[106] Even so, it affords no protection to the faculty member if the dismissal or termination is due to "noncausal" reasons such as the discontinuance of a program or financial exigency.

The faculty member may have a contract of employment for a definite period ... or the faculty member may be tenured ...

Although not as protective as tenure, a faculty member who has a contract of employment with the institution also enjoys the protection of "for-cause" only dismissals that might take place prior to the completion of the term of the contract. Moreover, if the nursing faculty member teaches at a public university or community college and is dismissed in violation of the contract of employment, he or she can sue alleging an entitlement in continued employment pursuant to the contract and a violation of due process rights.[107] If, however, a faculty's contract of employment was not renewed at the end of its term (e.g., 1 year), absent a discriminatory motive or an intent to violate the faculty member's constitutional rights, the institution could do so without liability.[108]

There have been a large number of cases involving faculty terminations in academic institutions. The cases involving terminations "for cause" include insubordination (*Hillis v. Stephen F. Austin University*[109]), sexual harassment (*Lehman v. Board of Trustees of Whitman College*[110]), and neglecting one's duties (*White v. Board of Trustees of Western Wyoming Community College*[111]).

Faculty challenges to for-cause dismissals by public institutions include some of the same grounds public students have used to challenge decisions by faculty. They include violations of the faculty member's liberty rights under the Fourteenth Amendment's Due Process clause (*Board of Regents v. Roth*[112]) and free speech under the First Amendment (*Connick v. Meyers*[113]).

Faculty challenges to for-cause dismissals by public institutions include some of the same grounds public students have used to challenge decisions by faculty.

Faculty members in private institutions have also mounted legal challenges to for-cause terminations that include breach of contract and discrimination. Both of these challenges have been used by faculty in public institutions as well.[114]

Faculty of nursing programs can avoid involvement in lawsuits surrounding employment termination by providing quality instruction to students. Adherence to the employment contract or requirements of tenured faculty is vital. Documented research and publication, as well as service on college or school committees can help the nursing faculty member retain his or her current faculty status or, if desired, obtain a promotion or tenure.

If the faculty member believes that a termination has occurred unfairly, or in violation of the employment contract or tenure, legal advice should be obtained as quickly as possible. At a minimum, the decision should be challenged through the established institutional procedures for dealing with decisions adverse to faculty. It may be, however, that legal action may be necessary to obtain a fair resolution of the issue. However, reminiscent of the decision in the *Horowitz* case, courts generally defer to the decisions of institutions when terminations of tenured faculty occur. As one court opined:

> The management of the university is primarily the responsibility of those equipped with the special skills and sensitivities necessary for so delicate a task. One of the most sensitive functions of the university administration is the appointment, promotion and retention of faculty. It is for this reason that the courts, and administrative agencies as well, should only rarely assume academic oversight, except with the greatest caution and restraint, in such areas as faculty appointment, promotion and tenure, especially in institutions of higher learning.[115]

SUMMARY OF PRINCIPLES AND APPLICATIONS

The world of academia is not an ivory tower insofar as legal issues go. Nursing students will continue to challenge faculty and institutional decisions. The findings of the study of suits filed against nursing education programs discussed earlier in this chapter indicated that of the 11 cases filed by students, 6 were decided in favor of the student.[116] Likewise, faculty will continue to challenge institutional decisions concerning their continued employment. As a result, student nurses and nursing faculty must remember that:

▼ Students do not leave their constitutional rights at the door of an academic institution.

▼ Students in public post-secondary institutions have constitutional protections afforded them that are not available to students in private academic institutions. They include due process rights for disciplinary actions; freedom from undue restraints on First Amendment rights; and equal application of constitutional rights to all students similarly situated.

▼ Students in private post-secondary institutions cannot be treated in an arbitrary, capricious or discriminatory manner by school officials. Rather, notions of fair play, notice, and equality should be guidelines under which faculty operate vis-à-vis the student body.

▼ Students in public or private institutions are not required to be given a hearing *prior* to dismissal from the school or program for academic reasons.

▼ Students in private post-secondary institutions can utilize the contract theory when they allege that a violation of some written document—a school catalog—or implied contract provision has adversely affected them.

▼ Any post-secondary institution receiving federal funds must conform to federal laws protecting handicap, age, religion, or sex.

▼ Generally faculty in schools of nursing have the ability and responsibility to evaluate students both academically and clinically. Those decisions will not be overturned by the courts unless they are found to be impulsive and without basis. Faculty are considered to be the "experts" in evaluating academic performance.

▼ The Buckley Amendment protects the release of student records and information in both public and private post-secondary schools.

▼ Drug testing of students in public and private post-secondary schools must be carefully evaluated.

▼ Should nursing negligence be alleged against a student, the standard applied to the student will be what the ordinary, reasonable, and prudent graduate *professional* nurse would have done in the same or similar circumstances.

▼ Student nurses must be familiar with their state nursing practice act throughout their career as nursing students as well as when they become a licensed practitioner.

▼ No suit against a faculty member for educational malpractice has been successful.

▼ Nursing faculty may, in some instances, be sued as employees of an academic institution and individually as well.

▼ An employment contract or tenure provides the nurse faculty member with more employment protection.

▼ Nonrenewal of a teaching contract may be challenged if the reason for nonrenewal is discriminatory or intentionally violates a constitutionally protected right.

TOPICS FOR FURTHER INQUIRY

1. Replicate the study of cases filed against school of nursing educational programs beginning with October 1989 until the present. Compare the findings with those of the first study. Identify differences, if any, and provide explanations as to why they exist. Suggest additional areas of research for future studies in this area.

2. Evaluate a school of nursing's clinical evaluation tool for a particular clinical rotation. Analyze the tool in terms of clarity, behaviorally defined objectives, and consistency of use among faculty. Suggest areas of improvement.

3. Analyze a public nursing education program's catalog concerning due process rights of students concerning grading. Suggest where improvements might occur.

4. Draft a contract of employment for a nurse faculty member in either a public or private nursing education program. Include provisions for termination of the contract, renewal of the contract, and faculty responsibilities.

REFERENCES

1. Henry Campbell Black. *Black's Law Dictionary*. 6th Edition. St. Paul, Minn: West Publishing Company, 1991, 542.

2. "Legal Relationships," *A Practical Guide to Legal Issues Affecting College Teachers*, Patricia Hollander, D. Parker Young, and Donald Gehring. Asheville, NC: College Administration Publications, Inc., 1995, 3 (The Higher Education Administration Series).

3. Ralph Chandler, Richard Enslen and Peter Renstrom. *Constitutional Law Handbook*. 2nd Edition. Rochester, NY: Lawyers Cooperative Publishing, 1993, 646 (with April 1995 Cumulative Supplement).

4. *Id*. at 697.

5. 294 F. 2d 150 (5th Circuit 1961), *cert. denied*, 386 U.S. 930 (1961).

6. D. Parker Young and Donald Gehring. *The College Students and the Courts: Cases and Commentary*. Asheville, NC: College Administration Publications, Inc., 1986, 13-6.

7. *Dixon v. Alabama State Board of Education, supra* note 5, at 158-159.

8. *Id*.

9. 95 S. Ct. 729 (1975).

10. Young and Gehring, *supra* note 6, at 13-8.

11. *Id*. at 13-8 and 13-9.

12. *Id*.

13. *Goss v. Lopez, supra* note 9, at 732.

14. 435 U.S. 78, 98 S. Ct. 948 (1978).

15. Abigail Petersen, "*Board of Curators v. Horowitz*," 6(4) *Hofstra Law Review* (Summer 1978), 1115.

16. *Id*. at 1116-1117.

17. *Id., citing Horowitz v. Board of Curators*, 74CV47-W-3 (W.D. Mo. November 14, 1975).

18. 538 F. 2d 1317 (8th Cir. 1978).

19. Petersen, *supra note* 15, at 1120.

20. 435 U.S. at 85-90.

21. 435 U.S. at 92.

22. *Dixon v. Alabama State Board of Education, supra* note 7, at 157.

23. Chandler, Enslen and Renstrom, *supra* note 3, at 1-1.

24. 42 U.S.C. Section 12101 *et seq*. (1992).

25. Michael Dowell, "The Americans with Disabilities Act: The Responsibilities of Health Care Providers, Insurers and Managed Care Organizations," 25(10) *Journal of Health and Hospital Law* (October 1992), 289.

26. Henry Perritt. *Americans with Disabilities Handbook*. 2nd Edition. NY: John Wiley & Sons, Inc., 1991, 163-188 (with 1996 Cumulative Supplement No. 1).

27. 42 U.S.C. 6101 *et seq*. (1975).

28. 835 F. 2d 1000 (2nd Cir. 1987).

29. *Id*. at 1001-1003.

30. *Id*.

31. *Id*. at 1005.

32. "Academic Affairs," *A Practical Guide to Legal Issues Affecting College Teachers, supra* note 2, at 9-11.

33. 565 F. 2d 2000 (1st Cir. 1977).

34. Young and Gehring, *supra* note 6, at 1-4-1-5.

35. *Id*. The Federal trial court decision is located at 422 F. Supp. 1354 (1976).

36. 449 N.Y.S. 2d 26 (1982).

37. 704 F. 2d 713 (1983).

38. *Id*. at 715.

39. *Id*.

40. *Id*. at 716.

41. 514 F. 2d 622 (10th Circ. 1975).

42. See also, *Clayton v. Trustees of Princeton University*, 608 F. Supp. 413 (1985) (student suspension for cheating during a lab practicum exam); *Boehm v. University of Pennsylvania School of Veterinary Medicine*, 553 A. 2d 575 (1990) (veterinary students accused by School of cheating; School decision upheld); *Abrahamiam v. City University*, 565 N.Y.S. 2d 571 (1991) (student suspended for cheating on physics exam; decision upheld).

43. An excellent resource for decisions involving students with emotional problems is *The Dismissal of Students with Mental Disorders: Legal Issues, Policy Considerations and Alternative Responses* by Gary Pevala. Asheville, NC: College Administration Publications, Inc., 1985 (The Higher Education Administration Series). See also, Henry Perritt, *Americans with Disabilities Handbook, supra* note 26; *Aronson v. North Park College*, 418 N.E. 2d 776 (1st District 1981) (student dismissed and denied readmission because of refusal to attend counseling required after testing indicated emotional problems; decision of College upheld).

44. "Academic Affairs," Hollander, Young and Gehring, *supra* note 2, at 10.

45. 359 N.Y.S. 2d 120 (1974).

46. *Id.* at 121.

47. 606 A. 2d 1239 (1992).

48. Chandler, Enslen, and Renstrom, *supra* note 3, at 1010.

49. 764 S.W. 2d 827 (1989).

50. *Id.* at 833.

51. 474 U.S. 214 (1985).

52. *Id.* at 837.

53. *Id.* at 838.

54. Pub. Law 93-380, 20 U.S.C. 1232g *et seq.* (1974).

55. U.S.C. 1232g (a) (1) (A).

56. *Id.* at 1232gC (4) (A).

57. *Id.* at 1232g (6) (b) (1) (A) through (I).

58. *Id.* at 1232g (5) (A) and (B).

59. *Id.* at 1232g (4) (A) and (B) and (5) (A) and (B).

60. The Fourth Amendment," Chandler, Enslen, and Renstrom, *Constitutional Law Handbook, supra* note 3, at 221–297.

61. Gary Pavela, "Constitutional Issues in the Residence Halls," *Administering College and University Housing.* Gary Pavela, Editor. Asheville, NC: College Administration Publications, Inc., 1992, 25-30 (Revised Edition). (The Higher Education Administration Series).

62. *Id.*; See also, entire text of *Administering College and University Housing.*

63. *Id.* at 25-30; See also, Stephen T. Miller, "Contracts and Their Use in Housing," in *Administering College and University Housing, supra* note 61, at 61-76.

64. *Id.*

65. Pavela, *supra* note 61, at 28.

66. See, for example, *People v. Lanthier*, 97 Cal. Rptr. at 297 (1971).

67. Pavela, *supra* note 61, at 26-28.

68. 469 U.S. 325 (1985).

69. *Id.* at 337-343.

70. *Id.*

71. Kevin Zeese, "Urine Testing of School Students," *Drug Testing Legal Manual.* Deerfield, Ill: Clark Boardman Callaghan, 1995, 7-1-7-18 (with regular updates).

72. 515 U.S., 132 L. Ed. 2d 564 (1995).

73. *Id.* at 573.

74. *Id.* at 574-575.

75. *Id.* at 577-579.

76. *Id.* at 582.

77. *New Jersey v. T.L.O., supra* note 68.

78. 20 U.S.C. 3171 (1986); 20 U.S.C. Section 1145g *et seq.* (1989).

79. *Id.* at 1145g(a).

80. *Id.* at 1145g (a) (1) (A), (2) (A) and (B). See also, Carolyn Palmer and Donald Gehring, Editors. *A Handbook for Complying with the Program and Review Requirements of the 1989 Amendments to the Drug-Free Schools and Communities Act.* Asheville, NC: College Administration Publications, Inc., 1992.

81. See, for example, Marilyn Asteriadis, Virginia Davis, Joyce Masoodi, and Marcia Miller, "Chemical Impairment of Nursing Students: A Comprehensive Policy and Procedure," (20)2 *Nurse Educator* (March/April 1995), 19–22. See also, generally, D. Polk, K. Glendon, and C. DeVore, "The Chemically Dependent Student Nurse: Guidelines for Policy Development," 41 *Nursing Outlook*, (1993), 166–170; E. Greenhill and K. Skinner, "Impaired Nursing Students: An Intervention Program," 30(8) *Journal of Nursing Education* (1991), 379–381.

82. *Id.*

83. See Kevin Zeese, *Drug Testing Legal Manual, supra* note 71.

84. Chandler, Enslen, and Renstrom, "First Amendment," *Constitutional Law Handbook, supra* note 3, at 75-219.

85. 393 U.S. 503 (1969).

86. *Id.* at 506-514.

87. 92 S.Ct. 2338 (1972).

88. *Id.* at 2340.

89. See, generally, Young and Gehring, *The College Students and the Courts: Cases and Commentary, supra* note 6.

90. Chandler, Enslen, and Renstrom, "Equal Protection and Privacy," *Constitutional Law Handbook, supra* note 3.

91. *Patterson v. Hunt*, 682 S.W. 2d 508 (1984); *Rosenberger v. Rector and Visitors of University of Virginia*, 795 F. Supp. 175 (1992).

92. University Hospital Consortium. *Nursing-Legal Survival: A Risk Management Guide for Nurses.* Oak Brook, Ill: University Hospital Consortium, 1992, 1118.

93. 681 P. 2d 15 (Kan. 1984).

94. Lelia Helms and Kay Weiler, "Suing Programs of Nursing Education," 39(4) *Nursing Outlook*, 158-161.

95. *Id.*

96. *Donahue v. Copiague Union Free School District*, 418 N.Y.S. 2d 375 (1979).

97. See, *Tolman v. Cencor Career Colleges, Inc.*, 851 P. 2d 203 (1993).

98. "Legal Liability," *A Practical Guide to Legal Issues Affecting College Teachers, supra* note 2, at 27.

99. *Id.*

100. Abigail Peterson, "Board of Curators v. Horowitz," *supra* note 15, at 1123, *citing Gasper v. Burton*, 513 F. 2d 843 (10th Cir. 1975); *Mustell v. Rose*, 211 SO. 2d 489, 498, *cert. denied*, 393 U.S. (1968); *Barnard v. Inhabitants of Shelburne*, 102 N.E. 1095 (1913).

101. *Id.*
102. Thomas Parrott, "Dismissal for Clinical Deficiencies," 18(6) *Nurse Educator* (November/December 1993), 14–17.
103. See generally, Delores Bower, Linda Linc, and Doreen Denega, "Part I—Evaluation in the Academic Setting," *Evaluation Instruments in Nursing.* NY: National League for Nursing, 1988, 3–82 (Pub. No. 15-2178).
104. Joseph Beckman. *Faculty/Staff Nonrenewal and Dismissal for Cause in Institutions of Higher Education.* Asheville, NC: College Administration Publications, Inc., 1986, 4. See also William Kaplin and Barbara Lee, "The College and the Faculty," *The Law of Higher Education: A Comprehensive Guide to Legal Implications of Administrative Decision Making.* 3rd Edition. San Francisco: Jossey-Bass Publishers, 1995, 150–370.

105. "Employment," *A Practical Guide to Legal Issues Affecting College Teachers, supra* note 2, at 23.
106. *Id.*
107. *Id.* at 5.
108. *Id.* at 8, *citing Hetrick v. Martin,* 480 F. 2d 705 (6th Circ. 1973); *Stebbins v. Weaver,* 537 F. 2d 939 (7th Cir. 1976).
109. 665 F. 2d 547 (1982).
110. 576 P. 2d 397 (1978).
111. 648 P. 2d (1982).
112. 408 U.S. 564 (1972).
113. 103 S. Ct. 1684 (1983).
114. See Beckman, *Faculty/Staff Nonrenewal and Dismissal for Cause in Institutions of Higher Education, supra* note 104.
115. *New York Institute of Technology v. State Division of Human Rights,* 386 N.Y.S. 2d 685, 688 (1976).
116. Lelia Helms and Kay Weiler, *supra* note 94.

21

The Nurse in Advanced Practice

Paula Henry, J.D., N.P.-C., B.S.N., R.N.

contents

The nursing profession has evolved to include several specialty practice areas in which the registered nurse has become a primary health care provider in the expanded role of advanced practice nurse (APN). An APN is a registered nurse who has successfully completed an additional course of study in a nursing specialty that provides specialized knowledge and skills to function in an expanded role. 1994 figures indicate that in the United States there are approximately 96,000 registered nurses who are qualified to function in the expanded role.[1] The majority of APNs fall into four categories: nurse anesthetist, nurse-midwife, nurse practitioner, and clinical nurse specialist. A 1990 Gallup poll conducted to determine the public's attitude toward health care and nursing showed that 86% of the public were receptive to having an APN as their primary care provider.[2]

Inherent in role expansion is the development of legal responsibilities that are unique to the advanced practice nurse. Understanding the important legal issues is necessary to fully comprehend the legal ramifications of an expanded role. The legal issues regarding role definition, scope of practice, standard of care, and overlapping functions will be discussed to provide a general framework for reference regarding advanced practice. Statutory authority and judicial recognition have addressed the definition of advanced practice and the nurse's ability to function fully in the expanded role.

DEFINITIONS OF ADVANCED NURSE PRACTITIONERS

Of the four main categories of advanced practice that are recognized within the nursing profession, the common denominator in each category is the fact that the individual is a registered nurse. The hallmark of the expanded role is the advanced educational training in an area of specialization with the concurrent increase in

---

KEY PRINCIPLES

Autonomy
Borrowed Servant Rule
Collaborative Practice
Independent Practice
Malpractice
Negligence per se
Overlapping Functions
Protocols
Respondeat Superior
Scope of Practice
Standard of Care
Vicarious Liability

---

responsibility, both professionally and legally. Role definition begins at the professional level with a review of the specific professional organization's policy statements and the nursing literature. Regardless of the category of advanced practice, the APN's focus is on the provision of quality nursing care in the promotion of health and the prevention of illness. The APN's goal is to be able to legally practice to the fullest extent of the APN's education, skill, and training. To obtain autonomy, the APN must achieve professional independence in decision-making and in defining the scope of practice.

Nurse Anesthetist

According to the American Association of Nurse Anesthetists, a nurse anesthetist is a regis-

---

RELATED TOPICS

Chapter 3	Concepts of Negligence and Liability
Chapter 4	Professional Negligence/ Malpractice: Prevention and Defense
Chapter 15	Licensure and Nursing Practice

tered nurse who has successfully completed an approved nurse anesthetist program from an accredited program.[3] In addition, to become certified, the nurse anesthetist must pass a national qualifying examination and then fulfill continuing education requirements every 2 years for recertification. In comparison, the American Society of Anesthesiologists in their 1982 statement defined the nurse anesthetist as a registered nurse who has satisfactorily completed an approved nurse anesthesia program.[4] Certified registered nurse anesthetists (CRNAs) provide anesthesia for dental, surgical, and obstetric procedures ranging from local to regional anesthesia.[5]

> *The APN's goal is to be able to legally practice to the fullest extent of the APN's education, skill and training.*

The American Association of Nurse Anesthetist in an amicus brief to the court in 1984 stated that nurses have been administering anesthesia for more than 100 years.[6] A recent survey shows that 65% of all anesthesia administered in the United States is administered by a certified nurse anesthetist; of that 65%, the nurse anesthetist is the sole provider of anesthesia in most rural hospitals.[7] Nurse anesthetists have the longest history of involvement with the legal profession, especially in the scope of practice arena.

Certified Nurse-Midwife

A certified nurse-midwife is a registered nurse with additional education in the independent management of the aspect of women's health care that pertains to pregnancy, childbirth, post partum, care of the newborn, and gynecology, including family planning.[8] This definition is consistent with the American College of Nurse-Midwives 1992 policy statement on nurse-mid-

wifery practice.[9] Certified nurse-midwives provide maternal-fetal services in the traditional settings of clinics and hospitals, as well as in the nontraditional settings of birth centers and clients' homes.

Nurse Practitioner

In the early 1970s, the American Nurses' Association identified the role of nurse practitioner. A nurse practitioner (NP) is a registered nurse, who with advanced educational preparation, is able to assess the physical and psychosocial needs of a patient through history taking, physical examination, ordering and interpreting diagnostic laboratory and radiographic studies, and implementing a therapeutic plan through the prescribing of appropriate medication and treatments, patient education, and applicable referrals.[10]

The NP's functions include, but are not limited to, annual health screening; the diagnosis and management of common acute health problems; and the monitoring of chronic long-term health disorders. The NP's practice encompasses the area of pediatrics, geriatrics, emergency medicine, family practice, obstetrics-gynecology, neonatology, adult medicine, and psychiatry, to name a few areas. Studies have shown that NPs provide safe, cost-efficient, and quality primary care.[11] A 1993 analysis of multiple studies done in the previous 10 years concluded that NPs provide care equivalent to or better than that of physicians.[12]

> *A 1993 analysis of multiple studies done in the previous 10 years concluded that NPs provide care equivalent to or better than that of physicians.*

Clinical Nurse Specialist

A lesser known APN is the clinical nurse specialist (CNS). The American Nurses' Association defines the clinical nurse specialist as a registered nurse who through graduate studies and supervised practice has become an expert in a defined area of knowledge and practice in a specific area of clinical nursing.[13] The CNS generally has a Master's degree or a Doctorate. He or she functions in the role of nurse practitioner providing direct primary care; as an educator of clients or other health care providers; as a researcher developing standards of practice; or as a consultant establishing competency levels through nursing case studies. The CNS also develops nursing care techniques and quality control measures in the clinical setting.[14] Of the four categories of advanced practice nurses, the CNS has had the least involvement with the legal system, perhaps because it is the least recognized as an advanced practice in nursing.

SCOPE OF PRACTICE OF ADVANCED NURSE PRACTITIONERS

Scope of practice refers to the legal parameters in which the nurse is authorized to practice.[15] Each state, through its constitutional police powers, has the authority to enact licensing laws that govern health care professionals. Physicians established their exclusive right to practice medicine, which included the right to diagnose, treat, and prescribe medication, and made it illegal for any other professional to carry out these functions. In the past 10 years, however, courts have recognized the overlapping functions of APNs and physicians. Therefore, there is legal recognition that APNs have the ability to competently perform and provide health care services that at one time were considered the domain of the medical profession.

APNs are held legally accountable for their own actions and are responsible for exercising independent and rational judgments based upon competent assessments of their patients when rendering nursing care.[16] Statutory law has established that the APN has the legal authority to practice under the individual nurse's license

and that authority does not flow from a physician's or any other health care provider's license. There are several sources of law to determine the APN's scope of practice and the legal authorization to practice. These are each state's nurse practice act; specific statutory rules and regulations; professional standards; and case law.[17] Attorney General opinions, although not binding upon the court, are utilized to interpret scope-of-practice issues. It is imperative that the APN have knowledge of the laws that affect his or her individual practice and that address the legal parameters in which the APN may provide health care services.

APNs are held legally accountable for their own actions . . .

Unfortunately there is no uniformity among the sources of law governing the APN. As of 1994, only 22 states have a nurse practice act that authorizes the advanced practice of nursing within that statutory framework.[18] Licensure regulations are the legal mechanism authorizing the practice of nursing, and they vary from state to state. Forty-two states have enacted rules and regulations that govern the scope of practice of the APNs, and only seven states recognize a clinical nurse specialist as an APN.[19] Many states rely on the national standards developed by each specialty when defining the scope of practice.

State regulations are another source of law defining the scope of practice. Most nurse practice acts establish a board of nursing to regulate APNs although some states establish separate boards, e.g., nurse-midwifery board or the board of medicine, that may regulate the APN.[20] There are also separate regulations establishing prescriptive authority or reimbursement for services, which will impact the advanced practice of nursing and may place extensive restrictions on the scope of practice.[21] California has separate statutes that regulate the scope of practice of nurse-midwives and nurse anesthetists. Arizona and Arkansas also have separate statutes regulating nurse anesthetists.[22] As of 1994, only two states, Alaska and New Mexico, authorize NPs to have a true independent scope of practice, defined as full independence without requiring physician supervision or collaboration.[23]

Independent practice is not defined by the fact that the APN functions "alone" or in collaboration with another or if the APN is reimbursed for the nursing services rendered. Independent practice is defined by the legal relationship of the APN within the health care arena. The Joint Commission of Accreditation of Health Care Organization's definition of a licensed independent practitioner as "an individual who is permitted by law and a health care institution to provide patient care services without direction or supervision within the scope of his/her license . . ." is applicable to APNs.[24] APNs have the educational preparation and clinical skills to function independently, because APNs are autonomous, responsible for their own judgment and actions, comply with national standards of practice, and function within their scope of practice.

APNs have the educational preparation and clinical skills to function independently. . . .

Case law is an additional source of law that can define the APN's scope of practice. In recent years, courts were required to define the scope of practice of nurses in expanded roles and had to determine if the nurse was practicing medicine without a license. In fact, as early as the 1930s, a court was asked to address the legal issue of nurses administering general anesthesia.[25, 26] In 1983, the Missouri Supreme Court in *Sermchief v. Gonzales,*[27] discussed later in this chapter, interpreted the Missouri Nurse Practice

Act to determine the NPs' scope of practice. The court held that their actions did not constitute the unlawful practice of medicine.[28] The current approach of the courts is to recognize that nurses and physicians perform overlapping functions and procedures that were once the exclusive domain of medicine.

STANDARD OF CARE OF ADVANCED NURSE PRACTITIONERS

Standard of care is the legal principle that underscores the premise that APNs must know the limits of their education, training, skills, and experience. The court in *Sermchief* stated that the hallmark of a professional is knowing the limits of one's professional knowledge.[29] The APN has the duty to render nursing services pursuant to the professional nursing standard of care. The APN's conduct is measured against that of a reasonably prudent professional nurse of similar knowledge and skill in similar or like circumstances.[30]

. . . the hallmark of a professional is knowing the limits of one's professional knowledge.

The APN's conduct is measured against that of a reasonably prudent professional nurse of similar knowledge and skill in similar or like circumstances.

Case law has addressed the issue of standard of care as it pertains to APNs and has determined, in some cases, that the APN should not be held to the standard of care of a physician.[31]

In *Whitney v. Day*,[32] the court of appeals held that a nurse anesthetist's standard of care is based upon the skill and care that a nurse anesthetist with the same education and training would possess, not an anesthesiologist's standard of care. The NA's standard of care is established by the testimony of a nurse anesthetist expert.[33] Similarly, the standard of care of a NP was a major legal issue in *Fein v. Permanente Medical Group*.[34] The APN is cautioned, however, that the preceding cases are fact specific and the rulings may not be followed in future cases.

Other sources that a court may consult to determine the standard of care of an APN are professional organization's policy statements, detailing the levels of performance in a given specialty. An example would be the publication of the American College of Nurse-Midwives entitled "Standards for the Practice of Nurse-Midwifery."[35] Written protocols or standardized procedures are guidelines that outline and authorize particular advanced practice functions and are generally developed in collaboration with a physician. The APN's written protocols are used to determine if the NP has met the standard of care.[36] Hospital policy and procedures[37] and collaborative practice agreements[38] can also be reviewed by the court to assist in identifying the standard of care of APNs.

To establish that there was a breach of the standard of care by the APN, expert testimony must be presented. In the *Fein* case, for example, a physician who was head of a cardiology department provided expert testimony on behalf of the defendant NP regarding the NP's standard of care.[39] A primary care physician, with experience in working with and supervising NPs, was the plaintiff's expert witness regarding the standard of care of the NP in the *Gugino v. Harvard Community Health Plan* case.[40] It is crucial for the future development of the role of APN that the standard of care be established by the testimony of a qualified APN expert, and APNs should strive to ensure that the legal community retains the appropriate expert on their behalf.

BARRIERS TO ADVANCED PRACTICE

In 1992, an economic study showed that an estimated $6.4 to $8.75 billion dollars could be saved annually if APNs were utilized to the full extent of their practice.[41] Practice barriers involving legal limitations of the scope of practice, prescriptive authority, and third-party reimbursement must be removed to permit consumers access to cost-effective and quality health care services. Organized medicine and restrictive legislation have created large obstacles preventing the APN from fully participating as a direct primary care provider in the health care arena. These practice barriers deny consumers their lawful right to choose their provider.

The legal authority to prescribe medications is the central barrier to the APN's legal and professional recognition as a primary care provider. The primary policy question is why there is failure to legally acknowledge the APN's ability and expertise to prescribe medications when APNs have been safely prescribing for the past 30 years.[42] APNs have, however, had to function among legal ambiguity and uncertainty to provide prescriptive services to their patients. The failure to have full legal prescriptive authority has caused delays in treatment and interruption in the continuity of care. Without clear legal authority, APNs have had to devise different mechanisms to implement their prescriptive treatment plan for their patients, which include (1) seeking out a physician to physically write the prescription; (2) utilizing presigned prescriptions; (3) phoning the prescription to the pharmacy under the physician's name; and (4) establishing written protocols delineating the drugs that can be furnished by the APN from a "laundry" list contained in a formulary.[43] These prescriptive practices severely limit APNs' ability to practice to the full extent of their legally recognized expanded role.

Although 42 states have enacted statutes pertaining to prescriptive authority for APNs as of 1994, all but three states, Washington, Alaska, and Oregon, contain very limited authority.[44] A positive step, however, was taken when the Drug Enforcement Agency (DEA) proposed regulations to allow APNs to apply for a DEA registration number to prescribe controlled substances, Schedule II through V, in federally run facilities.[45] Each state nonetheless has the authority to determine which provider can legally obtain a DEA number and prescribe a controlled substance in that state. Despite the fact that APNs have proven their ability to safely prescribe medications, they continue to be barred from full legal recognition by short-sighted legislation backed by organized medicine and insurance companies fearful of losing economic control over the health care marketplace.

Consumers are being denied access to the primary care services of the APN when the insurance industry refuses to directly reimburse the APN for services rendered or when regulations are established to limit any reimbursement to the APN. These regulations include a disproportionate reimbursement amount paid to the APN that is only a percentage of the reimbursement payment to the physician; limiting reimbursement based on geographic location or type of practice setting; or making reimbursement contingent on physician supervision.[46] Federal and state statutes must be amended to remove the statutory barriers to the APN's practice. Providing direct reimbursement to the APN for services rendered will directly increase consumers' access to the health care provider of their choice. Health care reform will not be achieved until the legal barriers to APN practice are removed. Reform can be achieved only through federal and state legislative changes that will promote access to cost-efficient and quality health care.

LEGAL ISSUES IN ADVANCED PRACTICE

A comprehensive review of the reported cases reveals that there are relatively few cases that have been filed against APNs, despite an increase of the expanded roles. Although some of the cases presented are examples including more of one category of advanced practice than the others, this basically reflects the fact that certain APNs have a longer history of practice. As a result, that group has had earlier involvement with the legal system regarding role definition and scope-of-practice issues. The cases selected for analysis were chosen on the basis of the important legal principles that the case presented within a certain time frame.

. . . there are relatively few cases that have been filed against APNs, despite an increase of the expanded roles.

Nurse Anesthetist

Negligence and Negligence Per Se

The majority of reported cases filed against APNs involve an allegation of negligence; that is, that the APN breached the standard of care. Malpractice actions are filed when the professional's failure to meet the standard of care directly causes harm to the patient. Of the four categories of APNs, the nurse anesthetist has the longest history of practice and also has the greatest number of reported cases. The practice issues relating to the nurse anesthetist's negligence generally concern the selection, administration, and management of anesthesia and to related procedures.

A 1985 Washington Appellate case, *Brown v. Dahl,*[47] addressed the plaintiffs' allegations against the nurse anesthetist for negligently administering the anesthetic; for failing to attempt corrective measures; and for the failure to seek help in a timely manner. The plaintiffs also sued Dr. Dahl, the anesthesiologist, for lack of informed consent during the preanesthesia evaluation and negligence for allowing the nurse anesthetist to administer the anesthetic when he represented that he would personally administer it. The morning of surgery, the nurse anesthetist informed Mr. Brown that she would be administering the anesthesia during his procedure. The nurse anesthetist testified at trial that Mr. Brown did not voice any complaints regarding the fact that the nurse anesthetist would be administering the anesthesia instead of Dr. Dahl.

During the initial induction, Mr. Brown developed a partially obstructed airway and difficulties in breathing. The nurse anesthetist attempted to counteract the reaction, and when that was unsuccessful, finally requested assistance. After several attempts by Dr. Dahl, an airway was established; however, Mr. Brown had sustained cardiac arrest and suffered permanent physical and mental disabilities. The trial court ruled that there was enough evidence of the nurse anesthetist's negligence to proceed to trial; the jury, however, found the nurse anesthetist not guilty. Plaintiffs appealed, and the appellate court reversed the lower court because the court failed to give a jury instruction on *res ipsa loquitur*,[48] and gave other improper instructions as well. The case was remanded back to the lower court for a new trial.

The nurse anesthetist has the affirmative duty to monitor the effects of an anesthetic agent and the patient's condition. Failing to properly monitor, which causes harm to the patient, will result in the nurse anesthetist being held liable for negligence. Besides the *Brown* case, two other cases are illustrative of these legal principles.

The first case is a 1985 North Carolina Appellate Case, *Ipock v. Gillmore*,[49] which upheld the jury's findings that the nurse anesthetist was negligent for failing to perform a proper preanesthetic evaluation and failed to properly monitor the patient during surgery. The patient underwent elective laparoscopy for sterilization, but because of medical complications, a total hysterectomy was performed. The patient suffered cardiac arrest during the procedure and suffered hypoxia and resultant brain damage caused by the nurse anesthetist's negligence during surgery.

The second case involves the failure of the anesthesiology team, which included an anes-

thesiologist, a nurse anesthetist, and a student nurse anesthetist, to properly monitor a patient's condition while she was undergoing a radiographic procedure under general anesthesia. In the Ohio case of *Lupton v. Torbey*,[50] the patient, at her request, underwent general anesthesia for a celiac axis radiographic study to confirm the diagnosis of arterial vascular constriction of the stomach, a condition that had caused her a long history of stomach pain. During the initial phase of the procedure, the anesthesiologist was supervising the nurse anesthetist; however, he left, leaving the nurse anesthetist and student to monitor the patient. Over the next 15 minutes, the nurse anesthetist failed to assess the patient's vital signs; however, he became concerned about how quickly the patient had responded to the anesthetic. The nurse anesthetist left to speak with the anesthesiologist, leaving the patient in the care of the student. Upon arrival, the radiologist discovered that the patient had no pulse, and emergency measures were instituted, but the patient suffered brain damage. Prior to completion of the trial, the anesthesiology team settled the case for $75,000.[51]

A fourth failure to monitor a case that resulted in a $1 million jury verdict is a 1985 Michigan case discussed in Key Case 21–1.

In a 1985 Georgia case, *Central Anesthesia Associates v. Worthy*[53] the doctrine of negligence per se was asserted to establish that negligence had occurred. Negligence per se is a legal theory that provides that when there is a statute or regulation that has been enacted and that establishes a standard of conduct, then a violation of that statute or regulation is assumed to be evidence that negligence did in fact occur.

In the *Worthy* case, a student nurse anesthetist (SNA) was under the supervision of a physician's assistant during the induction of anesthesia when the patient suffered cardiac arrest, resulting in brain damage. At that time, a Georgia statute required that CRNAs be under the direct supervision of a licensed physician with training or experience in anesthesia. Nonexpert testimony was presented at trial that established that

KEY CASE 21-1   Theophelis v. Lansing General Hospital (1985)[52]

Anesthetic death occurs

Parents and estate representative file wrongful death action against hospital and medical personnel; did not name CRNA

FACTS: Gary Schneider, a 7-year-old boy, was admitted to Lansing General Hospital for a tonsillectomy and bilateral tympanotomy. Anesthesia was initially administered by an anesthesiologist, Dr. Jack Gilmore, and a certified nurse anesthetist, Jane Palmer. However, the anesthesiologist was not present during the procedure. The patient suffered cardiac arrest. After resuscitative efforts he remained comatose, sustained a second cardiac arrest, and following an EEG which revealed no brain wave activity, was taken off the respirator. A diagnosis of anesthetic death was made by the pathologist.

The parents and the representative for the estate filed a wrongful death action alleging malpractice against the hospital and all the medical personnel involved, but did not specifically name the CRNA as a defendant. The plaintiffs alleged that the anesthesiologist and CRNA gave an overdose of anesthetic, failed to properly monitor the patient's condition, and failed to properly institute emergency resuscitative procedures. The allegations against the hospital were failure to have proper policies and procedures for the administration of anesthesia, for intensive care, and for emergency protocols, and failing to advise the parents that a CRNA rather than an anesthesiologist would be present throughout surgery.

Prior to trial, the plaintiffs settled with the CRNA and anesthesiologist and executed release agreements with them. The Anesthesiology Group and its members were dismissed. Plaintiffs proceeded to trial against the hospital, the surgeon, and treating pediatrician.

Trial court jury returned $1 million verdict against hospital

TRIAL COURT: A jury trial was held and returned a verdict against the hospital for $1 million dollars under the doctrine of *respondeat superior*. The judgment was reduced to $742,261 by the court to reflect an offset for the amount of settlement received from the CRNA and the anesthesiologist.

Hospital appeals court decision

APPEALS COURT: The Hospital filed an appeal arguing that its liability as a principal for the acts of its agents (CRNA and anesthesiologist) under the doctrine of *respondeat superior* was improper and that the settlement releases protected the hospital from liability for the acts of the CRNA and anesthesiologist. The hospital also argued that the evidence pertaining to actions of the CRNA and anesthesiologist should not have been introduced at the trial.

Appeals court upholds trial court decision

The appellate court upheld the lower court's decision and found that the trial court did not abuse its discretion in allowing evidence regarding the CRNA's and anesthesiologist's negligence as the evidence established the hospital's independent negligence for having improper policies and procedures (e.g., requiring use of precordial stethoscope during anesthesia). Furthermore, the appellate court held that in view of

KEY CASE 21–1   Theophelis v. Lansing General Hospital (1985)[52] Continued

the hospital's own independent and concurrent acts of negligence, liability under the doctrine of *respondeat superior* was proper.

ANALYSIS: The *Theophelis* case addresses the legal doctrine of *respondeat superior* in which the principal (the hospital) can and will be held liable for the acts of negligence by its agent/employees. Both the anesthesiologist's and CRNA's conduct in providing anesthesia was within their scope of employment. Although the CRNA was not named as a defendant in the case, it was her actions, along with anesthesiologist's and hospital's, that the jury considered in finding liability on the part of the hospital. An APN's action and the policies that govern that practice can be brought into question even though the APN is not named as a defendant.

---

the SNA was not supervised as required by the state statute, and more importantly, the plaintiff did not have to present expert testimony to prove that the SNA was negligent.[54] The Court ruled in favor of Mrs. Worthy under the doctrine of negligence per se.

In Key Case 21–2, the theory of negligence per se was used in a creative way.

Because negligence per se claims are filed against APNs when an injury occurs and the APN's conduct that allegedly caused the injury is not included in a state statute or regulation that defines the APN's scope of practice, APNs must be cautious when providing care outside state-established scope of practice parameters. This may be particularly important for those APNs who are not specifically authorized to prescribe medications and treatments by state law or regulation. The potential for future negligence per se claims against the APNs if an injury to a patient is alleged as a result of that prescribing is very real.

Res Ipsa Loquitur

This doctrine means "the thing speaks for itself." The essential elements that need to be proved in a *res ipsa loquitur* case are: (1) that the

plaintiff's injury that occurred would not have occurred under ordinary circumstances if someone had not been negligent; (2) that the injury was the result of defendant's action while plaintiff was under the exclusive control of defendant; and (3) that the plaintiff did not contribute to or voluntarily act in a manner to cause the injury.[57]

This theory was asserted in *Morgan v. Children's Hosp.*,[58] a 1985 case involving a nurse anesthetist's failure to adequately ventilate a patient undergoing a thymectomy procedure for the treatment of myasthenia gravis. The patient developed severe bradycardia, necessitating open cardiac massage, and although stabilized, he sustained global brain damage due to hypoxia as a result of the CRNA's negligence.[59] The trial court refused to give the res ipsa loquitur jury instruction, and a defense verdict was returned by the jury. The case was taken up on appeal, where the appellate court ruled that the lower court erred in failing to give the instruction and overturned the defense verdict and remanded it for a new trial.[60]

Vicarious Liability and Borrowed Servant

Vicarious liability is the legal doctrine that holds one person legally accountable for the acts

KEY CASE 21–2

Mitchell v. Amarillo Hospital District (1993)[55]

FACTS: The plaintiff, Michael Mitchell, was admitted to a Texas hospital in February 1987 with the diagnosis of cardiac tamponade. Emergency cardiac surgery was scheduled, and a CRNA employed by the hospital administered the anesthesia. During the administration of the anesthesia, the patient suffered cardiac arrest. Although resuscitation efforts were successful, the patient suffered brain damage and died 3 years after the incident.

Civil rights suit filed against CRNA and others for death of patient

The family filed a civil rights claim against the CRNA, the surgeon, hospital, and the medical director of the Department of Anesthesia.

CRNA and surgeon settled case with plaintiffs

TRIAL COURT: The plaintiffs settled with the CRNA and the surgeon. However, they pursued their claim against the hospital and the head of the Department of Anesthesia. A summary judgment motion was filed by defendant and granted by the trial court.

Trial court dismisses claims against remaining defendants

Plaintiffs alleged that under the legal theory of negligence and negligence per se, the hospital deprived Mr. Mitchell of his civil rights by permitting a nurse anesthetist to illegally practice medicine; make independent decisions; and prescribe controlled drugs. Plaintiffs alleged numerous violations of state and federal statutes under the theory of negligence per se. The trial court dismissed the claims against the hospital and head of the anesthesiology department, which were based on a constitutional challenge that Mr. Mitchell's rights under the Fifth and Fourteenth Amendments of the US Constitution had been violated.[56] The plaintiffs filed an appeal.

Plaintiffs appeal dismissal

APPEALS COURT: The Texas Court of Appeals upheld the trial court's decision and ruled that neither the acts of the CRNA nor the hospital's policy regarding nurse anesthetists constituted a deprivation of Mr. Mitchell's civil rights. It further upheld the finding that Texas law did not require a nurse anesthetist to be supervised by an anesthesiologist. Therefore, the actions of the CRNA did not violate any state statute.

Court of Appeals upholds trial court's decision

ANALYSIS: The *Mitchell* case represents a highly unusual case in which the action was based upon a claim for denial of civil rights under a theory of negligence per se. It should be noted that nowhere did the plaintiffs allege that the CRNA negligently administered the anesthesia or that there was improper supervision. Plaintiffs' focus was on the advance practice of the nurse anesthetist and the hospital's policy of permitting the nurse anesthetist to practice.

APNs should be aware that negligence and scope of practice allegations can and sometimes are clouded in unusual legal theories such as constitutional claims. It is equally significant that the *Mitchell* case was taken up on appeal from a summary judgment motion in which no evidence was introduced, but nonetheless procedurally resulted in the court determining the legality of the NA's practice and the hospital's policies regarding the expanded role of the CRNA.

of another person. Generally a principal/agent relationship must exist in which the principal has control over or directs the actions of the agent. The borrowed servant rule is when an employee is temporarily under the control of another with regard not only to the work to be performed, but also the manner in which the work should be performed. These theories are illustrated in the case of *Harris v. Miller*.[61]

Nurse-Midwives

A review of the legal literature reveals only a few reported civil cases involving nurse-midwives[64] and even fewer for nurse practitioners and clinical nurse specialists. However, APNs have been involved in criminal allegations for the illegal practice of medicine[65] and in antitrust cases.[66, 67]

RNs, who are functioning in an expanded role but lack the certification, have been charged and convicted of the illegal practice of medicine.[68] In *Bowland v. Municipal Court of Santa Cruz County*,[69] an RN who held herself out as a midwife was criminally convicted for failing to meet the California statutory requirement of certification. The *Bowland* case is illustrative of the legal premise that an APN who fails to comply with statutory certification requirements may be criminally prosecuted.

. . . an APN who fails to comply with statutory certification requirements may be criminally prosecuted.

A negligence per se theory was asserted against a nurse-midwife in *Lustig v. the Birthplace*[70] and was the basis for a $725,000 settlement for the wrongful death of a mother and child due to a nurse midwife's breach of the statutory duty to consult a physician when there was a significant change in either the mother's or child's condition.[71] The nurse-midwife, who followed the mother throughout her pregnancy and labor, failed to recognize changes in the mother's condition that were consistent with pre-eclampsia and that resulted in the stillbirth of the child and the death of the mother 2 days later.[72]

As of 1994, there were no reported cases in the United States that held a physician vicariously liable for negligence of the nurse-midwife,[73] although there may be unreported instances that a physician or a medical group has been found vicariously liable in circumstances in which the right of control had been established. The most important legal principle that the APN should understand is that each and every APN is responsible for his or her wrongful actions or omissions that cause harm to another.[74]

Vicarious liability is based upon the legal relationship of one party that has the right of control over another.[75] The APN has the responsibility to define the legal relationship with any other health care provider and must understand that vicarious liability will not be presumed, nor does it take the place of the APN's own liability.

In a 1990 malpractice case involving a nurse-midwife's failure to monitor and treat a mother's hypertension and pre-eclampsia a federal district court found the nurse-midwife negligent. That case is presented in Key Case 21–4.

Nurse Practitioner

Failure to inform a patient of known risks and delay in the proper treatment of an infection were two of the allegations against the nurse practitioner (NP) in *Gugino v. Harvard Community Health Plan*.[78] On the basis of medical expert testimony, the NP was held liable for the failure to inform the patient in 1975 of the known risk of infection associated with an IUD, the Dalkon shield, which the patient had had inserted in 1972. In addition, the NP was liable for the 48-hour delay in instituting the proper treatment, thereby necessitating the patient to undergo a

KEY CASE 21–3   Harris v. Miller (1991)

FACTS: In June, 1981, Etta Harris underwent back surgery for treatment of a ruptured disc. Dr. Miller, an orthopedic surgeon, performed the surgery, and the anesthesia was administered by a CRNA, William Hawks, who was employed by Beaufort County Hospital. The hospital did not have an anesthesiologist on staff, and its policy established that the nurse anesthetist would administer anesthesia under the responsibility and supervision of the surgeon performing the surgery. Dr. Miller was a private practitioner and not on the hospital staff. A preanesthetic evaluation was performed by the CRNA, but the CRNA failed to interpret the patients's chest x-ray properly and did not identify the enlarged heart that could lead to decreased heart function under certain anesthetic employed during surgery.

Nurse anesthetist administered anesthesia improperly and delayed administering needed blood to patient

At the beginning of the surgical procedures, the patient's blood pressure dropped and her heart rate was elevated to an abnormally high rate. The NA testified that he thought that these changes were the result of the fact that the patient was not responding to the anesthetic and increased the anesthesia. Approximately 1 hour later, while the operation was still continuing, the patient's blood pressure continued to remain low, and the surgeon noticed that the patient had lost 300 to 400 cc of blood, an amount twice the normal expected loss. The surgeon ordered the CRNA to administer blood; however, the CRNA delayed carrying out this order for approximately 40 minutes.

Meanwhile, the patient's blood pressure continued to remain at an extremely low level, and the CRNA failed to notify the surgeon of the patient's critical condition for approximately another 1½ hours. Resuscitative efforts were instituted, and a vascular surgeon was consulted who performed an exploratory laparotomy and found the aorta flaccid. The vascular surgeon clamped the patient's aorta so that blood flow would not enter the legs and the patient's blood pressure would return.

Patient's injuries include vocal cord paralysis, a permanent tracheostomy, and brain damage

The patient was admitted to the ICU where she remained comatose for an extended period of time. Upon regaining consciousness, the patient's vocal cords were paralyzed; she had a permanent tracheostomy and had residual disabilities as a result of the brain damage suffered because of improper ventilation during the procedure. A postoperative x-ray revealed that the endotracheal tube was improperly positioned in the right lung, leaving the left lung unventilated. Further evidence indicated that, during the procedure, the CRNA failed to listen for bilateral breath sounds after intubation.

Patient files a medical malpractice claim against the CRNA, doctor, and hospital

The patient spent 8 months in a rehabilitation center before being discharged home to be cared for by her husband. Mrs. Harris filed a medical malpractice claim against the CRNA, medical doctor, and hospital in 1983. She died 6 years later as a result of her injuries. The family was substituted in as the plaintiffs in Mrs. Harris' medical

KEY CASE 21–3   Harris v. Miller (1991) *Continued*

CRNA and hospital settle claim with plaintiffs

Trial court grants surgeon's motion for directed verdict

Plaintiffs appeal trial court decision

Appellate court affirms trial court decision

Plaintiff appeals court of appeals decision to Supreme Court of North Carolina

malpractice claim and it was amended to include a wrongful death claim against the doctor. In 1987 the plaintiffs settled their claim against the CRNA and the hospital.

TRIAL COURT: A jury trial was held. At the conclusion of the evidence, the defendant surgeon moved for a directed verdict. The trial court granted the surgeon's motion on the grounds that the undisputed evidence showed that the NA's negligence caused the injury and that the surgeon was not vicariously liable for the actions of the NA. The trial court's decision was based on the fact that plaintiffs failed to establish that the surgeon had a master–servant relationship under the doctrine known as the borrowed servant rule. Although the NA was employed by the hospital, plaintiffs argued that the NA was loaned to the surgeon and according to hospital policy was under the surgeon's control and responsibility.

Plaintiffs appealed by a writ of certiorari requesting the court of appeals to review the trial court's decision in granting the directed verdict.

COURT OF APPEALS: The Court of Appeals for North Carolina granted a hearing on the issue of whether the trial court erred in granting the directed verdict on the basis that the surgeon was not vicariously liable for the acts of the CRNA. It affirmed the trial court's decision.

The appellate court dealt with the issue of whether the evidence showed that the surgeon had sufficient control of the CRNA's acts and therefore he should be liable under the borrowed servant rule.

Although the appellate court interpreted the hospital's manual as evidence that the surgeon had the right of supervision, the court made a distinction between the power to supervise and the power to control. In addition, it rejected plaintiff's argument that the surgeon's testimony was evidence that he was ultimately responsible for the quality of care given to a patient and held that the surgeon did not have the right to control the CRNA's actions.

APPEAL TO SUPREME COURT OF NORTH CAROLINA: The plaintiff appealed the decision of the court of appeals to the Supreme Court of North Carolina. The supreme court on review held that there was sufficient evidence for the case to be heard by the jury under the doctrine of vicarious liability of the surgeon. The supreme court disagreed with the court of appeals' interpretation of the language of the hospital manual and interpreted the manual in the light most favorable to plaintiff, holding that the language could be interpreted that the surgeon was responsible for the selection and proper administration of the anesthetic agent.

Key Case continued on following page

KEY CASE 21–3   Harris v. Miller (1991) *Continued*

The supreme court believed that the surgeon, on the basis of the hospital policy manual and the doctor's testimony, held the right to control the CRNA's actions and in fact at one point in time ordered the CRNA to stop administering all anesthesia and give the patient 100% oxygen as a remedial measure.[62]

The supreme court reversed the court of appeals' decision and granted the plaintiff a new trial against the surgeon[63] on the theory of vicarious liability and negligent supervision of the CRNA. Plaintiffs could not retry their negligence claim against the surgeon for the bleeding problem.

ANALYSIS: The *Harris* case is illustrative of the legal principle that other health care providers may be liable for an APN's negligent actions if the supervising provider has control over the APN's acts. The right of control may be determined through an analysis of a facility's policy manuals. Whether an individual will be viewed as an employer and be held vicariously liable will depend on the facts of each case. Under the doctrine of vicarious liability, the right of control is two pronged—the right to control the result of an individual's action and the right to control the means to reach that result. In the *Harris* case, the policy manual established the surgeon's right to control the result of the anesthesia actions, and in fact the surgeon may have assumed that right when he ordered the CRNA to perform certain tasks.

The primary lesson contained in the *Harris* case is that when APNs develop their practice, they should not allow policies and procedures or hospital standards to create a legal relationship with other health care providers beyond that established by statutes or case law.

---

total hysterectomy for multiple abscesses.[79] The courts have held that the APN must keep abreast of the medical research regarding implanted devices. The APN has a continuing duty to inform his or her patients of any known risk associated with a course of treatment or a device, whether in the past or presently. It should be noted, however, that the APN will be held accountable only if the APN knew or should have known about the treatment or device.

Another case example of the NP's failure to warn of the known risks is the wrongful death claim filed against the county and the manufacturer of a polio vaccine for the actions of a

pediatric NP in the case of *Sheenan v. Pima County.*[80] The allegations claimed that the pediatric NP was negligent for failing to inform the parent of the danger of contracting polio after receiving the vaccine. Although the appellate court upheld the defense verdict on the grounds that the mother (the plaintiff), even if informed of the risk, would still have permitted her child to receive the vaccine, the court found that the pediatric NP, as a learned intermediary—the one most knowledgeable regarding the risks—had the duty to disclose to the mother the 1 in 5 million risk of contracting the disease. The legal premise that the APN has constructive knowl-

KEY CASE 21–4

Anderson v. United States (1990)[76]

Mother followed during pregnancy by nurse-midwife employed by Indian Health Service

FACTS: On September 12, 1984, the minor plaintiff, Casey Anderson, was born to Marie Anderson, an 18-year-old primipara at the Fort Yates Indian Health Services Hospital in North Dakota. During plaintiff's pregnancy, labor, and delivery, she was followed by a nurse-midwife, Dorothy Meyer, who was an employee of the Indian Health Services and was qualified to deliver babies in low-risk pregnancies. Plaintiff saw an obstetrician on one of her prenatal visits who informed her that she was progressing well.

Mother develops pre-eclamptic state, but staff does not intervene medically

During plaintiff's labor, the staff recorded elevations of her blood pressure, which were the presenting signs of pregnancy-induced hypertension. Although fetal monitoring was done on two separate occasions, the staff failed to recognize plaintiff's pre-eclamptic medical problem. Meconium staining was also present at the time plaintiff's membranes were ruptured, and there was evidence at the time of delivery that meconium aspiration had occurred. The baby was lethargic and required resuscitation at the time of his birth.

He is now 5 years old and is severely disabled. He is unable to walk, crawl, talk, see, or control his bowel movements, and he must be fed through a jejunostomy tube.

Mother files a malpractice suit alleging negligence to timely diagnose and treat pregnancy-induced hypertension and pre-eclampsia

Plaintiff filed a medical malpractice claim, alleging negligence in the failure to timely diagnose and treat plaintiff's pregnancy-induced hypertension and pre-eclampsia resulting in the minor plaintiff suffering from intrapartum asphyxia and being born with severe and permanent brain injuries and cerebral palsy.

U.S. FEDERAL DISTRICT COURT DECISION: This case was filed in the U.S. District Court, as the Fort Yates Indian Health Services Hospital in North Dakota is a medical facility operated by the United States in the Standing Rock Indian Reservation and pursuant to the Federal Tort Claims Act.[77]

Court rules the hospital, including nurse-midwife, negligent, and their negligence caused birth injuries

A bench trial was held, and the trier of fact ruled that the staff at the Fort Yates Hospital, including the nurse-midwife, was negligent in failing to timely diagnose and treat plaintiff's pregnancy-induced hypertension and pre-eclampsia, which proximately caused the minor plaintiff to suffer intrapartum asphyxia and severe permanent brain injuries.

The defendant, the United States, was held liable for approximately $3.4 million economic damages, and an additional $525,000 was awarded to the maternal grandmother on her loss of consortium claim under the doctrine of *in loco parentis* claim as she had assumed financial and physical responsibility of caring for the baby since his birth. A trust was established to handle the minor plaintiff's financial needs.

Key Case continued on following page

KEY CASE 21–4   Anderson v. United States (1990)[76] *Continued*

APPEALS COURT: No appeal was made by either party.

ANALYSIS: The significance of the *Anderson* case is that it was one of

APNs who are employees of government not immune from negligence suits

the very few reported cases that dealt with the expanded role of the nurse-midwife. It is also representative of the fact that APNs whose practice setting is a federal or government entity are not immune from allegations of negligence.

The *Anderson* case also reflects the deep-pocket theory and the doctrine of *respondeat superior*, as the action was brought against the United States as the principal for the actions of its agents who were acting within their scope of employment at the federally operated medical facility.

---

edge of the risks of treatment and drugs was established when the court acknowledged the advanced practice of professional nurses.[81]

The APN has a continuing duty to inform his or her patients of any known risk associated with a course of treatment or a device, whether in the past or presently.

There is a recognized affirmative duty to refer the patient to another health care provider or specialist if the patient's condition is beyond the advanced practice nurse's skill or knowledge.

In *Sermchief v. Gonzales*,[82] the court recognized that NPs who function in an advance role must

be aware of the limits of their knowledge and the limits contained in the written standing orders and protocols. There is a recognized affirmative duty to refer the patient to another health care provider or specialist if the patient's condition is beyond the APN's skill or knowledge.

Allegations of the APN's failure to institute proper treatment can be asserted against the APN, as illustrated in the well-known *Fein v. Permanente*[84] case.

Clinical Nurse Specialist

The title, clinical nurse specialist (CNS), has been recognized by the nursing profession since the 1930s, and historically, the role developed in the psychiatric nursing area. The role of the CNS has expanded into most facets of patient care. However, there is some confusion regarding the role of the CNS. Recently in California a task force was formed to investigate and review the role of the CNS to assist the legislature in addressing this area of advanced practice. In 1994 a new and exciting role for the CNS as a cardiovascular nurse interventionist was proposed in the nursing literature.[85] In the legal arena, however, a review of the reported case law does not reveal any cases involving the CNS. The CNS, however, is faced with similar practice hurdles

Text continued on page 513

KEY CASE 21–5   Sermchief v. Gonzales (1983)

Two NPs provided obstetric, gynecological and family planning care to patients via standing orders and written protocols developed by physicians

Complaint against nurses and physicians about services filed with licensing agency

Board of agency decides to seek criminal charges against NPs for practicing medicine without a license and against physicians for aiding and abetting that unauthorized practice

Nurses and physicians file suit asking for injunctive and declaratory relief

Court rules against NPs and physicians

The court reverses the lower court, holding that the NPs were practicing nursing as defined in the Missouri Nurse Practice Act

FACTS: Two NPs and five physicians were employed by the East Missouri Action Agency to provide obstetric, gynecologic, and family planning services to low-income patients. NPs Janice Burgess, a family planning practitioner, and Suzanne Solari, an obstetric-gynecologic practitioner, provided competent health care services pursuant to written standing orders and protocols developed by the physicians. In fact, there were no allegations that the NPs' actions had caused harm to any client.

In 1980, a confidential complaint was filed with the Missouri State Board of Registration for the Healing Acts alleging that the NPs were practicing medicine without a license and that the physicians, by developing written standing orders and protocols, were aiding and abetting unauthorized practice of medicine.

Upon investigation of the complaint, the Board decided to seek criminal charges against the NPs and hold a hearing to decide if the physicians' licenses should be revoked or suspended. Upon learning of the Board's actions, the NPs and physicians, through their attorneys, obtained a temporary restraining order against the Board, prohibiting the Board from acting further. An action for declaratory and injunctive relief was filed with the court, seeking a court order to permanently prohibit the Board from interfering with their practice, challenging the constitutionality of Missouri's Medical Practice Act, and for a determination that the NPs' actions constituted professional nursing.

TRIAL COURT DECISION: The trial court heard expert testimony from both sides, and ruled on behalf of the Board. The court held that the NPs' actions constituted the unlawful practice of medicine and enjoined them from performing any activities pursuant to their protocols unless a physician was on site at the time. The court further upheld the constitutionality of the Medical Practice Act, and thus the NPs had adequate notice that their actions were unlawful.

Regarding the physicians, the court ruled they were not immune from the Board's actions and would need to respond to the allegations of aiding and abetting the unauthorized practice of medicine.

The lower court's decision was appealed to the Missouri Supreme Court.

MISSOURI SUPREME COURT DECISION: The Missouri Supreme Court reversed the lower court's decision and ordered that judgment be entered for the NPs and physicians. The appellate court held that the NPs' acts were authorized under Missouri's State Nurse Practice Act, and therefore their acts did not constitute the unlawful practice of medicine.

The supreme court recognized that the legislature's intent was to authorize the expanding scope of nurse practice when the nurse practice act was revised, by having an open-ended definition of professional

Key Case continued on following page

KEY CASE 21–5   Sermchief v. Gonzales (1983) *Continued*

nursing and by eliminating the requirement that a physician directly supervise nursing functions. The court did not address the NPs' level of training or degree of skill, as the Board's challenge was directed only toward the NPs' legal right to act pursuant to the standing orders and protocols.

At the time of the appeal, the only basis of the court's review was the comparison of the medical practice act and the nurse practice act and the evidence presented at the time of trial, despite the fact that amicus briefs by advocates for the nursing profession were filed urging the court to rule in favor of defendants.

ANALYSIS: The *Sermchief* case is important, as it was the first legal challenge to address the legality of the APN's scope of practice. The Supreme Court of Missouri acknowledged that the state had recognized the expanded role of nurses when the nurse practice act was revised in 1975. The court applied the rule of statutory interpretation in comparing the medical practice act and the nurse practice act to determine the NP's scope of practice.

This case is also significant as the court, by recognizing the expanded role of nursing practice, articulated the legal premise that APNs also have the responsibility to act in a professional manner and know the limits of their professional knowledge. This would include the duty to act within the limits of standing orders and protocols and the duty to refer when a patient's needs exceed the APN's scope of practice.

However, it should be noted that the impact of *Sermchief* on APN's practice in other states may be diminished. Despite the fact that *Sermchief* was fortunately tried in a state that had an open definition of nursing and recognized the expanded role, future cases seeking reliance on *Sermchief* may need to be fact-similar to achieve a similar result.[83]

KEY CASE 21–6   Fein v. Permanente Medical Group (1985)

Patient experiences chest pain and calls Kaiser Health Plan physician who could not see him

FACTS: In February, 1976, a 34-year-old attorney, Lawrence Fein, experienced, over a 5-day period, brief intermittent episodes of chest pain while exercising and while working. As a Kaiser Health Plan member, he contacted his primary care physician on February 26, 1976, for an appointment, but his physician did not have an open appointment available, and he was given an appointment that afternoon with Family NP, Cheryl Welch, who was working under the supervision

KEY CASE 21–6 Fein v. Permanente Medical Group (1985) *Continued*

Patient sees NP, who, in consultation with physician-supervisor, determines chest pain due to muscle spasms

Chest pain still persists, so patient returns and sees a physician in Plan; diagnosis of muscle spasm also made by this physician

Pain still persists and ECG obtained on third visit

Myocardial infarction diagnosed and patient admitted to CCU

Suit filed by patient alleging failure to timely diagnose and treat heart attack

Jury returns negligent verdict against the Health Plan due to conduct of NP and physicians

Plaintiff loses appeal to fight reduction of noneconomic damages

of physician-consultant, Dr. Winthrop Frantz. Mr. Fein was aware that Ms. Welch was an NP and did not request to be seen by a doctor. After examining Mr. Fein, Ms. Welch consulted Dr. Frantz, who wrote a prescription for Valium, and Ms. Welch informed Mr. Fein that they believed his pain was due to muscle spasms.

At about 1 o'clock the next morning, the patient awoke with severe chest pains and was taken to the Kaiser Emergency Room where he was treated by Dr. Redding. After obtaining a chest x-ray and examining him, Dr. Redding concluded the patient was suffering from muscle spasms and ordered pain medication. The patient also continued to suffer from intermittent chest pain, which became more severe the next afternoon. He was again seen in Kaiser Emergency Room, where, after an ECG was obtained, an acute myocardial infarction was diagnosed, and he was admitted to the Cardiac Care Unit. The patient was able to return to part-time work within 8 months of the incident and full-time within 1½ years. At the time of trial, he was able to engage in all of his prior recreational activities.

In February, 1977, Mr. Fein filed a medical malpractice claim alleging failure to timely diagnose and treat his heart attack.

TRIAL COURT DECISION: A jury trial was held and expert testimony was presented. Plaintiff's cardiology expert testified that plaintiff's presenting signs and symptoms were consistent with an imminent heart attack, and at the time plaintiff saw the NP an ECG should have been ordered. Plaintiff's expert also testified that Dr. Redding should have ordered an ECG, and if an ECG had been obtained, the plaintiff's impending myocardial infarction could have been identified and medical intervention instituted to prevent or minimize the attack. Despite testimony by the NP and the emergency room physician and the defense experts, the jury ruled in favor of the plaintiff, and judgment was entered against the Permanente Medical Group for the negligent conduct of the NP and the two physicians (Frantz and Redding). The jury awarded approximately $1.2 million dollars for noneconomic and economic damages, which were reduced under statutory law.

Both parties appealed the lower court's decision.

APPEALS COURT DECISION: The plaintiff appealed the lower court's decision on the grounds that the judgment in his favor should not be reduced under the California statutes limiting noneconomic damages to $250,000 nor should receipt of any disability benefits reduce the amount of economic damages. The appellate court upheld the California statutes as being constitutional and affirmed the trial court's ruling to reduce the award.

Key Case continued on following page

KEY CASE 21–6   Fein v. Permanente Medical Group (1985) *Continued*

Health Plan appeals several issues, including the jury instructions regarding the NP standard of care

Appeals court ruled the lower court's applications of a physician standard of care to an NP in error

Even so, Appeals court upholds decision of lower court, as the use of the wrong standard of care did not affect judgment

The defendant medical group appealed the lower court's decision on several grounds pertaining to voir dire jury selection; causation and damage issues; denial of periodic payment; and the jury instruction regarding the standard of care of the NP.

The lower court had instructed the jury that the standard of care required of an NP when the NP examines a patient or makes a diagnosis is the standard of care of a physician and surgeon duly licensed to practice medicine in the State of California. The appellate court, based upon its review of California's Nurse Practice Act and the legislature's intent to recognize the existence of overlapping functions between physicians and RNs, held that the lower court erred in the NP's standard of care instruction to the jury.

However, although the trial court erred in its jury instruction, the appellate court upheld the plaintiff's verdict on the grounds that the lower court's error did not affect the judgment and would not warrant a reversal. In fact, the appellate court ruled that although there were errors by the trial court, none warranted a reversal, and therefore the judgment remained as entered.

It should be noted that the appellate decision was not unanimous, and several appellate justices dissented.

SECOND APPEAL REQUEST: The petition for rehearing filed by the plaintiff/appellant was denied on April 4, 1985.

ANALYSIS: The *Fein* case is the landmark case that addresses the standard of care of NPs and therefore is precedent in California that identifies the professional standard that the APN's conduct will be measured against in a negligence action.

An important issue in the legal recognition of the APN is the fact that in *Fein* a physician who was not an NP expert testified to the standard of care of the NP. To ensure that the appropriate professional standard is being applied, APNs should challenge any physician's expert qualifications in an action brought against them.

The *Fein* case is also significant for the principle that the NP standard of care will be applied only as long as the NP is functioning within the scope of the NP's practice. Because Ms. Welch consulted her physician-consultant and was acting within her scope of practice as a Family NP (even though her actions were found to be negligent), the standard her conduct would be measured against would be the NP standard. Functioning outside the scope of practice would expose the APN to be held to a non-nursing standard.

and liability issues that other APNs have had to confront. The legal issues pertaining to informed consent, especially in the research setting, and the duty to appropriately monitor and inform a patient of any known risks or dangers are applicable to the CNS's practice.

Inability to receive third-party reimbursement has prevented the CNS from being hired instead of another professional whose services are reimbursed.[86] Regardless of the practice setting, the CNS, along with the other APNs, is a provider of direct patient care, and is capable of functioning independently or interdependently in a highly competent and cost-effective manner.

SUMMARY OF PRINCIPLES AND APPLICATIONS

The APN's role in health care reform is slowly progressing. There are serious legal barriers preventing APNs from functioning to the fullest extent of their education, training, and skills. After 30 plus years, the APN continues to face legal obstacles regarding prescriptive authority, direct reimbursement, and scope of practice issues. Legal recognition must catch up to the realities of the APN's practice to allow patients full access to quality and cost-efficient health care by highly competent health care providers. The time has come for APNs to take their rightful and legal place in the promotion of health and reduction of health costs. It is imperative that to continue to provide competent and high-quality health care and to achieve a truly independent and autonomous practice, the APN must understand the legal principles pertaining to scope of practice, the standard of care, and the current legal theories. Therefore, the APN should:

▼ Be able to identify the practice issues that may expose him or her to allegations of malpractice

▼ Keep abreast of the changes in the laws that govern advanced practice

▼ Be familiar with the legal theories of *respondeat superior* and vicarious liability when the APN is acting in the role of employer or principal

▼ Adhere to the standards of care pertaining to the APN's area of specialty

▼ Develop written protocols and standardized procedures when required to comply with state statutes

▼ Identify the legal authority to perform overlapping functions

▼ Form collaborative practices with other health care professionals

▼ Identify the barriers to practice and the mechanism to achieve full prescriptive authority and reimbursement

TOPICS FOR FURTHER INQUIRY

1. Design a study to evaluate the consumer's knowledge and recognition of the APN's role in health care.

2. Help develop an APN national data base regarding unreported legal cases that involve an APN's practice but may not name the APN as a defendant.

3. Compare and contrast the effectiveness of collaborative practice agreements and employment agreements.

4. Analyze APN educational programs to determine the existence and amount of time spent regarding the legal aspects of advanced practice.

5. Design a study to evaluate insurance companies' recognition of the APN role.

6. Develop a marketing plan to improve the visibility of the APN's role in health care.

7. Draft a realistic proposal to educate legislators regarding the necessity for full prescriptive authority for APNs.

REFERENCES

1. O'Connor, K. ''Advanced Practice Nurses in an Environment of Health Care Reform,'' *MCN*, Vol. 19 (March/April 1994), 66.

2. *Id.* at 68, *citing* "Omnibus Poll," Lincoln, N.E. Gallup Organization, 1993.

3. Eskreis, T., "Health Law—The Legal Implications in Utilizing the Nurse Anesthetist in Place of the Anesthesiologist," *Whittier Law Review,* Vol. 7, 856 (1985).

4. *Id.* at 855.

5. Inglis, A. and Kjervik, D., "Empowerment of Advanced Practice Nurses: Regulation Reform Needed to Increase Access to Care," *The Journal of Law, Medicine & Ethics,* Volume 21 (1993), 194.

6. Eskreis, T., "Health Law—The Legal Implications of Utilizing the Nurse Anesthetist in place of the Anesthesiologist," *Whittier Law Review* (1985), 855, fn 1, *citing* "Brief Amicus Curiae," American Association of Nurse Anesthetist, *citing Jefferson Hosp, Dist. v. Hyde* 1045 S. Ct. 1551 (1984).

7. O'Connor, K. *supra* note 1, at 66.

8. Williams, D. "Credentialing Certified Nurse Midwives," *Journal of Nurse-Midwifery,* Vol. 39, (July/Aug. 1994), 258.

9. *Id.* at 259.

10. Brent, N., "The Nurse Practitioner after Sermchief and Fein: Smooth Sailing or Rough Waters," *Valparaiso University Law Review.* Vol 26, No. 2 (Winter, 1987), 221.

11. Schultz, J., Liptak, G., and Fioravanti, J, "Nurse Practitioners' Effectiveness in NICU," *Nursing Management,* Vol. 25, No. 1 (Oct. 1994), 50.

12. Brown, S. and Guno, D., "Nurse Practitioners and Certified Nurse-Midwives: A Meta-analysis on Process Care, Clinical outcomes and Cost effectiveness of Nurses in Primary Care Role," American Nurses Association, Publ. No. NP-85, (1993).

13. Askin, D., Bennett, K., and Shapiro, C., "The Clinical Nurse Specialist and the Research Process," *JOGNN,* Vol. 23, No. 4 (May 1994), 336.

14. O'Connor, K. *supra* note 1, at 66.

15. Inglis, A. and Kjervik, D., *supra* note 5, at 197.

16. O'Connor, K. *supra* note 1, 66.

17. Feutz, S., The Legal System: Past, Present, and Future, in *Nursing and the Law,* Professional Educational Systems. Third Edition. Eau Claire, Wis, 1989, 1–12.

18. Pearson, L. "Annual Update of How Each State Stands on Legislative Issues Affecting Advanced Nursing Practice," *Nurse Practitioner* (Jan. 1994), 22–53.

19. *Id.* at 22–53.

20. Williams, D., *supra* note 8, at 259.

21. Birkholz, G. and Walker, D. "Strategies for State Statutory Language Changes Granting Fully Independent Nurse Practitioner Practice," *Nurse Practitioner,* (Jan. 1994), 54.

22. Pearson, L., *supra* note 18, at 232.

23. Birkholz, G., *supra* note 21 at 54.

24. Williams, D., *supra* note 8, at 260.

25. *Chalmers-Francis v. Nelson* 6 Cal. 2d 402, 57 P. 2d 1312 (1936).

26. *State v. Borah* 51 Ariz. 318, 76 P. 2d 757 (1938).

27. *Sermchief v. Gonzales* 660 S.W. 2d 683 (Mo. banc 1983).

28. Brent, N., *supra* note 10, at 232.

29. 660 S.W. 2d 683, 690.

30. Feutz, S., Professional Negligence and Intentional Torts, in *Nursing and the Law,* Professional Education Systems. Third Edition. Eau Claire, Wis, 1989, 13–29.

31. Hirsch, H. and Studner, J., "The Nurse Practitioner (NP) in Action: Patient's Friend, Physicians' Foe?" in *Medical Trial Technique Quarterly,* Summer, 1984, pp 37–76.

32. *Whitney v. Day* 300 N.W. 2d 380, 382, (Mich. App., 1980).

33. Blumenreich, G., "Mitchell v. Amarillo Hospital District," *Journal of the American Association of Nurse Anesthetists,* Vol. 62 (Feb. 1994), 11.

34. *Fein v. Permanente Medical Group,* 38 Cal 3d 137, 695 P. 2d 665; 211 Cal. Rptr. 368 (1985).

35. Williams, D. *supra* note 8, at 259 and ftn. 5 at 264.

36. 38 Cal 3d 137, 695 P. 2d 665, 673, 211 Cal Rptr. 368, (1985).

37. *Czubinsky v. Doctors* Hospital 139 Cal. App. 3d 361, 188 Cal. Rptr. 685 (1983).

38. Sebas, M., "Developing a Collaborative Practice Agreement for the Primary Care Setting," *Nurse Practitioner,* Vol. 19 (March, 1993), 49.

39. 38 Cal. 3d 137, 695 P. 2d 665, 211 Cal Rptr. 368, (1985).

40. *Gugino v. Harvard Community Health Plan,* 380 Mass. 464, 403 N.E. 2d 1166, (1980).

41. Inglis, A., and Kjervik, D., *supra.* note 5, at 193.

42. *Id.* at 198.

43. *Id.*

44. Pearson, L., *supra* note 18 at 17.

45. Inglis, A., and Kjervik, D., *supra* note 5, at 201.

46. *Id.* at 198–199.

47. *Brown v. Dahl,* 705, P. 2d 781, (Wash. App. 1985).

48. Res ipsa loquitur is discussed in Chapters 3 and 4.

49. *Ipock v. Gillmore,* 326 S.E. 2d 271, (N.C. App., 1985).

50. *Lupton v. Torbey,* 480 N.E. 2d 464 (Ohio, 1985).

51. *Id.* at 464.

52. 141 Mich. App. 199, 366 N.W. 2d 249, (1985).

53. *Central Anesthesia Associates v. Worthy,* 254 Ga. 728, 333 S.E. 2d 829, (1985).

54. Blumenreich, G., "Supervision," *Journal of the American Association of Nurse Anesthetists,* Vol. 62, (Oct. 1994), 421.

55. 855 S.W. 2d 857, (1993).

56. Blumenreich, G., "Mitchell v. Amarillo Hosp. Dist.," *Journal of American Association of Nurse Anesthetists,* Vol. 62 (Feb. 1994), 11.

57. Blumenreich, G., "Supervision," *Journal of the American Association of Nurse Anesthetists,* Vol. 62 (October 1994), 421.

58. *Morgan v. Children's Hospital,* 18 Ohio St. 3d 185, 480 N.E. 2d 464, 18 Ohio B. Rep. 253, (1985).

59. *Id.* at 465.

60. *Id.* at 476.

61. *Harris v. Miller,* 103 N.C. App. 312, 407 S.E. 556, (1991).

62. Blumenreich, G., "Harris v. Miller," *Journal of American Association of Nurse Anesthetists,* Vol. 62, (June 1994), 210.

63. 335 N.C. 379, 438 S.E. 2d 731 (1994).

64. Jenkins, S., "The Myth of Vicarious Liability," *Journal of Nurse-Midwifery,* Vol. 39, (March/April 1994), 106.

65. 660 S.W. 2d 683, (Mo. enbanc, 1983).

66. *Bahn v. NME Hosp. Inc.,* 772 F. 2d 1467, (9th Cir. 1985).

67. *Nurse Midwifery Assoc. v. Hibbett,* 577 F. Supp. 1273, (D. Tenn., 1983).

68. *Bowland v. Municipal Court for Santa Cruz County,* 18 Cal. 3d 479, 556 P. 2d 1081, 134 Cal. Rptr. 630, (1976).

69. *Id.* at 480.

70. *Lustig v. the Birthplace,* No. 83-2-07528-9, Wash. King's

County Superior Crt., decided Sept. 9, 1983 as reported in 27 ATLA Law Rptr. 87 (March 1984).

71. 27 ATLA Law Rptr. 87 (March 1984).
72. *Id.* at 87.
73. Jenkins, S., *supra* note 61, at 99.
74. *Id.*
75. *Harris v. Miller*, 335 N.C. 379, 438 S.E. 2d 731, (1994).
76. *Anderson v. United States*, 731 F. Supp. 391, (1990).
77. 28 U.S.C. 2671 *et seq.*
78. *Gugino v. Harvard Community Health Plan*, 380 Mass. 464, 403 N.E. 2d 1166, (1980).
79. Hirsch, H., and Studner, J., *supra* note 31, at 64–66.
80. *Sheenan v. Pima County*, 135 Ariz. 235, 660 P. 2d 486, (1983).
81. Kelly, M., *supra* note 86, at 375.
82. 660 S.W. 2d 683, 690 (Mo. banc 1983).
83. Brent, N., *supra* note 10, at 221.
84. 38 Cal. 3d 137, 696 P. 2d 665, 211 Cal. Rptr. 368 (1985).
85. Engles, Mary, and Engles, Marguerite, "Cardiovascular Nurse Interventionist: An Emerging New Role," *Nursing and Health Care*, Vol. 15, No. 5 (April 1994).
86. Inglis and Kjervik, *supra* note 5, at 198–199.

22 The Nurse as Entrepreneur

contents

Perhaps one of the clearest examples of advanced practice for any nurse is owning and operating his or her own business. Whether that business be involved in the delivery of health care (e.g., a nurse staffing agency) or the selling of health care products such as operating room equipment designed by the nurse, there are important legal issues that must be analyzed and decided upon *before* the business is even initiated. Furthermore, there are many legal concerns that continue to be important long after the business is "up and running." This chapter will explore those issues within a general framework applicable to any business in which the nurse functions.

PRELIMINARY CONSIDERATIONS

Review of Professional Guidelines

An entrepreneur is defined as one "who assumes the total responsibility and risk for discovering or creating unique opportunities to use personal talents, skills, and energy, and who employs a strategic planning process to transform that opportunity into a marketable service or product."[1] A nurse entrepreneur is a nurse who performs those functions, not only to establish and maintain a successful business, but also to make quality nursing care and nursing more available to the public.[2] This dual role requires

RELATED TOPICS	
Chapter 3	Concepts of Negligence and Liability
Chapter 9	Contract Law
Chapter 15	Licensure and Nursing Practice
Chapter 16	The Nurse as Employee
Chapter 21	The Nurse in Advanced Practice

nurse entrepreneurs to be accountable and responsible not only to themselves, the profession, and employees, but also to consumers of health care. This accountability requires the nurse entrepreneur to be clear about adhering to professional guidelines, standards, and ethical principles. Therefore, one of the initial steps that must be undertaken by the future nurse entrepreneur is a thorough review of professional guidelines, standards, and ethical principles to ensure both philosophical and practical compliance with them.

One of the initial steps that must be undertaken by the future nurse entrepreneur is a thorough review of professional guidelines, standards, and ethical principles to ensure both philosophical and practical compliance with them.

Although the review may vary somewhat based on the nature of the nurse entrepreneur's business, the documents to be examined would include professional association standards, such as the American Nurses' Association's Code for Nurses with Interpretive Statements[3] and The Occupational Health Nurses' Association's Standards of Practice,[4] as well as scope of practice guidelines for particular specialties.

KEY PRINCIPLES
Sole Proprietorship
Partnership
Corporation
Professional Service Corporation
Professional Association
Antitrust Laws
Insurance

Community Analysis

Once the nurse thoroughly understands the professional underpinnings of the prospective business, the next stage in the preliminary phase is to consider carefully the prospective business idea. This includes evaluating the need for the future business, and should therefore involve a clear "needs assessment" in the geographic location where the business is to be. This can be done on a formal or informal basis. Formally, for example, the nurse could obtain statistics from the appropriate state department that compiles information concerning the prospective business being considered. If the nurse is considering a temporary staffing agency, for example, but it is discovered that the community is flooded with such agencies, it may not be in the best interest of the nurse or consumer to establish another there. Informally the nurse can review local telephone books to determine locations and numbers of current businesses identical or similar to the one being considered and can canvass them to obtain information concerning the services they provide.

In addition to evaluating competition, the nurse entrepreneur will also need to analyze such factors as available work force (if employees will be needed), location of the business (proximity to a hospital or clinic, if that need is present), cost of office space and whether renting or purchasing the space is best, and what options are available for marketing the business once it is established.

Initial Review of State and Federal Laws Affecting Business

The nurse also needs to evaluate what laws will pertain to the business. Although this step should also take place later in the formation of the enterprise, it is essential initially to ensure that the business can, in fact, be legally operated in the state. For example, if the nurse entrepreneur is contemplating establishing a home health care agency, a review of state licensing laws and respective rules and regulations, nurse practice and other professional practice acts, and reimbursement laws would be necessary to aid the nurse in determining if such a business can be legally and successfully established.

Financial Constraints

Because establishing a business takes an enormous amount of initial capital at the onset, the nurse entrepreneur will need to do an analysis of his or her financial status, not only for this initial outlay, but also for the time needed for the business to show a profit. Many experts in the field of consulting to entrepreneurs suggest that it may take as long as 3 years before a business begins to show a profit. Therefore, nurse entrepreneurs will need to evaluate how they will financially support the business and themselves during the time necessary for the business to grow. It may be, for example, that the nurse will have to work full- or part-time in a salaried position in addition to putting time into the business venture.

Many experts in the field of consulting to entrepreneurs suggest that it may take as long as 3 years before a business begins to show a profit.

Self-Analysis

The preliminary step of analyzing oneself is perhaps one of the most important. Traditionally, nurses have worked for others, either in a health care delivery setting, such as a hospital, or in a physician's office or clinic. Furthermore, until recently, professional nursing education has focused little attention on business concepts or principles. Also, because nursing is predominantly composed of women, society's expectations of women are that they will continue to maintain traditional roles, roles that do not include the establishment and running of a business.[5] Thus the nurse entrepreneur must carefully evaluate the personal and professional strengths and weaknesses that will help or inhibit the business' success. Strengths include:

▼ Resourcefulness

▼ Creativity

▼ Ability to withstand uncertainty

▼ Some experience in business

▼ Completion of a course or courses in business organizations, management, and/or finance

▼ Established social supports, including family

▼ A mentor or consultant who can be looked to for advice

▼ Flexibility

CONSULTING WITH EXPERTS

Once the preliminary steps have been completed, the nurse entrepreneur should put the business idea in writing, clearly outlining its nature, purpose, proposed general location, and other information decided upon during the preliminary phase. Then it is essential that the nurse consult with experts who can offer guidance through the maze of establishing and running the business.

It is essential that the nurse consult with experts who can offer guidance through the maze of establishing and running the business.

Consultation with an Attorney

The nurse entrepreneur will need to obtain accurate and up-to-date information concerning establishing the business consistent with the laws of the state where the business will be located. Many times, identifying an attorney well versed about a particular subject can be difficult, but not impossible. Information of this kind can be obtained from the state nurses' association, from local bar associations with lawyer referral services, from the national or local nurse attorney association, or from friends or colleagues who have established their own business.

It is important that the attorney selected is familiar with licensing laws, practice acts, business structures, and employment laws (if employees will be utilized). Equally important, however, is the nurse entrepreneur's comfort level with the attorney selected. The attorney should not only be viewed as an expert who will legally establish the business in the correct manner, but also as a resource the nurse entrepreneur can consult as the business changes. It is vital, then, that the attorney-nurse entrepreneur relationship be a solid one that can continue over time.

Business Structure

One of the first issues that will need to be determined when legal advice concerning the business is obtained is what organizational form the business will take. Generally there are three fairly universal organizational structures for businesses: the sole proprietorship, the partnership, and the corporation. These structures are governed by state law and may therefore vary slightly from state to state. Furthermore, some states have developed a fourth business structure option, the professional association. Variations on these four arrangements also exist, including the joint venture and the syndicate, but this chapter will focus on the four most common business models.

Sole Proprietorship

This business model is the least complicated of all of the business structures, and is excellent for the nurse entrepreneur who wants to establish a solo nursing practice, such as a private psychotherapy practice or a consulting service. In fact, a 1988 survey of 374 nurse entrepreneurs indicated that 186 identified themselves in this category.[6] The sole proprietor is, in effect, the business, and therefore any assets or liabilities belong to the owner. The nurse would declare income and expenses from the business as his or her own, and any profit would be taxed to him or her. In addition, the nurse would be required to pay estimated self-employment taxes, health insurance, and other costs normally paid by the business if it had been established under a different organizational structure.

If the nurse entrepreneur decides to utilize this form for the business, help such as secretarial services or additional nurses to provide client services may still be necessary. Usually those individuals are not considered employees, but are viewed as contractors who contract with the sole proprietor for the services. If they are independent contractors—that is, individuals working for themselves—they would be responsible for any and all taxes as a result of income paid to them by the nurse entrepreneur. If, however, the nurse contracted with a secretarial agency, for example, for typing services, then the agency would be responsible for paying the agency employee and reporting that income to the Internal Revenue Service.

In considering the sole proprietorship, the nurse entrepreneur will also want to obtain counsel from an attorney concerning the need to register the business with the state, city, or county office established to handle any business with an assumed or fictitious name. For example, if the nurse has decided to call the consulting business NURSE CONSULTANTS, then the nurse will need to register the business in the assumed or fictitious name index so that, if need be, the nurse can be readily identified as the owner of the business, and any additional information about the business, such as its starting date, can be obtained. If, however, the nurse decides to use his or her name as the business name, then there is usually no need to register the business with the assumed name office.

Partnership

A partnership is an arrangement, either formal or informal, whereby two or more individuals co-own a business for profit.[7] If formalized, the document is called the Partnership Agreement, and the nurse entrepreneur's attorney must represent the nurse's interests in developing and finalizing that agreement. If the partners decide not to formalize their business relationship in a written agreement, most states have a statute (e.g., the Uniform Partnership Act) that formalizes the relationship by governing the rights and responsibilities of individuals in the partnership to ensure that the owners fulfill obligations to themselves and the public. The nurse entrepreneur will want to seek a specific opinion from his or her attorney as to which approach is best to take for the proposed business.

Regardless of which option is selected, a partnership has legal implications that must be carefully evaluated by the nurse. To begin with, each partner can bind the other(s) in relation to the operation of the business, and each is personally responsible for the business debts incurred by the other(s). Moreover, the partnership arrangement is not a flexible one. If, for example, two nurses have established a nurse-managed center as a partnership, and one of them decides to leave the practice, then the partnership must be dissolved and a *new* one formed. And, each partner is responsible for his or her share of the business expenses and taxes according to the partnership agreement or partnership statute.

In addition to the general partnership arrangement, the nurse entrepreneur will want to explore with his or her attorney any advantages of establishing a *limited partnership*. Unlike the general partnership, a limited partner supplies money to the business but has no say in its operation, delivery of services, or any other aspect of the business. Moreover, the limited partner's share of liability is restricted to that which he or she has contributed to the business. This may be a valuable option for the nurse entrepreneur needing financial resources to begin the venture.

Again, as with the sole proprietorship, if an assumed name is utilized, it must be registered with the assumed name index, regardless of the type of partnership formed.

Corporation

A corporation is a very formalized business structure. Controlled by state, county, or national law, it is an entity established by incorporators to conduct business. The incorporators fill out and file articles of incorporation with the state, county, or national office empowered with granting corporation status. In a state, that office is the Secretary of State, and information required includes the name of the corporation, its purpose (e.g., to provide nursing care to the public), and the amount of financial backing initially available at incorporation.

The name of the corporation is an important piece of the filing process. To begin with, the name of the business cannot be identical to any other business name in the state, so the attorney will need to search the corporation list to determine if the selected name is available, and if it has not been used already, to reserve it for the nurse's use. In addition, if the name of the business will be an assumed one, it must also be registered as such with the Secretary of State.

When the appropriate office determines that the potential business has complied with all of its requirements, it will send the incorporators a certificate of incorporation and an incorporation number. In addition, the corporation is listed on the state's domestic corporation list, and to remain "in good standing" on that list, the corporation must file renewal papers and pay a filing fee on an annual basis.

Unlike the sole proprietorship and the partnership, the corporation must be managed by a board of directors who are elected by the owner/incorporators and the stockholders, if stock is issued. The board manages the business through established guidelines, called bylaws, and are accountable to the owners and stockholders for the decisions they make.

Unlike the sole proprietorship and the partnership, the corporation must be managed by a board of directors who are elected by the owner/incorporators and the stockholders, if stock is issued.

The corporation as a formal entity has interesting legal characteristics. To begin with, it has a "perpetual existence." In other words, once established, it survives any changes in ownership or purpose, although those changes must be communicated to the registration office and be consistent with its bylaws. In addition, the corporate structure protects the personal civil liability of the owners/incorporators and board of directors because it is a legal creature that can be sued and can accept financial responsibility for judgments entered against it.

Professional Corporation

The corporation the nurse entrepreneur will be establishing is usually not a general business corporation, but rather a professional service corporation. Also governed by state, county, or national law, the professional corporate structure is also very formalized, but is specific to professionals (e.g., nurses, dentists, and lawyers) establishing and rendering specific *professional* services to the public. Because the corporation is rendering a specific service, most state laws require the owners and shareholders of the corporation to be licensed in the same profession as the services provided by it. Also, a professional service corporation does not insulate its owners and shareholders from personal civil liability for malpractice, nor does it alter the professionals' ethical obligations and responsibilities to the clients.[8]

The opportunity to start a professional service corporation may not be readily available to the nurse entrepreneur, for its existence varies from state to state. The attorney consulted can advise the nurse on what availability there is for this form of business. For example, it may be that the statutory language of the professional corporation act does not expressly exclude nurses from incorporating, or it may clearly include nurses by referring to the state nurse practice act. Also important for the nurse and the attorney to evaluate is whether or not the corporation can render only one professional service, such as nursing, or can provide more than one, such as nursing and medical care.

Because of the traditional professional service corporation principle that all owners/incorporators must be licensed in the same profession, it has been only recently that multidisciplinary professional service corporations have been readily available to professionals. As a group, however, nurses have not been included in many of the up-dated state professional service corporation statutes. Therefore, if the nurse entrepreneur is contemplating a business that requires multidisciplinary services, and the option of incorporating such a business structure is not available, then the nurse will have to abandon the idea of a professional service corporation as the choice for that business, and utilize another organizational model for his or her business enterprise.

Professional Association

The professional association option may be available to the nurse entrepreneur in his or her state and, depending on the state statute, may provide an alternative to the prohibition against a multidisciplinary business entity. The attorney consulted by the nurse will need to review the state law to determine if this possibility exists, and if so, what if any restrictions are present. Generally, however, the alternative allows the formation of a professional *association*, as opposed to a corporation or partnership, by identified professional groups, such as nursing and

medicine; requires the establishment of a written association agreement that governs the business entity; and requires that the name of the business utilize the term *associates*, *associated*, or similar title.[9]

Insurance

The nurse entrepreneur will need to explore the various insurance needs he or she will have when initiating a business, and discussing this with the attorney is important. Moreover, the attorney can review policies of insurance being considered or purchased by the nurse and provide him or her with areas of concern that may need to be further explored in consultation with the insurance company and its agent. At a minimum, premises liability insurance and professional liability insurance will be required. Additional insurance concerns depend on whether or not the nurse entrepreneur will hire employees; for example, under state law, employers are mandated to contribute to workers' compensation and unemployment insurance for their employees. Also important to consider, whether or not employees are utilized, is the need for health insurance.

The nurse entrepreneur will need to explore the various insurance needs he or she will have when initiating a business . . .

Premises Liability Insurance

This type of insurance contract protects the physical plant of the business from loss that might occur from fire, water damage, flooding or other natural disasters, and theft. Also important to insure against loss will be the contents of the business office; that is, furniture, equipment, including computers and typewriters, and products, if any, sold or developed by the business. Many premises liability policies offer the replacement of business contents on a current market value basis, while others do not. It is important that the nurse be clear about what type of premises liability policy needs to be purchased.

In addition to protecting the business itself, a premises liability policy also covers injuries to clients that occur at the place of business. For example, if a nurse-midwife provides services at a clinic site, and a client should slip on the clinic floor, any injuries sustained that are found to result from that slip could be covered under the liability policy.

Other situations covered by these policies may include suits against the business owner for other injuries to clients, such as defamation and false imprisonment. Further, coverage may be available for injuries sustained while driving a motor vehicle if in connection with the operation of the business.

Specific exclusions vary from policy to policy, but most often the exclusions include professional liability coverage.

Professional Liability Insurance

Whenever the nurse is providing a *professional* nursing service, such as client counseling, client teaching, or direct nursing care, professional liability insurance is essential. As with premises liability policies, professional liability policies vary, and the nurse will need to be certain that the insurance purchased will adequately cover the nurse's role in the business venture. This will require a thorough review of the policy terms, not only with legal counsel, but with the insurance company and agent as well.

Specific points on which to seek clarification include the type of nursing service(s) covered by the policy; what types of nursing services, if any, are excluded; whether the policy is a claims-made or an occurrence policy (the latter being the better one to purchase if possible); what deductibles, if any, are applicable; and the coverage limits of the policy. Moreover, if the nurse entrepreneur utilizes employees who will provide nursing or other services, the nurse will need to consider providing professional liability insurance coverage for them as well. Conversely, if the business will be contracting with other professionals to provide such services, those professionals will need to be informed that they must carry their own liability insurance and show proof of coverage to the nurse entrepreneur.

Product Liability Insurance

If the nurse entrepreneur will be designing and/or marketing a product to be utilized in health care, such as an operating room instrument or an intravenous device, the state and federal product liability law will need to be carefully reviewed with counsel. An insurance plan also needs to be purchased to insure the nurse entrepreneur against lawsuits based on products liability law. Liability principles in products liability are based in "strict liability" or negligence theories. Because of the uniqueness of this area of law and the potential for culpability due to various roles the nurse entrepreneur may undertake, including a designer or supplier of health care delivery products, adequate and appropriate product liability insurance is a must.

Other Areas

Additional areas that need to be discussed with legal counsel by the nurse entrepreneur will depend on the nature of the business. For example, if employees will be utilized, the nurse must develop an employee handbook, job descriptions, and a policy and procedure manual to aid in establishing the working relationship between those employees and the nurse employer. In addition, mandatory compliance with any employee benefit packages, including but not limited to contributing to workers' compensation funds, will need to be explored. Furthermore, the nurse will want to consult with legal counsel on a regular basis to comply with changes in the law that might occur in relation to employee rights.

Consultation with an Accountant

Retaining an accountant is important to any entrepreneur or business executive, because the financial considerations in running a business are just as important as the legal considerations. As with the attorney consultant, the nurse entrepreneur should select an accountant with whom the many concerns of establishing and maintaining a business can be comfortably discussed and clarified. The accountant-client relationship will continue over time, and therefore it is essential that the accountant selected be accessible and responsive, and informed about the needs and concerns of the nurse entrepreneur. Identifying that type of accountant may be initially difficult if the nurse has not consulted with an accountant in the past, but referral sources to assist the nurse include the attorney consultant, professional associations for accountants, and colleagues or friends utilizing accountant services.

Although the exact topics to be discussed with the accountant will vary based on the nature of the nurse entrepreneur's business, there are several areas that should be explored regardless of the type of business. Those areas include tax implications of the business structure, implications of various financing options for the business, and establishing a bookkeeping system for the enterprise.

Tax Implications

Regardless of what form the organization of the business takes, there is no doubt that any and all income derived from the business must be declared to the Internal Revenue Service and state tax offices pursuant to federal and state tax laws. How these laws affect the business structures varies, however. For example, if the business is organized as a sole proprietorship, income is reported through the owner's social security number, and any income that remains after legitimate expenses are deducted becomes profit assessed to the sole owner. When operating a business as a sole proprietor, estimated

income tax payments may need to be paid to ensure that adequate tax payments are being made throughout the taxable year.

Regardless of what form the organization of the business takes, there is no doubt that any and all income derived from the business must be declared . . . pursuant to federal and state tax laws.

If the nurse entrepreneur decides to establish the business as a corporation, different tax rules apply. For example, any and all dividends paid to shareholders must be declared as income, in addition to any profit the corporation possesses. Of course, profit exists only after legitimate expenses are deducted, but federal tax laws have greatly decreased the ability of the corporation to fully deduct expenses.

The nurse entrepreneur will want to carefully evaluate the best business structure in light of the tax laws to enable the business to receive maximum benefit from the current law.

Financing the Business

Whatever form the business takes, financing it adequately is one of the most important aspects of establishing an enterprise. If the business is "undercapitalized," it may not be given the chance to prove itself in the long run. Therefore the nurse entrepreneur will need to carefully determine how much will be needed to get the business "up and running"; how income will be generated and where the income will come from; how much to pay in employees' salaries, if they are to be used; and how long, if at all, the nurse can exist without personal income from the business. The accountant can help the nurse estimate those costs and suggest the best way to deal with financing, especially as it relates to obtaining the maximum benefits in terms of tax liability. For example, it may be best for the nurse entrepreneur to combine a number of financing possibilities—a small bank loan and personal finances—rather than borrowing all of the money from a bank. Or, it may be best to explore financing from government agencies, such as the Small Business Administration. If any type of loan is received, the nurse entrepreneur will want the accountant and attorney to review the document for guidance as to how it will affect tax, and other, liabilities.

Bookkeeping

The nurse entrepreneur will save much time and anguish if a good system of bookkeeping is established from the start of the business and carried out faithfully as the business develops and grows. The accountant's advice can be invaluable. Documentation of income received, expenses paid, equipment purchased, and salaries of employees and the business owners or officers are just a few areas that must be explored. Detailed receipts of equipment purchased and expenses paid are vital. Documents supporting compliance with state laws requiring employer contributions to unemployment compensation and workers' compensation funds will also be necessary. Once established, the bookkeeping system stands as a ready defense should state or federal agencies request documentation of the business operation, and also provides a quick source of information needed by the accountant when preparing the business income tax returns.

Other Consultants

In addition to conferring with the consultants already discussed, additional support and information can be obtained through consultants specific to the nurse entrepreneur's needs. Additional ones to consider, either initially or at some future time in the business' growth, would include an employee benefits counselor, a marketing and/or advertising agent, if appropriate, an attorney specializing in patent, trademark, and copyright law, a financial planner, and a personal banker.

ANTITRUST CONCERNS

Assuming that the nurse entrepreneur is able to successfully master the maze of setting up a business, another obstacle will loom on the horizon—competition, or the resistance of other health care providers to allowing that business to flourish. Although professional groups other than nurses have begun to provide health care services in nontraditional roles and settings, this resistance is keenly felt by nurse entrepreneurs because of what has been termed their dependent role—that is, the delivery of health care under the direct or indirect supervision of a physician, regardless of the health care delivery setting.[10] This "dependent" status, coupled with the economic climate of health care delivery today *and* the positive impact that nurses functioning in nontraditional roles and settings have had on providing quality patient care at reasonable rates, has set the stage for attempts to limit, restrict, and/or boycott nurse-owned businesses.

Types of Barriers for Nurse Entrepreneurs

Many types of trade restraints on a nurse entrepreneur's practice have been identified. Four will be discussed: licensing constraints; limitations on, or nonexistence of, third-party reimbursement; inability to obtain admitting privileges to health care facilities; and inability to obtain physician supervisors or collaborators.[11]

Licensing Restrictions

Licensing restrictions effectively limit any nurse's practice. For the nurse entrepreneur, if the state nurse practice act does not provide for more "independent" practice on the part of the nurse, this restriction can quite literally sound the "death knell" for the nurse contemplating a nontraditional role if that role and the setting in which the care is to be delivered are inconsistent with the state statute. Facing a potential complaint filed by the state attorney's office alleging the unauthorized practice of medicine, for example, may simply be too much for many nurses to risk, even if the judgment ultimately favors the nurse, as was the case in *Sermchief v. Gonzales*, discussed in Chapter 21.

> *Many types of trade restraints on a nurse entrepreneur's practice have been identified . . . : licensing constraints; limitations on, or nonexistence of, third-party reimbursement; inability to obtain admitting privileges . . . ; and inability to obtain physician supervisors or collaborators.*

Reimbursement Concerns

Similarly, the inability of the nurse entrepreneur to count on payment of fees for nursing care from third-party payors, whether the services provided occur in a home, hospital, or clinic, effectively destroys the financial viability of the enterprise. Figures indicate that, for example, approximately six of seven Americans have some form of health insurance.[12] The types of health insurance plans include Medicare and Medicaid, employer-sponsored programs, and many managed care plans. Clearly, if a patient cannot utilize health insurance benefits to cover the cost(s) of being seen by a nurse, the patient will simply not consider seeking out those services regardless of the quality of care provided.

Inability to Obtain Admitting Privileges

To the nurse entrepreneur providing care to clients in an outpatient clinic, or to a nurse-midwife needing to utilize a hospital's services to deliver a patient's child, lack of admitting privileges effectively renders the nurse entrepreneur's services worthless. Although some institutions have granted admitting privileges to certain groups of nurse entrepreneurs, such as nurse-midwives, such privileges are clearly under the control of the medical staff, who continue to see *any* nontraditional health care provider of similar services as a potential threat to their own practice. As a result, those nurses who have obtained staff/admitting privileges are in the minority.

Lack of Physician Supervisors or Collaborators

Regardless of what state statutory framework exists in relation to expanded nurse roles, few, if any, allow the nurse to function independently of the physician. Thus, physician backup is essential to ensure that the nurse entrepreneur is practicing "nursing" as opposed to "medicine." This backup may take the form of a joint practice or a corporation. Or it may take the form of an arrangement with a physician for supervision, standing orders, and utilization of the physician for admissions to the appropriate health care facility. In either case, if no such physician collaboration or supervision exists, the nurse entrepreneur cannot deliver nursing services without risking liability for the unauthorized practice of medicine. Furthermore, many patients will not consider a nurse for the provision of nursing services unless there is clear ability to obtain access to whatever health care delivery system may be needed.

ANTITRUST LAWS AND THEIR IMPACT ON TRADE RESTRICTIONS

Antitrust laws, both on the federal and state level, prohibit anticompetitive measures, such as contracts, monopolies, boycotts, or other conduct that effectively constrains commerce or trade. The main federal antitrust laws are the Sherman Antitrust Act, the Clayton Act, and the Federal Trade Commission Act, all of which prohibit anticompetitive measures among states—that is, affecting interstate commerce—and among foreign nations. A proven violation of the federal laws may be enforced by one or both agencies empowered to administer and enforce the federal antitrust laws: the Department of Justice (Antitrust Division) and the Federal Trade Commission. Criminal and/or civil liability is possible for proven violations. Likewise, state antitrust laws ban anticompetitive measures within the respective state and, if proven, also result in civil and/or criminal sanctions.

Antitrust laws ... prohibit anticompetitive measures, such as contracts, monopolies, boycotts, or other conduct that effectively constrains commerce or trade.

The Sherman Act

The Sherman Act basically forbids any measure that effectively limits competition in interstate commerce and trade among foreign nations. Composed of Sections 1 and 2, it prohibits contractual relationships, "combinations and conspiracies" that restrain trade, and monopolies, "attempted monopolies and conspiracies to monopolize."[13]

The Clayton Act

This Act, and its Amendment known as the Robinson-Patman Act, bans price fixing and exclusive dealings involving contracts and tying arrangements that substantially lessen competition. Furthermore, it outlaws any merger, acquisition, or joint venture by corporate entities that

may result in a monopoly anywhere in the country by any line of commerce.[14]

The Federal Trade Commission Act

This federal law, enforced by the Federal Trade Commission, and empowered only to bring civil actions against alleged offenders, bans any and all unfair methods of competition and unfair deceptive practices or acts, which include false or misleading advertising or misrepresentations to the public.[15]

Specific Applications of Federal Antitrust Laws

In addition to prohibiting the above-described measures, other key factors must exist before one or more of the acts will apply. Often an "agreement" or "conspiracy" must exist between distinct individuals, groups of individuals, or entities that negatively affects competition. Once such an agreement or conspiracy has been found to exist, then the court must determine if the agreement is a *per se* violation of the Act; that is, if it is so potentially harmful to competition that nothing will justify its existence.[16] Price fixing, tying arrangements (one party sells a product—e.g., durable medical equipment—only on the condition the buyer purchase another product from the seller—e.g., home care intravenous equipment), and boycotts (attempting to refuse to deal with certain health care providers or provider groups to prevent their presence in the market place) have been found by the courts to be *per se* violations.[17]

If no *per se* violation exists, the court hears evidence concerning the intent of the agreement and its effect on competition and the marketplace. This has been called the "rule-of-reason" test, meaning that if the agreement does not "unreasonably" restrain trade, there is no violation of Section 1 of the Act.[18]

In the health care arena, the courts have critically analyzed whether conduct alleged to be anticompetitive really is so or whether it is motivated by "legitimate" objectives such as concern for quality patient care or safety, and whether there is an adverse effect on quality, price, or availability of services.[19] When the conduct can clearly be supported by a legitimate basis and does not adversely affect the marketplace, courts usually do not rule against the conduct.

In addition to the above analysis, the court also evaluates other factors, including the pertinent market for the product or service, the applicable geographic market for the product or service, and whether or not "monopoly power" (the power to control prices or exclude competition) is possessed by the alleged violation in the relevant market.

State Laws

If an agreement between two or more separate persons or organizations does not negatively affect interstate commerce, but does affect competition within a state, then a state's antitrust law may apply to that alleged limitation on competition and the marketplace. For example, Illinois' *Antitrust Act* was passed to promote the unhampered growth of commerce and industry within Illinois by banning restraints of trade, such as monopolies, price fixing, and allocating or dividing customers or supplies.[20] In addition to criminal sanctions, the Act provides for civil remedies against any person, corporation, or group, including injunctions, divestiture of property, and dissolution of domestic corporations or associations.[21]

Exceptions to Antitrust Laws

The federal and respective state antitrust laws both contain exemptions or exceptions to the general prohibition on restraining trade. In addition to the pivotal question of whether the alleged conduct affects interstate commerce (federal law) or competition within a state (state law), other general exemptions and exceptions include (1) activities of labor organizations or their members; (2) the purchase of stock for investment purposes not intended to lessen

competition; and (3) religious and charitable activities of not-for-profit organizations that are exclusively religious or charitable. Additionally, under the McCarren-Ferguson Act the "business of insurance," when regulated by state law and such regulation is not coercive, intimidating, or a boycott, is also exempt from the antitrust laws.[22]

The federal antitrust laws also provide an exception for application of those laws to peer review activities required under the Health Care Quality Improvement Act. However, it is important to note that the Health Care Quality Improvement Act's protection is narrowly defined in terms of its requirements for protection and the type of conduct it covers.[23] For example, a court would probably not grant immunity for alleged anticompetitive behavior by any professional association, such as the American Medical Association, that did not allow a physician membership in its organization because the physician had established a joint practice with a nurse-midwife.[24]

Implications for Nurse Entrepreneurs

At least one antitrust case involving nurses in independent practice has been decided that illustrates the concepts, principles, and theories discussed thus far. It is interesting that of all the antitrust methods possible to use against nurse entrepreneurs, two that seem to occur most often are the tying arrangement and the boycott. One well-known case that illustrates the illegality of a boycott against a nurse anesthetist is presented in Key Case 22–1.

The decision in the *Oltz* case is an exception to the general lack of success experienced by entrepreneurs challenging practice arrangements, including exclusive contracts with a group of providers, as an illegal boycott.[26] Even so, the nurse entrepreneur who believes that such illegal action may be occurring must obtain a legal opinion as to his or her possibility of success if a suit is contemplated under Section 1 of the Sherman Act.

KEY CASE 22–1   Oltz v. St. Peter's Community Hospital (1988)[25]

FACTS: The nurse anesthetist plaintiff, Tafford Oltz, was providing anesthesia services to St. Peter's Hospital in Helena, Montana, the only hospital of two in the city that provided services to the general public and was able to offer surgery services. The arrangement Mr. Oltz had with the hospital was an independent contractor arrangement; that is, he provided services, submitted his fee to the hospital—not the patient—and the contractual arrangement was on a month-by-month basis. When Mr. Oltz began his arrangement with the hospital, there were three anesthesiologists also working for the hospital, but that number increased to four shortly after Mr. Oltz began working with the hospital. It became clear that the plaintiff's services were in direct competition with the anesthesiologists' services because of Oltz's popularity with the surgical staff and his lower fees for the anesthesia services he rendered. During this period of discontent among the anesthesiologists, they decided to organize the anesthesia services into a Department of Anesthesia. With the hospital administrator and board apprised of the actions of the anesthesiologists, Oltz was taken off the anesthesia call schedule, and policies were adopted requiring supervision of anesthesia services solely by anesthesiologists (prior to the policy, they could be supervised by the surgeon or obstetrician). The hospital eventually cancelled his contract with the hospital.

Oltz's contract was reinstated, however, after Mr. Oltz's attorney and the State's Attorney General's Office wrote the hospital, threatening to sue if the contract cancellation was not rescinded. Although the contract was going to be reinstated, three of the four anesthesiologists threatened to leave, and the board then entered into an exclusive anesthesia contract with the anesthesiologists in Helena. Mr. Oltz was offered a salaried position at $40,000 a year, but he refused the offer, and filed suit against the hospital and the four anesthesiologists, alleging a violation of Section 1 of the Sherman Act in that the defendants had conspired to boycott his services and to exclude his services from the marketplace.

Hospital found to conspire to boycott nurse anesthetist's services

TRIAL COURT: The Federal Trial Court for the District of Montana, after the four doctors settled with Mr. Oltz and paid him damages, found for the plaintiff. Because the verdict also involved the awarding of damages to Mr. Oltz that were contested by both parties, both sought an appeal of the trial court's decision.

APPEALS COURT: The 9th Circuit Court of Appeals affirmed the trial court's decision and remanded the case back to that court on certain issues. Specifically, the appeals court held that competition for anesthesia services was severely restricted as a result of the actions of the hospital, as evidenced by increased prices for such services and by

Anesthesia services severely restricted because of

Continued on following page

KEY CASE 22-1   Oltz v. St. Peter's Community Hospital (1988)[25] Continued

exclusive arrangement with anesthesiologists

excluding Mr. Oltz's services from the marketplace; that the anesthesiologist and the hospital's interests were different enough to allow the application of the Sherman Act to the hospital; that the relevant market for anesthesia services was from the area around the hospital; that a conspiracy existed to exclude Mr. Oltz's services; and that a new trial on the damages awarded to Mr. Oltz should take place.

A conspiracy to boycott services did exist

At the trial for damages, Oltz was awarded a significant monetary award of three times his actual losses because of the defendants' conduct ("treble damages").

ANALYSIS: The Oltz case is an important one because it illustrates the successful application of the Sherman Act to a situation in which quality services were being offered at a lower price to the public, and it was that economic competition that affected two significant areas of anesthesia services in the marketplace—the anesthesia services provided by the nurse anesthetist and the anesthesiologists and the resulting contest for staff privileges. It is also important in that the case deals with a rural hospital, and it may be that in rural areas, competition must be more carefully safeguarded, especially when such competition is limited initially simply because the choices of services in the marketplace are fewer than in urban areas.

It is interesting that of all the antitrust methods possible to use against nurse entrepreneurs, two that seem to occur most often are the tying arrangement and the boycott.

The nurse entrepreneur must also keep in mind that litigation under the antitrust laws is difficult because of its highly technical and complex nature. For example, in a United States Supreme Court case, *Jefferson Parish Hospital v. Hyde*,[27] the Court held that an anesthesiologist's claim of the establishment by the hospital of an exclusive agreement for anesthesia services with a group of which he was not a member excluded him from the provision of those services and, in effect, established a tying arrangement, was not a violation of the Sherman Act. Specifically, Hyde alleged that because of the exclusive arrangement, patients could not obtain surgery at the hospital without selecting the anesthesiologist group the hospital exclusively contracted with to provide anesthesia services.

The Court, in ruling against Hyde, held that no *per se* violation of the Act had occurred because patients could be admitted to another hospital in the area if they wanted to. Because the exclusive arrangement was not a *per se* violation, the Court then applied the rule-of-reason test. The Court opined that because patients could seek hospitalization elsewhere, no reasonable restraint on competition existed, and no tying arrangement was proven.

For the nurse entrepreneur, the *Hyde* decision

clearly indicates that in order to challenge a consumer's inability to select the nurse as a health care provider because the nurse is not included in a group of providers the health care delivery system uses, he or she must show that (1) the market for the services provided is the same for both provider(s); (2) that market power is under the control of the target facility or group; and (3) that there is a clear, documented demand for the nurse's services.[28]

> *The nurse entrepreneur will need to stand ready to challenge conduct and arrangements that interfere with the nurse's right to provide quality, low-cost care to consumers and to practice in a manner consistent with the nurse's education, scope of practice, and experience.*

What impact the antitrust laws will ultimately have on managed care and the many health care delivery organizational arrangements that are developing remains to be seen. The nurse contemplating the establishment of a business within this ever-changing health care delivery environment will need to watch carefully for developments in this area. Because it is estimated that, as of July 1, 1995, 54 million Americans (21% of the population) are enrolled in HMOs,[29] the nurse entrepreneur must be able to provide care with or within these organizational structures in order to be successful in a business established to provide health care services. Will exclusive arrangements with certain providers continue to be upheld by the court? Will mergers of major hospitals eliminate competition in the selection of health care and health care providers by consumers? Will provider networks illegally

set fees in violation of the Federal Trade Commission mandates and the antitrust laws?[30]

Although the answers to these and other questions involving antitrust law cannot be easily answered, the nurse entrepreneur will need to stand ready to challenge conduct and arrangements that interfere with the nurse's right to provide quality, low-cost care to consumers and to practice in a manner consistent with the nurse's education, scope of practice, and experience.

SUMMARY OF PRINCIPLES AND APPLICATIONS

Although there are other areas of concern of which the nurse entrepreneur will also want to be cognizant, such as professional liability concerns when delivering patient care and insurance fraud and abuse if receiving third-party reimbursement under Medicare, Medicaid, or other contracts, the nurse entrepreneur will be well prepared to meet the obstacles facing him or her if preparation, hard work, and continued updating of information is obtained concerning the business established. Clearly the following principles are essential:

▼ A thorough assessment of self, the business structure, and the service to be provided is vital.

▼ Consultation with experts in the fields of business, law, accounting, and other identified areas is mandatory *before* one sets out to establish a business venture.

▼ Ongoing relationships with experts are necessary to ensure compliance with current, and changing, laws when maintaining a business.

▼ The organizational structure of the business—whether it be a sole proprietorship, partnership, professional association, or corporation—must be carefully decided after fully exploring the tax, accounting, and legal ramifications of that structure.

▼ The potential for antitrust concerns—whether through the establishment of a monopoly, a tying arrangement, or a conspiracy—must be kept in mind when establishing a business that may compete with other businesses or health care providers in the marketplace.

▼ The major federal antitrust laws include the Sherman Act, the Clayton Act, and the Federal Trade Commission Act. Generally all three prohibit any restriction of competition in the marketplace, with exceptions to that rule including activities that do not include interstate commerce, state action(s), and labor organizations' activities.

▼ In addition to federal antitrust laws, state statutes concerning preserving competition in the marketplace must also be reviewed. Although often similar, if not identical, to the federal antitrust laws, one area in which they are different is in the area of requiring *interstate* commerce to be affected by the alleged conduct.

▼ Nurse entrepreneurs must be ready to challenge obstacles to the establishment of their businesses not only in court, but through the legislative and other processes in which deterrents exist to the expansion and growth of autonomous practice.

TOPICS FOR FURTHER INQUIRY

1. Develop an interview guide for use with interviewing at least three nurse entrepreneurs currently in business in your state. Evaluate areas of difficulty for the nurse entrepreneur and how those areas of difficulty were resolved. Identify and analyze how each nurse entrepreneur obtained information to establish and run his or her business. Identify any anticompetitive experiences the nurses had to resolve, and how they did so.

2. Write a paper on the types of business structures available to a nurse in your state. Compare and contrast each type of structure and analyze how any limitations on a nurse's business may affect antitrust, or other, laws (e.g., state nurse practice act).

3. Develop a proposal to amend one of the federal antitrust laws in view of the changes in health care delivery. Include such areas as who would be affected by the proposal, how changes in initiating a case alleging a violation of the proposal would be handled, and the purpose of the proposed changes.

4. Conduct a confidential survey in your community to identify those health care delivery systems that allow advanced practice nurses to obtain admitting privileges in their facility. Analyze how that process is different, if at all, for other health care providers with admitting privileges. Also evaluate the nurse's ability to obtain admitting privileges in more than one facility. Suggest changes in current processes or propose procedures for initiation of admitting privileges in the facilities surveyed.

REFERENCES

1. Gerry Vogel and Nancy Doleysh. *Entrepreneuring: A Nurse's Guide To Starting A Business.* 2nd Edition. New York: The National League for Nursing, 1994, 4.
2. Laura Bernero Carlson. *The Nurse Entrepreneur: A Reference Manual for Business Design.* Kansas City, Mo: American Nurses' Association and Florida Nurses' Association, 1989, vii, *citing* New York State Nurses' Association, 1986.
3. American Nurses' Association, Washington, D.C., 1985.
4. American Association of Occupational Health Nurses, Atlanta, Georgia, 1994.
5. Vogel and Doleysh, *supra* note 1, at 9–10.
6. Myrtle Aydelotte, Mary Hardy, and Kathryn Hope. *Nurses in Private Practice: Characteristics, Organizational Arrangements and Reimbursement Policy.* Kansas City, Mo: The American Nurses Foundation, 1988, 30.
7. Henry Campbell Black. *Black's Law Dictionary.* 6th Edition. St. Paul: West Publishing Company, 1991, 773.
8. *Id.* at 238.
9. See, for example, 805 ILCS 305/0.01 *et seq.* (1992) (Illinois).
10. Bonnie Faherty, "Advanced Practice Nursing: What's All the Fuss?" 2(3) *Journal of Nursing Law* (1995), 9–17.
11. *Id.*
12. Ann F. Callard, "Paying for Health Care: Trends, Issues, Future Directions," *Current Issues in Nursing.* 4th Edition. Joanne McCloskey and Helene Grace, Editors. St. Louis: C.V. Mosby, 1994, 508.
13. 15 U.S.C. Sections 1 and 2 (1914).
14. 15 U.S.C. Sections 13, 14, 15, and 18 (1914).
15. 15 U.S.C. Section 45 (1914).

16. H. Guy Collier and James H. Sneed, "Exclusive Contracts between Hospitals and Hospital-Based Physicians: Recent Developments," *1993 Health Law Handbook.* Alice Gosfield, Editor. Deerfield, Ill: Clark Boardman Callaghan, 1993, 100–105.

17. *Id.*

18. *Id.*

19. David Marz and Christopher Murphy, "Antitrust Enforcement Encourages Health Care Providers to Cooperate Procompetitively," 3 *Annals of Health Law* (1994), 1–27.

20. 740 ILCS 10/3 (1982).

21. *Id.* at 10/7.

22. See, for example, U.S.C.A. Chapter 15 Section 17 (1914); 740 ILCS 10/5 (1987); 15 U.S.C.A. Section 10/2(b).

23. Ila S. Rothschild, "The Health Care Quality Improvement Act and the National Practitioner Data Bank: Current Issues and Emerging Legal and Operational Trends," *1993 Health Law Handbook.* Alice Gosfield, Editor. Deerfield, Ill: Clark Boardman Callaghan, 1993, 321–330.

24. Debra Gilmore, "The Antitrust Implications of Boycotts by Health Care Professionals: Professional Standards, Professional Ethics and the First Amendment," XIV *American Journal of Law & Medicine* (1988), 238–240.

25. 861 F. 2d 1440 (9th Circuit 1988).

26. Collier and Sneed, *supra* note 16, at 105.

27. 466 U.S. 2 (1984).

28. Karla Kelly, "Nurse Practitioner Challenges to the Orthodox Structure of Health Care Delivery: Regulation and Restraints on Trade," *American Journal of Law & Medicine* (1985), 196.

29. Emily Friedman, "Capitation, Integration, and Managed Care: Lessons From Early Experiments," *JAMA* 275 (March 27, 1996), 957.

30. For interesting overviews and implications of these questions, see, for example, Collier and Sneed, *supra* note 16; Marz and Murphy, *supra* note 19; James C. Dechene, "Application of Merger Guidelines to Hospital Consolidations," *1993 Health Law Handbook.* Alice Gosfield, Editor. Deerfield, Ill: Clark Boardman Callaghan, 1993, 29–45.

Interview Guidelines and
Assessment Criteria for
Choosing an Attorney

As this book illustrates, a nurse may be involved in various types of lawsuits. Whether a defendant in a professional malpractice suit or a suit involving another type of tort, or a plaintiff whose constitutional right of due process has been violated by a public academic institution, legal services are necessary to properly defend or initiate a suit.

A lawsuit, however, is not the only reason a nurse may need legal services. For a nurse entrepreneur, advice is necessary to establish and run a business. A nurse may need a contract developed or interpreted before signing, or a staff nurse may seek an opinion about practice concerns and liabilities.

Despite the many situations that require an attorney, nurses, and the general public, know little about the law, attorneys, or how to obtain legal advice or representation. Whether a clear legal problem exists, or when seeking advice and counsel before a problem arises, identifying an attorney to work with is essential. Competent representation is imperative if the nurse is involved in a specific case. Similarly, early competent counsel and advice are indispensable in a situation that might lead to future legal ramifications for the nurse.

This appendix provides general guidelines for the nurse in seeking legal counsel, regardless of the situation within which that need arises.

Some Information about Lawyers

A lawyer (also called an attorney, counselor, attorney at law, barrister, or solicitor) is an individual who has a minimum of a bachelor's degree *and* a law degree (J.D. or L.L.B.). Some attorneys, however, have additional degrees. Master's degrees in law (L.L.M.) are possible in

tax, patent, and health care law. Those attorneys who practiced another profession prior to law may have graduate degrees in that particular field. For example, lawyers who practiced nursing prior to law may have a Master's degree in nursing.

The basic law degree is granted after completion of law school, which generally takes 3 years if one attends full time. Master's programs in law are usually 1 to 2 years in length.

To practice law, the law school graduate must apply to sit for the state bar examination. The examination is given twice yearly (February and July) throughout the country. The application process to sit for the bar is detailed and includes the applicant providing information concerning education, jobs held, all addresses lived at, involvement in any lawsuits as a defendant or plaintiff, and character references.

Once completed, the application and the information contained in it are reviewed by the state supreme court (or its committee). Essentially the character and fitness of the applicant to sit for the bar, and ultimately to practice law in that state, are evaluated.

If the applicant is approved to sit for the bar examination and passes, the individual is issued a license to practice law in the state. Swearing-in ceremonies are held in which the attorney takes an oath to, among other things, defend the federal and state constitutions. The lawyer is then licensed to practice law in the state and must comply with state requirements concerning that practice, including, but not limited to, types of practice, advertising, license renewal mandates, and professional ethics.

The lawyer who is licensed to practice in a particular state may also want to practice in the federal court system. In some states, such as

Illinois, a specific application to the federal court system is necessary to do trial work in the federal courts located in that state. A lawyer may also choose to apply for admission to practice before the United States Supreme Court.

Identifying the Legal Problem

The first task for the nurse is to identify the legal problem that exists. This is important because it helps identify the type of attorney needed and also facilitates early intervention. For example, if a nurse is served with a summons and complaint naming him or her as a defendant in a professional negligence lawsuit, an attorney who concentrates his or her practice (or specializes) in the defense of malpractice suits is necessary. If, in contrast, the nurse employee is concerned about being disciplined by the employer for something that occurred at work, consultation with an attorney with experience in employment law is wise.

How to Find an Attorney

Once the legal problem is identified, the next step for the nurse is to find an attorney for the specific purpose of determining whether or not his or her services will be utilized. This is perhaps the most difficult step for the nurse. The local yellow pages and radio and television ads are several sources of identifying attorneys who practice in a particular state. Although readily available, these sources may not be the most efficient ways to locate an attorney.

Other sources that may be helpful used in conjunction with the above, or alone, include:

▼ Referral from a friend or colleague who has utilized an attorney for the same or similar problem

▼ Referral from another attorney whose services have been used for other legal advice or services

▼ Local or state bar associations (many operate lawyer referral services to the public)

▼ Other professional associations such as the American Association of Nurse Attorneys, state nurses' associations or organizations (See Appendix C)

▼ An attorney who has presented a seminar or presented a paper at a professional meeting

▼ Information services (directories, special yellow pages) about attorneys available in public libraries or law libraries (located at the local or state courthouse)

▼ A prepaid legal service plan, if a member

▼ Legal clinics or legal aid organizations, if low-cost legal services are needed and one is eligible

If the nurse is covered under a professional liability insurance policy and is named in a suit, contacting the insurance carrier is necessary, as discussed in Chapter 4. An attorney will be assigned to the case. Although the nurse may not have control over the attorney who is assigned to the case, an evaluation of the attorney utilizing the guidelines below can be made by the nurse. If the nurse is not comfortable with the attorney, the nurse should discuss this discomfort with the attorney and the insurance company. If the difficulties identified by the nurse cannot be resolved, another attorney can be assigned to the case.

How to Select an Attorney

Once the nurse has identified a potential source for an attorney, determination of *which* attorney will be utilized or retained is next. The selection process can occur either during a face-to-face meeting with the attorney or an initial telephone consultation, although a meeting is preferable. In either case, a fee may or may not be charged by the attorney for the consultation. This should be clarified by the nurse at the onset of the consultation.

The decision to select a particular attorney is best achieved by formulating certain questions concerning the attorney, the practice, the particular case or situation, the legal work required, and the nurse's role in the case. In addition, the nurse's impressions of the attorney and the ability to work with him or her are also important areas to explore.

These areas are important because the nurse will be paying the attorney to represent him or her in all dealings concerning the legal matter in question. Therefore, selecting an attorney whom the nurse trusts and is comfortable with is just as important as evaluating the attorney's skill and expertise.

The following are sample questions for the nurse to consider.

The Attorney

How long has the attorney been practicing law?

How many similar cases has the attorney handled?

Does the attorney represent individuals? Businesses and organizations? Both?

If the attorney cannot or will not take the case, can a referral be made?

When is the best time to contact the attorney during office hours?

If the case is taken, how does the attorney handle keeping clients abreast of developments (e.g., phone calls, letters)?

The Attorney's Law Practice

How much will the case and services cost? There are several fee arrangement possibilities listed in Table A–1.

Will the agreement be placed in writing and signed by both the attorney and the client?

Will a monthly bill (invoice) be sent indicating the time spent on the case or situation?

Will the attorney be the only lawyer working on the case or situation? If not, who else will be? What will be the additional cost to the nurse, if it exists?

What are the chances of success with the case or situation?

What strategies will the attorney utilize in the case or situation?

How long will a resolution of the particular problem take?

If an appeal is necessary, what additional costs will there be? What additional time frames can be expected? What are the chances of success on appeal?

If the situation involves criminal law or concerns, will the attorney (or firm) represent the nurse in that case? What additional costs/fees will there be?

When can the nurse expect the attorney to respond to calls or letters (e.g., within 24 hours, by phone, or written correspondence)?

The Nurse Client's Role

The nurse plays an important part in the overall success of any legal matter, whether during the initial consultation or during the progression of the case or legal matter. The attorney can do his or her job only if apprised accurately, completely, and honestly about the legal matter. Therefore, the following are questions for the nurse client to explore with the attorney concerning his or her role:

What information or additional documents does the attorney need, both at the initial meeting and afterward?

When should the nurse contact the attorney (e.g., when a new development arises, when documents are received)?

What should the nurse do when anyone in the case or situation contacts the nurse personally (e.g., the attorney for another party, the employer)?

How can the nurse help the attorney with the legal work needed (e.g., gathering information, supplying addresses)?

If the nurse is unclear about what to do in a particular situation after a case has been instituted or an attorney retained, the best approach

TABLE A–1	
Legal Fee Arrangements	
NAME OF ARRANGEMENT	**EXPLANATION**
Contingent fee	Used for civil cases in which the nurse is a plaintiff (e.g., when nurse sues employer for defamation); a percentage of money received for client goes to attorney; nurse must clarify if contingent amount to attorney is from gross amount awarded or deducted after expenses (e.g., court costs, subpoena fees); usual amount is 33⅓%, but some states regulate this arrangement in certain cases (e.g., professional negligence)
Hourly fee	Based on attorney's fixed hourly rate for any and all legal work done, including court appearances, drafting of documents, conferences; out-of-pocket expenses (e.g., court costs, delivery fees) are also billed to client; nurse should clarify if any legal work done is billed at a higher rate (e.g., court appearances)
Retainer fee	Utilized alone or in conjunction with hourly fee; nurse pays certain amount to attorney as initial payment on case or to have attorney available for legal work needed (e.g., establishing a patient care clinic); initial retainer will most probably be supplemented by additional retainers
Flat fee/fee for service	Amount is agreed to for services regardless of amount of legal work needed; used in "simple" or uncomplicated matters (e.g., review of documents or basic advance directive); out-of-pocket expenses billed to client

Data from: Barbara Repa, "When and How to Use a Lawyer," American Bar Association. *You and the Law.* Lincolnwood, IL: Publications International, Ltd., 1990, 8–34; Carmelle Cournoyer. *The Nurse Manager & the Law.* Rockville, MD: Aspen Publishers, Inc., 352–356; Henry Campbell Black. *Black's Law Dictionary.* 6th Edition. St. Paul, MN: West Publishing Company, 1991.

is to contact the attorney before anything is done. Something that the nurse sees as unrelated to the case or legal situation at the time may turn out to be intertwined in it. Therefore, seeking preventive advice from the nurse's attorney is always judicious.

The Nurse's Impressions/Ability to Work with the Attorney

This aspect of the selection process is very important, as discussed earlier. During the initial meeting or telephone conversation, the nurse should rely on what he or she thinks and feels about the attorney. For example:

Is the attorney clear in his or her explanation of the legal issues involved in the case or situation?

Is the attorney's full attention given to the nurse during that time or does the attorney allow other clients or staff to interrupt?

Does the attorney make the nurse feel at ease and appear interested in the case or legal situation?

Does the attorney "pressure" the nurse into making a decision about utilizing the attorney or provide time for the nurse to think about the choice?

Does the attorney interact with the nurse in a respectful manner?

If the nurse client decides to choose the attorney to represent him or her, then that agreement can be formalized and finalized. If, however, the nurse is not comfortable with the attorney, or wishes to explore other attorneys, the nurse should inform the attorney of her decision. The nurse can simply state that some time is needed to think about the information received before deciding whether to retain the attorney's services. As a courtesy, a call to the attorney concerning a decision not to retain his or her services is helpful to the attorney so that the consultation file can be closed.

Professional Responsibilities of the Attorney

An attorney, like any other professional, must conform his or her conduct to ethical rules that govern the practice of law and the representation of clients. The rules are included in a model Code of Professional Responsibility, adopted by the American Bar Association (ABA). Each state has adopted its own code of ethics. Those codes are either an adoption of the entire ABA model code or based on it. In either case, the state code is enforced by the state supreme court's disciplinary committee or commission.

The code of ethics establishes standards of conduct and lists prohibited conduct. If a violation of the code allegedly occurs, a complaint can be made to the committee or commission. The committee or commission investigates the complaint and, if appropriate, determines sanctions against the lawyer after a disciplinary proceeding or other procedures are completed.

Areas included in the code of interest to the nurse client include the requirements of:

▼ Maintaining confidentiality between the attorney and client with exceptions clearly delineated

▼ Representing the client fully, independently, zealously, and within the bounds of the law

▼ Avoiding conflicts of interest between a client and others, including the attorney himself or herself

▼ Withdrawing from representation of a client only in identified situations, with protections afforded the client

The last provision of a state code of ethics is important. Although the nurse client is able to terminate the attorney-client relationship at any time, the attorney is not able to do so. Rather, the attorney can end the representation only when, as examples, the client asks the attorney to do something illegal (e.g., destroy evidence) or utilize the judicial system inappropriately (e.g., to harass someone or obstruct justice). If a case is pending in court or other legal proceeding, withdrawal can occur only with permission of the court.

Regardless of the reasons for the withdrawal and when it takes place, every effort must be made by the attorney to avoid "unduly prejudicing" the client. This includes, of course, providing adequate notice to the client and the court or other tribunal and providing the client with his or her file, along with any original documents.

When Difficulties Arise between Attorney and Client

If the nurse client experiences problems with the selected attorney, a frank discussion with him or her should be initiated by the nurse. It is hoped that identifying the problems will aid in their resolution. If not, the nurse should terminate the relationship and obtain the services of another attorney if the legal case/situation has not been resolved.

If the nurse believes the attorney may have violated any of the ethical rules, the attorney should be reported to the state disciplinary committee or commission. In addition, if the nurse believes the attorney handled the case or situation negligently, then consultation with an attorney who handles professional liability suits against attorneys is advised. Moreover, if the attorney's conduct violates any criminal laws (e.g., personal use of the client's money, which constitutes theft), then contacting the police or state's attorney or state's attorney general's office is advisable.

The nurse who takes a course in law and nursing or who seeks out legal information for any other reason needs to have a basic understanding of legal research so that a particular law, regulation, or case can be easily located. Law libraries are organized differently than other libraries with which the nurse is familiar. In addition, legal research is also unique in comparison with the research the nurse does when preparing a paper or obtaining information for his or her clinical research project.

Although the most comprehensive source of legal information can be found in a law library (e.g., at a law school or court building), some legal references may also be found in local public libraries (e.g., state statute books, texts). Re-

gardless of location, certain basic information is necessary.

Legal References

Many types of legal references are helpful when one is doing legal research. Similar to nursing research, the sources can be described as *primary* and *secondary*. Obviously the use of primary sources is preferred and more scholarly than use of secondary sources. In fact, in the law, relying on secondary sources can be disastrous because laws and case decisions can and do change on a regular basis.

Some of the more common primary sources are listed in Table B–1.

TABLE B–1
Selected Primary Legal References

NAME	STATE/ FEDERAL	INFORMATION INCLUDED	SAMPLE CITATION
United States Code (U.S.C.)	F	Laws of federal gov't	42 U.S.C. S 1983 (1982 & supplement)
Code of Federal Regulations (C.F.R.)	F	Regulations promulgated by rule-making to enforce federal laws	40 C.F.R. S 405.53 (1980)
Illinois Compiled Statutes (ILCS)	S	Laws of the state of Illinois	401 ILCS 50/4 (1989 & supplement)
Illinois Administrative Code (IL. Ad. Code)	S	Regulations promulgated by rule-making to enforce state laws	68 IL. Adm. Code 1220.110 *et seq.*
United States Supreme Court Decisions (U.S.)	F	Supreme Court opinions	*Roe v. Wade,* 410 U.S. 113 (1973)
Federal Reporter (F. 2d)	F	U.S. District Courts of Appeals Decisions, Second Series	*Kranson v. Valley Crest Nursing Home,* 755 F. 2d 46 (3rd Cir.) (1985)
Northwestern Reporter (N.W. 2d)	S	Unofficial reporting system for most state appellate decisions in region covered (North and South Dakota, Nebraska, Iowa, Minnesota, Wisconsin, and Michigan), Second Series	*In re Kowalski,* 382 N.W. 2d, 862 (Minn. Ct. App. 1986)

Data from: *A Uniform System of Citation.* 14th Edition. Cambridge, Mass: Harvard Law Review Association, 1986.

TABLE B–2
Selected Secondary Legal Resources

NAME AND PUBLISHER	INFORMATION INCLUDED	SAMPLE CITATION
Black's Law Dictionary—West Publishing Co.	Definitions of legal terms and phrases	H. C. Black, Black's Law Dictionary (6th ed. 1991)
Journal of Health and Hospital Law—American Academy of Hospital Lawyers and DePaul University College of Law Health Law Institute	Articles on health and hospital law	Brent, The Impaired Nurse: Assisting Treatment to Achieve Continued Employment, 24 J. Health & Hosp. L. 112 (1991)
Personnel Law—Prentice-Hall	Textbook on personnel law	Sovereign, Personnel Law (3rd ed.) (1994)
Medicare and Medicaid Guide—Commerce Clearing House (CCH)	Unofficial compiling of materials from Medicare and Medicaid (also called a "service")	Medicare & Medicaid Guide (CCH) S 1401

Data from: *A Uniform System of Citation.* 14th Edition. Cambridge, Mass: Harvard Law Review Association, 1986.

Secondary sources are those that enhance the primary sources. Some of the more common ones are listed in Table B–2.

Understanding Legal Citations

In Tables B–1 and 2, examples of statute and case citations are listed. Citations must also be understood to find the specific case or statute of interest to the nurse. Samples of statute citations are listed in Table B–3, and examples of case citations in Table B–4.

It should be noted that the researcher may see both the "official" and "unofficial" reporting citations for a case in the citation. If so, the researcher can find the same case using either reporting system available. The following case citation gives both the state (official) and the regional (unofficial) citation:

In re Zagoras' Estate, 11 Ill. App. 3d 355, 296 N.E. 2d 641 (1973).

Also, the history of a case is seen in the case citation. The following citation tells the researcher the path the case has taken in the various courts of the judicial system:

United States v. Eller, 114 F. Supp. 384 (M.D.N.C.), *rev'd*, 208 F. 2d 716 (4th Cir. 1953), *cert. denied*, 347 U.S. 934 (1954).

Analyzing Statutes and Case Decisions

Statutes

When analyzing a statute, it is important to read the act in its entirety to get an overview of its intent and purpose. Most statutes contain the following sections: Title, Legislative Purpose, Definitions, Exceptions, and Penalties for Violations of the act. In addition, most statutes have cross-references, additional references, and cases decided under the act that can help with a more in-depth understanding of the act.

Because laws can change frequently, the nurse must also check the back of each volume of the statute book being used for the "pocket part." The pocket part is published in a thin, tissue-paper supplement that fits into the back cover of each volume. The pocket part contains any

TABLE B–3
Sample Statute Citations

NAME	VOL. NO.	TITLE OF SET	SECTION NO.	YEAR
Administrative Procedure Act (F)	5	U.S.C.	552 *et seq.*	(1946, as amended)
Illinois Nursing Act of 1987 (S)	225	ILCS	65/1 *et seq.*	(1987)

TABLE B–4

Sample Case Citations

NAME	VOL.	REPORTING SET/PAGE	COURT INFO	COMMENTS
Miller v. Spicer	822	F. Supp. 158	(D. Del. 1993)	Miller is the plaintiff, Spicer the defendant
In re Custody of a Minor	434	N.E. 2d 601	(1982)	"In re" means: "in the matter of," when court decides a matter without adversarial parties
People v. Osco Drug	298	N.E. 2d 753	(1973)	In criminal cases, the plaintiff is always the people of the state, as represented by the state's attorney or attorney general

recent changes in the laws contained in the volume (including new court decisions interpreting the particular statute) and must be consulted before research is considered complete.

Cases

Most case decisions are reported in a standard format. The arrangement of the information may vary somewhat, but most often includes:

▼ The case name

▼ Case citation information (e.g., the docket number, date of decision, name of court rendering decision)

▼ A brief case summary, which informs the reader of the facts of the case, lower court decision(s), and how the case came before the deciding court (judicial history)

▼ "Headnote" designations, which inform the reader of the specific points of law discussed in the case

▼ The names of the attorneys for each party in the case, the judge(s) who heard and decided the case, and the names of any judge(s) who did not take part in the decision

▼ The text of the opinion, which includes the facts, identification of the issue(s), the reasoning utilized, the court's decision/holding on each issue and the disposition of the case (e.g., reversal of the lower court decision, remand to the lower court with specific instructions)

▼ The text of any concurring and dissenting opinion(s) of the other judges (e.g., at appellate or state or federal supreme court level)

Any case decision cannot be relied on until it is checked to determine if it is still "good law." Changes in court decisions can occur when, for example, an appellate court (or other higher court) reverses a lower court decision, or an administrative agency decision is judicially reviewed by the appropriate state or federal court.

The process of checking case decisions is called "shepardizing" after the publisher of the soft-cover books that must be consulted (*Shepard's Case Citations*). The researcher must use current case citation and check it in all of the *Shepard's* volumes *after* the date of the decision for guidance as to the case's current status.

Computer-Assisted Legal Research

The use of computers and software in legal research has developed greatly over the past several years. For example, many state and federal statutes are now available on CD-ROM. Although the same principles exist when using the computer (e.g., making sure the case or statute relied on has not been amended, overturned, and the like), the method for doing so is different. Each law library or public library may have a different software package to do the research, especially if state and federal laws are involved. However, one common service for the reporting of cases is LEXIS[R]-NEXIS[R]. LEXIS[R]-NEXIS[R] is a software program for legal research.

appendix c

State Nurses' Associations, State Regulatory Agencies, and Selected Nursing Organizations*

STATE NURSES' ASSOCIATIONS AND
REGULATORY AGENCIES

ALABAMA

Alabama State Nurses Association, 360 N. Hull St., Montgomery 36104–3658

Board of Nursing, RSA Plaza, Suite 250, 770 Washington Ave., Montgomery 36130.

ALASKA

Alaska Nurses Association, 237 East 3rd Ave., Suite 3, Anchorage 99501

Board of Nursing Licensing, Dept. of Commerce & Economic Development, Division of Occupational Licensing, P.O. Box 110806, Juneau 99881

ARIZONA

Arizona Nurses Association, 1850 E. Southern Ave., Suite 1, Tempe 85282–5832

Board of Nursing, 2001 W. Camelback Rd., #350, Phoenix 85015

ARKANSAS

Arkansas Nurses Association, 117 S. Cedar St., Little Rock 72205

Board of Nursing, University Tower Bldg., Suite 800, 1123 S. University Ave., Little Rock 72204

CALIFORNIA

ANA/California, P.O. Box 225, 3010 Wilshire Boulevard, Los Angeles, CA 90010

Board of Registered Nursing, P.O. Box 944210, 400 R St., Suite 4030, Sacramento 95814

COLORADO

Colorado Nurses Association, 5453 E. Evans Place, Denver 80222

Board of Nursing, 1560 Broadway, Suite 670, Denver 80202

CONNECTICUT

Connecticut Nurses Association, 377 Research Parkway, Suite 2D, Meriden 06450

Board of Examiners for Nursing, 410 Capitol Ave., P.O. Box 340308, Hartford 06134

DELAWARE

Delaware Nurses Association, 2634 Capitol Trail, Suite A, Newark 19711

Board of Nursing, Margaret O'Neill Bldg., Federal and Court Sts., P.O. Box 1401, Dover 19903

DISTRICT OF COLUMBIA

District of Columbia Nurses Association, 5100 Wisconsin Ave. NW, Suite 306, Washington 20016

DC Board of Nursing, 614 H St. NW, Washington 20001

FLORIDA

Florida Nurses Association, Box 536985, Orlando 32853

Board of Nursing, 111 E. Coastline Dr., Suite 516, Jacksonville 32202

GEORGIA

Georgia Nurses Association, 1362 W. Peachtree St. NW, Atlanta 30309

Board of Nursing, 166 Pryor St. SW, Suite 400, Atlanta 30303

GUAM

Guam Nurses Association, P.O. Box CG, Agana 96910

Board of Nurse Examiners, Box 2816, Agana 96910

HAWAII

Hawaii Nurses Association, 677 Ala Moana Blvd., Suite 301, Honolulu 96813

*Every attempt has been made to ensure the accuracy of the addresses on this list. However, the reader is encouraged to verify any address listed before relying on it as a correct listing.

Board of Nursing, 1010 Richards St., P.O. Box 3469, Honolulu 96801

IDAHO

Idaho Nurses Association, 200 N. 4th St., Suite 20, Boise 83702

Board of Nursing, 2800 N. 8th St., Suite 210, Boise 83720

ILLINOIS

Illinois Nurses Association, 300 S. Wacker Dr., Suite 2200, Chicago 60606

Department of Professional Regulation, 100 W. Randolph St., 9th Floor, Chicago, 60601

INDIANA

Indiana State Nurses Association, 2915 North High School Rd., Indianapolis 46224–2969

Indiana State Board of Nursing, Health Professions Bureau, 402 W. Washington St., Rm. 041, Indianapolis 46204

IOWA

Iowa Nurses Association, 1501 42nd St., Suite 471, West Des Moines 50266

Board of Nursing, 1223 E. Court, Des Moines 50266

KANSAS

Kansas State Nurses Association, 700 S.W. Jackson, Suite 601, Topeka 66603–3731

Kansas State Board of Nursing, Landon State Office Bldg., 900 SW Jackson, Rm. 551S, Topeka 66612

KENTUCKY

Kentucky Nurses Association, 1400 S. First St., P.O. Box 2616, Louisville 40201

Board of Nursing, 312 Whittington Pkwy., Suite 300, Louisville 40222

LOUISIANA

Louisiana State Nurses Association, 712 Transcontinental Dr., Metairie 70001

Board of Nursing Examiners, Pere Marquette Building, New Orleans 70142

MAINE

Maine State Nurses Association, 295 Water St., P.O. Box 2240, Augusta 04338–2240

Board of Nursing, State House Station 158, Augusta 04333

MARYLAND

Maryland Nurses Association, 849 International Drive, Airport Square 1, Linthicum 21090

Board of Nursing, 4140 Patterson Ave., Baltimore 21215

MASSACHUSETTS

Massachusetts Nurses Association, 340 Turnpike St., Canton 02021

Board of Registration in Nursing, Rm. 1519, 100 Cambridge St., Boston 02202

MICHIGAN

Michigan Nurses Association, 2310 Jolly Oak Rd., Okemos 48864

Board of Nursing, P.O. Box 30018, Lansing 48909

MINNESOTA

Minnesota Nurses Association, 1295 Bandana Blvd. North, Suite 140, St. Paul 55108

Board of Nursing, 2700 University Ave. W, #108, St. Paul 55114

MISSISSIPPI

Mississippi Nurses Association, 135 Bounds St., Suite 100, Jackson 39206

Board of Nursing, 401 Robert E. Lee Building, 239 N. Lamar St., Jackson 39201

MISSOURI

Missouri Nurses Association, 1904 Bubba Lane, Box 105228, Jefferson City 65110

Board of Nursing, 3605 Missouri Blvd., P.O. Box 1337, Jefferson City 65102

MONTANA

Montana Nurses Association, 104 Broadway, Suite G-2, P.O. Box 5718, Helena 59604

Board of Nursing, Dept. of Commerce, Arcade Bldg. Lower Level, 111 N. Jackson, Helena 59620

NEBRASKA

Nebraska Nurses Association, 1430 South St., Suite 202, Lincoln 68502

Board of Nursing, Box 95007, Lincoln 68509

NEVADA

Nevada Nurses Association, 3660 Baker Lane, Suite 104, Reno 89509

Board of Nursing, Suite 116, 1281 Terminal Way, Reno 89502

NEW HAMPSHIRE

New Hampshire Nurses Association, 48 West St., Concord 03301

Board of Nursing, Department of Health and Human Services, 78 Regional Dr., Concord 03301

NEW JERSEY

New Jersey State Nurses Association, 320 W. State St., Trenton 08618

Board of Nursing, 124 Halsey St., P.O. Box 45010, Rm. 508, Newark 07101

NEW MEXICO

New Mexico Nurses Association, 909 Virginia NE, Suite 101, Albuquerque 87108

Board of Nursing, 4253 Montgomery NE, Suite 130, Albuquerque 87109

NEW YORK

New York State Nurses Association, 46 Cornell Road, Lantham 12110

NYS Board for Nursing, NYS State Education Dept., Cultural Education Center, Albany 12230

NORTH CAROLINA

North Carolina Nurses Association, P.O. Box 12025, 103 Enterprise St., Raleigh 27605

Board of Nursing, P.O. Box 2129, Raleigh 27602

NORTH DAKOTA

North Dakota Nurses Association, 549 Airport Road, Bismarck 58504

Board of Nursing, 919 S. 7th St., Suite 504, Bismarck 58504

OHIO

Ohio Nurses Association, 4000 E. Main St., Columbus 43213

Ohio Board of Nursing, 77 S. High St., 17th Floor, Columbus 43266

OKLAHOMA

Oklahoma Nurses Association, 6414 N. Santa Fe, Suite A, Oklahoma City 73116

Board of Nursing, 2915 N. Classen Blvd., Suite 524, Oklahoma City 73106

OREGON

Oregon Nurses Association, 9600 SW Oak St., Suite 550, Portland 97223

Board of Nursing, 800 NE Oregon St., Suite 465, Portland 97232

PENNSYLVANIA

Pennsylvania Nurses Association, 2578 Interstate Drive, P.O. Box 8525, Harrisburg 17105

Board of Nursing, P.O. Box 2649, Harrisburg 17105

PUERTO RICO

Colegio de Professionales de la Enfermeria de Puerto Rico, P.O. Box 3647, San Juan 00936–3647

Puerto Rico Board of Nurse Examiners, Call Box 10200, Santurce, 00908

RHODE ISLAND

Rhode Island State Nurses Association, 550 S. Water St., Unit 540B, Providence 02903

Nurse Registration and Nursing Education, Rm. 104, Cannon Health Bldg., 3 Capitol Hill, Providence 02908

SOUTH CAROLINA

South Carolina Nurses Association, 1821 Gadsden St., Columbia 29201

Board of Nursing, 2200 Executive Center Dr., Suite 220, Columbia 29210

SOUTH DAKOTA

South Dakota Nurses Association, 1505 S. Minnesota, Suite 3, Sioux Falls 57105

Board of Nursing, 3307 S. Lincoln Ave., Sioux Falls 57105

TENNESSEE

Tennessee Nurses Association, 545 Mainstream Dr., Suite 405, Nashville 37228–1207

Board of Nursing, 426 5th Ave. N., Cordell Hull Building, 1st Floor, Nashville 37247

TEXAS

Texas Nurses Association, 7600 Burnet Rd., Suite 440, Austin 78757–1292

Board of Nurse Examiners, 333 Guadalope, Tower 3, Suite 460, Austin 78701

UTAH

Utah Nurses Association, 455 East 400 South, Suite 402, Salt Lake City 84111

Division of Occupational and Professional Licensing—Board of Nursing, Heber M. Wells Bldg., 4th Fl., 160 E. 300 S., P.O. Box 45805, Salt Lake City 84145

VERMONT

Vermont State Nurses Association, 26 Champlain Mill, 1 Main St., Winooski 05404

Board of Nursing, 109 State St., Montpelier 05602

VIRGIN ISLANDS

Virgin Islands State Nurses Association, P.O. Box 583, Christiansted, St. Croix 00821

Board of Nurse Licensure, Kongens Gade #3, P.O. Box 4247, St. Thomas 00803

VIRGINIA

Virginia Nurses Association, 7113 Three Chopt Road, Suite 204, Richmond 23226

Board of Nursing, 6606 W. Broad, Richmond 23230

WASHINGTON

Washington State Nurses Association, 2505 2nd Ave., Suite 500, Seattle, WA 98121

Washington State Board of Nursing, P.O. Box 47864, Olympia 98504

WEST VIRGINIA

West Virginia Nurses Association, 2003 Quarrier St., Charleston 25311

Board of Examiners for Registered Nurses, 101 Dee Drive, Charleston 25311

WISCONSIN

Wisconsin Nurses Association, 6117 Monona Drive, Madison 53716

Board of Nursing, Rm. 174, P.O. Box 8935, Madison 53708

WYOMING

Wyoming Nurses Association, Majestic Bldg., Suite 305, 1603 Capitol Ave., Cheyenne 82001

Board of Nursing, 220 Carey Ave., Suite 110, Cheyenne 82002

SELECTED NURSING ORGANIZATIONS

American Nurses' Association, 600 Maryland Avenue, SW, Suite 100 West, Washington, DC 20024

American Academy of Nurse Practitioners, Capitol Station, LBJ Bldg., P.O. Box 12846, Austin, TX 78711

American Association of Colleges of Nursing, Suite 530, One Dupont Circle, Washington, DC 20036

American Association of Critical-Care Nurses, 101 Columbia, Aliso Viejo, CA 92656

American Association of Neuroscience Nurses, 218 N. Jefferson, Suite 204, Chicago, IL 60661

American Association of Nurse Anesthetists, 222 South Prospect, Park Ridge, IL 60068

The American Association of Nurse Attorneys (TAANA), 3525 Ellicott Mills Drive, Suite N, Ellicott City, MD 21043

American Association of Occupational Health Nurses, Inc., 50 Lenox Pointe, Atlanta, GA 30324

American College of Nurse-Midwives, 818 Connecticut Ave. NW, Suite 900, Washington, DC 20006

American Organization of Nurse Executives (AONE), 1 North Franklin St., Chicago, IL 60606

American Psychiatric Nurses' Association, 1200 19th St. NW, Suite 300, Washington, DC 20036

Association of Nurses in AIDS Care, 704 Stonyhill Rd., Suite 106, Yardley, PA 19067

Association of Operating Room Nurses, 10170 E. Mississippi Ave., Denver, CO 80231

Association of Rehabilitation Nurses, 5700 Old Orchard Rd., 1st Fl., Skokie, IL 60077

Association of Women's Health, Obstetric, and Neonatal Nurses (AWHONN), 700 14th St. NW, Suite 600, Washington, DC 20005

Emergency Nurses Association, 230 E. Ohio, Suite 600, Chicago, IL 60611

Intravenous Nurses Society, Inc., Two Brighton St., Belmont, MA 02178

The National Alliance of Nurse Practitioners, 325 Pennsylvania Ave. SE, Washington, DC 20003–1100

National Association of Pediatric Nurse Associates and Practitioners, 1101 Kings Hwy. North, Suite 206, Cherry Hill, NJ 08034

National Association of School Nurses, Inc., P.O. Box 1300, Scarborough, ME 04074

National Black Nurses Association, Inc., 1511 K St. NW, Suite 415, Washington, DC 20005

National Council of State Boards of Nursing, Inc., 676 N. St. Clair, Suite 550, Chicago, IL 60611–2921

National Gerontological Nursing Association, 7250 Parkway Drive, Suite 510, Hanover, MD 21076

National League for Nursing, 350 Hudson St., New York, NY 10014

National Student Nurses' Association, 555 W. 57th St., New York, NY 10019

Sigma Theta Tau International Honor Society of Nursing, 550 W. North St., Indianapolis, IN 46202

Society of Gastroenterology Nurses and Associates, Inc., P.O. Box 809156, Chicago, IL 60680

Data from: BRB Publications, Inc. *State Public Records: A Definitive Guide to Searching for Public Record Information at the State Level.* 2d Edition. Tempe, AZ: BRB Publications, Inc., 1995; American Nurses Foundation. *American Nurses Publishing Catalog-1996.* Washington, DC: ANA Foundation, 1966.

Annotated Listing of Selected Legal Columns in Nursing Journals

NAME OF JOURNAL; PUBLISHER	NAME OF LEGAL COLUMN	AUTHOR(S)	COLUMN FREQUENCY	COMMENTS
American Association of Nurse Anesthetists Journal (AANAJ); AANA Publishing, Inc.	Legal Briefs	Gene Blumenreich, JD (AANA General Counsel)	6 times a year	Author examines one issue per column; includes case citations and key words in each column; writes in an easy-to-understand style; topics include malpractice issues and employment concerns.
American Association of Occupational Health Nurses Journal (AAOHNJ); Slack, Inc.		Varied	Monthly	Authors examine varying topics each month; short articles give brief overviews of topics; topics include AIDS, environmental issues, new laws affecting OHN practice
American Journal of Nursing (AJN); American Journal of Nursing Co.	The Legal Side	Varied	Every other month	Question-and-answer format; writing style clear and easy to understand; topics include informed consent, death and dying issues, employment concerns.
Association of Operating Room Nurses Journal (AORNJ); Association of Operating Room Nurses	OR Nursing Law	Ellen K. Murphy, RN, JD, CNOR, FAAN	Monthly	One topic per column is presented and discussed; topics clearly pertain to OR nursing; columns are in-depth yet easy to understand.
Home Healthcare Nurse (HHCN); Lippincott-Raven Publishers	Legalities of Home Care	Nancy J. Brent, RN, MS, JD	4 times a year	Each column takes one issue of importance to the home health nurse and agency and succinctly discusses it; topics include confidentiality issues, new laws affecting the home health care nurse and practice, and liability concerns.
The Journal of Nursing Administration (JONA); Lippincott-Raven Publishers	Legal Insights	Ann Scott Blouin, RN, MA, PhD and Nancy J. Brent, RN, MS, JD	4 times a year	Topics geared to nurse administrator; writing style clear and concise; series topics include job transition and various board memberships of nurse administrators.
Nursing '96; Springhouse Corp.	Legal Questions	Varied	Monthly	Question and answer format; general topics are presented in a question format with responses.
Nursing Management; S-N Publications, Inc.	Law for the Nurse Manager	Janine Fiesta, RN, BSN, JD	Monthly	Each column presents a legal topic of interest to nurse managers; utilizes case law; applies law to practice; topics include workers' compensation, delegation issues, and liability concerns.

Abortion: Termination of pregnancy before the fetus reaches the stage of viability. Abortion can be spontaneous or induced, therapeutic or nontherapeutic.

Abuse: Mental or physical maltreatment.

Acceptance: When there is a voluntary, clear, definite communication to accept the offer as specified by the offeror.

Administrative Law: Deals with the body of law of governmental agencies, whether federal, state, or local.

Administrative Procedure Act: A statute that governs respective federal and state administrative agencies. This act defines the types of rules that can be passed and the process of rule making and its scope.

Advance Directive: A written statement that directs health care providers concerning consent or refusal for treatment when the individual patient does not possess decision-making capacity.

Advanced Practice Nurse: A registered nurse who has successfully completed an additional course of study in a nursing specialty that provides specialized knowledge and skills to function in an expanded role.

Affirmative Action Plan: A program established to overcome the effects of past discrimination against groups protected by antidiscrimination laws.

Alternative Dispute Resolution (ADR): Includes but is not limited to mediation, arbitration, conciliation, and screening panels. The ADR movement began in 1979 for the purpose of identifying alternatives to litigation when legal conflicts arose among parties.

AMA: Against medical advice.

American Board of Nursing Specialties (ABNS): A peer review program established in 1991 to set standards and establish policies and procedures concerning certification and to educate the public concerning certified professional nursing care.

Americans with Disabilities Act: A federal antidiscrimination law that, among other things, prohibits a nurse and other health care providers from discriminating against disabled persons in the provision of health care services.

Answer: Defendant's written assertion either denying the plaintiff's allegations in the complaint or admitting them, but then setting forth defenses against them.

Antitrust Laws: Both on the federal and state level, prohibit anticompetitive measures such as contracts, monopolies, boycotts, or other conduct that effectively constrains commerce or trade.

Appellant: The party who initiates an appeal.

Appellate Courts: These courts sit in review of cases appealed from the state or federal trial courts.

Appellee: The party against whom the appeal is taken.

Arbitration: A process in which a dispute is submitted to a third neutral party, or a panel of arbitrators, to hear arguments, review evidence, and render a decision.

Arrest: When a person is taken into custody in order to obtain an answer to a criminal charge or charges.

Artificial Insemination: Process of artificially inseminating a female via the introduction of viable sperm into the vagina, cervical canal, or uterus by artificial means.

Assault: This tort protects an individual's interest in the freedom from the apprehension of harmful or offensive contact. There is no requirement of an actual touching of the plaintiff; the intent to spur apprehension and the resultant fear that contact might occur in the victim satisfies this requirement.

Assisted Suicide: The inducing, aiding, or forcing of another to commit suicide.

At-Will Employment Doctrine: Protects both the employer or the employee's right to terminate their relationship at any time for any reason.

Automation Defense: Rests on the fact that because the behavior that comprised a criminal act was done in an unconscious or semiconscious state, it could not be the result of a voluntary act.

Autonomy: A moral principle generally referring to individual freedom of choice or liberty interests.

Bail: Consists of money and is used to ensure the court that the accused will remain in the state and be present in court for the trial of the alleged crime(s).

Battery: This tort protects an individual's interest in freedom from an affirmative, intentional, and unpermitted contact with his or her body, any extension of it (e.g., clothing), or anything that is attached to it and identified with it. Unlike assault, actual contact is essential.

Best Interest of the Individual Test: A test used to evaluate competing personal and state interests when an incompetent person is involved and a decision concerning treatment or nontreatment must be made. In its pure form, it takes into account only the present welfare of the person and ignores societal, familial, or other secondary concerns that do not focus on what is best for the person at that time.

Booking Procedure: Involves recording identifying and other information (e.g., name, address, age) about the person arrested in the police "log" or "blotter"; notation of the crime committed; fingerprinting and photographing of the arrestee.

Borrowed Servant Doctrine: When an employee is temporarily under the direct control and supervision of someone other than the employer, thereby becoming the "temporary employee" of the other person.

Brain Death: Occurs when all vital functions of the brain, brain stem, and spinal reflexes are irreversibly nonexistent as determined by accepted medical standards.

Breach of Confidentiality: This tort protects a patient's sharing information with a health care provider without fear that the information will be released to those not involved in his or her care.

Breach of Contract: When one party to a contract fails to perform, without a legal justification, any major promise or obligation under the contract.

Buckley Amendment: Passed by Congress to ensure a consistent approach to the release of a student's school record.

Burden of Proof: Means the obligation to affirmatively convince the judge or jury that the allegations contained in the complaint, which form the basis of the suit, are true.

Certified Nurse-Midwife: A registered nurse with additional education in the independent management of the aspect of women's health that pertains to pregnancy, childbirth, post partum, care of the newborn, and gynecology, including family planning.

Charge Bargain: An example of plea bargaining in which the defendant pleads guilty to a lesser crime.

Civil Rights Act: Passed in 1871 after the Civil War, Section 1983 of this act protects all of the rights encompassed in the Constitution (including life, liberty, property, privacy, due process, and equal protection) as well as federal statutory and administrative rights.

Civil Rights Violations: Occur when an individual's rights are transgressed by the government or a governmental entity.

Civil Service Reform Act: Passed in 1978, this federal act regulates rights and responsibilities concerning collective bargaining and unionization for Veterans' Administration Hospitals.

Claims-Made Policy: Only covers a claim if injury occurs and the claim is filed while the policy is in effect.

Clayton Act: An act and its Amendment known as the Robertson-Patman Act that bans price fixing and exclusive dealings involving contracts and tying arrangements which substantially lessen competition.

Clinical Nurse Specialist (CNS): The American Nurses Association defines the CNS as a registered nurse who, through graduate studies and supervised practice, has become an expert in a defined area of knowledge and practice in a specific area of clinical nursing.

Common Law: "Judge-made" or "court-made" decisions; based on precedent, custom, usage, and tradition; also called "case law."

Complaint: The pleading required to initiate a case.

Completion of Contract: When the contract is

adhered to, performance occurs, and the obligations under the contract are met.

Conciliation: An example of an alternative dispute resolution (ADR) mechanism in which the purpose is to improve communications and decrease tensions between the parties to a dispute.

Constitution: The primary law of a nation or state which establishes the character and organization of its government, limits and distributes power within the government, and establishes the extent of the government's power.

Contingent Fee: Used in civil cases; the attorney and client agree that a certain percentage of any money obtained by way of judgment or settlement for the client is paid to the attorney for the attorney's legal fees.

Contract: A voluntary agreement between two or more individuals that creates an obligation to do or not do something and that creates enforceable rights or legal duties.

Contract Law: Deals with promises and the enforcement of them where a legal right has been created.

Corporation: A very formalized business structure controlled by the state, country, or national law. It is an entity established by incorporators in order to conduct business.

Counterclaim: A pleading in a civil case used by a defendant when a denial of the allegations in the complaint occurs and the defendant alleges his or her own causes of action against the plaintiff in the same case in order to defeat the plaintiff's case.

Covenantal Relationships: A type of nurse-patient relationship characterized by the mutual exchange of gifts, entrustment, and endurance.

Criminal Procedure: Defined as the procedural steps through which a criminal case must pass.

Cross-Claim: A pleading in a civil case used when co-parties—either co-plaintiffs or co-defendants—assert allegations against each other that are germane to the case and may avoid liability for that party.

Defamation: A tort which occurs when an individual's good name or reputation is damaged because of something that is written (libel) or said (slander) about the person that is untrue.

Defendant: The individual, individuals, corporation, governmental agency, or state or federal government sued. In a civil case, the allegations against the defendant may include causes of action for personal injury, loss of money, or an invasion of a protected right. In a criminal case, the defendant is accused of committing a certain crime or crimes.

Defense: The defendant's answer or response to a claim or suit that sets forth the reasons why the defendant is not liable and why the relief requested should not be granted. The defense of a case includes, but is not limited to, the filing of an answer, raising specific, affirmative defenses against the allegations, obtaining evidence to support one's position, and identifying the best strategic overall approach to the case.

Deposition: A type of pretrial discovery method whereby a party or witness statement is taken under oath and the individual gives his or her statement concerning the case with all parties and their attorneys present.

Discovery Motions: Used during the discovery phase of a case when the parties are experiencing difficulties with each other in obtaining requested material or taking a deposition, for example; may also be used when unique discovery is needed or is not consistent with civil practice rules.

Domestic Violence: Conduct of a family member or a member of a household toward another family or household member so that the result is physical, psychological, or developmental injury or damage. Domestic violence includes abuse, neglect, or exploitation.

Due Process of Law: The Fifth and Fourteenth Amendments to the United States Constitution state that no federal or state government can deprive an individual of life, liberty, or property without due process of law. The courts have defined due process as what is fair under the circumstances.

Early and Periodic Screening, Diagnosis, and Treatment Program: A federally funded program that provides preventive health care to children of low-income parents.

Emergency Medical Treatment and Active Labor Act: Prohibits facilities receiving Medicare and Medicaid funds from "dumping" patients out of their emergency rooms when they cannot pay. Requires hospitals to medically screen a patient for an emergency condition; stabilize the patient's condition; and if transfer of the patient is required, the transfer can occur only after stabilization of the patient's condition.

Employee Polygraph Protection Act: A federal law prohibiting private employers from using a lie detector test or its results to make employment decisions listed in the act.

Employee Retirement Income Security Act (ERISA): ERISA sets minimum protections in the area of pension plans and mandates that most employers, with the exceptions of governmental employers and some church-sponsored plans, comply with its requirements, including nondiscrimination, the provision of a summary plan description to employees, the vesting of benefits, and plan terminations.

Endorsement: The process of granting a license after an evaluation as to whether an individual already granted a license in another state satisfies the requirements in the state where the application is pending.

Entrapment Defense: Can only be used against

law enforcement officers or individuals cooperating with law enforcement officers or agencies who overstep their role in "encouraging" another to commit a crime and instead initiate the criminal act and convince an otherwise uninterested individual to participate in that crime.

Equal Employment Opportunity Laws: Also called antidiscrimination laws. Their purpose is to proscribe employment policies and practices that result in different treatment of, or a disparate impact on, any protected class of applicants or employees.

Equal Pay Act: No employer can discriminate in the payment of wages on the basis of gender/sex when equal work of equal skill, equal effort, and equal responsibility is done under similar working conditions; amended the Fair Labor Standards Act of 1938.

Equal Protection Clause: Located in the Fourteenth Amendment to the United States Constitution; prohibits state governments from making unreasonable classifications in its laws. The federal government is also prohibited from doing so in the Fifth Amendment's Due Process Clause.

Equal Protection of the Law: Means that no one person or persons shall be denied the protections of the law given other persons or individuals in like or similar circumstances.

Euthanasia/Mercy Killing: Both terms mean mercifully putting to death people who suffer from painful, incurable, and distressing diseases.

Ex Parte Motion: Means "one side only"; may be used in rare circumstances where giving notice to the other party may not be possible or helpful; is often used when one party seeks an injunction or restraining order against another.

Express Consent (for Treatment): Manifested by an oral declaration concerning a particular treatment ("yes") or by a written document (a consent form) that the patient signs.

Expert Witness: An individual who, by training, education, and/or experience is qualified by the court as able to assist the jury in understanding subjects not within the knowledge of the average lay person.

Exploitation: Taking unjust advantage of another for one's own benefit or gain.

Fair Labor Standards Act: A federal law passed in 1938 that established minimum wages, overtime pay, and maximum hours of employment.

False Imprisonment: Freedom from a restriction of one's choice of movement is the interest protected by this tort.

Family and Medical Leave Act: This act, effective in 1993, requires employers with 50 or more employees to grant an employee up to 12 weeks of unpaid leave annually for the birth or adoption of a child, to care for a spouse or immediate family member with a serious health condition, or when the employee is unable to work due to a serious health condition.

Federal Constitution: Composed of 7 Articles and 23 Amendments, the first 10 of which traditionally have been called the Bill of Rights. All 23 Amendments focus on individual rights that are protected against governmental intrusion.

Federal Trade Commission Act: This federal law, enforced by the Federal Trade Commission and empowered only to bring civil actions against alleged offenders, bans any unfair methods of competition and unfair deceptive practices or acts.

Flat Fee for Service: The amount for legal services is agreed to between the lawyer and client, regardless of the amount of legal work needed.

Fraud: Conduct involving an individual falsely

representing a fact (by conduct, words, false or misleading allegations) or concealment of that which should have been disclosed to another person.

Good Faith and Fair Dealing: In contract law, the duties of good faith and fair dealing is an implied term of all contracts. Therefore, all parties to a contract are expected to conduct themselves accordingly once the contract has been entered into.

Grievance Procedures: Any process by which an employee may question or appeal a superior's decision affecting job security.

Guardian: A person or organization judicially appointed to make decisions for the person; may be a "personal" guardian (making decisions concerning the care, support, comfort, health education, and maintenance of the ward) or an "estate" guardian (making financial decisions concerning the ward and ward's assets).

Guardian Ad Litem: A court-appointed position made during the course of the proceeding in order to protect the interests of the alleged disabled adult or minor. Serves as the court's investigator; that is, providing information to the court as to what is in the best interest of the alleged disabled adult or minor concerning the appointment of a guardian.

Health Care Quality Improvement Act (HCQIA): A federal law passed by Congress in 1986 in response to the increasing occurrence of malpractice in the United States and society's concern about the quality of health care. The purpose is to improve the overall quality of health care; limit the ability of incompetent physicians to move from state to state without disclosure; and to encourage good faith involvement by physicians in peer review activities.

Hourly Fee: A legal fee arrangement based on the attorney's fixed hourly rate for any and all legal work done, including court appearances, drafting of documents, conferences, and out of pocket expenses.

Immunity from Suit: Protects an individual or entity from liability in certain circumstances.

Impeach: To question a witness's credibility during a witness's testimony at trial or during a deposition.

Implied Consent: Consent given by an individual's conduct rather than verbally or in writing.

In Vitro Insemination: Involves the removal of an ovum from the female, fertilizing it in vitro, and then replacing the fertilized egg back into the uterus.

Incident or Occurrence Screening: A systematic institution-wide process for identifying adverse patient care situations.

Informed Consent: A patient's right to know and understand what health care treatment is being undertaken.

Intent: In relation to intentional torts, a state of mind about the results of a voluntary act (or the results of a voluntary failure to act) and includes not only having a desire to bring about the results but also knowing that the results are "substantially certain" to occur.

Intentional Torts: Ones most often seen in health care are assault, battery, false imprisonment, and conversion of property.

Judicial Review: A means by which parties affected by an agency decision can challenge the decision if it is believed to be arbitrary (unreasonable), not based on the law, illegal, or not based on the agency's power, procedures, or policies.

Judiciary: The branch of the government that interprets, construes, applies, enforces, and administers the laws of state or federal governments.

Jurisdiction: The authority by which a court

recognizes and decides cases; can be applied to one particular court or the particular court system as a whole.

"Just Cause" Termination: An exception to the at-will employment doctrine whereby the employee's conduct must violate the rules and conduct established by the employer in order for the employee to be terminated from his or her position.

Justice: A moral principle referring to fairness; receiving one's due.

Legal Precedent: The American system of determining legal rights and responsibilities by the court based on prior case decisions, rulings, rationale, and custom.

Liability: Responsibility for a possible or actual loss, penalty, evil, expense, or burden for which law or justice requires the individual to do something, pay, or otherwise compensate the victim.

Liberty Interest: In administrative law, this interest has been expanded to include the right of the individual to contract, engage in any of the common occupations of life, to acquire useful knowledge, to marry ". . . and generally to enjoy those privileges recognized . . . as essential to the pursuit of happiness by free men." Example: the possession of an occupational license in good standing.

Limited Partnership: A limited partnership is one in which the limited partner supplies money to the business but has no say in its operation, delivery of services, or any other aspect of the business.

Living Will: A document that establishes a written mechanism for an individual to specify wishes concerning the withdrawing or forgoing of life-sustaining treatment.

Manslaughter: Homicide not bad enough to be murder but too bad to be no crime whatever. Categories of manslaughter include voluntary manslaughter (killing another in the heat of passion or when provoked), involuntary manslaughter (killing another when committing an unlawful act), or criminal negligence involuntary manslaughter (conducting oneself in a lawful manner but without proper care or necessary skill).

Mediation: Usually an informal process in which the parties involved in a dispute will attempt to voluntarily resolve their differences by utilizing a private mediator or a mediation service.

Medical Directive: A non–statute-based advance directive that is designed as a "comprehensive" document; specifically, it can be used for various treatment and patient condition situations and also provides for the appointment of a proxy decision-maker.

Moral Principles: Serve as a foundation for moral conduct and reference points for ethical decision-making in nursing.

Moral Reasoning: The interpretative process that helps to connect one's moral values with one's ethical choices.

Motion for Directed Verdict: Requested by either party during trial; asks that a verdict in his or her favor be granted because the party with the burden of proof did not meet that burden.

Motion for Judgment Notwithstanding the Verdict: Requested by either party after the judge or jury reaches a decision.

Motion for Mistrial: Requested by either party before the jury's verdict or judge's decision in order to render the trial void.

Motion to Strike: Used when a party requests that biased material, or harmful information included in a pleading or in oral testimony, be removed from the pleading or record and disregarded.

Motion for Summary Judgment: When a party in a case asks the court to dismiss the case because there is no contest about the facts and the moving party is entitled to a ruling in his or her favor as a matter of law.

Motion to Dismiss: Usually done before a hearing or trial; attacks the suit by alleging insufficient legal basis to sustain the suit.

Mutual Assent: In contract law, requires one or more parties to approve, ratify, and confirm something; is also called "a meeting of the minds."

National Council of State Boards of Nursing Data Bank (NDB): Established as a voluntary reporting system for member state boards of nursing to convey data concerning disciplinary actions taken against nurses by the particular state board.

National Labor Relations Act (NLRA): Also known as the Wagner Act. Specifies employee, employer, and union rights, responsibilities, and expected conduct when collective bargaining is contemplated or undertaken in the workplace; protects the public from interruptions in commerce that might occur due to unfair labor practices and strikes; and encourages free private collective bargaining.

National Mediation Board: Established to promote and select arbitrators for contract disputes in, for example, the railroad and airline industries.

National Organ Transplant Act: A federal law passed by Congress to address many problems of organ donation.

Neglect: The failure or omission to do something one could do or what one is required to do.

Negligence: Conduct that falls below the standard established by law for the protection of others against unreasonable risk of harm.

Nonmaleficence: A moral principle of doing no harm.

Nurse Anesthetist: According to the American Association of Nurse Anesthetists, a registered nurse who has successfully completed an approved nurse anesthetist program from an accredited program, passed a national qualifying examination, and fulfilled continuing education requirements every 2 years for recertification.

Nurse Entrepreneur: A nurse who establishes and maintains a successful business and also makes quality nursing care and nursing services more available to the public.

Nurse Practitioner (NP): A registered nurse who, with advanced educational preparation, is able to assess the physical and psychological needs of a client through history taking, physical examination, ordering and interpreting diagnostic laboratory and radiographic studies, and implementing a therapeutic plan through the prescribing of appropriate medication and treatments, patient education, and applicable referrals.

Occupational Safety and Health Act (OSHA): A law passed by Congress in 1970 to ensure a healthy and safe workplace for workers. This law imposes two duties on covered employees: to provide a workplace free from recognized hazards that are causing or likely to cause death or serious physical harm to employees (also called the employer's "general duty") and to comply with regulations promulgated by the Occupational Safety and Health Administration of the Labor Department.

Occurrence Insurance: Covers a claim regardless of when it was filed so long as the incident arose while the policy was in effect.

Occurrence Witness: Someone who will be able to support or refute respectively allegations in the case.

Offer: A clear, direct, and precise communication in any form (in writing or orally) to another (the offeree) that the offerer intends to enter into a contract.

On-Call Duty: Where the employee is required to be available, either at the work site or nearby so that reporting to work is swift when needed.

Parens Patriae Doctrine: Meaning "the parent of the country." This doctrine, in the United States, is used to protect those individuals who cannot protect themselves, such as children and incompetent adults.

Parole Evidence Rule: Rule of contract interpretation that is important when challenging a contract and its terms.

Partnership: An arrangement, either formal or informal, whereby two or more individuals co-own a business for profit.

Patient Self-Determination Act: Effective in 1991, this federal act requires hospitals, nursing homes, health maintenance organizations, and home health care agencies receiving Medicare and Medicaid funds to, among other things, have written policies and procedures concerning adult patients and their ability to provide informed consent and refusal for treatment.

Peer Review: A component of quality assurance carried out by the entity's practicing health care providers, including nurses. The purpose is to examine the quality of care provided by the health care provider group (e.g., physicians or nurses) and the group's adherence to established standards of practice.

Penumbra Doctrine: States that when implied governmental powers exist in a charter, those powers can be "engrafted" on another.

Period of Discovery: A time during which all the parties to a suit are given the chance to obtain information concerning the issues contained in the suit from the other parties, witnesses, or other sources.

Personal Liability: This rule holds everyone responsible for his or her own behavior, including his or her own negligent behavior.

Plaintiff: The person (also called the petitioner) who initiates the suit; the person who has the burden of proving the case.

Plea Bargaining: The process in which the accused, through his or her attorney, and the prosecuting attorney agree to a mutually satisfactory resolution of the case.

Pleadings: The formal, written allegations by parties in a case of their respective claims and defenses.

Professional Association: A type of business structure which allows professionals such as nurses and physicians to form a professional association; requires the establishment of a written association agreement that governs the business entity and requires that the name of the business utilize the term "associates," "associated," or similar title.

Premises Liability Insurance: Protects the physical plant of the business from loss that might occur from fire, water damage, flooding, or other natural disasters and theft.

Pretrial Conference: The final step in the pretrial phase of the trial process; its purpose is to clarify and fairly resolve any pending issues in the controversy prior to trial or, if possible, to settle the case.

Professional Corporation: Governed by state, county, or national law, the professional corporate structure is a formalized business organization specific to professionals (e.g., nurses, dentists, lawyers), who establish and render professional services to the public.

Professional Liability Insurance: A contract whereby an insurer agrees to enter into a policy of insurance with the insured (e.g., the hospital or the nurse) in order to provide coverage for delineated professional activities.

Professional Negligence: Also called professional malpractice; involves the conduct of professionals (e.g., nurses, physicians, dentists, and lawyers) falling below a professional standard of due care.

Property Interest: In administrative law, property interest is interpreted as any "legitimate claim of entitlement" to a benefit that may be adversely affected by an administrative action.

Quality Assurance: The planned, internal process of a health care delivery system established to continually and systematically monitor, assess, and improve the quality of patient care.

Quash Service of Summons: To render void the service of the summons and complaint of a party; if granted, requires another try at service because the court does not have power over the party unless the summons is properly served.

Quasi-Intentional Torts: Torts where the intent of the actor may not be as clear as with the intentional torts, but a voluntary act on the defendant's part takes place as does the subsequent interference with an individual's interest. Common quasi-intentional torts seen in health care are defamation, breach of confidentiality, invasion of privacy, and malicious prosecution.

Reciprocity: The process of granting a license to an applicant who is already licensed in another state, when that state's licensure requirements are the same as in the state in which the applicant is seeking licensure.

Reply: Plaintiff's response to the defendant's counterclaim; can also be used after a motion is filed in a case or at any other time the court orders either party to file one.

Res Ipsa Loquitur: Means literally, "The thing speaks for itself." It is a rule of evidence that allows for an inference of negligence on the part of the defendant due to the circumstances surrounding the injury.

Res Judicata: Once a final decision in a case has been made by a court having jurisdiction, it is binding on all of the parties and is therefore an absolute bar to any further legal action that involves the same claim, demand, or cause of action.

Respondeat Superior: Latin term meaning "Let the master speak"; based on vicarious liability. For the employer (master) to be vicariously liable for the negligent acts of employees (or its agents), the act must have occurred during the employment relationship and have been part of the employee's job responsibilities.

Retainer Fee: A legal fee arrangement utilized alone or in conjunction with an hourly fee; the client pays a certain amount to the attorney as an initial payment on a case or to have the attorney available for legal work that is needed.

Right: A power or privilege to which a person is entitled.

Risk Management: The internal process of a health care delivery system aimed at procuring liability insurance, improving patient care, and reducing financial loss for the health care entity.

Risk Treatment: Includes controlling risks/losses and risk financing; may also include loss prevention, reduction, and avoidance.

Rule-Making: The process of an administrative agency to deal with its responsibilities in carrying out a particular piece of legislation with clarity and efficiency.

Rules of Contract Interpretation: Guidelines adopted by the law in order to provide a set of rules for clarifying a contract when there is a challenge to its language.

Screening Panels: Established in some states to aid in reducing the number of cases that are filed in court by evaluating whether the proposed case has merit.

Sentence Bargain: An example of a plea bargain when the defendant pleads guilty to some of the counts of a multicount complaint or indictment, and in return, receives a lesser sentence.

Separation of Powers Doctrine: Dividing the powers of a government among its constituent parts in order to avoid a concentration of power in any one part, which could lead to abuse.

Sherman Act: Basically forbids any measure that effectively limits competition in interstate commerce and trade among foreign nations.

Sole Proprietorship: A business model that is the least complicated of all the business structures. The sole proprietor becomes the business and therefore any assets or liabilities belong to the owner.

Standing Orders: Commonly written for procedures and medications.

Stare Decisis: Means "to stand by cases decided" and refers to the court following its own principles of law and those of inferior courts as applied to a particular set of facts.

State Supreme Court: The final court of appeal in a state judicial system.

Statute of Frauds: Requires certain contracts be in writing and signed by the party who must perform it. Its purpose is to ensure reliable, objective evidence of agreements.

Statute: A law passed by Congress (federal), state, or local legislative bodies.

Statute of Limitations: Establishes the time periods within which a claim may be filed or within which certain rights can be enforced.

Strict Liability: A tort liability theory whereby the manufacturer and others will be held responsible for an injury without regard to the fault or intent of those individuals to harm or injure another.

Subpoena: Used for a deposition or at trial to ensure the presence of the person who is not named in the suit but whose testimony as a witness in a particular case is needed.

Substituted Judgment Test: A test used to evaluate competing personal and state interests when an incompetent person is involved and a decision concerning treatment or nontreatment must be made. It takes into account what the incompetent person would decide if he or she were able to make the decision personally. The test has been called the "subjective test."

Suicide: The deliberate termination of one's life by one's own hand.

Summons: The official notification to the defendant that a suit has been filed against him or her.

Surrogate Motherhood: An arrangement whereby one woman (the "surrogate") conceives and bears a child under an agreement to surrender the child to another person or persons, who must then adopt the child as their own.

Testimony at Trial: The process of providing evidence, through one's statement under oath, for the purpose of establishing or providing a fact or facts in a judicial inquiry.

Third-Party Complaint: Used by the defendant to bring a third party into the suit not originally sued by the plaintiff because the third party may be liable for the plaintiff's injury.

Tort: A civil wrong other than a breach of contract, where the law will provide a remedy by allowing the injured person to seek damages.

Total Quality Management (TQM): Also called continuous quality improvement (CQI). A structured system for involving an entire organization in a continuous quality improvement process targeted to meet and exceed customer (patient) expectations.

Triage: The screening and classification of emergency department patients to determine their priority of treatment.

Uniform Anatomical Gift Act: Allows an adult "of sound mind and body" to donate all or part of his or her body as a gift, which takes effect upon his or her death.

United States Supreme Court: The Supreme Court of the land; the final court to which a case can be appealed.

Utilization Review: An internal process of an institution to evaluate the provision of health care services in terms of medical necessity; the appropriate use of resources for the level of care needed; and, if the care met adopted standards of care for both care professionals and quality care generally.

Venue: Involves the place or geographic area where a court with jurisdiction can hear and determine a cause.

Vicarious Liability: Also called imputed liability or imputed negligence; refers to the responsibility one is found to have for the actions of other individuals because a special relationship exists between those individuals.

Violence: The unjust and unwarranted exercise of force, often physical (but also psychological) and accompanied by outrage, fury, or vehemence. The use of violence is a deliberate act(s) that can result in abuse, injury, or damage.

Wage Garnishment: When a court enters an order requiring an employer to pay a portion of the employee's (debtor's) paycheck to a creditor until the debt is paid.

Workers' Compensation Laws: Requires employers to cover all employees (not independent contractors) who are injured while doing their job by providing compensation for those injuries.

Written Interrogatories: A type of pretrial discovery method whereby questions are directed at one party concerning information needed by the party who files them with the court and sends copies to all the other parties. The answers to the questions must be in writing and sworn to under oath.

It is difficult to know what the future holds for nursing. Today's health care practice climate is supersaturated with change. Most of those changes directly impact upon the nursing profession, its members, and the clients nursing serves. Managed care alone has drastically affected the way in which nursing care is delivered. Whether in home health, ambulatory care, or acute care settings, the focus of managed care is on the careful and efficient use of health care services, procedures, and treatment modalities in a cost-effective manner.[1] This focus has resulted in potential threats, opportunities, and challenges for nursing.[2] The long-overdue use of the registered professional nurse as a case manager, the utilization of advanced nurse practitioners to provide primary care to patient populations, and the advent of entrepreneurial opportunities for business-minded nurses are just a few of the many opportunities and challenges for nurses. Even so, potential threats do exist in terms of job loss, control over the delivery of patient care to a particular client, and increased liability for injury to a patient when less care—or no care—is given due to noncoverage for services.[3] Nursing must meet these potential threats through continued active involvement in the legislative and political arena of managed care. Moreover, constant updating as to common law decisions and statutory changes dealing with liability issues for nursing will be essential.

Work redesign and the increased use of assistive workers has also created an impact on nursing and nursing practice, if in no other way than by acutely increasing the concern about the future of nursing.[4] However, little information has been generated to support the concerns of nursing surrounding job loss and decreases in salaries as examples. In fact, the statistics included in the Institute of Medicine's report, *Nursing Staff in Hospitals and Nursing Homes: Is It Adequate?* indicate that from 1983 to 1993 the absolute numbers of employed registered nurses increased to 1.9 million from 1.3 million.[5] The report also indicates that during the "aggressive era of hospital restructuring," full-time equivalent nursing personnel in community hospitals rose 2.7% from March of 1994 to March of 1995, which includes a 3.5% increase for registered nurses.[6] Moreover, salaries for nurses have increased 46% in comparison to those of the average U.S. worker.[7]

Clearly, nursing will need to carefully evaluate these data and conduct studies and compile statistics in order to identify future trends and outcomes of continued restructuring and use of assistive personnel and nurse staffing.[8] Because no challenge to the very existence of nursing can be taken lightly, continued use of the judicial system to evaluate patient care restructuring and any subsequent alleged threat to nursing practice will probably be necessary.[9]

The profession will continue to wrestle with informed consent and refusal for treatment issues, including the newest development in this arena—health professional–assisted suicide. Although there has been a flurry of court challenges and legislative action concerning this subject (17 states considered some form of assisted suicide legislation in 1995),[10] it will take the United States Supreme Court to resolve the legal issues that abound concerning this very real patient care and health care delivery issue. Until then, professional associations such as the American Nurses' Association are already attempting to guide their members concerning the legal and ethical ramifications of participating in assisting a patient to commit suicide.[11]

It is my belief that the future holds a place for nursing and it will continue to exist as a profession. However, nursing is at a crossroads, and it cannot rely on its past in order to continue into the future.[12] Rather, the profession will need to become increasingly more proactive, more provocative, more political, more unified, and more legally sophisticated. At the same time, it will need to be more flexible, more compromising, and more collaborative, not only with outside "forces" but also with those within the ranks of nursing. If the nursing profession can blend these roles and move in a forward direction, it will survive and grow, albeit in a differet way from yesterday.

Perhaps Judith Viorst in her book *Necessary Losses* characterized loss and growth best:

> As for our losses and gains, we have seen how often they are inextricably mixed. There is plenty we have to give up in order to grow. For we cannot deeply love anything without becoming vulnerable to loss. And we cannot become separate people, reasonable people, connected people, reflective people without some losing and leaving and letting go.[12]

Godspeed, nursing. It should be an interesting future.

NANCY J. BRENT

---

1. Lanis Hicks, Janet Stallmeyer and John Coleman, "Overview of Managed Care," *Role Of The Nurse in Managed Care*. Washington, DC: American Nurses Publishing, 1993, 1.
2. "The Nurse's Role," *Role of The Nurse in Managed Care, supra* note 1, at 45.
3. See generally, Christopher Kerns and Carol Gerner. *Health Care Liability Deskbook*. Deerfield, IL: Clark Boardman Callaghan, 1995.
4. Institute of Medicine. Division of Health Care Services. *Nursing Staff in Hospitals and Nursing Homes: Is It Adequate?* Gooloo Wunderlich, Frank Sloan and Carolyne Davis, Editors. Washington, DC: National Academy Press, 1966, 4–8.
5. *Id.*
6. J. Duncan Moore, "IOM Study Shows Jump In Nurses' Wages," *Modern Healthcare* (February 12, 1996), 40.
7. *Id.*
8. See, Charlene Harrington, "Nurse Staffing: Developing A Political Action Agenda For Change," 2(3) *Nursing Policy Forum* (May/June 1996), 15–16, 24–27.
9. One case already pending which includes allegations concerning the use of unlicensed assistive workers and the detrimental effects the hospital's restructuring plan has on nursing practice in that institution is *California Nurses Association v. Alta Bates Medical Center et al.*, No. 740798-5, September 13, 1994, Superior Court of Alameda County, CA.
10. "Assisted Suicide Controversy Rages On," 2(3) *Nursing Policy Forum* (May/June 1996), 8 (NEWS BRIEFS SECTION).
11. See, American Nurses' Association. *Position Statement On Assisted Suicide*. Washington, DC: American Nurses Association, 1994; American Nurses' Association. *Position Statement On Active Euthanasia*. Washington, DC: American Nurses Association, 1994.

12. For example, in its Nov. 1995 Third Report, the Pew Health Professions Commission recommended, among other things, that nursing utilize a single title for each level of nursing preparation and service, reduce the size and number of nursing education programs by 10–20% (mainly in associate and diploma degree programs), and utilize nurses with masters degrees in the acute care setting and independent practice as primary care providers. Pew Health Professions Commission, University of California, San Francisco, San Francisco, CA, 1995, Third Report, vi. The Commission's full report, *Critical Challenges: Revitalizing the Health Professions for the Twenty-First Century,* was published in Dec. 1995.

13. Judith Viorst. *Necessary Losses: The Loves, Illusions, Dependencies And Impossible Expectations That All Of Us Have To Give Up in Order To Grow.* New York: Fawcett Gold Medal Books, 1986, 368.

ISBN 0-7216-3463-X